1 & 2 KINGS

Smyth & Helwys Bible Commentary: 1 & 2 Kings

Publication Staff

Publisher and President
Cecil P. Staton

Executive Vice-President
David Cassady

Senior Editor
Mark K. McElroy

Managing Editor
Lex Horton

Art Director
Jim Burt

Graphic Design
Mary Frances Burt, Vickie Frayne

Copy Editors
Laura Shuman, Erin Smith, Jennifer Whiteley

Editorial Assistance
Amelia Barclay, Jackie Riley, Edd Rowell, Jean Trotter

Smyth & Helwys Publishing, Inc.
6316 Peake Road
Macon, Georgia 31210-3960
1-800-747-3016
© 2000 by Smyth & Helwys Publishing
All rights reserved.
Printed in the United States of America.

The paper used in this publication meets the minimum
requirements of American National Standard for Information
Sciences—Permanence of Paper for Printed Library Materials.
ANSI Z39.48–1984 (alk. paper)

Library of Congress Cataloging-in-Publication Data

Brueggemann, Walter.
1 & 2 Kings: a commentary / Walter Brueggemann
p. cm. – (Smyth & Helwys Bible Commentary; 8)
Includes bibliographical references and index.
ISBN 1-57312-065-0
1. Bible. O. T. Kings–Commentaries.
I. Title: 1 and 2 Kings. II. Title: First and Second Kings.
III. Title. IV. Series

BS1335.3. B7894 2000

222'.5077–dc21
00–46372

SMYTH & HELWYS BIBLE COMMENTARY

1 & 2 KINGS

WALTER BRUEGGEMANN

PUBLISHING, INCORPORATED   MACON, GEORGIA

PROJECT EDITOR
R. SCOTT NASH
Mercer University
Macon, Georgia

OLD TESTAMENT
GENERAL EDITOR
SAMUEL E. BALENTINE
Baptist Theological Seminary
at Richmond, Virginia

NEW TESTAMENT
GENERAL EDITOR
R. ALAN CULPEPPER
McAfee School of Theology
Mercer University
Atlanta, Georgia

AREA
OLD TESTAMENT EDITORS
MARK E. BIDDLE
Baptist Theological Seminary
at Richmond, Virginia

AREA
NEW TESTAMENT EDITORS
R. SCOTT NASH
Mercer University
Macon, Georgia

KANDY QUEEN-SUTHERLAND
Stetson University
Deland, Florida

RICHARD B. VINSON
Averett College
Danville, Virginia

KENNETH G. HOGLUND
Wake Forest University
Winston-Salem, North Carolina

ART EDITOR
HEIDI J. HORNIK
Baylor University
Waco, Texas

ADVANCE PRAISE

No scholar of our time probes the heart of biblical faith more profoundly than Walter Brueggemann. With the passion of rhetorician and preacher, he interweaves interpretation and appropriation as so releases the power of ancient speech to inform and transform contemporary life. In turning his talents now to the books of Kings, he has given us a remarkable commentary.

—Phyllis Trible
Professor of Biblical Studies
Wake Forest Divinity School
Winston-Salem, North Carolina

This book is vintage Walter Brueggemann. He is the consummate scholar. Yet, he writes in ways that make his work congenial to the pulpit. Brueggemann is a reminder that the academy and the parish, the scholar and the preacher, work together to offer the church our very best.

—Charles B. Bugg
Kenneth L. Chafin Professor of Preaching
Director, Chevis F. Horne Center for Preaching and Worship
Baptist Theological Seminary at Richmond
Richmond, Virginia

Brueggemann has the rare gift of making biblical texts understandable to general readers. In 1 and 2 Kings, he uses that gift well, enriching it with illustrations from art, current events, and popular culture. The result is a readable commentary that will evoke both surprise and pleasure.

—James L. Crenshaw
Robert L. Flowers Professor of Old Testament
Duke University
Durham, North Carolina

This book is a great read, a delicious treat, but no surprise from the master writer, Walter Brueggemann. Brueggemann's potent prose makes the two books of Kings more interesting than they ever were alone. He finds the human drama and the divine pathos behind the thrones of Israel's mostly tragic monarchs, who are too much like us, and he uncovers the resistance and merciful fire of Israel's prophets, who are too unlike us.

Then there is the elegant visual art from across the ages that adds aesthetic commentary upon power, betrayal, and salvation.

This book will serve the general reader, the believing reader, the preacher, the student, and the scholar. The books of Kings may even join the lists of people's favorite biblical books.

—*Kathleen M. O'Connor*
Professor of Old Testament
Columbia Theological Seminary
Decatur, Georgia

Those of us both in the academy and in the parish have come to anticipate with relish any announcement of a forthcoming book by Professor Brueggemann. In the case of this particular commentary on 1 and 2 Kings, hope does not disappoint. Brueggemann provides both creative exegesis of the biblical text (i.e., he does more than simply rephrase or retell the story) and powerful applications of that text (that always flow out of the exegesis rather than bypass it). Such applications (personal, ecclesial, national) appear consistently under the title *Connections.* Having just completed a commentary on 1 and 2 Kings as part of a larger manuscript, I only wish I had had access to this commentary. Thank you, Walter, for sharing with us once again from your vast storehouse of biblical insight, wisdom, and evangelical zeal for the Church to hear afresh from Scripture the powerful message of who God is and who God's people are to be.

—Victor P. Hamilton
Professor of Religion
Asbury College
Wilmore, Kentucky

In these volumes, Brueggemann gives the reader the benefit of his many years of reflection on the issues of violence and power in relation to the Scriptures. He approaches the text with his characteristic attention to literary nuance and shading, treating it as a connected narrative and interpreting it as such. He does not leave the text as a dead artifact, but shows its intriguing connection to both the New Testament and the modern world.

—John N. Oswalt
Research Professor of Old Testament
Wesley Biblical Seminary
Jackson, Mississippi

Most of the preaching and teaching I've heard has been from the New Testament. I know Jesus and Paul pretty well. When I move into the Old Testament, I'm unsure of myself. I suspect a lot of people are like me.

Walter Brueggemann's commentary on 1 and 2 Kings does not presume I am an Old Testament scholar. He takes me by the hand and leads me through violence and intrigue, strange names and places, and a plot line that is hard to follow. In short, he makes sense of it. I can use that kind of help.

—Cecil E. Sherman
Professor of Pastoral Ministries
Baptist Theological Seminary at Richmond
Former Coordinator, Cooperative Baptist Fellowship
Former Pastor of churches in Texas, North Carolina,
Georgia, New Jersey

CONTENTS

2 KINGS

ABBREVIATIONS USED IN THIS COMMENTARY

Books of the Old Testament, Apocrypha, and New Testament are generally abbreviated in the Sidebars, parenthetical references, and notes according to the following system.

The Old Testament

Genesis	Gen
Exodus	Exod
Leviticus	Lev
Numbers	Num
Deuteronomy	Deut
Joshua	Josh
Judges	Judg
Ruth	Ruth
1–2 Samuel	1–2 Sam
1–2 Kings	1–2 Kgs
1–2 Chronicles	1–2 Chr
Ezra	Ezra
Nehemiah	Neh
Esther	Esth
Job	Job
Psalm (Psalms)	Ps (Pss)
Proverbs	Prov
Ecclesiastes	Eccl
or Qoheleth	Qoh
Song of Solomon	Song
or Song of Songs	Song
or Canticles	Cant
Isaiah	Isa
Jeremiah	Jer
Lamentations	Lam
Ezekiel	Ezek
Daniel	Dan
Hosea	Hos
Joel	Joel
Amos	Amos
Obadiah	Obad
Jonah	Jonah
Micah	Mic

Nahum	Nah
Habakkuk	Hab
Zephaniah	Zeph
Haggai	Hag
Zechariah	Zech
Malachi	Mal

The Apocrypha

1–2 Esdras	1–2 Esdr
Tobit	Tob
Judith	Jdt
Additions to Esther	Add Esth
Wisdom of Solomon	Wis
Ecclesiasticus or the Wisdom of Jesus Son of Sirach	Sir
Baruch	Bar
Epistle (or Letter) of Jeremiah	Ep Jer
Prayer of Azariah and the Song of the Three	Pr Azar
Daniel and Susanna	Sus
Daniel, Bel, and the Dragon	Bel
Prayer of Manasseh	Pr Man
1–2 Maccabees	1–2 Macc

The New Testament

Matthew	Matt
Mark	Mark
Luke	Luke
John	John
Acts	Acts
Romans	Rom
1–2 Corinthians	1–2 Cor
Galatians	Gal
Ephesians	Eph
Philippians	Phil
Colossians	Col
1–2 Thessalonians	1–2 Thess
1–2 Timothy	1–2 Tim
Titus	Titus
Philemon	Phlm
Hebrews	Heb
James	Jas
1–2 Peter	1–2 Pet
1–2–3 John	1–2–3 John
Jude	Jude
Revelation	Rev

Other commonly used abbreviations include:

BC	Before Christ
(also commonly referred to as BCE = Before the Common Era)	
AD	Anno Domini ("in the year of the Lord")
(also commonly referred to as CE = the Common Era)	
v.	verse
vv.	verses
C.	century
c.	*circa* (around "that time")
ed.	edition or edited by
trans.	translated by

Scholarly works cited by abbreviations include:

AB	*Anchor Bible*
ABD	*Anchor Bible Dictionary*
ANET	*Ancient Near Eastern Texts*
BZAW	Beiheft zur *Zeitshrift für die alttestamentliche Wissenschaft*
FRLANT	Forschungen zur Religion und Literatur des Alten und Neuen Testaments
ICC	International Critical Commentary
JBL	*Journal of Biblical Literature*
JSOT	*Journal for the Study of the Old Testament*
JSOTSup	Journal for the Study of the Old Testament— Supplemental Series
NIB	*New Interpreters Bible*
NRSV	*New Revised Standard Version* of the Bible
OBT	Overtures to Biblical Theology
OTL	Old Testament Library
TDOT	*Theological Dictionary of the Old Testament*
ZAW	*Zeitshrift für die alttestamentliche Wissenschaft*

AUTHOR'S PREFACE

In the preparation of this commentary, I have collected many debts. Above all, I am grateful to Fred Whitehurst who handled the complexities of the artwork in an able and persistent way. Tim Simpson helped prepare the final form of the manuscript, and the indefatigable Tempie Alexander, one more time, worked her magic of transformation over my work. I am grateful to my friend, Sam Balentine, who invited me to participate in the series, and to Scott Nash, who dealt with matters of manuscript preparation for the press. Beyond all of that, I am fortunate to be among colleagues and students who foster an environment for sustained reflection and writing.

Walter Brueggemann

SERIES PREFACE

The *Smyth & Helwys Bible Commentary* series is a visually stimulating and user-friendly series that is as close to multimedia as possible in print. Written by accomplished scholars with all students of Scripture in mind, the primary goal of the *Smyth & Helwys Bible Commentary* series is to make available serious, credible biblical scholarship in an accessible and less intimidating format.

Far too many Bible commentaries fall short of bridging the gap between the insights of biblical scholars and the needs of students of God's written word. In an unprecedented way, the *Smyth & Helwys Bible Commentary* series brings insightful commentary to bear on the lives of contemporary Christians. Using a multimedia format, the volumes employ a stunning array of art, photographs, maps, and drawings to illustrate the truths of the Bible for a visual generation of believers.

The *Smyth & Helwys Bible Commentary* series is built upon the idea that meaningful Bible study can occur when the insights of contemporary biblical scholars blend with sensitivity to the needs of lifelong students of Scripture. Some persons within local faith communities, however, struggle with potentially informative biblical scholarship for several reasons. Oftentimes, such scholarship is cast in technical language easily grasped by other scholars, but not by the general reader. For example, lengthy, technical discussions on every detail of a particular scriptural text can hinder the quest for a clear grasp of the whole. Also, the format for presenting scholarly insights has often been confusing to the general reader, rendering the work less than helpful. Unfortunately, responses to the hurdles of reading extensive commentaries have led some publishers to produce works for a general readership that merely skim the surface of the rich resources of biblical scholarship. A visual generation of believers deserves a commentary series that contains not only the all-important textual commentary on Scripture, but images, photographs, maps, works of fine art, and drawings that bring the text to life.

The *Smyth & Helwys Bible Commentary* makes serious, credible biblical scholarship more accessible to a wider audience. Writers and editors alike present information in ways that encourage readers to gain a better understanding of the Bible. The editorial board has worked to develop a format that is useful and usable, informative and pleasing to the eye. Our writers are reputable scholars who participate in the community of faith and sense a calling to communicate the results of their scholarship to their faith community.

The *Smyth & Helwys Bible Commentary* series addresses Christians and the larger Church. While both respect for and sensitivity to the needs and contributions of other faith communities is reflected in the work of the series authors, the authors speak primarily to Christians. Thus, the reader can note a confessional tone throughout the volumes. No particular "confession of faith" guides the authors, and diverse perspectives are observed in the various volumes. Each writer, though, brings to the biblical text the best scholarly tools available and expresses the results of their studies in commentary and visuals that assist readers seeking a word from the Lord for the Church.

To accomplish this goal, writers in this series have drawn from numerous streams in the rich tradition of biblical interpretation. The basic focus is the biblical text itself, and considerable attention is given to the wording and structure of texts. Each particular text, however, is also considered in the light of the entire canon of Christian Scriptures. Beyond this, attention is given to the cultural context of the biblical writings. Information from archaeology, ancient history, geography, comparative literature, history of religions, politics, sociology, and even economics is used to illuminate the culture of the people who produced the Bible. In addition, the writers have drawn from the history of interpretation not only as it is found in traditional commentary on the Bible but also in literature, theater, church history, and the visual arts. Finally, the *Commentary* on Scripture is joined with *Connections* to the world of the contemporary Church. Here again, the writers draw on scholarship in many fields as well as relevant issues in the popular culture.

This wealth of information might easily overwhelm a reader if not presented in a "user-friendly" format. Thus, the heavier discussions of detail and the treatments of other helpful topics are presented in special-interest boxes, or Sidebars, clearly connected to the passages under discussion so as not to interrupt the flow of the basic interpretation. The result is a commentary on Scripture that focuses on the theological significance of a text while also offering the reader a rich array of additional information related to the text and its interpretation.

An accompanying CD-ROM offers powerful searching and research tools. The commentary text, Sidebars, and visuals are all reproduced on a CD that is fully indexed and searchable. Pairing a text version with a digital resource is a distinctive feature of the *Smyth & Helwys Bible Commentary* series.

Combining credible biblical scholarship, user-friendly study features, and sensitivity to the needs of a visually-oriented generation of believers creates a unique and unprecedented type of commentary series. With insight from many of today's finest biblical scholars and a stunning visual format, it is our hope that the *Smyth & Helwys Bible Commentary* series will be a welcome addition to the personal libraries of all students of Scripture.

The Editors

HOW TO USE THIS COMMENTARY

The *Smyth & Helwys Bible Commentary* series is written by accomplished biblical scholars with a wide array of readers in mind. Whether engaged in the study of Scripture in a church setting or in a college or seminary classroom, all students of the Bible will find a number of useful features throughout the commentary that are helpful for interpreting the Bible.

Basic Design of the Volumes

Each volume features an Introduction to a particular book of the Bible, providing a brief guide to information that is necessary for reading and interpreting the text: the historical setting, literary design, and theological significance. Each Introduction also includes a comprehensive outline of the particular book under study.

Each chapter of the commentary investigates the text according to logical divisions in a particular book of the Bible. Sometimes these divisions follow the traditional chapter segmentation, while at other times the textual units consist of sections of chapters or portions of more than one chapter. The divisions reflect the literary structure of a book and offer a guide for selecting passages that are useful in preaching and teaching.

An accompanying CD-ROM offers powerful searching and research tools. The commentary text, Sidebars, and visuals are all reproduced on a CD that is fully indexed and searchable. Pairing a text version with a digital resource also allows unprecedented flexibility and freedom for the reader. Carry the text version to locations you most enjoy doing research while knowing that the CD offers a portable alternative for travel from the office, church, classroom, and your home.

Commentary and Connections

As each chapter explores a textual unit, the discussion centers around two basic sections: *Commentary* and *Connections*. The analysis of a passage, including the details of its language, the history reflected in the text, and the literary forms found in the text, are the main focus of the *Commentary* section. The primary concern of the *Commentary* section is to explore the theological issues presented by the Scripture passage. *Connections* presents potential applications of the insights provided in the *Commentary* section. The *Connections* portion of each chapter considers what issues are relevant for teaching and suggests useful methods and resources. *Connections* also identifies themes suitable for sermon planning and suggests helpful approaches for preaching on the Scripture text.

Sidebars

The *Smyth & Helwys Bible Commentary* series provides a unique hyperlink format that quickly guides the reader to additional insights. Since other more technical or supplementary information is vital for understanding a text and its implications, the volumes feature distinctive Sidebars, or special-interest boxes, that provide a wealth of information on such matters as:

- Historical information (such as chronological charts, lists of kings or rulers, maps, descriptions of monetary systems, descriptions of special groups, descriptions of archaeological sites or geographical settings).

- Graphic outlines of literary structure (including such items as poetry, chiasm, repetition, epistolary form).

- Definition or brief discussions of technical or theological terms and issues.

- Insightful quotations that are not integrated into the running text but are relevant to the passage under discussion.

- Notes on the history of interpretation (Augustine on the Good Samaritan, Luther on James, Stendahl on Romans, etc.).

- Line drawings, photographs, and other illustrations relevant for understanding the historical context or interpretive significance of the text.

- Presentation and discussion of works of fine art that have interpreted a Scripture passage.

Each Sidebar is printed in color and is referenced at the

appropriate place in the *Commentary* or *Connections* section with a color-coded title that directs the reader to the relevant Sidebar. In addition, helpful icons appear in the Sidebars and link to a word or phrase of the same color within the text. These hyperlinks provide the reader with visual cues to the type of material that is explained in each Sidebar. Throughout the commentary, these four distinct hyperlinks provide useful links in an easily recognizable design.

AΩ

Alpha & Omega Language

This icon identifies the information as a language-based tool that offers furthers exploration of the Scripture selection. This could include syntactical information, word studies, popular or additional uses of the word(s) in question, additional contexts in which the term appears, and the history of the term's translation. All foreign terms are transliterated into the appropriate English characters.

Culture/Context

This icon introduces further comment on contextual or cultural details that shed light on the Scripture selection. Describing the place and time to which a Scripture passage refers is often vital to the task of biblical interpretation. Sidebar items introduced with this icon could include geographical, historical, political, social, topographical, and economic information. Here, the reader may find an excerpt of an ancient text or inscription that sheds light on the text. Or, one may find a description of some element of ancient religion such as Baalism in Canaan or the Hero cult in the Mystery Religions of the Greco-Roman world.

Interpretation

Sidebars that appear under this icon serve a general interpretive function in terms of both historical and contemporary renderings. Under this heading, the reader might find a selection from classic or contemporary literature that illumines the Scripture text or a significant quotation from a famous sermon that addresses the passage. Insights are drawn from various sources, including literature, worship, theater, church history, and sociology.

Additional Resources Study

Here, the reader finds a convenient list of useful resources for further investigation of the selected Scripture text, including books, journals, Web sites, special collections, organizations, and societies. Specialized discussions of works not often associated with biblical studies may also appear here.

Additional Features

Each volume also includes a basic Bibliography on the biblical book under study. Other Bibliographies on selected issues are often included that point the reader to other helpful resources.

Notes at the end of each chapter provide full documentation of sources used and contain additional discussions of related matters.

Abbreviations used in each volume are explained in a List of Abbreviations found after the Table of Contents.

Readers of the *Smyth & Helwys Bible Commentary* series can regularly visit the Internet commentary support site for news, information, updates, and enhancements to the series at **<www.helwys.com/commentary>**.

Several thorough Indexes enable the reader to locate information quickly. These Indexes include:

- A *Sidebar Index* groups content from the special-interest boxes by category (maps, fine art, photographs, drawings, etc.).

- A *Scripture Index* lists citations to particular biblical texts.

- A *Topical Index* lists alphabetically the major subjects, names, topics, and locations referenced or discussed in the volume.

- A *Modern Authors Index* organizes contemporary authors whose works are cited in the volume.

INTRODUCTION

The books of First and Second Kings constitute the great "royal history" of Israel in the Old Testament. They trace the ups and downs of kingship all the way from the death of David (962) to the destruction of Jerusalem (587), with a brief addendum linked to the death of the Babylonian king Nebuchadnezzar in 562. I have used the term "royal history" to recognize at the outset that this literature is concerned with "royal" data, that is, the policies, actions, and destinies of the several rulers of these two ancient states. In such an ancient patriarchal-royal society, it is clear that the future of the state and all of its members is linked to and largely determined by the future of its kings.

The phrase "royal history," however, also includes the term "history." And, indeed, in Christian accounts of the Old Testament, these two books are regularly reckoned to be "history." No doubt these books form the most reliable timeline we have for the monarchy in these ancient states and articulate the primary shape of that ancient past through which this ancient community in two states is most commonly understood. Indeed, the timeline of this material has largely been adopted as normative, as we lack any alternative presentation. We have no better sustained data than is provided in these books. At the same time, to term this literature "history" in any modern sense of an accurate "factual" account of that past is widely recognized to be deeply problematic. Thus it is a difficult question to determine in any particular instance whether this "historical" report in the text is "factually" reliable. The problem in part is that the data is confusing and unclear and does not always confirm what we think we know from other, albeit sparse, sources. That is, taken as "history," the detail of this account is not consistently reliable.

The greater problem, however, is that the narrative does not intend to be "history" as we, in our modern modes, understand the term. This narrative is not and does not purport to be a "factual account" of the monarchial past. Rather consistently the narrative "footnotes" its text in order to alert readers who want detailed "history" that they can go to the "sources" to check out the facts. These "sources"—now lost to us—are often specified:

The Book of the Annals of the Kings of Judah (see 1 Kgs 15:7).
The Book of the Annals of the Kings of Israel (see 1 Kgs 16:20).

This narrative then is under no obligation to provide a full account of the "factual data," but assumes that the curious reader can check that out in the library.

Thus our text is not "history." It is, rather, an *interpretive commentary* upon that royal history or, as we might say, it is a "theology of history," an attempt to understand the vagaries of lived public experience in that world with particular reference to YHWH, the God of Israel. This God is seen to be an active and decisive player in this lived history. This narrator has no interest in "royal history" as it might be articulated without reference to YHWH, and indeed the narrator believes that such an account is nonsensical and meaningless precisely because YHWH is decisive at every turn. For that reason, in the Jewish order of books in the Hebrew Bible these books are among the "Former Prophets" (along with Joshua, Judges, and Samuel) and are not offered at all as "history."[1] Thus our text eschews any positivistic responsibility or option and wants to bear witness to the ways in which the God of Israel matters for the life and future of Israel.

Because these books are "prophecy" and not "history,"—that is, theological commentary and not factual reportage—it is important that we understand, as best we can, the perspective from which the theological interpretation is offered. We may identify four reference points in this interpretive perspective:

(1) The defining "fact" is that, in the end, the Holy City of *Jerusalem was destroyed* by an assault of the Babylonian armies. That is, the huge reality of this text—and of the entire Old Testament that cannot anywhere be avoided—is the ending of the city, the monarchy, and the temple. While Babylon is the proximate agent of that destruction, this interpretation presents Babylon (and Nebuchadnezzar, its ruler) as agents acting on behalf of Yahweh who wills that destruction of Yahweh's own holy city.

(2) The defining "fact" of the destruction of Jerusalem reminds us that the subject of this long narrative is finally Jerusalem, the people, the government, and the God who abides there. In addition to the obvious subject of the monarchy that inhabits the city (to which the northern regime has no legitimate access), the other core symbol of the city's holiness is *the Jerusalem temple*. The temple is crucial for the interpretive perspective of this narrative. At the end of the narrative we learn of the destruction of that temple (2 Kgs 24–25). At the beginning of the narrative, we have a long, careful report on its construction and dedication as a place of presence and forgiveness (1 Kgs 5-8). Between the glorious beginning of the temple and its pathos-filled ending, the temple—investing

the city with divine presence—is a major preoccupation of the narrative. Positively, we learn of temple reforms undertaken by pious Judean kings as a way to prize and enhance the temple for pure Yahwistic religion, thus replicating Solomon's major achievement. Negatively, we learn of several instances when foreign intruders rob the temple, thus anticipating its brutal end. The narrator pays considerable attention to the temple as an indicator of Yahweh's inclination toward the city.

(3) It is unmistakably evident, however, that the temple is a penultimate agenda for the narrator, for in the end, it is *Torah* that primarily occupies the interpretive energy of the narrative. The Torah—presumably the teaching tradition of Deuteronomy—is the norm and measure of what is good and evil in the public process. Indeed, 1 and 2 Kings are a Torah-focused assessment of the royal history. At the outset, the dying King David counsels his son Solomon to adhere to Torah:

> Be strong, be courageous, and keep the charge of the LORD your God, walking in his ways and keeping his statutes, his commandments, his ordinances, and his testimonies, as it is written in the law of Moses, so that you may prosper in all that you do and wherever you turn. Then the LORD will establish his word that he spoke concerning me: "If your heirs take heed to their way, to walk before me in faithfulness with all their heart and with all their soul, there shall not fail you a successor on the throne of Israel." (1 Kgs 2:2-4)

His son, however, is seen to be indifferent to Torah, is warned about land loss (9:6-9), and in the end is judged harshly as a Torah-violator (1 Kgs 11:1–11).

In complementary fashion, King Josiah at the end of the narrative is presented as the quintessential Torah-keeper who functions as an alternative to Solomon (2 Kgs 23:25). The narrator works his case about monarchy, temple, and city in order to insist that power finally is not the arbiter of public life. What counts is Torah obedience as the measure of prosperity or trouble. Thus Torah relativizes all the royal claims of dynasty and all the sacerdotal claims of the priesthood to make a determined claim about the true character of Israel's public history as the rule of Torah.

(4) In close connection to the Torah, this narrative account of royal history allots huge amounts of space to *the prophets* who are seen to be advocates of Torah requirements. When this literature is termed "latter prophets," it may mean that the material itself is "prophetic" in submitting real life to Torah criteria. It also means, however, that we expect the cast of characters in the royal history to

include prophets, as indeed it does. In the reign of Solomon, Ahijah the prophet brings the near-death warrant to Solomon (1 Kgs 11:31-34). An unnamed "man of God" delivers the initial judgment against the Northern Kingdom (1 Kgs 13). In the long central section of the books, the report is especially interested in the Omri dynasty in northern Israel—except that the long account of the Omri dynasty is in fact primarily concerned with the prophets who dominate the narrative. In the latter part of the books, the prophet Isaiah is pivotal for King Hezekiah (2 Kgs 19:20-34). Jeremiah, by contrast, is not visible in the same way at the end of the seventh century, but as my exposition will detail, the narrative account of the final days of Jerusalem is intimately linked to the tradition of the prophet Jeremiah.

All of this means that the reader of these books must not expect too much "royal history," but can watch as royal history is variously enhanced by the *temple*, critiqued by the *prophets*, and judged by the *Torah*. The clue to the whole is that Yahweh is the definitive actor in the public life of Israel; therefore all claims for *Realpolitik* are in fact provisional and penultimate.

The narrative is conventionally divided into three unequal parts. 1 Kings 1–11 narrates the reign of Solomon, marking his huge success, his singular achievement of the temple, and the serious Torah judgment lodged against him for his careless, disobedient self-indulgence.

1 Kings 12–2 Kings 17 is a long and fairly complex account of the two modest states of Israel and Judah, an account ending with the demise of the Northern state. This narrative account is distinguished in three principal ways. First, the narrative has adopted a complex scheme whereby the story line of the Northern and Southern governments are told in tandem, with periods of close interaction between the two and periods of hostility. Second, the two small states live in the real world of geopolitics; as a consequence these states are in turn under threat from the Syrian and Assyrian governments. The domiant feature of the demise of the Northern Kingdom is the presence of Assyria in whose path of ambition sits the capital city of Samaria. Third, this middle part of the books is dominated by prophetic figures—Elijah, Micaiah, and Elisha—so that in important ways, the kings are only context and setting for prophetic accounts. In any case, the Northern state is terminated, thus permitting a major interpretive marker in 2 Kings 17.

2 Kings 18–25 completes the account of the continuing state of Judah after the demise of the Northern state until the end in

587 BC (with the already mentioned addendum). The centerpiece of this section is "the Reform of Josiah" (2 Kgs 22–23) in which the king enacts Torah requirements for his realm in the face of heavy Torah sanctions (covenant curses). In this latter piece, the narrative apparently has opportunity, finally, to present a full-scale statement of the dominant interpretive agenda. That agenda is profoundly theological; thus the narrator has found a way in which to retell the public life of Israel and Judah, featuring Yahweh as the decisive factor, even in a world of menacing and unavoidable superpowers. Readers will do well to notice the interpretive angle of the piece and the artistic finesse whereby the interpretive agenda is brought to realization.

Finally, I should note that the chronology of the kings—even if in large part reliable—is complex and fractured in detail. I have elected to present two kinds of data for the royal chronology that are not compatible with each other in detail. First, in commenting on different kings, I have reported the length of years of rule as given in the text. Second, at the same time, I have situated each king according to a critical chronology.[2] In more than a few cases, it will be evident that the biblical and the critical numbers do not coincide. Both kinds of data are important, but it is not crucial for our purposes to reconcile them. Because the narrative is a sustained act of interpretation, the precise "facts" of chronology have no particular bearing on the account or its proposed meaning.

NOTES

[1]On the characteristic problem of the category of "history" for interpreting this material, see Yosef Hayim Yerushalmi, *Zakhor: Jewish History and Jewish Memory* (Seattle: University of Washington Press, 1982).

[2]I have chosen to follow the chronology utilized by John Bright, *A History of Israel*, 3rd ed. (Philadelphia: Westminster Press, 1981).

OUTLINE FOR 1 & 2 KINGS

1 KINGS

I. Solomon's Rise to Power, 1 Kings 1:1-53
    A. David as an Old Man, 1:1-4
    B. Solomon's Victory, 1:5-53

II. Solomon's Consolidation of Power, 1 Kings 2:1-46
    A. David's Divided Advice to His Son, 2:1-12
    B. Solomon's "Obedience" to His Father, 2:13-46

III. Beginnings as a Pious, Wise King, 1 Kings 3:1-28
    A. An Initial Tale of Legitimacy and Piety, 3:1-15
    B. Royal Wisdom Enacts Justice, 3:16-28

IV. Royal Impressiveness, 1 Kings 4:1-34
    A. An Emerging Bureaucracy, 4:1-6
    B. Internal Revenue Service in Jerusalem, 4:7-19
    C. Benefits of the Global Economy, 4:20-21
    D. Nothing Lacking, 4:22-28
    E. Royal Wisdom, 4:29-34

V. Temple Preparations, 1 Kings 5:1-18
    A. Solomon's Request, 5:1-6
    B. Hiram's Response, 5:7-12
    C. Solomon's Builders, 5:13-18

VI. Temple Construction, 1 Kings 6:1–7:51
    A. Building Solomon's Temple, 6:1-38
    B. Building Solomon's House, 7:1-12
    C. Furnishing the Temple, 7:13-51

VII. The Temple Dedicated and Made Operational, 1 Kings 8:1-66
    A. The Inaugural Procession and Anthem, 8:1-14
    B. Interpretive Commentary on Temple Significance, 8:15-26
    C. A Second, Different Wave of Significance, 8:27-53
    D. A Concluding Blessing, 8:54-66

VIII. An Interface of Theological Warning and Self-Congratulations
    1 Kings 9:1-28
    A. A Theological Notice, 9:1-9
    B. Achievements of an Impressive Kind, 9:10-28

IX. The Global Economist, 1 Kings 10:1-29
    A. The Visit of the Queen of Sheba, 10:1-13
    B. Solomon's Successes, 10:14-29

X. When the Chickens Come Home to Roost, 1 Kings 11:1-43
    A. The Theological Verdict, 11:1-13
    B. The Judgment Enacted, 11:14-43

XI. An Urgent Political Settlement, 1 Kings 12:1-33
    A. Failed Negotiations, 12:1-19
    B. Accommodating New Realities, 12:20-33

XII. Ominous Prophetic Inscrutability, 1 Kings 13:1-34
    A. A Sign Against Bethel from Judah, 13:1-10
    B. A Countervoice from Bethel, 13:11-19
    C. An Obedient, Devouring Lion, 13:20-25
    D. A Judgment Confirmed, 13:26-34

XIII. Rival Kings, in Failure and in Death, 1 Kings 14:1-31
    A. The Death and Judgment of Jeroboam, 14:1-20
    B. The End of Rehoboam, 14:21-31

XIV. A Series of Undistinguished Monarchs, 1 Kings 15:1-32
    A. The Short Career of Abijam, 15:1-8
    B. Asa, a Long Reign, a Short Narrative, 15:9-24
    C. Nadab for Two Years, 15:25-32

XV. Northern Upheavals, 1 Kings 15:33–16:34
    A. Baasha Gone Quickly, 15:33–16:7
    B. Elah Murdered after Two Years, 16:8-14
    C. Zimri, Defined by Violence, 16:15-20
    D. Omri the Winner, 16:21-28
    E. Ahab, Son of Omri, 16:29-34

XVI. Elijah, Man of Power for Life, 1 Kings 17:1-24
    A. Wilderness Beginnings, 17:1-7
    B. Life for Widow and Orphan, 17:8-16
    C. New Power for Life, 17:17-24

XVII. Troubler of Israel, 1 Kings 18:1-46
    A. Preparation for Life and Death Struggle, 18:1-19
    B. No More Limping on Two Opinions, 18:20-40
    C. The Triumph of Rain, 18:41-46

XVIII. Letdown and Revival, 1 Kings 19:1-21
    A. A Wanted Man, 19:1-3
    B. Despair and a Ministering Angel, 19:4-10
    C. New Confrontation, New Commission, 19:11-18
    D. Elisha Recruited, 19:19-21

XIX. War, Diplomacy, and Prophetic Zeal, 1 Kings 20:1-43
    A. Diplomacy and Posturing, 20:1-12
    B. A First Victory, 20:13-21
    C. A Second Victory, 20:22-30
    D. A Royal Exemption, 20:31-34
    E. A Prophetic Assault, 20:35-43

XX. A Clash over Land, 1 Kings 21:1-29
    A. Naboth against the Crown, 21:1-16
    B. Prophetic Judgment on Land-Grabbing Royalty, 21:17-29

XXI. Ahab's Last Venture, 1 Kings 22:1-53
    C. Prophetic Intervention against Royal Plans, 22:1-28
    D. Military Implementation of Prophetic Verdict, 22:29-40
    E. The Good King Jehoshaphat, 22:41-50
    F. The Quick Reign of Ahaziah, 22:51-53

2 KINGS

I. Once More, King over Prophet, 2 Kings 1:1-18
    A. The Initial Prophetic Sentence, 1:2-4
    B. The Drama of Confrontation, 1:5-16
    C. The Word Enacted, 1:17-18

II. A Transition in Prophetic Authority, 2 Kings 2:1-25
    A. Preparatory Interaction, 2:1-8
    B. The Ascension, 2:9-12
    C. The Newly Authorized Prophet, 2:13-25

1 KINGS

SOLOMON'S RISE TO POWER

1 Kings 1:1-53

AN INTRODUCTION TO 1 KINGS 1–11

These chapters begin with an account of David's death. That death is important for the characterization of the brutal way in which Solomon came to royal power. The chapters summarize the reign of Solomon. They artistically hold together an account of his economic success as judged by conventional political standards and an ominous critique of Solomon's disregard for Torah that evokes heavy and enduring judgment. In a general way, the narrative is organized with the positive materials in chapters 3–4 under the rubric, "Solomon loved Yahweh" (3:3) and the negative parts in chapters 9–11 under the rubric, "Solomon loved many foreign women" (11:1). Between these two stand chapters 5–7 concerning the construction of the temple, culminating in the dedication of chapter 8. In the judgment of this narrative, Solomon is quite a mixed bag of worldly success and Torah failure.

COMMENTARY

David as an Old Man, 1:1-4

As the books of Kings begin, David is "old and advanced in years" (1:1), then "very old" (1:15). The books of Kings begin with the demise and death of David and the struggle for the throne. The books of Samuel are dominated by David. He is there a wily, ruthless, blessed man of God. The story of his rise to power is saturated with violence, culminating in a series of "necessary and convenient" deaths (2 Sam 2-4). Because his reign is scarred by violence, it does not surprise us that this chapter about demise and succession is permeated with an undercurrent of violence. The old king is surrounded by ambitious sons and advisors, each of whom seeks advantage. The narrative, in subtle and understated ways, lets us see the workings of aggressive power cloaked in all the niceties of royal protocol.

The beginning point is David's failure (1:1-4). He has been a powerful, virile force, unafraid of violence, no stranger to the manipulation of sexual politics (see 1 Sam 25:42-44). But now "he could not get warm." We might take the phrase as a hint of poor circulation, except the antidote to his problem is a "very beautiful" young virgin. Her presence in the narrative (and in the king's bed) is not simply as a hot water bottle. Her role rather is to arouse the king sexually. Because of the last phrase of v. 4, "did not know her sexually," it is probable that "not get warm" means not to have an erection. Thus the point of the opening paragraph is to report the king's sexual impotence, his loss of virility, and therefore his disqualification as king. The end of David's virility, tested by a very "beautiful young virgin," opens the way for the following narrative, for there is now a functional vacancy on the throne. One senses the vultures around the court, circling for the kill.

Solomon's Victory, 1:5-53

There are, so the story runs, two candidates for successor to David, each with determined supporters in the court. [Parties to the Conflict] One candidate is Adonijah who takes aggressive action to seize the throne (1:5-10). He seems a plausible candidate for kingship. He is very handsome, a trait that runs in the family (1:6; see 1 Sam 16:12; 2 Sam 14:25). He looks like a king! Moreover, he is next in birth order to the tragic Absalom (see 2 Sam 3:3-4) and so has a

Parties to the Conflict

Clearly the competition for the throne between Adonijah and Solomon is not simply a personal rivalry, though it is surely that. Rather each of these sons of David is surrounded by a palace entourage that is jealously supportive of its candidate and for each member. A great deal is at stake professionally and personally. The adherents to Adonijah apparently are the established "ins." But more than that, they are likely the theological conservatives who take more seriously the old covenantal traditions. Conversely, the followers of Solomon are more likely those who want to see royal policies of a more "developmental" kind that will move Israel more into international trade and prosperity, a move that also implies important theological accommodations. Thus the dispute is a *policy* dispute expressed as a *leadership* struggle.

The party of Adonijah:

Joab, the military man;
(2 Sam 3:23-39; 11:14-25; 18:9-19:8)

Abiathar, the priest
(1 Sam 22:20, 2 Sam 15:24-29)

The party of Solomon:

Benaiah, the military man;
(2 Sam 8:18; 20:23)

Zadok, the priest;
(2 Sam 8:17; 15:24- 37)

Nathan, the prophet.
(2 Sam 7:1-16; 12:1-15, 24-25)

In this sketch, Nathan does not appear as a prophet of the Lord. Though it has not been confirmed as to which meeting with David this sketch refers, here Nathan is markedly different in his demeanor in meeting with David as compared to their meeting on the aftermath of Uriah's death. On this occassion, he is shown humble and "deferential" before David, perhaps very aware of the importance of political timing. They are both couched in the bleariness of old age which is captured so succinctly by Rembrandt with his use of a variety of line techniques ranging from parallel strokes, bold outlines, and light and dark contrasts. Rembrandt was intrigued by the aging countenance as seen in many of his works, i.e., the *Mother as a Prophetess*, the self-portraits, and numerous biblical illustrations.

Rembrandt van Rijn. *Nathan before King David*. 17th century. Pen and brush drawing. Kupferstichkabinett, Staatliche Museen, Berlin, Germany. (Credit: Foto Marburg/Art Resource, NY)

---

legitimate claim to the throne (see 1 Kgs 2:22). Indeed, his actions echo the royal pretensions of his brother Absalom (2 Sam 15:1-7): (a) he gathers for himself a showy royal entourage (1:5); (b) he engages in quite extravagant ritual activity (1:9); (c) he hosts a banquet for the royal family. These are all actions designed to evoke support for his candidacy. He seems to have learned nothing from his failed brother Absalom, for like him, he asserted himself without reckoning with the still formidable power of David to make or break his ambitious sons.

The narrative puts us immediately on notice of trouble to come. The would-be successor to David consults with two deeply established forces in the Jerusalem power structure, Joab, David's military chief of staff, and Abiathar, one of David's primary priests

(1:7). The two are leaders of the old guard. But ominously, he lacked the support of the other primary priest (Zadok), the number two military man (Benaiah), the prophet Nathan (who has no counterpart in his company), and the palace guard ("David's own warriors"). From the outset it is clear that Adonijah has impressive resistance. The roster of resisters in v. 8, however, is intensified in the brief note of v. 10: "He did not invite…his brother Solomon." This is the first mention of Solomon since the birth note of 2 Samuel 12:24-25. He has been kept in abeyance all this time by the narrator.

The plot of succession takes on poignancy with the narrative account of David's resistance to Adonijah (1:11-37). This narrative relates a carefully choreographed strategy by which David, apparently now feeble and easily manipulated, is recruited as the decisive legitimator of Solomon, the second candidate for the throne and Adonijah's serious rival. As we read on, it is clear that the impulsive efforts of Adonijah were rash and without the careful plotting needed in such a court dense with cunning. The role of the old king in securing the throne for Solomon is offered in five scenes (1:11-37).

Scene 1 (1:11-14). Nathan takes the initiative. This is the same Nathan who pronounced the decisive oracle legitimating David and "your offspring after you" (2 Sam 7:12), the one shrewd enough to confront and condemn David (2 Sam 12:1-15), and the one present at the naming of Solomon (2 Sam 12:24-25). He has heard of Adonijah's coup and takes immediate steps to counter it. He recruits Bathsheba, mother of Solomon, as his foremost ally in intrigue. His urging to her suggests that if Adonijah's claim to the throne succeeds, Solomon will lose not only the throne. As primary rival, his life will be in jeopardy; such is the ruthlessness of royal aggression. Nathan gives Bathsheba her lines to speak to David; he scripts the entire scenario. His words in her mouth are to be put to David in pretend-innocence: "Did you not?…" The form of a question is subtle, for in fact it implies that David had made a promise to Bathsheba which, so far as the narrative goes, David had not uttered. That is, the leading question introduces to David something hoped for but never promised.

Scene 2 (1:15-21). Bathsheba performs her role dutifully as instructed by Nathan. She goes to David, into the very room where David is now with the "very beautiful young virgin." The meeting is perhaps a grating one for Bathsheba, to see the virgin now occupying her place.

For whatever reason, she modifies the lines Nathan had given her. Now it is not, "Did you not?..." as in v. 13, but "You swore..." The question has become a fact. The ruthless mother generates new political reality. [The Queen Mother Petitions] The alleged oath of David to Bathsheba now becomes the premise for the rest of the story. According to the "revised version," Solomon is designated, but "now suddenly..." (1:18) Adonijah's preemptive acts are characterized with particular notice of the exclusion of Solomon (see v. 10). In v. 20, Bathsheba puts it squarely to David: David must act promptly and decisively and for Solomon...or Solomon and his mother will be "offenders," that is, enemies of the new king whose lives are endangered (see v. 12). The speech of Bathsheba is a daring and imaginative one, creating a political crisis from which David can extricate himself in only one way, for he dare not renege on his vow!

> **The Queen Mother Petitions**
> As we will see more clearly in 1 Kgs 2, Bathsheba will occupy the powerful office of "queen mother" with great aplomb. In this narrative, however, she is not yet queen mother. She is only the vigorous advocate for her son who is top candidate for king. And while she will soon be "elevated" in power and prestige, here she is only a suppliant. The narrative presents her as a humble petitioner, perhaps on her knees before the king.

Scene 3 (1:22-27). On cue, Nathan intrudes in order to support Bathsheba's urging, as planned in v. 14. Whereas Bathsheba had moved Nathan's ploy of two questions to an indicative in v. 17, Nathan returns to a mode of questioning that is more deferential, less risky. Nathan recites for the king, as Bathsheba has just done, the aggressive acts of Adonijah. But his recital is framed in vv. 24 and 27 by two questions. The questions suggest a reprimand to the king, not a reprimand about what the king ostensibly has done, but a scolding that David allegedly has acted without telling Nathan. The prophet subtly shames the king for acting without his counsel; Nathan's tone is as if the prophet believes David has indeed authorized Adonijah, even though Nathan knows better.

Scene 4 (1:28-31). The feeble king has now been effectively assaulted on two fronts, by Bathsheba whose indicative holds the king to an oath neither he nor the narrator can remember and by the soft reprimand of Nathan who shoves the king away from Adonijah and toward Solomon. The double strategy works. David is now resolute. He addresses Bathsheba and promises to act on his vow that he had not remembered but now remembers clearly and with great determination. David—reminded and reprimanded—is still the key player, still master of his own house, still capable of an act of great authority. Bathsheba's concluding response in v. 31 is perhaps ironic. On the face of it, it is a conventional court formula. In this context, however, she can see that the king is dying; she is

In this depiction, the trumpets call attention to the anointing of an individual, framed more by personality and the royal moment than by the power of collective ritual and the sacramental act of anointing.

Julius Schnoor von Carolsfeld. *Solomon Named to Succeed David*. 19th century. Woodcut. from *Das Buch der Bucher in Bilden*. (Credit: Dover Pictorial Archive Series)

ready to have him die with the new Solomonic legitimacy in hand. Thus her wish that the king "live forever" is less than earnest.

Scene 5 (1:32-37). All that remains to be done is royal drama. David summons "the other side" to create "the other king." Zadok and Benaiah, leaders of the high court party, are to do the deed. David knows the power and cruciality of royal theater. Solomon is to ride "my own mule," to be seen in the king's limo, like arriving on "Air Force One." The new king is to arrive at the river Gihon, perhaps the same source of water for Jerusalem where life-and-death political decisions are enacted. There the "churchy types," the ones in Yahwistic roles—priest and prophet—are to administer the sacramental oil of anointing, even as David had long ago received Yahweh's designation by oil (1 Sam 16:13). The sacramental act is to be matched by public drama: trumpets, acclamation, royal procession, enthronement. David knows how to make a king! In the end, "I have designated." David's nod is decisive. This is David's throne, and he will assign it as he chooses.

The end of the drama gives the last word to Benaiah who is now about to replace Joab as top military man (1:36-37). The military man sounds the name of Yahweh. The military man dares to expect that Yahweh will "ordain" what palace intrigue has evoked and what the duped David has enacted. Moreover, the military man

---

AΩ Royal Sacramental Theater

The act of anointing as a visible, observable act is simple and unexpressive. It consists simply of putting oil on the head of someone. It may be that originally anointing was taken to be an act of *healing*. But then it also became an act of *empowerment*.

But what is important is not simply the act of oil, but the *sacramental* understanding of the act whereby it was trusted that something *theologically effective* is done that decisively impinges upon the recipient of the oil. In this regard, the act is like every sacramental act: it bears powerful significance only for those who trust the act and read out of it symbolic, effective power.

We may imagine that such anointing has two intertwined dimensions. On the one hand, it is taken as a *deeply freighted theological act*. Thus it is understood that with the *oil* comes the *spirit*, that is, the "force of God," to do important things and the authority to enact them. This theological enactment is powerful even if it is done in secret or in private, as with the young boy David (1 Sam 16:12-13). But the deeply theological act comes readily to be understood as *royal theater*, that is, a public relations device to make visible power and authority that is to be received by the king. While such a theatrical performance of course can be manipulated and cynical, at its best the visible drama of the act and its theological significance cannot be separated from each other.

The verb "anoint" is in Hebrew *mashah* This is no special theological term, but simply means to "smear." Characteristically the Old Testament has no special, privileged theological vocabulary, but uses ordinary words that take on special meanings. The verb simply mean "to apply oil." But the same Hebrew term is used as a noun (*mashah*), "the one anointed," that is, designated and empowered. When the proper vowels for the noun are supplied, the term is "messiah," the one anointed. But one must be clear that in its early narrative use, the noun only refers to the king (or later the priest) who is designated for office. Although the term indicates entry into special power, it does not carry any very heavy theological overtone. Only slowly and belatedly, the noun "messiah" (anointed) came to have theological, anticipatory significance, so that the "messiah" is the one anointed who will eventually come to enact God's will on earth. But the thick, theological dimension is not yet present in our text.

For Christians, it is important to recognize that the noun "messiah," derived from the verb *mashah*, translated into the Greek as "Christ." That is, Christ is the one empowered by special oil. In older traditions, there could be many messiahs (even a Persian one in Isa 45:1), who were empowered to do God's will in the earth, and only late does the term develop into exclusive particularity as "the (one) Messiah," that is, the Christ. Our text evidences an early usage that precedes the development of the term so common in later Christian usage.

The term is used for a variety of kings in the Old Testament, including the non-Israelite king, Hazael, in 2 Kings 9:15-16:

Royal anointings:

The anointed king in anticipation (1 Sam 2:10).

Saul (1 Sam 9:16; 10:1; 15:1, 17; 24:6, 10; 26:9, 11, 16, 23; 2 Sam 1:14, 16).

David (1 Sam 16:12-13; 2 Sam 2:4, 7; 5:3, 17; 12:7; 19:21).

Solomon (1 Kgs 1:34, 39, 45; 5:1).

Hazael (1 Kgs 19:15-16).

Jehu (2 Kgs 9:3, 6, 12).

Joash (2 Kgs 11:12).

Jehoahaz (2 Kgs 23:30).

Solomon in the Midst of Adonijah

Narrative arrangements in the Old Testament are characteristically done with sensitivity and shrewd design, and never by accident. In the present case, it is clear that the narrative about Solomon in vv. 11-40 is the decisively important part of the narrative. It begins with the intrigue of Nathan and Bathsheba in v. 11 and it concludes with the public acclamation of the new king in vv. 39-40.

But the dramatic tension of the narrative depends upon the Solomonic account of anointing being situated in the midst of the Adonijah narrative. In vv. 5-10 Adonijah assertively takes the initiative toward the throne, and in vv. 41-53 Adonijah

must deal with the fearful residue of Solomon's achievement. From the perspective of Adonijah's party, Solomon interrupts the story of Adonijah. From Solmonic perspective, however, the true account of anointing is surrounded by an upstart who must be overcome, intimidated, and squelched. The juxtaposition of narrative sections makes the tension keen, until it is resolved into the exaltation of Solomon and the humiliation of Adonijah:

    a vv. 5-10 Adonijah
      b vv. 11-40 Solomon
    a' vv. 41-53 Adonijah.

---

dreams of expansion (military?) so that Solomon's throne will outdo David. We do not know, of course, if Benaiah's blessing is to be taken at face value, or if it is ironic. The subtlety of this manipulative drama suggests that none of the words by any of the speakers is quite what it appears to be.

The narrative legitimacy of vv. 11-37 is quickly enacted in vv. 38-40. Everything goes as planned. The principle players are, again, Zadok, Nathan, and Benaiah. They occupy the royal role. They arrive at the river of royal drama. Zadok administers the oil and so creates a "messiah" (1:39). [Royal Sacramental Theater] The trumpets are blown; Solomon is acclaimed king, as per David's instructions. The account mentions one other presence, "Cherethites and Pelethites," "David's own warriors" (see 1:8). They are the hired mercenaries who supply the muscle for the throne as popular support ebbs. The whole is an in-house drama. The public ritual dramatizes the agreements made in private.

The people come late to the deal and the narrative does not pretend otherwise (1:39-40). The public celebration is enormous; perhaps the public is easily managed by royal drama. Perhaps there really was devotion to the new king, though that seems improbable. Perhaps the public is so devoted to the old king that his designation is enough. In any case, the public has no voice in what has been enacted.

The anointing of Solomon constitutes the central material of this chapter. It is, however, framed by an Adonijah narrative. [Solomon in the Midst of Adonijah] Before the Solomonic episode, we have seen Adonijah's self-assertion (1:5-10). Now, in the wake of Solomon's enthronement, we return to Adonijah (1:41-53). First there is the public report to the king's sons (1:41-48). The party is still going on from v. 9. Now the revelry is decisively interrupted. The son of Abiathar, one of Adonijah's stalwarts, brings the news. Jonathan is expected to bring "good news" (gospel; v. 42). But the news is not good. He reports in detail the drama of Solomon (1:43-48). He names the principles of Solomon's enterprise, names surely capable of evoking fear; he mentions the royal role; he characterizes the sacramental act of anointing. He summarizes the public acclaim. The narrative is skillful in reiterating in familiar detail and sequence the decisive turn of affairs. The entire process is sanctioned by David who, in the feebleness of his bedridden state, provides a Yahwistic endorsement of it all (1:48). Nathan's question is answered. Bathsheba's alleged vow from David is enacted. Jerusalem's throne is redeployed. It is a done deal.

The public report is followed by a response of profound fear (1:49-53). The crowd disperses frantically (1:49). Nobody wants to be seen in public with Adonijah. But the narrator is not interested in the crowd. The object of attention is Adonijah. Earlier it had been acknowledged that if Adonijah won, Solomon and his mother are dead ducks (1:12, 21). Now the shoe is on the other foot. Adonijah is now the one in mortal danger. He flees to the altar as a place of sanctuary. [Solomon on the Horns of a Dilemma] Solomon promises a "safe conduct" for

Solomon on the Horns of a Dilemma

The altar of Israel in the pre-temple period was perhaps not much developed, as it was to be later under Solomon. It was, nonetheless, a place of sanctuary, a place to be safe and protected from any who would hurt or kill. "The horns of the altar" refers to a construction whereby at the corner of the altar, horns protruded. Archaeologists have found such altars, for example at Megiddo. The "horns" were a place to "grab on," as a source of physical connection to the security of the altar.

While Adonijah held to the horns, it is Solomon who faces a dilemma. Either he may respect the place of sanctuary and so let Adonijah live, who will surely be a continuing threat to him. Or he can violate the holy sanctuary and seize his competitor and dispose of him. Neither is a good choice. For the moment, Solomon manages to circumvent his dilemma. But only for the moment. It will not take long, in the second chapter, before Adonijah is dispatched (2:25), and Solomon has no more dilemma. This king, like every king, must deal with such dilemmas promptly and ruthlessly. But that is, in this narrative, deferred.

Horned altars have been discovered at many Iron Age sites in Israel and were prevalent in biblical accounts. The Meggido stratum in which this altar was found was characterized by large public structures and is generally thought to have been built by King Solomon. It included a four-entryway gate and a well-built double wall.

Four-Horned Incense Altar. Palestine. Megiddo, Stratum VA-IVB. Iron Age IIA, 10th century BC. Limestone. Height 67.5 cm. University of Chicago. Excavated by the Oriental Institute, 1926. Chicago, Illinois. (Credit: Courtesy of the Oriental Institute of the University of Chicago)

his brother that is hedged by a harsh, demanding condition: "*if* he is worthy." That is, if he is completely loyal to Solomon and is no longer a rival and threat. Adonijah has no option. He knuckles under to the new king. He swears allegiance and is tersely dispatched out of court. Solomon is the winner in the deathly contest. David has willed it; Yahweh has blessed it; the military has guaranteed it. Judah has a new king; the throne is now assigned by choreographed intrigue, sacramental acts that smack of cynicism, and guaranteeing military power. We are ready for the story of "the kings" to unfold. Adonijah has "gone home."

CONNECTIONS

The beginning chapter of the books of Kings already plunges us into the most interesting and most difficult issue faced in this account of Israel's monarchy: the interplay of *raw, crude politics* and the insistence that this particular history is *an arena for God's purposes*. It is not easy to hold together in tension raw, crude politics and the sense of God's purposes, but this narrative is agile and subtle in doing just that.

The primary story line of the chapter is readily governed by the practice of politics that is calculating, manipulative, and at the brink of violence. Awareness of these features in the narrative makes clear that biblical faith—especially royal faith—takes place in the real world where the stakes are high and players will go to great lengths and run great risks to acquire their goals. The Bible has too often been treated and read as a sweet story of men and women of faith acting in the world according to their faith. In reality, however, things are much more complicated. One of the hallmarks of the Bible is that its primary characters are men and women who face reality and live as best they can. They pay some attention to the claims of faith but at the same time are quite unromantic about the dangers, threats, and options that are grounded concretely. We may notice in this chapter three aspects of such raw, crude politics.

1. The political life of the royal court in Jerusalem is deeply disputed, as the court is divided in its leadership into clear factions. We are accustomed in the Bible (as in the neat royal history of Great Britain, for example) to recite the time line of monarchs as though they are easily and obviously one after another. But the time line is only a thin summary of winners, behind which, in detailed narrative, are the messy realities of struggle and rivalry.

On Political Sex

David, a military man as well as a political leader, is well schooled in the practice of exploitative sex. I have commented elsewhere on "military sex" in relation to David in 2 Samuel 11:

The immediate context of military culture, moreover, is sustained by a larger context of greed and exploitation, brutality and economic promiscuity that is without neighborliness, a culture into which we are all more or less inducted. David, Uriah, and Joab are not actors in a vacuum, but participants in a military culture that the narrator lets us see.

Walter Brueggemann, "Abuse of Command," *Sojourners* 26/4 (July-August, 1997): 24.

In this narrative, the factions are clear, with the Adonijah party perhaps representing the old tribal conservatism and the Solomonic party, led by Nathan, an ambitious coalition of those eager for "social development" and public advance. Clear to all parties, moreover, is that a struggle to control the future is a serious one in which playing for keeps is the name of the game. The dispute is partly a struggle between persons who lust for power. But the two parties also embody important ideological commitments that involve more than simply personal ambition.

2. The entry point of the narrative suggests that this politics is never far from sexuality. [On Political Sex] Politics and sexuality, in a macho society, represent twin possibilities for domination. It is evident in vv. 1-4 that we are here into the "politics of virility." David had been, in his long life, no stranger to virility of a crude kind, as we are told in terms of his readiness to "take" the wife of Nabal (1 Sam 25:39-44), and more notably the wife of Uriah the Hittite (2 Sam 11–12). Moreover, the tale of Amnon his son in 2 Samuel 13–14 and the report of the eagerness of Absalom, his rebellious son, to seize his father's concubines indicate that a part of royal legitimacy is the endless demonstration of a capacity for macho domination (2 Sam 16:20-22).

It is this history and aura of domination that make the David of vv. 1-4 so pitiful. Indeed, his "failure to get warm" evokes the savage contest among his sons to see which son will replace the failed father.

Attentiveness to such a theme permits an important link, in our own time and place, to our own "politics of virility" as we are beset with the sexual exploits of public leaders, or as we learn increasingly about the endless exploitation of "military sexuality," or as we notice professional sports that trade in virility complete with "cheer leaders." All such marketing of sexuality is in the interest of domination, as it was in that ancient society.

3. Beyond partisan dispute and the politics of virility, however, we notice that the struggle for succession is close to the edge of violence in a sustained way. Reading this text is not unlike watching the film *The Godfather*. The ominous music that accompanies the film means to suggest that violence can break out at any moment. This chapter should be read with a background of such ominous music.

In the narrative observe that if Adonijah wins, the lives of Bathsheba and Solomon are jeopardized (1:12, 21). On the other hand and more importantly, we are privileged to witness a scene of deep anxiety among the party of Adonijah when Solomon's coup is announced. The guests "tremble" and flee (1:49). Adonijah, moreover, flees to the safety of the sanctuary (1:50). Nobody among the losers is safe! It is as though all parties accept that their lives will be exterminated if they do not prevail. This story turns upon the near threat of violence, neither the first nor the last time the shape of public life is rooted in violence.

The plot line moves through partisanship, virility, and the deep threat of violence, soon to be enacted. We do not read this text for the sake of these accents. We read, rather, because we take this text in some definitive way as *scripture*, as revelatory of God's ways in the world, as God moves in and through and beyond the violence and virility.

As suggested by this illustration from *The Godfather* movie, the calm of hushed communication and scheming was often a prelude to unspoken violence and power clash.
(Credit: Barclay Burns. Graphite illustration.)

This chapter, taken by itself, does not give us much to go on. In Bathsheba's cunning suggestion (1:17) and in David's trusting, bewitched response (1:30), it is as though Solomon receives the throne on the basis of an oath in the name of Yahweh, the God of Israel. As we have seen, however, such a claim is not very secure. Beyond that, all we have is the affirmation of Benaiah, the military officer with most to gain (1:36-37), and the utterance of the feeble David that echoes the dynastic promise of 2 Samuel 7 (1:48). These are thin claims. Nevertheless they suggest that the players themselves, or the players as offered by the narrative, understand that there is more to the tale than crude self-promotion. Another purpose is at work here, perhaps larger than all of the manipulation. The narrative itself barely provides grounds for such a claim, but it is a claim deeply held by the faithful who always find clues to God at work in our lived world. Most to be noticed, I submit, is the thinness of the evidence and the daring quality of the theological claim.

Beyond that, we may notice two specific features of the story. First, David commands *the anointing* that is implemented by Zadok the priest (1:34, 39). The notion of anointing—sacramental designation by the pouring on of oil—is a very special act in biblical faith. Anointing is reckoned in 2 Kings 9:12 as a dangerous, subversive, revolutionary act that evokes political activity. In our context, such an act recalls the personal designation of David who, by anointing, is filled with power and given a future that culminates in kingship (1 Sam 16:13). For Christians, of course, the verb "anoint" (*mashah*) becomes the noun "messiah" that in the Greek is "Christ." And so we dare conclude that in the midst of these raw acts of politics, we are set toward the messiah of Bethlehem and Nazareth. It is a stretch of interpretation but one long made in Christian reading.

Finally, we pay attention to "Solomon" who is here no major actor, but a passive recipient of events. He is the beloved of Yahweh (2 Sam 12:24-25), as though predestined for rule. He is "great David's greater son" (see v. 37). As we shall see, there is something ironic about his name (Solomon=*shalom* "peace"), for his ways of governance are rooted in violence scarcely linked to *shalom*. A Christian reading, nevertheless, takes this Solomon as a link in the coming of great David's greater son who will indeed bring shalom. Such a reading is made in faith, but it does not deny or nullify the realism of the narrative.

SOLOMON'S CONSOLIDATION OF POWER

1 Kings 2:1-46

This extended chapter marks the transition of power from father David to son Solomon, reporting David's death and Solomon's ruthless consolidation of royal power. The chapter divides into *David's speech* of counsel to his son (2:1-9) and *Solomon's actions* that only partly correspond to David's counsel (2:13-46), between which is the terse notice of David's death (2:10-11).

COMMENTARY

David's Divided Advice to His Son, 2:1-12

David's speech is a characteristic farewell address placed on the lips of a dying person, a speech that is a legacy remembered and treasured (2:1-9; compare the farewell speech of Samuel, 1 Sam 12:1-25). The most interesting aspect of this speech on the lips of the old king is the clear incongruity between vv. 1-4 and vv. 5-9. In vv. 1-4, David's speech is a presentation of Torah theology reflective of the book of Deuteronomy. [Deuteronomic Theology] The opening imperatives of vv. 2-3 echo the imperatives given to Joshua in Joshua 1:6-7. The phrasing appears to be military, but it is used to urge devotion to the Torah as the explicit will of Yahweh. The charge speaks of the "Torah of Moses," likely referring to the book of Deuteronomy. The little

---

Deuteronomic Theology

A dominant assumption of many biblical interpreters is that the entire history of Israel from the land-entry in Joshua 1 to the exile in 2 Kings 25 constitutes one long, coherent account of Israel's life in the land. That history—comprising the books of Joshua, Judges, Samuel, and Kings—is governed by theological-interpretive assumptions derived for the book of Deuteronomy. Thus the whole is called "Deuteronomic Theology." This interpretive account of Israel's past is evident in these texts, partly by the way the material is juxtaposed and arranged, partly by the insertion of key interpretive statements of which 2:1-4 is a primary example.

These kinds of texts—that we will have occasion to identify throughout 1 and 2 Kings—are infused with "Torah theology." That is, the texts affirm that prosperity or adversity in the life of Israel is directly determined by whether or not Israel (and its kings) obey the Torah of Moses. In our text David echoes this theology in order to say that everything for Solomon's future depends upon Torah obedience. The long-term estimate of this history is that Israel's life, overall, is one of disobedience; and therefore exile is its inescapable outcome. The books of 1 and 2 Kings are the slow telling of the tale of Israel that culminates in exile as a consequence of Torah violation.

For further study, an excellent resource is Terence E. Fretheim, *Deuteronomic History* (Nashville: Abingdon, 1983).

connecting phrase "so that" links *obedience to Torah* and *prosperity*. This tradition teaches that obedience to Torah is the requirement and condition that makes prosperity possible.

In v. 4, the conditional quality of the royal promise is intensified by the word "if." [The "If" of Faith] This is an exceedingly important turn in the royal theology of Israel. The initial promise by God to David in 2 Samuel 7:11-16 is quite unconditional. The king may be punished, but will always be loved. In Psalm 132:11-12, however, the initial promise of 2 Samuel 7 is decisively changed to make it conditional. The introduction of "if" into the royal promise makes the monarchy of David subject to the conditions of Torah, thus reinterpreting the monarchy that had been an offer of free grace. This "if" is very old in Mosaic teaching, present already in Exodus 19:5-6. Perhaps its fullest presentation is voiced in Deuteronomy 30:15-20, where it is affirmed,

> If you obey…then you shall live,…
> But if your heart turns away…you shall not live long.

David's instruction in this utterance is peculiarly important, because in much of the royal narrative, David is not attentive to the Torah, but seems to assume that he is exempt from Torah requirements. In the dramatic story of Uriah and Bathsheba (2 Sam 11–12), David acted beyond Torah. Moreover, in what follows in this speech of David, the rigorous "if" of Torah is not operative. But in these verses monarchy for the future is held to severe

---

The "If" of Faith

Parts of the Davidic tradition express God's *unconditional* love for Israel (and for the family of David). But the larger framing of Israel's faith is in terms of covenantal *conditionality* expressed in Torah commandments. Everything depends upon Torah obedience. In the rhetoric of Deuteronomy, this conditionality is an uncompromising "if" rooted in Moses and his teaching. That tradition of conditionality serves both to warn Israel and to invite Israel to passionate obedience to the Torah. Among the more important texts of "if" are the following:

Now therefore, *if* you obey my voice and keep my covenant….(Exod 19:5)

If you obey the commandments of the LORD your God that I am commanding you today, by loving the LORD your God, walking in his ways, and observing his commandments, decrees, and ordinances….(Deut 30:16a)

As for you, *if* you will walk before me, as David your father walked, with integrity of heart and uprightness, doing according to all that I have commanded you, and keeping my statutes and my ordinances. (1 Kgs 9:4)

If your sons keep my covenant and my decrees that I shall teach them….(Ps 132:12)

demands, insisting that royal power must be devoted to divine purpose.

David's continued counsel to Solomon now goes in quite a different and unexpected direction (2:5-9). Here the issue seems to be not Torah requirements, but political prudence. David mentions three specific persons who have been important to his governance who survive David, with whom Solomon must deal. [David's Enduring List]

First, he names *Joab*, his trusted general and hatchet man who has been very close to David and upon whom David has endlessly relied (2:5-6). Indeed, Joab has been the key player in "resolving" the "Uriah question" for David (2 Sam 11:14-22) and the Absalom rebellion (2 Sam 18:9-23, 19:1-8). While David has depended upon Joab to do his dirty work, David is also exasperated with Joab and his brothers (2 Sam 16:10; 19:22) and at a pivotal point, pronounced a curse against him:

> May the guilt fall on the head of Joab, and on all his father's house; and may the house of Joab never be without one who has a discharge, or who is leprous, or who holds a spindle, or who falls by the sword, or who lacks food! (2 Sam 3:29)

In our text, David explicitly mentions Joab's murder of Abner (2 Sam 3:27) and Amasa (2 Sam 20:9-10). Both Abner and Amasa were political rivals of Joab for the top military job so that Joab's actions are self-protective. But one should also notice that the death of Abner is a very "convenient" one for David, for Abner is a political threat to David as well.

In any case, David declared that "the guilt fall on the head of Joab," and now the old man remembers. He knows that Joab is a

In this illustration, Shimei is depicted on higher ground, a hillside apart from David and his followers. He is in the act of throwing another stone as other stones are shown having been cast at the feet of David. The wild look in his eyes along with the gesture of his arm are in contrast to the Christ-like calm of David as he restrains his men, namely, Abishai. As seen in 1 Kgs 2:9, this portrayal of David as a man of great peace and beneficence is certainly not the king that would utter to his successor in the last days of his life, "you must bring his gray head [Shimei's] down with blood to Sheol."

Julius Schnoor von Carolsfeld. *Shimei's Curse*. 19th century. Woodcut. From *Das Buch der Bucher in Bilden*. (Credit: Dover Pictorial Archive Series) threat to Solomon. David urges Solomon to "act according to your wisdom," that is, according to prudence that will eliminate Joab.

The second name remembered by the dying king is *Barzillai*. Solomon is to act in "fidelity" toward Barzillai, because Barzillai has previously acted in "fidelity" to David. That is, Solomon is obligated to continue to pay what the royal family owes this man who intervened on behalf of David at a poignant and dangerous moment. The remembrance refers to the brief narrative of 2 Samuel 17:27-29. In that episode, Barzillai, wealthy landowner in Gilead, provided food provisions for David as he was fleeing from his son Absalom. This was an immense act of generosity; it was also an act of courage, for by it Barzillai publicly took sides with David in the civil war. We may imagine that Barzillai is a weighty figure whose public demonstration of support for David would have evoked support from other landed families as well, the support David required for survival as king.

Barzillai's pivotal public act of support is already recognized in the narrative of 2 Samuel 19:31-40. David invites Barzillai to join his Jerusalem entourage, likely an offer of an important post in the government. A settlement is made that one of Barzillai's "servants" will go to Jerusalem, thus assuring David an influential ally and giving Barzillai continuing representation of his interests in David's court. In his counsel to his son, David is aware that the throne does not exist in a political vacuum, but depends upon strategically placed, powerful allies among the landed. Thus the urging of "fidelity" is not only an obligation, but a practical act as well.

The third name recalled is *Shimei* (2:8-9). This mention refers back to the peculiar episode of 2 Samuel 16:5-14, wherein Shimei publicly assaults David, throws stones at him, and accuses him of murder, specifically murder of the house of Saul. (Some think the charge against David refers to the narrative of 2 Samuel 21:1-14.) In the narrative of 2 Samuel 16, David is magnanimous toward Shimei, relies upon Yahweh's protection, and vetoes the passion of Abishai (brother of Joab) who wants to kill Shimei.

The threat of Shimei to David is twofold. First, the pronouncement of a curse against the king is itself a dangerous political act (see Exod 22:28). While the curse itself may or may not be a powerful word of "magic," it does linger and echo in damaging ways in public memory. But more important, Shimei embodies the continuing threat of Benjamin, Saul's people, the northern faction in Israel that is never securely integrated into David's realm. Thus Shimei's seemingly out-of-control act is in fact a gesture behind which lurks a powerful political sentiment hostile to David.

2 Samuel 19:18b-23 already dealt with the Shimei incident. When David defeats the threat of Absalom, Shimei is the first to come seeking reconciliation with the victorious king. Because the coup of Absalom did not succeed, Shimei knows that he is a wanted man, and so he acts promptly to confess his affront and to seek protection. As in the initial encounter of chapter 16, David is again generous. Because he is newly secure, he is forgiving and accepting, not willing to make any new enemies in his moment of triumph, and not needing to.

In our text, however, it is clear that the old man has forgotten nothing and, indeed, has forgiven nothing. And so in v. 9, he gives the same counsel to Solomon concerning Shimei as he did concerning Joab in v. 6: Solomon is "wise," that is, able to do what is necessary to consolidate power. Perhaps the "death sentence" on Shimei is because of a personal grudge against a detractor. Perhaps Shimei still embodies the old northern threat that will resurface in the time of Rehoboam, son of Solomon (1 Kgs 12). Either way, the state has its reasons!

David died a peaceable and honorable death (2:10-12). As we shall promptly see, however, just below that surface of peaceableness was the violence that David has bequeathed to his son.

Solomon's "Obedience" to His Father, 2:13-46

Solomon's action follows David's speech (2:13-46). Solomon has perhaps listened well to his father just as David died. But as many sons and daughters in such a context, Solomon acts upon his father's advice selectively, picking and choosing his own way. What strikes one in these verses is the utter ruthlessness and uncompromising resolve of Solomon on his way to power. In these episodes, Solomon deals with four characters out of David's past, but only two of which are on David's "short list" in vv. 5-9.

Adonijah, brother and rival to Solomon, is dealt with first (2:13-25). He was not mentioned by David; but we already know from chapter 1 that he is an enduring problem for the new king. In 1:52, Solomon had ordered him to "go home," with the proviso that he could live "if he is worthy." But of course a competitor for the throne will remain under rigorous surveillance and is not likely to be found "worthy."

The most remarkable element about this narrative is that Adonijah seems to make things easy for Solomon. That is, he "volunteers" his "unworthiness." Adonijah comes to the queen mother, Bathsheba, to make a daring, foolish request. We know that queen mothers in Israel are characteristically powerful court players. [The Queen Mother] The request of Adonijah to Bathsheba, staggeringly, is that he be given the very beautiful young virgin who has last serviced old, failed David (1:1-4). He makes his pitiful request to Bathsheba by reminding her that he was "supposed" to be king, and receiving Abishag would be a splendid consolation prize.

The request for the young virgin reminds us that we are back into characteristically Davidic sexual politics. On the first level, this is unembarrassedly a men's world in which women are taken and given (see 2 Sam 12:10). But beyond that, we must recognize that power is a contest of virility in which the one who can dominate the concubines (harem) sends a public signal of virility and therefore royal legitimacy. [Concubines as Political Gestures] Already in 2 Samuel 12:11-12, Nathan's threat to David is the redeployment of "your wives" in a public exhibition that signifies David's loss of power. And in his failed coup against David, Absalom seizes the concubines of David in a public display of blatant virility in order to evoke the rebellion (2 Sam 16:21-22).

Given the symbolic significance of concubines and the cruciality of controlling the royal concubines, we may indeed wonder at Adonijah's request. Did he think the request of one concubine, perhaps the prize woman, was a small, modest petition not to be noticed? Or did he think that Solomon's position was not yet secure and that this was a deliberate act of defiance? Or did he, like some modern political leaders, become so intoxicated with the royal office that he acted irrationally? We do not know; from our vantage point, it is evident that by this act Adonijah seals his own death warrant.

Bathsheba dutifully relays the request to Solomon, perhaps with rolling her eyes (2:19-22). She seems an indifferent message carrier. But surely she understood, as Adonijah apparently did not, the

---

Concubines as Political Gestures

In that ancient world, the collection of royal concubines was not uncommon. The practice was not so much an articulation of sexuality as it was the politics of virility, that is, the way in which the king made visible and public his own potency. That is, his capacity to keep many women indicated his strength and energy, and so his legitimacy as a ruler who is "king of the mount." It seems evident that such a practice might have been precluded by the public vision of Mosaic covenantalism. That the early kings of Israel subscribed to the practice of concubines likely indicates development in a theory of kingship that was increasingly distant from the Mosaic vision and, conversely, more congruent with common non-

Israelite practice. That is, royal concubines were one more way to be "like the other nations" (1 Sam 8:5, 20).

It is noteworthy that the number of concubines steadily increased:

Saul: one (2 Sam 3:7)

David: ten (2 Sam 5:13; 15:16; 20:3)

Solomon: three hundred (1 Kgs 11:3)

This increase surely corresponded to the growth of royal claims and ambitions. It is to be noticed that Rehoboam, son of Solomon, had sixty concubines (2 Chr 11:21), perhaps reflecting a diminished governance.

The Queen Mother

It is noteworthy that in presenting basic material about each of the kings of Israel and Judah, the data characteristically includes the name of the queen mother, especially for Judah. This mention makes it unmistakably clear that the queen mother was a most formidable presence in that ancient world of royal intrigue, and perhaps even held a recognizable "office" in court. But then, we must suppose such prominence in a patriarchal society, for the one who "produces" the winning son has also "won" over all the other mothers whose sons were wannabes.

In this narrative, we are able to see that Bathsheba has ready access to the king and is a decisive player in the events that bring her son to power. She is, of course, only the first in the long line of queen mothers who in varying ways may have influenced royal policy in ancient Israel.

King/Son	Mother	Mother's Father	Mother's Home	Reference
Solomon	Bathsheba	Eliam	?	2 Sam 11:3; 12:24
Israel				
Jeroboam	Zeruah			1 Kgs 11:26
Ahaziah	Jezebel	Ethbaal	Tyre	1 Kgs 16:31; 22:52
Jehoram	Jezebel	Ethbaal	Tyre	2 Kgs 3:2; 9:22
Judah				
Rehoboam	Naamah	?	Ammon	1 Kgs 14:21
Abijah	Maacah	Abishalom	?	15:2
Asa	Maacah	Abishalom	?	15:10
Jehoshaphat	Azubah	Shilhi	?	22:42
Jehoram	?	?	?	....
Ahaziah	Athaliah	Omri/Ahab(?)	Israel	2 Kgs 8:26
Joash	Zibiah	?	Beersheba	12:1
Amaziah	Jehoaddin	?	Jerusalem	14:2
Azariah	Jecoliah	?	Jerusalem	15:2
Jotham	Jerusha	Zadok	?	15:33
Ahaz	?	?	?	....
Hezekiah	Abi	Zechariah	?	18:2
Manasseh	Hephzibah	?	?	21:1
Amon	Meshullemeth	Haruz	Jotbah	21:19
Josiah	Jediah	Adaiah	Bozkath	22:1
Jehoahaz	Hamutal	Jeremiah	Libnah	23:31
Jehoiakim	Zebidah	Pedaiah	Rumah	23:36
Jehoiachin	Nehushta	Elnathan	Jerusalem	24:8
Zedekiah	Hamutal	Jeremiah	Libnah	24:18

Linda Shearing, "Queen," *The Anchor Bible Dictionary*, 6 vols. (New York: Doubleday, 1992) 5:585.

As we shall see, particular attention should be paid to the role of Athaliah as queen mother (2 Kgs 8:26). And in the final, confused days of Judah, among the rival offspring of Josiah, it is possible that pro-Babylonian and pro-Egyptian policy is reflected in the grouping of political players around rival queen mothers. In any case, the role is not unimportant nor to be treated lightly.

inevitable outcome of the request. Solomon's response is prompt and unambiguous (2:22). He understands the full political import of the request: Ask for Abishag?! Why not ask for the entire kingdom?! That is, asking for her is tantamount to requesting the whole, because if Adonijah is seen to control the female favorite, he makes a visible claim for his power to rule. And besides, he is older and already has his own legitimacy.

The force of Solomon's response likely indicates his awareness that he is still more than a little vulnerable. After all, not only Adonijah, but also Joab and Abiathar still live. The party of Adonijah is still alive and well (see 1:7). The royal refusal is massive. And besides that, Adonijah has now unmistakably demonstrated his "wickedness" (1:52), that is, his refusal to accept the rule of Solomon. Solomon did not need any explicit mandate from David in this case. He acts in his "wisdom." He concluded that

Typical of medieval illustrations, the convention of continuous narration is used in this illustration as King David is shown on the left in the act of being buried, and, to the right, Bathsheba appears before Solomon; an event that occurs just after the death of King David. The artist has used the two prominent trees and the makeshift throne to bracket the scene changes, which move from left to right.

In the illustration, no sooner is David in the ground then Solomon begins to carry out David's charges against his enemies. Here, Bathsheba has appeared before her son, Solomon, to inform him of Adonijah's request. In this 15th-C. book illustration, the queen mother is shown humble and obedient before the newly crowned King. The image seems to imply that she is truly appearing on behalf of Adonijah. However, in the text, Bathsheba is received with her son, the king, "rising to meet her and bowing down to her." Also, in the text, Bathsheba, the queen mother, sits on a throne brought to her by Solomon.

1 Kings 2: 10-11, Death of David and *2 Kings 19–25, Bathsheba Asks Solomon for Abishag to Marry Adonijah.* (Printed book). *Nuremberg Bible* (Bibla Sacra Germanica). 1483. Private Collection. (Credit: Bridgeman Art Library)

Adonijah has knowingly gambled his life on this ploy. And now he has lost! And now he must die!

Solomon's speech in v. 24 voices, for the first time, his claim that he is king by Yahweh's action. And since Adonijah has not only threatened Solomon but has failed to accept Yahweh's will, he must die. The self-righteous, self-serving decree of vv. 23-24 is promptly enacted (2:25). Benaiah, the hatchet man of the new regime, is dispatched. The outcome: Solomon one, Adonijah zero!

As Adonijah is terminated, it is time to secure Adonijah's foremost allies. *Abiathar* the priest also is not mentioned in the last speech of David, but is nonetheless a continuing threat to the new regime (2:26-27). Solomon, however, will not kill a priest. This priest is spared even though he has been on the wrong side and so deserves to die. He is spared both because of his office as a priest and because of his long devotion to David (see v. 26). But if not death, then banishment, house arrest, and continuing surveillance.

Abiathar was allied early with David in his rise to power. As long ago as 1 Samuel 21–22, his father Ahimelech had sheltered David as fugitive from Saul, and had given him food. When the desperate Saul came to his place, he killed all the priests and family of Ahimelech...except that Abiathar escaped. And because Saul was such a threat and Ahimelech had risked so much for David, David accepted Abiathar into his company:

> Stay with me, and do not be afraid; for the one who seeks my life seeks your life; you will be safe with me. (1 Sam 22:23)

Thus there is some irony in the early assurance of David to Abiathar together with the hostility of David's son toward Abiathar.

But as the text recognizes, from the outset the narrative has known that the family of Abiathar is not the wave of the future. Verse 27 alludes to the oracle of 1 Samuel 2:27-36 in which the death sentence apparently refers to the family of Abiathar:

> No one in your family shall ever live to old age. The only one of you whom I shall not cut off from my altar shall be spared to weep out his eyes and grieve his heart; all the members of your household shall die by the sword. (1 Sam 2:32b-33)

It was the destiny of Abiathar, who backed the wrong candidate, to weep and grieve forever. [Echoes of the Banished Priest] In his place will be "a faithful priest" (1 Sam 2:35), now presumably Zadok (1 Kgs 1:8), that is, faithful to Solomon!

After the killing of Adonijah and the banishment of Abiathar (whom David had not mentioned), Solomon deals with *Joab*, whom David had on his "wanted list" in vv. 5-6 (2:28-35). It is impossible to overstate the importance of Joab for early monarchial politics. For that reason, Joab's name inevitably comes next after Abiathar, for he is the other primal resister to Solomon. Like Adonijah before him (1:50), Joab seeks sanctuary from the king at the altar. In a hint of what is to come, Solomon has no respect even for the traditional sanctuary of the altar. Reasons of state override ancient religious custom: "Go strike him down!" The centerpiece of the Joab episode is the command of Solomon to Benaiah. Echoing the charge of his father, Solomon takes great pains to indict Joab of guilt and, in passing, to acquit his father and himself.

As David before him, Solomon mentions two spectacular murders, those of Abner and Amasa (2:32). But of course things are not as straightforward as the royal account might suggest. The more important case is the death of Abner that has been reported in 2 Samuel 3:26-29. We are told first of all that Abner is killed in retaliation for the death of Asahel, Joab's brother, thus redefining the death. Second, in response to the death of Abner, David issues an extravagant disclaimer, taking great care to assign the death to Joab (2 Sam 3:28-29). Third, the narrative adds:

> So all the people and all Israel understood that day that the king had no part in the killing of Abner son of Ner. (2 Sam 3:37)

The rhetoric at least invites suspicion. Apparently some thought David was implicated in the death. If we notice the careful and seemingly exaggerated rhetoric of 2 Samuel 3, we may then

---

Echoes of the Banished Priest

Abiathar of course is never heard from again. That is what happens to persons excluded by ruthless power. We do notice, however, that he is banished to the village of Anathoth, of the tribe of Benjamin.

It is conspicuously important that many centuries later, the prophet Jeremiah appears in Jerusalem and is said to be "of the priests who were in Anathoth" (Jer 1:1, see 32:6-15). Because the village locus is the same for the later prophet as for the banished priest, it is plausible that the priestly line in which Jeremiah is situated is the line of the banished Abiathar. That connection, which is plausible but cannot be proven, is of interest in terms of genealogy and pedigree. But it is much more important that Abiathar represents a sociotheological perspective resistant to the development of a self-aggrandizing monarchy such as Solomon embodies. The importance of this is that the same perspective is articulated by Jeremiah much later, when he is profoundly critical of temple and monarchy, as in Jer 7:1-15, 22:13-19.

Among the more helpful discussions of the issue is Jon D. Levenson, *Sinai & Zion: An Entry into the Jewish Bible* (New York: Winston Press, 1985).

appreciate the comparable exaggerated rhetoric of Solomon in our chapter, wherein the new king goes to some length to be clear about guilt. The cadences of the royal speech in 2:33 again assert the innocence of David and the legitimate expectations of *shalom* for the realm.

As in v. 25, the expressed will of the king takes little time to enact. Apparently the killing is at the altar, perhaps a juxtaposition that tells all we need to know about the "wisdom" of Solomon. The action parallels v. 25, but now with an important addendum. Benaiah is now made commander in place of Joab; Zadok is priest in place of Abiathar. A quick review of the parties to dispute in 1:7-8 makes clear that the old guard is now eliminated; space is opened for the new appointees. Benaiah is as ruthless for Solomon as was Joab for David. And he is duly rewarded for his brutality with promotion.

The elimination of Adonijah, Abiathar, and Joab makes the new regime secure. But there is still one more settlement to be made from David's list (2:36-46). We have already considered *Shimei* and David's advice about him (2:8-9). Solomon is not precipitous, perhaps because Shimei is not so great a threat as the others. Solomon transfers him to Jerusalem and places him under house arrest. The action is likely a part of monitoring the continuing threat from the north. Shimei accepts the restriction, surely aware that was his best choice among the available options.

But the restriction does not hold. Shimei violates parole. There is no suggestion in the narrative that Shimei's departure from Jerusalem was anything but innocent. There is no hint that he was engaged in subversion against the king. More likely, he was compelled, as we often are, by economic risk, in this case the loss of slaves.

Innocent or not, he violated parole. Perhaps Solomon was waiting for an excuse to enact David's advice. Perhaps he had to act in order to demonstrate to others his seriousness. Either way, Solomon reviews the history of the case for Shimei, in order to make clear that the king is in the right and Shimei legitimately deserves to die. It may be worth noting that Solomon's phrase, "the Lord will bring back your evil" (2:44), is closely paralleled to David's earlier statement, "The Lord will repay me with good" (2 Sam 16:12). The verbs "bring back/repay" both attest that the outcome is not a human determination, but is an enactment of God's governance. Moreover, as in v. 33 when Joab's condemnation is matched by a dynastic affirmation, so here Shimei's condemnation is matched by another sweeping dynastic affirmation (2:45).

"The force" is with Solomon and will not be stopped. As in vv. 25, 34, the royal verbiage is followed by Benaiah's quick sword, the sword that enacts Solomon's "wisdom."

The concluding statement is terse and tells all (2:46). Solomon is now in charge. The transfer of power is complete. The king named *Shalom* sits on the throne in the city named Jeru-*shalom*. That is all the sentence tells us. But if we trace the entire chapter, it is clear that this is and will be a troubled *shalom*, for we can still hear the butchering echo of the sword of Benaiah:

> He struck him down, and he died. (2:25)
> [He] went up and stuck him down and killed him. (2:34)
> He went out and struck him down, and he died. (2:46)

This is what David has destined for Joab and Shimei—perhaps not needing to mention Adonijah. The rebellious party of Adonijah, Joab, and Abiathar has been overcome and defeated. The enduring threat from the north is decisively silenced. Karl Marx may be right that every state is founded on violence. In any case, this one is surely secured in that way.

CONNECTIONS

The tension in royal theology between *unconditional free promise* and *conditional requirement* is an acute and recurring one. When exalted claims for the royal court are made, Israel celebrated the unconditional promise of Yahweh. But when Israel reflects on the cruciality of Torah commandments and the sordidness of the monarchy, it thinks about God's commandments and the consequent blessings and curses that arise from obedience or disobedience.

This issue of *unconditional and conditional* is a difficult one that I believe admits of no easy or obvious resolution. [The Riddle of Unconditional / Conditional Love] Christian tradition has a great tendency to focus upon "the free grace of God." And yet, because the Christian community is morally serious and believes that actions have important consequences, it is also theologically necessary to consider the conditionality of our life with God, an accent especially important to the eighth- and seventh-century prophets of ancient Israel who gave a critique of the monarchy.

The issue of conditionality and unconditionality is an interesting one when considered in terms of psychology. Some children are nurtured in an environment of ready affirmation that is experienced as unconditionality; that nurture can result in either joyous self-acceptance or in an exaggerated sense of self-importance. Some children are raised in a context of endless moral insistence and implied disapproval; that can result in either a robust sense of duty or in a deep notion of failure and inadequacy. And so it is important to maintain the tension between the two accents.

📖 **The Riddle of Unconditional/Conditional Love**
While it is possible to see that some biblical texts articulate God's unconditional love and some other texts show its conditionality, in truth things do not sort out so clearly. The inner connection of the two accents is evident in Jesus' parable in Luke 16:19-31. In that parable of judgment, the poor man is "carried away by the angels to be with *Abraham*" (v. 22). Conversely the rich, uncaring man is given only Moses: "They have *Moses and the prophets*; they should listen to them" (v. 29). In much biblical interpretation, Abraham is seen to be a carrier of God's unconditional love, whereas Moses keeps the uncompromising "if" of Torah front and center. Thus in the use of these traditions, Jesus skillfully takes up both traditions and judges the two protagonists in the parable in terms of the *unconditional acceptance* of the poor man and the *conditional requirement* of the rich man.

In the larger world of political-economic power, it is possible, given such inordinate power as the U.S. now has, to imagine that such power is unconditional and therefore nation-states (like ancient imperial superpowers) can do whatever they like. The tradition of conditionality (the prophetic tradition), however, insists that even such raw power that seems beyond challenge is, soon or late, subject to the moral conditions that curb and limit and question such power. The issue is a difficult one and an important one. The Torah tradition here expressed by David recognized that power never finally can escape the ethical conditionality of God.

These three statements concerning Joab, Barzillai, and Shimei constitute a very large appeal to David's past history: concerning *Joab*, 2 Samuel 3, 20, concerning *Barzillai*, 2 Samuel 17, 19, and concerning *Shimei*, 2 Samuel 16, 19. That entire memory is now focused and mobilized in this moment of the death of the king. This appeal to the narrative past is a powerful affirmation that the past lingers into the present with enormous authority. The past must be served and honored and resolved.

In recent decades, we have been able to observe conflicts among peoples and nation-states that are deeply rooted in old—even ancient—memories. In many of these struggles, an outsider might think that the power of the past—especially when it is so destructive—ought to be relinquished. But it is not! And so the past lingers in many places, as it did for David, like stones crying out for justice of ancient grievances (Luke 19:40). David's appeal is a reminder that our unsettled pasts continue to exercise authority among us.

David's counsel clearly concerns a settling of old scores; even the positive statement about Barzillai is the payment of an old debt. It is equally clear, however, that David's urgings to his son are not simply a passion for revenge. Also operative here are prudential "reasons of state." Thus Solomon is twice urged to act in "wisdom," that is, to do what is prudent for the new regime. And the reason for prudence is that those old unsettlements will linger with implications for the future. Joab constitutes a threat to Solomon because, as we have seen, he has sided with Adonijah (1:7) and perhaps represents a well-articulated ideology that opposes Solomon's emerging urban bureaucracy. Shimei may represent a continuing Northern resistance that the dynasty of David never effectively overcame. By contrast, Barzillai represents those great landed families upon which Solomon may still be dependent in time to come. A focus upon "reasons of state" and the need for prudence beyond passion reminds us that the Bible is not to be read simply as a tale of private individuals acting in personal motivations. Always implicit in these narratives are larger ideological issues and powerful systemic forces at work that require a certain alertness in reading.

The most important point to notice, in my judgment, is that in the advice of vv. 5-9, we are a great distance away from the Torah urging of vv. 1-4. The noble claims of Torah are not present in vv. 5-9 that are driven by passion and prudence. Possibly this odd interface reflects different editorial hands at work. Taken as it stands, however, it is enough to recognize that David on his deathbed is a person of deep contradiction and incongruity, caught between the clear claims of faith and the obvious requirements of raw power. As we shall see, this tension between faith and power pervades the books of Kings. And if *characters in the biblical narrative* are so beset by contradiction, it does not surprise us that we, as *readers of the Bible*, know about the same contradictions. As we recognize the quality of irony in the text, we may follow Reinhold Niebuhr in recognizing the ironic quality in our own lived history, an irony that asserts that nothing is ever quite as it seems to be.

We may identify one major theme as a "connection" in this text, and three lesser motifs. The major theme is that in this narrative we are watching the establishment of *shalom* by the king whose name is *Shalom* (Solomon). In verse 33, it is anticipated that there will be *shalom* for the house of David "forevermore." This emphasis invites us to ponder the establishment of "peace on earth" and the way in which political-military power is an imperfect instrument of such peace.

The peace that Solomon will provide, as we shall see, is a guarantee of "peace and prosperity," order and abundance for all those who benefit from his regime. Indeed, the king's capacity for abundance and stability in his context matches any we might imagine in our belated U.S. superpower that dominates the global economy.

It is, however, a "peace" that is no real peace at all. For it is founded in violence, sustained by force, and marked by extravagant self-indulgence for some, made possible by exploitation and manipulation of others. This text, in anticipation, presents this "peace" in an ironic way, knowing that there is less of peace here than meets the eye.

Indeed the tone of the text is as ominous as the film *The Godfather* with its endless music of threat. We expect, in our narrative, that Marlon Brando or Al Pacino will at any time order yet another killing, the slow, steady process of the violent elimination of all those who are not "worthy," whose allegiance is doubtful, and who must therefore pay the price. The instrument of elimination is the sword of Benaiah, aggressive and ambitious new military leader. Benaiah, however, is only a tool of state. Behind that tool of state lies the enduring verdict of Nathan on David:

> Now therefore the sword shall never depart from your house, for you have despised me, and have taken the wife of Uriah the Hittite to be your wife. (2 Sam 12:10)

The sword lingers massively in this family. As it had taken Absalom (2 Sam 18:14-15), so now it has taken *Adonijah* and *Joab* and *Shimei*, with *Abiathar* still under threat. According to the tradition, it is the initial act of autonomy and rebellion on David's part that has fated this dynasty to self-devouring violence. The narrative is a window upon our own violence as a community, a violence rooted in unrestrained autonomy and now worked against any and against all who are in the way of private acquisitiveness, whether of wives or of other property. The music is not as loud in our history as in the film, but it as ominous. And much of it is in the name of *shalom*.

This section also contains three lesser points.

1. The request for Abishag by Adonijah invites reflection upon the politics of virility. It is of course clear in any sober reflection that good governance does not depend upon virility. But we are endlessly seduced by that option. And so the U.S. voting public is treated, in sequence, to the jogging of Jimmy Carter, the wood chopping and riding of Ronald Reagan, the boating of George Bush, and again the jogging of Bill Clinton, all attempts to demonstrate vitality and virility, enough strength to intimidate and keep the market up. That sustained exhibition is accompanied, at least

in John Kennedy and Bill Clinton, by data and/or rumors of sexual adventurism, partly a cause of embarrassment, but also partly cause for macho self-regard. The required demonstrations are of a kind parallel to that of the "concubine-market" in ancient Israel, a process in both cases not remote from policies of violence. One can imagine readiness to trade concubines in our contemporary world, if we did not have a thin veneer of piety as a screen against such scandal.

2. We have seen that Solomon acted on his father's counsel toward Joab and Shimei and added, logically enough, Adonijah and Abiathar to the list as primal offenders. What may give us most pause is the absence of Barzillai from Solomon's duty-list after the commendation of David in vv. 6-7. Solomon's list is all negative— one banishment and three executions. Barzillai was, in David's list, the single case of positive fidelity toward a long-term ally.

That one positive case of fidelity is absent from Solomon's list, perhaps because Solomon never did understand about fidelity, never could engage in generosity or gratitude toward anyone about anything. If, as I have suggested, Barzillai is a representative of that landed-body need for consensus government, then his absence here suggests a changed theory and practice of government. Under Solomon, a tightly centralized bureaucracy replaced a consensus practice fostered by David. If things are tightly enough controlled, there is no need for consensus allies. As we shall see, tight control by the bureaucracy almost immune from popular support pre-dictably ends in exploitative oppression, for there is no need for consensus or for consultation or for concession. The disregard of Barzillai is an ominous sign of changed theories of power.

3. We may notice two trajectories of faith represented by the two priests in the narrative. Zadok is the winner, the one allied with Solomon's theory of tight social control. We know very little about Zadok. But we know about the derivative priesthood of the Zadokites, named for him. The Zadokites emerge as the preeminent priests in a closely ordered hierarchy of holiness, that is, a scheme of blessed privilege.

By contrast, we hear no more of Abiathar. Except we notice that his place of banishment, the village of Anathoth (as has often been noticed) many centuries later, is mentioned again. Jeremiah the prophet is identified as "son of Hilkiah, of the priests that were in Anathoth" (Jer 1:1). The linkage has suggested that Jeremiah belongs to the old theological, covenantal tradition of Abiathar, and so emerges as a powerful critique of high Jerusalem theology embodied by the Zadokites. Thus the competing priests, Zadok and Abiathar, seem to be representatives and embodiments of competing theological traditions, one embodying radical Torah obedience and the other featuring protected privilege in the name of holiness. It takes no great imagination to see these same tendencies alive and well in current church disputes and in the practice of socioeconomic theory in current public discourse. The disputes in this narrative are models of the enduring disputes about the focus and claims of this theological memory.

BEGINNINGS AS
A PIOUS, WISE KING

1 Kings 3:1-28

In this chapter we are offered the beginning point of Solomon's newly established regime. The unit divides into two unequal but perhaps cunningly related parts (3:1-15, 3:16-28).

COMMENTARY

An Initial Tale of Legitimacy and Piety, 3:1-15

Verses 1-2, presented as Solomon's very first royal act, report Solomon's marriage to the daughter of Pharaoh. Taken alone, this might be considered as nothing more than a historical note. But given its placement in the text, we may appropriately suggest that its function is more than informative. The note about the marriage is surely designed as a marker to indicate the primary tendency of King Solomon. On two counts, Pharaoh must be considered a threat and a contrast to everything Israelite. First of all, Pharaoh embodies a concentration of imperial wealth and power, a center of commerce whereby security for the state consists in trade and military policy. As such, the Egyptian enterprise surely is a powerful contrast to the simple, covenantal horizon of Israelite faith that relied upon Yahweh and tended in the direction of neighborly equality.
[The Egyptian Connection]

The Egyptian Connection

No doubt Solomon deliberately imitated the great royal enterprises of the states around him. It is most plausible to conclude that one of the most attractive models in this regard was the "grandeur of Egypt." Thus scholars have noted that Solomonic replication of Egypt may have included (a) appropriation of Egyptian wisdom as an intellectual achievement of importance, (b) participation in commerce that in turn produced stratified society and eventually exploitation that sounds like an echo of the role of Pharaoh in the Exodus narrative (Exod 5:4-19), (c) imitation in the administrative structure of Solomon's government that seems to have the same titles and functions as Egyptian officials, and (d) implementation of building projects that are not unlike those of Pharaoh. This may include the design and theology implied in the architecture of the temple and, more importantly, the more general state building projects that parallel the very state building projects in Egypt that required the slaves of the Exodus narrative (see Exod 1:11). The marriage to the daughter of pharaoh is a signal for engagement with Egypt, an engagement that led Solomon into the political "big time," but conversely, also led Solomon away from old Mosaic roots. The narrative before us is primarily attentive to this strange tension in the account of Solomon that so shaped the future of Israel in terms of both glory and disaster.

This image of King Solomon by Gustave Doré seems to capture something of the responsiveness to God at this time in his reign. As the caption in the text that Doré illustrated reads: *Thus King Solomon excelled all the kings of the earth in riches and in wisdom. The whole earth sought the presence of Solomon to hear his wisdom, which God had put into his mind. 1 Kgs 10:23-24*

Gustave Doré. *Solomon* from the *Illustrated Bible*. 19th century. Engraving. (Credit: Dover Pictorial Archive Series)

Beyond that, "Egypt" is a term in Israelite memory and tradition that bespeaks brutality, exploitation, and bondage, the demeaning of the human spirit, and the suppression of covenantal relations. Indeed, Israelite memory concerning Yahweh is that the taproot of faith and life is emancipation from Pharaoh. Notably the Pharaoh is not identified. Historical calculations suggest that the Pharaoh of the moment is perhaps Siamun. [Candidates for Pharaoh] It is, however, crucial that he is not named, for in his anonymity he is emotionally connected to the ancient pharaoh of the Exodus narrative, also left unnamed (Exod 1:8). All Pharaohs are the same in Israelite imagination, and they are all a threat to Israel. But now, through the wedding, they have become "family."

Solomon has allied himself with Pharaoh, the antithesis of everything Israelite. There is no doubt that it was a political marriage, designed to serve political interests. The marriage signals Solomon's deliberate departure from what traditional Israel treasured the most. The remainder of vv. 1b-2 may be only a note to indicate that this marriage is situated in the pre-temple phase of Solomon's administration. Because there was no temple, of course they worshiped elsewhere in shrines called "high places." [The High Places] More than that, however, these verses likely contain a polemic that this worship was not loyally Yahwistic, but that Jerusalem was seduced by other gods (see 11:4). Thus the *marriage* and the *worship* together indicate a readiness to compromise or depart from Yahwism.

The thesis sentence for what follows in vv. 3-15 is given in v. 3: "Solomon loved

Candidates for Pharaoh

It is not at all clear which pharaoh may have been so connected to Solomon. The reconstructed sequence of pharaohs includes Siamun (978–959) and Psusennes II (959–945) from the XXI dynasty and Sheshonk I (945–924) from the XXII dynasty. It is likely, however, that in our text, the pharaoh is to be taken as paradigmatic, so that the precise identity of the pharaoh is not important for the point of the text.

In Egyptian art, there is also a tendency to minimize the aspects of portraiture and the specific identity of a particular pharoah, and emphasize instead, the symbolic office of pharoah, the unifier of upper and lower Egypt; the earthly equivalent to Horus, mythic son of the miraculous union of Isis and Osiris. The pharoah was always larger than life and eternally perpetuated through the dynasties. In this example, the frontal stare and cubic rigidity negate a portrait reading of the statue. However, with lesser personages, the Egyptian sculptors were more predisposed to capture the details of the individual.

Chefren from Giza, c. 2500 BC. Rose Granite. Private Collection, France. (Credit: Erich Lessing/ Art Resource, NY)

the Lord." The term "love" does not refer to romantic sentimental-ity, but rather to the practice of singular and obedient loyalty. Solomon begins his reign as a determined adherent to Yahweh and to Yahweh's Torah. Thus at the outset he practices the obedience urged by David in 2:1-4.

Solomon's loyalty to Yahweh is expressed in highly visible acts of public piety. He offered many sacrifices at many high places, and an especially extravagant offering at Gibeon, a most prominent place of royal worship. Solomon's behavior is not unusual. Because kings in that ancient world ruled at the behest of the gods and were taken to be the primary servants of the gods, it was important to be seen in devotion to one's god, thus enhancing royal legitimacy.

The divine response to these acts of public devotion is a dream (3:5-14). In that ancient world, a dream is understood not as a ran-dom offer of the unconscious but as an intrusion of the deity into one's affairs. [Dreaming beyond the Given] The dream reported is a power-ful claim for legitimacy, because what God gives in a dream is

---

AΩ The High Places

The phrase "high place" seems to refer generally to elevated locations that were claimed and dedicated as places as worship, perhaps as places where God or the gods were thought to be present. The statement in our verse simply rec-ognizes that prior to the temple, other kinds of places were used for worship. The text on its own terms seems to regard this as normal and acceptable. In other strands of the Old Testament, reference to "high places" is polemical, regarded as an aberration and departure from Yahwism of a most objectionable kind (2 Kgs 14:4; 15:4,35). Most likely no such polemic is intended or to be inferred here, except that given the negative judgment to be given on Solomon in chapter 11, it is not impossible that this "innocent" text is placed to pre-pare the way for the later polemic. This is one of many evidences to suggest that theological judgments about divine "presence" were in flux in Israel, in tension, and at times contradictory.

As depicted in this rendering of the Ziggurat Temple at Ur (mod-ern Muqaiyir, Iraq) from 2100 BC, it is common in the ancient Near East to locate temples and altars in prominent elevated locations. In fact, the ziggurat temples of the Sumerians were called moun-tains and actually simulated the gradual ascent of a mountain. A shrine or altar was located at the top and offerings would be made to the god of the city-state. It was believed that the god or god-dess of a particular city-state would enter and exit the land through this prominent, "high place" on a daily basis.

(Credit: Jim Burt)

beyond human control or exploitation or manipulation or resistance. It is, so to speak, the real thing!

The dream consists in three parts, each of which is a speech. In the first brief speech, Yahweh asks what Solomon needs or wants (3:5). The implication is that Solomon can have from Yahweh whatever he asks (see Matt 7:7). This is an amazing offer of generosity in which Yahweh is immediately and generously available to the king.

The second part of the dream is Solomon's well-crafted prayer response (3:6-9). The prayer-speech is divided into two parts. In the first part, Solomon reviews Yahweh's past generous acts toward David (3:6). At the beginning and end of the verse, the king thanks Yahweh for "great and steadfast love," that is, Yahweh's utter reliability toward David. The sign of that enduring fidelity, moreover, is the gift of an heir, Solomon himself, thus keeping the royal, dynastic promise intact. That is, Solomon begins in gratitude for past gifts from God.

But the middle portion of the verse rather inverts matters. As expressed, the gift of Yahweh's enduring fidelity toward David is not free gift. It is given to David in response. It is given as a quid quo pro, because David has been obedient. We shall see later that David's obedience is more complicated than this, but here it is direct and complete. The inference to be drawn is that both David and Yahweh have been faithful; but it is David's fidelity that has evoked and required Yahweh's fidelity. There is a bit of a coercive hint here: You owed us this much!

The second part of Solomon's response, introduced by "and now," turns from past review to present circumstance. The "and now" regularly introduces a petition like the one forthcoming in v. 9. But prior to v. 9, in the proper protocol of piety, Solomon states his own modesty, vulnerability, and need. The prayer aims to convey the mismatch between the work of the king and the resources of this king. The petition is that Yahweh should overcome the mismatch by special endowments to the king.

In the petition itself, the king asks for an "understanding mind." This conventional translation is scarcely adequate; it would be better to render "a hearing heart," or even "an obedient heart." The principle work of a king in the ancient world is to serve as judicial officer, to sort things out, to render verdicts, to determine what is good and evil, just and unjust. The prayer for "a listening heart" is

Dreaming beyond the Given

It is important to recognize that in that ancient world, dreams are not to be understood in terms of psychological unrest, as they are in our post-Freudian world. Well before the emergence of such psychological categories of interpretation, dreams are understood as messages from the gods that are given in sleep, when conventional human controls are at rest and the hovering and haunting of God has a chance. It may well be that dreams are of special interest and importance when dreamed by royal persons. The two primary foci on dreams in the Old Testament concern the dream of Pharaoh interpreted by Joseph (Gen 41) and the dream of Nebuchadnezzar interpreted by Daniel (Dan 4). The dream is also a political statement that important decisions are made by God well beyond the control or even understanding of the royal person. That is, the dream subverts the certainty of royal control.

With great tumult, Giordano has opted for Baroque theatricality to convey the image of Solomon's dream. This interpretation demonstrates the Old Testament understanding of dreams as instructional access to God's presence.

Luca Giordano. *Solomon's Dream.* 17th century. Oil. Prado, Madrid. (Credit: Bridgeman Art Library)

not simply that he should be made clever or discerning, but that he be attuned to Yahweh's guidance and purpose for justice. Thus the new king wants to have the sensitivity and wisdom to order Israel's life by the will of Yahweh.

The third element of speech is Yahweh's answer to Solomon's petition (3:10-14). Solomon's prayer commends him to Yahweh. We might have expected the son-in-law of Pharaoh to ask for long life, riches, and military success. These are the items Pharaoh characteristically champions and, indeed, they are the conventional goals of every royal claimant. But Solomon did not ask these. He did not ask what he may have been tempted to ask—because he is serious about being a good, Yahweh-oriented, Torah-informed king.

In response, Yahweh will give two gifts to Solomon. He will give what Solomon has asked. The king will be given the sensitivities of a good judge. But he will also be given what he might have asked and did not...riches and honor. He is given what he had not asked. We may infer that had he asked for these things now to be given, he would have brought trouble upon himself with Yahweh. As the dream concludes, Solomon has the best of both: *gifts for rule* and *gifts for well-being.* No wonder the assurance is interrupted by a lyrical affirmation of Solomon's incomparability: None like him!

Before Yahweh's response is ended, however, the glorious promise is qualified with a condition, echoing 2:4 (3:14). It is not enough that Solomon makes a good choice at the outset. He must make a good choice all along the way, the choice of listening and obeying, for it is in choosing obediently that Israel and its king choose life.

The upshot of the dream in v. 15 is that Solomon is motivated to even greater public piety in Jerusalem than he had enacted in Gibeon. He is intensely Yahweh's king and now gives visible evidence of it.

We may consider the juxtaposition of vv. 1-2 and vv. 3-15. I suggest that vv. 1-2 are placed as a foil to help us understand and appreciate vv. 3-15. In the dream Solomon chooses against Pharaoh and rejects that way of kingship. One might expect Pharaoh (or his son-in-law) to choose riches, long life, and victory. In this faithful choice at least, Solomon rejects all of the "pharaoh-options." He remembers who he is as a subject of Yahweh.

Royal Wisdom Enacts Justice, 3:16-28

This well-known story is straightforward and not difficult to understand. While it may be the sort of story that was popular and reiterated in many cultures, here its function is to exemplify Solomon's wisdom, thus confirming the gift of Yahweh promised in the dream. The story intends to present the king as a shrewd judge whose cleverness makes the doing of good possible in difficult and unclear cases.

The narrative is arranged around a problem (3:16-22) and the royal solution (3:23-27), together with a reflective conclusion (3:28). *The problem* is not difficult to understand. Because both mothers passionately yearn for a live, healthy baby, they charge "baby snatching." Both mothers claim the live baby as their own.

The solution offered by the king is an act of shrewdness that falls outside any ordinary judicial procedure (3:23-27). Apparently there was no data upon which to base a decision, no testimony from any attendant, no markings on the babies that would identify their proper mothers. The king has nothing to work with, except the presence and attitude of the two mothers. Obviously the king must be an attentive observer of their conduct and aptitude, out of which he forces the issue. The response of the two mothers, once the issue is forced, permits an easy determination of the case.

In the context of the larger Solomon narrative, the editorial comment of v. 28 must be fully appreciated. Solomon's decision is recognized by his political constituency as dazzling. He has done something they would not have conceived. His wisdom is to reach outside perceived options, to engineer some fresh data that permits a knowing verdict. We are told that the popular response to the king is twofold: (a) they know that such wisdom was *from God*, a gift beyond human cleverness. Indeed, such awareness of God's gift of wisdom for the king evokes lyrical affirmation of David, the king's father:

The word of my lord the king will set me at rest; for my lord the king is like the angel of God, discerning good and evil. (2 Sam 14:17)

(b) They discern that such wisdom from God was *to implement justice*, that is, to enhance the fairness and trustworthiness of the community. Solomon now is equipped for the most characteristic work of the king, whose primal responsibility is public justice. [Royal Justice]

Royal Justice
Give the king your justice, O God,
  and your righteousness to a king's son.
May he judge your people with righteousness
  and your poor with justice.
May the mountains yield prosperity for the
  people and the hills,
  in righteousness.
May he defend the cause of the poor of the
  people, give deliverance to the needy, and
  crush the oppressor.
  (Ps 72:1-4)

CONNECTIONS

Verses 1-2 may only be an offer of information. If they are an intentional theological polemic, they raise questions about the purity and discipline of faith in a seductive situation. The seduction is not narrowly religious. Given Egypt's role in that ancient world, the seduction may be in terms of military and economic aggrandizement that depends upon and produces social relations alien to Israel's notion of covenant.

Such a polemic against compromise and seduction may raise important issues for a community of faith (synagogue or church) that must seek its way in an ocean of attractive economic offers. [Faith Seduced] There is enough evidence that the Western Church in broad sweep has easily colluded with economic practice and economic theory that in fact contradict its own faith claims. This negative practice of Solomon, however, is only a preface for the positive foundational narrative that follows next.

In these verses Solomon must choose. He must choose the fundamental direction of his reign. The choice is between self-aggrandizement and self-giving for his realm. The choice is between *usual forms of power* (riches, long life) and *power obedient*

Faith Seduced

There can be little doubt that Solomon "in all his glory" embodies the temptation of Israel to "be like the nations," to imitate the power and splendor and grandeur of other great states. There can also be no doubt that such a temptation entails a sharp departure from the old faithfulness to Yahweh commanded in the simplicities of Sinai. And while that temptation in the Solomonic enterprise has theological rootage, it is articulated in economic categories of self-indulgence that inevitably ends in exploitation.

While the overlap of throne and religion makes the situation somewhat complex, it takes no great imagination to see how such patterns of temptation are addressed to ecclesial communities, Jewish and Christian. That is, both the synagogue and the church face the endless temptation of accommodating the more attractive values of surrounding culture. And as with Solomon, such a seduction has theological rootage but shows up especially in economic categories. That is, the church can benefit economically by being allied with dominant cultural forces, and the leadership of the church can thereby live a more comfortable, albeit compromised life. Solomon is surely offered in the text as a paradigm for such a sellout in ancient Israel.

---

to Yahweh (wisdom to determine good and evil, right and wrong, justice and injustice). Because of vv. 1-2, perhaps the choice is to act like Pharaoh, his father-in-law, or against Pharaonic power. It is a choice that Solomon must make and must continue to make, as must every person who administers great power.

The choice before Solomon is a characteristic choice in Israel, made characteristic because of the character of Yahweh. This characteristic choice is made clear in Jeremiah 9:23-24 which sounds like a report on the options facing Solomon: [Control or Fidelity: Drastic Options]

> Thus says the LORD: Do no let the wise boast in their *wisdom*, do not let the mighty boast in their *might*, do not let the wealthy boast in their *wealth*; but let those who boast boast in this, that they understand and know me, that I am the LORD; I act with *steadfast love, justice*, and *righteousness* in the earth, for in these things I delight, says the LORD (see 1 Cor 1:26-31).

On the one hand one may choose worldly *wisdom* (as in 2:6, 9), worldly *might*, and worldly *wealth*. On the other hand one may choose *steadfast love, justice, and righteousness*, the characteristic marks of Yahweh and the things Yahweh most delights in. The first choice is a decision to serve self at the expense of everyone else. The alternative choice is to serve the well-being of the community and to enhance it through fidelity and just dealings.

This is the choice that Israel must always make again. It is the choice commanded by Deuteronomy (Deut 30:15-20) and faced by Joshua (Josh 24:14-15). It is the choice required by the prophets (Amos 5:4-15; Isa 1:16-17) and the summons made in the exile (Isa 55:6-9). It is the choice to which Jesus calls his disciples (Matt 6:24).

Control or Fidelity: Drastic Options

The matter is put as a stark choice in the text. In practice, the choices are no doubt more often complex and less than clear. But the literature is trying to trace the dominant storyline of Solomon and the monarchy, and so regards the fundamental options for kingship as clear and simple. One option that endlessly haunts Israel since Sinai is the practice of fidelity that relies completely upon the faithfulness and reliability of Yahweh. That choice, however, is a deeply difficult and demanding one, for it leaves everything open. And so Israel is tempted, as are we all, to exercise some control, to be able to predict and administer and manage. But as the text has it, such efforts at control are seen to be diminishments of trust that is too risky. The same contrast of control or trust permeates the entire life of faith, for trust of that sort means going where we cannot see. The dilemma of those entrusted with great power is that it often seems foolish and unnecessarily risky to trust where control can be exercised. But then, to be open for trust rather than control is indeed the mystery of faith, a mystery endlessly demanding and endlessly healing whenever we are able to trust.

The choice Solomon makes in his dream is a decision for *wisdom*, true discernment that can sort out the things that make for life. The choice of wisdom is an urging long made by Israel's wisest teachers:

> My child, do not let these escape from
>   your sight:
>   keep sound wisdom and prudence,
> and they will be life for your soul
>   and adornment for your neck.
> Then you will walk on your way securely
>   and your foot will not stumble. (Prov 3:21-23)

> Get wisdom; get insight: do not forget,
>   nor turn away
>   from the words of my mouth.
> Do not forsake her, and she will keep
>   you;
>   love her, and she will guard you.
> The beginning of wisdom is this: Get
>   wisdom,
>   and whatever else you get, get insight. (Prov 4:5-7)

While this wisdom clearly has a prudential aspect, it is oriented to Yahweh. To be wise is to understand what Yahweh wills and to practice it. And clearly Yahweh does not will the greedy pursuit of riches or preoccupation with one's own life. What God wills is the enhancement and well-being of community neighbors in faithful and just relations. The wisdom urged in Proverbs is practiced in the narrative of Joseph.[1] Joseph is seen to be a man "wise and discerning" (Gen 41:38-39), who is given authority for the good ordering of the household. In our text, Solomon chooses in his dream to align himself with that practice of caring government for the enhancement of the realm, a readiness to look beyond himself for the good of others.

He had "all other things" (what he had not asked) added as well (3:13). The phrasing of this verse seems to anticipate the promise of Matthew 6:33:

> But strive first for the kingdom of God and his righteousness, and *all these things* will be given to you as well.

Seek God's rule, God's righteousness! "All these things will be added," that is, food, clothing, housing. Or in Solomon's world, riches and honor and long life. But they are not more than by-products of a good choice of Yahweh's wisdom.

Because Solomon is a large commercial, entrepreneurial success, we pause over his choice to notice that the choice he makes also faces us as his later readers. Those of us who live in a postindustrial, consumer society that is endlessly greedy for more can of course choose to pursue riches and self-security. We can do that at the expense of others. Indeed, the market policies of the U.S. increasingly concentrate wealth in the U.S. while the world around grows more poor and more desperate and therefore more violent. The dominant choice is to choose for self at the expense of all the others.

But we in the community of faith are like Solomon. [The Choice Continues] We can make another choice, a choice of wisdom that is both practical and neighborly. To make such a choice is not popular, but it is urgent. The hard choice we now face about our economy and what it does to our neighbors may help us to

---

The Choice Continues

The kinds of choices lined out in this text are precisely the kinds of choices facing the church in our season of disestablishment in the West. It is now clear that the church in the U.S. has been allied with dominant economic interests for a very long time. Thus the gospel has been largely privatized, and the assumptions of the market economy have been assumed by the Church and largely left uncriticized. But now we are able to see in fresh ways that there is an immense gap between what passes now for "The American Dream" and the claims of the gospel. While the gospel celebrates a neighborly ethic, the ideology of the American Dream is in large part a way of rugged individualism that regards the neighbor as a competitor. The choice is grounded in adherence to the God of the covenant. But the choice is effected in neighborly zones of life, specifically in economic values and transactions. It would be extravagant to say that Solomon embraced a "global economy," but that is more or less the case in that ancient world of limited horizon. The analogue now seems to me to be the values of "The Global Economy" that is capable of producing enormous wealth while it also displaces and exploits in harsh ways. An alternative to that economic practice is not obvious, just as it was not obvious that Solomon could choose otherwise. It is my estimate that the choices now facing the community of faith are as difficult and complex and obscure as those Solomon refused to make. Now, as then, the community of faith faces temptations of social power that obscure and contradict its true identity.

understand the choice that Solomon dreamed of making. The text is an invitation to choose against the choices of Pharaoh, the model exploiter.

This narrative account evokes a major accent and a suspicious footnote. It may suggest to us the cruciality of a reliable, discerning, imaginative judiciary. Finally, the ordering of society in a workable way depends upon a judiciary that is not only reliable and credible, but that has the freedom to move outside conventions to offer new dimensions of the rule of law never before perceived. [Beyond Strict Constructionism]

In the U.S., we have recently witnessed the retirement of Justices Harry Blackmun and William Brennen. While their work has been disputed (and thought too "liberal" by some), none can doubt that they managed the trust of law with great *imagination* and courage, and thereby produced fresh dimensions of justice in our society. Great jurists must not only have a grasp of law and legal precedent, but an uncommon human passion that makes decisions that are rooted in something like God's purposes that serve the well-being of community.

Clearly great judicial actions are not done by rote and reiteration. Martha Nussbaum has carefully argued that great jurists characteristically live by emancipated imagination that dares to rearticulate social reality in new categories. [Nussbaum on Imagination] This is what Solomon does in this narrative, an act perceived by his contemporaries as more than human cleverness.

Having said such positive things about Solomon, I add one important dissent. His way to a solution was by way of *a sword*:

> So the king said, "Bring me a sword," and they brought a sword before the king. The king said, "Divide the living boy in two; then give half to the one, and half to the other." (3:24-25)

Solomon seems to have the sword excessively on his brain, the sword as a tool of control, coercion, and intimidation. In chapter two, his father David twice urges him to act wisely, to kill (3:6, 9). Solomon's regime, in that chapter, is three times to *enact the sword* (2:25, 34, 36). This is a strange *wisdom* that governs by *violence*.

To be sure, the sword in this narrative is only a ploy. But it is a severe ploy, one that was perfectly credible to the real mother. That is, the real mother could imagine that the king would proceed in that way, a notion that must have deeply terrorized her. One may wonder about what the king would have done with his threat of violence had the real mother not flinched. Would he have escalated the threat? Would he have "divided" the child? We of course will

---

📖 Beyond Strict Constructionism

Recent history of the judiciary in the U.S., and in the Supreme Court in particular, has evoked dispute about interpretation of the U.S. Constitution. Specifically, those who want a minimalist government (generally those who are privileged by the status quo) insist on "strict constructionism," that is, no judicial decision except those warranted by the "initial framers of the Constitution." But of course such a notion is an illusion, because almost none of the great issues before the court at the end of the twentieth century could have been on the horizon of the "initial framers." Good judges and jurists must always interpret, imagine, and construe from tradition in the face of new issues. Solomon is no "strict constructionist," but must decide afresh.

Nussbaum on Imagination

In a formidable and suggestive book, Martha Nussbaum has argued persuasively that sound administration of justice in the courts requires a disciplined, emancipated imagination, whereby judges make connections and interpretive maneuvers not evident to a less generative perspective. It is evident in our text that Solomon commits an overt act of imagination. In the same way, Nussbaum cites cases where the same "leaps of interpretation" are made. It is instructive that the judges she quotes from time to time explicitly acknowledge appeal to imagination. Solomon is a case study of shrewdness that permits his ruling to be *generative* and *constructive* in a way that is not "strict."

Martha Nussbaum, *Poetic Justice: The Literary Imagination and Public Life* (Boston: Beacon Press, 1996).

---

never know. We do not know that about the king in this act, but we now know a great deal about this king.

It is sufficient to notice that Solomon's "wisdom" from God is not "nice." It is marked by prudence; but it is also, it seems, marked by a kind of crudeness that can damage. Perhaps wisdom that governs must always be a compromised wisdom with coerciveness behind it. As we shall see, Solomon's wisdom, here narrated, becomes increasingly compromised and finally dubious in the narrative that follows. Indeed, in the end this wisdom turns out to be self-destructive foolishness in masquerade. That, however, is not yet evident in our text.

NOTE

[1]Gerhard von Rad, "The Joseph Narrative and Ancient Wisdom," *The Problem of the Hexateuch and Other Essays* (New York: McGraw-Hill, 1966) 292-300.

ROYAL IMPRESSIVENESS

1 Kings 4:1-34

This extended chapter is a summary report on the development, success, and extravagance of the Solomonic regime. That regime must have been enormously successful and deeply impressive to Israelites who were only two generations removed from hill-country subsistence living. The chapter is divided into five sections. The first four sections concern economic development and are complemented in the fifth section by an account of one of Solomon's cultural interests.

In this chapter Solomon is evidently changing the foundations of social relationships in Israel decisively, away from egalitarian, communitarian modes and toward a much more highly organized arrangement. For such an ambitious government, two general mechanisms are required, a *bureaucratic ordering* of administrative power and an adequate *system of taxation* to finance the new ambitions. As we shall see, both needs are reflected in this text.

COMMENTARY

An Emerging Bureaucracy, 4:1-6

At the outset, we are told of Solomon's "cabinet," the responsible administration officials who oversee the necessary branches of government. It is important to remember that only forty years earlier, under Saul's leadership, Israel had no such roster of officials. The beginnings of such administrative arrangements appear under David (2 Sam 8:15-18; 20:23-26), but are much more fully developed in our present text. This list clearly reflects "the next generation" of elites after David, the heirs of the founding generation of David's company who continue to be the privileged and powerful into the next generation. Thus the list includes a son of Zadok and two sons of Nathan, so that the leaders of the Solomonic coup continue to be represented in places of influence (see 1:34).

In addition to the priests, this "new order" includes secretaries, a recorder, and a military commander. Evidently there is some confusion in the list, for along with the "son of Zadok" as a priest, "Zadok and Abiathar" are listed as priests. Most likely neither of the older

AΩ Friend of the King

Perhaps the "friend of the king" was simply the most intimate confidant of the king. But because the phrase occurs in a list of officials, it may have been a formal post. Kyle McCarter writes:

> We should probably assume that the title was first used as an honorific, as in Egypt, later becoming the designation for an officer of state, a sort of privy counselor.

Hushai is designated as David's "friend of the king" (2 Sam 15:37; 16:16; 1 Chr 27:33). In Isaiah 41:8, remarkably, Yahweh terms Abraham "my friend."

Kyle McCarter, *2 Samuel* (AB9; Garden City: Doubleday, 1984) 372.

priests belongs on this list, certainly not Abiathar who has been banished by Solomon (2:26-27). Additional officers of the crown include a "friend of the king," likely to be understood as an official role, perhaps the king's most confidential adviser, and then an agent "in charge of forced labor." [Friend of the King] While the particulars of the list are of interest and while we do not understand all of their functions, much more important is the cumulative force of the list, suggesting a well-formed "coverage" of every aspect of public life. Such an ordering of royal power is likely an import into Israel from elsewhere, an import that is surely something of a departure from earlier Israelite practice. It has been suggested that some of these offices reflect Egyptian influence, an unsurprising possibility in light of 3:1-2.

I may comment upon two aspects of this list. First the presence of "secretary and recorder" suggests that this is a "writing government" of a formal kind with many records and statistics. Moreover, a government with a lot of paper is one that plausibly has "state secrets" so that worry about security and protection of governmental workings likely come next. This seems matched by the "secretary of labor." The mention of this official is sure to raise questions in the face of Israel's egalitarian tradition. Indeed, "forced labor" accurately describes the program of state slavery in Egypt from which Yahweh emancipated Israel in the Exodus [On Forced Labor] To find such an officer in Solomon's cabinet is a measure of how drastically Solomon has abandoned Israelite tradition and embraced new modes of administrative power. It is impossible to know to what extent this list is a mere inventory and to what extent the narrative is an ironically critical comment, exposing the

The Egyptian division of labor in ancient ties included the viziers, which were arthitectural overseerers, scribes, and other administrative officials. This ordering of royal power in Egypt may be appreciated in the example of the scribe. The scribe was an important official in the Egyptian social system and the office was a valued profession. As scholars, the scribes studied and organized sacred and scientific texts. Training for this profession started in childhood and was passed down through the generations. Because of their importance, they were often granted their own tombs, and statues of them were often carved to insure the sanctity and safety of their own afterlifes.

Egyptian Scribe, from Saqqara, Egypt. Old Kingdom. 5th dynasty c. 2400 BC. Limstone, alabaster and rock crystal. Musée du Louvre, Paris. (Credit: Giraudon/Art Resource, NY)

On Forced Labor

Israel's memory is permeated with notions of "forced labor," requirements imposed by the throne. There is no doubt that the Exodus deliverance was emancipation from forced labor (Exod 1:11-14; 5:4-19), pressure to meet state production quotas. Samuel recognized such state practice as a threat to the covenant community (1 Sam 8:12-17). Already in the time of David there are hints of the practice in Israel (2 Sam 20:20). But it is with Solomon, perhaps imitating Egypt, that forced labor becomes critically important in Israel. The evidence is ambiguous. 1 Kgs 9:15-22 claims that Israelites were exempt from service, but 5:13-18 suggests otherwise. Either way, Solomon imposed demands that caused the resistance movement of chapter 12. The memory of emancipation makes Israel endlessly resistant and vigilant against such exploitative practice. Solomon, however, seems not to notice.

---

hazardous political commitments of Solomon. Specifically the mention of a "secretary of labor" is a clear anticipation of 1 Kings 12 and the events through which the Solomonic regime fell apart in a labor dispute.

Internal Revenue Service in Jerusalem, 4:7-19

The bureaucratic listing of vv. 1-6 has prepared us for this longer, more complex list of tax officers in vv. 7-19. It is telling indeed that this is the longest list, suggesting that the regime was most needful of and therefore most attentive to a complex arrangement for tax collections. Already in the severe warning of 1 Samuel 8:11-17, the crusty old seer had warned that the primary quality of the new monarchy would be to "take," a harsh term for taxation. This accent upon taxation suggests (a) that the government lived exceedingly well and needed revenue to do it, and (b) such an emphasis upon taxes no doubt evoked, over time, hostility from the citizenry.

The listing itself is geographically complex. There is an old suggestion that the new tax districts deliberately cut across old tribal lines in order to nullify what might have been tribal resistance to the new arrangement. [Map: Royal Tax Districts] It is evident that being a tax officer was a privileged role and not at all a menial chore. Among the tax officers are Ahimaaz (son of Zadok who had become Solomon's son-in-law; see 2 Sam 18:27), a son of Hushai (see 2 Sam 15:37), and a second son-in-law of Solomon (Taphath, v. 11). The collection process seems to have been in the hands of those most trusted, most closely linked to Solomon, and likely those who most benefited from the process. Tax collectors characteristically have been resented and viewed as exploitative; these tax officers are likely no exception to that rule. [The Urge to Tax Reform]

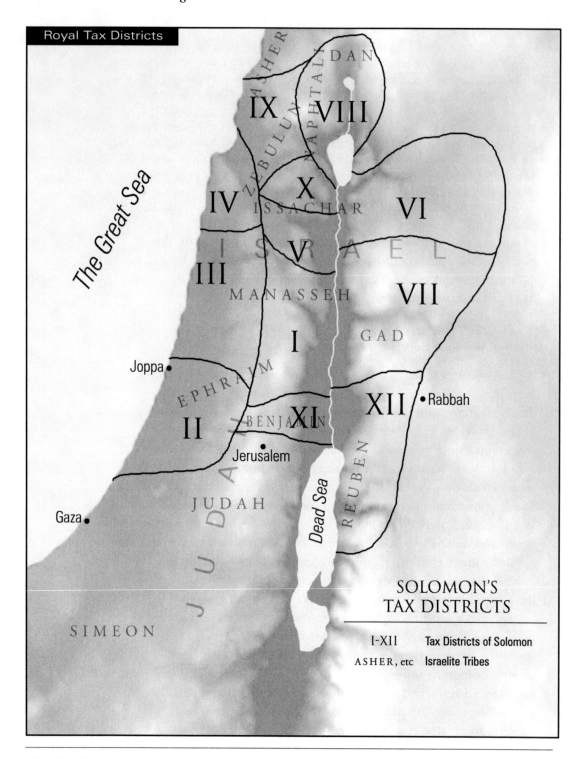

Royal Tax Districts

SOLOMON'S
TAX DISTRICTS

I–XII	**Tax Districts of Solomon**
ASHER, etc	**Israelite Tribes**

Royal Tax Districts

While such a sketch is admittedly hypothetical, it is clear that the proposed boundaries transgress old tribal boundaries.

This three-part narrative painting or *istoria* is consistent with the scriptural account. In the center of the composition, Christ tells St. Peter that he will find the tax in the mouth of the fish. The left section of the fresco depicts St. Peter's retrieving the coin from the mouth of the fish. Then, as shown on the right side of the painting, St. Peter hands the tax to the collector. Consistent with the observations made in the commentary text, this visual narrative shows the tax collector standing apart from the crowd and dressed differently than all the other figures. In the central portion of the composition, the tax collector's back is to the audience and his heels extend over the edge of the painted frame. When he receives the tax from St. Peter, he is again set apart, this time from the apostle, through the orthogonals created by the architecture. The tax collector is on the other side of the threshold, reinforcing this ongoing trend of alienating the tax collector from the people. In the two places in the painting where St. Peter is shown with the tax collector, it is illuminating to note how they are compositionally arranged as mirror opposites.

Masaccio. *The Tribute Money*. Fresco in the Brancacci Chapel. Santa Maria del Carmine, Florence. c. 1421–1428. (Credit: Alinari/Art Resource, NY)

The following two verses are an interpretive pause in the report of the details of government (4:20-21). They assert that the regime of Solomon really works! It produces the abundant life through the channels of administration (4:1-6) and taxation (4:7-19).

But the texture of these two verses is more complex than appears at first glance. We may notice two features that will help us read the text more closely. First, we may notice the juxtaposition of v. 20 and v. 21. Verse 20 focuses on the internal life of Judah and Israel as the people of God. It is this people that enjoys a high standard of living. But the claims for Judah-Israel are supported by the very different assertion of v. 21, namely, that Solomon presides over a vast, imperial economic enterprise. That enterprise stretches from the Euphrates River in the north to

The Urge to Tax Reform

Tax collectors do not have it easy in our contemporary world; for there is always a case to be made for "tax reform." It was no different in that ancient world where the entire taxation enterprise was saturated with exploitation:

Do not even the tax collectors do the same? (Matt 5:46)

Many tax collectors and sinners came and were sitting with him and his disciples. When the Pharisees saw this, they said to his disciples, "Why does your teacher eat with tax collectors and sinners?" (Matt 9:10-11)

If ... the offender refuses to listen even to the church, let such a one be to you as a Gentile and a tax collector. (Matt 18:17b; see also Matt 21:31; Luke 19:2-9)

Some of the objections to taxation, ancient and contemporary, concern corruption. Some are opposed to the finance of the public enterprise on principle. Solomon's grandiose schemes must have evoked immense hostility from those who paid for them.

Egypt, Israel's farthest imaginative expansion of territory. [Map: Empire of David and Solomon] Moreover, it is not said of these lands that they "eat, drink, and rejoice." Rather, they "bring tribute," that is, they pay taxes that are characteristic of colonies paying to the imperial power. Solomon's imperial government has become a "money machine," not money willingly brought but taxation imposed in what must have been coercive ways. Thus the *coercive taxation* of colonies in v. 21 permits the *affluence* at home in v. 20.

Second, unlike the rather sober descriptions of vv. 1-19, we may notice that these two verses are freighted with interpretive commentary that appeals to biblical tradition. Three allusions show that Solomon has fulfilled all the old promises of God made to the ancestors: [Promises Now Fulfilled] (a) "As many as the sand of the sea" is an old promise of fruitfulness and fertility made to the ancestors (Gen 22:17; 32:17). (b) The boundaries of "Euphrates ... to the border of Egypt" voices the boldest vision of "Greater Israel" promised by God (Gen 15:18-21), a vision never actualized but the basis of dreams of power, prestige, and security, given by the God who keeps promises. (c) The term "happy" refers to exuberant festival celebration. Such celebration asserts the effectiveness of Solomon, but the "subtext" asserts that this well-being is a gift wrought by God.

On the surface the verses are exuberant about Solomonic Israel. In that regard the text expresses a self-congratulatory innocence. The makers of the text, however, already knew that Solomon's mighty kingdom will collapse in chapter 12 in a labor dispute. The labor dispute suggests that, while Israel and Judah "ate, drank, and were happy," glad affirmation included only some in Judah and Israel. A more informed reading may take this text with some irony, already recognizing that the appearance of well-being is mostly appearance, while the seeds of destruction that come with self-indulgence are already sown. They are not voiced in the text because they are not yet visible in the community. But the reader of the larger text is on notice. There is more here than meets the eye.

Nothing Lacking, 4:22-28

Verses 22-26 seem to detail the claim of v. 20. The picture of the royal household is one of extravagance and self-indulgence. When we remember that Israel had only recently had a simple subsistence economy, the transition to Solomonic opulence is striking indeed. It is equally telling that the inventory of the royal household specializes in *meat* of many kinds, food only dreamed about in a peasant economy.

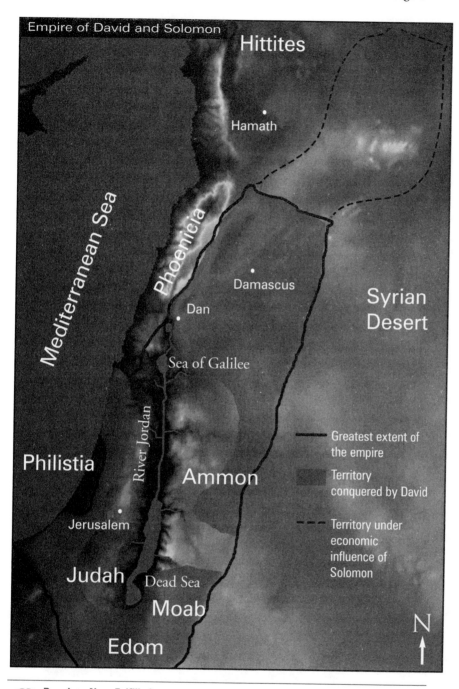

Empire of David and Solomon

Hittites

Hamath

Mediterranean Sea

Phoenicia

Damascus

Dan

Sea of Galilee

Syrian Desert

River Jordan

Philistia

Ammon

Jerusalem

Judah   Dead Sea

Moab

Edom

—— Greatest extent of the empire

Territory conquered by David

- - - Territory under economic influence of Solomon

N ↑

Promises Now Fulfilled

The text is arranged to assert that Solomon is the means by which Israel's most treasured promises from Yahweh are now fulfilled. The promise of God is asserted, for example, in Gen 15:18-21:

> To your descendants I give this land, from the river of Egypt to the great river, the river Euphrates, the land of the Kenites, the Kenizzites, the Kadmonites, the Hittites, the Perizzites, the Rephaim, the Amorites, the Canaanites, the Girgashites, and the Jebusites.

Other texts also echo the fulfillment theme (Isa 10:22, Hos 1:10; Rom 9:27; Heb 11:12).

In this painting by Tanner, the viewer is given a glimpse into the humble abode of an elderly African-American gentleman. The bare necessities are seen in what could be a tenant house as evidenced in the old coffee pot, the iron skillet and the creaky floors. Yet, echoing the sense of Matt. 6:25, 29, in the midst of such downtrodden conditions, there is the quiet glow of love and peace. Though with tattered clothes, the arms of the elderly man frame the young boy, and, though eye contact is not being made between them, there is the sense of real presence in the midst of this shared experience. The holiness of this moment is underlined with the inclusion of sacramental objects on the back table, bathed in a warm, glowing light—the bread and the pitcher.

Henry Ossawa Tanner. *The Banjo Lesson.* 1893. Oil on canvas. Hampton University Museum, Hampton, Virginia. (Credit: Hampton University Museum)

Anxiety and Beyond

Undoubtedly Solomon's extravagant self-indulgence generated anxiety, for such a visible, ostentatious enterprise is bound to evoke hostility among those who are deprived and yet must sacrifice for it. The anxiety is perhaps signalled by the large military establishment the king maintained.

A powerful and ironic contrast to Solomonic well-being with anxiety is voiced by Jesus who offers well-being without anxiety:

Therefore I tell you, do not worry about your life, what you will eat or what you will drink, or about your body, what you will wear…. Yet I tell you, *even Solomon* in all his glory was not clothed like one of these. (Matt 6:25, 29)

The interrelation of these verses is not unlike that of vv. 20-21. Verses 22-23 describe the affluence of the internal life of the community and v. 24 asserts Solomon's "dominion" over a vast territory, a territory that produces great tax revenues (tribute) that finance the royal apparatus. The term "dominion" is the same as in Genesis 1:28, suggesting that Solomon is the "real Adam" who exercises God's governance over all of creation, that is, over the controllable zone of productivity.

The same pairing of internal security and external exploitation is reiterated in vv. 25-26. It is asserted that Israel and Judah lived "in security," a phrase closely parallel to "happy" in v. 20. But the assertion of "security" is matched in v. 26 by an inventory of Solomon's great military system anticipated in 1 Samuel 8:11-17. [Anxiety and Beyond]

We may note in these verses one other irony. In vv. 22-23 we have an extravagant enumeration. In v. 25, however, a peasant view of well-being is "vine and fig tree," a modest agrarian expectation. [The Leanness of "Vine and Fig Tree"] Thus the juxtaposition of texts provides a contrast between urban affluence and rural modesty. Perhaps "all is well" in city and in country. It may more likely be that the narrative report hints at a growing disproportion that is not yet visible, but that soon or late will erupt in revolutionary anger.

Verses 27-28 are a reflective reprise on the long report of vv. 1-26. More specifically they connect to vv. 7-19 and the effectiveness of the royal taxation system. Thus "the officials" refers to the "twelve officers" of v. 7. Their duty was to keep the demanding royal enterprise afloat, no small responsibility given its ambitious and ostentatious way of life. The conclusion, "let nothing be lacking"—a phrase congruent with "happy" (4:20) and "in safety" (4:25)—indicates that the system works. No royal desire or appetite failed to be satisfied.

Pastoral images of peasants epitomize the work of Jean-François Millet. A sense of nostalgia informs this depiction of peasants gathering the remnants of the harvest; their lives are seen as inextricably immersed in the life of the land. Millet and other artists of the Barbizon school of landscape painting in France were reacting against the modernization of Paris by the city planning of Georges-Eugene Haussmann. This was taking place not far from the village of Barbizon on the edge of the Fountainebleau Forest.

Jean-François Millet. *The Gleaners*. 1857. Oil on canvas. Musée d'Orsay, Paris, France. (Credit: Giraudon/Art Resource, NY)

AΩ **The Leanness of "Vine and Fig Tree"**
"Vine and Fig Tree" is a set phrase in Israel to refer to an adequate, secure economic existence in a peaceful environment. The phrase evokes a pastoral note that lacks the aggressive, conflictual drive of Solomon's "money machine." It may be that the phrase is thus used here ironically, for if there is anything Solomon will be unable to provide, it is secure economic existence in a peaceful environment. Solomon's governing values and policies in principle preclude such an environment. Other uses in 2 Kgs 18:31-32, Isa 36:16, Hos 2:12, Mic 4:4, Hab 3:17-18, Zech 3:10, and Joel 1:12 greatly illuminate the phrase. It is not clear if our usage intends to celebrate or subtly criticize Solomon.

It is as though v. 28 is an incidental addendum referring back to the defense policies of v. 26. "Barley and straw" is the military energy necessary to maintain control of the territories (4:21, 24) that in turn supply the income making affluence possible. Thus the government is preoccupied—as governments usually are—with taxes and defense. Later on it will be apparent that Solomon's neglect of the human infrastructure of his realm could only have deleterious and destructive outcomes.

Royal Wisdom, 4:29-34

Solomon is presented as the model embodiment of wisdom (4:29-34). He had prayed for and been granted the wisdom to rule over Israel responsibly (1 Kgs 3:9, 12). That wisdom, moreover, had been evidenced in concrete decision making (3:16-28). And now, in lyrical summary, God's gift of wisdom is celebrated in an international context.

The gift from God is articulated in three synonymous terms, "wisdom," "discernment," "breadth of understanding." The first two terms are conventional, as in 3:12. The third term that might be translated "wide heart" is parallel to the "hearing heart" of 3:9, and refers to an expansive capacity to comprehend all knowledge. [A Wide Heart] This wisdom, however, is not the accumulation of data. It is rather the capacity to understand all of life in its depth and in its God-given mystery…and Solomon is best at it. [Fear at the Outset]

The impressive scope of his wisdom is characterized in three ways:

1. His learning is contrasted with all other centers of learning, especially those of Egypt and "the East," the most remote and respected and awesome centers of learning. (It is important to remember that much later, in the story of Jesus, the wise men "came from the East" (Matt 2:12). After these zones of

---

AΩ **A Wide Heart**
The phrase used for Solomon's responsiveness to Yahweh is a curious one. Gerhard von Rad comments:

> To be able to handle such knowledge, really required a *rohab leb*, a "width," "a breadth" of heart and mind (1 Kgs 5:9). In this concept, what was both the task and, at the same time, the presupposition of Israel's humanity found admirable expression.

Gerhard von Rad, *Wisdom in Israel* (Nashville: Abingdon Press, 1972) 310.

The phrase refers to largeness of vision and perspective beyond self-interest.

Fear at the Outset

Solomon's pious response to Yahweh is a showcase for the right kind of wisdom in Israel. Wisdom is not technical information at all, but the depth capacity to discern the workings of Yahweh in the midst of daily life. The posture of Solomon here echoes the pious urging of the book of Proverbs: "The fear of the Lord is the beginning of knowledge" (Prov 1:7). Von Rad observes:

> The statement that the fear of the Lord was the beginning of wisdom was Israel's most special possession…. [Israel's] thinking had to operate within spheres of tension indicated by the prior gift of the knowledge of God.

Gerhard von Rad, *Wisdom in Israel* (Nashville: Abingdon Press, 1972), 68.

The radicality of Yahwistic wisdom, in contrast to the technical competence of knowledge without faith, is fully affirmed by Paul:

Has not God made foolish the wisdom of the world?…For God's foolishness is wiser than human wisdom, and God's weakness is stronger than human strength. (1 Cor 1:20, 25)

For the wisdom of this world is foolishness with God. (1 Cor 3:19)

And if I have prophetic powers, and understand all mysteries and all knowledge, and if I have all faith, so as to remove mountains, but do not have love, I am nothing. (1 Cor 13:2)

The beginning of Solomon's reign is marked by attentiveness to the ways in which Yahweh will give well-being. Too bad Solomon suffered from acute memory loss!

inscrutability, the comparison goes so far as to name competing examples of wisdom (4:31). We are unable to identity those named in any way, but they must have been learned people with international reputations. Finally, we are told that Solomon's reputation for wisdom is so spectacular that it is something of a tourist attraction (4:34; see 10:1). In Solomon this hill-country people has now reached the "big leagues" and is no longer second class. Its king is better than the best.

2. Solomon's international reputation is further celebrated in terms of the quantity of his production of wisdom sayings (4:32). It is impossible to assess these numbers as to their reliability. But if one has tried to create a proverbial saying that will withstand the test of accumulated experience, one will know that it is very difficult to formulate even one such saying. Thus 3,000 sayings plus songs is an extraordinary number, surely in keeping with his already stated international reputation.

3. Solomon's wisdom, moreover, embraces all branches of scientific learning, trees and every species of animal life. It is evident that the list in v. 33 is congruent with the primary categories of Genesis 1:20-25. That is, Solomon's learning is commensurate with all of creation. He is indeed a "renaissance man."

This exuberant affirmation of the king would suggest that he is represented and celebrated as the true, judicious, all-knowing manager of all creation. That is, the king is understood as "the true Adam," the *real* human being. And he is treated so in later Israelite development which attributes to him the wisdom materials of Proverbs, Ecclesiastes, and Song of Solomon.

This picture may be the one we are supposed to receive from the text. However it is to be noticed as well that these verses are a

---

Ambivalence about Royal Authority

All through the Bible, the faithful are ambivalent about governmental authority. In the end, one must be context-specific about the question. The two commonly cited passages make the point. In Rom 13:1, Paul is fully dependent upon the government of Rome and so affirms government:

Let every person be subject to the governing authorities; for there is no authority except from God, and those authorities that exist have been instituted by God.

On the other hand, Rev 13:7 emerges from a context in which Rome was persecuting Christians who could not think that the government was given by God:

It was allowed to make war on the saints and to conquer them. It was given authority over every tribe and people and language and nation.

The government may protect or it may slaughter. No doubt the rule of Solomon evoked opposing notions of its legitimacy. The verdict in any particular context is never innocent or disinterested.

conclusion to a long account of (a) Solomon's bureaucracy, (b) Solomon's taxation arrangements, and (c) Solomon's effective military policies. Thus it may be suggested that wisdom is a practice of "the arts" designed primarily to enhance the monarchy's efforts to be "like the other nations" (1 Sam 8:5, 20), only better than they are. Such a recognition allows us to conclude that Solomon may not have been so much a voicer of actual proverbs as a *patron* of the arts of wisdom, who authorized and financed a community of wisdom scholars to produce learning that is imaginative, judicious, and clever in order to compete with the like enterprise in rival monarchies. Thus the phrase "wiser than anyone else" may not so much express awe at the king as assert that "we're number one!" Seen in this way, any romantic notion of Solomon is called into question. Wisdom may be presented here as "an offer of the state," as are taxation and defense.

CONNECTIONS

Solomon is into serious government (4:1-6). By such a list as this, the text raises questions for us about the nature of government and how it relates to faith. In fact, of course, government cannot be discussed theologically in the abstract; one must focus upon particular governments.

In general we may say that biblical faith has a most ambivalent attitude toward government than the biblical text seems to have toward the government of Solomon. [Ambivalence about Royal Authority] From one perspective, government is a necessary and God-given good, whereby public order and well-being may be assured and maintained. In the Bible, the clearest positive statement about government is made by Paul in Romans 13, where he urges acceptance of governmental authority. By contrast, the most extreme negative statement about government is made in Revelation 13, in an apocalyptic vision of the government as a rapacious beast. It is important and ironic that both Romans 13 and Revelation 13 speak of the Roman empire: the quintessential government may be seen variously as good or as vicious beast.

There is no doubt that Solomon's regime is viewed with the same ambivalence. Solomon is indeed a guarantor of *shalom*, as is evident in v. 20. At the same time, equally evident is that Solomon's regime is subsequently viewed as an oppressive, exploitative operation. Every government benefits some at the expense of others. No doubt a verdict depends upon whose interests are served positively or negatively. It is astonishing, but completely understandable, that the same government can be viewed in both ways. The key question of every government—including that of Solomon and including Rome and our own governments—concerns whose interests are enhanced or diminished.

These verses focus on taxes, an endless preoccupation of every government, an endless bone of contention, the cause of many foolish policies, the source of endless political unrest and resistance (4:7-19). The fact that identifiable members of the Jerusalem elite were responsible for the system suggests that it was a lucrative enterprise. While we have no data, it is plausible that this tax collection system was not unlike the one known in the Roman period, when collectors had to produce for the government but were free to collect beyond their quotas for their own benefit. It is entirely plausible that this tax system was greatly exploitative.

This text is lean and leaves us with only bare data. But when we recall the ominous words of son Rehoboam a generation later, we may appreciate the tax burden imposed by his father:

> My father made your yoke heavy, but I will add to your yoke; my father disciplined you with whips, but I will discipline you with scorpions. (1 Kgs 12:14)

The yoke under Solomon is already heavy!

The ambivalence toward taxes derives from the larger ambivalence toward government we have already noted. Governments are entitled to fair support. Indeed, even Jesus authorized, "Render unto Caesar what belongs to Caesar" (Mark 12:17). But we are also able to notice that Jesus commented about burdens and yokes and their easement (Matt 11:28). To be sure, there is nothing explicit in this saying about taxes except that the saying occurs in the Gospel of Matthew, the text (and the evangelist?) most closely concerned with taxation (see v. 19 in the same chapter). It is not impossible that Jesus' revolutionary words about easement also suggest a revolutionary reappraisal of taxation imposed by exploitative governments. And indeed, whether Jesus intended so or not, this issue is clearly on the minds of some of the critics of Solomon.

If the text is read ironically (as I suggest), then these voices of exuberant self-congratulation are to some great extent voices of self-deception (4:20-21). What Solomonic Israel learns is that such "eating and drinking" (=self-indulgence) that does not include everyone cannot be sustained. Already Solomonic eating and drinking excluded some. On two counts, trouble is intrinsic to the enterprise, both because of internal exclusion and because of external coercion.

The triad "eat, drink, be happy" is closely echoed in the parable of Jesus in Luke 12:16-20. In Luke 12:19, the same triad of terms occurs, where the subject of the story, a rich land owner, is portrayed as self-indulgent, unnoticing, and uncaring. Insofar as our text may be linked to that parable, Solomon is cast as the rich man destined to death. The parable of Jesus appears in the context of teaching on covetousness that brings death. Solomon may be taken as a very effective coveter, though none of that is on the surface of our text.

The hints at a built-in contrast between royal affluence and peasant subsistence provides entry for an interpretive comment (4:22-26). On the surface, Solomon's narrative in 1 Kings seems to be a tale of boundless success, prestige, power, and wealth, all the things for which the king did not ask in chapter 3 but that God gave him anyway. If we remember the outcome of the Solomon narrative in chapters 11 and 12 and if we pay attention to the subtle detail of the text, however, we may notice, below the surface success, the rumblings of troublesome things to come.

The imagery of *surface appearance* and *hidden rumblings* is a way to comment on the future of society in which visible wealth and real poverty exist side by side. The Solomonic achievement of dominion may offer a parable for the affluent success and dominion of the U.S. as the last superpower. The surface appearance of our society, like that of Solomon, is impressive; barely hidden, however, is the dangerous and growing gap between wealth and poverty, between access and exclusion, between privilege and subsistence. The text is no ground from which to anticipate "an eruption of revolutionary anger" among us, as the Bible does not make specific predictions.

The reader can decide, as I have decided, whether this portrayal of Solomon carries an implicit critique and whether, as critique, it illuminates our own distorted economy dependent on bloated military expenditure to maintain a consumer economy of seemingly limitless indulgence...all the while disregarding the costs of neglect of the human community and the basic attentiveness necessary for a viable society (4:27-28). [War against the Poor]

If wisdom—here understood as the practice and articulation of proverbial sayings in huge quantities—is seen not so much as discernment as public relations, then these verses might suggest to us the issue of *government funding of the arts* (4:29-34). Such a construal of Solomon's greatness brings the matter of "arts and higher education" closer to our own issues.

War against the Poor

An explosion of technological, economic, and social transformations is creating a new world order in which the gap between rich and poor is widening virtually everywhere. [Richard J. Barnet, *The Global War Against the Poor* (Washington: The Servant Leadership School) 6.]

The globalization of advertising creates a monoculture of consumerism and insatiable desires. This process was aptly called a colonization of consciousness. Biblically speaking, this situation can be compared to the unleashing of the idol Moloch (1 Kgs 11;7; Acts 7:43). [Milan Opocensky, "Address of the General Secretary" (World Alliance of Reformed Churches), 4.]

It is not to be contended that Solomon reflects all of the threats and risks now before us in our economy. But a contemporary reading of this text cannot avoid noticing how readily the text makes contact with this key dimension of current faith issues.

We may first of all observe, positively, that the practice of wisdom as an aesthetic, imaginative, artistic, intellectual venture is seen to be an essential ingredient of good government. It takes no special insight to see that where the arts are not fostered, public life is more likely to have the texture of boorish primitivism.

On the other hand, negatively, when we consider that Solomon's regime is all-encompassing, we may also wonder if the arts (here wisdom) are so embedded in the ambitions of state that they do not in fact embody the kind of liberated expression so crucial to the nurture of the human spirit. It is not difficult to imagine that wisdom teachers in Solomon's enterprise were in some sense "kept," and required to tilt wisdom insights toward royal definitions of reality and monarchial interests. We have no direct evidence of such a requirement. In a deeply suspicious opinion, however, George Mendenhall can suggest:

> As in so many other cases, the eminence of his wisdom, whatever it may have been, was much more a product of his social and political power at the time than of any lasting, intrinsic value. Furthermore, all wise men subsequent to his reign would be obligated by the social system to "update" his archaic observations. Whatever conclusions may eventually be agreed upon by biblical scholars, it is at present virtually impossible to conceive of a grandiose power structure of the time of Solomon that did not produce and support a gamut of technical specialists. It is equally impossible to imagine that the king would not have been *ex officio* the "king of the mountain."[1]

The data is not at all clear. The text, nonetheless, is grounds for rethinking the arts, emancipated imagination, and ideological constraints. These issues are endless problems in our own time as in ancient time.

NOTE

[1]George Mendenhall, *The Tenth Generation: The Origins of the Biblical Tradition* (Baltimore: Johns Hopkins University Press, 1973) 355.

TEMPLE PREPARATIONS

1 Kings 5:1-18

Chapters 5–8 of 1 Kings concern the building of the Jerusalem temple, the primary contribution for which Solomon is remembered in Israel. This larger unit may be divided into three parts: chapter 5 concerns *preparation* for the building of the temple, chapters 6–7 concern the actual work of *construction,* and chapter 8 is an extended *theological reflection* upon the significance of the temple. In reading this material, it is important to recognize that the temple is a radical innovation in the life and faith of Israel. Never before has Israel had a permanent place in which to worship Yahweh. We can assume that such a changed notion of worship decisively impacted Israel's self-understanding and Israel's sense of Yahweh in its midst.

COMMENTARY

Chapter 5 concerns preparation for the temple that consists in securing building materials (lumber and stones) and an adequate work force for the task. While Solomon could supply an adequate work force, he could not from Israel's own territory secure proper lumber. For that reason he entered into a trade pact with Hiram, king of Tyre. While this narrative account appears to be a straightforward report, we will observe two ominous notes just beneath the surface of the text.

Solomon's Request, 5:1-6

Prior to this narrative, we have only the brief note of 2 Samuel 5:11 to indicate that this same Hiram of Tyre had been an ally and partner of Solomon's father, David. In that previous scenario, Hiram had supplied cedar for David's own place. Now Hiram does parallel work for Solomon in the temple construction. But before the work can be undertaken, royal protocol must be observed. When a king dies, treaty agreements must be renewed with the successor ruler in order to assure continuing cooperation. [Attending Royal Funerals] In verse 1, Hiram and Solomon must reaffirm the treaty that existed with David. On the basis of that treaty now renewed, negotiations can

Attending Royal Funerals

Hiram had to renew his alliance with Solomon when David died in order to assure that the alliance would function reliably into the next generation. The same renewal of alliance was enacted by Hanun the Ammonite after his father Nahash had died (2 Sam 10:1-2). Such alliances were not automatic, but required intentional, interpersonal engagement. Thus Solomon and Hiram made a "new peace" (5:12) that was to their mutual advantage and likely at great cost to their subjects.

For a comparable reason we witness "world leaders" in our own time flocking to the funerals of other "world leaders." In fact grieving the death is a minor reason for such gatherings. The purpose is much more to meet the successor of the dead and affirm mutual assurances for the continuing status quo. Thus is power kept in place so that "the haves" continue to have.

proceed concerning the temple. The negotiation consists of parallel speeches by Solomon (5:2-6) and by Hiram (5:7-9). Evidently they agree to exchange goods to the mutual advantage of both regimes. Solomon's speech, however, is not mere trade talk, but is loaded with theological affirmation. The point of his speech is to secure cedar for the building and to assure a common working agreement. (v. 6). But that arrangement is given theological impetus by reference to both David and to Yahweh.

It is more than a little problematic that David did not build a temple. The reason given here is that David was too busy with the war effort. The earlier reason given is that Yahweh is too set free to want to be boxed in a house, but here the reason is domesticated. [A God Too Liberated] Solomon's situation is very different from David's. Whereas David is endlessly vexed by enemies, Solomon has "rest on every side," that is, he has no military

The nomadic lifestyle of the Bedouins comes to mind as an alternative understanding to the construction of a permanent place in which to worship God. (Credit: Barclay Burns. Graphite illustrartion.)

challenges (see 4:21, 25-28). [The Rest-Giving God] Moreover, already in the great announcement of 2 Samuel 7 where Yahweh said he wished no temple, v. 13 affirms that David's own son will indeed build a temple. The theological tradition is evidently ambiguous on the temple, reflecting its disputed, unsettled notion of Yahweh's character. Solomon, in any case, resolved the ambiguity: He will build! But having said that, we should notice that even with this firm resolve that is enacted, the tradition is unsettled enough to caution that it is a house for Yahweh's "name," not for Yahweh's full, personal presence. The "name" is a way of speaking about the presence without overcommitting Yahweh

AΩ **The Rest-Giving God**
The formula of Solomon in v. 4 is traditional: "Yahweh has given me rest on every side." David used it already in 2 Sam 7:11 as the impetus for planning a temple. Before David, moreover, the phrase is used in the old traditions of Moses (Deut 25:19) and Joshua (Josh 21:44). The formuia refers to a social situation free of military threat and political challenge. The phrase is an equivalent for *shalom* that comes only when Yahweh's full rule is established and Yahweh's full purpose enacted. It is such freedom from threat that evokes thoughts of a temple.

and compromising Yahweh's freedom. [A House for a Name] This rich array of freighted theological phrases opens a way for the practicality of what comes next. On the basis of these themes of rest, name, and the oracle of 2 Samuel 7:13, Solomon is prepared to proceed with lumber and manpower (5:6).

A God Too Liberated

The temple texts of 1 Kings 5–8 have 2 Samuel 7:1-17 as their backdrop. In that text, Nathan authorizes a temple for Yahweh (v. 3). Subsequently Yahweh declares, through Nathan to David, that Yahweh does not want a temple, precisely because it violates Yahweh's freedom:

> I have not lived in a house since the day I brought up the people of Israel from Egypt to this day, but I have been moving about in a tent and a tabernacle. Wherever I have moved about among all the people of Israel, did I ever speak a word with any of the tribal leaders of Israel, whom I commanded to shepherd my people Israel, saying, "Why have you not built me a house of cedar?" (vv. 6-7)

Yahweh wants no temple because Yahweh is on the move, completely unfettered. And certainly Yahweh wants no cedar house, because cedar smacks of affluence and indulgence. After 2 Sam 7: 6-7, ironically, the text proceeds to authorize a temple in v. 13, an authorization taken up and implemented in our text. It is clear that royal Israel had to navigate carefully through the difficult theological question of a temple. A king must have a temple, even if Yahweh is opposed to the notion. The question for institutionalized forms of faith endlessly concerns Yahweh's capacity for "moving about among all the people."

AΩ **A House for a Name**
The phrase "a house for the name of Yahweh" is an important attempt in ancient Israel to make theological sense out of the presence of Yahweh in a place of worship. The phrase is properly placed within the tradition of Deuteronomy:

> Then you shall bring everything that I command you to the place that the LORD your God will choose as a dwelling for his name…If the place where the LORD your God will choose to put his name is too far from you…. (Deut 12:11, 21)

The phrase is an attempt to make an affirmation that lives between two theological dangers. One danger is to make Yahweh so remote that the worship place is no place of real presence. Such a conclusion may be drawn if it is affirmed that Yahweh is far away, in heaven and not at all in the designated place of worship (see Deut 26:15). The other danger is the opposite, to affirm that Yahweh is *fully and without reservation present* in the worship place, and therefore completely available and on call. The formula of the name seeks to avoid both excessive remoteness and presumptuous availability.

When we consider the formula and Solomon's use of it, we may marvel at the shrewdness and delicacy of the formulation. We may also ponder how difficult the question of Presence is, and how ambiguous every claim about God's "Real Presence" in our worship must be. It is the difficulty and ambiguity that have been present in the church's long dispute about "Real Presence" in the Eucharist.

Hiram's Response, 5:7-12

Hiram's response to Solomon is fully cooperative. Notably, Hiram's initial doxology of verse 7 is not addressed to Solomon. He speaks rather of the praise of Yahweh and Yahweh's gift of a son of David. Even this outsider (Gentile!) is smitten with this wise king and with the God who has given such wisdom. Clearly, according to the text, the alliance is completed on Solomon's terms, so overwhelming is Solomon and so overwhelming is the God who empowers and legitimates Solomon.

As a consequence, Hiram accepts the terms of agreement. Hiram will provide cedar timber for Solomon, which Solomon did not otherwise have. Solomon will provide for Hiram food that Hiram apparently did not have. Solomon will provide food because of the vast tax-collecting, food-producing apparatus we have seen in chapter 4. It should be noted that in vv. 8-9 the term "needs" is *hephets*, elsewhere rendered "pleasure." There is a tone of affluence and self-indulgence in the royal rhetoric. The trade agreement is to serve the large ambitions of both kings.

The remainder of the chapter narrates the implementation authorized by the two speeches (5:10-18). The exchange is long-term, "year by year" (5:11). The notice of "wisdom" in v. 12 matches Hiram's recognition of Solomon's wisdom in v. 7, making clear that his wisdom consists in skill in statecraft and in international economics, a very different use from the references in chapters 3 and 4.

AΩ **Stones Treasured and Rejected**
The stones quarried for the temple are clearly beautiful; they are called "great, costly stones." The phrase indicates that the supervisors selected only the very finest materials for the temple. That provision for the temple is picked up in the poetry of Isaiah where the stonework for the temple has become metaphorical:

See, I am laying in Zion a foundation stone,
    a tested stone,
    a precious cornerstone, a sure foundation. (Isa 28:16)

In this verse, the "precious cornerstone" would seem to be the utter reliability of Yahweh in whom Israel may trust completely. That is, architecture has been made a vehicle for a faith assurance.

The Isaiah text, moreover, is quoted in Mark 12:10, Acts 4:11, and 1 Pet 2:6-7. Only now the imagery of "stone" refers to Jesus, who has been rejected (crucified) and then become the head of the corner (resurrection). The imagery of temple has been redeployed to speak of Jesus (see John 2:19-22). The effect of such a transposition is that in the story of Jesus the temple itself has ceased to be the center of attention and is regarded as profoundly problematic. The ongoing utilization of the temple imagery suggests how biblical language is endlessly in process and underway and not settled. It also attests to the uneasiness Israel characteristically senses about the temple. While the temple is indispensable for a great state such as Solomon has founded, it is theologically problematic. It was never as easy for Yahweh as it was for Solomon.

Solomon's Builders, 5:13-18

In verse 13, the narrative account takes a turn. Now the subject is no longer building supplies, but a labor force. The labor force for this public works project is from "all Israel," that is, from every tax unit in the kingdom, a huge work force. The project consists in a work assignment in Lebanon where Tyre is located and where the cedars are to be cut. Moreover, we have already seen in 4:6 that Adoniram is in charge of forced labor. The large number of workers and supervisors is likely designed to impress the reader with the scope and significance of the project; at the same time, however, it also indicates what an all-consuming enterprise this is, surely impinging upon every aspect of the economy, so that the capacity of Israelites to enjoy their own produce is likely placed in deep jeopardy. Along with timber, now we are told of quarrying stones for the temple, stones that are costly and that are handled with great artistry. [Stones Treasured and Rejected] One gains the impression of great enterprising activity with passion, care for effectiveness, and brilliant organization.

CONNECTIONS

We may observe two more ominous aspects of the entire temple venture. We cannot be sure they are intended by the text, as we do

Julius Schnoor von Carolsfeld. *Solomon Builds the Temple*. 19th century. Woodcut. *Das Buch der Bucher in Bilden*. (Credit: Dover Pictorial Archive Series)

not know how ironically the text may be taken. But if the text is more than a simple report, two items require our attention.

First, following the lead of his father David, Solomon eagerly and without hesitation entered into a trade pact with Hiram the Phoenician. On the face of it, that would seem to be innocent enough, except that on two counts, the tradition invites serious reservation.

First, cooperation with Hiram and Tyre (Phoenicia) is entry into a world of trade and commerce viewed as fundamentally alien to the covenantal identity of Israel. The strong indictment of Isaiah 2:6-22 specifically focuses upon "clasping hands with foreigners" (v. 6), an image of making economic agreements. Moreover, the "cedars of Lebanon" are named in v. 13 as an emblem of pride and arrogance. More extensively, Isaiah 23 and Ezekiel 26–28 view Tyre, later on, as a trading operation modelling autonomy, arrogance, self-indulgence, and indifference to any moral, covenantal dimension of reality. Solomon's engagement with Hiram, in the context of prophetic faith, is to be viewed with deep alarm, as sure to distort the community.

This ominous prospect is reinforced by the awareness that "cedar" is taken in the prophets as a sign of affluence that invites autonomy and indifference. In addition to Isaiah 2:13, see Isaiah 37:24, Jeremiah 22:14-15, and Zephaniah 2:14. [Cedar as Social Symbol] "Cedar" is a sign of commoditization that turns a community away from genuine neighborly care. With respect to both *Tyre* and *cedar*, Solomon may be perceived as turning Israel away from its true Yahwistic identity. And since the engagement with Tyre and the investment in cedar are both in the context of the temple, it is necessary to view the temple of Solomon as, at best, an ambiguous achievement. While the temple is apparently to the honor of Yahweh, this text seems to hint that in important ways, the temple is also a dangerous distortion of Yahwism.

The second critical aspect of this text is the recruitment of "forced labor" in the interest of this grand state project. Something disastrous happens to the economy when it is largely devoted to such a grandiose project. Moreover, the reality of forced labor in such huge numbers is surely reminiscent, in faithful Israel, of the great state building projects of Egypt (Exod 1:11) whereby early Israel was forced into labor and treated harshly. More specifically, the organization under three hundred supervisors recalls the "taskmasters and supervisors" that abused the Israelite slaves long ago (Exod 5:10-14). The text suggests that Solomon has forgotten that ancient torment and has radically shifted Israel to a commodity culture that specializes in oppressiveness and exploitation.

Cedar as Social Symbol

The prophet Jeremiah castigates the dynasty and particularly Jehoiakim for attachment to cedar as a symbol of power, prestige, and importance:

> Woe to him who builds his house by unrighteousness,
>   and his upper rooms by injustice;
> who makes his neighbors work for nothing,
>   and does not give them their wages;
> who says, "I will build myself a spacious house
>   with large upper rooms,"
> and who cuts out windows for it,
>   paneling it with cedar,
>   and painting it with vermilion.
> Are you a king because you compete in cedar?
> Did not your father eat and drink
>   and do justice and righteousness?
>   Then it was well with him.
> He judged the cause of the poor and needy;
>   then it was well.
> Is not this to know me? says the LORD. (Jer 22:13-16)

Such a royal self-assessment, from prophetic perspective, is completely misinformed. The prophetic poem reflects an awareness that such an embrace of "conspicuous consumption" characteristically tells against justice and righteousness. At the end of the royal line, Jehoiakim embraces what is already underway in Solomon's ostentatious temple.

In such a seemingly innocent report there is much for us to ponder if we are to receive this text as scripture. The convergence of a *trade pact* and *forced labor* may invite us to rethink a global economy (for that is what Tyre sponsored) in which the needs and yearnings of citizen-subjects are completely submerged in ambitious royal schemes. Indeed, the focus is now not even on the

In Doré's engraving, the mass organization of forced labor is evident through the tremendous effort required to fell and transport the cedars to Jerusalem. The illustration refers to the biblical passage 1 Kgs 5:16-24.

Gustave Doré. *The Cedars of Lebanon Destined for the Construction of the Temple*. 19th century. Engraving. From the *Illustrated Bible*.

(Credit: Dover Pictorial Archive Series)

AΩ **Worship as Self-Indulgence**

A long time after Solomon, a prophetic poem voices a polemic against worship as self-indulgence:

> Yet day after day they seek me
>   and delight to know my ways,
>   as if they were a nation that practiced righteousness
>   and did not forsake the ordinance of their God;
> they ask of me righteous judgments,
>   they delight to draw near to God.
> "Why do we fast, but you do not see?
>   Why humble ourselves, but you do not notice?"
> Look, you serve your own interests on your fast day,
>   and oppress all your workers....
> If you refrain from trampling the sabbath,
>   from pursuing your own interests on my holy day;
>   if you call the sabbath a delight
> and the holy day of the LORD honorable,
>   if you honor it, not going your own ways,
>   serving your own interests, or pursuing your own affairs....
>   (Isa 58:2-3, 13)

In this text, the term *haphets* is used five times, variously translated as "delight" and "interest." The poem concerns worship that suits the whim of the worshiper without reference to the reality of God (see also Amos 5:4). The text on Solomon's temple is not explicitly about such self-preoccupation, but the aura of satiation that pervades the Solomon narrative suggests such a dimension of self-indulgence in the temple in all its splendor.

"needs" of Solomon and Hiram, but rather their "delight" in self-aggrandizing ways. [Worship as Self-Indulgence]

That convergence of *trade pact* and *forced labor*, moreover, is in the service of the temple. Such a convergence may suggest that ambitious, ostentatious religion can indeed collude with the forces of economic oppression. Surely such a religious enterprise has lost its sharp edge of critical awareness and energy. Nobody suggests here that Solomon is "wicked." Rather, the economic-temple project takes on a life of its own, makes its own demands, and enacts its own appetites in uncaring ways. It takes little imagination to see that such a trade pact, with its necessary state supports, puts the religious enterprise firmly on the wrong side of what are Israel's characteristic human questions.

TEMPLE CONSTRUCTION

1 Kings 6:1–7:51

With the completion of preparations for the building of the temple (supplies and manpower), these two chapters now take up the actual construction of the temple. The chapters trace the building of the temple (6:1-38), other buildings in the royal complex (7:1-12), and the internal furnishings of the temple (7:13-51). The apparent purpose of this entire report is to articulate the splendor of Solomon's achievement as a builder, presented to establish Solomon's ostentatious piety or perhaps to lead the reader to awe, amazement, and gratitude for Solomon's achievement.

At the same time, however, one cannot help but notice the opulence of the enterprise made possible only by forced labor (cheap labor) and what must have been coercive tax policies required to help pay for the project. And if one entertains the thought, perhaps suggested by the text, that the entire project has as much to do with the glorification of Solomon as it does with the honoring of Yahweh, then one may return to wonder about the tension in the authorizing text of 2 Samuel 7:5-7 precluding a temple, while v. 13 authorizes it. From the ground up, the temple in Jerusalem is seen in the tradition as an ominously ambiguous undertaking. If we keep that issue in focus, then we will not be too upset by the fact that the text at many points is unclear and inconsistent. One has a very difficult time reconstructing or understanding the actual detailed situation of the temple from the text. But then we may surmise that such a specific architectural gain is not the primary interest of the text. It is enough either to *exult in the achievement* or to *critique the indulgence*, depending on how the text is understood.

COMMENTARY

Building Solomon's Temple, 6:1-38

Chapter 6 is bound by two interesting affirmations. At the outset, the project is situated with a very precise chronological notation (6:1). The date is likely a theological attempt to situate the building of the temple at what was regarded, from the perspective of the framers of the text, as the "midpoint" of Israelite history. [A Theological Chronology] Thus the date, like much else in the text, is to be understood not in terms of historical accuracy, but as a theological reference point. If the text is perhaps framed or composed in the exile, then it may be that the temple building is offered at the midpoint between *Exodus* and *Exile*.

The chronological orientation of v. 1 is matched in v. 38 by a concluding statement that the temple building was finished (*kalah*), that is, completed, in a perfect way. It is noteworthy that the building project lasted seven years, a number that, like the chronology of v. 1, is to be understood theologically and not chronologically. The verb "finish" is, not incidentally, the same verb used for the *completion of creation* (Gen 2:1) and the *completion of the tabernacle* (Exod 39:32; 40:33). Because the temple, like the tabernacle, is a place of worship and, like creation, is an ordered cosmos, we may imagine that the three uses are parallel and intentional [On Sevens for Completeness] The references in vv. 1 and 38 seem to put us on notice that this text is theologically self-conscious and not so much concerned for historical-architectural accuracy.

The basic plan for the temple is sketched out in vv. 2-10. The floor plan is in three parts. [A Borrowed Floor Plan] The terms used in the NRSV for the three parts are "vestibule," "nave" (*hekal*), and "inner sanctuary" (*debir*). The older terminology characterized the last two chambers as "Holy Place" and "Holy of Holies." Interestingly, NRSV uses terms that are available from contemporary church architecture. The older terminology paid attention to the "degrees" of holiness expressed architecturally, so that movement from vestibule to nave to inner sanctuary represented an increasing measure of holiness requiring an intensification of exclusiveness. That is, the vestibule had relative open access, the nave was more exclusive, and the inner sanctuary was off limits except for the

A Theological Chronology
There are a variety of ways to understand the chronological note with which the chapter begins. [See the summary statement of John Gray, *1 & 2 Kings*, OTL (Philadelphia: Westminster Press, 1963) 150-51.] None of these possible explanations, however, is to be taken as historically accurate. Once we are freed of that connection, it is possible to consider the date given for its theological import, in relation to Exodus, Exile, and the larger shape of the history of Israel.

AΩ **On Sevens for Completeness**
Of course seven is regarded in Israelite tradition as a sign of perfection. Thus the number here need not be taken literally, but may be a way of speaking about the perfection of the temple. The use of seven in this way is paralleled in the work of creation in seven days. It is, moreover, noteworthy that the construction of the tabernacle by Moses is directed in seven speeches, surely designed to parallel the seven days of creation (Exod 25–31).

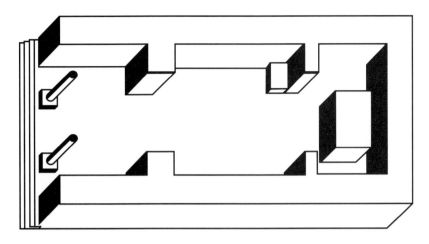

An isometric drawing of the eighth- or ninth-century Tainat shrine found between Aleppo and Antioch in Syria. Two free-standing pillars were located in the porch area. This drawing is based on a sketch that initially appeared in *The Biblical Archaeologist,* IV (1941):21.

A Borrowed Floor Plan

It is commonly agreed that the floor plan of the temple with its division into three rooms with graded levels of holiness is not unique to Israel. "This tripartite plan is similar to that of many of the Canaanite temples excavated in Palestine and also to the Neo-Hittite temples in N Syria." The closest parallel is at the site of Tell Tainat. That there are so many parallels means that the builders and designers utilized copies of other temple plans, clearly not designing temple space according to the distinctiveness of Yahweh. Such an architectural procedure worked powerfully against theological claims of distinctiveness made for Yahweh.

Carol Meyers, "Temple, Jerusalem," *The Anchor Bible Dictionary, 6 vols. Si-Z* (New York: Doubleday, 1992) 6:355.

highest form of priestly entry on special occasions. This arrangement of holiness reflects a hierarchical understanding of public access, public privilege, public significance, and, in the end, public worth. It must not be thought that this architectural arrangement was primarily *theological* to enhance the deity nor *aesthetic* to provide an impressive order. It was also aggressively *sociological,* to sort people out and control *access* to holiness in ways reflective of a carefully guarded hierarchical social order. The more "upper-class" elite, the greater access and nearness to God. The less socially valuable, the sooner came the prohibitive barriers to access. It was a way of sorting out social relationships in the name of God's holiness [Degrees of Holiness]

Moreover, it is commonly thought that this three-room arrangement was a rather conventional Near Eastern (Canaanite?) arrangement imported into Israelite Jerusalem; perhaps Hiram the Phoenician brought his own architect along with the building materials (see 7:13). Thus it would appear that Solomon utilized

Degrees of Holiness

The priestly presentation of all things cultic in the Old Testament is concerned for the holiness of Yahweh, that Yahweh's holiness should be recognized, honored, and not infringed upon. That holiness, moreover, is regarded as almost a physical, palpable substance that occupies space. While Yahweh's holiness is everywhere effective in the cultic life of Israel, according to priestly discernment there are relative intensities of that holiness, so that Yahweh's palpable presence is more acute, dangerous, and powerful in some places than in others. In the floor plan of the temple with its three distinct chambers, the three rooms are arranged so that as one goes from the vestibule, to the nave, to the inner sanctuary, one moves to greater and greater intensity of holiness so that the "Holy of Holies" is the most holy place where Yahweh's holiness is most concentrated, most powerful, and most dangerous.

See Walter Houston, *Purity & Monotheism: Clean & Unclean Animals in Biblical Law,* JSOT Supp. 140 (Sheffield: Sheffield Academic Press, 1992) and Philip P. Jenson, *Graded Holiness: A Key to the Priestly Conception of the World,* JSOT Supp. 140 (Sheffield: JSOT Press, 1992).

conventional practices that are no particular reflection of a Yahwism rooted in egalitarianism, but likely reflects a hierarchical ordering of society that is inimical to Yahwism. If that is correct, it is not difficult to understand the initial resistance to a temple in 2 Samuel 7:5-7 and the ongoing critique of the temple in the prophets. [Jeremiah on the Temple]

We may notice several other features of the temple that witness to its glory and splendor: (a) It is perfectly symmetrical in terms of cubic measures. That is, it enacts and communicates a deep sense of *orderedness,* thus asserting that the temple and the God of the temple are an alternative to chaos and disorder. Such an equation of *presence* and *order* in the religious practice of the privileged and the powerful will not surprise us. Such a practice serves, along the way, to substantiate all the vehicles for social order and social control that are administered by the power classes, royal and priestly.

(b) The *orderedness* of the enterprise is matched by the *poshness* of the construction. That is, no expense is spared to make it the finest, thus glorifying the God of the temple and enhancing the sponsoring monarchy. This is reflected in the complexity of "stories" to the building (though the matter is not very clear in the text). That the building has "stories" suggests a rather elaborate form of architecture. This, moreover, is matched by "windows," an elegant and expensive architectural element available in the ancient world only

Jeremiah on the Temple

The great prophets of Israel, rooted as they appear to be in the Torah traditions of Moses, take a consistently critical stance toward the temple. They regard the temple as a temptation for Israel to deny its own distinctiveness and to distort the radicality of Yahweh. None of the prophets offers a more trenchant critique of the temple than does Jeremiah. Most specifically, chapter 7 of Jeremiah, called by scholars "The Temple Sermon," is a massive attack on the pretensions of the temple as a place of worship where the Torah demands of Yahweh have been silenced so that Yahweh is seen to be a God who offers only security without requirement. Thus in v. 4 the prophet mocks routinized temple chants. In v. 11, he accuses Israel of violating commandments and then treating the temple as a place in which to hide, like "a den of robbers." And in v. 12, he warns that the temple in Jerusalem is not immune from the threat of Yahweh, but that in the end it will be devastated like the old shrine in the North at Shiloh. Obviously such a critique is well beyond the horizon of the temple texts of Solomon. Indeed, it may be suggested that Solomon introduced into Israel the very understandings of the temple against which the prophets protest.

The luxurious appearance of the temple has captured the imagination of artists for centuries. This illustration shows the overall epic grandeur of the temple.

Reconstruction of the Temple of Solomon. (Credit: Foto Marburg/Art Resource)

to the powerful and the wealthy. [Conspicuous Royal Consumption] The construction of stories and windows is further enhanced by the use of cedar (6:9-10). We have already seen in chapter 5 that cedar is likely a coded signal in this narrative both for financial extravagance and for glad cooperation with non-Israelite forces (Hiram) who do not understand Yahweh or take Yahwism with any seriousness.

(c) Along with orderliness and poshness, v. 7 suggests an intentional effort at *dignity* befitting a royal enterprise. We already know in 5:15-18 that skilled stonecutters were involved in the building project. But now we are told that the act of stonecutting that involves hammers and chisels and inevitably noise is done at the quarry and not at the temple site in order to avoid disturbance at

Conspicuous Royal Consumption

Thorstein Veblen was a classical sociologist who in the early part of the century analyzed U.S. wealth. He arrived at the phrase "conspicuous consumption" to characterize the wealth of very rich people who needed to spend their money in ostentatious ways, because having wealth was reenforced by *being seen to have wealth through expenditure*. Veblen's phrase, "conspicuous consumption," may be pertinent to the "costly" aspects of Solomon's temple. It is evident in the report of the temple that Solomon lavished the temple with expensive fixtures, surely in part to be seen as having wealth and as pious in the devotion of that wealth to the temple. As Veblen saw, such consumption is a contradiction to genuine human values. In the same way, such consumption in ancient Israel is a contradiction to the claims of covenant. On such conspicuousness in ancient Israel, see Jer 22:14-15a.

Thorstein Veblen, *Theory of the Leisure Class* (New York: Viking Penguin, 1994).

the holy place. This is an astonishing notation suggesting that the process of building is understood as a tactic for enhancing the final product. But noticeably, the idea of *silence* is likely incongruent with the vigorous, boisterous praise of Yahweh on other occasions (as in Exod 15:20-21). The embrace of silence likely reflects the royal desire of the power class that is enhanced and reassured about power by having no disruptive intrusions or disturbances in the arranged ordering of worship life. Thus the summons of Habakkuk 2:20 is not a politically directed statement; it nonetheless serves a certain notion of worship along with a certain practice of social control:

> But the LORD is in his holy temple;
>   let all the earth keep silence before him! (Hab 2:20)

The convergence of *orderliness*, *poshness*, and *dignity* produces a temple suitable for a certain kind of Yahweh and fit for a king. Not surprisingly, the construction of a royal chapel [A Royal Chapel] reuses the term "finished" to assert its perfect completion. Such a structure must guarantee both divine presence and special access to holiness for the royal establishment.

In this chapter, vv. 11-12 are odd and merit special attention. They are sandwiched between the term "finish" in v. 9 and "finish" in v. 14 that sounds like a reiteration of v. 9. The two verses between, commonly termed Deuteronomic because they reflect the stern covenantal requirements of Deuteronomy, echo the "if" of 3:14 and are argued in an "if-then" pattern making the presence of Yahweh in Israel deeply *conditional*. The "if" condition concerns obedience to the Torah commandments. The "then" consequence of obedience is the fulfillment of the promise that Yahweh will "dwell" in the midst of Israel and not "forsake." The negative counterpart to this assertion is that *disobedience* will lead to the *absence of Yahweh*. That is, Yahweh's presence to save is not at all assured by the temple, but depends upon Torah obedience.

We may ask why these verses are situated just here, since they are in deep tension with the context that offers a high view of temple. These brief verses in

A Royal Chapel

Kings in the ancient world characteristically built temples to honor god(s), whereby honor accrued to the king as well. Such temples constructed by the king and for the worship of the king are not to be understood as public churches. Rather they function as royal chapels and serve "reasons of state." They may be carriers of values and commitments offered to the public, but the access and purpose is for the royal enterprise. In the Old Testament, the most obvious case of the "royal chapel" is the warning given by the priest Amaziah to the prophet Amos who had uttered harsh judgment against the royal house:

Never again prophesy at Bethel, for it is the king's sanctuary, and it is a temple of the kingdom. (Amos 7:13)

In similar fashion, we may judge that the temple in Jerusalem was primally a royal chapel to serve reasons of state.

Temple and Torah

The juxtaposition of themes makes clear that in the difficult theological adjudications of the Old Testament, the claims of Temple and the claims of Torah are in deep dispute and are indeed the primal faith options available to Israel. The temple is linked to the entire royal enterprise and appeals to the unconditional promises of Yahweh prefigured to Abraham and uttered to David. The Torah tradition, rooted in Moses and echoed by the prophets, focuses upon the commands of Yahweh. While biblical faith takes both claims seriously, in the end the principles carried by Temple and Torah are not readily harmonized. And so the several traditions, as this one, work at the tension. The texts of Kings in the end are the theological achievement of the Deuteronomists who seek to hold these claims together, the tension notwithstanding. In my judgment, however, this tradition rooted in the book of Deuteronomy finally comes down on the side of Torah. Thus it is important that the most explicit promise of presence is stated in the midst of Torah; the statement makes clear that the presence of Yahweh in the temple is not easy or automatic, but depends upon a community of Torah keepers.

---

fact reflect the defining tension in Israel's faith between *temple theology* and *Torah theology*. In large measure these chapters are unqualified in offering the temple as a guarantee of Yahweh's presence. These two verses, however, reflect a dissenting opinion that is deeply rooted in Israel's core memory. [Temple and Torah] This tension likely reflects a deep social tension as well, so that the urban elites gathered around Solomonic trust in the temple, but the peasant population remained deeply suspicious of a religious enterprise that seems self-indulgent and that patently lacks the sharp edge of a critical ethic. It is evident, moreover, that the two perspectives cannot be easily harmonized or compromised. Israel's yearning for Yahweh is framed as a profound either/or that continues to vex and enliven Israel's faith.

The remainder of the chapter concerns the completion of the temple and its furnishings (6:14-38). The unit begins with yet another statement, he "finished" it (see v. 9). The first part of the unit describes the completion of the walls and the ceilings. In addition to the ordered symmetry of the whole, we may notice four specific elements:

1. The reference, yet again, to cedar and to the carving of gourds and open flowers suggests great attention to aesthetic detail. The old Torah tradition focuses upon ethical requirements, an accent that is common in Protestant and especially Puritan traditions. By way of the same contrast, the temple traditions of ancient Israel prize the aesthetic and artistic alongside the ethical. The temple is indeed devised for "the beauty of holiness" (see Pss 27:4; 29:2; 90:17; 96:6, 9). God is known through and mediated by beauty. Again the temple may be linked to traditions of creation and tabernacle. In the creation liturgy of Genesis 1, it is likely that the verdict, "It is good, it is very good" (Gen 1:10, 12, 18, 21, 31) refers to an aesthetic assertion, "It is lovely." The tabernacle

tradition, moreover, pays great attention to the materials required for loveliness (Exod 25:3-8 and generally in chapter 28). There is in the tabernacle tradition, as in our text, no restraint about expenditure for loveliness where Yahweh's presence may dwell, a loveliness quite contrasted with the ugliness or ordinariness of that which lies outside the sanctuary.

2. While we have seen the extravagance of cedar in the preceding, now the whole of the inner sanctuary is overlaid with gold. In vv. 20-22, "gold" is mentioned six times, creating an impression that this most costly, most extravagant, rarest, most lovely commodity creates a suitable environment for the dwelling of Yahweh. Again the provision is consistent with the tabernacle that is completely decorated with gold (see Exod 25:3, 11, 12, 13, 17, 18, 24, 26, 28, 29, 31, 36, 38, 39, etc.). Nothing is too good for Yahweh! Obviously one may recoil at the extravagance, not unlike the building of great cathedrals overlaid with gold taken off the backs of peasants in "underprivileged" parts of the world. Alongside that easy and obvious criticism, however, we may notice what this extravagance means to affirm about Yahweh. This God is a royal personage for whom these great extravagances are only barely good enough. When the king or the queen comes, only the best can be utilized. And this God is the God of Solomon, greater than the king who himself lives in a world of finery. This greater-than-Solomon must receive all that Solomon can muster.

3. The most holy place (inner sanctuary, Holy of Holies) receives special attention (6:16, 20-22). This is the small, limited-access recess at the back of the nave where the holiness of God is most intense. It is indeed the place of "real presence." And therefore it is the part of the temple most luminously dominated by gold (6:20-22), which makes it a suitable habitation for "the Holy One." This small room becomes the pivot point of the entire temple. It is, in other traditions, apparently curtained off to provide a screen of

---

An Exilic Retelling

Most scholars think that the material in Kings was finally shaped as we have it in the Exile. It was, moreover, shaped as a pastoral response to the needs of exiles who felt abandoned by Yahweh. The temple is one offer of the presence of God that is available to the exiles, albeit at a distance. If this way of understanding the text is valid, then it is important that the Torah requirements are not accented in the presentation. The notion that the temple is "perfect" suggests that it is a perfect and sure offer of Yahweh's presence without qualification or reservation. The pastoral dimension of such an assertion is that the perfect offer of presence is not in doubt, even for exiles. Thus the notion of "perfect" is neither architectural nor theological but pastoral in import. According to this reading, the account of the temple is retold with attentiveness to the acute pastoral needs and sensitivities of the exiles in their season of absence.

privacy for the holy one, to prevent access and prying eyes (Exod 40:3). And it is a place for God alone, to be intruded upon only annually by the High Priest (Lev 16:3-4, 11-16). The details of this arrangement are not clear in the text, but great reverence for Yahweh's presence is unmistakable.

4. Into this special place has come "the ark of the covenant of Yahweh" (6:19). The ark is the most ancient and most treasured instrument of Yahweh's presence, perhaps to be understood as a vehicle upon which the invisible deity rides (see 1 Sam 6:10-12; 2 Sam 6:12-19).

The work is completed and pronounced "perfect" (*tôm*) (6:22). Every possible preparation has been completed. Yahweh will now "dwell" there. Notice that in this exultant summary, the Torah strictures of vv. 11-13 are not acknowledged. All is in readiness. [An Exilic Retelling]

Having said that, the narrative description continues with even more refinements (6:23-26). These verses consider the matter in great detail, again the symmetry of cubits, again gold, and again cedar. The primary new element in these verses is the cherubim that are richly decorated temple objects. They are apparently wood carvings of winged creatures, carvings that decorate the Holy of Holies and represent courtly attendants upon the royal presence. While the wood carvings are only decorations, with any sacramental sensitivity they become visible reinforcements of presence, for this Royal Presence is never alone, but always with attendants. In the later liturgical fantasy of Ezekiel, the winged creatures are imagined to be live creatures (not wood carvings) who either transport or accompany the mobile deity, both in departure from the temple into exile (Ezek 10:1-22) and perhaps aiding in the return to the temple from exile (Ezek 43:1-7). This liturgic fantasy helps us appreciate the splendor and power of the decor of the temple that is deeply linked to the sense of Yahweh's presence. Alongside Ezekiel 10 and 43, attention may be given to Isaiah 6, wherein the prophet in the temple is confronted by seraphs who attend to the awesome, holy one in a regal environment. The seraphs of Isaiah 6 and the cherubim of Ezekiel 10 and 43 are closely linked. In both cases what might have seemed mere carvings are, in sacramental context, lively attendants to the Holy One. Clearly the residence of the Holy One, the Holy of Holies, is a lively, peopled place, made possible by careful, generous, attentive preparation.

The chapter concludes with another declaration of completeness (6:37-38). The temple is completed, in a sense exactly parallel to the period required to complete creation.

AΩ **Finish**

Remarkably, the report of the temple construction uses the term "finish" repeatedly (1 Kgs 6:9, 14; 7:1; 9:1, 25). The repeated use of the term suggests a sense of completeness. All is now ready for the habitation of Yahweh in the temple. The term moves the awareness of Israel from the physical construction to the theological occupation, thus assuring presence. It is important to see the completion of the temple in relation to the completion of creation (Gen 2:1) and completion of the tabernacle (Exod 39:22; 40:33). In each case the completion is a sign of well-being with God. In the great hymn of Charles Wesley, "Love Divine, All Loves Excelling," the verb "finish" is an imperative expressing a hope for what God has not yet completed:

> Finish then the new creation,
> Pure and spotless let us be;
> Let us see thy great salvation
> Perfectly restored in thee!

Whereas the hymn awaits God's final work, the temple texts celebrate that the work is now fully accomplished.

Recognized as working in the style of the French Renaissance, Fouquet's style also reflects the late Gothic tradition in northern Europe. Not only the subject of a French cathedral, but his inclusion of a minute detail reflects this Gothic influence. In Fouquet's cityscape many figures operate in a broad space that is defined by a foreground, middle ground, and background—a development associated with the redefining of pictorial space in the Italian Renaissance. Fouquet incorporates elements of medieval and Renaissance styles. It is somewhat ironic that this manuscript illumination was entitled, "Building the Temple of Jerusalem." It is as if the paradisal Temple of Jerusalem is coming to fruition in the present time of the artist. The temple is depicted in the form of an elegant Gothic cathedral. It is worth noting that the idea of completion, so important in the biblical text, is perhaps at work in the artist's expression in this illumination. The entire "cosmos" of the medieval world of France is involved with this building as a variety of stone craftsman labor in the lower section of the illumination, replete with stonecutters, sculptors, and mortar mixers. Laborers move to and fro into the building and townspeople are also visible. The King of France, as Solomon, is shown blessing the crowd and, simultaneously perhaps, identifying himself with the completion of the cathedral. The artist may have had the same intention as King Solomon in identifying the will of the King with the will of God. Fouquet depicts the ascending gold facing on the facade of the cathedral. This is possibly a symbol of the "heavenly Jerusalem" in the medieval Gothic world. By association, the Solomonic temple was depicted as an embodiment of the completeness of the work of Yahweh.

Jean Fouquet. *Building the Temple of Jerusalem*. c.1475. Illumination on vellum. Bibliotheque Nationale, Paris, France. (Credit: Giraudon/Art Resource, NY)

Building Solomon's House, 7:1-12

The tale of the temple began in 6:1-38 and continues in 7:13-31. It is, interrupted, however, in 7:1-12 by an account of Solomon's completion of "his own house." The phrasing of 7:1 indicates that "his house" is in fact an extended complex of buildings, of which the temple is only one element. Indeed, the entire complex required thirteen years to build, contrasted with only seven years for the temple. The two numbers suggest that in terms of effort—and perhaps appearance—the temple is not the central building and perhaps not the most noticeable. The introductory formula of v. 1, moreover, uses the verb "finish" yet again. Solomon is one who can "finish." [Finish]

The royal complex, according to this list, includes five buildings. We know almost nothing about these buildings. From vv. 2-5 we may generalize that they were, like the temple, lovely in their symmetry and constructed from the finest, most expensive materials. While the buildings no doubt had important functional value, they were also a "showcase" for the success and prosperity of the regime, unprecedented in Israel. That success and prosperity, as we have already seen, are based on an effective *internal system* of tax collection and forced labor, coupled with an *external system* of tributes from colony states. All the wealth of the royal apparatus permits an enormous self-exhibition by the king, the one "greater than David" (2:37).

Of the five buildings, we may comment on only two of them. The "Hall of Justice" likely refers to the "supreme court" building where the king's judiciary functioned. We have no data about the administration of justice under Solomon, though it is clear that justice is a major responsibility of the king. In order that we may be prepared for the harsh culmination of the Solomonic era, we may pay attention to two strands of royal justice in other texts. On the one hand the liturgical claims of Psalm 72 indicate that justice is the task of the monarch. Moreover, "justice" in this liturgical piece consists in intervention on behalf of the poor who have no other leverage in public affairs. [Royal Responsibility] In this Psalm the role of the king is parallel to or an imitation of the role of the true God in Psalm 82.

> **Royal Responsibility**
> Give the king your justice, O God,
> and your righteousness to a king's son.
> May he judge your people with righteousness,
> and your poor with justice.
> May the mountains yield prosperity for the people,
> and the hills, in righteousness.
> May he defend the cause of the poor of the people,
> give deliverance to the needy,
> and crush the oppressor....
> For he delivers the needy when they call,
> the poor and those who have no helper.
> he has pity on the weak and the needy,
> and saves the lives of the needy.
> From oppression and violence he redeems their life;
> and precious is their blood in his sight. (Ps 72:1-4, 12-14)

[Psalm 82 as a Charter for Justice] Moreover, according to Ezekiel 34, it is precisely the failure of the monarchy in its judicial function that brought about the Exile and loss of land:

> Ah, you shepherds of Israel who have been feeding yourselves! Should not shepherds feed the sheep? You eat the fat, you clothe yourselves with the wool, you slaughter the fatlings; but you do not feed the sheep. You have not strengthened the weak, you have not healed the sick, you have not bound up the injured, you have not brought back the strayed, you have not sought the lost…. (Ezek 34:2b-4)

The king is the "shepherd" of the Israelite flock. And it is the neglect of the king that causes the sheep to be "scattered" into exile.

A second trajectory concerns the institution of the judiciary reflected in narrative texts. Jehoshaphat, a later Davidic king, is credited in 2 Chronicles 19:5-11 with a significant judicial reform that suggests that heretofore the judicial was less than effective. The royal decree to the newly constituted judges exhorts,

> Let the fear of the LORD be upon you; take care what you do, for there is no perversion of justice with the Lord our God, or partiality, or taking of bribes. (2 Chr 19:7)

Indeed, the judges are to operate with integrity:

> This is how you shall act: in the fear of the lord, in faithfulness, and with your whole heart. (2 Chr 19:9)

The provision is designed especially to protect the weak from the pervasive, intimidating power of the strong.

It is often thought that the institution of judges by Moses at the behest of Jethro historically linked to the reform of Jehoshaphat that was just cited. In any case, the concern for reliable judges is expressed in parallel cadences:

📖 Psalm 82 as a Charter for Justice

The king implements the will of the sovereign God. Thus behind the "Hall of Justice" stands the intention of Yahweh that is nowhere more clearly stated than in Psalm 82. The Psalm is reckoned to be a very old declaration that begins with a vision of God holding court in the heavenly realm:

God has taken his place in the divine council;
in the midst of the gods he holds judgment.

The Psalm then portrays Yahweh as the one who commands that justice be given to the weak and the orphan, the lowly and the destitute. At its best the monarchy in Jerusalem replicated this vision of Yahweh. At its best we may imagine that "the Hall of Justice" was an arena for such activity. We may also imagine, given what we know of Solomon, that such a procedure was seldom "at its best."

You shall also look for able men among all the people, men who fear God, are trustworthy, and hate dishonest gain. (Exod 18:21)

It is evident that Israelite tradition regarded the maintenance of credible courts as a cornerstone of a viable society.

The royal mandate for justice, reflected in both the tradition of the Psalms and in the narrative, is clear about royal responsibility. The royal mandate, according to Ben Ollenberger, is matched by the temple traditions wherein Zion is the place of Yahweh's residence and Yahweh is the great defender of the poor.[1] Thus the king, in the administration of justice, replicates and acts for the true guarantor of justice, Yahweh. All of this, I suggest, is signalled in Solomon's "Hall of Justice."

The other building about which we may comment is the house built for the daughter of Pharaoh (7:8). It is evident that Solomon maintained an active harem, likely for political purposes (11:3). Possibly the pharaoh's daughter was the dominant force in the harem, commensurate with her father's standing as the most prestigious of foreign kings. Perhaps this house was unique, so that Pharaoh's daughter was the only royal wife with such a private edifice; or perhaps the house is regarded as a representative of the construction necessary to house the royal wives. Either way, the preeminence of foreign princesses indicates Solomon's openness and commitment to non-Israelite contact, contacts subsequently regarded in a powerfully negative way (11:4). At the very least, the mention of the house stands in an ironic relation to the "Hall of Justice," if justice here signifies, as I have suggested, the old, traditional commitments of covenantal Yahwism. Indeed, we may take these two royal structures as emblematic of the tension in the Solomonic project between the *old Israelite tradition* that was communitarian and the newer openness to *non-Israelite practice* that was less passionate about communal justice. It is in any case clear that this inventory of royal structures is no mere list of architecture but is put together in order to reflect the powerful and dangerous tension that defined royal power in Israel.

Finally concerning these structures, vv. 9-12 draw a pragmatic conclusion: they cost lots of money! These verses suggest that the construction is careful and symmetrical, that the use of cedar is expensive. But most important, three times we are told that the stonework is "costly"…because it is rare. No expense is spared. This is the best! But isn't it odd that this should be the conclusion drawn? The tone of these verses reminds me of a visit to a fabulous well-known independent church on the West coast. The tour guide pointed out many features to the edifice, but did not comment on the function or aesthetic quality of anything. Rather we were told only how much each item cost. Like our text, this was an extreme expression of commoditization, that is, the readiness to treat everything as a commodity to be bought and sold, to be priced and valued only by the market. What disappears in our text is any sense of royal function or royal obligation or the sustenance of any religious dimension of political power. Indeed, the entire account of Solomon in 1 Kings 3–11 suggests a pervasive commoditization in which human values and purposes are accidental and receive no attention. Such a social horizon for public policy, as Solomon administered it, could only lead to indifference and exploitation. Surely this commoditization parallels that of pharaoh in the book of Exodus, to which Solomon has ideological links through his marriage to the Egyptian princess.

Furnishing the Temple, 7:13-51

After the interlude concerning the other buildings in the royal complex, 7:13-51 resumes a report on the temple, now concerned with the more particular furnishings of the temple. This long unit is well and deliberately framed, beginning with the identification of the master craftsman, Hiram, who will oversee the project (7:13-14) and concluding with a final "formula of completion" (7:51). It is worth noticing that at the outset *Hiram* is the one who acts and at the end it is *Solomon* who is credited. The interplay of Hiram and Solomon is a characteristic example of "double agency," whereby in different ways the craftsman and the king are each fully credited with the project. Such is the nature of "royal" accomplishment.

The identification of Hiram, the artisan, is a bit curious. If his pedigree is to be taken with historical seriousness, then he is "from Tyre," but he is from a family of the Israelite tribe of Naphtali. The text seems concerned to establish his Israelite identity, but acknowledges he is from Tyre. This might suggest that he is bicultural, intermingling Phoenician and Israelite components. That mix, moreover, is exactly what might be most appropriate to Solomon, who conducts a bicultural reign and builds a bicultural temple. That is, there are traces and elements of old-fashioned Yahwism in the temple, perhaps traces the artisan Hiram preserved from his Israelite roots. But there is a preponderance of non-Israelite, seemingly Pharaonic or Canaanite influence in the temple, perhaps reflective of the artisan's Phoenician context. This bicultural enterprise, reflecting the pedigree of the builder, is both the glory and the dilemma of Solomon's temple, for it is purported to be a temple for Yahweh, and yet it is an elaborate, hierarchally ordered sanctuary that is in principle inimical to Yahweh. But whatever Israelite peasants (whose voice sounds in 2 Sam 7:5-7) might have thought about the compromise, Solomon proceeds undaunted in his practice of compromise and accommodation. The outcome is a lovely, extravagant structure shot through, as we shall see in chapter 8, with awkwardness and ambivalence for Yahwism.

In the end, what counts for this report, however, is not Hiram's pedigree, but his competence. He is full of "skill, intelligence, and knowledge," that is, he is peculiarly qualified to complete this "state of the art" project. His credentials are not unlike those of Bezalel and Oholiab, artisans who completed the tabernacle (Exod 36:1-7). Indeed it is almost certain that the texts on tabernacle and temple are interrelated, reflecting a generic way of speaking in Israel about such matters. Notably, moreover, in both texts, the competence of the artisan is celebrated as "wisdom," that is, a technical capacity for the assignment. Such a use of the term "wisdom" is of course very different from the "wisdom of Solomon" already noted. Except that in both cases the term refers to special competence that includes a theoretical base and practical insight. The two facets of wisdom include statecraft and craftsmanship. Finally, it may be that the naming of the lead craftsman is a fictive construal and that the name Hiram is simply reiterated from the Phoenician king of 5:1ff. It is clear in the text, of course, that the two Hirams are quite distinct and not at all confused with each other. But in the building of the tradition (memory), the name may have been reused. In either case, we have a Phoenician doing good work in an Israelite context.

The artistic achievements of Hiram are four. He cast and erected the two pillars with capitals (7:15-23); he made a "molten sea," that is, he formed a metal bowl that was shaped and large enough to symbolize a sea (7:23-26); he erected ten "stands" (7:27-37); and he completed the incidental equipment of pots, shovels, and basins, equipment necessary for the ritual work of the temple (7:38-44). The subsequent list assigned to Solomon in vv. 48-50 suggests that the list of incidentals assigned to Hiram is representative and not exhaustive.

We observe, first, that the several achievements of Hiram were elegant and lovely, with nothing spared to achieve artistic perfection. The temple must reflect not only the affluent capacity of Solomon but also the splendor appropriate to the character of Yahweh who, in this process, is transformed into an urban resident

AΩ **Strength and Stability**

The names of the pillars—"Jachin" and "Boaz"—are enigmatic. There is, however, a strong scholarly inclination to take the two names as the first word in two parallel sentences. One conjecture is that they are sentences that witness to the strength of Yahweh, for Boaz is the word strength with a preposition, thus, "in strength," and Jachin may come from the verb *kûn* which means "established." The two terms, if so understood, witness to the formidable quality of Yahweh, the God celebrated in the temple. But because the temple is not only for Yahweh but also propaganda for the monarchy, the same claims of strength and stability, derivatively, refer to the king. Thus God and king are bound together in this highly freighted liturgic gesture. As the God of the temple is "refuge and strength," so at its best is the monarchy.

The two-pillar columns are frequently shown in model reconstructions of other temples in the land of Israel. Above, columns found at Hazor (100 years after Solomon) may be similar to the two columns at the entrance of Solomon's temple. Also seen, a clay model of a temple from Trans-Jordan from this period shows two prominent decorated columns. (Credit: Zeev Redovan)

commensurate with the other royal, urban elites who now become Yahweh's primary constituency.

Having observed the artistic achievement of the temple, it is most likely that this is not "art for the sake of art," but that the artistic achievement is freighted with immense symbolic significance, much of which is lost to us. We may comment only upon the first two artistic productions of Hiram, the pillars and the sea.

The two pillars, exact duplicates, are elaborately decorated, suggesting their great importance to the enterprise. What clues we have about their significance are likely expressed in the names assigned to them (7:21). While the two names "Jachin" and "Boaz" are not self-evident in their meaning here, one plausible explanation is that the two terms, which appear to be proper names, are in fact Hebrew words from which a sentence may in each case be extrapolated. They assert on the one hand the *stability* of the temple (and therefore the stability of the royal house...*yakin*) and on the other hand the *strength* of the temple (and therefore the strength of the royal house...*boaz*). [Strength and Stability] Thus the names assert what is also evident architecturally, for the pillars embody stability and strength. The pillars thus may be seen as characteristic phallic symbols (stelae) such as power regimes are wont to present in order to make a claim for authority rooted in virility and perhaps something like sexual energy. [The Washington Monument] If this interpretation is correct, then it is clear that the *claims of Yahweh* and *the claims of Solomon* are intentionally linked, perhaps fused in liturgic imagination.

The molten sea was an elaborate figure of immense proportion, extravagantly decorated. Again it exudes a sense of stability, power, and reliability in that it is mounted on the backs of twelve oxen (7:23-26). The oxen are surely articulations of durable power and their number matches the old tribal confederation of Israel (or more recently the number of tax districts in 4:7). It is plausible that the great sea was involved, either in practice or in symbolic invitation, with the rituals of washing and purification that seem to have been assigned to the temple. In that sense, there may be some linkage with later Christian baptismal fonts. [From Sea to Font]

The Washington Monument

The appearance of the pillars must have suggested strength and solidarity. It may be too much to argue that such upright stelae are also emblems of virility—that is, phallic symbols—except that the claims of virility and the interface of sexuality and religion in the ancient world are amply clear. It is not necessary, however, to imagine that such a stela of virility is gross or decadent in itself. We may perhaps suggest a parallel to the Washington Monument, also a formidable upright stela that exudes messages of strength and durability. But of course, one can hardly pay attention to the monument without also associating with it images of virility. Whether the monument is deliberately phallic is not important, although it may bespeak the interface of virility and reliability necessary for the foundation of a great state. It was ever thus.

The Washington Monument
(Credit: Barclay Burns)

Also plausible, however, is that the "sea" has cosmic symbolism and refers to the chaotic waters that were known to be all around the stable earth and that were an ominous, threatening force endlessly jeopardizing created order. If that is so, then this huge basin evidently *contains* the waters of chaos and so *contains* the forces of chaos that threaten. From that linkage, we may deduce two important claims for the temple. First, the temple itself is an embodiment of and an enactment of creation order that is a reliable line of resistance against the threat of cosmic chaos. Worshipers might regularly go to the temple for escape from and assurance against the threat of chaos. Indeed, this claim of order amidst chaos is exactly the claim voiced from the temple city in Psalm 46:

> God is our refuge and strength,
>> a very present help in trouble.
> Therefore we will not fear,
>> though the earth should change,
>> though the mountains shake in the heart of the sea;
>> though its waters roar and foam,
>> though the mountains tremble with its tumult....
> God is in the midst of the city;
>> it shall not be moved;
> God will help it when the morning dawns. (46:1-3, 5)

At the same time, the king is cast as the chief bearer of order whose task it is to service and guarantee the well-being of the community and to fend off the forces of chaos. The primary way in which the king undertakes this task is by the administration of justice that fends off social disorder and unrest that can be an earnest of cosmic disorder and unrest. For this reason Solomon's wisdom is so important, for the capacity to enact social order is congruent with the very character of God's created order. The linkage also indicates why there is the "Hall of the Throne" in the royal complex from where the king enacts judgment in "the Hall of Justice" (7:7). Thus it is plausible to imagine that "the sea" is a generative reference point for claims of temple and monarchy as agents and sources of coherence and justice in a world that is marked by a deep jeopardy. [Ollenburger on the Temple]

We are able to say less about the "stands." But one may notice two facets of the description (7:27-37). First, the artistic presentation of lions, oxen, and cherubim makes clear that the stands are duly freighted with liturgical significance (7:29). Plausibly "lion and oxen" may bespeak the strength and solidarity of the sponsoring monarchy; the cherubim, on the other hand, are artistic assertions of the presence of Yahweh, for they portray subordinate attendants in the royal court gathered around the invisible Presence. Thus the triad of terms again voices the deep connection of temple and monarchy. The second point to observe is "the wheels" (7:30-33). This reference of course calls to mind the more familiar vision of wheels in the initial presentation of Ezekiel (Ezek 1:15-21). That vision is equally enigmatic, but the wheels there are often understood as assertions of Yahweh's mobility, for Yahweh sits on a throne capable of movement. The mention of wheels in our text that seeks to articulate stability and permanence seems less appropriate than in a text designed for exiles who yearn for a God as "portable" as their own deportation. Possibly, however, in ancient Israel, a rather generic characterization of temples exists, so that this characterization of the presence, even if stated differently, may be deeply interdependent with that of Ezekiel. The truth is that we do not know the meaning of the wheels, but they are surely linked to a claim of Presence.

This extensive and elusive characterization concludes with a series of closing statements (7:45-51).

1. Curiously, the elaborate description locates the place of work on the bronze equipment "in the plain of Jordan" (7:46). Older archaeological studies permitted a claim that the metal works of Solomon could be located in the East Jordan territory. It is not

From Sea to Font

The great basin at the temple may have been an emblem for purification for those seeking to enter the holy place. If the basin is understood in relation to purification and washing, then we may reflect on a development of the imagery in Christian tradition into a baptismal font, one meaning of which is ritual washing and purification to qualify for a new life in Christ. The linkages to the great Mormon baptistry in Idaho Falls is especially powerful, for that basin is also mounted on the back of animals. Of course religious imagery has its own wayward development, and a close connection must not be posited. But the linkages are nonetheless evident. As with the pillar, the basin so mounted bespeaks power and reliability, precisely the qualities that might be sought in a new life.

Baptistry in Idaho Falls Temple. Salt Lake City, Utah. (Credit: Barclay Burns)

⌀ **Ollenburger on the Temple**

Special attention may be paid to the study of Ben C. Ollenburger, the most comprehensive statement we have that the temple in Jerusalem was an expression of the governance of Yahweh as king over all of creation. It was a guarantee of order and a promise of justice willed by Yahweh. The temple must not be reduced in importance to something spiritual, for it had decisive impact on the capacity to found a great state on reliable theological foundations. The state and the regime are safe because they rely upon and are authorized by the one who orders, guards, and guarantees all of creation.

Ben C. Ollenburger, *Zion, the City of the Great King: A Theological Symbol of the Jerusalem Cult,* JSOT Supp. 41 (Sheffield: Sheffield Academic Press, 1987).

clear why that datum is given here. Perhaps the note parallels that of 6:7 to indicate that the "heavy lifting" of production was done away from the temple site so as to respect the aura of holiness proper to the temple site.

2. The note in v. 47 is of a very different kind, more in keeping with the claim of 6:20-22, asserting that it was all very grand, very exotic, and very expensive. Indeed, the bronze was so extravagant that it was impossible to keep proper account of the sums. Such a notation could, as we say, redound to the glory of Yahweh. I am, however, suspicious enough to imagine that the note really served to give Solomon "bragging rights" for the most expensive temple. The claim sounds like "conspicuous consumption."

3. Verses 48-50 express a penultimate conclusion for the building, crediting Solomon (not Hiram) with the accomplishment. But what strikes one in these verses is not the primacy of Solomon, but the primacy of "gold." Six times the term is used to apply to every item in the temple construction, including especially the "Holy of Holies." The text with its sixfold "gold" parallels vv. 9-12 with its threefold "costly." It is the same act of commoditization. What most impresses is how *expensive* it all is, so that the provisions for Yahweh's presence are transposed into a celebration of market value. It is odd indeed that in this entire tale of the building of the temple, the only direct statement about Presence is in 6:13, where Yahweh's dwelling with Israel is linked to Torah obedience and not to temple loveliness or grandeur. Obviously, the connection between presence and temple is a vexed and ambiguous one. This vexation and ambiguity are already signalled in Yahweh's "second opinion" given to Nathan in 2 Samuel 7:5-7. As we shall see, this same vexation and ambiguity reemerges in 1 Kings 8, the long, complex reflection on temple presence. That is, the elaborate, extravagant construction of the temple turns out to be only oddly related to Yahweh's presence. Yahweh's very character makes the temple problematic. Solomon proceeds with his royal grandeur, but he cannot overcome this dangerous, unadministered freedom of

Yahweh at the heart of Israel's faith. The very text that celebrates the temple seems subtly to be warning us not to take the temple with excessive seriousness.

CONNECTIONS

The immense care taken with the temple and the great attention to detail indicate that the temple is highly important to Israel. The community must be able to *host the holy*, for unless the holy is intentionally hosted, human life is diminished and cheapened. It is all very well to claim that God "is present everywhere." Without denying that, however, Israel understood from the outset that it is essential to give durable, concrete, institutional expression to God's presence. And it must be done with care. In many "mainline" interpretations of the Old Testament, the emphasis upon the *prophetic* and the *ethical* accents has resulted in disregard of the *cultic* life of Israel. This community well understood the importance of disciplined, regular, reliable access to Yahweh.

This preparation for hosting accentuates the artistic and the aesthetic. This neglected side of biblical faith recognizes that Yahweh is mediated to Israel in and through beauty. And therefore nothing is to be spared in the preparation.

Having said that, we may note three complexities in this preparation. First, it is possible to so accent the artistic that the ethical conditionality of Yahweh's presence is ignored. For this reason 6:11-12 are pivotal in the whole. Clearly an intrusion, these verses remind the advocates of beauty that there is a bedrock of covenantal commandment that cannot be disregarded or overcome. Because ethical passion is so elemental for Yahweh, presence depends upon taking ethical requirements seriously. Without that dimension, risks are taken toward self-indulgence that offend Yahweh.

Second, there are hints that the temple construction tends toward self-indulgence for the sponsoring regime. The endless preoccupation with gold and what is "costly" suggests that some in Israel were more interested in what was spent than in the intrinsic liturgic quality of the temple as a place of encounter and communion. Preoccupation with expenses suggests the commoditization of religion whereby everything about Yahweh's holiness is for the sake of and capable of cost analysis. [Temple as Commodity] In the process, the claims, needs, and expectations of Yahweh become instrumental only in serving the needs of the dynasty. The regime of Solomon needed to spend its way into respect, security, and impressiveness. The seduction of commoditization is enormous in an affluent society, then or now. Thus Yahweh and the worship of Yahweh become objects for sale, management, and manipulation. Once begun, the process is not limited to religious practice; instead, all of life—including the life of the neighbor—becomes a priceable commodity. One can see that happening in Solomon's Israel. One can, moreover, surely see it in contemporary society. The first casualty of such objectification is neighborliness whereby the neighbor ceases to be a partner or a responsibility and becomes a mere inconvenience.

Third, the silencing of the ethical and the focus upon the aesthetic linked to commoditization mean that the temple readily becomes a tool for dynastic aggrandizement. By placing 7:1-12 at the center of the temple report, the text skillfully shows that the temple is a part of the royal complex, situated where it is to legitimate and propagandize for the monarchy.

In the end, we are able to see that religious passion, when institutionally expressed, is essential for a community but is at the same time deeply open to distortion. Solomon—and some after him—have lacked the discipline and resolve whereby the cruciality of institutional forms of faith can resist the distortions so readily at hand. It is exceedingly difficult to give *due attention* to cultic presence without giving *undue attention* that reifies the cult. The dangers are visible in Solomon's project.

Temple as Commodity

Solomon's temple is constructed according to the "gold standard":

The construction is "gold, gold, gold, gold, gold." The stones are "costly, costly, costly." The accoutrements—even the pans for the fire and the hinges on the doors—are "gold," "golden," and "pure gold." Then the reason for all this hit me: Solomon is showing off!

Given the immense, unfettered power of the global economy in our day, this wearisome report of the temple in Jerusalem is a warning of how religion can, and does, become a commodity. The practices of communal life are priced out according to an alien standard: *money* value, not *theological* value. Once this standard is entrenched, the tendency to "weigh" everything religious casts a shadow over courageous expressions of faith within the community.

Walter Brueggemann, "Faith with a Price," *The Other Side* 34/4 (July & August, 1998): 33.

NOTE

[1]Ben C. Ollenburger, *Zion, the City of the Great King: A Theological Symbol of the Jerusalem Cult*, JSOT Supp. 41 (Sheffield: Sheffield Academic Press, 1987).

THE TEMPLE DEDICATED
AND MADE OPERATIONAL

1 Kings 8:1-66

The long account of chapters 6–7 details the construction of the temple. Except for 6:13, we have encountered no explicit theological statement about Yahweh's presence in the temple. In the present long chapter, we move from the *architecture* of the temple to its *theological-liturgical* significance, a move accomplished by a dramatic, extravagant event of dedication, whereby the royal achievement of the building is handed over to Yahweh. This chapter is made up of a series of quite distinct literary and liturgical pieces that, as we shall see, give voice to quite different and competing notions of the theological significance of the temple.

COMMENTARY

The Inaugural Procession and Anthem, 8:1-14

The initial processional entry into the temple is characterized in vv. 1-13. These verses appear to be a carefully crafted statement designed to comprehend in temple ideology a broad variety of theological interests and traditions. The sweeping horizon of these verses suggests that the temple is presented in a great ecumenical vista, intended to include but also to transcend earlier, more local theological traditions. We may notice the following elements:

1. The text is at some pains to include the cadences of the old tribal traditions in order to assert that the temple is the continuation and culmination of ancient tribal memories. Thus "elders of Israel" and "leaders of the ancestral houses" are included in the procession, representatives of the various tribal traditions that Solomon in fact wanted to eradicate (8:1). And along with them comes the ark and the tent, surely treasured symbols of an earlier, less complex, pre-monarchial way of worship (8:4).

2. But the allusions to old traditions are set down in royal context. Thus the action is in "the city of David," never a "city of Israel" (8:1). The extravagance of sacrifice reflecting royal affluence (8:5) and the

references to the cherubim (8:7) attest to a high temple theology that overrides simplicity and makes an impressive show of Presence.

3. It is the remarkable achievement of Solomon to hold these quite different theologies together. One can nonetheless see the tension still visible in the grand rhetoric of the occasion. On the one hand, high temple theology with its claim to the palpable presence of Yahweh is primary. That is, given the preparation and the procession, Yahweh is *really here*. This is made explicit in two ways. First, the coming of the cloud of glory is a priestly way to voice the concrete and overwhelming presence of Yahweh in the sanctuary (8:10-11). It is evident that this rhetoric is closely linked to Exodus 40:34-38, the culmination of the tabernacle tradition. [Temple and Tabernacle] In that account, the careful preparation and implementation of Moses make it possible for Israel to host Yahweh. It is evident in the juxtaposition of the two texts that in Israel's liturgic imagination, Mosaic tabernacle and Solomonic temple clearly are intimately interconnected.

Second, the poetic lines of vv. 12-13 are commonly thought to be a very old, perhaps authentic expression of temple theology. The words are set on the lips of Solomon, but they are likely a hymn of the chancel choir. The lines are loaded with powerful theological claims. The identification of "thick darkness" as Yahweh's dwelling place refers to the ominous, inscrutable atmosphere of the "Holy of Holies" where Yahweh abides in solemn, lonely splendor. We note, moreover, that Solomon is identified as the key actor in v. 13, the "I" who positions Yahweh; in contrast to Solomon, Yahweh does not act but is the passive recipient of Solomon's action, the *object* commensurate with Solomon as *subject*. Finally, the last line makes two important points. The verb "dwell" is *yashar*, "to sit permanently." This verb contrasts with the more usual *shaken*, "to sojourn, or "inhabit provisionally." [Verbs of Presence] The temple is presented as Yahweh's "final resting place." The permanence affirmed in the verb, moreover, is reinforced by the final plural term "forever." Thus the liturgy claims that Jerusalem is now Yahweh's final, permanent residence, with Yahweh as a patron for the royal regime.

Temple and Tabernacle

As the Bible is arranged, the plan and construction of the tabernacle in Exod 25–31, 35–40 predates and anticipates the temple of Solomon. The term "tabernacle" (mishkan) is a noun derived from the verb "sojourn" (shaken), a verb of presence we have seen in 6:13. That is, the tabernacle is a traveling place for Yahweh's occasional presence. The temple is seen to replicate the tabernacle in important ways.

According to scholarly judgment, however, the tabernacle in the book of Exodus is a projection backward from Solomon's temple and is a later textual construct. While the canonical and the scholarly presentation differ on the relationship of the two, it is inescapable that the two are connected to each other. To these two should be added the temple vision of Ezek 40–44 as a third scenario. What is clear in considering all these texts is that there is a shared tradition of cultic, institutional presence. It is, moreover, evident that the assured presence of Yahweh is problematic, admitting of no certain or settled articulation.

On the other hand, however, v. 9 recalls the resistance to temple voiced in 2 Samuel 7:5-7. This dissenting observation means to debunk high claims of presence. Alternatively, it asserts that the ark does not "contain" Yahweh. Indeed, the ark is *empty*...except for the Torah tablets! This low view of presence is a vigorous reassertion of old Mosaic tradition that Yahweh's presence is known primally as *commandment* and Israel's reception of Yahweh's presence is primally in *obedience*. The juxtaposition of v. 9 with vv. 10-13 exhibits the classic tension of *Torah faith* and *temple-royal faith*. We may be astonished that even in this most glorious, ecumenical provision of presence, Israel is determined to remember that the issue of presence is deeply disputed and endlessly problematic. Yahweh's presence among Yahweh's people is much desired, but never easy, never obvious, always a problem.

Interpretive Commentary on Temple Significance, 8:15-26

Solomon now makes two addresses to introduce an affirmation of the temple. In the first address, Solomon speaks to the congregation of Israel in the temple (8:15-21). In the second address, Solomon prays to Yahweh (8:22-26). Both addresses have the purpose of justifying the temple, rooting it in Davidic authority, and summoning Yahweh to full commitment to the temple. The speeches are freighted with the ideological claims of the dynasty, so that we can see the close linkage between temple and dynasty here made liturgically.

The address to the community asserts that Yahweh has kept a promise in the completion of the temple. In vv. 15-19, the promise from 2 Samuel 7 is reiterated. But the reference to 2 Samuel 7 is partial and selective. In 2 Samuel 7, Yahweh had at first asserted that no temple was desired; that initial prohibition of temple-building, however, refers only to David and not to his son. Our

---

AΩ **Verbs of Presence**

The several verbs used to characterize Yahweh's presence in the holy place may appear to us to be synonyms. It is clear, however, that there is a great deal at stake in the different terms. The most dynamic sense of presence is offered in Exod 20:24: "I will come (*bo'*) to you," suggesting an active intrusion. The most used term, *shaken*, "sojourn," affirms that Yahweh is present but not permanently committed: Yahweh is free to come and go. This verb maintains Yahweh's freedom beyond cultic, institutional control. A third term, used noticeably in 8:12-13, is *yashav*, "to dwell, sit, or inhabit." This term expresses a permanence, as when a king sits on a throne. This verb is not used as much; when used it presumably makes a high claim of presence. The semantic field suggests that Israel paid great attention to the nuance of verbs, because the ways of presence concern both Yahweh's *availability* and Yahweh's *freedom*.

text makes primary appeal to 2 Samuel 7:13, where it is anticipated that son-Solomon would build the temple. The "now" of v. 20 is the fulfillment of the Solomonic enterprise. While the diction speaks of Yahweh's upholding the promise, in fact the verses congratulate Solomon on his achievement. That is, the whole is a self-serving royal statement, capable even of preempting the Exodus-Sinai tradition for the king.

The prayer of vv. 23-26 reiterates the same themes. The prayer begins in doxology (8:23-24). Yahweh the creator is celebrated for the qualities of covenantal loyalty. These are the most characteristic features of Yahweh's way in the world. But that large characterization is immediately transformed in v. 24 into Yahweh's commitment to the dynasty. In v. 25, the doxology is abruptly transformed into a petition organized around two imperative verbs: "Keep...confirm." That is, the particular aspect of Yahweh's covenantal fidelity is loyalty to the Davidic house and the oath to keep an heir on the throne. It is important to notice that while the general appeal in this prayer is to 2 Samuel 7, the specific oath of Yahweh quoted back to Yahweh in v. 25 is not from 2 Samuel 7, but occurs more precisely in Psalm 132. But an examination of Psalm 132 makes clear that the Psalm has once more introduced the Deuteronomic, Torah-focused "if" not present in 2 Samuel 7. [The Dynastic Promise]

Two observations about this combination of Solomonic utterances are appropriate. First, it is important to see that the *occasion of the temple* is broadly turned to *royal advantage*. While, in theory, *Zion theology* may be quite distinct from *royal theology*, in practice they are deeply intertwined. How could it be otherwise! The temple is from Solomon and by Solomon and inevitably for Solomon. Thus the temple becomes an extravagant arena from which to exhibit and verbalize and insist upon royal claims.

View of *Solomon's Temple*, Haggadah from Moravia. 1729. Manuscript illumination. Museum of the Old Jewish Cemetery, Prague, Czech Republic. (Credit: Scala/Art Resource, NY)

Solomon's Prayer at the Consecration of the Temple. II Chronicles VI. Oleograph. c. 1870. Private collection. (Credit: Image Select/Art Resource, NY)

The Dynastic Promise

It is commonly thought that the promise of longevity to the house of David is rooted in 2 Sam 7:11-16. That remarkable promise, anticipated in 1 Sam 25:28, is unconditional and without limit. That promise is echoed in the more extended exposition of Ps 89:19-37. Israel counts heavily on that promise, the taproot of messianic hope for both Jews and Christians.

There are, however, two large problems with this unconditional, limitless commitment. The first is theological. The old Torah tradition of Moses— reiterated by the Deuteronomist—is uncompromising in its insistence that Yahweh's commitment to Israel is profoundly conditioned by Torah obedience. This understanding is reflected in the covenantal "if" of Exod 19:5, an "if" introduced into the Davidic promise in Ps 132:12. The second problem is historical: as things turned out in the sixth century, the dynasty was ended for all practical, political purposes in the Babylonian incursion, a reality acknowledged in Ps 89:38-51 (see Jer 22:30). It may be that the theological and historical misgivings about the unconditional problems converge in these texts. In any case, Israel is clearly as unsettled about dynastic durability as it is about temple presence. See Ps 78:68-72 where the two are intimately linked.

Second, a modest but insistent qualification to this seemingly shameless dynastic preemption of the temple is, in turn, the conditional formulation of v. 25, echoing Psalm 132 that is a revision of 2 Samuel 7. In this verse, the lean Torah promise of v. 9 is again visible. The "if" makes clear that the presence is mediated in, with, and under Torah obedience.

A Second, Different Wave of Significance, 8:27-53

According to the form of the text, Solomon's petition in vv. 22-25 continues in vv. 27-53. That is, Solomon seizes the occasion to enunciate a full theological function for the temple. Probably, however, vv. 27-33 are to be understood as a quite distinct rhetorical offer: First, it is clear that vv. 27-30 resist the royal claims for the temple just made, thus suggesting a different perspective; Second, the list of troubles and situations culminating in the Exile (8:46) suggests a context different from that of Solomon. These verses are aware of the problematic character of divine presence and likely reflect an exilic situation that left people both physically separated from the temple and for good reason profoundly unsure about temple guarantees. These verses exhibit Israel engaged in bold pastoral theology (cast as liturgical formulation) precisely when more conventional guarantees have failed. [Theology as Pastoral Care]

Whereas the liturgic utterance of vv. 10-13 had placed Yahweh visibly and physically in the temple, vv. 27-30 issue a protest against such a claim and offer an alternative. The opening question of v. 27 requires a decisive "no" in response. No, Yahweh will not dwell on earth…because Yahweh is *too free,* but also because Yahweh is *too big.* The earth is not large enough for the splendor of Yahweh. Indeed, Yahweh is so unutterably massive that even heaven, the large open space above the earth, is not adequate to hold Yahweh. No container is adequate for holding Yahweh. Conclusion: this little temple should not have such pretensions and therefore the song of vv. 12-13, perhaps the entire dedicatory anthem, is a cozy, misguided illusion. What a dash of cold water tossed into the dedicatory text! The entire claim of the temple is abruptly and uncompromisingly rejected!

Theology as Pastoral Care

The long section of vv. 35-53 with its accent on forgiveness is an important departure from the earlier preoccupation with presence. It is worth noting that the continually developing tradition of the text can move in quite new interpretive directions in response to the needs of the community. These verses purport to be a comment about temple presence, that is, a theological statement about the temple. But in fact the verses are a pastoral response to the crisis of exile. Jews in exile pondered the failure of the Jerusalem enterprise and accepted the failure in terms of a deep sense of guilt. Given that context, the needed and welcome word is one of forgiveness that will permit a future for faith. (See also Isa 40:2; 55:6-9.) In these verses then, the text is no longer focused on the temple, but on the community of exiles awaiting an opening to a future with Yahweh. That future is given in and through forgiveness.

But then, if v. 27 obliterates any conventional claim for temple presence, does it follow that the temple is null and void, without theological significance? No, and vv. 28-30 promptly articulate an alternative notion of temple that we may regard as highly significant, but distinctly "low church." The alternative rationale for temple is organized around the "name theology" of Deuteronomy that we have already seen in 5:5. That is, Yahweh is not there, but Yahweh's name is there. Yahweh's "dwelling place" is in heaven (8:30), but Yahweh's "eyes" are endlessly attentive to the Jerusalem temple (8:29). This careful wording nicely sorts out the way *Yahweh in heaven* is present *to* the temple but is not present *in* the temple. The formula seeks to adjudicate the tricky affirmation of *presence* in the midst of Yahweh's *freedom.*

The practical outcome of this formulation is that the temple becomes a primary meditation through which Israel's prayers are channeled to the attentive God of heaven. Thus this countertheory

of presence, with it pastoral focus, is summarized in the three petitionary verbs of v. 30: hear, heed, forgive. The accent is on the last
of these verbs. The religious significance of the temple now is that
it is a *vehicle for forgiveness*, thus pushing quickly beyond royal ideology and temple pretension to the intimate, powerful pastoral
needs of those who want to live in covenantal communion with
Yahweh.

The following section of vv. 31-53 is a long pastoral reflection
upon the need for forgiveness and the assurance of forgiveness,
enumerating the characteristic cases in which forgiveness is needed
and offered. [The Waiting God] In this sequence of cases, the first case in
vv. 31-32 differs from the others. In this case, the plea is only that
Yahweh will be a just judge. The text imagines a court case in
which a verdict must be rendered concerning an alleged wrong.
Here petition includes only the first of the verbs of v. 30, "hear."
Hear the case; be the judge. The judgment to be given by Yahweh
is from the options always faced by the judge, to condemn or to
vindicate. This is a bold liturgical claim that finally Yahweh is the
real judge, though it is not at all clear how judgment in heaven is to
be received on earth, for this rhetoric is not at all otherworldly or
apocalyptic. Perhaps in context we may say only that this petition
serves as a foil for what is to be voiced in the coming cases that
plead only for forgiveness. In this case, the one who hears in heaven
may indeed condemn or vindicate. But the subsequent petitions
are no longer evenhanded. They are, rather, requests for *vindication*
of the *unworthy*. [Vindication without Condemnation] That is, this is not an
appeal for "justice" but a prayer for grace-filled mercy. In context,
the temple is an arena and vehicle for the generous, forgiving
benevolence of Yahweh.

We may take the petition of vv. 33-34 as characteristic and exem-
plary for the series that follows. The petition is premised on an
admission of sin (8:33). Here there is no need to adjudicate that
matter as in vv. 31-32; the premise is conceded. Indeed, Israel has
not only sinned, but has suffered defeat as a consequence. Israel
prays out of its suffering. The sequence of the approach to Yahweh
is important: turn, confess, pray, and plead. Hans Walter Wolff has
shown how the term "turn" (=repent) is decisive for Deuteronomic
theology in exile.[1] Israel's only way into the future is to reverse
course and reembrace Torah obedience. The verb "turn" is reenforced by "confess your name." In the public naming of Yahweh,
Israel acknowledges its linkage to Yahweh, its obedience to Yahweh,
and its reliance upon Yahweh; in most elemental form, Israel's characteristic sin is to deny that defining relationship. It is on the basis

AΩ **The Waiting God**

The characteristic verbs of these verses concern Israel's required approach to Yahweh: turn, confess, pray, plead. What is remarkable are the verbs of petition addressed to Yahweh: hear and forgive. While Israel is fully aware of its failure and sin, the more important awareness is that Israel nonetheless has full confidence in Yahweh. It is assured that Yahweh, for all the failure of Israel, is continually attentive to Israel, ready to hear, prepared to respond, able to forgive. That is what is meant by "your eyes may be open day and night" (8:29). There is here no easy forgiveness or cheap grace. But Yahweh is fully ready to receive the turning of Israel. This stance of Yahweh is echoed in the parable:

> But while he was still far off, his father saw him and was filled with compassion; he ran and put his arms around him and kissed him. (Luke 15:20)

Notice, as Yahweh's *eye* is watching, so the father *saw* and was filled with compassion. (On compassion from Yahweh, see 1 Kgs 8:50.)

Rembrandt van Rijn. *Return of the Prodigal Son*. 17th century. Oil on canvas. Hermitage, St. Petersburg, Russia. (Credit: Giraudon/Art Resource, NY)

of a turn to Torah and a confession of Yahweh that Israel may pray and plead. The entire sequence is an embrace of covenantal existence that Israel had sought to evade.

On the basis of this sequence Yahweh is now urged to hear and forgive (the term from v. 30). The text affirms Yahweh's capacity and readiness to set aside the alienation evoked by Israel and enacted as exile. Thus this is a pastoral theology for Israel in exile, anticipating homecoming, premised on repentance, and enacted by Yahweh who graciously regards from heaven. The practical outcome of forgiveness and reconciliation is restoration to the land lost by sin. These verses detail an entire theological scenario of *exile and homecoming*, a dominant pattern of Israel's faith, exemplified in the wayward son welcomed home in Luke 15:11-32. Everything depends upon the "turn." But everything is completed in the resolve of Yahweh who hears and forgives.

With some variation, the following episodes present Israel's classic recital of divine threats (curses), in each case with an approach of "turn" and a resolution in forgiveness. [The Pattern of Curse]:

> vv. 35-36 drought: turn…forgive;
> vv. 37-40 famine, siege, plague: stretch out…forgive;
> vv. 41-43 foreigner: prays…hear;
> vv. 44-45 war: pray…hear.

There are important variations in these petitions. But they are all to the same effect. Return to Yahweh with serious intention may lead to restoration and well-being.

The last case in vv. 46-53 follows the same pattern, but is more complex and burdened with heavy phrasing. The problem is exile (8:46). The action begins with the call to "come to their senses" (8:47). [A Moment of Self-Awareness] Verses 47-48 concern repentance; a response of compassion is assumed in vv. 49-51. Thus a theology of confession and obedience is transposed in terms of exile and home-coming. This is followed—beyond the stereotypical pattern—with an additional petition in vv. 52-53 that passionately seeks well-being for Israel. The defining verb "separate," with an appeal to Moses, asserts that from the outset Israel has been peculiar (see Exod 19:5-6; Deut 7:7-11). The petition is that Yahweh should now act to make that separateness visible after Israel has almost

Vindication without Condemnation

In judicial language (as in v. 32), the court always has two options, condemnation and vindication. But after v. 32, this text no longer sees condemnation as an option. The prayer through v. 53 is all about vindication, about acceptance, pardon, and affirmation. Cast in the language of prayer, these verses sound a primal claim of biblical faith especially celebrated in Reformation traditions: Yahweh is prepared to vindicate (justify):

> …He who *vindicates* me is near.
> Who will contend with me?
>   Let us stand up together.
> Who are my adversaries?
>   Let them confront me.
> It is the Lord GOD who helps me;
>   Who will *declare me guilty*? (Isa 50:8-9)

It is God who *justifies*. Who is to *condemn*? It is Christ Jesus, who died, yes, who was raised, who is at the right hand of God, who indeed intercedes for us. Who will separate us from the love of Christ. (Rom 8:33-35)

Yahweh yearns for Israel to *turn and live*. (Ezek 18:32)

The Pattern of Curse

The prayer of vv. 33-53 recites a long list of troubles that may come upon Israel: defeat, drought, famine, exile. While the list is perhaps a new composition, it is useful to recognize that Israel has a stock list of such troubles, albeit with variations, to which appeal can be made. See what are perhaps old lists in Lev 26:14-39 and the elaborated list of Deut 28:15-68. A variation is utilized in the prophetic poem of Amos 4:6-13. The theological import of the list, in all its variations is to regard every calamity as a means of Yahweh's governance. In our text, moreover, every calamity is subject to Yahweh's positive readiness to forgive.

AΩ **A Moment of Self-Awareness**
The phrase "come to their senses" is the pivot point for rescue of the exiles (8:47). The Hebrew, literally, is "return [bring back] to their heart." The phrase apparently means to call to mind their failure and sin. But beyond the focus on sin that the verse seems to require, the phrase may mean to recover the commitment that has set their heart toward Yahweh. In any case, the phrase anticipates the term in the parable when the son "came to himself" (Luke 15:17). That is, the son remembered who he was and to whom and with whom he belonged. The parable illuminates the intention of v. 47.

---

disappeared among the nations. Thus forgiveness is in the interest of reenacting Israel's peculiar destiny in the world as the people of Yahweh. It is more than a little ironic that the most fervent petition concerning Israel's peculiar identity is placed in the mouth of Solomon, the one who did the most to undo Israel's peculiar identity in order to be "like the nations."

A Concluding Blessing, 8:54-66

The concluding utterance of Solomon is a benediction to the community, a blessing that matches the blessing of vv. 15-21 (8:54-61). Yahweh is celebrated and identified as the one toward whom Israel's life is devoted. Two accents sound through the blessing. First, there is an affirmation of what Yahweh has done and what Yahweh will yet do, articulated in familiar formulae. The acknowledgement of "rest," peaceable security in the face of all enemies, recalls 5:4 and appeals to the affirmation of David in 2 Samuel 7:1. Behind David's statement lies the old conclusion of the Joshua narrative (Josh 21:44). That usage, moreover, is matched by the additional claim, also echoed in our text, that:

> Not one of all the good promises that the LORD had made to the house of Israel had failed; all came to pass. (Josh 21:45)

In Joshua 21:45 this statement refers to the settlement of the land and the work of Joshua. In our text, the same sense of completedness, rooted in Yahweh's fidelity, refers to the completion of the temple and the work of Solomon. The temple is the supreme act of Yahweh's fidelity. On that basis, the blessing of Solomon focuses on what Yahweh will yet do, to "be with us" and to "maintain the cause." That is, Yahweh is to give stability and durability to Solomon and through him to the people of Israel.

Second, the appeal to Yahweh's fidelity, past and future, is matched by a powerful bid for Israel's obedience (8:58, 61). The language is surely Deuteronomic. It is stated, however, so that obedience is seen to be a gift of Yahweh, not a condition of Yahweh's favor. The short-term purpose of the blessing-wish is the enhancement of Israel. The long-term intention, however, looks beyond Israel to the world of the nations:

> So that all the people of the earth may know that the LORD is God; there is no other. (8:60)

The well-being of Israel is seen as testimony to the nations that Yahweh is the reliable (and only) God. The same motif is stated earlier in v. 43:

> ...so that all the peoples of the earth may know your name and fear you, as do your people Israel, and so that they may know that your name has been invoked on this house that I have built.

The enterprise of Solomon, in Deuteronomic formulation, intends that all nations should acknowledge and obey Yahweh. Jerusalem centers faith not only for Israel but for all the nations that may yet embrace this God.

With the final blessing of vv. 54-61, the speaking is finished. But the king must enact yet one more superb royal gesture, a concluding sacrifice to match the initial sacrifice of v. 5. In keeping with the extravaganza of Solomon's achievement from which nothing is held back, now in the sacrifice Solomon holds nothing back as a liturgical gesture. This is what kings do in that ancient world; they exhibit both their immense *piety* and their equally immense *success*, for in royal circles, piety and success are easily conflated. [Echoes of the Conflation]

The extravagance of the sacrifice—22,000 oxen and 120,000 sheep—is a clear reflection of huge wealth, even surpassing the royal expenditures of 4:22-23. Like that in-house expenditure, this

---

Echoes of the Conflation
It is the easiest thing in the world to connect *piety* and *success*. Indeed, the core theology of ancient Israel invites that linkage in its teaching that the righteous will prosper. When the connection is reversed, success is taken as a sign of piety. That association of the two seems operative in the characterization of the scribes who exercise immense social power (Mark 12:38-39) and in the Pharisee who is caricatured in terms of self-congratulations (Luke 18:11-12). The same mistaken equation is a powerful seduction in a market economy like ours where it is easily thought that wealth is a virtue and negatively, that poverty is a moral failure. At its best, biblical faith knows better than to make the equation. The book of Proverbs nicely distinguishes wealth from virtue:

Better is a little with the fear of the Lord than great treasure and trouble with it. (Prov 15:16)

Better is a dry morsel with quiet than a house full of feasting with strife. (Prov 17:1)

liturgic gesture is made possible by the efficient tax collection and uncompromising insistence upon foreign tribute. Apparently v. 63 depicts the primary act of sacrifice, but v. 64 echoes a second act presented as unusual for "the middle court." The act of sacrifice is a gesture of gratitude to Yahweh and an acknowledgement that Yahweh has given what is offered; the human act is a return to the generous creator. The act of Solomon perhaps echoes the gesture of David, [A Churchly Echo] also one of extravagance, whereby David makes a visible theological affirmation:

> For all things come from you, and of your own have we given you.
> (1 Chr 29:14)

A Churchly Echo

The statement of David is closely echoed in a standard stewardship affirmation of the church:

We give thee but thine own,
whate'er the gift may be;
all that we have is thine alone,
a trust, O Lord, from thee.

(William H. How, c.1858)

The point is paralleled in Paul:

What do you have that you did not receive? And if you received it, why do you boast as if it were not a gift? (1 Cor 4:7)

The acknowledgement is at the core of creation theology; all creatureliness is a gift of the creator. The claim, however, is exceedingly difficult in a market economy of rank individualism wherein everything held is viewed as private property to be kept exclusively for self.

Whatever may have been Solomon's mixed royal motives, this gesture is theologically powerful on its own terms.

The narrative then adds a concluding summary (8:65-66). This was a "great assembly," a representative gathering of all parts of a mixed population, all for the moment in grateful adherence to Yahweh, all for the moment in solidarity with their unqualifiedly successful king. The festival of dedication is a perfect liturgy, punctiliously done in every detail, lasting the required seven days of perfect duration. The focus is on the *goodness* of Yahweh in which all rejoice. But we notice, yet again, that the narrative is not quite innocent. It is an affirmation of "his servant David," that is, of the dynasty. Moreover, the people are drawn "from Lobohamath to the Wadi of Egypt." These geographical points allude to the far northern and far southern borders of Greater Israel, thus voicing the geopolitical grandeur of Solomon (see 4:24). God is good, and Solomon is the immediate beneficiary of that goodness.

CONNECTIONS

As we have seen, this text is a rich, dense one that exhibits both the achievements and the problems of Israel's established religion. The temple is (a) a vehicle to make visible Yahweh's commitment to and presence in the host community, (b) a gesture of political propaganda for the sponsoring dynasty, and (c) an announcement to the surrounding nations that Israel has moved into the big leagues of theopolitics. Thus the temple, inevitably, is a religious symbol fraught with ambiguity.

1. It is a great enactment of ecumenism, whereby the city of Jerusalem is able to gather in festive affirmation all the disparate populations of the United Monarchy. While there are no doubt urban elites who guided the entire process (and had likely negotiated matters with Hiram), the narrative takes care to specify the participation of "the heads of tribal leaders of the ancestral houses of Israel" (8:1), that is, the old tribal structure that treasured the ark and never fully accepted monarchy nor the urban elites who came with the monarchy. The temple is an act of ecumenism because it offers a shared vision of reality that transcends separateness and that encompasses all the different elements of the community. It is a large pluralism that did not try to force agreement on particulars. As we shall see subsequently, this large embrace finally faltered on economic disparity that could not be covered over by liturgy.

2. The temple is a place of presence, a guarantee that Yahweh is now "resident" in Jerusalem, thus assuring the well-being of the city and the realm. It is, however, massively clear in the text that this pluralistic assembly was not at all agreed about Yahweh's presence. We are able to identify two powerful expressions of Yahweh's presence that make Yahweh in some way materially available in the temple. In vv. 10-11, the text echoes the Priestly theology of glory (Exod 40:34-38), so that Yahweh's presence is known only in some inscrutable way. But in vv. 12-13, what is likely an ancient temple song makes the presence much more flatly palpable. The double use of the term "dwell" (*yashav*) means to sit or abide permanently, suggesting that Yahweh is there and will never leave. The verb *yashav* is a considerable advance (or distortion) of the verb *shaken* we have seen in 6:13, in which the quality of presence is not so durable or flat. Our verb in this text makes Yahweh nearly a prisoner in the royal chapel. And later on in the life of Israel, this claim proved to be too much for Yahweh when the temple failed.

Perhaps vv. 10-11, 12-13 voice royal "orthodoxy," a claim necessary to the state. But the "heads of the tribes," practitioners of old-fashioned covenantalism, would have their counterway. And so vv. 27-30, in what is perhaps Deuteronomic theology, affirm that the Priestly claims of presence assert too much. Only Yahweh's name is there, not Yahweh. But v. 9 is even more bold in its debunking assertion. I like to imagine this is the sober report of a custodian who had examined the holy furniture and discovered that the ark contained nothing (surely not Yahweh) except the tablets of Torah. Now that may be too naive, but this report echoes a theology that Yahweh is only present in Torah commandments and only known through obedience, not through liturgic operations. [Obedience as Knowledge]

The theological issues, important as they are as theological issues, are never innocently theological; we are bound to notice here that dynastic enhancements permeate the text. This is most evident in the words of vv. 15-21, but see also vv. 56-61 and the concluding formula of v. 66. Church edifices are never socially neutral and never politically indifferent. More broadly, the "public influence" of the church is never innocent, which is why the church endlessly disputes who shall control its future. It is clear in Psalm 78 that the *choice of Zion* by Yahweh is intimately entwined with the *choice of David* by Yahweh:

> He chose the tribe of Judah,
>   Mount Zion, which he loves.
> He built his sanctuary like the high heavens,
>   like the earth, which he has founded forever.
> He chose his servant David,
>   and took him from the sheepfolds...
> to be the shepherd of his people Jacob,
>   of Israel, his inheritance. (Ps 78:68-71)

📖 Obedience as Knowledge

Biblical faith is singularly committed to the conviction that "knowledge of God" is not cognitive but practical. That is, Yahweh is known and communed with through obedience:

> He judged the cause of the poor and needy;
>   then it was well.
> Is not this to know me? (Jer 22:16; see Hos 6:6)

The point is reiterated and affirmed in both Jewish and Christian tradition:

> To be is to obey...to be is to obey the commandment of creation.... Being is obedience, a response.... Living involves acceptance of meaning, obedience, and commitment.

Abraham Heschel, *Who is Man?* (Stanford: Stanford University Press, 1965) 97-98.

All right knowledge of God is born of obedience.

John Calvin, *Institutes of the Christian Religion I* (The Library of Christian Classics; Philadelphia: Westminster Press, 1960) 72.

The dispute elemental in Israel and central to this text is echoed in the church's long dispute over the Eucharist and the way in which Jesus is present in the elements of communion. Of course the options in the history of Church interpretation run from transubstantiation to a thin notion of memorial that denies "presence." And as in the ancient temple, the Eucharistic dispute was conducted over important and fine theological points. But they are never merely theological points, for *presence* is characteristically linked to *power* of a crass political kind. Where God is present, those who control access to such a valued presence are immediately major players in politics. All parties in this text, I dare say, understood that the stakes were very high. And now these same questions devolve, in the church, into questions of eligibility for ordination, for everyone understands that eligibility for ordination concerns control of access.

It could not be otherwise. Thus the assertion of royal ideology and the excessive concern for presence put one on notice to take this temple—every temple establishment—with a grain of salt, as perhaps the tribal elders did. The narrative account of 1 Kings 8 seems clearly to be the interpretive center of the long history of Joshua, Judges, Samuel, and Kings. From here on, it is all downhill. Thus even in giving us this exuberant narrative, the historians know that the royal-temple establishment does not quite work. The narrative is the story of the collapse of that establishment. It does not quite work even according to its own best rhetoric.

The protest against excessive presence in vv. 27-29 deftly moves in v. 30 to the theme of forgiveness, a theme then expounded in vv. 34-52. The move from *presence* to *forgiveness* is perhaps a genuinely evangelical interpretive maneuver whereby the temple is drastically redefined and its function is redescribed. Of course it may be that forgiveness is a theological matter in a religion of grace that does not require liturgical structure. Every theological tradition knows, however, that the claim of forgiveness must be given visible locus and shape. And so in these verses, the temple is the clear access point to heavenly forgiveness. (This does not mean that forgiveness cannot happen elsewhere.) We are thus able to see at work in this grand festival a second, very different theology preoccupied with forgiveness, an expectation Israel has that Yahweh will sustain Israel and is indeed "for us" as the coldness of temple might not acknowledge. For this reason, the Psalter includes songs of joy over forgiveness:

> Happy are those whose transgression is forgiven,
> whose sin is covered.
> Happy are those to whom the LORD imputes no iniquity,
> and in whose spirit there is no deceit....
> Then I acknowledged my sin to you,
> and I did not hide my iniquity;
> I said, "I will confess my transgression to the LORD,"
> and you forgave the guilt of my sin. (Ps 32:1-2, 5)

> If you, O LORD, should mark iniquities,
> Lord, who could stand?
> But there is forgiveness with you,
> so that you may be revered. (Ps 130:3-4)

The regime that built the temple for reasons of state may have had little interest in forgiveness. But around the edges of the royal claim of presence, Israel's true yearning for communion and the true gift of Yahweh have their say.

3. The massive sacrifice of vv. 62-64 again bespeaks the *commoditization* of religion that Solomon seemingly cannot resist (see 6:21-22; 7:48-50). It is most remarkable that in this context, *claims of covenant* can emerge, for *covenantal faith* lives in deep tension with a *religion of commoditization*. The covenantal cadences of vv. 57-60 culminate in the sweeping exclusive theological claim of v. 60:

> ...so that all the peoples of the earth may know that the LORD is God; there is no other.

The temple does indeed enunciate the claim of "onlyness" for Yahweh, a claim beyond the usual claims of Deuteronomy (see Deut 6:4-5). It may be that the lust for grandeur on the part of the regime can transpose the exclusiveness of covenant into a programmatic theological conclusion.

4. Finally, we may notice that in the Christian tradition Jesus has a deeply ambiguous relation to the temple. The temple of the first century, of course, is not the one Solomon built. But the one then standing still embodies the same ambiguous claims that must be reckoned with. The terse note of Mark 11:11 is likely an assertion that Jesus is the Lord of the temple:

> Then he entered Jerusalem and went into the temple; and when he had looked around at everything, as it was already late, he went out to Bethany with the twelve.

Indeed, in vv. 15-19 Jesus seems to "preside" over the temple as his own, in a way that evokes lethal hostility. Moreover, in the Fourth Gospel, Jesus seems to displace the temple (John 2:19-22), and so to deny the claim of presence for the temple (John 4:20-24). It is astounding that the church, as quickly as possible, replicated the Solomonic act of "establishment," thereby assuring at the core of its life the same ambiguity that clearly haunts the Solomonic enterprise. The ambiguity cannot be expelled or overcome; but it is of great importance that the ambiguity be recognized, to prevent us from assigning ultimate importance to claims—architectural, liturgical, doctrinal, moral—that can never be more than penultimate.

NOTE

[1]Hans Walter Wolff, "The Kerygma of the Deuteronomic Historical Work," *The Vitality of Old Testament Traditions*, by Walter Brueggemann and Hans Walter Wolff (Atlanta: John Knox Press, 1975) 83-100.

AN INTERFACE OF
THEOLOGICAL WARNING
AND SELF-CONGRATULATIONS

1 Kings 9:1-28

This chapter consists of a rigorous theological reflection on the reign of Solomon (9:1-9) and six textual fragments that characterize his governance (9:10-28). The juxtaposition of these two textual units suggests some sense of irony that amounts to an understated but clear critique of the monarchy.

COMMENTARY

A Theological Notice, 9:1-9

The theological reflection of vv. 1-9 is an odd response, surely deliberate, to the great temple event of chapter 8. This unit is divided into two parts and is presented as a dream that is a counterpart to the initial dream of 3:5. It is commonly held that while the initial dream of chapter 3 may have been regarded as an authentic royal experience, in the present chapter the dream is likely a rhetorical device for one more restatement of Deuteronomic theology. In the first part of the dream, Yahweh answers the petition of 8:29: Yes, Yahweh's attentive eye will be on the temple, ready to hear prayers and forgive (9:1-3). Indeed, Yahweh's answer goes beyond the prayer; not only the *eye* of Yahweh, but the *heart* of Yahweh will be there, along with the *name*...for all time. Verse 3 is a weighty and complete legitimation of the temple. The temple will be all that Solomon intended and all that Israel dared to hope. The dedication of the temple to Yahweh has "taken." Yahweh receives the temple given and will be present there, albeit in Deuteronomic ways.

Verse 4, however, is an abrupt rhetorical surprise: "But you." The speech sharply distinguishes temple and king. Just because Yahweh swears devotion to the temple does not mean the same unconditional commitment of Yahweh applies to Solomon or to the dynasty. Then follows in vv. 4-9 the most complete and symmetrical statement of the Torah-conditioned theology of the Deuteronomists. The positive deed-consequence statement is given in vv. 4-5. The conditional "if" concerns Torah obedience (9:5). [The Double "If" of Torah] The outcome of such obedience is a reiteration of the dynastic promises of 2 Samuel 7, now governed by Torah. The negative counterpart concerns the condition of disobedience (9:6), with horrendous consequences for disobedience (9:7-9). Obviously in the double "if-then" of vv. 4-9, the negative consequence receives more verbiage, as though this is the accent of the whole. This long statement of threat reiterates much of the stylized rhetoric of covenantal curses (as in Deut 28). The risk of disobedience is first of all exile from the land, but this includes destruction of the temple and the derivative ridicule of Israel for being connected to a failed project. The rejection of the temple is more fully stated in v. 8.

The passage culminates with a new rhetorical pattern of "Why...Because" in vv. 8b-9 that reiterates the earlier "if-then." The question of "why" is proportionate to the anticipated destruction. Why would such a terrible thing happen? The answer is "because" of disobedience that Yahweh will not tolerate.

The immediate effect of this freighted passage is that it fully and without qualification brings Solomon and the monarchy under the Torah. Clearly the king will be tested by Torah criteria; the temple presence, moreover, grants to the king no exemption from the Torah. The statement, however, is not aimed primarily at Solomon. It is rather a long-term principle that brings exile to the horizon of Israel. The phrase of v. 7, "cut Israel off from the land," is an unambiguous signal that this account of the life of Israel knows where it will end. Its life will conclude in 2 Kings 24–25 in Babylon. According to this narrative interpretation, moreover, service to the

---

AΩ **The Double "If" of Torah**

We have already noticed the "if" of Torah in 2:4; 3:4; 6:12; 8:47. Our text voices that same teaching, except that here the matter is symmetrical and complete:

9:4 if (obedience)
9:5 then (establishment)
9:6 if (disobedience)
9:7 then (exile).

The alternatives are simple and clear. It is not self-evident that a great state lives by neighborly obedience. But that is the case asserted here. The case is not made up on the spot. It derives from Israel's oldest teaching of blessing and curse:

If you will only obey the LORD your God, by diligently observing all his commandments that I am commanding you today, the LORD your God will set you high above all the nations of the earth; all these blessings shall come upon you and overtake you, if you obey the LORD your God....

But if you will not obey the LORD your God by diligently observing all his commandments and decrees, which I am commanding you today, then all these curses shall come upon you and overtake you. (Deut 28:1-2, 15)

The either/or is simple and direct, not at all complicated or qualified by Solomon's many achievements.

other gods, in violation of the Sinai command, leads to exile. The "why" question of v. 8 entertains the thought that such exile from land and from temple may be Yahweh's failure. The "because" response of v. 9, however, makes it abundantly clear that the failure belongs to Israel. Thus vv. 1-9 enunciate a comprehensive philosophy of history for which Torah is the key and clue.

Achievements of an Impressive Kind, 9:10-28

The second part of this chapter presents six brief statements that characterize the reign of Solomon (9:10-28). For the most part, these notes are connected to earlier narrative elements in the Solomon report. [Earlier Motifs Reiterated] Each literary unit in this report exhibits some dimension of Solomon's long and impressive reign:

1. *Negotiations with Hiram* (9:10-14). We have seen already in 5:1-12 that Solomon has negotiated a mutual trade agreement with Hiram the Phoenician. Clearly Solomon is a big-time investor and commercial trader and his paramount trading partner is Hiram.

Verse 10 is something of an editorial connector: The temple took seven years (see 6:38); the royal complex, thirteen years (7:1). The total, plus one for a new beginning, is twenty years. These numbers likely serve editorial, rhetorical purposes and need not necessarily be taken literally. These verses report on the unfinished business between the two royal traders. Solomon gives Hiram twenty cities in the north of the kingdom, close to Hiram's own territory (9:11).

This routine sentence contains a hint of astonishing royal power in which whole populations are viewed as pawns of royal wish. The two kings are engaged in map making (remaking), completely unconcerned for customary ethnic arrangements (see Prov 22:28; 23:10). Presumably Solomon was paying a trade debt. But the payment is less than satisfactory to Hiram (9:13). We are not told why Hiram objected to the offer, but the villages clearly did not meet his expectations. Nor do we know why the area is renamed *Cabul*. There are proposals for the etymology of the term suggesting that

Earlier Motifs Reiterated

The Solomon narrative of chapters 3–11 is arranged so that the great account of the temple dedication in chapter 8 is the pivot point of his entire reign. It appears that the materials prior to chapter 8 and after chapter 8 are arranged thematically and symmetrically, so that the material in 9:10-28 constitutes a rough reprise on motifs introduced earlier in the narrative. The correlations are only approximate, but they are worth noting:

—Negotiations with Hiram 5:1-12…9:10-14
—Recruitment of forced labor 5:13-18…9:15-22
—A roster of officials 4:1-6…9:23
—Reference to the daughter of Pharaoh 3:1; 7:8…9:24
—Acts of sacrifice 3:3; 8:5, 62-63…9:25
—International commerce 4:21, 24…9:26-28.

The narrative is designed to show that the great act of piety in temple construction and dedication is situated in an ambitious, prosperous, seemingly self-aggrandizing enterprise.

the name means "worthless," but we cannot be sure of that. The surprising outcome of the transaction is that Solomon receives yet more gold from Hiram. This is an odd outcome since Hiram was displeased at the trade. The intention of the whole may be to communicate that Solomon clearly had the upper hand in the relation: (a) He receives as much as he desired (9:11); (b) He passed to Hiram unacceptable cities and made the deal stick (9:12-13); (c) He received yet more gold. He is an effective trader. He can compete with the great ones and win. He is indeed "wise" in the ways of the world.

2. *The economy of state projects* (9:15-22). We have already seen in 5:13-18 that Solomon employed forced labor on state building projects, a fulfillment of the anticipation of 1 Samuel 8:11-17 that the royal government would "take." But this text is more finely nuanced than the earlier report in chapter 5. Here we are told that the forced labor was in the service of great building projects. The text mentions the "houses" of chapters 6–7 (9:15), plus buildings in Jerusalem and the Millo. [The Millo] The building projects included what must have been fortifications at the three strategic cities of Hazor, Megiddo, and Gezer, plus other locations for military resources—chariots, horses, and troops. [The Great Fortified Cities] One gains the impression of a vast growth economy fueled primarily by state investments.

Beyond what this text tells about the ambitions of the regime, the passage is of interest especially because of the important and insistent qualifier of v. 22. The manpower for state projects is not drawn from Israel, but only from conquered peoples. On the one hand, this text contradicts 5:13 that includes Israelites among the state force. On the other hand, the text identifies in some detail the conquered peoples who were reduced to state slavery. The distinction between Israelites and "outsiders" forced into slavery reflects an "enlightened policy" of protecting a home base of political support. It is clear that neither Solomon nor the textual report raises any question about such a state procedure. Indeed we may identify a triad of state necessity in vv. 10-23: (a) ambitious internal commerce, (b) elaborate buildings in the interest of military security, and (c) the work force to make such security possible.

3. *Organization of the work force* (9:23). In the bureaucratic roster of 4:1-6, we have already seen the penchant for good organization in the Solomonic enterprise. Among the chief officers of the regime was a "secretary of labor, Adoniram." In our present verse, we are given a clue as to the more specific organization of the labor force. It is clear that organizational genius is at work in the deployment of

AΩ **The Millo**
The "Millo" refers to a specific geographical part of the city of Jerusalem, though its location or significance is obscure. It is referred to in connection with construction not only under Solomon but also David (2 Sam 5:9) and Hezekiah (2 Chr 32:5). Perhaps the name comes from the Hebrew term *mal'* "fill," so that it may have been a landfill among the deep terrace ravines of the city.

Walls and city gates at Meggido, Israel. (Credit: Erich Lessing/Art Resource, NY)

The Great Fortified Cities

Two observations about the three fortified cities of v. 15—Hazor, Megiddo, Gezer—may be made. First, they are each strategically located on the main trade routes that would also be the access points for intruding armies. Thus they are natural choices for fortification. Second and more interesting, archaeologists have found at the three sites precisely the same design for a great city gate. (Compare the famous Lion Gate at Mycenae, Greece.) This a remarkable result of archaeological recovery that suggests that the same builders and planners were at work on the three cities. It is plausible, moreover, that the three gates were from the time of Solomon. If that is so (and it is disputed), this is a concrete and remarkable interface of excavation and textual notation.

Lion Gate. 1250 BC. Mycenae, Greece.
(Credit: Foto Marburg/Art Resource, NY)

human resources (see 5:14). Now we are told that the chief officers number 550, a huge number of supervisors reflective of a large work force. The scheme exudes competence and efficiency, without reference to humane treatment.

4. *Pharaoh's daughter* (9:24). We have already noted Solomon's marriage to the Egyptian royal house (3:1), plus the building of a special house for Pharaoh's daughter in the royal complex (7:8). Moreover in 9:16 we are told of the military action of Pharaoh in

The Temple of Solomon is depicted amidst other identifiable and contemporary buildings.
View of the walled city of Jerusalem showing the Temple of Solomon. 1493. Woodcut. *Nuremburg Chronicle* by Hartmann Schedel. Fol 17. (Credit: Foto Marburg/Art Resource, NY)

Religion as State Function

The terse reference to Solomon's public piety in v. 25 is likely one more act of royal exhibition. Nothing special is made of it, and the narrative does not seem especially interested in it. The situating of sacrifice in the midst of many royal preoccupations is paralleled to the impression of chapter 6, that the temple is simply a part of a larger royal complex of buildings.

The locus of piety and temple along with other things royal suggests a quite functional approach to the practice of worship. That is, according to the social theory of Emile Durkheim, religious claims signified by church buildings do not need to be *true* in order to be *functionally important* for the community. Emile Durkheim, a most important French sociologist (1858–1917), offered a "functional" view of religion. That is, whether the faith claims of any religion are true or not, they perform an important *function* as the "glue" that provides social coherence and stability.

The most accessible form of this approach is offered by Peter Berger, *The Sacred Canopy: Elements of a Sociological Theory of Religion* (New York: Doubleday Anchor, 1967) and Peter L. Berger and Thomas Luckmann, *The Social Construction of Reality: A Treatise in the Sociology of Knowledge* (New York: Doubleday Anchor, 1966.

That is, the temple performs an important *social function* without making any larger theological claim. In our own time, such a functional approach to worship, made explicit by Talcott Parsons, provided that new suburban communities need a church, just like they need a shopping mall, a hospital, a library.

Talcott Parsons is Durkheim's most important U.S. student and follower. Among his important books is *Structure of Social Action 1 and 2* (New York: Free Press, 1967). It was Parsons who provided the sociological learning for new, planned communities in the U.S. that needed a *church* as it needed a number of indispensible, visible social institutions.

Such an approach avoids any theological claim for the edifice. In Solomon's time, the temple is a necessary ornament of the dynasty. Others may assign weightier significance to it, but that is a matter of judgment outside the purview of royal planners and propagandists.

securing the city of Gezer as a dowry. The "Egyptian connection," state buildings, and security measures are all clearly intertwined. That convergence is perhaps epitomized in the house that Pharaoh's daughter now occupies. The Egyptian connection would seem to be the counterpoint to the Hiram connection. Solomon is a major international player, undeterred by any old-fashioned, homegrown notion of covenantal community.

5. *Solomon the High Priest* (9:25). The Torah traditions have long specified three special festal occasions per year (Exod 23:14; Deut 16:16-17). In our text, there are no specifics about the liturgical calendar. We know only that Solomon was dutiful about this role in the temple. Because the temple is the "royal chapel," the king is clearly the high priest responsible for the right celebration of the great state festivals. The king's regular appearance at the festivals surely lent legitimacy to the temple, claimed legitimacy for the dynasty, and gave evidence of the true piety of the king. We may notice only how terse this comment is. There is no narrative report; we are perhaps permitted the conclusion that this is simply one more event on the prescribed royal calendar; it is important to be seen going through the motions. [Religion as State Function]

6. *Solomon the Entrepreneur* (9:26-28). The final note of this chapter seems to refer back to vv. 10-14 and the negotiations with Hiram, plus the earlier dealings reported in 5:1-12. Solomon and Hiram deeply needed each other and perhaps had complementary resources and strengths. Clearly, Solomon was heavily committed to a growth economy that depended upon international trade. The two geographical reference points in this text concern Ezion-Geber, Israel's access point to the Red Sea, and the trade routes of the south and Ophir, apparently a location in Southern Arabia, perhaps in present-day Yemen. In any case, Solomon and Hiram were engaged in trade in gold. It is suggested in v. 14 that while the two rulers were allies, Solomon characteristically got the better of the deal.

This long recital of the achievements of Solomon, detailed as (a) trade that produced gold (9:10-14, 26-28), (b) forced labor that provided for security measures and building projects (9:15-22), (c) organizational competence (9:23), (d) connections to Pharaoh (9:24), and (e) a facade of piety (9:25), provide a rich portrayal of a successful king. (The portrait is continued in 10:1-19, but I have divided the material according to chapters for more manageable focus.) On the face of it, the text is a celebration of the king and his remarkable achievements. If we remember that Israel, only two generations before, was a disadvantaged hill country with a peasant population, the work of Solomon must necessarily be received as exotic and astonishing. Thus the text is indeed celebrative.

If, however, we consider vv. 10-28 in juxtaposition to vv. 1-9, we may reconsider such a celebrative reading. The criteria of a "successful king" in vv. 1-9 indicates nothing about trade or buildings or alliances or organization. It all turns on the single point of Torah obedience, that is, upon the ordering of social relationships according to the covenantal vision of Moses. If we take this seriously, we may suggest that the Torah-principle functions in the final form of the text as a severe critical principle that regards Solomon's considerable achievements not as admirable but as deeply opposed to the demands of Torah. If Torah has to do with *love of God* and *love of neighbor*, then the massive expansionist enterprise of Solomon is to be judged harshly as a deep failure.

It is difficult to imagine that the critique of Torah could receive much of a hearing in the actual context of Solomon, for such criticism would have struck those on the make as old-fashioned and irrelevant. But of course we are reading "canon." We are reading Solomon as a creation of scripture. Given in its belated form, the entire chapter voices the deep tension in Israel between *Torah principle* and *the royal growth economy*. Since the two elements in the text are only placed back-to-back and not commented upon

---

A Postcare Society

In a critique of the global economy, the postcare process of greed is referred to as a "tunnel society."

In a tunnel, traffic must travel through as quickly and as safely as possible and then depart out the other end; traffic must reach the light at the end of the tunnel. However, in order to achieve a maximal flow of traffic, only some vehicles suitable for tunnel traffic are welcome in the tunnel…. In principle, the trademark of a tunnel society is a ceaseless expansion of production and productivity, the purpose of which is to transport us to the light at the end of the tunnel: a rising standard of living, along with a substantial enough increase in prosperity to permit us to fund environmental protection, social and medical care, and development aid for poor countries. But entering and maintaining the process of the tunnel requires "sacrifices." Because some people do not have the capacity to work as efficiently as others, they are *excluded* from the production process. Some become unemployed; others, such as some who are physically or developmentally challenged, cannot handle the demands of the production process. Likewise, maintaining the process of the tunnel requires *expulsion*. Because increased efficiency requires us to ignore the persistent demands of the environment and of people who have been ostracized, in a tunnel economy we find it necessary to expel environmental and social burdens onto other sectors of society, including the state…. Finally, the tunnel process requires *extraction*. In a competitive climate, business finds it necessary to extract as much as possible from the services that land, labor, and capital provide. But this extraction gives rise to the need for society to remedy the distress caused by unemployment, environmental destruction, and workplace stress. The tunnel society is therefore a postcare society…. With a kind of tunnel vision, we then appeal for *more* production to finance *more* postcare expenditures…. Perhaps we will continue to produce and produce, but the promised prosperity will never arrive.

Bob Goudzwaard and Harry de Lange, *Beyond Poverty and Affluence: Toward an Economy of Care with a Twelve-Step Program for Economic Recovery* (Grand Rapids: Eerdmans, 1995) 135-36.

(9:1-9, 10-28), no explicit judgment is made for us in the text. But since the narrative and we (belatedly) know that the story ends in exile, the critique kept implicit is nonetheless palpably available for our reading.

CONNECTIONS

It may be that the characterization of Solomon's effective governance is simply a historical narrative about how this people moved quickly to phenomenal success. The report is almost an exemplar of how to make a great society work and a great economy hum. As such, Solomon is an anticipation of later oppressive international economies, of the capacity to make useful alliances and deploy manpower effectively.

Likely, however, we need no ancient models or lessons in the development of a great economy. We do better to pay attention to the remarkable juxtaposition of *Torah warning* (9:1-9) and the *royal, urban achievement* (9:10-28) and ask about their relationship to each other. Because the final form of the text is Deuteronomic, we may assume that vv. 1-9 bear the signature and judgment of the later editors, and provide a clue to how the text is to be read.

The Torah warning seems feeble in the face of the booming enterprise of Solomon, so feeble that it could hardly get a hearing. By any practical, worldly-wise criterion, Solomon is a success and needs no chastening. And yet, the feeble voice of Torah persists, in the end to declare the great economic and military achievements of Israel irrelevant, if one asks about either joy or security.

The analogue to our own situation is remote, but it is not difficult to construe. Ours is an international economy on the make, booming and prosperous. The International Monetary Fund and the World Bank, servants and functions of the economy, rush to the aid of failed economies, but with aid that demands as well as gives. The parallels to Solomon are suggestive in terms of trade, security, buildings, and manpower. In the midst of such prosperity, moreover, this unaccommodating tradition still raises issues about long-term viability, about viability that is seemingly immune to human questions. [A Postcare Society]

It is important that the Torah principle not be understood as some old, quarrelsome legalism. Rather Israel insists that Yahweh has factored into the structure of creation some inescapable givens that have to do with human quality and covenantal neighborliness. [On Human Capital] These givens cannot be defied, not because there is an angry God waiting somewhere to punish, but because the

On Human Capital

Cash value is easy enough to measure. Jon Gunnemann, however, contrasts such "cash value" with "human capital":

It can be argued that much of the modern economy depends on religious capital in more than one form. It depends, for example, on individuals being renewed in their worship and community life in order to face yet another week of work. Singing a hymn builds capital by virtue of its potential for replenishing exhausted individuals. So does prayer and meditation…from the standpoint of the traditional economy, you can't generate this human capital.

Jon P. Gunnemann, "Capital Ideas: Theology Engages the Economic," *Harvard Divinity School Bulletin* (1999): 6-7.

The Solomonic venture is long on "cash value," short on "human capital, a fact that bore costly consequences in 1 Kings 11–12.

givenness includes consequences not noticed by Solomon but endured by his successors. The great aims of state are happiness and security. The Torah principle insists upon human questions, making the obvious point that there is *no happiness* in the long run without neighborliness (contra 4:20); in parallel fashion there is *no security* without obedience to common humanity authorized by Yahweh's governance. The Torah principle here is not oppressive or chastening or actively insistent. It is simply stated. It sits there waiting and monitoring.

In our global economy, preoccupied with trade, security, and deployment, the Torah principle still sits and monitors. It is odd and noteworthy that the steps taken toward security produce *more anxiety*. The provisions for happiness produce *more tension*. The Torah tradition knows why…and waits. Every generation, including our own, is much like that of Solomon, always redeciding whether the Torah principle is an irrelevance or whether, as some thought, that Torah decisively declares most of our efforts at joy and security fundamentally mistaken, incapable of producing that for which we most hope. Israel waited a long time for evidence. We ourselves may notice their painful learning, or wait long for our own. [An Alternative to Greed]

An Alternative to Greed

The prophets of Israel envisioned a human society of just economics. They are echoed in the visionary statement of Pope John Paul II:

True development must respect and promise personal, social, economic, and political human rights, including the rights of nations and of people. Mere economic development makes the human person prisoner of economic planning and selfish profit…. True development must be based on love of God and neighbor.

Encyclical Letter of Pope John Paul II on Social Concerns (1987) 20-21.

THE GLOBAL ECONOMIST

1 Kings 10:1-29

This chapter picks up themes of chapter 9 and provides an ebullient report on Solomon's specialization in "riches and wisdom" (10:23), the very things he had *not* asked for in the dream of 3:10-13. According to this report, Solomon is successful on every front, has no negative element anywhere in his dossier, and is the marvel of all the earth. The chapter divides into a narrative concerning the visit of the Queen of Sheba (10:1-13) and a more generalized list of Solomon's successes (10:14-29).

COMMENTARY

The Visit of the Queen of Sheba, 10:1-13

The meeting of the Queen of Sheba with Solomon in Jerusalem was surely a summit meeting to work out a trade pact, not unlike recent meetings of "The Seven Industrial Powers" (10:1-13). [Sheba] The preoccupation of the meeting concerns Solomon's two foremost "claims to fame," wisdom and riches. As I have suggested in 4:29-34, wisdom may here propose Solomon as "a patron of the arts."

The narrative is staged as the great royal retinue of Sheba enters Jerusalem, perhaps in formal procession (10:1-2). The purpose is surely to impress, as these two negotiating monarchs engage in a game of "chicken" to see who would blink first. The queen is impressive, but she is no match for Solomon!

[The Visit]

AΩ **Sheba**
Almost nothing is known of "Sheba." It is common guesswork to conclude that it was a kingdom located somewhere in the Arabian peninsula. Because Sheba is so rarely mentioned in the Old Testament, it is clear that it was not normally in the assumed world of Israel. This suggests that Solomon's connection to Sheba is an extravagant reach, possible only at the pinnacle of economic success. It is perhaps to be concluded that Sheba was selected as representative for the textual account, precisely because it is remote and little known. This adds to the wonder of the encounter.

The first order of business is to match wits, to test wisdom (10:2b-5). The queen surely brought her most learned advisors with her. They had done their homework, but were nonetheless dazzled by Solomon's impressiveness. The commanding phrase for Solomon, "nothing hidden," indicates that he had a resolution for every problem posed. In the telling of the narrative, the report can not refrain from offering the entire index of royal achievements in vv. 4-5, all of the themes we have previously considered: wisdom, building complex, extravagant food, bureaucracy, and sacrifices to Yahweh. The whole is a royal package from which no single item can be separated. The sum of Solomon is more than the parts. The queen is so impressed that she violates royal urbanity and is left speechless and breathless. The final phrase of v. 5 is, literally, "he took away her breath (*rûaḥ!*)"

The queen's response to Solomon in vv. 6-9 is a wonderfully crafted celebration of the king. The queen admits that Solomon is even better than his formidable reputation. And while she is impressed with his wisdom, what counts is the

The Visit

In the many visuals that focus upon the Queen of Sheba's visit to King Solomon, interpretations vary as to the nature of the queen's humility before Solomon. For example, in the painting by Peter van Lint the queen's swooning theatricality portrays her as emotionally overcome in the presence of the King.

On the other hand, the queen's attitude and demeanor is much more aristocratic and composed in the painting by Claude Vignon (see next page). Completed in 1624, this Baroque painting captures the dramatic grandeur of the court

Peter van Lint. *The Queen of Sheba Before Solomon.* 17th-C. Oil on leather. Museé Crozatier, Le Puy-en-Velay. Paris, France. (Credit: Giraudon/Art Resource, NY)

prosperity to make everyone "happy." The double use of the term "happy" echoes 4:20; but we should notice the restrictions on "happiness" that may be suggested. The first group of happy ones, "wives," may refer to a very well outfitted harem. Notice, however, that the Hebrew has "men," perhaps referring to the royal entourage. The term "men" is a better parallel to the second happy constituency, "servants." The terms together refer to those who regularly attend to Solomon and not to the populace. The queen is reporting on a well-ordered, well-satiated royal entourage, a "palace cliché." What is to be observed is the narrow range of the queen's horizon, no doubt the same narrow range of Solomon. The populace is nowhere on the queen's screen of perception as it was not on the king's monitor either. The others do not count, and nobody cares if

with the queen shown approaching the king in a processional manner as her entourage remains in tow and moves with a similar processional cadence, replete with tribute. The queen's head is bowed and her hand is placed over her breast as if he "…took away her breath." The grandiosity of the occasion is captured by Vignon as the two persons of royalty meet face to face with their corresponding entourages. Vignon's depiction stresses the theatricality of the setting with his use of a *tenebroso* lighting that highlights and contrasts with lights and darks the features of the foreground figures. The diagonal dominance of the composition contributes to a sense of movement with its strong directionality.

Claude Vignon the Elder. *King Solomon and the Queen of Sheba*. 1624. Museé de Louvre, Paris, France. (Credit: Alinari/Art Resource, NY)

they are "happy." This is royal, hegemonic thinking at its most seductive and dangerous.

Most remarkably, the reported speech of the queen turns her into a good Yahwist, with an awareness of the preferred slogan of Israelite kingship. The speech, of course, is exactly the kind of rhetoric of mutual congratulations with which the powerful salute each other. Moreover, the queen uses the wonderfully dynastic term "forever," for the royals cannot imagine that the splendor will ever end. In the midst of such cadences of privilege, however, the queen is made to utter the most demanding of all royal mandates, "justice and righteousness," terms used in the royal poetry of Isaiah 9:7 (see 11:3b-5), and what must have been the liturgy of Psalm 72.

[Justice and Righteousness]

Whether deliberately or not, the speech of the queen offers a powerful irony. As we have seen, v. 8 is shockingly exclusionary, but the phrasing of v. 9 includes on the horizon of royal responsibility precisely those who are excluded from the present royal "happiness." Now all of this may be no more than conventional rhetoric by a queen who knew the proper Israelite slogans. If, however, the text is as intentional as I take it to be, then "justice and righteousness" placed here become an ominous anticipation of what is to come in chapters 11 and 12.

Upon completion of the speech in v. 9, the narrative adds a note on the huge tribute the queen had brought, tribute that is exotic and therefore of immense value (10:10). The report intends us to see that Solomon is the senior, stronger party in this negotiation, and the queen substantively enacts her subordinate position in willing deference. Trade pacts between unequal trading partners require special gestures that amount to significant cash (see 4:21; 9:14). If the gestures of the queen here and of Hiram in 9:14 are coupled, the impression is given that all roads and all gold lead to Jerusalem.

AΩ Justice and Righteousness

This word pair on the lips of the queen is astonishing, because it is a word pair that seems to embody the primary demands of Israel's Torah-prophetic traditions. The terms are used together in some royal texts. But the characteristic usage is prophetic: see Isa 5:7, Amos 5:7, 24; 6:12; Jer 22:13, 15. The terms together bespeak a political-economic practice of *social solidarity* whereby all members of the community are afforded the resources necessary for a viable existence of well-being, security, and dignity. The two terms, moreover, are understood as being grounded in Yahweh's covenantal will for a community of well-being wrought through neighborly obedience. The word pair, when understood in prophetic perspective, constitutes a major critique of the kind of acquisitive aggrandizement embraced by Solomon.

The mention of gold and other exotic gifts in v. 10 leads to a digression in vv. 11-12 that has no direct connection to Sheba, but takes up the theme of Ophir from 9:28. The picture given in these two verses is a vast commercial enterprise that was complemented by Hiram (see 9:27), but that accrued to the benefit of Solomon and Jerusalem.

After the interlude and digression of vv. 11-12, the narrative provides a summary of the queen's visit. The queen now departs so that the scene may end. But she does not go empty-handed. She receives "every desire." The term is the same word used in 5:8-9 with reference to Hiram where the NRSV renders "need." It is telling that in their royal transactions, one cannot be sure if the term is "need" or "desire," because in such self-indulgent affluence everything "desired" is a need to be met. In any case, it is to be noted that nowhere in this narrative, not even in the report of her departure, does Solomon give her anything. She gave him gold and spices and precious stones. He gives her not a single tangible gift. What then did he give her in v. 13 that satisfied her "desire"? We may imagine that what he gave her was a trade agreement, perhaps "most favored nation" status, or some such guarantee for her commercial interest. In any case the visit and the agreement were clearly much more important to her than to him. For Solomon, this was another day at the office being feted and admired and honored. We may imagine the agreements served him well…as does everything else!

Solomon's Successes, 10:14-29

With the completion of the narrative report, the remainder of the chapter is an inventory of Solomon's unparalleled successes (10:14-29). The list concerns three items:

1. Solomon wanted the world to know, "I'm rich!" (10:14-23). Solomon is clearly at the center of a huge commercial enterprise in which wealth from every transaction came to Jerusalem from every direction. The Queen of Sheba must have been only one representative of a number of foreign agents who were tied to Solomon in ways that produced immense wealth for Jerusalem. The preoccupation with gold is evident. The gold, moreover, is used in ostentatious ways to decorate one of the royal edifices, the House of the Forest of Lebanon (see 7:2-5) that in 7:1-12 receives the most detailed description. This building must have been the formal throne

From Sea to Shining Sea

The geopolitics of Solomon are nicely voiced by reference to Tarshish. We have already seen in 4:24 the tracing of the borders of "Greater Israel." Here the scope of Solomonic influence is even more extensive. The reference to Tarshish in these verses likely indicates a settlement to the West, perhaps as far as Spain at the extreme West of the Mediterranean Sea. (The location is not certain but plausible.) The reference to Ezion-Geber indicates access to the Red Sea and the South (9:26). If we take the two references to Tarshish and Ezion-Geber, we have a suggestion of an economic, commercial network dominated by Solomon. It is evident, according to the text, that Solomon's reach is the entire known world. No wonder he abounded in wealth!

---

room designed in detail for the enhancement of the monarchy. The report intends to leave us awed by the wealth, gold supplied by a fleet of ships that transport endless valuable commodities (10:22). [From Sea to Shining Sea]

The report of wealth offers two telling phrases to impress. The positive phrase of v. 20 parallels the hyperbole of the queen in v. 7: "Nothing like it was ever made in any kingdom." The negative phrase of v. 21 accents the gold even more: silver "was not considered as anything in the days of Solomon." When silver is that completely devalued and disregarded, there is more than enough gold!

2. The queen had also been smitten with Solomon's wisdom, so the concluding summary cannot neglect wisdom (10:23-25). But then these three verses are carefully put together. Only v. 24 is about wisdom: It is a gift of Yahweh to Solomon. That is, it is put in "his heart." This echoes 3:9:

> Give your servant therefore an understanding mind [heart] to govern your people, able to discern between good and evil.

The purpose of wisdom is to rule well. The reference, however, is framed in vv. 23 and 25 by yet another reference to wealth. It is clear that wisdom is a function of wealth. In v. 23, the two are paired. But in v. 25, the paragraph designed for wisdom moves yet again to wealth. The term rendered "present" is the term *minhah* rendered "tribute" in 4:21. Solomon's subjects did not bring valuable and exotic "gifts" because they were *awed*, but because they *owed*, owed to the dominant and insistent power in the region.

3. The mention of tribute/present in v. 25 leads directly to the third facet of the royal inventory namely the convergence of commerce and military power (10:26-29). It may be that here, as in vv. 14-22, the accent should be on commerce. Except that commerce of this kind is almost always firmly

linked to military domination. The opening reference to "chariots and horses" suggests that Solomon had an immense security force, likely stationed in Hazor, Megiddo, and Gezer plus a number of other strategically placed cities (9:16, 19). That opening mention of horses and chariots in v. 26 is matched in vv. 28-29 by reference to his trading activity. Solomon is an *arms dealer*, who moves horses and chariots from the South (Egypt) to the North (Hittites and Syria/Aram). Solomon is strategically placed as the middle man who supervises all overland commerce, and takes his cut.

No wonder the queen had her breath taken away. The convergence of *wealth, power, and wisdom* is awesome. Israel had never seen anything like it and would never again. It is a moment for Solomon, a moment of *shalom*, a moment for Jeru-*shalom*.

CONNECTIONS

The celebration of Solomon here employs the most extravagant terms possible. The visit of the Queen of Sheba is emblematic and representative of the pivotal place Solomon had come to occupy, if not in the actual world of royal competition and commercial success, then at least in the imagination of Israel. This is no casual visit between friends. This is a formal visit of state designed to secure mutually beneficial trade agreements, although beyond trade agreements the propaganda gains of such a visit are always an important, calculated by-product. The visit is carefully choreographed for mutual enhancement.

Having said that, there is no doubt that Solomon is the stronger party and stands to gain the most. It is important that the queen comes to him and not the other way round, for the client state always honors the patron state by a visit. Israel is only recently a peasant economy. And therefore to be the host of a visit by an exotic queen signals that Solomon has now joined the powerful of the earth. More than that, the visit articulates that Gentiles (=non-Israelites) are suppliants who must seek the approval, protection, and generosity of the state of Israel.

The notion of a Gentile visiting as suppliant is exploited in the great promissory piety of Isaiah 60. [Anticipated Economic Recovery] The poet addresses a defeated postexilic community of Jews, but anticipates recovery as a fully functioning economic power.

📖 **Anticipated Economic Recovery**
Hope for Jerusalem is voiced as the image of prosperous Gentiles come to Jerusalem, bringing their tribute as a salute to the primacy of Jerusalem:

Then you shall see and be radiant;
　　your heart shall thrill and rejoice,
because the abundance of the sea shall be brought to you,
　　the wealth of the nations shall come to you.
A multitude of camels shall cover you,
　　the young camels of Midian and Ephah;
　　all those from Sheba shall come.
They shall bring *gold and frankincense*,
　　and shall proclaim the praise of the Lord.
All the flocks of Kedar shall be gathered to you,
　　the rams of Nebaioth shall minister to you;
they shall be acceptable on my altar,
　　and I will glorify my glorious house....
Your gates shall always be open;
　　day and night they shall not be shut,
so that nations shall bring you their wealth,
　　with their kings led in procession.
For the nation and kingdom
　　that will not serve you shall perish;
　　those nations shall be utterly laid waste. (Isa 60:5-7, 11-12)

Jerusalem is envisioned as a place of well-being in which the shipping lines and loading docks are overextended, all *unloading* tribute and booty "day and night." Note well that the goods elsewhere termed "spices" (10:10) are here specified as "frankincense...along with gold" (Isa 60:6).

The Gentile offer of "frankincense and gold" is readily taken up by the Gospel of Matthew for the enhancement of Jesus:

They knelt down and paid him homage. Then, opening their treasure chests, they offered him gifts of gold, frankincense, and myrrh. (Matt 2:11)

The visit of the "magi" is yet one more visit of Gentiles who come in obeisance to the Jewish king. Thus Jesus, in the wake of Solomon, is the true Jewish king who receives Gentile tribute. Or conversely, in Christian tradition, Solomon and the Queen of Sheba become the types that anticipate the rule of Jesus who will be given exotic gifts from the East. In both texts, large, successful cultures and economies submit to the rule of the one authorized and legitimated by the rule of Yahweh.

This account of Solomon is indeed the portrayal of a fabulously effective economy, one paralleling what we of late have come to call "the global economy." A primary feature of the global economy is that it has such capital strength and leverage that it is able to dictate the terms of all other economies, so that no local economy can finally resist or stand outside its purview. Such an economy, moreover, is completely insulated from human questions, questions about the maintenance of human fabric and the sustenance and dignity of those who fail to compete and produce according to expectation. In our own time and place it is, of course, not yet known whether such an uncaring, massive force can in the end sustain itself when the quality of human community has been completely destroyed by unrestrained acquisitiveness. The situation of our global economy at the end of the twentieth century is not unlike the portrayal of chapter 10. Everything works! There is not "a discouraging word" uttered about the wonder of Solomon; and were such a word uttered, then or now, it would be thought odd and irrelevant.

We do not know how cunning the narrative is. But it remains for the queen in v. 9 to utter a signal that must have been ill received. One can imagine that in all the palaver of trade negotiations with pleasant behavior, cleverness, and many cocktails, when the queen said "justice and righteousness" there came an embarrassed silence into the room. For the phrase immediately poses all the difficult human questions that the ideology of profits means to deny. In that ancient text, the queen's phrase is a peek over into chapters 11 and 12 where human questions, grounded in Torah requirements, bring a devastating end to the Solomonic enterprise that is said in v. 9 to be forever. So in our time and place, the surfacing of "justice and righteousness" may be an unwelcome peek into tomorrow, for the poetic-prophetic traditions know that the human questions cannot be forever silenced while the forces of greed run wild. Those questions and demands will sound in their savage way. And they will keep sounding until acknowledged. In our time, such issues are almost invisible…but not quite. In our text they are, in the same way, almost invisible…but not quite. The queen says more than she knows. She departed for home to her own land without a second thought about the matter. But the text remembers what she quickly forgot and what the king perhaps never noticed.

Paul Kennedy has surveyed the rise and fall of great nation-states in the modern European world from the Hapsburgs to the Netherlands, to Britain, and finally to the U.S.[1] Kennedy notices how oddly nation-states appear in their supremacy and then fade rather abruptly. Kennedy's thesis is that every nation-state has a calculus of territory, population, and resources that it must keep in balance. And where that balance is disregarded, as in military adventurism, decline happens quickly and inescapably.

The analysis of Kennedy is not directly linked to our text nor to any theological sensitivity, but it gives pause. Solomon's ambitious, exhibitionist policies did not stay connected to or informed by the social reality of Israel on the ground. Kennedy makes clear that a great state cannot be sustained by show or will if attention is not paid to the indispensable homework of the economy. As we move beyond chapter 10, it will be clear that attention has not been paid in Jerusalem to the human dimension of the economy. The move into chapters 11–12 is abrupt and unexpected. The "if" of Torah requirement will not go away, even if chapter 10 manages nicely without it...except for the queen's passing comment.

NOTE

[1]Paul Kennedy, *The Rise and Fall of the Great Powers: Economic Change and Military Conflict between 1500 and 2000* (New York: Random House, 1987).

WHEN THE CHICKENS COME HOME TO ROOST

1 Kings 11:1-43

The change of mood, as we move into chapter 11, is abrupt and ominous. Chapter 10 had been a celebrative account of Solomon's enormous success on every front, without any hint of negativity. Now, suddenly, at the end of the Solomon narrative, we receive a theological verdict on Solomon according to the Torah-criteria of the Deuteronomists. The chapter consists of a *theological verdict* (11:1-13), together with three accounts of would-be opponents of Solomon (11:14-22, 12-25, and 26-40), and a concluding literary footnote (11:41-43).

COMMENTARY

The Theological Verdict, 11:1-13

The Torah verdict against Solomon is cast in a characteristic prophetic *lawsuit speech* (11:1-13). The editorial practice of the book of Kings is to provide a *theological* assessment of each king by the criterion of Torah-obedience, a criterion in which kings characteristically are not at all interested. Thus the kings are evaluated by norms that they themselves would have taken to be irrelevant.

The characteristic lawsuit speech follows a conventional pattern of *indictment* and *threat*. In this passage, the indictment against Solomon (11:1-8) is extensive and insistent. It is introduced by the presenting problem in v. 1: "Solomon loved many foreign women." The phrase is clearly juxtaposed to the introductory formula of 3:3: "Solomon loved the Lord." According to editorial arrangement, we are meant to conclude that the change from Solomon's first love to his later, decadent love is a matter of the aging process: "When Solomon was old." (11:4). We have, however, seen enough to know that Solomon, all along, kept these two loves alive. This evaluative account indicates that Solomon, by marriage, was related to hosts of other countries and other regimes, so that the total, according to this negative assessment, is 700 wives and 300 concubines. One could conclude from this data that the king is completely preoccupied by sexuality. It is more likely the case, however, that the many women in his court reflect endless political arrangements that are sealed and made visible by political marriages. And since we have seen that Solomon in his exhibitionism must operate on a vast scale in order to impress, it does not surprise us that Solomon (or the narrator) must offer an enormous number of women to match the vastly exaggerated scale of everything else in Jerusalem.

In any case, the theological evaluation of Solomon does not linger over marriages to foreign women per se. Rather the affront is that along with the foreign wives came the gods they worshiped in their own countries. This connection between *wife* and *god* can be taken on a personal basis, so that the newly wed princess brings her religion with her (see Ps 45:12-15 on such a royal marriage). More likely, the intermarriages bespeak not simply a personal attachment to other gods, but a broad cultural exchange in which values, symbols, and practices are interchanged, so that the clarity and singularity of Yahwism is lost in the shuffle.

Either way, as an intimate personal or as a broad cultural development, intermarriage that leads to interreligious contact is viewed in this assessment as a sorry departure from Yahwism. The Torah prohibition quoted in v. 2 apparently cites Deuteronomy 7:3-4:

Do not intermarry with them, giving our daughters to their sons or taking their daughters for your sons, for that would turn away your children from following me, to serve other gods. Then the anger of the LORD would be kindled against you, and he would destroy you quickly.

Thus the key issue is that the heart of the king was diverted from Yahweh so that he no longer had the "discerning heart" requested in 3:9. That is, the splendid establishment of Solomon that we have seen described and celebrated in detail was no longer reflective of Yahwistic

---

Many Gods

The charge against Solomon, under the influence of his many foreign wives, concerns the presence of "many gods" in Jerusalem violating the exclusive claims of Yahweh. This indictment names four deities, Astarte (of Sidon), Milcom (of the Ammonites), Chemosh (of Moab), and Molech (of the Ammonites). Likely the names as such are not to be taken here with any precision; rather the text simply gathers together representative names of gods as typical of the betrayal of Solomon. In the judgment of many scholars Astarte (Asherah) was a goddess who in some forms of heterdox Yahwism was considered Yahweh's consort, a claim firmly rejected in Deuteronomic theology. The gods Milcom and Chemosh were known to be the gods of neighboring peoples, and Molech is perhaps a confusion with and derivation from Milcom. The point of the passage does not depend upon any clear identification of the deities.

One of the earliest examples of Asherat, "The mother of the gods," or the "holy one." She was the spouse of El, the "Father of men," and in Ugarit, a maritime city, she was associated with the sea.

Asherat, 1900–1300 BC. Terracotta figurine, 16.4 cm. Lebanon (Byblos). (Credit: The Barakat Gallery, Beverly Hills, CA)

AΩ **Echoes of Davidic Judgment**
The image of "tearing" as a way of speaking about the abrupt and violent transfer of power from one leader to another is twice stated (11:11, 31). Whereas this son of David is the loser in this subversive transaction, the same rhetoric is earlier employed on David's behalf:

The LORD has torn the kingdom of Israel from you this very day, and has given it to a neighbor of yours, who is better than you. (1 Sam 15:28)

The LORD has torn the kingdom out of your hand, and given it to your neighbor, David. (1 Sam 28:17; see 1 Sam 13:14)

What the family of David receives as a gift from Yahweh (in the time of Saul) is taken from them by the same action of Yahweh. The parallel rhetoric is surely deliberate. The powerful in Israel are always again relearning respect for the overriding claim of Yahweh:

…until you have learned that the Most High has sovereignty over the kingdom of mortals, and gives it to whom he will. (Dan 4:25)

---

loyalty, neither in terms of its actual cultic practices nor in terms of its social policies that had little contact with the neighborly covenantalism of Moses.

The essential indictment against Solomon is stated in v. 4: the king has departed from Yahweh and from Torah obedience. Verses 5-8 only supply the particularities with reference to Astarte, Milcom, Chemosh, and Molech. [Many Gods] It is important to note that this catalogue does not fully correspond to the list of foreign wives in v. 1; missing is the name of any god associated with Pharaoh's daughter or with the Hittites. Such a difference suggests that the list of foreign gods is not precise or particular, but is a conventional list of the primary and recurring threats to Yahwism. In sum, Solomon has violated the first commandment of Sinai (Exod 20:3) from which all else in Yahwism derives. The love of Yahweh assures well-being (3:3); the love of many foreign wives brings massive trouble on the regime of Solomon and upon the long-term prospects of the Jerusalem establishment.

The sentence against Solomon is brief and uncomplicated (11:9-13). In fact the bald, direct sentence is only v. 11b: "I will surely tear the kingdom from you and give it to your servant." [Echoes of Davidic Judgment] In this terse statement, the theological verdict on Solomon is complete:

Indictment: His heart was not true to the LORD. (11:4)

Sentence: I will tear the kingdom from you. (11:11)

This theological perspective dares to assert that the rise and fall of power and the turn of public destiny depends singularly upon Torah obedience. In what follows this clear, simple theological conviction is clearly only worked out in the vagaries of the public process. The statement itself, however, concedes nothing to these complications. Israel is now on notice that everything depends upon Torah, a truth remote from the horizon of the great regime of Solomon.

The verdict of v. 11 effectively ends the regime of Solomon from a theological perspective. But of course such theological judgments, no matter how passionately entertained, cannot override the reality that takes place on the ground. For that reason, vv. 12-13 must add two important qualifications to the devastating announcement. First, the kingdom did not end in Solomon's lifetime, but persists in its Solomonic form into the reign of his son Rehoboam (11:12). Second, the loss of the kingdom did not entail the loss of Jerusalem, Judah, or Benjamin that the Davidic house retained for a very long time. Thus the severe judgment is tempered by lived reality. The mitigating grace is expressed theologically in a double "for the sake of," for David, for Jerusalem, Yahweh's two great loves (11:13). Here we are able to see the deep tension within Israel's faith between *severe Torah theology* and *affirming royal theology*. This tension is expressed in the books of Kings as though Jerusalem, Yahweh's special love, is somehow exempt from Torah judgment...at least for a long time.

The Judgment Enacted, 11:14-43

The remainder of the chapter reflects the realities that are to be faced concerning the public, historical implementation of the lawsuit just uttered (11:14-40). It is important to recognize that in the horizon of the books of Kings, Yahweh does not characteristically act in transcendental, supernatural ways. Rather, Yahweh's purposes are enacted in and through historical agents and events. These verses offer three candidates who will implement the devastation of Solomon's kingdom intended by Yahweh. The data of the narrative makes clear that the exploitative regime of Solomon had provoked a great deal of opposition and hostility on every side. The narrative suggests that Solomon is surrounded by those who wait impatiently for a chance to attack and destroy Israel.

Verses 14-25 report on two "adversaries" who despise Solomon but who in fact never take any action against him. They are termed "adversaries," for which the Hebrew word is *satan*, the negative tester. The first such potential opponent is Hadad of the royal house of Edom (11:14-22). We are told that Hadad's hostility toward the house of David is very old, rooted in the inflammatory, abusive activity of Joab on behalf of David (11:15-16). The slaughter here sounds much like the earlier notation on Pharaoh (Exod 1:22) and the subsequent devastation of Herod (Matt 2:16). Hadad barely escaped the killing by Joab, fled to Egypt, and there became, by marriage, a member of the royal household. Not unlike Solomon himself, Hadad is closely attached to Pharaoh. The most interesting point of this account is that Hadad was ready to end his exile and return home to Edom when David died, but Pharaoh restrained him. We are not told why, only that Pharaoh did so. It is not impossible that Pharaoh did so as a protective measure for Solomon. In any case, by v. 22 the regime of Solomon has one smoldering antagonist held in check by the persuasiveness of Pharaoh.

We are told even less about the second "adversary," Rezon (11:23-25). He is a fugitive from the government of Zobah, and he eventually becomes king of Syria (Aram). Though he takes no action against Solomon, the narrative refers to the "slaughter by David," perhaps appealing to the action reported in v. 15. In any case, Rezon's rise to power in Syria is not unlike that of David in Israel, for David also was something of a terrorist who eventually rose to power in Hebron and then in Jerusalem (see 1 Sam 22:3). The portrayal of Rezon, brief as it is, makes clear that this is a political world in which power is highly personal and deeply volatile. Staying on top of the heap must have required endless vigilance.

The reports on Hadad (11:14-22) and Rezon (11:23-25) are, in the end, inconclusive, beyond communicating the environment of hostility all around Solomon. The narrative's interest, however, is in the third adversary, Jeroboam (11:26-40). Jeroboam is reported as a man of some political leverage, a functionary in Solomon's court (11:28). Because he was in charge of forced labor, one might have expected him to be committed to Solomon and perhaps despised by the populace. But perhaps he lived so close to exploitative practices that he saw their evil and was repelled by them. We are told he "rebelled" ("raised his hand") against the king (11:26).

The narrative, however, attributes no political initiative to Jeroboam. Rather he is "recruited" by prophetic designation (11:29-39). We are not told why he was selected for such a role. What counts is the intrusive activity of Ahijah, a prophet not known before this episode; he appears abruptly and decisively. That he is the "Shilonite" is important; that is, he belongs to the shrine of Shiloh. This old northern shrine, prominent in early Israel, is often reckoned to be a seat for older, radical Mosaic notions of social organization. Thus it is plausible that Ahijah is not to be

A Tearing
This scene is based upon 1 Sam 15:27-29 and illustrates the symbolism of tearing. In this situation, the kingdom of Israel is being torn away from Saul whereas in the confrontation in 1 Kgs between Jeroboam and Ahijah, Solomon's kingdom is symbolically being torn from him and divided into 12 pieces.

Julius Schnoor von Carolsfeld. *Saul Tears Samuel's Robe.* 19th century. Woodcut from *Das Buch der Bucher in Bilden.* (Credit: Dover Pictorial Archive Series)

understood simply as a lone, odd prophet, but that he acts on behalf of a community of opinion that was deeply opposed to the character of Solomonic governance. Such marginalized communities as those that opposed Solomon must work with "the weapons of the weak," since they are denied normal political or military means. [The Weapons of the Weak] The "weapons of the weak" are symbolic, prophetic actions that enact a political statement with lingering authority and force.

Ahijah *acts* and then he *speaks* (11:30-41). His act is a simple one (11:30). He tears a new garment into twelve pieces, utilizing the verb "tear" (*qara*) from v. 12. It is a dramatic, highly visible act, sure to catch attention. [A Tearing] But the act requires explanatory speech (11:31-41). The speech of the prophet is an echo and exposition of the judgment of vv. 11-13. The decisive act refers to *tearing* tribes out of the kingdom of Solomon, twelve pieces for twelve tribes. The prophet in v. 32 must make the same allowances as in v. 13 that not all twelve tribes will be taken, for Jerusalem will be kept for David. Thus the "Jerusalem exemption" is again acknowledged. The qualifier of v. 32 does not, however, tone down the massive harshness of v. 33 that echoes the indictment of vv. 5-8. Thus vv. 31 and 33 offer *sentence* and *indictment* in reverse order, the same assertions we have seen in vv. 5-8, 11. The same qualifiers as in vv. 12-13 are acknowledged in vv. 32, 34-36, recognizing both the exception of Jerusalem and the continuation of the dynasty into the next generation. The prophet is a mouthpiece for the theological verdict given earlier in the chapter.

Only in vv. 37-38 does the prophetic speech break new ground with direct address to Jeroboam. The assurance given to the erstwhile administrator of forced labor is not unlike the assurance given to David in 2 Samuel 7. Two things in particular are to be noticed. First, the promise to Jeroboam is clearly conditional (11:38). The rhetoric is rooted in the Torah requirements of Deuteronomy as it had not been for David. Second, Jeroboam is promised a "sure house," exactly the phrasing of Abigail to David in 1 Samuel 25:28, and the promise to David in 2 Samuel 7:16. Jeroboam is summoned to be the *new David*, the carrier of Yahweh's best promises. This is a direct, staggering, precise displacement of one dynasty by the authorization of another, a deeply subversive act (see 1 Sam 16:1-13 for a parallel).

The final line of the prophetic speech is odd indeed (11:39). The statement makes clear that the core theological tradition of Israel can never have done with David. Already in v. 36, the same subversive prophet had allowed a "lamp" in Jerusalem "all the days," and now in v. 39, the punishment of David's heir is "not for

---

The Weapons of the Weak

The contest between entrenched royal power and dissenting prophetic advocacy is unmistakably clear. It is a contest between deep resources and no resources at all, clearly an unequal match. In the language of Robert R. Wilson, it is a transaction between "center" and "periphery." [Robert R. Wilson, *Prophecy and Society in Ancient Israel* (Philadelphia: Fortress Press, 1980).] By any measure the vision of the prophet should never prevail. And yet it does occasionally. James C. Scott studied the shrewd and daring "weapons" that the poor use to challenge the powerful. [James C. Scott, *Weapons of the Weak: Everyday Forms of Peasant Resistance* (New Haven: Yale University Press, 1987).] Ahijah is a case in point. His only "weapons" are speech and drama. They are used to good effect. In some cases—perhaps this one in chapter 11—these weapons are enough to initiate a counterpolitics. There is something inscrutable and irresistible about such challenges that defy the ordinary means of governance. Read theologically, such inexplicable turns of affairs are termed "miracles":

No wisdom, no understanding, no counsel,
    can avail against the LORD.
The horse is made ready for the day of battle,
    but the victory belongs to the LORD. (Prov 21:30-31)

all days," not to perpetuity. It is as though the well-established ideological claim of David places a check on the revolutionary venture of the prophet. Thus the promise to Jeroboam is a full one...but not quite. This speech thus reiterates the earlier verdict on Solomon. But then it moves beyond the earlier verdict in two more venturesome statements: (a) this can be *a new dynasty;* (b) *the old dynasty is not abandoned.* The prophetic speech ends; Jeroboam does not respond.

The daring chapter that renounces Solomon and seems to dispose of him has a realistic ending (11:40-41). For all the revolutionary expectation of the prophet, Solomon is still in power. He is still dangerous and not to be toyed with. But then, oppressive governments are like that. Just when "the handwriting is on the wall" and it is everywhere visible that the regime has failed, it often happens that the regime becomes most ruthless and most dangerous in self-defense. Solomon knows about Ahijah and Jeroboam. He knows, because it is his necessary business to know, and he has ways of finding out. He is not deterred for an instant by prophetic resistance. At the end of his long reign, he is prepared to maintain himself in the same way he has secured his throne at the outset: by the sword (see chapter 2). Jeroboam flees to Egypt as had Hadad earlier (11:18). Pharaoh is a port of refuge who hosts the enemies of Solomon. Jeroboam must wait. And we must wait a chapter longer for the word of the prophet to become fleshed in politics.

The concluding editorial note in vv. 41-43 will become, from now on, standard in the review of the kings of Israel and Judah. The summary statement gives the essential data for the reign concluded. Especially noteworthy is that these summaries characteristically offer a citation to a reference book presumably available to the reader, here "The Book of the Acts of Solomon." We do not have such a book, but apparently it was available, offering more complete, reliable historical data. The importance of the citation here is that it makes clear that the biblical text does not intend to provide "the full story." This account is at best selective, designed to argue a theological case and advocate a theological verdict. It would be a great mistake, says the footnote, to take this material as either complete or objective. It is neither, and it intends to be neither.

The summary data on subsequent kings regularly concludes with a stylized verdict...good or bad. This element is missing here, because the entire chapter has as its purpose and function a verdict on Solomon. Solomon is a *failed* king. The theological perspective given here is completely unimpressed by the data of chapters 9 and 10, or even the temple rendition of chapters 5–8. What counts is only Torah obedience. On that count the data is not ambiguous. "His heart was not true." And because the God who gives commands is the God who governs Israel's future, big trouble is under way for the monarchy.

CONNECTIONS

The great claim in this chapter that writes the sorry end of Solomon is that there is an *overriding obligation* in the historical process that cannot be evaded. That is, public power and public policy are not, in the end, a matter of luck or prudence, or nerve, or power. Beyond any human posturing and human strategies, there is yet another dimension to the public process.

In the parlance of ancient Israel, that *overriding obligation* is expressed as *the will and purpose of Yahweh* that finally will have a say in the deployment of power. The Solomonic narrative is amazing in how long it can tell its tale without reference to the purposes of Yahweh. Indeed, in his wealth and power, one might conclude that Solomon is a free, autonomous agent who can do all that he desires. Perhaps the king himself, and those around him, had drawn that misguided conclusion. But unfortunately for him, says this text, such a judgment is premature and disastrous.

The narrative is at some pains to identify the dimensions of this obligation that are not simple and one-dimensional. We may identify three aspects of this *inscrutability* that are very different from each other, but that oddly converge in a single conclusion.

1. The overriding focus is on *the commandment of Yahweh*. Yahweh has, from early on, asserted the requirements of a viable public life. The core requirement is "Yahweh alone." But we must not misunderstand this command. To be sure, it is a cultic restriction, so that other gods and powers may not be honored or celebrated in Israel. But the command pertains no more to cultic life than it does to the life of politics and economics. In those dimensions of life, devotion to Yahweh is transposed into concern for the neighbor. Thus to "know Yahweh" is to serve neighbor through public policy (see Jer 22:15-26). This daring claim of obligation implies that a public practice that violates Yahweh by violating neighbor is sure to end in ruin.

2. After the focus on command, attention to the adversaries— Hadad, Rezon, and Jeroboam—suggests that such *disgruntled opponents* are a means whereby Yahweh's disestablishing purposes are enacted. The text is careful to make no connection at all

between the first two of Solomon's adversaries and the command of Yahweh. It does seem clear, however, that Jeroboam is presented as a means of Yahweh's governance. The "tearing from Solomon" is not only a gift to Jeroboam, but is accomplished through his agency.

This is an odd claim that no hegemonic power can ever acknowledge in time. That is, that opposition forces, dissenting parties, revolutionary challenges—even terrorists?—may be the means whereby power organized in disobedience may be terminated by Yahweh. The claim does not seem very likely, if one thinks of Gerry Adams's resistance to the Ulster government, or perhaps if one notices Arafat against Israel, or if one pays attention to disgruntled vigilantes in the U.S. But then the case is more clear if one ponders the long-term resistance of the African National Congress leaders to apartheid in South Africa. All of these movements, some more obviously than others, seem a good distance remote from prophetic, covenantal verdicts, except that the tale of the revolutionaries occur on the same page with the theological verdicts!

3. The obligation is also expressed through *some odd characters* such as Ahijah the prophet who has no credentials and no visible authorization. Ahijah may have a sound critical tradition behind him. But he appears "on the road" as something of a nut, wearing a new garment. He enacts a "symbolic act," a parable that calls conventional assumptions about power into question. We may have a more disciplined notion of prophets in mind, but here the prophet is a weird guy who injects into public consciousness a dramatic alternative possibility. Perhaps as close as we come to such prophetic acts are symbolic subversions such as those undertaken by the Brothers Berrigan who specialize in acts of blood poured on armament installations. Such acts are absurd in the face of established power, as the Berrigans readily

Obligation Made Strategy

The demand of Torah, reinforced by prophetic insistence, is a simple one: socioeconomic power must keep on its horizon *the face of the neighbor*, a requirement Solomon did not honor. That simple insistence, however, must be enacted in ways that are wise, strategic, and complex, if they are to impact a complex economy. Thus neighbor love must be enacted as economic policy, an enactment completely refused by Solomon. In our own time, some guidelines emerge in a free-market economy; they urge that the economy must be managed differently if it is to be sustained and made generative of community health. For one such proposal, see Herman E. Daly and John B. Cobb, Jr., who discuss a redirected economy under six headings:

(1) University Reform,
(2) Building Communities,
(3) Changing Trade Policies,
(4) Establishing an Optimum Scale,
(5) Measuring Economic Progress,
(6) Attitudinal Change.

The important point is that a resolve *to obey* must be matched by a *visionary wisdom* concerning how to obey in effective, transformative ways. It is crucial for Daly and Cobb that the pages following these recommendations are concerned with "religious vision."

Herman E. Daly and John B. Cobb, Jr., *For the Common Good: Redirecting the Economy toward Community, the Environment, and a Sustainable Future* (Boston: Beacon Press, 1989) 355-75.

acknowledge. Except that such acts do cause establishment power everywhere to tremble, for strange "counter power" is released through such acts that seems to be authorized in ways that the establishment cannot control.

The convergence in our chapter of *commandment, revolutionary alternative, and prophetic symbolization* serves to put the regime on notice. The actual "end" of the regime comes in chapter 12, in a more routine political act. But who knows to what extent the oddness of chapter 11 evokes and nourishes the determined resistance of chapter 12!

Of course all of this is "unlikely." It must have been unlikely then, and it is certainly so now, given our power arrangements secured in technology and hidden in bureaucracy. It seemed unlikely to the Shah in Iran and to the apartheid government in South Africa. But the text is not intimidated or silenced by our rational dismissal of such raggedness. The text simply sits there, rather regularly making it impossible to remove from our thoughts and our awareness this sense of obligation that relativizes our best inventiveness. [Obligation Made Strategy] By the end of the chapter, Jeroboam is "on hold." Indeed, much of the time this ominous obligation is on hold. But that gives little comfort, for "on hold" status is not the same as nullification.

AN URGENT
POLITICAL SETTLEMENT

1 Kings 12:1-33

THE TWO STATES, 1 KINGS 12–2 KINGS 17

This long section of narrative offers a parallel account of the regimes in the North and the South. The southern regime of David's dynasty in Jerusalem is a tale of amazing continuity, being momentarily disrupted only by the break around the heterodoxy of Athaliah (2 Kgs 11). By contrast the Northern Kingdom, finally situated in Samaria, is a study of discontinuity featuring four distinct dynasties, plus a tail end of stopgap rulers who variously submit to and defy the empire. The narrative renders theological verdicts upon each of the several kings. In the North all are condemned for having departed, as did Jeroboam, from the legitimacy of Jerusalem; in the South the judgments are more varied and nuanced, but all are according to a rigorous theological criterion of Torah.

The defining feature of this narrative, however, is the dominant presence in the narrative of the prophets, Elijah, Elisha, and Micaiah. All of these odd voices are situated in the midst of the Omri dynasty that is used by the narrator primarily as a mounting platform for these prophets. The Omri dynasty is judged by the narrative to be the worst by the Torah standards of the narrative. That dynasty, however, is simply symptomatic and paradigmatic of the entire northern account that culminates in 2 Kings 17 in the Assyrian onslaught and deportation. That devastation means the end of the northern state is readily understood by this narrative in Yahwistic categories.

COMMENTARY

The shift from royal father to royal son is often a perilous transition for an undemocratic regime (see Exod 2:23; Isa 6:1). It was by no means clear that the North (Israel) would adhere to the Judean son of Solomon (see 2 Sam 20:1). David had first become king of Judah (2 Sam 2:4), and only later king of Israel by a separate process of negotiation (2 Sam 5:3). The northern allegiance to the dynasty of David had never been secure. And now it threatens to end completely. Rehoboam must hurry to Shechem to save his northern constituency—to Shechem the traditional rallying place of tribes with long Mosaic, pre-Davidic memories.

Jeroboam, moreover, like Charles DeGaulle, waits in Egypt to be summoned home as leader (11:40). The occasion of crisis is an opportunity for negotiation but also a chance for rebellion and

This scene depicts the moment in the text when King Rehoboam decides in favor of a "heavy yoke" for the people of Israel.
Julius Schnoor von Carolsfeld. *Jeroboam Petitioning the King.* 19th century. Woodcut. From *Das Buch der Bucher in Bilden.* (Credit: Dover Pictorial Archive Series)

secession. The narrative of this chapter divides into two parts: failed negotiations with Rehoboam (12:1-19) and the establishment of Jeroboam's new regime (12:25-33). Between the two sections stands a prophetic anticipation concerning the ongoing tension between the two new regimes (12:20-24).

Failed Negotiations, 12:1-19

The chapter begins with the tale of failed negotiations (12:1-19). The narrative proceeds in a clear fashion with an offer to negotiate (12:1-5), the double consultation of Rehoboam with "older men" and "younger men" (12:6-11), the response of Rehoboam to his northern partners (12:12-15), and the rejection of Rehoboam and the rule of Jerusalem by the North (12:16-19).

The North is prepared to continue allegiance to the Davidic crown. But because of its covenantal traditions and the lessons it has learned from Solomon about centralized government, it will not immediately cede its own bargaining rights. Jeroboam comes home from exile in order to lead the negotiations. The key point in the parlay is a "heavy yoke" (12:4). The term "yoke" is not here explicated, but it refers to an imposed burden or obligation. [An Easy Yoke] In this context, the term undoubtedly refers to governmental impositions under Solomon of either tax requirements or labor requirements ("forced labor"), or both. As we have seen, Solomon's ambitious programs required ample supplies of both (5:13-18; 9:15-22). Israel in the north is unwilling to continue under the son the same heavy requirements of the father.

The demand of the North is not an easy one for the new king, for an agreement to a "light yoke" will require great budget cutbacks, a curtailment of Solomon's showy accomplishments. Rehoboam must take council and count the costs of his beginning (12:6-11). The new king parlays in turn with "the older men" and "the younger men." There is a scholarly suggestion that these labels refer to two governmental bodies, but that is unlikely. More plausibly, the king conferred with different sectors of his government. The "older men" perhaps have longer memories, or perhaps they themselves had grown doubtful of Solomon's acquisitive policies. Either way, they urge the young king to adopt a conciliatory policy in which the new king takes the role of "servant," as one with but not over the people. Such counsel bespeaks a certain attitude toward government as well as a good deal of common sense. [On Servanthood and Power]

An Easy Yoke
The yoke of social expectation and requirement, like the demands on a work animal, can be made lenient or severe. Rehoboam missed his chance. The term "yoke" turns up in two other quite familiar uses. In Isa 58:6, it is Yahweh's will to,

let the oppressed go free
and to break every yoke.

In Matt 11:18, Jesus offers an easy yoke that is contrasted to more conventional social expectations that cause weariness. What Rehoboam refused is a major offer of the gospel, an offer with immediate economic implications.

The king explores all of his options. The young men who advise the young king lack experience and common sense and an awareness of the inherent limitations of power. They are like officials who come newly elected to power in Washington and imagine that they now have the capacity to do anything they want; and they learn otherwise only painfully. They do not understand the cruciality of the consent of the governed. The young men may be the new generation of power elites in Jerusalem who have no memory other than Solomon's opulence. They likely are the ones who are so "happy" under Solomon (4:20; 10:8), who have never known anything but extravagant privilege and a heavy sense of their own entitlement. They likely take their affluence as normal and have never known anything other than a standard of living supported by heavy taxation. Their advice to the king grows out of their self-preoccupation (12:10-11). They urge that governmental burden be made heavier and more stringent, more aggressive and exploitative.

Rehoboam is as young as his young advisors, as foolish as his foolish young advisors (12:12-14). His response is offered as a direct quote of the worst advice imaginable. He declares outright that his coming governance will be more demanding—more yoke, more discipline, more taxes, more labor quotas. Not a good beginning!

At a practical level, the king could not be more shortsighted. Indeed, we may wonder why he is so foolish. Our text, however, has a word of explanation for the king's self-destructive conduct (12:15). No doubt the king is free in his irresponsible decision. That freedom for royal initiative, however, is in the context of Yahweh's large oversight of public affairs that Israel never completely forgets. In this verse, the narrative nicely ties together the practical policies of chapter 12 and the theological verdict of

---

On Servanthood and Power

The "older men" advocate a kingship that serves the populace. This is the proper relation of people and their rulers. Rulers exist in order to enhance the realm and those who occupy it. In Ezek 34, however, one can observe the process of governance by which the ruled come to exist for the rulers, so that political power exists only to enhance those already powerful. It is unmistakably clear that such a theory of governance now dominates the U.S. political scene.

In Mark 10:35-45, it is evident that the disciples deeply misconstrue Jesus' intention, for they are disputing about thrones, that is, about power. Against that distortion, Jesus tersely redefined power as servanthood in a statement echoing the advice of the old men that the young king rejected:

You know that among the Gentiles those whom they recognize as their leaders lord it over them, and their great ones are tyrants over them. But it is not so among you; but whoever wishes to become great among you must be your servant, and whoever wishes to be first among you must be slave of all. (Mark 10:42-44)

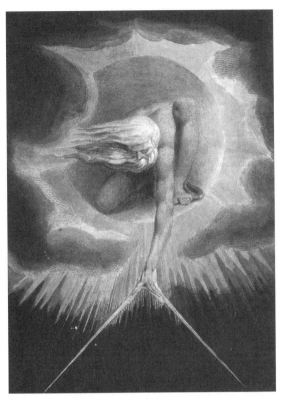

ΑΩ **A Note on Providence**

"Providence" refers to the hidden, decisive ways in which God governs for our good. The most spectacular example of providence is in Gen 22, in which God, at the last moment, "provides" a ram as an offering, thereby rescuing Isaac from death. The theme of that narrative is, "God will provide." Karl Barth has noticed that the term "provide" in Hebrew is *ra'ah*, "to see." He suggests that "to see" is "to see ahead," pro-video…provide…providence…. Such a casting of the narrative asserts that there is a hidden governance at work for our good. So for Israel, God has "seen ahead" that the destruction of the Solomonic enterprise of acquisitiveness is a good to be accomplished through the course of public life.

God's planned creation is suggested in this print with the compass functioning as a direct extension to project God's designs upon the world. The compass comes from medieval representation of the Lord as Architect of the Universe.

William Blake. *The Ancient of Days*. 1794. Etching. Library of Congress, Washington, DC.

---

chapter 11. In chapter 11, the prophet Ahijah had announced forfeiture of the North (11:31-32). In that chapter, however, the loss is only prophetic rhetoric. Now it becomes practical politics, a fulfillment accomplished by the king's foolishness. The Bible has no clear formulation concerning how *divine purpose* is practically implemented. If we emphasize the practical, we may say that the divine decree is an interpretation of the political. If, however, we are more theologically attentive, we will say that these two chapters together articulate Yahweh's providence, Yahweh's hidden way of shaping reality for the sake of Yahweh's purposes. [A Note on Providence] The clearest parallel known to me for this text occurs in the David narrative, wherein Absalom chooses the destructive advice of Hushai rather than the wise common sense of Ahithophel. Again we may wonder why the young prince Absalom is so obtuse. The narrative knows:

> For the LORD had ordained to defeat the good counsel of Ahithophel, so that the LORD might bring ruin on Absalom. (2 Sam 17:14)

According to this narrative, public history is not reduced to human choices and stratagems. In the midst of human choices there is another "choosing" at work to which human agents have no access. (The same assumption finally governs the book of Job.) In our case, Yahweh had already, in the utterance of Ahijah, determined matters. Yahweh had willed the division of the Solomonic kingdom. It remains for human agents like Rehoboam to choose, unwittingly, the choices of Yahweh.

The response of the North to the policy declaration of the new king is quick and decisive, and not unexpected. Verse 16 reiterates a political slogan of the North, a formula of secession asserting that the North never owed David allegiance in any case. The formula is already sounded in 2 Samuel 20:2 in the Saulide rejection of

The Uprising

Rehoboam's first act, after the statement of secession, stunningly was to send his agent for forced labor to reassert control. It is more than a little ironic that he was killed by stoning, for it suggests that the peasants of the North lacked conventional military means but that even with only stones, the force of their resentment was incalculable and could not be put down by conventional military force.

The act of stoning calls to mind the Palestinian "uprising" in recent years against the power of the state of Israel. The state of Israel clearly held complete military advantage. For the Palestinians, stoning was the chief means of aggression, an *up*rising not put *down* by the government. The parallel strikes me as odd but worth noticing. I cite this example of peasants against government not because it is peculiar, but because the means of stoning was the weapon at hand. In many other cases, the same dynamics operate, but not usually with stones.

Scythes are the weapons of the workers in this revolt of German workers.

Käthe Kollwitz. *March of the Weavers* from the series *The Weavers' Revolt*. 1897. Etching. Fine Arts Museums of San Francisco, CA (Credit: Fine Arts Museums of San Francisco, Achenbach Foundation for Graphic Arts, 1963.30.867)

David. The North pulls away from Jerusalem, which of course means a great loss of tax money and human resources for the throne of David. Rehoboam did not give up so easily. In an attempt to defy the rebellion, he sends Adoram—of all people—to reactivate the draft of forced labor. The dispatching of Adoram must have been especially inflammatory to the North, but it also indicates the real agenda of the throne. The head of "forced labor" is prepared immediately to make the yoke heavier. The obduracy of the Jerusalem regime is answered appropriately by the North (12:18). The government official is stoned to death. [The Uprising] The government of Jerusalem has no credibility in the North. The officers of state receive no respect or deference. Rehoboam in his foolishness has enacted the ominous notice of Ahijah. The king had to flee for his life. The dream of David and the ambitions of Solomon, in a quick process, are all down the drain. Verse 19 adds a laconic notice: Things remained in a failed condition. The "transgression" of the North here begins and has persisted. Rehoboam did irreversible damage to his own cause.

Accommodating New Realities, 12:20-33

The fateful separation of North and South requires adjustments on both sides (12:20-24). For the North, a new beginning must be made. Jeroboam, who led negotiations and who has been in our purview since the prophetic incentive of chapter 11, readily becomes king of the new enterprise. The authorization of the prophet in 11:37-38 means that Jeroboam has a chance for greatness. Indeed, he begins with a promise almost as sweeping as that made to the house of David.

Matters are not so simple for the South, for the loss smarts. For a Jerusalem king to "lose" the North may be like a U.S. president who "loses" China or Southeast Asia. It must not happen! And so Rehoboam is ready to end the secession by means of a strong and massive military force. Perhaps he would have prevailed, for we are told nothing of Northern military preparedness. Rehoboam is deterred, not by any practical matter, but by a prophetic utterance. The prophet Shemaiah stops the Southern venture by a declaration echoing the word of Ahijah (11:31) and the dark disclosure of 12:15:

This thing is from me. (12:24)

That is, the division of North and South is authorized and caused by Yahweh. What God has rent asunder, the king will not seek to join together. The division of the kingdom is willed by God. Remarkably Rehoboam who would not listen to good political counsel accepts the prophetic word. The split becomes accepted political reality. [A Divine Rationale?]

Jeroboam, by this point, has received prophetic affirmation (11:37-38) and popular public acclaim (12:20). But he has no visible props necessary for the exhibit of royal authority, certainly nothing to compete with the well-established Jerusalem operation.

A Divine Rationale?

The "turn of affairs" given in our verse yields no rationale for divine resolve. We are not told how this overthrow happened; we are also not told why it happened, but are only left to conjecture. Clearly Yahweh wants the government of Rehoboam to fail. We are left to conclude that the Solomonic enterprise with its failure to honor either God or neighbor has exhausted Yahweh's patience. The judgment, as given in chapter 12, is not just because of religious offenses but perhaps also has an economic dimension. But of course, none of that is said. The Holy One need not explain. We are left to ponder. Was the "turn of affairs" reasonable according to divine logic?

For that reason, he must immediately undertake building projects that show him publicly acting the way kings act (12:25-33). First, he "builds" Shechem and Penuel, two old Israelite shrines that now are claimed as royal focal points (on Shechem, see Gen 35:4; Josh 24:1, 25, 32; 1 Kgs 12:1; on Penuel, see Gen 32:31). Of the two shrines, Shechem is the far more important traditional locus of the community. But the narrative is not in fact interested in either building site beyond the general observation that the king was a builder. The narrative comes to its topic only in vv. 26-27, wherein Jeroboam acknowledges that he must take steps to compete with the magnetic pull of Jerusalem, a pull that, if not countered, could terminate this secession and end Jeroboam's brief day in the sun. According to the text, the matter of rival shrines was a purely pragmatic issue, not at all impinged upon by piety, a judgment not difficult to accept given the calculating prehistory of Solomon.

While Jeroboam recognizes the need for such an arrangement in vv. 26-27, the actual installment of the two "calves" is a creative step presented, in the first instance, with no hint of censure (12:28-29). It is commonly thought that the calves are not themselves embodiments of any god but are vehicles upon the back of which sits the invisible God. Thus the calves function in the North the same way the ark does in the Jerusalem temple, as a throne for the present but invisible deity (see 1 Kgs 8:3-13). The calves are set up at the two shrines that presumably mark the boundary limits of Jeroboam's inchoate governance. They are guarantees and assurances of God's presence and availability to Israel, apart from the

Jerusalem establishment. Read in this way, the two calves are unexceptional and unobjectionable.

We must remember, however, that we are dealing with a Northern installment that will rival Jerusalem, while the literature we have before us in 1 Kings is a Southern account of faith and history that has weighty commitments to Jerusalem's claims. Thus what may have been an innocent and well meaning liturgical alternative to Jerusalem is promptly subjected to a heavy-handed theological caricature and critique. Thus immediately we are told, "this thing became a sin" (12:30). Note well, we are not given any theological reason for the judgment that it is a sin, except that it caused the people to worship elsewhere, other than in Jerusalem.

When the account reaches a polemical tone, careful attention must be paid to Exodus 32 and the story of the "Golden Calf." The story of the golden calf represents Aaron as an unauthorized rival to Moses and the calf as an unacceptable rival to Yahweh. Possibly, as many scholars think, the narrative of the golden calf is a projection back into the Moses tradition of the story of 1 Kings 12, in order to submit the act of Jeroboam to a massive critique as fundamentally resistant to the tradition of Moses. Thus a neutral, pragmatic act is transposed into a massively negative act by the process of polemical interpretation.

We may notice in our text two seemingly deliberate references to Exodus 32. First, the statement of Jeroboam in 12:28, "Here are your gods, O Israel,..." is closely parallel to the statement of Aaron in Exodus 32:4. The theme is presented as though Aaron and Jeroboam, in turn, simply manufactured "gods" for their own convenience. Second, 1 Kings 12:31 observes that the priests of Jeroboam were "not Levites," a statement that tilts toward the Aaronide priesthood of Exodus 32 that is submitted to the harsh treatment of the Levites in Exodus 32:25-29. Thus from the narrative of Exodus 32, the priests of Jeroboam are taken to be heterdox. The religious enterprise of Jeroboam, necessary to the political establishment of the North, is condemned in principle by the normative Deuteronomic opinion that governs 1 Kings 12. As we shall see, the "sin of Jeroboam" becomes an enduring reference point and cause of condemnation of the North. His founding act seals the judgment of the North through all its different dynasties.

The remainder of the chapter (12:32-33) presents Jeroboam as aggressively active about worship in high places. We may understand his zeal for worship from the pragmatic perspective of vv. 26-27; we may also notice how the text is saturated with polemical rhetoric, with reference to "high places," a phrase we have already encountered in 3:2. By the end of this narrative unit, the kingdom of the North, renegade though it may be, is well under way. The dismantling of the Solomonic achievement is nearly completed.

CONNECTIONS

This chapter cannot be understood apart from chapter 11. When the two chapters are taken together, it is evident that *faith* and *politics* are deeply intertwined in the horizon of Israel. It is striking that 12:1-16, an account of the breakup of the kingdom of Solomon, is cast completely in political categories...except for the notice of v. 15. That account, moreover, is perfectly credible on its own terms. It concerns the interplay of dominant political force (that is completely insensitive to the realities of life in the community) in relation to the hopes, expectations, and insistences of those who are no longer willing to be exploited. It is perfectly credible that the insistence of the community should grow out of hopes too long deferred. Equally credible is that the self-indulgent Rehoboam, with his equally self-indulgent "young men," should miss the point of the protest and invite the loss of the royal power base. What interests us, however, is the notation of v. 15 that places Yahweh at the center of the political exchange and makes clear that the political process is the working out of a profound theological conviction already evident in chapter 11.

The juxtaposition of religious and political reality on the one hand makes clear that from the perspective of this account, politics is not an autonomous zone of life where the working of power has a life of its own. Conversely, the juxtaposition makes clear that Yahweh can never be understood as simply a transcendent force concerned with spiritual matters, for Yahweh is engaged in the midst of power and oppression. Such an intertwining of religion and politics is a deep challenge to our secularized ways of thinking. Moreover, the religious dimension here is fundamentally emancipatory, working against the closure of the political process in absolute control.

Perhaps the most dramatic case of this intertwining in recent memory is the overthrow of the apartheid regime in South Africa. No one can doubt that the overthrow, albeit democratic, was an exercise in power, planning, and propaganda of the most clear-headed kind. And yet, anyone who pays attention to the rhetoric of transformation will know that the political cause was deeply grounded in theological passion of the most elemental kind, affirming that the God of all truth will not be indifferent to exploitation and oppression.

If we take this juxtaposition from the ancient texts, via the example of South Africa, into our own U.S. context, the juxtaposition invites renoticing what we may prefer not to notice. No doubt, our economy, in which the gap between haves and have-nots grows exponentially, is commonly regarded as an autonomous operation with a life of its own. But the logic of our text indicates otherwise. It asserts that the God of the covenant is deeply enmeshed in such public processes and, soon or late, will see to it that there is an answering for the pain that some cause to others by systemic arrangement, an answering that entails the radical redeployment of power and the transfer of goods from some to others. Of course such an upheaval is nowhere visible, just as it was not visible in Israel at the death of Solomon. But as we have seen, the convergence of political revolutionaries, prophetic utterance, and popular unrest is an awesome enterprise, especially if it knows itself invested with the force of the God of the covenant.

AΩ **The Calf**

The "calf" becomes a recurring reference in the judgment of Israel. In addition to the incidental polemic in our verses and the anticipatory polemic of Exod 32, see also Deut 9:13-21. In Hosea, moreover, the "calf" is a reference for all that is distorted in North Israel:

> Your calf is rejected, O Samaria.
> My anger burns against them.
> (Hos 8:5; see 10:5-6)

> "Sacrifice to these," they say,
> People are kissing calves! (Hos 13:2)

Finally, 2 Kgs 17:16, the final statement of judgment on the failure of the Northern Kingdom, recalls the calves. Clearly the installation of the calves is taken as emblematic of a deep distortion of life. Because the calves are designed to rival Jerusalem, the polemic seems always to contain a pro-Jerusalem tone.

Because the calves are said to be "manufactured," they come to represent defiant autonomy that refuses to submit to life on Yahweh's terms. The manufacture of life for self belongs to virile money-making; but of course, that project always fails, as it did in this ancient venture.

Young Bull. 900-600 BC. Bronze. Syria.
(Credit: The Brakat Gallery, Beverly Hills, CA)

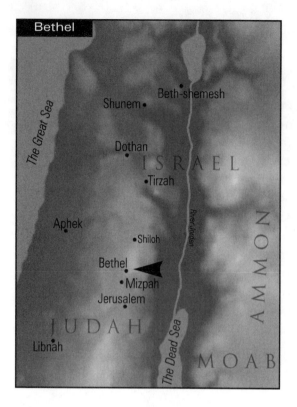

We may ponder briefly the "calf" of Jeroboam. We have seen that it may have been an innocent innovation that only subsequently was comprehended in a massive polemic. As we have it, in any case, the installation of the North is now treated polemically. If we associate this calf with Exodus 32 and that polemic (as seems required by the final form of the tradition), we may consider afresh the phrase "golden calf." [The Calf] The phrase includes two parts. First, the term "calf" might also be "bull," thus a symbol of virility, generative power, and reproductivity. The term "golden" of course refers to an obsession we have seen in Solomon for the most expensive and ostentatious decor. The two terms together, *golden* and *calf,* readily add up to the interface of *virility* and *money*, a combination that makes for aggressive, ambitious domination and control of a most ostentatious and determined kind.

The combination of *virility* and *money* may be taken as emblematic of the powers of free market aggressiveness and acquisitiveness nowhere more clearly enacted than in professional sports that knows no restraints concerning money and macho, seconded by all sorts of gross hints of sexuality. Professional sports in our society, moreover, have become a metaphor for free market aggressiveness in which neighborly questions disappear and human issues become invisible. This of course is a far reach from Jeroboam at Dan and Bethel. [Map: Bethel] But given the polemical character of the narrative, it keeps reaching toward all the distortions, ancient and contemporary, that lead away from Yahwistic covenantalism. Taken at its baldest, we may imagine that the later critique of Karl Marx is already implicit here:

> Money is the universal, self-constituted value of all things. It has therefore robbed the whole world, human as well as natural, of its own values. Money is the alienated essence of man's work and being, this alien essence dominates him and he adores it.[1]

NOTE

[1]David McLellan, *The Thought of Karl Marx: An Introduction* (London: Macmillan Press, 1971) 21.

As mentioned in the commentary, the sanctuary at Bethel is also shown in this painting as embodying all that is "wayward as a shrine." The golden bull shrine looms above at the center of the painting, providing a fulcrum by which the painting is split between worshiping God and idolatry. On the left, the man of God is shown proclaiming against the altar (1 Kgs 13:1-10). King Jeroboam is shown reeling in shock amidst the smoky incense. According to the text, Jeroboam is powerless against the man of God and even depends on him to restore his withered hand. The king's attendants are perhaps holding his injured right arm as he recoils with dismay. The French Rococo artist, Fragonard, has masterfully composed this painting to deliver the full force of the narrative. The king is shown in the brightest area of the painting, amidst the hazy and diaphonous lighting so characteristic of the rococo style. The man of God is shown with his hands pressed together in prayer, creating an upward directionality toward the bull shrine. The entire composition forms a triangle with the bull at the apex. Dramatically, the aghast King Jeroboam, in pointing back toward the man of God, contributes to maintain the energy and movement. The emphasis upon dramatic movement and theatrical lighting, established in the Baroque period, is blended with the characteristic Rococo hazy flood of backlighting. This tends to merge the forms into each other and blur the distinct edges.

Jean Honore Fragonard. *Jeroboam Sacrificing to the Idols*. 18th century. Oil on canvas. Ecole des Beaux Arts, Paris, France. (Credit: Giraudon/Art Resource, NY)

OMINOUS PROPHETIC INSCRUTABILITY

1 Kings 13:1-34

This remarkable and enigmatic narrative chapter is all of one piece, with each part contributing to the whole. Obviously, several themes operate in the narrative in a variety of overlays and interrelations. We may divide the narrative into five distinct units; all of them, however, seem fully focused on the theme of *judgment against Bethel,* as our chapter is situated between 1 Kings 12:33 and 2 Kings 23:4-20.

COMMENTARY

A Sign against Bethel from Judah, 13:1-10

Jeroboam, the new king in the North with the new shrines in Bethel and Dan, has just celebrated a festival at Bethel. [Bethel] Immediately, a "man of God" from Judah comes to pronounce judgment against that shrine. The speaker is unidentified and completely without credentials. We are not told that he is commissioned by Yahweh. We only know he is "out of Judah." At the outset we may surmise that this is a Judah-David polemic against the Northern establishment that serves primarily to detract from the claims of Jerusalem.

The work of this "man of God" is twofold. First, he announces that a future Davidic king, Josiah by name, will come and slaughter the priests of the high places on the altar (13:2). Second, he offers a

---

Bethel

The town of Bethel, located on the border between northern Israel and southern Judah is strategically placed as contested territory. It is, moreover, invested with special importance as a prominent shrine in the history of Israel. Its choice by Jeroboam as a royal shrine may be in part dictated by tradition and in part by location.

In order to appreciate its significance and therefore the poignancy of the oracle against it, attention should be paid to Jacob's dream at Bethel (Gen 28:10-22) and the prominence of Bethel in the time of the Judges (Judg 20:26-28). According to prophetic conviction, perhaps congruent with our narrative, Bethel stands under acute judgment for its waywardness as a shrine (Hos 10:15; Amos 3:14). There is no doubt that the town and sanctuary become something of a metaphor for all the departures from true faith as understood in the final form of the biblical text.

"sign" to vouchsafe for the anticipation of Josiah namely that the altar will be destroyed. This then is a long-term anticipation and a short-term action, both of which are destructive acts against Bethel. Concerning the double speech itself, we may marvel that the narrative is arranged to connect with Josiah, a king who will not appear until 300 years later. [Josiah] This pivotal reference to Josiah suggests the artistic and deliberate way in which the entire narrative of Kings is arranged with great theological self-consciousness.

The king's response to the double threat is also twofold. First, the king rightly discerns that this "man of God" is a deep threat to the new regime and must be stopped. He orders his arrest, but his gesture of authorization for the arrest stops halfway, as his hand withers. The king is shown to be powerless before the "man of God." The immobilization of the king, moreover, is matched by a report that the altar at Bethel is torn down, just as the "man of God" had said. The king may be evil, but he is no fool. He promptly recognizes the superior power of the "man of God," and so he appeals to him to have his damaged hand restored…which the "man of God" immediately does, yet another manifestation of his immense power. Now the king makes his second response to his erstwhile foe. He extends hospitality and invites him to eat with him, a grand royal offer. But the "man of God" is bound to resist the invitation. He is under command from Yahweh (we are now told, but not heretofore). He is commanded by Yahweh to avoid any fraternization with any of the Northerners. Thus his business is finished and he must depart.

This first scene already alerts us to the odd incongruity between style and substance. The style of the narrative is that of a regular,

---

📖 Josiah

Probably Josiah, the last effective king in the Davidic line, was a most formidable figure in the political and military life of Judah. It seems clear that he was able to undertake, in the wake of the waning and collapse of Assyrian power, a vigorous political and military recovery of the northern territory lost under Rehoboam. While this may be presented as an act of peculiar piety, the king was surely no stranger to the reality of governance.

But whatever may be the facts of the case, there is no doubt that Josiah looms large in the interpretive proposal of this Deuteronomic history (see 2 Kgs 22–23). Indeed, it is difficult to overstate his cruciality for a philosophy of history centered in Torah obedience. Josiah is portrayed as the ultimate Torah-keeper who gives closure to the historical narrative, a closure that corresponds to the Torah-keeping piety of Moses at the outset of the history.

This Josiah, in this literature, is not only an impressive historical figure, but he functions as a theological model. Given that interpretive commitment, it is no wonder that he is presented in 2 Kgs 23:15-20 as the one who completes the divine oracle of judgment in 1 Kgs 13:2. Such a presentation operates with the important convergence of a theology of Torah piety and military reality. In the face of that convergence, Bethel has no chance.

straightforward story. But the content is neither regular nor straightforward. Indeed, the narrative bristles with signs and signals that something extraordinary and freighted with divine power is at work here. The "man of God" appears abruptly. The reference to Josiah is odd. The altar is destroyed in ways not told us. The king's hand is damaged and healed inexplicably. The "man of God" is deeply inscrutable. The story offers a weighty announcement of a judgment stronger than any of the human characters. This enigmatic appearance from the South puts the Northern regime on notice and in jeopardy.

A Countervoice from Bethel, 13:11-19

But the Judaic "man of God" is immediately countered. There was an "old prophet" in Bethel…Bethel again! He seems to embody all the claims of the North that are determined to subvert the prominence of the South. Indeed, the meeting of the two characters—Judean "man of God" and Israelite "old prophet"—seems to embody the regional tension that is always at the brink of war. We are not told why the "old prophet" takes an initiative; certainly no Yahwistic mandate is voiced.

The "old prophet" issues an invitation of hospitality to the "man of God," exactly as had the Northern king (13:15; see 13:7). The "man of God" a second time refuses the imitation, for the same reason (13:16; see 13:8-9): he is under Yahweh's command to avoid fraternization. Thus far this second meeting replicates the first.

But then the "old prophet" advances beyond the royal invitation by appealing to his own prophetic credentials (13:18). He offers the "man of God" a "second opinion," vouched for by an angel, that overrides the initial prohibition of Yahweh (13:18). On the basis of this "second opinion," the "man of God" violates his own mandate from Yahweh and accepts Northern hospitality (13:19). Only we know—the "man of God" does not know—that he is being deceived. We are not told whether the deception is the strategy of the "old prophet" or whether he does so on divine command. It does not matter. Either way, the "man of God" has been unable to keep to his own mission, and thus much is discredited. We are struck by the power of prophetic utterance, even if it is a deliberately false utterance. [Prophetic Deception]

> **📖 Prophetic Deception**
> The deception worked by the "old prophet" against the "man of God" leads to the death of the latter (13:18). We might wonder about the ethics of such a prophetic stratagem. We may notice, first of all, that nowhere is this "old prophet" authorized by Yahweh (though he makes that claim in his deception, v. 17), and nowhere is the ploy authorized. Thus it is possible to regard the "old prophet" as a dishonorable man in the service of Northern ideology, and the ethical problem evaporates.
>
> We may notice another case, however, in which Yahweh is directly engaged in such subterfuge. In 1 Kgs 22:19-23, a stratagem is devised by "the gods" to deceive King Ahab that will lead to his death. In this account, Yahweh is clearly at the center of the death-dealing ruse and gives approval. Moreover, in 1 Sam 16:2, Yahweh is the one who devises the deception for the safety of Samuel. The cases are enough to make clear that the cunning of divine purpose cannot be held to our belated ethical norms. One must ask difficult questions of such narratives, even if in our case the issue is plain old deception.

An Obedient, Devouring Lion, 13:20-25

The deception of v. 18 appears to be simply a human ploy. As the narrative advances, however, a human ploy triggers Yahwistic engagement (13:20-25). Now the "old prophet," the one who had deliberately deceived, receives "the word of the Lord." In the prior conversation with the "man of God," no claim is made that his utterance is the word of Yahweh. But now he utters a divine oracle that bears the form and gravity of a prophetic speech of judgment:

> *Indictment*: Because you have disobeyed the word of the LORD, and have not kept the commandment that the LORD your God commanded you…(13:21)

> *Sentence*: Your body shall not come to your ancestral tomb. (13:22)

This is a most remarkable speech of judgment. The "man of God" is condemned as guilty, even though the one who gives the speech of condemnation is the one who has devised and brought him to guilt. The sentence pronounced against him is that he will not be well and safely and respectfully buried "with his fathers," that is, in his home territory. The phrasing reflects the close-knit connection of tribal society, in life and in death. His fate is that his death will be away from his people, abandoned and dishonored. [Dishonored in Death]

📖 Dishonored in Death

The ancient world of Israel and Judah cared a great deal about *honor* and felt a great dread about *shame*. It was perhaps the case that the final honor for a person—especially a male—was an honorable death in the midst of one's ancestors. Conversely, to be buried (or abandoned) in death elsewhere is a profound shame. Thus the curse pronounced in v. 22 is severe. The alternative plan of v. 30, that the "man of God" should be given the honor of burial in the tomb of the "old prophet" is a partial redress of the shame, but only partial (see Matt 27:57-61).

We may cite two proximate parallels to this drama of shame and honor. David petitions Saul to desist from his relentless pursuit of him:

> Do not let my blood fall to the ground away from the presence of the LORD. (1 Sam 26:20)

If Saul pursues David, he must flee from his people and may die among the Philistines. Thus he is away from "the presence of the Lord," but also away from his own people. David's appeal evidences the ignominy of such a final fate.

A more immediate parallel is the curse pronounced by Jeremiah against King Jehoiakim:

> They shall not lament for him, saying,
> "Alas, my brother!" or "Alas, sister"
> They shall not lament for him, saying,
> "Alas, lord" or "Alas, his majesty!"
> With the burial of a donkey he shall be buried—
> dragged off and thrown out beyond the gates of Jerusalem.
> (Jer 22:18-19)

Here the sentence is even more dreadful, for he will not even be grieved with "alas" as is our "man of God" in 1 Kgs 13:30. Moreover, the king will receive no burial at all—unlike the "man of God" who at least will be buried—but will be abandoned as refuse outside the city.

The parallels suggest both the weightiness of the curse in v. 22 and the importance of the redress in vv. 29-31.

The prophetic sentence is uttered in v. 22 and immediately and decisively enacted in v. 24. There is no delay, no slippage, no chance to misconstrue the death. *Disobedience* evokes commensurate *punishment*. As in other matters, the narrative is not forthcoming about the lion. There is no suggestion that the lion is mandated by Yahweh, even as the "old prophet" initially is not explicitly committed to Yahweh. This narrative is about the strangeness of Yahweh's inscrutability in the public process. But of course, none can doubt that the lion is the work of Yahweh to enact the prophetic sentence.

But the outcome of the killing is odd indeed, as odd as everything else in this narrative. The lion killed but did not eat. The lion devoured neither the man nor his donkey, but stood as in some regal watch over them. (The image that comes to me is much like the concluding scene in Isak Denesin's *Out of Africa*, wherein the lions watch the grave of Denys.) The astonishing public sight was a thing to behold. It is as though the lion signifies that the "Lion of Judah" is not yet finished with this "man of God." Even in death, there is more to this event, so that neither the Northern "old prophet" nor the prophetic curse he spoke can terminate the significance of this "man of God." [A Lion's Share]

A Judgment Confirmed, 13:26-34

In vv. 26-32, the narrative takes yet another curious turn. Upon learning of the lion's watch over the slain "man of God," the "old prophet" comments upon the death, reiterating the severe speech of judgment he had uttered:

Indictment: It is the man of God who disobeyed the word of the LORD. (13:26; see 13:21)

Sentence: Therefore the LORD has given him to the lion. (13:26b; see 13:22)

This interpretive comment, that in fact tells us nothing we did not already know, twice focuses upon "the word of the Lord." The sentence is because of disobedience "to the word"; the sentence enacts "the word." The whole is because of the word that had mandated the entire confrontation in the first place (13:2).

But then the "old prophet" acts in a completely unexpected, unexplained way (13:27-30). As in v. 13, he mounts his donkey and rides to where the now dead "man of God" is. There he finds what "people" had found in v. 25: the lion by the body of the "man

A Lion's Share

In the imaginative rhetoric of the Old Testament, the lion is often cited as the most dangerous threat to human safety and human life (see 1 Kgs 20:37). Sometimes, the lion is especially dispatched by Yahweh as an instrument of divine wrath (2 Kgs 17:25-26). Sometimes the lion is cited as a metaphor to characterize the extreme danger of other threats (Pss 7:2; 10:9; 17:12; 22:13; Jer 4:7; 5:6). On occasion, it is Yahweh who is like a lion (Hos 11:10; Amos 1:2).

In the context of the imaginative use of the term, we can better understand the usage in our narrative. The lion who kills the "man of God" is a ferocious adversary, perhaps dispatched by Yahweh, though no such claim is made in the narrative. It is clear that characteristically, the "lion's share" is huge, whatever the devastating animal might want. All the more reason for us to be dazzled by the odd, restrained conduct of this lion. It kills, but it does not eat. The odd behavior of the lion, unlike almost every other lion, is yet another sign that this narrative is peculiarly freighted. As the "old prophet" finally (begrudgingly?) honors the "man of God," so in the end the lion will not eat the "man of God," because he has spoken a word of Yahweh.

---

of God" and the carcass of the donkey. That the lion had torn or eaten neither again testifies to the odd inscrutability of the story. The prophet who had declared that the "man of God" would not be well buried in his own community (13:20) now enacts an alternative burial. He brings the body of the "man of God" to his own grave, there buries him and publicly grieves him: "Alas" ("Woe"). While in life he had been his dread adversary, in death he knows him and articulates profound solidarity with him, for in the end he wants "my bones beside his bones." This is an uncommon gesture toward an outsider who has threatened the Northern establishment and who in turn has been placed under curse. All of that hostility, in this remarkable moment of death, is overcome.

Immediately, we are told why this odd reversal appears in the narrative and a new attitude toward the intruding "man of God" is articulated:

> For the saying that he proclaimed by the word of the LORD against the altar in Bethel, and against all the houses of the high places that are in the cities of Samaria, shall surely come to pass. (13:32)

The "old prophet" refers to the ultimatum of v. 2 that has been signed in v. 5. There is evidence that the initial utterance of the "man of God" continues in effect. But the "old prophet" here does not rely only upon the sign. He is convinced in more elemental ways (we know not how) that the initial threat to the North is valid and will come to pass. It is difficult to portray the emotional force of v. 32. It begins with a grammatical maneuver in Hebrew (infinitive absolute) that underscores "will come to pass" with a most emphatic "surely."

The "man of God" who has been cursed by "the old prophet" deserves honor and respect, and receives them belatedly from his curser. The narrative, however, is only incidentally interested in the destiny of "the man of God" who carried the word. What counts, rather, is the oracle of v. 2 itself that continues in effect. In order to appreciate the shaping significance of the oracle for the total royal history of Israel as presented in these texts, our attention turns to the work of King Josiah in 2 Kings 23, the same Josiah anticipated in our text in 13:2.

In the subsequent report on Josiah, the darling of this interpretation of Israel's history, is the one who defiles and destroys all the fixtures of disobedient religion with which Jerusalem teems (2 Kgs 23:4-14, 19-20). This report of wholesale reforming passion is the context for the "fulfillment" of the oracle of 13:2. In 2 Kings 23:15-18, it is reported that King Josiah pulled down the altar at Bethel, and burned the bones from the tombs on the altar,

> ...according to the word of the LORD that the "man of God" proclaimed. (2 Kgs 23:16)

That is, the text makes clear that Josiah's acts of profanation are the completion of the oracle. More than that, however, King Josiah observes the tomb of the "man of God" where his bones lie beside the bones of the "prophet who came out of Samaria." As the lion paused in respect for the "man of God," so the king leaves the tomb undisturbed, thus honoring the "man of God," replicating the "old prophet" who has buried and honored him. Thus the oracle of 13:2 and the verification of 13:32 are vindicated.

The strange life and odd death of the "man of God," however, did not effectively disrupt the Northern regime (13:33-34). King Jeroboam and his priests at the high places continued undeterred, with business as usual. But of course, the failure of the North to respond to the "man of God" is completely predictable. For the only meaningful response that could have been made, had they taken the oracle seriously, would have been to go out of business and return in loyalty to Jerusalem. This, of course, they would never do.

The verdict of the narrative is as unambiguous as it is predictable: "This matter"—the worship arrangements in the North—is a sin...from the perspective of the Southern Deuteronomists. That sin, the sin of rebellion and secession, is enough to cause the termination of Jeroboam's dynasty. The matter would seem to be a Catch-22 for Jeroboam. He had received a prophetic promise of an "enduring house" (11:38). But in principle the illegitimate shrines of the North fate his dynasty to oblivion. The sin of separation from Jerusalem, moreover, becomes the criterion by which, in

In Doré's illustration of this scene, the man of God lies face down, having just been slain by the lion. The old prophet of Bethel emerges out of the shadows, guiding the donkey that will carry the body to its proper burial. Silhouetted on a hillside mound, the iconic, yet enigmatic, presence of the lion resounds against the backdrop of the skies as it looks outward in the direction of the old prophet and, at the same time, faces the heavens.

Gustave Doré. *Prophet of Bethel* from the *Illustrated Bible*. 19th century. Engraving. (Credit: Dover Pictorial Archive Series) unvarying consistency, all Northern rulers are deemed illicit and placed under judgment. The devastating oracle from the "man of God" continues to reverberate to the deep trouble of the North.

CONNECTIONS

This enormously enigmatic tale does not admit of any easy or obvious point of "relevance" for us. There is in the narrative a deep struggle between the rival shrines of Jerusalem and Bethel, between the rival reigns of Rehoboam (not mentioned here) and Jeroboam. There is, moreover, a deep struggle between the two oracle speakers who contend for the truth.

In the context of 1 and 2 Kings, however, there is no true contest. The narrative account of the rival participants is not only told from a Southern, Jerusalem perspective, with a conviction that the South is Yahweh's true intention and the North is a false start, but the narrative is also from a chronological perspective that has seen the North collapse in 722 under Assyrian pressure (see 2 Kgs 17). There was every reason to conclude with such a judgment.

Thus the narrative embodies the Jerusalem establishment's claim for the cruciality of the Davidic line, which in Christian interpretation becomes a claim for Jesus.

Beyond that, we may notice the deep, inscrutable quality of the narrative at many points:

1. The "man of God" comes out of Judah, so far as we are told at the outset, without any divine mandate (13:1). He simply appears.
2. The hand of the pretending king withers (13:4).
3. The altar condemned is torn down, but we do not know how (13:5).
4. The hand of the pretending king is restored (13:6).
5. The "man of God," in the end, is talked out of his mandate of obedience to Yahweh by deception, and brings judgment upon himself (13:19).
6. The lion, instrument of judgment, does not devour, but stands guard (13:24-25).
7. The "old prophet" oddly changes course and honors the "man of God" with his own tomb (13:30-31).

None of this is explained. None of it is reasonable. The narrative wants to say that in the course of contested theological-political interaction, there is a deep current of meaning and purpose to which human agents have no access, namely, the intention of

Yahweh. Without regard to any human utterance or any human agent, the outcome of the prophetic oracle is sealed, even if not visible until 2 Kings 23. We are put on notice that the story of 1 and 2 Kings is not a narrative of human conduct, but a portrayal of the hidden purposes of Yahweh that will in the end prevail.

The most magisterial comment known to me on this text is by Karl Barth who provides a compelling, intriguing interpretation:

> According to Isa 40:8, this addition can only be: "But the word of our God endureth forever." It may well be said that this is in fact the beginning and end, the sum and substance of 1 Kgs. 13—that the Word of God endures through every human standing and falling, falling and standing on the left hand and on the right.

Barth then makes his characteristic move to Jesus:

> But this story, too, does point to the real subject if Jesus Christ is also seen in it, if at the exact point where this story of the prophets breaks off a continuation is found in the Easter story. The Word of God, which abides forever, in our flesh.[1] [Barth on the Narrative]

Barth on the Narrative

Karl Barth was the greatest Protestant theologian of the twentieth century; in his dense theological discourse, he often engages in detailed, stunning biblical exposition. Among his most characteristic and most impressive biblical interpretations is that on our passage. Readers who want either a full consideration of the text or a wondrous example of theological method may wish to consult Barth's unparalleled discernment of the text. Before Barth pushes on to a Christological accent—as he always does—he sees in this text a tension between Judah and Israel reflective of ninth century politics and sixth century hope:

The peculiar theme of the chapter is the manner in which the man of God and the prophet belong together, do not belong together, and eventually and finally do belong together; and how the same is true of Judah and Israel.

Karl Barth, *Church Dogmatics* (Edinburgh: T.& T. Clark, 1957), II:2, 393-409.

Public history is a working out of Yahweh's hidden intention. The outcomes are beyond the accomplishment of any human agent or any human utterance, or any lion. In context, the fulfillment comes in the good king Josiah. The Jerusalem enterprise is vindicated. Later on, even that will not hold; it is too transitory to endure as does the Word of God. But God's verdict for a time cohabits human projects, while the raging of curse and honor, of life and death, have their way. Everything changes; underneath, everything from God is reliable and steadfast, and will not be defeated.

NOTE

[1]Karl Barth, *Church Dogmatics* (Edinburgh: T. & T. Clark, 1957) II:2,409.

RIVAL KINGS, IN FAILURE
AND IN DEATH

1 Kings 14:1-31

With the kingdom of Solomon brought under judgment (11:1-13), the split of the kingdom into North and South (12:1-24), and the establishment of a Northern regime with shrines in Bethel and Penuel (12:25-33), the narrative account of royal history in Israel and Judah is now ready to proceed in a fairly stereotypical way. 1 Kings 14–16 summarize an extended piece of that history and rely on recurring formulae to frame the interpretive interests of the history. [The Royal Chronology] The present chapter may be divided into two parts, the concluding narrative account of the rule of Jeroboam (14:1-20) and the parallel concluding account of the reign of Rehoboam (14:21-31).

COMMENTARY

The Death and Judgment of Jeroboam, 14:1-20

The reign of Jeroboam ends with a massive prophetic judgment (14:1-20). Indeed data concerning the whole of Jeroboam's twenty-two years in power (922–901) is sparse in this account: he received prophetic authorization (11:37-38), established alternative shrines

---

The Royal Chronology

This historical account of the two states is organized by reference to the kings. The strategy of the material is to cross reference the two kings lists, so that there is a rough alternation of Northern and Southern kings. For chapters 14–16, the royal chronologies are fairly clear and not much in dispute:

North	South
Jeroboam 922–901	Rehoboam 922–915
Nadab 901–900	Abijam 915–913
Baasha 900–877	Asa 913–873
Elah 877–876	Jehoshaphat 873–849
Zimri 876	
Omri 876–867	
Ahab 869–850	

(12:25-33), and received a prophetic denunciation (13:2). That is all.

In the present text the illness of Abijah, son of Jeroboam, is offered as a framing narrative for the prophetic announcement to follow (14:1-6, 17-18). Because the child is sick, the king seeks counsel and aid from the prophet of Shiloh, Ahijah. [Map: Shiloh] He has great confidence in Ahijah, for he authorized the kingship of Jeroboam in the first place (11:29-39). Ahijah is a prophet of Shiloh, a great Northern shrine, a great Israelite shrine long before the prominence of Jerusalem. [The Force of Shiloh] The king might therefore expect support from the prophet that could take the form of healing for his son. We are not told why he dispatches his wife in secret to the prophet, but in any case the ploy does not work. The prophet recognizes her and immediately declares that he is instructed (sent) by Yahweh to announce "severity" (14:6). The "severity" is that "the child shall die" (14:12). And indeed the child does die, is buried and mourned (14:17). It is all "according to the word of the Lord" (14:18).

Clearly, the narrative has no particular interest in the welfare of the child, for the encounter moves quickly past the illness of the child to the long prophetic speech of vv. 7-16. The prophet is sent, authorized by Yahweh, and the king has no option apart form prophetic declaration. The purpose of the entire narrative is to make clear that the future of the regime is completely determined by the will of Yahweh that takes the form of prophetic utterance.

This long speech is a characteristic "speech of judgment," not unlike the speech of judgment against Solomon in 11:1-13. It is divided into two parts, *indictment* and *sentence*. The indictment begins with "because" and states the grounds for judgment (14:7-9). Jeroboam's condemnation is that he did not behave like David, but has done evil, violating commandments and disregarding Yahweh. The prophetic judgment is completely generic and lacks

---

📖 The Force of Shiloh

A case can be made that Shiloh was not only a great sanctuary at one time, but that it was also a center of considerable political influence and authority. Thus it is not impossible that the initial oracle of Ahijah of Shiloh (11:29-39) was of some political force against the claims of Jerusalem that were both cultic and political. The statement of Ps 78:60-72 indicates some continuing rivalry between the shrines of Jerusalem and Shiloh, though that Psalm gives theological victory to Jerusalem. For a belated appeal to the lessons of Shiloh that might be important to Jerusalem, see Jer 7:12-15. On the suggestion of an enduring claim for Shiloh, see the discussion of Martin Cohen.

On the Shilonite priesthood, see "The Role of the Shilonite Priesthood in the United Monarchy of Ancient Israel," HUCA 36 (1965): 59-98. For a suggestion on a U.S. analogue, see Walter Brueggemann, "When Jerusalem Gloats Over Shiloh," *Sojourners* 19/6 (July 1990): 24-27.

any specificity. Because Jeroboam is here completely contrasted with David, this may mean that in general Jeroboam was not Yahwistic and disregarded Torah commandments, a crucial concern for the Deuteronomists. Or it may mean that the singleness of Jerusalem worship is violated, thus it represents a Southern assault on Northern heterodox worship as in 12:30-33. If the latter, then, of course, the matter is a Catch-22 for Jeroboam, for no Northern king can survive with Southern worship. It is likely that the judgment is a stereotypical dismissal and has no particular content.

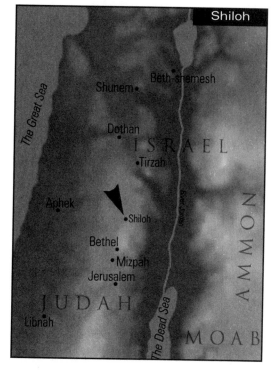

The *sentence*, beginning with a characteristic "therefore," is massive and perhaps hyperbolic (14:10-16). The judgment is not only against the king, but against what might have been a dynasty. This is indeed a projected "slaughter of the innocents" (see Exod 1:22; Matt 2:16-18), for dynastic politics, ancient and modern, is violent indeed. The heirs of Jeroboam will be treated like excrement, left for the dogs to devour in ultimate dishonor. Indeed it is Yahweh's own work to instigate a coup and summon one who will displace the regime (14:14). Yahweh continues to tamper with dynastic politics, an old practice of Yahweh (see 1 Sam 16:1-13; 1 Kgs 11:29-39). As the story goes, Yahweh will try new candidates for king to see whether there is an acceptable one. Yahweh causes Northern dynastic politics to be endlessly unstable.

In the midst of this massive dismissal of the dynasty, there is a pause to give attention to the young son Abijah, whose illness has triggered this entire encounter (14:12-13). Even that son will die! There are no exceptions in the family. But he will be buried and mourned, that is, given an honorable death (14:17-18). He is the only one who will escape the ultimate shame. The reason given for this remarkable exception is completely enigmatic. There is in him "something pleasing" (good) to Yahweh. But we are not told what. Perhaps he is young, and innocent, and vulnerable—but we have no clue from the text.

The exception for the young prince, however, does not detract from the primary, negative point. Now, in vv. 15-16, the speaker of judgment becomes more extreme and more expansive. Verses

15-16 constitute yet another self-contained speech of judgment. The indictment is because of idolatrous, heterodox worship. The sentence is a striking, a rooting up, a scattering of Israel. The verbs bespeak exilic displacement. The text anticipates the dispersion of northern Israel in 722, when the Assyrians conquer the territory and relocate many of the people (see 2 Kgs 17:5-40). These verses look beyond the particularities of Jeroboam and his short-term regime to the large sweep of northern Israel that will end in the Assyrian debacle. The sweeping condemnation of v. 16 makes the "sins of Jeroboam" the defining and irrevocable act of Israel that seals the fate of the state well beyond the dynasty itself. As we shall see, according to this interpretation of Northern history, this failure at the outset continues to work for generations, to negate the entire Northern enterprise. The whole of the North is under massive judgment. The decent burial of the young son is an exception that only witnesses to the dread verdict on all the rest of the North.

Verses 19-20 add a footnote to tell the reader where to look for more data on the regime in a reference now lost to us. That he "slept with his ancestors" only means that the announced devastation is on hold for now. But only for now.

The End of Rehoboam, 14:21-31

Having disposed of the Northern regime, the narrative now gives closure to the reign of Rehoboam, son of Solomon (14:21-31). We have even less on him than we do on Jeroboam, and the narrative clearly has no enduring interest in him. This account is framed in vv. 21, 29-31 with the characteristic data of kingship. We are told, in what will become a familiar pattern, his age when he came to power, the length of his reign, a reference to a fuller literary account of the reign, an allusion to his wars with the North, his burial, and the name of his successor; none of this is exceptional. It is noteworthy that his mother, Naamah, is twice mentioned, at beginning and end (14:21, 31). I have already suggested, with reference to Bathsheba, that queen mothers are key figures in this account of royal history. [The Queen Mother] Perhaps the most telling feature is that his mother is an Ammonite. Nothing is made of that here, but we are not unaware of the judgment made on Solomon that included among his distorting wives an Ammonite (11:1). It is not impossible that the queen mother is

The Queen Mother
The double reference to Naamah, mother of Rehoboam, suggests attention again to the role of the queen mother, even though nothing is explicit in this text.

See Christopher R. Seitz, *Theology in Conflict: Reactions to the Exile in the Book of Jeremiah* (BZAW 176; Berlin: de Gruyter, 1989) 52-55 on the role of the queen mother.

Shishak

Shishak was ruler in Egypt 931–910, thus overlapping significantly with the reigns of Jeroboam and Rehoboam. There is no doubt of his assertion of Egyptian control over Palestine. A contemporary text from the shrine in Karnak describes his successful venture into the north, and a triumphal stela at Megiddo indicates his important installation there. The more expanded account of 2 Chr 12:2-12 indicates a continuing awareness of his impressiveness in Israelite memory.

It is possible, in light of Shishak's characteristic thrust North, to appreciate more fully the decision to settle geopolitical reality differently in the bold peace initiative of Anwar Sadat toward the contemporary state of Israel. Given enduring geopolitical realities, imaginative policy options may vary. In Shishak, however, there is no variation from conventional strategy.

---

twice mentioned in order to call quiet attention to the enduring judgment against that distortion.

The summary account of the reign of Rehoboam is given in two separate parts. In vv. 22-24, a theological verdict is rendered, and it is not good. The phrasing of v. 21b, "the city that the Lord has chosen," is a high claim for Jerusalem made in the characteristic rhetoric of Deuteronomy, with reference to "name theology" (see 8:29). That is, Jerusalem is singularly Yahwistic and so resistant to any heterodox practice. But vv. 22-24 tell us precisely that Judah engaged in heterodox practices, seemingly as much so as the North under Jeroboam. Indeed the rhetoric is more extreme here than in the condemnation of Jeroboam in v. 9. In two regards the rhetoric is extreme, first with reference to "male prostitution" (see Deut 23:17-18). While this phrasing suggests a religious practice that offended Yahweh, the actual meaning of the phrase is deeply disputed.[1] Second, along with "male prostitution," the narrative uses the term "abomination," a term reserved for the most affrontive, offensive practices thinkable. The astonishing feature with this rhetoric is that the indictment of vv. 22-24 is followed by no sentence. Perhaps such a sentence is delayed in deference to David, Yahweh's true love.

In vv. 25-28, the rhetoric leaves off theological reflection and offers what must have been an actual historical report. Shishak, founder of the twenty-second Egyptian dynasty, engineered an important revival of Egyptian international influence. [Shishak] Characteristically when Egypt asserts itself, it aims at control of the land bridge of Palestine in order to protect itself from the major powers of the North. Thus we may understand his assault on Jerusalem in terms of geopolitical reality, though we may also notice in 11:40 that he had hosted Jeroboam as a fugitive, and may have had special animosity toward Jerusalem and the Davidic house.

In any case, the threat to Jerusalem is real. The pharaoh took away much of the gold that Solomon had installed in his temple, thus causing Judah real material loss as well as deep humiliation. The Jerusalem king is incapable even of protecting his own central shrine! Indeed, as a result of the loss, the king is forced to "fake it" with bronze decorations instead of gold, and even they must be kept under lock and key.

It is remarkable that the shift of rhetoric from vv. 22-24 to vv. 25-28 is a move from direct theological rhetoric to what appears to be historical reportage. Its placement, however, makes plausible that the report of vv. 25-28 is to be understood as a *prophetic sentence* linked to the *prophetic indictment* of vv. 22-24. Thus the sentence occurs within the historical process. As is characteristic in prophetic faith, Shishak may have been motivated by geopolitical considerations of his own, but his northern venture is understood as the enactment of Yahweh's harsh governance of Jerusalem. The narrative, by placement, suggests a theological element to the historical process that needs not be made explicit.

CONNECTIONS

The narrative takes considerable care with the account of these two founding kings of the small states of Israel and Judah. The founding events are clearly decisive for all that follows, as though Jeroboam and Rehoboam set matters in motion that will keep turning up in destructive ways. It is important to read these "events" with long-term significance, as though the historical-theological process that constitutes Israel's public life forgets nothing and forgives only reluctantly.

We may understand such a theological claim if we consider an analogue in U.S. history. Much is made of the fact that high minded founders of the United States—Washington and Jefferson among them—were slaveholders and were to some extent haunted by that contradiction. They did not act to free their slaves, and it worked no hardship on them to keep them. It takes little imagination, however, if one raises long-term moral issues, to see that founding reality continues to haunt and vex the republic with what has been rightly termed "The American Dilemma."[2] That is, racism is not one of many dilemmas in the U.S., but it is *the* defining, seemingly insoluble public contradiction of U.S. history. That defining dilemma of course worked its powerful will in the War between the States, in the sorry vengefulness of Reconstruction, and in the enduring violence that still visits urban life, against which "Civil Rights" makes only modest progress. It is the judgment of our text, that such disobedience at the outset has long-term power to distort. And if we embrace the analogue, who is to dispute the claim?

The haunting power of such distortion may lead us to these derivative insights. First, these defining judgments, harsh against both regimes, illuminate why the political process in North and South is deeply unstable. The political process is permeated by theological-moral judgment. In the North, this judgment entails a frequent overthrow of power; in the South it culminates in the exile to Babylon. The interpretive judgment made here is that the public process was never simply about knowledge and power, for the issues of public ethics cannot be expelled. Every political process, compromised as it is, stands under judgment.

Second, it is clear that the judgments, given differently in North and South, are understood as Yahweh-authorized, though the case is less explicit concerning the South. These claims, explicit or implicit, are what has been meant by the phrase, "God acts in history." The phrase, it turns out, is deeply problematic and is now in some disfavor. The phrase is nonetheless an attempt to insist upon and affirm that the claim of prophetic faith warrants attention, even if it cannot be articulated with any precision. [The Prophetic Claim] The sustained claim of this account of royal history and of all of Israel's faith is that public power is not finally an autonomous process, but that power must answer to truth. [What Is Truth?] That of course is a lesson that power must always relearn, always in painful ways.

The Prophetic Claim

The claim of "God Acting in History" is an awkward one in modernity, because the reality of history and the assertion of God strike moderns as completely incommensurate. But of course it is precisely the incommensurabilty that makes the linkage as important as it is difficult. One eloquent statement of the linkage, unbothered by the doubts of modernity, is that of Martin Buber:

> But the world of prophetic faith is in fact historic reality, seen in the bold and penetrating glance of the man who dares to believe. What here prevails is indeed a special kind of politics, theopolitics, which is concerned to establish a certain people in a certain historical situation under the divine sovereignty, so that this people is brought nearer the fulfillment of its task, to become the beginning of the kingdom of God.

Martin Buber, *The Prophetic Faith* (Harper Torchbooks; New York: Harper & Brothers, 1949) 135. For a more general discussion of the interface of politics and theology in theopolitics, see H. Graf Reventlow et. al. (eds.), *Politics and Theopolitics in the Bible and Postbiblical Literature* JSOT Supp. 171 (Sheffield: Sheffield Academic Press, 1994), and Walter Brueggemann, "The Prophetic Word of God and History," *Interpretation* 68 (1994): 239-51.

What Is Truth?

The inescapability of *power* answering to *truth* leads finally, in a Christian trajectory, to the vexed question Pilate put to Jesus: "What is truth?" (John 18:38). The answer is enigmatic in that narrative, but the question lingers to haunt. Of the encounter, Paul Lehmann has written:

> Thus the nocturnal conversation between Jesus and Pilate turns into a confrontation. In this confrontation, the ambiguity of power and the ambiguity of Presence are juxtaposed....The point and purpose of the presence of Jesus *in the world*, and now before Pilate, are to bear witness to the truth, that is, "to make effective room for the reality of God over against the world in the great trial between God and the world.

Paul Lehmann, *The Transfiguration of Politics: The Presence and Power of Jesus of Nazareth in and over Human Affairs* (New York: Harper & Row, 1975) 53.

Third, the claim of Yahweh's judgment in the historical process is easy to misunderstand. It would be simple if divine judgment worked by God's swooping in with supernatural force. That, however, is not a main claim of the Bible. Rather, God's judgement works through human agents. And so Shishak, in context, does more than he knows. Indeed, Shishak may be understood in context as a harbinger of Nebuchadnezzar, the one at the end of this historical account, the final enactor of Yahweh's judgment on Jerusalem (see 2 Kgs 24:10–25:12). It is easy to speak of the supernatural, and such speech satisfies a certain religious propensity. But of course the Soviet Union did not fall and South African apartheid did not end because of supernatural intrusion. They ended because of the stirrings of justice and freedom in the small places of history. Such endless testimony may give us pause in our own U.S. social setting where technological, military power is without rival. The working of God is slow, not highly visible. But, so says the narrative, that working is very sure.

NOTES

[1]See Phyllis A. Bird, *Missing Persons and Mistaken Identities: Women and Gender in Ancient Israel,* OBT (Minneapolis: Fortress Press, 1997).

[2]Gunnar Myrdahl, *An American Dilemma: The Negro Problem & Modern Democracy* (Transaction Publications, 1996).

Tintoretto's painting is an intense expression of the juxtaposition of power with Presence. The Roman governor's court is depicted amidst Greco-Roman architecture with great heights and ambiguous spaces. Appearing as an elongated ethereal phantom, Christ stands before Pilate, who "washes his hands" of the whole affair. The calm, unemotional Presence of Christ is contrasted with the overall air of disturbance of recoiling figures and a disturbed, grimacing Pilate.

Jacopo Tintoretto. *Christ Before Pilate*. 1566–1567. Oil on canvas. Scuola Grande di San Rocco, Venice, Italy. (Credit: Cameraphoto/Art Resource, NY)

A SERIES OF
UNDISTINGUISHED
MONARCHS

1 Kings 15:1-32

The recital of royal history continues, featuring two Judean kings, Abijam (15:1-8) and Asa (15:9-24), and one king of northern Israel, Nadab (15:25-32). The narrative of each particular king is brief and focuses upon the theological verdict rendered from the perspective of the Deuteronomic theology.

COMMENTARY

The Short Career of Abijam, 15:1-8

Abijam, son of Rehoboam, ruled in Jerusalem for only two years, 915–913 (15:1-8). (A variant spelling of his name is Abijah, and he is listed in some reference books with that spelling.) The report on this short-lived reign is largely presented in stereotypical biographical data in vv. 1-2, 7-8. In this data, we may note especially the name of his mother Maacah and that of his grandfather, Abishalom. The latter name is of interest because it may be a thoroughly Yahwistic name, and as a variant of "Absalom" is perhaps linked to the Davidic memory. If this is so, it is quite in contrast to the mother of Rehoboam who is a foreigner (14:21, 31).

Beyond this data, we are told only two things regarding this king. First, he receives a negative theological verdict in v. 3. Second, we are twice told of the ongoing civil war between North and South (15:6, 7). That the war is twice reported may indicate its seriousness as an historical fact, or it may be a part of the theological verdict against a royal policy, for the war has been prohibited by Yahweh in 12:24.

The most noteworthy item in this paragraph summary, however, is not about Abijam, but about David to whom appeal is made as a contrast to the current king (15:4-5). David is the looming royal "Nevertheless" in Jerusalem (see 11:12, 34) who protects the dynasty from its own self-destructiveness. [The Davidic "Nevertheless"] The verdict against Abijam, like the recent verdict against Rehoboam, is enough

AΩ **The Davidic "Nevertheless"**

In this theological tradition, David stands as a divine commitment that permits faith to withstand every circumstance and hope to override every defeat. In this text, the reality of Abijam is negative, but because of David something other is possible that is not derived from circumstance. While the "nevertheless" is concretely linked to David, in fact the same "nevertheless" of divine commitment, more broadly, is the primal claim of biblical faith. A clear case for the "nevertheless" of faith in the Old Testament is the realism of Hab 3:17 overcome by the "yet" of v. 18:

Though the fig tree does not blossom,
   and no fruit is on the vines;
though the produce of the olive fails
   and the fields yield no food;
though the flock is cut off from the fold

and there is no herd in the stalls,
yet I will rejoice in the LORD;
   I will exult in the God of my salvation.

The best-known case of the "nevertheless" of the gospel is the lyrical affirmation of Paul:

No, in all these things we are more than conquerors through him who loved us. For I am convinced that neither death, nor life, nor angels, nor rulers, nor things present, nor things to come, nor powers, nor height, nor depth, nor anything else in all creation will be able to separate us from the love of God in Christ Jesus our Lord. (Rom 8:37-39)

Something of the same resolve is reflected in the "nevertheless" of our text.

---

to terminate the Davidic dynasty, for the verdict is as severe as the one against the North that does terminate the dynasty there (14:10-17). But, of course, the termination does not happen in Jerusalem, at least not for a long time. And the reason for the durability of the dynasty, we are told, is Yahweh's promise to David. Because of David the dynasty endures in spite of his pitiful successors. The appeal to David, however, is stated in a most curious way. It would perhaps have been enough to reference the unconditional promise made to David for the dynasty in 2 Samuel 7:11-16. But this theology is oriented to Torah; for that reason, David's "nevertheless" is rooted in David's Torah righteousness and not simply in Yahweh's fidelity. The obedience of David counts.

But then, in a remarkable moment of candor, the narrative must add a huge "except" regarding David (15:5). The exception, for which allowance is made, is the Uriah-Bathsheba episode in 2 Samuel 11–12 that is too prominent to be denied or overlooked. David's Torah righteousness is deeply compromised in that event, as the prophet Nathan has made clear (2 Sam 12:10-11). The important matter for our text, in any case, is that the "except" of Uriah-Bathsheba does not trump the "nevertheless" of Yahweh's fidelity upon which the regime can continue to count. In the end, the fidelity of Yahweh is decisive. And yet the "except" continues to loom. It does not defeat God's fidelity, but it is an enormously important qualifying footnote. By the rhetorical juxtaposition of "nevertheless" and "except," our narrative manages to hold together the two governing themes of interpretation that are kept delicately and shrewdly in tension throughout this royal narrative.

Asa, a Long Reign, a Short Narrative, 15:9-24

Asa, grandson of Rehoboam, was on the throne in Jerusalem for forty-one years, 913–873 (15:9-24). It is remarkable that he receives only a few more verses of coverage than does his father who lasted only two years. The report on Asa is divided into two more or less characteristic parts, a theological verdict (15:9-15) and what appears to be a factual historical report (15:16-24).

The theological verdict, on the whole, is positive, thus a contrast to that of his predecessors. He did "what was right" by purging heterodox worship, notably the practices of his grandfather, Rehoboam (15:23-24). Among other things, he negated the heterodox practices of his mother who, incidentally, has the same name as the mother of his father, apparently intended as the same woman. The quintessential act of religious departure from Yahwism is the Asherah, perhaps a symbol of pagan fertility religion, perhaps at one time Yahweh's female consort. [The Asherah] Asa is a reforming king, taking steps to assure a singular focus on Yahweh. And therefore he is celebrated by this theological perspective: "His heart was true!" (15:14). He devoted royal energy and royal resources to the temple, again a contrast to his grandfather who dismantled the decor of the temple (15:15; 14:25-28). We may notice that the temple loss under Rehoboam is because of his political weakness; conversely, Asa's restitution of the temple may be a measure of political stability, so that the fate of the temple is intimately connected to the political-economic condition of the state.

The assessment of Asa is positive—except for the note in v. 14a. The high places, still a measure of infidelity to Yahweh, endured (see 3:2). This is a small note that does not by much diminish the positive valuation made of Asa; except that it is there. We may wonder if Asa was neglectful and indifferent, or perhaps it was politically not prudent to go "all the way" in reform. Either way, the narrative confirms the fact that the theopolitical enterprise in Jerusalem is characteristically a compromise. Most remarkably, it is a compromise that this theological perspective can tolerate. In any case, Asa is a vast improvement over what has gone before.

The historical account of Asa's reign is preoccupied with the civil war, the war precluded by Yahweh (12:24), but prosecuted by Asa's

The Asherah

The term "Asherah," already used as condemnation of Solomon in 11:5, refers to a cult symbol, perhaps a pole. But the cult symbol signified and referred to a Canaanite goddess who is situated, in Canaanite lore, as a consort to the god, Baal. Thus it is likely that the term, when used polemically in the Old Testament, refers specifically to a goddess, but more generally to an entire religious practice and religious understanding that were opposed by the ethical covenantalism of Deuteronomy. The embrace of that alternative system of faith in Israel is likely not a deliberate alternative choice, but a slow, gradual, unwitting compromise, so that Yahwism is distorted by the alternative in its environment. Such a practice has no analogue among us, unless we imagine that ideologies of autonomous selves who can secure self lead to a compromise and distortion of biblical faith.

Asherah. 1300 BC. From Minet el Beida. Ugarit, Syria. Louvre, Paris, France. (Credit: Giraudon/Art Resource, NY)

Baal with Thuderbolt. 1700-1300 BC. Bas-relief on limestone stele. From Ugarit Syria. Louvre, Paris France. (Credit: Erich Lessing/Art Resource, NY)

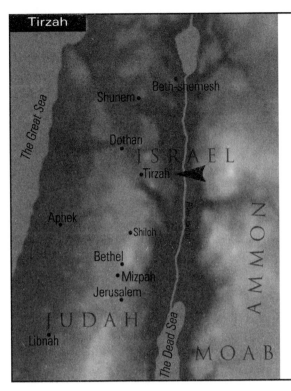

Tirzah
This city (for a time the seat of government in the North) figures only briefly in the biblical record. Its location is uncertain, but archaeological judgment provides a provisional consensus that it is the site of Tell-el-Far'ah to the northeast of Samaria. The site lasted as capitol from the time of Baasha (15:21) until Omri moved his operations to his new city of Samaria (16:24).

predecessors (14:30; 15:6-7). But Asa takes an important strategic initiative, either because he is more desperate or because he is more imaginative. He negotiates with Syria (Aram) to form a defense pact that will separate Syria from its previous cooperation with Israel and make Syria, along with Judah, an adversary of Israel. That is, Asa intends by the alliance to put Israel in a vice, to be squeezed into submission. This is the first entry of Syria into the orbit of Jerusalem politics, a position it will occupy for the long term.

The remarkable feature of this pact is what the narrative tells us about its terms. In fact Asa purchases an ally by cashing in temple resources, on which see v. 15. It is, however, important that the term "present" is almost everywhere else in the Old Testament translated as "bribe." Asa bought an ally and, as a consequence, he must mobilize the work force of his nation in state projects (15:22). The report does not use the term "forced labor" that had such a bad press under Solomon and Rehoboam; but that is what it is. For reasons of "national defense"—almost always a good excuse—Asa reconstitutes the policy of forced labor that was decisive in the collapse of the great Solomonic achievement. The forced labor policy is to build fortifications at Geba and Mizpah, in order to protect the northern border of Judah. These installations are juxtaposed to Ramah, the fortification on Israel's southern boundary

(15:17). The alliance worked! The Syrian king moved against the Northern Kingdom, as Asa had anticipated. The outcome is that the Northern king, Baasha, had to pull back and relocate at a safer place, Tirzah (15:21). [Tirzah]

The narrative provides us with one other notation about Asa. He was "diseased in his feet" (15:23). This is an exceedingly odd notation that permits speculation about the king. The terse comment may mean simply to report an old age infirmity as a detail toward death. Or it could refer to a serious ailment such as leprosy that would impede his rule. Or it is possible, since "feet" is elsewhere a euphemism for genitalia, that he is impaired in his "virility" that matters so much in royal ideology (see 1:1). Nothing is made of the point. But since the narrative may hint and suggest, the way is left open for theological speculation. It remained for later theology to bring Asa under judgment in a verdict that seized upon the hints of negativity made here. [An Alternative Report]

Nadab for Two Years, 15:25-32

Nadab, son of Jeroboam, reigned two years, 901–900 (15:25-31). The report is stereotypical; he receives a negative verdict from the narrator, an unvarying judgment upon Northern kings (15:26, 30). The core of his report concerns his assassination by Baasha, an upstart with no credentials offered. Upon the murder of Nadab, Baasha became king (15:28). Upon becoming king, he murdered the entire house of Jeroboam (15:29). The report is uncommonly violent, reflective of the violent overthrow:

An Alternative Report

The narrative account of Asa is offered as descriptive report. On two counts in the subsequent theological reflection of 2 Chr 16:7-12, Asa's "data" is turned to negative theological judgment. First, the alliance he initiated with Syria is interpreted there as an act of unfaith, trusting in allies rather than trusting Yahweh:

Because you relied on the king of Aram, and did not rely on the LORD your God, the army of the king of Aram has escaped you....You have done foolishly in this; for from now on you will have wars. (2 Chr 16:7, 9)

The judgment parallels the foreign policy of "trust" advocated by the prophet Isaiah.

Second, Asa's foot disease is presented in our text simply as a fact. In 2 Chr 16:12, the king is condemned for seeking healing from a doctor rather than from Yahweh, thus a parallel to the political alliance. In both acts, Asa is judged for lacking the kind of faith in Yahweh that would shape his actions. It may be that in the Chronicles account the foot disease is a consequence (punishment) for not trusting Yahweh in the political arena. The version given in the Chronicles indicates yet another attempt to state the tricky relation of faith to power and power to faith.

He left to the house of Jeroboam not one that breathed, until he had
destroyed it.

The important point is that Baasha enacts and fulfills the prophetic
anticipation of 14:10-14. The child of 14:13, 17-18 was fortunate
indeed, for he was the only one who died a death short of violence.
Our text deliberately alludes to the oracle of Ahijah in chapter 14,
proposing that the overthrow of the short dynasty of Jeroboam is
indeed the work of Yahweh. It is important for the narrative that
Baasha in v. 27 is given no theological warrant for his action. He is
not initiated by Yahweh. He acts on his own as a political schemer
and terrorist. The theological interpretation offered here readily
links his violence and divine intention, a nervy theological
maneuver.

The final note on Nadab is terse (15:32). The verse folds Nadab
into a reflection in Asa and an anticipation of Baasha in v. 33. The
civil war goes on and on; the context of governance is endless war
that produces an ambience in which everything brutal is possible.

CONNECTIONS

What strikes me most about this narrative in three episodes is the
delicate and ambivalent connection made between the purposes of
Yahweh—for good or for ill—and the brute realties of power
politics. Yahweh is at the center of each report:

1. Abijam is given room to rule because of Yahweh's commitment
   to David (15:4-5).
2. Asa has a heart true to Yahweh, has a long reign, and is a man
   of power (15:23). [The Mighty One]
3. Nadab and his clan are destroyed at the behest of Yahweh
   (15:29).

The narrative is bold to affirm that Yahweh is secretively at work in
the affairs of state.

And yet, in spite of such a claim, the narrative is permeated with
policies of violence that took on a life of their own:

1. Abijam is in a hopeless war precluded by Yahweh (15:6-7, see
   12:24).
2. Asa is a more imaginative wager of war, but he ends with bad
   feet (15:33).
3. Nadab is victimized by a ruthless coup (15:29).

The narrative places side by side explicit theological rationale and the brute reality of aggressive actions. The text, however, is not able to probe this mystery of juxtaposition with any precision, only warning us against two easy temptations: (a) the theological temptation of *fideism* that credits everything directly to God and (b) the political temptation of *cynicism* that takes the public process to be void of meaning. The interface of these two facets

AΩ **The Mighty One**
The verdict on Asa includes a curious note: "all the acts of Asa, all his power, all that he did" (15:23). In this triad, the reference to power is most uncommon, even though some subsequent kings receive the same conclusion. The term "power" is *gibbor* and bespeaks massive human capacity of a quite masculine kind. Here it likely refers to Asa's military capacity. The same term is used in the familiar recital of royal titles, "Wonderful Counsellor, Mighty God" (Isa 9:6). Asa fulfills royal expectation. He is a mighty one...except for his feet!

of the narrative anticipate the Niebuhrian perception of "critical realism" that holds public power in the context of faith but misses nothing of the reality on the ground. [Niebuhr on Faith and Power] Such a balancing act of *realism* that is *critical* permits neither romanticism nor cynicism, but endless attentiveness to a hiddenness that is only visible late, although it cannot be disregarded in the meantime.

In this illustration, Asa's forces are moving against Baasha's troops; the forces of Israel are retreating en masse.

1 Kings 15:16, War between Asa and Baasha. 1483. (Printed book). *Nuremberg Bible* (Biblia Sacra Germanaica). Private Collection. (Credit: The Bridgeman Art Library)

Niebuhr on Faith and Power

Reinhold Niebuhr was the most influential U.S. Christian ethicist in the twentieth century. In a series of important essays and books, he critiqued soft, liberal Christianity and its romantic view of public power that failed to reckon with its brutality. Faithful to his theological roots in Augustine and Calvin, he faced the huge potential of power for destructive evil, and yet witnessed to the mystery of God that permeates human power. As a believing man, his prayers acknowledged the deep ambiguity of power, reason, and religion. An example of his public prayer is reported by Richard Fox:

> Eternal God, Father Almighty, maker of heaven and earth, we worship you. Your wisdom is beyond our understanding, your power is greater than we can measure, your thoughts are above our thoughts; as high as the heaven is above the earth, your majesty judges all human majesties. Your judgment brings princes to naught, and makes the judges of the earth as vanity; for before the mountains were brought forth or ever the earth and the world were made, even from everlasting to everlasting you are God. Give us grace to apprehend by faith the power and wisdom which lie beyond our understanding; and in worship to feel that which we do not know, and to praise even what we do not understand; so that in the presence of your glory we may be humble, and in the knowledge of your judgment we may repent; and so in the assurance of your mercy we may rejoice and be glad.

Richard Fox, "Reinhold Niebuhr-the Living of Christian Realism," *Reinhold Niebuhr and the Issues of our Time,* ed. Richard Harries (Grand Rapids: Eerdmans, 1986) 21. The prayer is reported without a primary citation.

NORTHERN UPHEAVALS

1 Kings 15:33–16:34

Unlike chapters 14 and 15, chapter 16 (introduced by 15:33-34) is concerned only with a series of Northern kings: Baasha (15:33–16:7), Elah (16:8-14), Zimri (16:15-20), Omri (16:21-28), and Ahab (16:29-34). The sequence bespeaks, from the perspective of this presentation, a sorry tale of violence and instability.

COMMENTARY

Baasha Gone Quickly, 15:33–16:7

While we have already seen an allusion to Baasha in 15:17, only now is he properly presented according to the protocols of this royal narrative (15:33–16:7). He lasted twenty-two years (900–877). Though he is an uncredentialed rebel, he is presented as having (unwittingly?) executed Yahweh's will in overthrowing the failed dynasty of Jeroboam (15:29). Beyond the stereotypical data including a predictable negative verdict as a Northern king, we know nothing of his twenty-two years of power.

It is telling that in the text, immediately upon the verdict, an oracle is presented that declares the end of Baasha and his dynasty. That is, the only thing we know of Baasha is that he is the object of an oracle of judgment. The oracle in the mouth of Jehu is a characteristic speech of judgment. The *indictment* of v. 2 is general and stereotypical. It is introduced with a reminder of Yahweh's initial graciousness to Baasha. He was a nobody, made somebody only by Yahweh. The formula of exaltation, "out of the dust of the earth," suggests that coronation is like creation in its miracle of divine gift of something from nothing (see Gen 2:7).[1] The *sentence* of vv. 3-4 is equally characteristic, but intensely strong and violent. The dynasty of Baasha (brief as it is) will be treated like the house of Jeroboam that was condemned by Yahweh in 14:10-14 and destroyed by Baasha in 15:28-29. A parallel fate now concerns Baasha, wherein the destroyer will promptly be the destroyed. Again a concern is expressed for an honorable death. The sentence is an inclusive parallelism of "in the city…in the country," exposure of the royal bodies to "dogs and birds" (see 14:11). That is, no escape, no honorable burial, no public grief (unlike 14:18). The sentence is total in its devastating dismissiveness...the word of the Lord! The closing formula is predictable; but as with Asa (15:23), Baasha has his power mentioned, that is, he is someone with whom to reckon (16:5-6).

Verse 7, however, is a curious concluding notation. It seems to reiterate the indictment of v. 2, again referring to the oracle of Jehu. The odd factor, according to the NRSV translation, is that Baasha is condemned both (a) because he was *like* the house of Jeroboam, and (b) because he *destroyed* the house of Jeroboam. The oddity is twofold. First, the double judgment is a Catch-22 for Baasha, for the condemnation of the house of Jeroboam seems qualified by a hidden desire to protect it, as though the destruction is disapproved; second, the destruction was at the behest of Yahweh and Baasha's action appears obedient (15:29). Baasha is in any case in a no-win situation. [An Alternative Reading]

Elah Murdered after Two Years, 16:8-14

Baasha's son, Elah, lasted only two years, 877–876 (16:8-14). Between the introductory formula of v. 8 and the concluding formula of v. 14, we are told nothing of his brief reign. Folded into this framework, the narrative concerns the overthrow of Elah, son of Baasha, "according to the word of the Lord." The human agent of the overthrow is Zimri, an army commander, so that this is a military coup. But the coup is framed by a prophetic speech of judgment. The *indictment* is generic in its reference to idols (16:13). The sentence concerns the violent action of Zimri:

He did not leave him a single male of his kindred or his friends. (16:11)

Again the enactment of the harsh judgment of Yahweh is massively violent, an echo of the earlier royal massacres. Again human agents (unwittingly?) perform the intention of Yahweh, an intention that is always negative with reference to the North.

Zimri, Defined by Violence, 16:15-20

Zimri, tool of Yahweh's judgment, did not wear well (16:15-20). He lasted seven days. He of course has no legitimacy for the office of king. He is, in vv. 16 and 20, accused of "conspiracy," even though his actions are "according to the word of the Lord." His brief trace of power is nothing more than military opportunism. It is answered by the more effective opportunism of Omri, also a military man who seems to be higher ranking and certainly more efficient. With Elah a failed leader, the vacuum for power is filled with competing, violent military men. Zimri, it turns out, is no match for Omri, and so he commits suicide and tries to take the entire apparatus with him by fire. He is indicted in a conventional way for sin (16:19), except that it is difficult to imagine how much evil and how much causing of evil in Israel it was possible to do in seven short days. The judgment on him is formulaic, but the end results are the same. Zimri might be useful for an instant, but he is without enduring significance in the life of Israel. [Zimri Remembered]

Omri the Winner, 16:21-28

The death of Zimri, however, does not end the violent dispute for leadership among the military men (16:21-28). The people are divided, half and half, half for Tibni, half for Omri whom

---

Zimri Remembered

Zimri's public time was brief—seven days. But 2 Kgs 9:31 suggests that his name became a cliché referring to political treachery. In that later narrative, when Jehu the rebel comes to kill the despised queen, she says to Jehu, "Is it peace, Zimri?" That is, she refers to her murderer as another Zimri, likening his violent treachery to his antecedent. She no longer refers to a person, but to a slogan:

To be a "Zimri" may have connoted someone who conducts his treachery behind the screen of supposed good will and with the help of insiders who ply the victim with hospitality until he is incapable of defending himself…. Such is the way "Zimris" always come.

Rod R. Hutton, "Zimri," *Anchor Bible Dictionary*, 6 vols. (New York: Doubleday) 6:1095.

we have just seen as the one who eliminates Zimri. We know nothing of either of these two contenders, except that they are products and perpetrators of violence—no doubt in the name of military responsibility—that endlessly destabalized the society of northern Israel. In the end Tibni died and Omri prevailed. We are given no reason for this outcome to the dispute, no strategic reason and, more important, no theological justification.

Omri the winner is, for the writer, without theological legitimation. It is all power and Omri is the winner in a power game. It has been conventional to credit Omri with seven years of governance (876–869), but the chronology followed in the NRSV allows him twelve years. During that time he emerged as a powerful and shaping force, establishing a dynasty that lasted, for the first time in northern Israel, to the third generation (16:24-27) [The House of Omri]

The theological verdict on Omri by the Deuteronomists is predictable. He is stereotypically condemned. It is striking that no punishing action is proposed or taken toward him, the condemnation notwithstanding; as a consequence, he is permitted a peaceable death, an uncommon ending among Northern kings. No doubt Omri's central historical significance is little reflected in this polemical biblical summary. While his recognition by other powers testifies to his competence, the only clue we are given in the Bible concerning his importance is the establishment of a new royal city, as the capital is transferred from Tirzah to Samaria, "city of Omri."

Omri established a city that had no antecedents, no tribal claimants or disputes, built on land the new king had purchased. One cannot but notice the parallel to David's achievement in building the "city of David" where there were no tribal antecedents, with a purchase of land (2 Sam 5:6-10; 24:18-25). Just as Jerusalem is never "the city of Israel" but always "the city of David," so we may imagine that Samaria is always properly and peculiarly Omri's own property, a base from which to mount powerful royal initiatives. The theological verdict on the historical reality (as best as we have it) diverges completely from what we may take as historical data

The House of Omri

Omri himself lasted only briefly. His dynasty of one son and two grandsons lasted until 842. It is remarkable, however, that even after the overthrow of his dynasty by Jehu in 842, the Assyrians continued to refer to Israel as "The House of Omri," and to Jehu, of another dynasty, as "son of Omri." So great is the impression that Omri left in the power circles outside Israel

"At that time I (Shalmaneser III, 840 BC) received tribute of the inhabitants of Tyre, Sidon, and of Jehu, son of Omri." Annals of Shalmazar III

James Pritchard, *Ancient Near Eastern Texts.* 277-281.

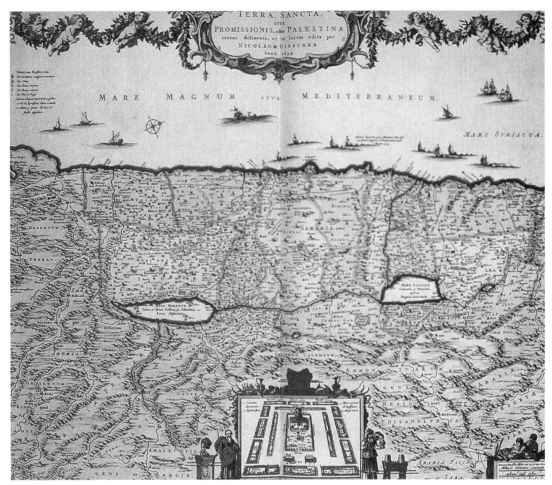

The Dutch mapmakers were very concerned about the Holy Land being depicted accurately. This map shows the city of Samaria. The establishment of Samaria is described in 1 Kgs 16:24.

Dutch Map of the Holy Land. 18th century. (Credit: Planet Art)

about Omri. The narrative escalates the judgment against Omri, "more evil" than all who were before him. Perhaps the greater condemnation of this Northern king is commensurate with his greater political effectiveness, for this Davidic historian already looks askance at any Northern well-being of any sort.

Ahab, Son of Omri, 16:29-34

Omri is the founder of the dynasty; but his son Ahab is more influential, more provocative for this account, and better known (16:29-34). In this chapter we are given only the introduction and verdict on Ahab; his conclusion must await the enactment of many prophetic tales, and is given to us only in 22:37-40.

God Baal of the Thunderstorm. 2nd–1st mill. BC. Gilded bronze idol with an Egyptian-style crown. Louvre, Paris, France. (Credit: Erich Lessing/Art Resource, NY)

Ahab is presented as an extreme case of evil. His father Omri did "more evil" (16:25). But now Ahab does "more evil" than even Omri. The general indictment of v. 30 is detailed in the following verses. We may see in vv. 31-34 two quite distinct elements. In vv. 31-33 the target of theological polemic is Jezebel, a Sidonian princess. In the critique of Solomon in 11:1, the Sidonian "foreign women" are already included among the distorters of Israel's covenantal faith, so that here Ahab is a specific case of the general critique of Solomon. While in popular lore Jezebel has been portrayed as erotic and seductive, there is no ground for such a notion. Rather she embodies the social ideology of her upbringing that came along with the theological commitments she embraces. Her theological commitment to Baal, we are told, is enacted by the building of an altar and an Asherah (see "The Asherah," pp. 190, 429). The worship of Baal is reflected in the famous "conflict on Mt. Carmel" (chapters 18–19), a contest between Yahweh and Baal. The social ideology that accompanies Baalism is not at all reflected in that episode, but is evident in 1 Kings 21, wherein Jezebel holds to and practices a theory of land ownership that privileges royal claims.

Both the theological practice and the social ideology are deeply inimical to covenantal Yahwism. Moreover, the two—theological commitment and social ideology—are deeply intertwined so that theological Baalism is the legitimating force for a social theory of exploitation against which Yahwism stands. The deep either/or of Yahwism and Baalism reflects a profound divide between social theories and worldviews only thinly coded in our verses. That either/or helps us understand the urgency and forcefulness of the polemic made against Ahab via Jezebel. [An Alternative View of Ahab and Jezebel] Thus the entire sequence of Northern kings, their instability and violence, builds toward Ahab. He is the quintessential distortion of Yahwism according to this presentation, a distortion that has theological and social spin-offs, a distortion that evokes, in turn, the prophetic polemics and alternatives that follow in 1 Kings 17–22 and 2 Kings 1–9.

The second theme of polemic against Ahab is offered in the enigmatic v. 34. The external issue is the building of Jericho, perhaps as a restored military installation given its strategic location in the Jordan valley. The concern of the text is not the restoration of Jericho, but the involvement of two sons of the builder, Abiram and Segub, in the process of rebuilding. The exact meaning of this reference to the sons is unclear, but the formula "according to the word of the Lord which he speaks by Joshua, son of Nun" is a reference back to Joshua 6:26:

> Cursed before the be anyone who tries
>   to build this city—this Jericho!
> At the cost of his firstborn he shall lay its foundation,
>   and at the cost of his youngest he shall set up its gates!

An Alternative View of Ahab and Jezebel

There is no doubt of the massive polemic in the biblical text concerning Ahab and Jezebel. If, however, we step outside that heavy polemic, it is possible to see the matter differently, rather against the grain of the biblical text. Winfried Thiel proposes that Omri's policies—continued by Ahab—were to deal with social tension between "the Israelite tribes and the traditional Canaanite elements of the populace." [Winfried Thiel, "Omri," *Anchor Bible Dictionary*, 6 vols. (New York: Doubleday) 5:20-21.] In response to these tensions, Thiel suggests, the king initiated a "policy of parity," in order to give voice to traditional Canaanite concerns. Such a redress in that direction was of course perceived by Yahwists as a sellout. If Thiel is right, here is a clear example where wise public policy is at odds with the insistent passions of Yahwism.

From a very different perspective, Phyllis Trible proposes that Elijah and Jezebel be understood as counterparts who may be judged differently from different standpoints:

Elijah and Jezebel, beloved and hated. In life and in death they are not divided. Using power to get what they want, both the YHWH worshiper and the Baal worshiper promote their gods, scheme, and murder. A reversal of the context in which their stories appear illuminates the bond between them. In a pro-Jezebel setting Elijah would be censured for murdering prophets, for imposing his theology on the kingdom, for inciting kings to do his biding, and for stirring up trouble in the land. The epitaph for him would be, "See now to this cursed male." By contrast Jezebel would be held in high esteem for remaining faithful to her religious convictions, for upholding the prerogatives of royalty, for supporting her husband and children, and for opposing her enemies unto death. [Phyllis Trible, "Exegesis for Story-Tellers and Other Strangers," JBL 114 (1995): 17-18.]

In the narrative of Joshua, Jericho is a hated and feared Canaanite city leveled by Joshua and the Israelites. As a conclusion to the story of its destruction, Joshua utters a poetic curse, intending that Jericho must never be rebuilt, for the Israelites want the Canaanites never to have that much concentrated urban power again. If it is rebuilt, moreover, the new builder shall do so at the cost of his sons, that is, shall lose his sons as a penalty. This utterance is a standard, stylized curse stated in poetic parallelism to mean "all," foundations/gates, firstborn/youngest. It is, however, nothing more than an emotive act of rhetorically generic condemnation.

In 1 Kings 16:34, our verse, however, the generic curse of Joshua that has no particular reference is now applied concretely and specifically to Ahab's rebuilding project. Now "firstborn/youngest" is made specific, so that actual children are named. It seems evident that the narrative here has misunderstood and misconstrued the intent of the curse in Joshua 6:26. But even given that misunderstanding, it is not clear what is meant, for the phrase that NRSV translates "at the cost of" is an interpretive rendering of a simple Hebrew preposition. It is possible, though not certain, that the verse alludes to the practice of "foundation sacrifice" wherein a child was killed and entombed into the foundation of a new building as an act of piety to assure the well-being of the new structure. If that is intended, then the function of this verse is to make clear how Ahab has degraded covenantal practice, how cheap life is, and how arrogant royal practice has become.

CONNECTIONS

This chapter continues the sorry tale of royal failure, wherein royal power is an endless distortion of covenantal Yahwism. This chapter continues the tale of chapters 14–15, and therefore the "connections" already made in those chapters pertain here. Only here the account is exclusively of the North, and therefore the Southern theological perspective can condemn and dismiss without restraint, for no Northern king can be a carrier of anything positive.

The text offers a critique of *power politics* about which we may make four interpretive comments:

1. Three times in the chapter (16:7, 12, 34), the narrative pivots on "according to the word of the Lord." In each case, the

act legitimated by Yahweh is a negative, destabalizing, destructive one. This formula is a device in the narrative for asserting that there is a powerful, even if hidden, Holy Purpose at work in public history that cannot be mocked or circumvented.

2. The particular force of that Holy Purpose in this account is essentially negative and subversive. That is, the God of the Torah is impatient with every ordering of public power that is unresponsive to the demands of covenantal neighborliness. It is possible for managers of public power—like Omri and Ahab—to have their way for a very long time…but not finally. In the end, all of the cunning and power of established authority cannot sustain itself in the face of Yahweh who wills otherwise. The text shows that such aggressive and self-indulgent practices of power are penultimate, and give way soon or late, in the end, to the intention of Yahweh.

3. In this slice of biblical faith, it is clear that the rule of Yahweh does not concern piety, private morality, or careful theological formulation. It concerns, rather, the ordering and reordering of public power. That is, according to these texts, the primal agenda of the God of Israel. Much church usage of the Bible is simply a gross misreading of the claims of faith, for finally the issues are the Torah claims of God and neighbor, for which Jezebel functions as the perfect foil.

4. In this presentation, biblical faith is a counterdiscernment of public power, the same counterdiscernment we have seen concerning Solomon in chapter 9. The powers that be may be mightily impressed with their power, wealth, knowledge, and capacity to control. But this theological perspective is not for an instant impressed, because it focuses on other claims. Thus Omri may have been a large figure in the international politics of the day, but he receives here only six verses, and those to condemn him. In Torah perspective, he is an irrelevance. Similarly Ahab must have been a much-noted leader in his time, but here he is only context for the prophets who are the real makers of history.

The radicality of this view of public history is so odd for us that a "connection" is not easy or obvious. Since the emergence of modern theories of "autonomy" in the Enlightenment, now enhanced by unprecedented advances in technology, the political-economic process does indeed seem to be handed over completely to key human players. Indeed, the dealers who manage political power by image manipulation and the controllers of the global economy appear to be "on their own." In

The Endless Reopening of History

The theological perspective of this text insists that whenever established power is entrenched, the God of Israel may, in violent ways, destabilize and reopen the public process of politics. It occurs to me that this lesson may be current for us. With the collapse of the Soviet Union, Francis Fukuyama, then a functionary of the U.S. State Department, wrote a gloating book on "The End of History," wherein he concluded that the deep historical battle for control of public history is over and U.S. democratic capitalism has won. [Francis Fukuyama, *The End of History and the Last Man* (New York: The Free Press, 1992).] His phrase "The End of History" means the end of elemental ideological conflict. Such a view, of course, does not reckon with the restless, subversive holiness of Yahweh who permits no absolutizing of human power, not even the claims of U.S. democratic capitalism. The kings in that ancient time were always surprised to find their own establishment less than absolute.

---

their face, however, come these tales of inscrutability. The writers of our text cannot "explain" how dynasties rise and fall, how secure power is overthrown, how respected authority is vetoed. The text in any case bears witness to this reality in that ancient world that we are able to see, even now in our own time. The text may give us pause even in our Enlightened self-regard. [The Endless Reopening of History]

NOTE

[1]On the formula of enthronement, see Walter Brueggemann, "From Dust to Kingship [1 Kings 16:2; Genesis 3:19]," ZAW 84 (1972): 1-18.

ELIJAH, MAN
OF POWER FOR LIFE

1 Kings 17:1-24

With this chapter we arrive at an abrupt and decisive interruption of the royal narrative, a pause to consider the *prophetic counterforce* in Israel's life. It is impossible to overstate the historical, literary, and theological significance of this intrusion that features, in turn, Elijah (1 Kgs 17-21 along with 2 Kgs 1-2), Micaiah (1 Kgs 22), and Elisha (2 Kgs 3-9). The three are completely unexpected, uncredentialed, and uninvited characters in the royal history of Israel. According to the tale told, they enact the raw, unfiltered power of Yahweh that lies completely beyond the command of the royal houses. Indeed, their presence in the narrative serves to expose the inadequacy and lameness of the kings as shapers of history, in order to assert that real authority and real energy for historical reality lie outside the legitimated claims of monarchy.

In the present chapter, Elijah is featured in three narrative accounts: his summons to prophetic vocation (17:1-7), his care for an alien widow (17:8-16), and his power for life against death (17:17-24). The latter two episodes are connected, but they offer very different dramatic actions and claims.

COMMENTARY

Wilderness Beginnings, 17:1-7

The prophet appears to the king in the narrative unannounced and unexplained. His name, Elijah, means "Yah(weh) is my god (el)." His very existence is as assertion that counters the report of 16:31-33 that situates Ahab amidst other gods. Elijah embodies a summons to Yahwism and a dismissal of all other options.[1] His opening assertion concerning a drought sets the confrontational tone for his entire sojourn in Israel (17:2). The assertion of drought may be understood in two ways. First, drought is widely understood in that ancient world as a divine curse. [Drought] When God is displeased, rain is withheld. Moreover, the assertion that Yahweh will cause a drought is a

This fresco offers the viewer a simple, large image of Elijah in contemplative pose given to meditation and prayer, often accompanied with a raven.

Saint Elijah, c. 1252. Byzantine fresco. Mary's Assumption Church. Moraca, Serbia. (Credit: Erich Lessing/Art Resource, NY)

Drought

The Bible lives in a world of water scarcity, always with the threat of drought. The promise of biblical faith is that Yahweh, the creator, has guaranteed an ample water supply to sustain all of life:

> You make spring gush forth in the valleys;
>   they flow between the hills,
> giving drink to every wild animal;
>   the wild asses quench their thirst.
> By the streams the birds of the air have their habitation;
>   they sing among the branches.
> From your lofty abode you water the mountains;
>   the earth is satisfied with the fruit of your work.
> (Ps 104:10-13)

Yahweh is a reliable sustainer who looks after the land of Israel, but also all of creation:

> Who has cut a channel for the torrents of rain,
>   and a way for the thunderbolt,
> to bring rain on a land where no one lives,
>   on the desert, which is empty of human life,
> to satisfy the waste and desolate land,
>   and to make the ground put forth grass?
> (Job 38:25-27; see Deut 11:11-12)

The creator guarantees all that is necessary for a luxurious, abundant life.

But because the Old Testament is relentlessly committed to the *moral shape* of creation, it insists in many places that water for life is given in a context of covenantal obedience to the commands of Yahweh. The negative counterpart is that rain withheld is a punishment for disobedience; thus drought is a curse in response to covenantal violation. The point is evident in the two great curse recitals of Lev 26:18-20 and Deut 28:23-24; see Amos 4:7-8). The point is succinctly made in Hos 4:2-3 wherein *disobedience* causes "*languishing*" (drought), so that all of creation shrivels up (see Jer 14:1-6).

In our text, Yahweh is fully in control of rains and drought. The assertion of drought in v. 1 is in response to the Baalism of 16:31-32. As we shall see subsequently, Elijah has the capacity to bring rain, to turn curse to blessing. Our narrative take place in the midst of an immediate theology of creation. The world depends upon Yahweh; Elijah is Yahweh's agent in the management of creation.

deliberate refutation of Baal whom Ahab worships, because Baal, a "fertility god," is a rainmaker (see 16:31-32). But the prophetic assertion challenges that claim by insisting that rain and drought are completely in the governance of Yahweh, and certainly not in the power of Baal. Thus the announcement of drought is a deeply theological affirmation and polemic.

Second, it is the work of the king to assure fertility (and therefore rain). In that ancient world royal responsibility for rain is not unlike contemporary presidential responsibility for the economy. The measure of an effective king is rain that produces corps. In this simple assertion the capacity to administer rain and therefore life is taken from the king. The king is made a political irrelevance, void of any critical function for society. The king is being robbed of his *raison d'etre*.

Elijah is a man at the behest of Yahweh's word. Yahweh commands, Elijah is completely and immediately obedient (17:3-6). He is directed by Yahweh to enter the wilderness, to distance himself from all normal life-support systems, to live in a context of extreme vulnerability, to be deeply at risk. He is east of the Jordan, outside the zone of administered life, beyond the sphere of royal control.

He is immediately obedient. He has no regular food supply. He is at the mercy of the elements. He will eat nothing of the luxury of royal food, but subsists on the lean diet that ravens can fly in, matched by water only from the unreliable wadi. The narrative makes nothing of this food arrangement. Perhaps it is a discipline and a testimony. Perhaps it is an exhibit of his obedience. Perhaps it is a narrative strategy for placing the prophet beyond the reach of the king. The narrator tells us none of that.

All that we are told is that the "wadi dried up" (17:7). Even this primitive arrangement of sustenance failed. The concluding sentence may indicate the extremity of Elijah's situation, and consequently the extremity of royal Israel. Or the verdict may be a verification of the thesis of v. 1. A drought is declared and now a severe drought is enacted. Elijah speaks the truth! The realm is endangered. Clearly the king is in jeopardy, because he is no reliable provider of well-being. The narrative is so straightforward that we may not easily notice how ominous and how subversive it is. We now follow this power-laden figure who lives completely outside royal categories.

Life for Widow and Orphan, 17:8-16

The second episode begins with equal abruptness (17:8-16). Again Elijah is commanded by "the word of the Lord," for he is a creature of that word (17:8). He is dispatched by Yahweh to Sidon, a territory outside Israel. This note not only asserts Yahweh's governance beyond the territory of Israel (more territory than King Ahab administers), but Sidon is the home territory of Jezebel (16:31). It is as though this is a counterthrust on the part of Yahweh against the incursion of Jezebel into Israel. Elijah is sent, moreover, to a nameless widow who functions in the narrative as a cipher for the powerless, uncredentialed, disadvantaged, and hopeless. [On Widows] The prophet asks her for water—his wadi has dried up and he needs water! He asks for bread (bread only for the day), for Yahweh has promised that the widow would feed him (17:10-11; cf. v. 9). Her response to the prophet is a measure of her destitution (17:12). She has neither drink nor food to spare. Indeed, she is starving to death; her statement would seem to suggest a critique of king Ahab, for widows and orphans, poor and needy, are the peculiar charge of the king.

Thus far, our narrative is only setting the stage for the drama in which the prophet takes command of the scene. His work is in two parts. He makes a lordly speech (17:13-14), and then he enacts the wonder he has just announced (17:15-16). The speech is a characteristic speech of promise. It begins with an assurance: "Do not

---

AΩ **On Widows**

In a patriarchal society, a widow—without a husband as protector and guarantor—is vulnerable and endangered. It is for that reason that the covenantal laws of Deuteronomy regularly enjoin protection of widows, along with orphans and aliens, as people deeply at risk (Deut 24:17-18, 19-22). Paula Hiebert offers this verdict:

The Hebrew *'almanâ* [widow] then, like the *ger*, [alien, sojourner] existed on the fringes of society. In a society where kinship ties gave one identity, meaning, and protection, both the *almanâ* and the *ger* had no such ties. Unlike, the *ger*, however, the *almanâ* lived in this liminal zone as a woman. Not only was she bereft of kin, but she was also without a male who ordinarily provided a woman with access to the public sphere.... The wicked take advantage of the *almanâ* because they fear no reprisals from outraged family members. Yahweh takes special care of the *almanâ*, supplying the role of the missing male kin who would have been concerned for her well-being and economic support. [Paula S. Hiebert, "'Whence Shall Help Come to Me?' The Biblical Widow," *Gender and Difference in Ancient Israel?"* ed. Peggy L. Day (Minneapolis: Fortress Press, 1989) 130, 137.]

In our narrative, Elijah appears as the advocate of the widow on behalf of Yahweh. He effects abundance in a society where her status has resulted in acute deprivation. The concern is not different in the New Testament; see Mark 12:40-44; Jas 1:27. Elijah enacts a wonder whereby the widow is included back into the world of Yahweh's abundance.

AΩ Do Not Fear

This formula has been identified as introducing a "salvation oracle." Its utterance assures Yahweh's active engagement on behalf of the addressee who is otherwise bereft of resources (see Isa 41:10, 13, 14; 43:1; 44:2). That is, it is utterance that is circumstance altering. While some scholars have thought the phrase is peculiarly linked to assurance in battle (as in Deut 20:3), Edgar Conrad has shown that it can be an assurance in many other circumstances as well. [Edgar W. Conrad, *Fear Not Warrior: A Study of* 'al tira' *Pericopes in the Hebrew Scriptures*, Brown Judaic Studies 75 (Chico: Scholars Press, 1985).]

In our narrative, utterance of the formula by the prophet is a declaration that Yahweh's resources for life are present, and therefore the circumstance of death will not prevail. This stereotypical formula is a profound assurance to the widow and makes a high claim of authority for Elijah. It is instructive that in the parallel account of Mark 5:36, the formula, to the same effect, is expanded: "Do not fear, only believe." The same formula is used by Jesus for the same purpose in John 6:20. This authorized utterance creates a new circumstance and a new prospect for well-being, especially among those who have no alternative resources or hope.

---

fear." This "salvation oracle" is a characteristic formula whereby an utterance of powerful presence alters circumstance. [Do Not Fear] It is spoken against death in order to assure life. It is spoken against exile to assure homecoming. It is spoken against despair in order to assure hope. The speech mobilizes the life-giving power of Yahweh. The assurance is followed by a specific promise of meal and oil that reverses the destitution of the widow and her son. In a circumstance of extreme scarcity, the prophet speaks lavish abundance.

Elijah is, moreover, as good as his word (17:16). No, he is as good as Yahweh's word, for it is "the word of the Lord" that vetoes circumstance and guarantees abundant life. Note well, that the narrative does not explain. It has no curiosity about how this has all happened. It is a wonder! It is an act that draws amazement like a magnet. The story keeps being retold, and the astonishment of the act abides from generation to generation, endlessly amazed that God, through this human agent, can override killing scarcity with lavish abundance. [Abiding Astonishment]

📖 Abiding Astonishment

This capacity of Elijah to produce an enduring, reliable abundance of oil and meal is indeed a "miracle," a wonder that resituates the widow. The narrative does not explain. But it testifies to the wonder. We may imagine, moreover, that this story of testimony was cherished and restated many times, each time evoking a sense of amazement and gratitude, an awareness that daily life is invested with God's inscrutable blessing. We cannot understand or be addressed by the Elijah narrative as an offer of good news, unless we see how the prophetic miracle rests at the center of the action.

Martin Buber, in an elegant phrase, has characterized miracle as a happening of "abiding astonishment," an event retold in the life of the community with an enduring capacity in each rehearing to reopen life to the gifts of God.

On the formula, see Walter Brueggemann, *Abiding Astonishment: Psalms, Modernity, and the Making of History*, Literary Currents in Biblical Interpretation (Louisville: Westminster/ John Knox Press, 1991) 30-33.

New Power for Life, 17:17-24

The feeding miracle of vv. 8-16, however, only creates a context for the more urgent, more conflicted engagement of the widow and the prophet (17:17-24). The presenting problem now is the illness of the son (17:17). We do not know why he is ill, but we notice that the narrative rather carefully avoids the bald statement that he was "dead." In any case, the mother is beside herself about her son, and lashes out at Elijah with an accusation (17:18).

The prophet, however, does not respond to her accusation. He disregards it; instead he takes command of the situation. His action is bracketed by "Give me your son" (17:19) and "See, your son is alive" (17:23). Between these two statements he has *taken* the son and submitted him to the life-giving power of Yahweh, and then has *given* the son back to the mother. Between these two utterances to the mother, his action consists in two prayers addressed to Yahweh. In the first of these, he speaks an accusatory question to Yahweh, something of a parallel to the mother's initial comment to him (17:20). In the second petition, he prays for life for the boy, an insistent demand that is answered by Yahweh (17:21). The narrative reports, without making any special fuss, that the prayer is answered. The boy lives again! Yahweh answers the prayer! But all attention is focused on Elijah, this powerful man of Yahweh who can summon Yahweh's gift of life into a scene of death. As in v. 14, the narrator offers no explanation and expresses no curiosity about the wonder just enacted. It is a wonder that defies explanation. It is a gift of life that the king could never grant. It is a pastoral transformation that the mother could not have anticipated.

The return of the revived son to the mother evokes a grateful response from the mother as intense as her initial accusation. She recognizes the power and significance of Elijah (17:24). He is a man of God! He is a carrier of "the word of the Lord." Of course, the narrator has known this all along (17:2, 5, 16), but now the needy woman knows as well. Indeed, as it is represented, the purpose and gain of this latter "wonder" is the credentialling of Elijah as a force from Yahweh in the life of Israel. In our modern reading, we may be preoccupied with the "miracle." In the shaping of the text, however, the "miracle" is a sign that points beyond itself to signify about the miracle worker, Elijah. [Miracle as Sign] The reader is now on notice, as the king is now on notice, that this is one greater than he who will now shape Israel's life, before whom the king is helpless. The credentialling of Elijah is rooted in these two miracles of oil-meal and revived son. The two narratives, however, are placed in the context of wilderness food that avoids any collusion with royal resources and of the widow as the social habitat of counterpower. The newness Elijah will enact for Israel from Yahweh is a newness completely outside the bounds of established power. He will do so by a counterpower that endlessly subverts establishment

In this painting, thanksgiving and recognition of God are paramount. The mother of the revived child is kneeling in prayerful humility, transfixed by the sight of her son who returns from the upstairs room with Elijah. The widow functions in a space apart from the others. By isolating her at the foot of the stairs, the artist is able to use the stairway wall as a backdrop by which to accentuate and clarify her gestures of recognition and praise. The shadow of the ornamental bird above her praying hands perhaps underscores the real Presence of her transcendental recognition echoed in 1 Kgs 17:24: "Now I know that you are a man of God, and that the word of the Lord in your mouth is truth." This poignant mother-child reunion is reiterated by the motif of the baby chick perched on the mother hen's back, seen at the bottom right of the painting. This painting is filled with esoteric signs and intimations that are symptomatic of the mind-set of the Pre-Raphaelite brotherhood with which Brown associated.

Ford Maddox Brown. *Elijah Restoring the Widow's Son.* 1868. Oil on canvas. Victoria & Albert Museum, London, England. (Credit: Victoria & Albert Museum, London/Art Resource, NY)

Miracle as Sign

The modern world is excessively fascinated by "miracles." For the most part, what we call "miracles" in the Bible are signs that point past the act itself to assert the *authority of the agent*. Thus the "miracle" of oil and meal and the miracle of restoration are narrated to witness to the awesome authority of Elijah. The widow (and we) are able to recognize that "You are a man of God." Thus v. 24 ends the narrative but in fact is the premise for what follows about Elijah.

Miracle as authorizing *sign* is evident concerning Jesus in the Fourth Gospel. His action against the temple in John 2:13-22 is a sign of his authority over against the authority of the temple system.

Of this action, Gail O'Day comments:

Jesus, a complete outsider to the power structure of the Temple, issues a challenge to the authority of the Temple that quite literally shakes its foundations.... Jesus challenges a religious system so embedded in its own rules and practices that it is no longer open to a fresh revelation from God, a temptation that exists for contemporary Christianity as well as for the Judaism of Jesus' day.... He issued a radical challenge to the authority of the religious institutions of his day. [Gail R. O'Day, "The Gospel of John: Introduction, Commentary, and Reflections," New Interpreter's Bible (Nashville: Abingdon Press, 1995) 9:545.]

His challenge to the system closely parallels the dramatic challenge to the royal system enacted by Elijah.

power. The narrative invites us to amazement at this completely inexplicable happening in the midst of ordinary life.

CONNECTIONS

One is struck by the abruptness of the appearance of Elijah. He comes from nowhere, completely without any credentials or authority. He breaks in upon the royal history that abhors abruptness and that overflows with credentials and protocol. The narrative is arranged to dramatize the collision course of king and prophet in which the prophet regularly prevails. The confrontation between king (Ahab) and prophet (Elijah) is an intensely personal meeting. Two factors, however, point beyond a personal confrontation. First, the name of the prophet, "Yah is my God," indicates that the central protagonist against the king is not the prophet, but the God who sends the prophet. Second, Elijah carried "the word of the Lord," almost a palpable force set loose in the midst of Israelite history. The effect of the intrusion is to destabilize and delegitimate royal claims that have endured this long only because of the restraint of Yahweh. The name of the prophet and the power of the word attest that this is a challenge of Yahweh to the proponents of Baal (see 16:31-32).

The narrative makes clear that Elijah is one filled with irresistible authority. The reason for his uncommon power, moreover, is that he refuses any conventional nourishment that may be provided by the royal system. That is, he lives and relies upon sustenance from outside everything Ahab administers, for taking royal nourishment diminishes undomesticated authority. Israel is endlessly aware of the capacity of established power to rob and sap faithful people of alternative power. See Isaiah 55:1-2 where Israel is invited to bread, water, and wine that are alternative to Babylonian offers, and especially Daniel 1, wherein a model Jew refuses imperial food, to great effect:

> In every matter of wisdom and understanding concerning which the king inquired of them, he found them ten times better than all the magicians and enchanters in his whole kingdom. (Dan 1:20)

The narrative of John the Baptist carries a distinct echo of Elijah's practice of resistance (Luke 3:1-2). That narrative describes the entire Roman apparatus of bureaucratic rule; then, abruptly, it announces over against that apparatus the singularity of John who is marked by "the word of God" that creates an alternative in the face of established authority. Moreover, John is marked by emblems of the dangerous outsider:

> Now John was clothed with camel's hair, with a leather belt around his waist, and he ate locusts and wild honey. (Mark 1:6)

He is indignant that anyone would expect otherwise, and is determined to remain in his chosen way of life, itself a huge contrast to the established apparatus.

Elijah—and John after him—are extreme cases, to be sure. In their extremity, however, they embody disengagement, resistance, and alternative as a mark of faith that yields transformative power.

The testimony of Elijah offered in this opening account invites a reconsideration in a community of faith that has too easily come to terms with its social environment. Specifically, the U.S. church, in a deeply indulgent consumer economy, is invited to rethink and reconsider its own embrace of such "junk food" that erodes peculiar identity and robs of energy for vocation. Elijah is a figure uneroded and unrobbed, who mounts a ministry of subversive power for life.

Elijah's encounter with the widow—on Jezebel's home turf!—makes clear that his ministry is not among the powerful and the credentialed. That he conducts his opening scene of ministry in such a context asserts that the power for life that he bears will not be administered through the usual channels of privilege. In this regard, his sojourn with the widow parallels Jesus' ready engagement with "publicans and sinners," the social rejects who are devalued and who will diminish all those who spend time with them (see Luke 5:30-32). But Elijah's work is not simply to rescue the debilitated, though he does that.

His work, rather, is to enact the *reality of abundance* in a world seemingly *governed by scarcity*. [The World of Abundance] The encounter between the two is a lesson in distribution. The widow—and her entire social class with her—are left out of the distribution of worldly goods in royal Israel. She is hopelessly deprived and so has

As mentioned in the connections, John's presence as a "dangerous outsider" is conveyed in this depiction of the Baptist as a man of the wilderness. The artist's Mannerist style further emphasizes the hagard and elongated figure of John.

El Greco. Detail from *Saints John the Baptist and John the Evangelist*. c. 1600. Oil on canvas. Museo de Santa Cruz, Toledo, Spain. (Credit: Erich Lessing/Art Resource, NY)

no capacity to sustain her own life or the life of her son. In despair, she accepts her disastrous disadvantage.

The prophet, however, refuses the conventional arrangement of advantage and disadvantage. He enacts a world of guaranteed abundance for the widow, in defiance of more conventional arrangements of scarcity. Thus the encounter is not a "do-good" act of charity; it is rather a revolutionary act that rejects the myth of scarcity fostered by the privileged, a myth accepted by the widow who has no available alternative. The prophet is able to enact this "wonder" of meal and oil, because there is *more than enough*. This narrative then is affirmative testimony to the generosity of the creator who has given enough gifts for all and critical testimony against the monarchy that has arranged the abundance of the creator through a practice of scarcity.

There is no doubt that the contemporary world, like that ancient royal world, subscribes to a myth of scarcity.[2] But such scarcity is not a given of creation. It is an imposed power arrangement whereby some have too much so that, consequently, some have too little (see Exod 16:17-18 for a counteraffirmation). Prophetic faith refuses to accept that power arrangement and appeals behind it to

---

⌕ The World of Abundance

There is no doubt that biblical faith witnesses to the wondrous abundance of the creator who has provided creation as a food-producing, life-sustaining system. This is evident in the creation narrative, in the wonder of manna (Exod 16), and culminates is the assertion of Jesus:

I come that they may have life, and have it abundantly. (John 10:10)

There is also no doubt that since the confiscation and hoarding of Pharaoh in Genesis 47, the world has been organized around coveting that produces scarcity, a scarcity that deeply negates Yahweh's gift of abundance (see Luke 12:13-21).

The issue of *abundance versus scarcity* is at the heart of the Elijah miracles, whereby the prophet releases the abundance of creation, thereby overruling royal scarcity. The same issue is still at work in the modern economy. On the issue in contemporary life, M. Douglas Meeks concludes:

The work of the Holy Spirit is about *access* to God's economy.... A trinitarian understanding and experience of the Holy Spirit occasions a conflict between the economy of God and the economic ethos of our society: the conflict between scarcity and what the New Testament calls the *pleroma* or the fullness of God's blessing and gifts in the Holy Spirit.

M. Douglas Meeks, *God The Economist: The Doctrine of God and Political Economy* (Minneapolis: Fortress Press, 1989). 171

In a different perspective Regina Schwartz suggests that a theological basis for scarcity is rooted in a singular God and produces the pervasive forms of violence that occupy the Bible and continue to haunt contemporary life in destructive ways. [Regina Schwartz, *The Curse of Cain*] In the face of ancient and contemporary scarcity, Elijah stands as a powerful sign of Yahweh's astonishing, overwhelming, life-giving plenty.

the will and gift of the creator. A case can be made that contemporary economics—even the booming so-called "global economy"—works from scarcity so that some enjoy huge resources at the expense of others who can only "eat and die." The narrative intends to expose such an immobilizing myth and to invite an embrace of an alternative that is expressed as praise and practiced as redistribution.

The final act of this chapter—the restoration of the son—is of course more dramatic and more elemental than the narrative of oil and meal. The narrative dramatizes Elijah's power to bring life into a world of death. Characteristically the narrative points beyond the prophet to the God who authorizes him and answers his prayer. That is, the pivotal point of the narrative is this second petition of the prophet in v. 21. Elijah is a man who prays, who refers the crisis at hand beyond himself; Yahweh is a God who hears and who has the power of life and of death (see Deut 32:39; 1 Sam 2:6; Isa 45:7; Job 5:18). Yahweh is the God of all power who is mobilized by the prayer of Elijah.

As is commonly recognized, this episode is replicated in Mark 5:21-43 in the life of Jesus. Jesus raises the dead daughter of a leader of the synagogue, Jairus. There is, however, an important difference. Whereas Elijah prays to Yahweh to give life, Jesus simply addresses the child and orders her to "get up." That is, Jesus does not refer the crisis beyond himself, but is presented as the one who can raise the dead. Jesus is given the role of Elijah, but also has the role of Yahweh to whom Elijah prays.

Both the narrative of Elijah and Jesus attest that we are here in the presence of life-giving power that can transform situations of defeat, despair, and death. The raising of the child is an earnest of Jesus' resurrection, whereby the church triumphantly mocks the power of death:

> Death has been swallowed up in victory.
>   Where, O death, is your victory?
>   Where, O death, is your sting? (1 Cor 15:54-55)

It is important in making the move from Elijah to Jesus that the miracles of raising the dead not be taken as isolated miracles, nor simply as dazzling acts of transcendence. They are rather engagement with the powers of death who seek to rob the vulnerable of life and well-being. In the larger Elijah story, Ahab is an agent of death who cannot produce rain and who will finally destroy Naboth. Thus Elijah challenges the way in which social power is organized; he unleashes an alternative possibility in the world. The narrative intends us to be dazzled, not by a religious oddity, but by the redefinition of the daily reality of life around us in God's creation.

This entire chapter, in all three episodes, poses the question, where is the power for life vested? In its deep "unreason," the narrative asserts that the power for life is outside royal administration, for the king cannot cause rain, cannot give oil and meal, cannot raise the dead. In our own context, the same question lingers. It is easy, now as then, to imagine that the power for life is among the powerful, beautiful, and privileged, controlled by scientific sophistication and technological finesse, knowledge about power, about food, about medicine. Such a perspective, of course, produces competition, conflict, and finally war over control of the resources and organs for life.

And yet—so this narrative makes clear—the real gift of life, concretely, daily, on the ground, wells up elsewhere, in ways not administered, inscrutable, amazing, subversive, transformative. The narrative explains nothing. But it puts us on notice. Life possibilities are not contained in our control. While the widow may have welcomed the prophet, it is no wonder that many others found him to be a profound inconvenience.

NOTE

[1]See Regina M. Schwartz, *The Curse of Cain: The Violent Legacy of Monotheism* (Chicago: University of Chicago Press, 1997).

[2]M. Douglas Meeks, *God The Economist: The Doctrine of God and Political Economy* (Minneapolis: Fortress Press, 1989).

TROUBLER OF ISRAEL

1 Kings 18:1-46

I have suggested that Elijah's "pastoral care" of the widow in chapter 17 is an implicit challenge to the royal apparatus in Israel. Now that challenge becomes public and explicit. This long narrative can be divided into three parts: an initial confrontation (18:1-19), the public contest (18:20-40), and the culmination in rain (18:41-46). Elijah is the key character in every scene. Playing opposite him, Ahab appears in scenes 1 and 3, but is absent in the central scene where he is represented by the prophets of Baal who are executed at the end of the scene.

The entire narrative, presented in a leisurely, playful way, concerns the deep dispute between explanatory systems of religion (Yahwism and Baalism) with Elijah and Ahab cast as representatives of the two systems. That the meetings are so acrimonious and the outcomes so violent indicates the heavy stakes in the issue. There is no doubt that in the Bible, and especially in this cluster of narratives, Baalism is heavily caricatured in Yahwistic representation. Indeed, we have only the caricature so that the narrative is not, and does not intend to be, an evenhanded exposition. The caricature that dominates Israel's imagination is that Baalism is a socioreligious system rooted in the capacity to secure life for self by the manipulation and control of the gifts of the creator, by self-centered management that inevitably leads to an antineighbor ethic. Thus it must not be thought that the contest concerns mere religious symbols or slogans; it is rather a deep and costly conflict between two contrasting perspectives on reality that are deeply rooted theologically and highly visible in the life and social practice of the community.

COMMENTARY

Preparation for Life and Death Struggle, 18:1-19

The narrative prepared for the contest by a dramatic preliminary meeting between king and prophet (18:1-19). The issue, continuing from 17:1, is the drought. As indicated in that chapter, the drought is a curse; the business of the king, moreover, is to deliver rain, to bring

Domenico Beccafumi. *Elijah Sending Out Obadiah*. 16th century. Marble intarsia on pavement. Duomo, Siena, Italy. (Credit: Scala/Art Resource, NY)

a blessing (see Ps 72:16). In the narrative Ahab clearly cannot produce rain in the face of Yahweh's resolve, and therefore he is a discredited king.

This new narrative begins as abruptly as 17:1, only now with a reversed message (18:1). Now there will be rain, but it is rain linked to Elijah who must carry the new message of rain to the king. The rain depends upon meeting the king, and that takes some careful choreographing.

In the context of that divine decree for rain, the drought continues to be severe enough to produce famine, yet another curse from Yahweh (18:2). In order to counter drought and famine, Ahab devises a plan together with his major domo, Obadiah. [Obadiah] The two of them together will seek for water, in order to save the realm (18:3-6). The imagery of the search for water is designed to dramatize the extremity of the situation, but also, I suggest, to portray the king as a ludicrous, desperate man whose realm is now out of control.

The encounter between Elijah and Obadiah does not advance the plot, but only portrays something of Elijah's constituency (18:7-16). The exchange between them indicates that there are serious Yahwists (at least one) in the very house of Ahab, that is, those who passionately disapprove of Ahab and who act in daring ways for their faith. The encounter intensifies the dispute upon which the entire narrative turns.

The exchange between prophet and royal servant, framed by vv. 7-8 and 16, is Obadiah's speech of protest, wherein he voices his devotion to the prophet and the consequent risk he runs. He describes the frantic royal pursuit of Elijah to indicate how bloodthirsty the king is. He reports on his own pious actions whereby he has protected Yahwistic prophets against the violence of Jezebel. And finally, because he knows Elijah is something of a phantom figure, he fears that his role is a setup that will expose him without any support. The substantive gain of this speech is to make clear that the prophet, for all his singular visibility, is not a lone figure, but is in a context of what must have been an important community of support. [A Supporting Cast]

The rhetoric of this speech is most carefully rendered. It turns on a threefold "go tell your lord," first as the command of Elijah (18:8), second as sarcastic refusal (18:11), and then as a reiteration (18:14). The command is too risky. But Obadiah does finally obey (18:16). There is a meeting.

AΩ Obadiah

This "servant of the king" appears in the Bible only in this narrative, and is not to be confused with the prophet by the same name. The name "Obadiah" means "servant of Yahweh," indicating an assertion of faith and devotion to Yahweh. His formal position in the royal apparatus is "in charge of the palace," suggesting that he holds a very prominent and influential position in the government, perhaps second only to the king.

The narrative, however, presents him in a way that is congruent with his name. He is a deeply devoted Yahwist and a loyal follower of Elijah, that is, holding to the "Yahweh-alone" faith of the prophet. Thus he is for the prophetic movement an insider figure, ostensibly serving Ahab but in fact serving precisely the cause that means to subvert and delegitimate the king who practices Baalism. His odd and important position as an undercover agent for Yahwism is never explicitly stated but only given us in the process of the narrative. To be a "servant of Yahweh," according to this narrative, is to resist the king and his policies.

A Supporting Cast

Obadiah plays a covert but exceedingly important role as supporter of Elijah. Our usual reading of the Bible pays attention to the "headliners." But clearly the star characters are not lone actors but are embedded in and dependent upon communities of support that they represent. Robert R. Wilson has shown how such figures as Elijah have "peripheral social functions" for a dissenting community. That is, prophetic traditions bespeak determined, risk-taking communities. Perhaps a close parallel to Obadiah is the role played by Shaphan in the ministry of Jeremiah. Jeremiah is the star character who is much exposed to royal opposition. But in the pivotal narratives, Shaphan and his family are always strategically placed to provide quiet but crucial support in dangerously contested circumstances (Jer 26:24; 36:11). We may well reread the Bible with attention to "minor" figures who live at the edge of the narrative in dangerous, faithful ways.

Robert R. Wilson, *Prophecy and Society in Ancient Israel* (Philadelphia: Fortress Press, 1980), 194-201.

AΩ **Prophetic Troublemakers**

The prophet and the king dispute about who is the troublemaker. The term "troubler" (*'ker*) refers to actions that disrupt the peaceableness of the community:

> Those who are greedy for unjust gain *make trouble* for their households,
> but those who hate bribes will live. (Prov 15:27; see 11:20)

In this proverb, the trouble is greediness that disturbs proper social arrangements. The best-known usage of the term is in Joshua 7–8, wherein Achaan covets and withholds from the community two hundred shekels of silver as private gain. The result is that his community is defeated. The place where he acted against the community is named, "The Valley of Achor Trouble" (Josh 7:26).

The "troubler" is one who disturbs the well-being of the community by acting for self against healthy social relationships. The prophets were often perceived as troublers because they dissented from conventional reality and raised awkward questions. Thus Hosea is dismissed as a "fool" who is "mad" (Hos 9:7); Jeremiah is reckoned to be a traitor for undermining the war effort (Jer 38:4). And surely Elijah is a profound social disturbance. The work of prophets is to raise questions and expose what is taken for granted when it is in fact destructive.

The prophet turns the tables on the king: The king is the one who troubles Israel by policies of Baalism that hinder the full functioning of adequate social relationships. The charge against the king is remarkable, for the king is responsible for workable social relationships. The exchange is not unlike the civil rights protests of the 60s in the U.S. The protesters were thought to be disturbers of the peace, when in fact it was accepted, distorted social relationships that caused trouble of a deep, unnoticed kind.

The meeting is a dramatic confrontation that consists in only one quick exchange (18:17-19). The king speaks first (18:17). He should, because he is the king. He asks a question that parallels the question of Obadiah in v. 7. But whereas Obadiah's question is an act of deference, Ahab's is an accusation. He identifies Elijah as a disturber of Israel. [Prophetic Troublemakers] The implication is that the realm would not be in trouble if it were not for the prophet; that is, there would be no drought. The accusation is not unlike the ill-informed statement of the widow in 17:18.

Elijah's response is denial and countercharge (18:18-19). It is the king who in fact troubles Israel. This is an amazing charge against the king, that the king is a disturber of the peace. The charge concerns not only the king, but the king's family, that is, the House of Omri. We have seen that the dynasty is formidable (16:23-34); but we have also seen that the dynasty, from Yahwistic perspective, is evil. The consequence is the contest at Carmel that will involve 450 prophets linked to Baal, 400 with Asherah, all under the patronage of Jezebel. The issue is joined! There is no doubt that Israel is "troubled." We will see who is to be blamed.

No More Limping on Two Opinions, 18:20-40

The actual contest is wondrous street theater with everything dramatized and overstated (18:20-40). [The Contest] Mt. Carmel may indeed be simply a convenient location, or it may be that as a "high place" it is appropriate to divine presence. Or it is possible that the name "Carmel" is appropriated as "vineyard of God," thus alluding to fertility. Elijah sets the issue of the meeting in his initial address to the people (18:21). The purpose is to force a decision among the people who have refused to decide. [On Having It Both Ways] "Limping" means to engage in a cultic dance in celebration of Baal while

The Contest

The narrative offers a contest between gods presented in graphic and dramatic form. The same sense of conflict, however, is given elsewhere in the text of the Old Testament. In Isa 41:21-29, a characteristic expression of disputation, the poet presents an imagined court case (v. 21) in which other gods give testimony about their claim to be gods (vv. 22-23) that leads to a verdict of "nothing" (v. 24). Conversely, Yahweh gives testimony that vindicates the God of Israel (vv. 25-27). The poem is not as clear as the narrative, but both texts offer a sense of Israel's disputatious way of faith. The conflict of the gods is a dispute about the character of the world, the shape of morality, and the requirements of public policy. Our narrative is the most dramatic presentation of a standard way of theological thought and speech in Israel. Clearly a bland monotheism is no adequate alternative to such a way of dispute.

In this Renaissance mosaic, one-point linear perspective is defined by the overall proportionality of the scale of the figures. There is a clear delineation of a foreground, middle ground, and background. The vanishing point falls on the horizon line between the two sacrificial bulls. As Elijah gestures toward the altars and bulls, the ground rules are being established, "Let's Rumble!"

Domenico Beccafumi. *Pact between Elijah and Ahab*. 16th century. Marble intarsia on pavement. Duomo, Siena, Italy. (Credit: Scala/Art Resource, NY)

On Having It Both Ways

The famous phrase "limp along on two opinions" dramatizes Israel's perennial attempt to have it both ways. To choose against Yahweh is impossible in Israel; but to choose singularly for Yahweh appears to be excessively radical and costly. The issue is endlessly a life-or-death issue for Israel. The same issue is expressed in Rev 3:16:

So, because you are lukewarm, and neither cold nor hot, I am about to spit you out of my mouth.

When the faithful are neither hot nor cold, there is no clear passion in any direction.

Among the more visible cases of indecision is the example of the "German Christians" (*Deutsche Christi*) in the days of Hitler. These were Church people who thought they could live faithfully without choosing between the dominant ideology of National Socialism and the claims of Christ. This settlement of both-and as a majority opinion was sharply challenged by the Confessing Church and its Barman Declaration with its sharp either/or. I cite this case only because it is highly visible, not because it is any worse than the endless lukewarmness of the church in the face of real issues. The settlement of both-and—both faith and consumerism, both faith and capitalism, both faith and militarism, both faith and racism, etc., etc.—is most often not a deliberate decision but rather a slow erosion of awareness. Prophetic faith always disrupts such irenic settlements and forces the issue.

---

professing Yahweh. The prophet insists that the two loyalties are mutually exclusive and one cannot have it both ways. The response of silence may indicate the resistance of the people. The last thing they want is to decide. Elijah directs the preparation for the contest with bulls and fire. He lays down the ground rules so that there will be no doubt when the scores are tallied.

Now Elijah engages the prophets of Baal directly, the ones under the protection of Jezebel (18:25). The contest is arranged so that each side offers its evidence for the god it champions. The Baal team goes first (18:26-29). The narrative reports their passionate appeals to Baal, interspersed with Elijah's dismissive mocking of them in v. 27. Baal does not answer. There is only silence. Elijah, in vigorous sarcasm, begins to make excuses for a god who fails to appear. He portrays an indifferent and unresponsive god. The clincher, however, is not the loud taunting of the prophet, but the negative conclusion of the narrative:

no voice, no answer; (18:26)
no voice, no answer, no response. (18:29)

The Hebrew has the flat negative particle *'ain* five times! None, not any ever! Baal is absent, silent, indifferent, unresponsive, uncaring, unwilling to answer. His devotees are abandoned and on their own. They cried aloud, they cut themselves, they raved…nothing! The Yahwists have known since the outset of the contest that Baal will not answer:

The events leading up to the annihilation of the prophets of Baal exposed the powerlessness of these prophets against God. In this print by Nolpe, Elijah is shown immersed in intense prayer with God, seeking God's will as a witness to the people. The moment of ignition is captured while the masses exclaim and gesticulate in bewilderment. In prayer, Elijah calmly remains focused upon God. The defunct altar in the middle ground of Nolpe's etching implicitly signals the imminent death of the prophets as their powerlessness is revealed.

Pieter Nolpe. *Elijah Praying to God to Extinguish the Fire on Bull being Sacrificed*. 17th century. Etching. Fine Arts Museums of San Francisco. (Credit: Fine Arts Museums of San Francisco, CA. Achenbach Foundation for Graphic Arts, 1963.30.11375.)

Then he will say: Where are their gods,
  the rock in which they took refuge...?
Let them rise up and help you,
  let them be your protection! (Deut 32:37, 38)

Now it is Elijah's turn, that is, Yahweh's turn. It is time for Yahweh to "do his stuff," to demonstrate both sovereignty and responsiveness. Elijah makes preparation, taking care to link Yahweh to the twelve tribes of Israel, thus situating the contest in the framework of Israel's core memory (18:31). He makes the circumstance of Yahweh's performance as difficult as possible: "fill and pour...do it a second time...do it a third time." There is no chance of a hoax or a deception. If it works, it will be the real thing, and everyone will know it is such.

On Killing Prophets

It is an old practice to kill prophets who are unacceptable (see Luke 13:34). Already in Exod 32:28, the sons of Levi kill 3,000 adherents of Aaron; though not prophets, they are religious advocates. Hananiah is not killed, but he does die on schedule as a false voice (Jer 28:17). In our case, Elijah, fresh from victory, kills the prophets of Baal, perhaps as many as 450 (see v. 22, but see also 400 additional ones in v. 19). The narrative seems to accept the legitimacy of killing the losers in this winner-take-all context.

It is remarkable that in victory Elijah does what Jezebel had earlier done. Phyllis Trible has observed the parallel:

Every move of Elijah—chiding the people for their equivocation, proposing generous terms for the context, taunting the Baal prophets in their failure to elicit fire, building suspense through deliberately paced measures that eventuate in the consuming fire of YHWH—every move of Elijah is calculated to destroy Jezebel.

Yet in a peculiar way his incendiary victory exalts her. After all, her blatant actions occasioned the contest. Now they presage the aftermath. Elijah emulates Jezebel …Winner and loser exchange identities to expose the futility of the contest.

Phyllis Trible, "Exegesis for Storytellers and Other Strangers," *JBL* 114 (1995): 7-8.

The episode underscores the severity of the issue and the lack of any sense of compassion.

It is not for us to criticize the narrative, but to notice how the same juices of death operate even now. The assassination of Martin Luther King, Jr. is only the most dramatic case in recent time of the need to silence those who threaten our schemes on behalf of a larger vision.

And then he prays (see 17:20-21)! Here the address to Yahweh is through the ancestors of Genesis. The address is formal and solemn, congruent with the urgency of the moment. The petition is twofold: that Yahweh shall be seen as God, that Elijah be seen as intimately linked to Yahweh. The credibility of both is at stake as the two are completely intertwined (18:36). The petition continues in v. 37, asking that Yahweh do what Baal did not do in v. 29. The moment is cast as a life-or-death occasion for Yahweh, when everything will be decisively settled. Yahweh's response in v. 38 is completely congruent with the prayer. Yahweh does what is asked; Yahweh is vindicated and Elijah is made credible.

The response is decisive. The people drew the only conclusion that could be drawn (18:39): "Yahweh is God, Yahweh is God." The verdict is inescapable. There are no more "two opinions." There is one opinion. Yahweh is acknowledged, Baal is routed and eliminated from consideration. But the response is more than affirmation. As Elijah is vindicated, so the prophets of Baal, the ones linked to Jezebel, who worked in vv. 22-29, are thoroughly discredited. This is a contest for "keeps" and they have lost. Within the context of the narrative, they are likely not surprised at their fate. They are executed as Elijah surely would have been had things gone otherwise. Perhaps ironically, they are killed in the wadi, the gully that is now dry, but that will, by the gift of Yahweh, soon surge with water. Yahweh is known to be God, but Yahweh must always and again demonstrate power and defeat rivals who endlessly challenge. [On Killing Prophets]

The narrative culminates with the overwhelming gift of rain, thus exhibiting the outcome of Yahweh's victory, Yahweh's sovereignty, and Elijah's confirmation (18:41-46). Importantly, Yahweh's victory is over Baal, for it is Baal who is reckoned in Canaanite religion to be the rainmaker. The announcement of drought (17:1) and of rain (18:1) are defiant claims on the part of Yahweh; it is Yahweh and not Baal who makes rain. The contest and victory over Baal in vv. 20-40 are now a harbinger that Yahweh will give rain, the firstfruits of the rule of Yahweh in an arid, drought-ridden context. This is Yahweh the creator, the maker of heaven and earth, the guarantor of fruitfulness who now gives rain as gift and as sign of sovereignty.

The Triumph of Rain, 18:41-46

This concluding paragraph is dramatically presented as anticipation (18:41-44) and finally as implementation (18:45-46). In the anticipation, Elijah is no longer hostile toward Ahab. Perhaps he does not need to be, because he (along with Yahweh) is the winner. Elijah's word to the king seems to reassure: "Relax, enjoy, everything will be all right." The prophetic imperative is "go up," first to the king (18:41), then to the servant (18:43), then to the servant seven times (18:43). The wait is worth it: "Look ("behold")! a little cloud." But the prophet knows. He warns the king to run for his life. He knows the rain is coming; he knows Yahweh is on the move and thus he knows the outcome (18:45). There was wind, the same *rûah* that ordered chaos (Gen 1:2), the sure sign of Yahweh's powerful activity. And there was a heavy rain. The God who withheld rain and caused drought now gives rain. The rain is given at the behest of Elijah. Ahab is no player. Ahab has done nothing to turn curse to blessing. Ahab is irrelevant to the future of the realm. It is all Yahweh…and all Elijah. The concluding verse asserts that Elijah now is freshly empowered by the hand of Yahweh (18:46). He runs in front of the king's chariot with almost superhuman power. He is the prophetic agent who now makes new life possible. He is exultant as is his God.

CONNECTIONS

The narrative is about the radical transformation of the realm of Israel from drought to rain, from curse to blessing, from death to life. In an arid climate where all vegetation is vulnerable because of

The Canaanite Option

This narrative has been most influential in shaping several generations of Old Testament interpretation in terms of the profound contrast between Israelite faith and Canaanite religion. Outside of the Bible, our knowledge of Canaanite religion is primarily derived from Ugarit, an ancient Phoenician city where scholars have found a rich deposit of library resources from one practice of that religion. More recent scholarship suggests that in many ways, Israelite faith and Canaanite religion had very much in common.

Older scholarship was preoccupied with the contrast between the two. Two titles may suggest an oppositional approach, the work of G. Ernest Wright and Norman Habel. [G. Ernest Wright, *The Old Testament against Its Environment* (SBT 2; London: SCM Press, 1950); Norman C. Habel, *Yahweh versus Baal: A Conflict of Religious Culture* (New York: Bookman Associates, 1964).] It is likely that in different circumstances the interface between the two took a variety of different forms, our narrative text being the most antagonistic. For a different approach that hints at more positive linkages, see Walter Harrelson, *From Fertility Cult to Worship: A Reassessment for the Modern Church of the Worship of Ancient Israel* (Garden City: Doubleday and Co., Inc., 1969).

---

water shortage, this transformation is nothing short of a resurrection. The deep turn to life is evoked by Elijah, but it is enacted solely by Yahweh, so that the narrative as a whole, in its dramatic force, is a doxology to Yahweh newly acknowledged, acknowledged through the process of the drama. In the end, the entire narrative moves toward the acclamation of the people:

> Yahweh, it is he who is God;
> Yahweh, it is he who is God. (18:39)

In its primitive articulation, the "contest" reads like a showdown between neighborhood bullies that revolves around shows of raw power. It is important to reconize, however, that "Yahweh vs. Baal" is not simply "between the gods," but the names of the competing gods bespeak competing social systems and alternative accounts of the world. There is no doubt that "Baalism" has been much caricatured in modern scholarship, and there is no doubt that Baalism is caricatured in the biblical account itself. [The Canaanite Option] "Baal" functions in these texts as a deathly alternative to the life-giving will of Yahweh. While interpretive caricature has been extensive, an important contrast between the two loyalties came to be decisive for Israel's self-understanding.

"Baalism" must be reconstrued from what we know in the Bible and from nonbiblical texts. No doubt as affirming readers of the Bible, our sense of "Canaanite religion" is skewed. Israel's perception is that Baalism is a system of religious belief and practice that takes the impulses for life and fertility and fruitfulness to be embedded in the processes of creation itself. As a consequence, this religious perspective believes that the processes of life can be managed and controlled by human technique. That is, the "secrets of life" can be tamed. A second, related consequence is that there seems to be no compelling ethical dimension to this possibility of control, so that the control of life is indeed open to abuse and exploitation.

Insofar as Israel's faith can be contrasted with such a perspective, the affirmation that "Yahweh is creator" is an insistence that the "powers for life" are not embedded in the processes of life themselves, but that they are held in the hand of the creator who is deeply committed to creation but not identified with it. This creator thus withholds ultimate control of life from human management so that the mystery of life finally cannot be overcome. This creator, moreover, is a righteous God so that living well in creation depends upon a neighbor ethic that ultimately precludes abuse and exploitation. (In the Elijah narratives, this point is on exhibit in the Naboth narrative of 1 Kings 21.)

The contest at Carmel thus is an argument and dispute between two rival perspectives on reality. To be sure, such a dispute seems remote from us. If this characterization of Baalism is correct (and it may be excessively polemical), then we may see that we are not far removed from the same issues, if "Baalism" should be understood as a Promethean attempt to reduce the mystery of life to knowable, manageable techniques, so that life come under our control. If this interpretive connection is valid, then we may see that a sense of the world as a *mystery from God marked by a neighborly ethic* is in deep dispute, in our own day, with *the reduction of life to a manipulation of technical knowledge.* I state the contrast most baldly to see that our dispute is as focused as that ancient contest. There is, in the end, no middle ground, just as there was not at Carmel. There are indeed "two opinions" that fully require a decision. I should imagine that medical research, the potential of military devastation shamelessly embraced, the industrial destruction of the ecosystem, the cheapening of the life of those who are not productive, all suggest that this profound contest is replicated and reenacted often among us in policy disputes as well as in more daily decisions about neighbors.

Theologically this narrative attests to the rule of Yahweh as creator. This is creation theology, wherein the world of shrivelled Israel is taken to be Yahweh's world, dependent upon Yahweh, receptive of the gift of life than can be given only by Yahweh. [The Emancipation of Creation] It is confession of the world *as creation* that sets limits on human exploitation. In our own time this theological limit is largely disregarded in the mad effort for control.

Politically, Ahab the king, who here is a cipher for public power committed to Baalistic technique, is fundamentally irrelevant to

Rubens has perhaps conflated the reference in scripture where the angel feeds Elijah just prior to his 40-day trek to Mt. Horeb and the arrival on the mountain. The setting is in a cave. In the interpretation by Peter Paul Rubens, Elijah's cave comes complete with stairs and spiral columns. Consistent with the Baroque, the figures are intermeshed in blurred contours, dramatic lighting and movement as the angel is in the act of handing Elijah both bread and water. Here, Rubens' associations with the Eucharist are unavoidable, an association that is all the more plausible given his contact with Rome and Catholic Flanders in the 17th century.

Peter Paul Rubens. *The Prophet Elijah Receives Bread and Water from an Angel*. 17th century. Oil on canvas. Musée Bonnat, Bayonne, France. (Credit: Giraudon/Art Resource, NY)

the future of the world. Ahab is portrayed as a helpless, passive spectator to the contest. We may anticipate from this radical narrative the thought that the great managers of public and corporate power in our own time who are bewitched by technical, amoral control are in the end irrelevant to the future of the world. The impetus for life is elsewhere, among those who attend to the neighborly will of the true creator. Thus the contest of chapter 18 is linked to the neighborly acts of 17:8-24. Both attest to the power for life that lies outside royal administration. Ahab cannot make it rain. Ahab cannot give meal and oil. Ahab cannot restore the boy. There is no need for two opinions, no need for "the second opinion of Baalism." Yahweh is enough. The affirmation of the people in v. 39 invites the radical reorientation of public power and public policy according to a new core conviction. No wonder Elijah could run as a horse. Because the world had been turned back to its life-giver. It is enough to give energy!

The Emancipation of Creation

As a result of this contest, Yahweh's creation is permitted to function fully again. We may anticipate that the rains sent by Yahweh would cause "the desert to rejoice and blossom" (Isa 35:1). Until Yahweh's victory, it is possible to think that creation was prevented from being its fully fruitful self.

With huge adjustments from that ancient crisis to our own crisis of ecology, we may suggest that the rule of Yahweh permits the flourishing of creation. Gibson Winter has transposed the crisis of "Yahweh versus Baal" to a question about the meaning of "nature" in a technological society:

> Land in a technologized world is merely a means for making money. Land is an exploitable, alienable resource. It can be bought and sold like any other commodity.... In the mechanistic paradigm, this is considered a "rational" approach to land, since land like anything else may be scarce in one place and plentiful in another.... The spirituality of the technosociety is at war with the spirituality of peoples in the organicist heritage who aspire to self-determination and sovereignty. This is the shape of the struggle of decolonization in the third world.
>
> Gibson Winter, *Liberating Creation: Foundations of Religious Social Ethics* (New York: Crossroad, 1981).

Wendell Berry has written passionately about the crisis of technological agriculture and its abuse of creation. He describes the agriculture of native Americans (Papago) in Southwest U.S.:

> The Papago communities were at once austere and generous; giving and sharing were necessarily their first principles. The people needed each other too much to risk individualism and dissent.... "The man who hoarded, who saved, who said he and his blood would make it on their own.... such a man led his kin to extinction.... The poverty of our own "affluent society" never existed among them.... And they lived in harmony with their place: they lived the net yield of the desert's hydrologic budget.
>
> Wendell Berry, *The Gift of Good Land: Further Essays Cultural and Agricultural* (San Francisco: North Point Press, 1981) 51.

But then Berry characterizes Pancho, an heir to that tradition:

> Pancho is a man with two minds: one, a flashy invention known as "the consumer mentality," which he shares with all modern Americans; the other, the traditional pattern of knowledge, ceremony, and community, which was the way of his ancestors for a thousand years. He is a modern man with a thousand-year-old mind.
>
> Wendell Berry, *The Gift of Good Land: Further Essays Cultural and Agricultural* (San Francisco: North Point Press, 1981) 60.

The *double-mindedness* links the current crisis to the old Carmel contest. As always a decision must be made again.

Quotation from the poem *Dover Beach* by Matthew Arnold.

> Ah, love, let us be true
> To one another! for the world, which seems
> To lie before us like a land of dreams,
> So various, so beautiful, so new,
> Hath really neither joy , nor love, nor light,
> Nor certitude, nor peace, nor help for pain;
> And we are here as on a darkling plain
> Swept with confused alarms of struggle and flight,
> Where ignorant armies clash by night.

LETDOWN AND REVIVAL

1 Kings 19:1-21

Elijah (and Yahweh) have won a huge, perhaps decisive victory in chapter 18 over Baal, Ahab, and Jezebel. The struggle, however, was not yet finished. Elijah is still in jeopardy, a hunted man. In this narrative Ahab and Jezebel are present only in v. 1, but they are a heavy and ominous threat that drives the entire narrative. Ahab, moreover, defers to and appeals to Jezebel as the more dominant voice. Her resolve is to pronounce a royal death sentence over Elijah (19:1). [Anything They Can Do...] The motivation for her resolve is surely political as Elijah threatens the authority of the crown. He has destroyed the prophets of Baal, surely legitimators of the crown (18:40). The affront to the crown cannot go unanswered. But the threat is also theological, for the political and theological are deeply intertwined. It is no wonder that Elijah flees for his life. He flees south to Judah, out of the territory of Jezebel and Ahab (19:3; see Amos 7:12).

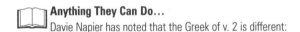 **Anything They Can Do...**

Davie Napier has noted that the Greek of v. 2 is different:

> Now Jezebel sent word to Elijah: "If you are Elijah, I am Jezebel."

The statement is a defiant put-down, whereby Jezebel tops Elijah. It suggests to me, "Anything you can do, I can do better." Napier exposits the defiant line. [Davie Napier, *Word of God, Word of Earth*, (Philadelphia: United Church Press, 1976) 58-59.]

> An insistence that he must practice the piano:
> > "If you are Davie, I am Mrs. Wilson."
> Eye trouble during graduate school:
> > "If you are Davie, I am adversity."
> On a put-down for engagement in civil rights protest:
> > "If you are Davie, I am Bill."
> On scholarly discipline:
> > "If you are Davie, I am Egbert."
> On war protest that offended his university president:
> > "If you are Davie, I am the president."

The royal line seeks to belittle the prophet. The narrative will have it otherwise, and overcomes the belittlement of the prophet at the hands of the queen.

COMMENTARY

A Wanted Man, 19:1-3

Verses 1-3 provide the ominous context for what follows for the fugitive who must run for his life. The following narrative concerns Elijah's retreat from royal threat even further south into the wilderness (19:4-10) and his encounter at Horeb where he receives a new mandate from the God he champions (19:11-18). Verses 19-21 are something of an addendum wherein Elijah implements one of Yahweh's commands by securing Elisha as his follower.

Despair and a Ministering Angel, 19:4-10

The fugitive is on the run, because the crown is playing hardball (19:4-10). As those entrenched in power often do, Ahab and Jezebel will stop at nothing to protect themselves and their advantage. But of course Elijah himself is not naive (innocent), for he also has engaged in terrorist politics. For that reason, he must run. The wilderness to which he flees is beyond the control of the crown. But of course, it is also a place of risk, for there are none of the usual life supports. Such a circumstance of wilderness risk, to be sure, is no new venture for Elijah (see 17:1-7). He arrives in the wilderness completely spent. He has mustered enormous energy for the dispute at Carmel. And though he has won, he is permitted no chance of exultation. His wish-prayer of v. 4 is for death. He is distressed and dismayed. And then he sleeps. He has no energy for anything else. The sleep is loss of control.

It is, however, more than that. Sleep (when the guard is down) is a time when the inscrutable powers of God work their will with us. Verses 5-7 are bracketed by the narrator. These verses happen while he is asleep. Perhaps it is a dream, but a dream reckoned as an effective divine disclosure. A messenger (angel) comes. Nothing is explained and the narrator has no curiosity. It happens "suddenly" (*hinneh*). The messenger from God touches him, commands him, feeds him. Food is given, a warm cake and water, everything needed, a reminder of what he had done for the widow (17:16). He is fed, surely comforted. He is, nevertheless, exhausted. He sleeps a second time. The angel feeds him a second time. Now he regains his strength, strength enough for a long sojourn at Horeb, the great mountain of confrontation. The text is somewhat unclear: he is at the mountain, yet he is in a cave. He is fed and strengthened, but his despair is not yet overcome.

He is addressed by "the word of the Lord." The phrasing is curious. It is not "the Lord," but more likely a mediation parallel to "the messenger." He is in an odd place, "…Horeb…cave." It is an unnatural place for a prophet, to be sure, since he has been dispatched against the crown. The prophet issues his defense, giving reason for his plight. The reason is that he has been "very zealous." The grammar employs an intensifying form of a verb that is already intense. He has been passionately, singularly, utterly devoted to Yahweh, without qualification. That very passion has now put him at risk. He is at risk because Israel (not to say the crown) is disloyal and on a rampage against the prophets of Yahweh. He is where he is because his faith and courage have made him a wanted enemy of the state. His jeopardy is intensified by his sense of profound isolation. He is the only one left, without companion or support. In his response to the divine mediator, he does not count even on the angel who has ministered to him.

New Confrontation, New Commission, 19:11-18

The movement of the narrative is odd and jumps from theme to theme. There is feeding (19:5-8) and self defense (19:9-10). But now, in v. 11, the response of the word to the prophet is odd. God meets discouragement and self-pity with a massive theophany (19:11-18). The narrator clearly intends to offer a parallel here to Moses at Sinai (Exod 33:21-23). Elijah is about to experience the peculiar confrontation that was heretofore granted only to Moses. Elijah, like Moses, is at Horeb. Elijah, like Moses, is there forty days and forty nights (Exod 24:18). Elijah, like Moses, now experiences an overpowering, forceful coming of Yahweh marked by the massiveness of storm, for Yahweh is, among other things, the irresistible force of a storm God. The parallel is intentional. Israel is once again at Horeb, with theophany, to be met by the overwhelming presence of Yahweh.

The actual narrative account employed from the Moses tradition, however, functions here only as a foil, in order to give a very different account. Davie Napier has nicely cast vv. 11-12 in terse poetic form:

> There was a mighty wind
> Not in the wind was Yahweh
>
> After the wind earthquake
> Not in the earthquake was Yahweh

And after the earthquake fire
Not in the fire was Yahweh

And after the fire—
A sound of gentle silence.[1]

The great wind that split mountains and broke rocks is like the time of Moses. The earthquake is replicated from Moses. The fire belongs to the tradition of Moses. These are all the characteristic features of theophany, God's coming marked by cataclysmic disruption of natural phenomena. The tradition of theophany strives to voice in effective ways the sheer power of Yahweh's irresistible coming.

The triad of wind, earthquake, and fire, however, is all preliminary and is made completely irrelevant by the disjunctive entry at the end of v. 12. The bombast now is no adequate vehicle for Yahweh. Now Yahweh is known in "a sound of sheer silence." [A Sheer Silence] The precise meaning of the phrase is difficult, permitting a field day of speculation among translators, often moving in a mystical direction. The main point may be to contrast whatever it is with the *loud* tradition of theophany. The familiar KJV rendering, "still small voice," suggests a sound that is soft and intimate. More recent opinion suggests no voice, no sound, but an eerie silence laden with a sense of holiness. The phrasing is open to speculation and we can reach no definitive judgment on its meaning.

AΩ **A Sheer Silence**
   The phrase reporting the way in which Yahweh comes to Elijah is endlessly enigmatic. The NRSV has "a sound of sheer silence," suggesting real silence. The Contemporary English Version has "a gentle breeze," that seems highly unlikely and somewhat romantic. The familiar KJV translation is "still small voice." James Montgomery, following C. F. Burney, proposes, "voice of a light whisper." [James A. Montgomery, *The Books of Kings* (ICC; Edinburgh: T. & T. Clark, 1951), 313-14.] In the end, it is evident that the phrase is beyond us. Care must be taken that one does not take the phrase out of context; for in context, it is prelude to a demanding confrontation. It is not the offer of intimate solace, for such an offer would seem incongruous to both parties in the narrative.

Whatever may be intended by the peculiar wording, it did indeed elicit Elijah's full attention. He stood "at the entrance of the cave," a parallel to Moses in Exodus 33:21-23. Elijah presents himself, exposes himself to the threatening intrusion of Yahweh, and is prepared to be addressed. Whatever may have been the "sheer silence" with its freighted holiness, Elijah is now addressed by "a voice" that is profoundly authoritative. The exchange of vv. 13b-14 is a reiteration of vv. 9b-10. While there may be some confusion in the transmission of the text, more likely the repetition is to characterize the angular relation between Elijah and Yahweh. Elijah is passionate and therefore endangered. But Yahweh, in response, shows no pity or sympathy for him. [A Response to Complaint] The response made

A Response to Complaint

Elijah's description of his sorry state may constitute something of a complaint to Yahweh. It is not cast as a prayer, but it is surely a bid for compassion, if not for rescue. While not precisely the same, the response of Yahweh comes elsewhere as a characteristic response to complaint. It is conventional that the response to complaint on the part of a faithful, attentive God is a salvation oracle. [See Patrick D. Miller, *They Cried to the Lord: The Form and Theology of Biblical Prayer* (Minneapolis: Fortress Press, 1994), 141-77.] The divine oracle is characteristically an announcement of presence and help: "Do not fear" (see Isa 41:8-13; 43:1-5; 44:1). The response is designed to transform a situation of need and trouble by divine intervention. Thus the conventional rhetorical form is a powerful vehicle for theological assurance.

It is evident that the response Yahweh makes to Elijah is scarcely assurance of help or presence:

> Go, return on your way to the wilderness of Damascus; when you arrive you shall anoint Hazael as king over Aram. Also you shall anoint Jehu son of Nimshi as king over Israel; and you shall anoint Elisha son of Shaphat of Abel-meholah as prophet in your place. (1 Kgs 19:15-16)

Instead of assurance, he receives mandate. Thus the narrative breaks conventional form and does not offer what the prayer of Elijah might normally evoke from Yahweh. The violation of the form is poignant in context.

The daring transposition of complaint-response in this text has most in common with the Lamentations of Jeremiah. In parallel fashion, Jeremiah's use of the form breaks convention. [On the complaints of Jeremiah, see Kathleen M. O'Connor, *The Confessions of Jeremiah: Their Interpretation and Role in Chapters 1–25*, Dissertation Series 94 (Atlanta: Scholars Press, 1988).] Thus in Jer 12:1-4 the prophet states a deep bewilderment and need. Where we expect assurance and consolation, the prophet receives from Yahweh only a more demanding commission:

> If you have raced with foot-runners and they have wearied you,
> > how will you compete with horses?
> And if in a safe land you fall down,
> > how will you fare in the thickets of the Jordan? (Jer 12:5)

The starchiness of prophetic use of the rhetorical convention is not surprising in the midst of the rigors of prophetic faith.

---

by Yahweh is fully focused on public mission and is not at all interested in the suffering or fear of the prophet.

The address to the prophet who is still licking his wounds is a massive imperative: "Go" (19:15). *Go back* to the conflict, *go back* to the trouble, *go back* to the risk. The mission given him is to enact three anointings: Hazael as king of Syria, Jehu as king of Israel, and Elisha as successor prophet (19:15-16). There are problems with this mandate (a) because nowhere does Elijah ever anoint anyone, and (b) because we have no evidence that prophets were anointed. (On royal anointing, see 1 Kgs 1.) If, however, we take the address to Elijah as it stands, we will not linger over critical problems. We will, rather, see more clearly how dangerous is the prophetic office, how subversive the role of the prophet is to be! The anointing of the two kings is a maneuver whereby political coups are instigated. Of these imperatives, the only one we know about is the anointing of Jehu (accomplished by Elisha and not by

In the woodcut, the creative forces of nature—earth, wind, and fire—catastrophically catapult before a bowed Elijah. The "sheer silence" of God's Presence is communicated through the artist's deployment of a series of pietistic cherubs shown accompanying God, all surrounded in a cocoon of light.

Julius Schnoor von Carolsfeld. *The Lord Appears to Elijah*. 19th century. Woodcut. From *Das Buch der Bucher in Bilden*. (Credit: Dover Pictorial Archive Series)

Elijah) that brought a bloody end to the dynasty of Omri and Ahab (2 Kgs 9:1-13). It is not necessary to attribute any "magical" significance to an anointing, but only to see it as a powerful symbolic gesture that evokes a radical political vision and a due sense of "sacramental" legitimation for the coup. The oracle, moreover, knows that this authorized action only escalates the conflict, so that it is anticipated that there will be more killing. The expectation and authorization of killing echoes 18:40 and plays upon the zeal of Elijah that signals radical revolutionary, ideological activity that refuses any compromise (see vv. 10, 14). The theophany of vv. 11-12 yields revolutionary politics that are not rooted in any pragmatic calculation but are understood to be rooted in Yahweh's radical insistence that has its setting in the deep struggle of Yahwism with Baalism. It is difficult to imagine a more singular vision that is completely convinced of its own righteousness, so convinced that the "Yahweh party" will surely take no prisoners.

Almost as an afterthought, v. 18 seems to allude to and counter the self-preoccupation of Elijah in vv. 10, 14. Twice Elijah has complained, "I, I only am left." Verse 18 is a response: "Oh, by the way, you are wrong." You are not the only one left. There are 7,000 left who are loyal Yahwists and who have not given in to Ahab's new state religion. The number is a clear refutation of Elijah's sense of himself. He has no reason for self-pity. The Yahweh party is strong and vibrant. The refutation may also serve as an assurance. The movement is alive and well.

Elisha Recruited, 19:19-21

The final paragraph of vv. 19-21 is a bit enigmatic, but its intent is clear. Elijah has been mandated to anoint Elisha (19:16). But he does not. Instead he throws his mantle over him, the same mantle he used to protect himself from the theophany (19:19; see 19:13). We may simply take the two dramatic actions—anointing, wrapping in a mantle—as synonymous in their significance. Either way, Elisha is recruited as the follower and successor of Elijah.

It is not clear why the narrative presents the "call of Elisha" as it does. The call itself is nonverbal (19:19). There is only a dramatic act that both parties understand. Elisha understood it as a summons to "follow" (19:20); in the end he does "follow" and becomes Elijah's aide (19:21). But between his acknowledgement and his response, Elisha must set things right at home (19:20-21a). He asks leave to kiss his parents farewell and he offers a great feast. We are not told why, only that Elijah permits him to do so. No judgment is passed on his action, and it does not really seem to matter. What counts is that he "left" (everything) and "followed." He is, by the end of the unit, fully Elijah's recruit and, by implication, Yahweh's man. He has been inducted into the revolutionary party of Yahweh, perhaps to join the killing, certainly to share the risk. There is no small irony in the movement of the chapter: at the outset Elijah is afraid and filled with self-pity; he has withdrawn. At the end, he is prepared to carry on. He recruits Elisha without a word about the risk or the cost. The transformative events that move him from fear to resolve are only two: He is fed by an angel, and he is addressed by a voice. He is compelled by a mandate and an assurance that are beyond his comprehension and certainly beyond the horizon of the king. The God who feeds and addresses is on the move; the prophets of that God are consequently underway with their dangerous alternative.

CONNECTIONS

Immediately after the contest at Carmel, this chapter features a deeply exhausted prophet at risk for his courageous act of faith that entailed a showdown with his opponents, the opponents of Yahweh. The narrative concerns the restoration of a man of faith who, through the dramatic movement of the chapter, is carried from despondency to fresh energy and militancy. That dramatic restoration, however, is not accomplished here through psychological attentiveness, for if anything the narrative is psychologically unconcerned. Rather the transformation wrought through the narrative is by the theological, that is, God-rooted ministrations that are inscrutable and beyond comprehension. Elijah does not need to "understand"; he needs only to receive.

We may identify several remarkable incidents in this drama of restoration. In his fear Elijah is alone in the wilderness, a place without life supports. Indeed, he wishes for death. But his death-wish (we might say depression) is met by the attentiveness of an angel (19:5-7), an agent of God who comes to be a resource for life where none is available. Twice the angel commands him to "get up and eat." Twice he eats and is restored. The narrative exhibits no curiosity about the angel. It tells and is prepared to accept that Yahweh dispatches agents and representatives who bring resources of sustenance into places where there are none. It is a recurrent affirmation of Israel's faith that Yahweh's visitation makes contexts of death into arenas of life. And if Yahweh has been declared victor over Baal, then it does not surprise us that such angels may come where death seems regnant.

The closest parallel to this ministration, perhaps, is the visitation of the angel to Hagar (Gen 16:7-13; 21:17-19). In this story as well, the angel embodies and bestows life support in the wilderness. In Christian extrapolation, Matthew 4:11 notes that when Jesus was in the wilderness, "angels came and waited on him," so that his wilderness became a place of sustenance. It is evident that in faithful Israel, angels as ministering presences are assumed as a normal part of Yahweh's sustenance. Indeed, Israel's trustful poetry offers protection by Yahweh's angels in the most dangerous places:

> For he will command his angels concerning you
> > to guard you in all your ways.
> On their hands they will bear you up,
> > so that you will not dash your foot against a stone.
> You will tread on the lion and the adder,
> > the young lion and the serpent
> > you will trample under foot. (Ps 91:11-13)

The landscape of life for the faithful is laden with Yahweh's good resources.

Elijah replicates the life of Moses (19:8), being forty days and nights in Horeb (Exod 24:18). He is indeed presented as the new Moses, reconstituting Israel as a distinctive community in his own context. Moreover, the theophany of vv. 11-12a is reminiscent of the theophany at Sinai in Exodus 19:16-25. The deliberate references to Moses make the departure from the Sinai narrative in the "sheer silence" all the more drastic and dramatic. [Forty Days of Exposure]

The zeal of Elijah for the cause of Yahweh concerns his unqualified devotion and passion against the forces of Ahab and Baalism (19:10, 14). The wording in both statements involves an infinitive absolute, a grammatical stratagem that bespeaks enormous intensity. That same uncompromising passion for Yahweh is attributed to Phineas, grandson of Aaron and a priest (Num 25:11). Numbers 25 says that the zeal of Phineas for Yahweh has turned away the anger of Yahweh and protected Israel from destruction. In our text this rhetoric contributes to the intensity of the battle with Baalism and the indispensable role of Elijah in sustaining Yahwism. The effectiveness of Yahweh is carried by people like Elijah who refuse compromise and who appear to others as genuine fanatics.

It is evident that in this zeal, as often happens to the zealous, Elijah has overvalued his own significance. His zeal seems to

AΩ Forty Days of Exposure
Elijah's sojourn at Horeb for forty days and nights is intentionally parallel to that of Moses (Exod 24:18). The number is surely conventional. The same motif is taken up for Jesus (Matt 4:2; Luke 4:2). Forty days and nights in the wilderness becomes a figure for extreme testing to find out if the subject can live without normal life supports. We are not told of either Moses or Elijah that they did not eat. But clearly the period is a dangerous rendezvous with Yahweh testing what resources are available and what resources must be resisted with a characteristic consequence of renewed and vigorous obedience. Thus with Moses, the consequence is the episode of the Gold Calf (Exod 32) and the reconstitution of Israel. With Elijah it is reengagement with Ahab after a season of self-pity. With Jesus it is preparation for his entire destiny in the face of resistant authority.

be commensurate both with the urgency of the conflict and with the power of the theophany. Nevertheless, the final utterance of Yahweh checks Elijah's (self-serving?) zeal. In fact, it is not true that "I, I only am left." In truth there are 7,000 uncompromised, 7,000 unacknowledged by Elijah. His sense of his own importance has blinded him to the political shape of the conflict. There are allies he has not noticed.

The zeal of Elijah is not a mere theological, cognitive passion. The commitment to covenant comes to mean that Yahwistic loyalty in Israel has deep and—as we shall see—bloody political implications. Elijah is indeed deeply subversive. Ahab has in fact not misunderstood him as a troubler, at least for his dynasty. Faith-driven political passion is difficult to contain in conventional politics.

Yahweh's refutation of Elijah is taken up by Paul in Romans 11:4-5 in a "divine reply":

I have kept for myself seven thousand who have not bowed the knee to Baal. So too at the present time there is a remnant, chosen by grace.

The usual rendering of v. 18 as "I will leave" is weak, for the verb is "I will *provide* a remnant" (*sh'ar*).

Paul understands the theological significance of the verb and so understands a theological remnant of people who remain true to the gospel, a remnant "chosen by grace." Paul exposits a larger meaning of the text in his vexed argument about Jews and Christians, about law and grace. Thus the combative situation of

Elijah is transposed into a different contest, wherein "law" in Pauline terms becomes the new cipher for Baalism.

In the end, the several movements of angel visitation and theophanic dialogue serve a larger "either/or," for which Elijah is the front man. That either/or characteristically sets the deep, radical claims of Yahwism over against every religious accommodation. Elijah is a brutal, overassertive model of resistance, not terribly winsome or attractive. Characteristically those of his ilk who conduct such warfare on behalf of Yahweh are not winsome or attractive. We do not easily understand the either/or if we make it into a pretty picture. It is a stance that is faithful, so the narrative insists, but it is not pretty.

Elijah's uncompromising insistence comes to include Elisha as his disciple. It is useful to ponder, consequently, recruitment into the radical cause whereby we may consider the "Cost of Discipleship."[2] Signing on to radical Yahwism was not, in that ancient context, less than dangerous. It is, moreover, not difficult to spot contemporary contexts of such danger. Indeed, it may be, finally, that even our own context is dangerous for obedience, if we see things honestly enough.

The brief paragraph on Elisha is at best enigmatic (19:19-21). Curiously, Elijah throws a mantle over him, but does not anoint him (see v. 16). What counts is that he left his oxen and followed. The language is anticipatory of the rhetoric of Jesus' disciples in the Gospel of Mark:

Peter began to say to him, "Look, we have left everything and followed you." (Mark 10:28)

The same rhetoric evokes a profound assurance from Jesus:

Truly I tell you there is no one who has left house or brothers or sisters or mother or father or children or fields, for my sake and for the sake of the good news, who will not receive a hundredfold now in this age—houses, brothers and sisters, mothers and children, and fields *with persecutions*—and in the age to come eternal life. But many who are first will be last, and the last will be first. (Mark 10: 29-31)

The other parallel that may be suggested is the request of Jesus' disciple to finish business at home before discipleship (Matt 8:21). Jesus, in this case, is more demanding than Elijah:

Follow me, and let the dead bury their own dead. (Matt 8:22)

Whereas Elisha is permitted to finish at home, the respondent to Jesus is granted no such slack. Either way, the either/or of faith makes discipleship urgent. Elisha enacts that urgency.

NOTES

[1]Davie Napier, *Word of God, Word of Earth* (Philadelphia: United Church Press, 1976) 62.

[2]See Dietrich Bonhoeffer, *The Cost of Discipleship* (New York: Macmillan, 1955). Bonhoeffer's risky discipleship in oppositon to National Socialism is not unlike the theo-political system opposed by Elijah and Elisha.

WAR, DIPLOMACY, AND
PROPHETIC ZEAL

1 Kings 20:1-43

By the time we finish chapter 19, Elijah has been through what we might call his vocational crisis. We may expect him to reenter the conflict with Baalism. That reentry, however, is put on hold until chapter 21. In the present chapter 20, Elijah is absent, so that the chapter is something of an interruption in the larger narrative. As we shall see, however, the chapter is dominated by "a prophet" (20:13-14), a "man of god" (20:28), and "a company of prophets" (20:35-42). These odd characters are not named, but they surely are not unlike Elijah in their vision and in their function vis-à-vis the king. Thus the chapter, like the several Elijah narratives, serves the claim that prophetic authority and prophetic alternative continue to intrude upon and vex royal history.

The presenting problem of the chapter is Israel's endless conflict with Aram (Syria) that from time to time breaks out in combat. It is useful to recognize that Israel, presided over by King Ahab, and Syria are small companion states that have much in common, but that also, for the same reason, have much in dispute. In passing it is worth noting that the geopolitics of Israel vis-à-vis Syria remains unchanged until the present day. And therefore the current dispute between Israel and Syria over the Golan Heights is roughly a continuation of a very old dispute reflected in the present narrative.

COMMENTARY

Diplomacy and Posturing, 20:1-12

The chapter concerns a season of disputatious international negotiations (20:1-12), an Israelite victory over Syria (20:13-21), a second defeat of Syria (20:14-30), a treaty between victor and loser (20:31-34), and a concluding prophetic narrative that brings King Ahab under prophetic judgment (20:35-43). At least on the surface, the powerful internal dispute between Yahwism and Baalism is put on hold, except that the prophets, in the end, continue to be hostile to Ahab.

The narrative opens with negotiations between Ben-hadad of Syria and King Ahab (20:1-12). This is the first active sighting of Syria in our narrative, reflective of the rise of that state as an active player in the ninth century. For a long time after this initial intervention, Syria continues to be a factor in Israel's life, sometimes enemy, sometimes ally. Clearly the Syrian king, "Son of Hadad," is the aggressor. The continuing negotiations between the two kings is conducted in imaginative, hyperbolic language that likely characterizes the practice of that region. [When Hyperbole Is Misunderstood]

In the first round of negotiations, Ben-hadad threatens and Ahab concedes everything (20:1-6). Ben-hadad is the leader and spokesperson for a huge coalition of minor states, perhaps very modest city-states, that are fully armed and come against Samaria, Israel's capital city. For openers, Ben-hadad makes a sweeping threat concerning not only the royal treasury but also the royal family. Kings tend always to be after silver, gold, and women (see Deut 17:17). This may only be an opening bluster; or with such a coalition, it may be the real thing. Apparently Ahab is a much weaker party, for in his response, he concedes everything and resists nothing (20:4). But this may also be overstatement, and on the face of it does not yet amount to surrender. Ben-hadad, in a sweeping response to Ahab, must answer once more to say, "No, I really mean it" (20:5-6). The first round of negotiations leaves Ahab in a weakened position before Syrian bluster.

The king of Israel, however, is not a one-man show. He leads a government and he must consult with his major supporters, the elders (20:7). [Kingship Modified by Elders] For that reason there is a second round of negotiations that is not defined by the concessions of v. 4 (20:7-12). In the second round, Ahab reports to the elders that he did not "refuse" Syrian belligerence. But the elders veto the appeasement policy of the king (20:8). The relationship is not

---

When Hyperbole Is Misunderstood

It seems clear that Ben-hadad engages in the luxury of political hyperbole in vv. 5-6, 10. He threatens, in extreme language, complete confiscation and annihilation of Ahab's realm. Perhaps such braggadocio is to be expected in his environment, but it needs to be separated from policy. As it turned out, Ben-hadad was weaker then he sounded, not much of a threat to Israel.

I mention this piece of the narrative because it seems to me that U.S. foreign policy is regularly gullible and taken in by the hyperbolic rhetoric of small, renegade states whose rhetoric never matches reality. These leaders of small, under-developed states know this is an effective way to conduct policy that is short on real power.

unlike cases when the U.S. federal administration negotiates a treaty, only to have it rejected by the Senate. The elders are not so intimidated, not so ready to surrender as the king. As a result the king must return to announce to the Syrian king, "This I cannot do" (20:9). That is, "I cannot secure the support of the government for surrender."

In vv. 10-11, the two kings bluster in rich rhetoric. Ben-hadad dismissively declares that Samaria is as nothing and will not even provide dust—the emblem of complete diminishment—for the Syrians (20:10). Not to be outdone, Ahab must answer to show that he is not intimidated (20:11). He asserts that what counts is not initial braggadocio, but the one still alive at the end; that one, he implies, will be Ahab and not Ben-hadad. The second round of negotiations does not in fact advance anything, except our awareness of defiant rhetoric. In the end, Ben-hadad proceeds with the siege and keeps Samaria under threat. The narrative adds in passing, "He had been drinking on the job." He is, the text implies, out of control and therefore acting foolishly.

> **Kingship Modified by Elders**
>
> It is worth observing that Ahab, in the face of a Syrian ultimatum, must consult with the leaders before he makes war-policy commitments. Such consultation may be only political posturing to gather public support for the war effort. It may be a wise recognition, evident at least since the parley in 1 Kings 12, that the "consent of the governed" matters deeply to political Israel. The king in Samaria had to deal with political reality and was not free to conduct policy in a wish-world of rhetoric. This is perhaps a point not often understood by the prophetic community.

A First Victory, 20:13-21

Enough of talk! Now military action (20:13-21). But the battle is not sheer military operation (see Prov 21:30-31). It does not surprise us, given the perspective of the narrative of Kings, that the key element in the battle narrative is prophetic announcement (20:13-14). Indeed, the utterance of a "certain prophet" is decisive and contradicts our anticipation. We had been led to believe that the king of Syria was the stronger party. The word of Yahweh, however, is decisive, more than "The Equalizer." The prophet asserts tersely, "I will give it into your hand." The prophet, moreover, offers strategy: "By the young men." The prophet summons necessary leadership: "You." The king is dispatched to battle by the prophet. The entire mandate, moreover, is so that "You shall know that I am the Lord" (20:13). The promised victory is not to enhance Ahab nor even to protect Israel. It is to demonstrate the sovereignty of Yahweh, who will defeat Syria and the Syrian gods. [You Shall Know]

Ahab is responsive to prophetic initiative. He musters the leadership of "district governors" as the prophet directs. The king musters 7,000 soldiers. It is surely no coincidence that the number is equivalent to the 7,000 who in 19:18 have not given in to Baal. This is the irreducible core of Yahwists who will fight the battles of Yahweh. [District Governors]

The battle itself is simply implementation of prophetic assurance (20:16-21). It is in fact no contest. The king of Syria is still drinking to excess and is no worthy adversary. He orders the capture (not killing) of the Israelites. But Israel plays for keeps, seemingly more vicious and brutal than the Syrians. While the king of Syria himself escapes, his troops are routed. Israel wins and knows that Yahweh is the real winner. This victory parallels the one in 18:39, so that we may imagine doxological echoes in Israel of 18:39: "The Lord indeed is God, The Lord indeed is God."

AΩ **You Shall Know**

The formula repeated in vv. 13 and 28 is a most significant theological affirmation. Walther Zimmerli has seen how the formula, which becomes a crucial tag word in the prophecy of Ezekiel, is deeply rooted in the oldest traditions of Israel's faith. [Walther Zimmerli, *I Am Yahweh* (Atlanta: John Knox Press, 1982) 39-58.] To "know Yahweh" is to acknowledge Yahweh's governance and to respond obediently to that governance. Israel's endless theological work is to come to terms with the distinctive, uncompromising character of Yahweh.

A Second Victory, 20:22-30

The victory of Israel, however, is only provisional, and another round of combat is sure to come (20:22-30). The prophet warns the king of the need for continued military preparedness (20:22). The narrative shifts promptly to a Syrian strategy meeting (20:23-25). Perhaps the strategic analysis of the Syrians reflects the demographic reality of Israel. Israel is a hill-country people, and Yahweh is a hill-country God. The Syrian analysis imagines a severe limitation in Yahweh's capacity for governance and in Israel's military capacity.

The battle resumes (20:26-30). Again the contest is uneven. Again Syria is the stronger party, for Israel is "like two little flocks of goats," insignificant and vulnerable. Again a man of God speaks, in close parallel to v. 13 (20:28). The message is the same: Israel will win and Israel will know that "I am Yahweh." The battle serves the enhancement of Yahweh. But unlike v. 13, this time the

District Governors

The translation in the NRSV makes these soldiers sound like administrators. More likely, following John Gray and Roland de Vaux, these are a standing army (perhaps mercenaries) consisting of "shock troops" that are exceedingly mobile, quick, and effective. [John Gray, *I & 2 Kings: A Commentary*, OTL (Philadelphia: Westminster Press, 1963) 376-77; Roland de Vaux, *Ancient Israel: Its Life and Institutions* (New York: McGraw-Hill, 1961) 221.] A parallel occurs in the "Republican Guard" of Syria's Saddam Hussein. The verse seems to suggest crack troops who immediately carry out royal policy in effective and decisive ways.

prophet gives a theological rationale. The reason for Israelite victory and Syrian defeat in this second confrontation is that Syria has slandered Yahweh.

The Syrian judgment that Yahweh is disabled and vulnerable in the valley evokes Yahweh's ferocious intent. The limitation voiced by Syria is a claim that Yahweh's capacity is restricted. In response, Yahweh must vigorously execute the battle to demonstrate power and to teach Syria a lesson it is slow to learn. Again, as in v. 13, the issue is theological concerning Yahweh's unassailable reputation. The battle again enacts the oracle, and again Israel is victorious. Again Yahweh is vindicated. Indeed the battle is a rout and the Syrian army is massacred. Everyone either died or fled. There is no doubt about the outcome of the battle or its significance.

A Royal Exemption, 20:31-34

The single exception to the slaughter, the exception that concerns the narrator, is that the Syrian king escapes (20:30a-34). The conflict between Israel and Syria was long-standing, vigorous, and, when possible, brutal. (So it continues to be even now.) But kings are another matter. Quite often royal protocol dictates friendlier behavior among kings than policy permits. There is a bond between kings that causes personal consideration, perhaps because regicide may know no limits once it is begun.

In any case, these verses suggest a personal confrontation that is outside established war policy. The defeated and escaped king of Syria must run the risk of protection from Ahab. Partly as a ruse and partly as a genuine act of deference to the winner, he presents himself as a penitent loser. The narrative offers a highly choreographed negotiation between the two kings that may be understood through three particular phrases:

1. The advisors of Ben-hadad anticipate that the Israelite king is "merciful." This is the premise of the action. The Hebrew term is *ḥesed*, which means that he honors treaty commitments. The notion may strike us as odd, because it does not mean that the Israelite king acts out of emotional sensitivity; rather, the mutual interest of the two kings, perhaps grounded in old treaties, is more important than the present conflict. If we seek precedent for such *loyalty* on the part of Israelite kings, we may consider 2 Samuel 10:1, where David resolves to "deal loyally" (*ḥesed*) with the king of Ammon. But of course the ensuing narrative makes clear that such loyalty has limits. It is, in our narrative, the bet of Syria that these limits have here not been violated. [Royal Loyalty]

2. Ahab's response to Ben-hadad is, "He is my brother" (20:32). Again this response is not to be taken with any emotional overtone. Rather it is an acknowledgement of an older, already existing treaty arrangement. [The Royal Brotherhood] The king's judgment is that the old treaties transcend present conflict. For that reason, he is willing to make an accommodation.

3. The outcome is a treaty (*b'rîth*) between the two, a term we often render as "covenant" (20:34). The treaty is designed to create a pause in hostilities in the interest of both parties. It is evident, however, that Ahab has enormous leverage in the relationship, for (a) Ahab receives towns back (like an adjustment of boundaries after the last conflict when Syria claimed disputed territory), and (b) Ahab is given trade rights in Damascus. The gain for Ben-hadad is the preservation of his life and of his capacity to govern. The gain for Ahab is the recovery of territory and extended influence in the region. (On returned cities, see the parallel in 9:10-14).

In the world of *Realpolitik*, this is a commonsense deal. Seen theologically, the Israelite victory in the face of heavy odds is seen in prophetic formulation as a victory for Yahweh. Out of it, Israel is to know "I am Yahweh." There is no hint in the text that Ahab—masterful compromiser that he is—can look past himself to see the working of Yahweh. The king, characteristically, is unable to enter the perceptual world of prophetic discernment. The tension between sheer pragmatism and the principled, radical claim of prophetic Yahwism is fully apparent here.

A Prophetic Assault, 20:35-43

In the final episode of this complex chapter, we are back into the world of prophetic drama far removed from royal pragmatic (20:35-43). The episode, staged "by a certain [unnamed] member" of the prophetic guild, is, in fact, something like street theater. [Street Theater as Peasant Strategy] The narrative moves in

Royal Loyalty

We are dealing with "personal diplomacy" between kings. Such diplomacy is neither as cold or as formal as we know it, but it also is not a practice of intimacy. It is a world in which personal loyalty counts for a great deal. On the practice of loyalty in this text, Katharine Sakenfeld comments:

English speakers simply are not accustomed to thinking of loyalty as a category relevant to relationships between military archenemies. Since the connection between the parties appears to be based only in hostility, mercy may seem the more appropriate rationale for explaining what happens in this story. But the narrative leaves much unsaid. Could Ahab have achieved the resulting economic and territorial hegemony for Israel if he had slain Ben-hadad? Possibly not. Was the economic arrangement between their predecessors one made only under duress, or was it one involving mutual agreement and advantage? The text is not clear on this point. It does appear that despite the current warfare the narrator presupposes some prior history of relationship between heads of the two peoples. And even though the context is one of hostility, one characteristic feature of biblical loyalty is clearly present: appeal is made to one in power on behalf of one who is in desperate need.

Katharine Doob Sakenfeld, *Faithfulness in Action: Loyalty in Biblical Perspective*, OBT (Philadelphia: Fortress Press, 1985) 24-25.

three scenes, each exceedingly odd when seen from the perspective of state policy.

1. The "certain member" prepares himself for confrontation with the king (20:35-37). He needs to be beaten up so he can appear as a wounded war veteran. In fact this initial part of the narrative is rather incidental to the plot. He requires a colleague to beat him up, but the colleague refuses. As a consequence of his refusal, he is killed by a lion. The episode parallels 13:24-28, where it is equally clear that the lion is an instrument of prophetic enactment. The reference to the lion only indicates how odd and

AΩ **The Royal Brotherhood**
In addition to the pragmatics of cooperative diplomacy that checks ideological destructiveness, there is no doubt that kings practice a distinctive kind of solidarity with each other that overrides some other considerations. The appellation "brother" may bespeak some prehistory to the relationship, but it also refers to the formal relations of those bound in treaty. Michael Fishbane, in a study of Amos 1:11, has shown how "brothers" refers to treaty partners. [Michael Fishbane, "The Treaty Background of Amos 1:11 and Related Matters," JBL 89 (1970): 313-18.] In that text, the violating regime has "cast off all pity" (*raham*) that belongs to treaty obligations. In our text, the term *hesed* functions in the same way. Thus Ahab acts upon a treaty obligation that must be honored. It is this honoring of treaty obligations that, in the next paragraph, the prophetic figure condemns.

remarkable this account is, freighted beyond royal rationality. In light of the lion, a second colleague is readily persuaded to assault the certain member in order to create a necessary appearance. The lead character is now prepared to meet the king.

2. Upon meeting the king, the prophet tells the king a parable, not unlike the stratagem of Joab in 2 Samuel 14:1-11 and Nathan in 2 Samuel 12:1-5. He presents himself as a wounded soldier who has failed in his assignment of guarding a prisoner, of letting him escape through negligence. He is aware, inside the ruse against the king, that his failure of duty carries heavy penalty. The king, in response, need announce no judgment. The heavy judgment is

---

Ω **Street Theater as Peasant Strategy**
The ruse enacted by the prophet is something like "street theater," that is, conduct outside conventional expectation that is in part play. Such conduct is, however, not mere entertainment. Amos Wilder comments on the odd conduct reported in the New Testament:

We seem to see a movement devoted to soul saving, indifferent to politics, slavery, and other social patterns. But actually it was a guerilla operation which undermined social authority by profound persuasion. What no overt force could do it did by spiritual subversion at the level of the social imagination of the polis and provinces of the empire.

Amos Niven Wilder, *Theopoetic: Theology and the Religious Imagination* (Philadelphia: Fortress Press, 1976) 28.

The same subversive, carnivalesque quality of drama is, in more contemporary categories, enacted in Korean Minjung Theology that acts playfully against established authority. [*Minjung Theology: People as the Subject of History,* ed. Kim Yong Bock (Singapore: The Commission on Theological Concerns, 1981).] See James C. Scott, *Weapons of the Weak: Everyday Forms of Peasant Resistance* (New Haven: Yale University Press, 1987.) While such actions are playful, they may have profound and dangerous political consequences.

AΩ **Devoted to Destruction**

This phrase, "devoted to destruction," translates the Hebrew term *ḥerem*. While the term bespeaks violence, it is important to understand that it is an ideological violence, driven by a singular devotion to Yahweh. The term itself is etymologically linked to "harem," wherein wives are singularly devoted to "the king" who holds a monopoly of access and guards it as a life-and-death matter.

Thus according to radical Yahwistic ideology, Ben-hadad should have been executed as a way of offering a devotee of Baal to Yahweh. The term is reflected in the war ideology of Deut 20:17 that the NRSV renders as "annihilate," and especially in 1 Sam 15, where Saul is condemned and removed from office for sparing Agag and thereby violating *ḥerem*. Indeed, it is possible to see that Ahab's rescue of Ben-hadad parallels Saul's action in that chapter. By implication, Ben-hadad should be removed from the office of kingship as was Saul. It is not possible to voice in a more succinct way the radical Yahwistic ideology of an uncompromising sort than by the use of this term *ḥerem*.

---

already given in the very telling of the failure: The one remiss in duty either dies or pays. The king sees the case clearly.

3. Now the parable is translated for the king in order to apply to his own case. The king is taken up into the imaginative world of the parable. This is the only possible way to communicate truth to power when power refuses direct address. The parable lets the king see his own actions afresh. He is the one assigned to guard "this man" = Ben-hadad. He is the one who let him escape. He is the one derelict in duty. He is, therefore, the one under severe judgment. The culmination of the exchange is the utterance of prophetic judgment against the king (20:42):

Indictment. The king let escape a man "devoted to destruction." The phrasing in English hides the crucial Hebrew term *ḥerem* that designates a person or people to be annihilated in military action in order to eliminate a threat to the purity or separateness of Israel. [Devoted to Destruction] By the use of the term, the prophetic indictment draws the matter of the king of Syria into the most demanding, most brutal ideology of Israel, thus echoing yet again the harshest, most exclusive Yahwism that Elijah embodies. Ahab has compromised this ideology and so is on the wrong side of ideological warfare.

Sentence. The violation of that rigorous ideology will cost Ahab both his life and the life of his people. It turns out that the entire chapter and certainly vv. 35-43 exist solely in order to voice this hard condemnation of the crown. Ahab is placed under a prophetic death sentence. His death is as sure as that of Ben-hadad should have been.

It is no wonder that the king left "resentful and sullen" (20:43). The terms describing the king are not easy to render, suggesting not only vexation and upset but perhaps also defiance. His resistance to a prophetic rendering of reality is enormous. The prophetic confrontation, as part of the larger prophetic confrontation, is at least an unhappy nuisance. It is a nuisance, perhaps, like the Berrigan brothers who are resilient and incorrigible and refuse to quit. Over time such a visible nuisance can become a public relations problem for the crown, can take on political life and significance until it becomes a real threat to the government. One might not expect prophetic theater to have such force. But while such "public demonstrations" are irrational and outside policy channels, they occasionally become dangerous. When that happens, as in this case, the established authorities tend to have few options and little maneuverability.

CONNECTIONS

This chapter is part of the Elijah tradition, even though Elijah himself never appears in the narrative. The purpose of the narrative is to further the deep ideological struggle out of which Israel will be defined for the future. The presenting problem is the war with Syria that culminates in a political accommodation to the defeated Ben-hadad. Such a political accommodation very often would seem to be wise pragmatic policy, for in the real world of power, winners and losers must always deal with each other the next day, after the war.

That political accommodation, however, is the trigger for a countertheme. Woven into the narrative is another scenario of Israel's history, advocated and enacted by "a company of prophets" who seem to be a free, roaming collection of folk who are invested with odd (Yahwistic?) power and who owe no allegiance to established authority. Taken politically, they are a troublesome lot for all established authority. Taken theologically, they practice what Klaus Koch terms "metahistory," a sense of public reality not derived from royal authority, but governed in hidden ways by the immediate force of Yahweh.[1] Such a counterforce, championed by the narrative, is endlessly problematic for those who must govern.

The pivot points of this counterperspective are voiced in v. 13 and 28, which assert a victory of Israel beyond the expectation of military realism in order that Israel may *know Yahweh*, that is, acknowledge Yahweh's victory and sovereignty. Thus, theologically, the point is to advance the views of extreme Yahwists against an accommodating, compromising political perspective that is willing to deal in the real world with those who are not passionate Yahwists.

This chapter, as much as anywhere in the Elijah materials, may help us think clearly about the singleminded ideology of Yahwism. Taken as a theological statement, the claims are singular and appropriate to convinced faith. They assert that Yahweh counts decisively and that Yahweh's will will be enacted in public issues, established royal authority notwithstanding. Taken politically, however, we are able to see how demanding, how problematic, and perhaps how objectionable such ideology is, for the insistence of this prophetic, carnivalistic company is that the enemy should be killed—no

---

Faith Become Politics

The clash of prophet and king in this chapter is a model for the inescapable tension between faith and politics. The king practices "loyalty" toward his "brother" king, but there is no explicit theological dimension to the gesture. The prophet invokes the ideology of *ḥerem*. but gives no thought to the pragmatics of diplomacy or the enduring political realities. The ideological temptation to move in a simple, straight line from faith to politics is indeed hazardous. It represents the posture of a "true believer" who wants no slippage from belief-ful passion to public action. During the 1990s, a vigilante mentality in the U.S. wanted Saddam Hussein in Iraq "taken out." The same simplemindedness was present in many during the Cold War in the need to "Kill Commies."

The primary effort to counter such destructive ideology in recent time has been the work of Reinhold Niebuhr who understood that political "realism" must temper ideological zeal with the facts on the ground. Niebuhr endlessly warned against "The Children of Light" who know too readily and completely what must be done and what is right. In a sermon on Matt 13:24-30, on "wheat and tares," he writes:

> Winston Churchill, for example, was a very ambitious young man. His ambition gave him the chance to accomplish much. What he achieved was not only great statesmanship but had a quality of magnanimity that reminds us of the wisdom of the wheat and the tares.
>
> Thus human history is a mixture of wheat and tares. We must make provisional distinctions, but we must know that there are no final distinctions. "Let both grow together until the harvest." Man is a creature and a creator. He would not be a creator if he could not overlook the human scene and be able to establish goals beyond those of nature and to discriminate between good and evil. He must do these things. But he must also remember that no matter how high his creativity may rise, he is himself involved in the flow of time, and he becomes evil at the precise point where he pretends not to be, when he pretends that his wisdom is not finite but infinite, and his virtue is not ambiguous but unambiguous.
>
> From the standpoint of biblical faith we do not have to despair because life is so brief, but we must not pretend to more because we are so great. Because we are both small and great, we have discerned a mystery and a meaning beyond our smallness and our greatness, and a justice and a love which completes our incompletions, which corrects our judgments, and which brings the whole story to a fulfillment beyond our power to fulfill any story.

Reinhold Niebuhr, *Justice & Mercy,* ed. Ursala Niebuhr (Louisville: Westminster/John Knox Press, 1974) 57, 59.

The prophet in our narrative had less patience with "the tares" from Damascus.

compromises, no prisoners. No objection can be made to the theological claim. When taken with political literalness, however, such a perspective contributes endlessly to ever fresh cycles of brutality.
[Faith Become Politics]

In our own time, there is a kind of simplistic, vigilante politics of extremism that wants public policy to be organized by the mandates of "pure faith." There are no conclusions here, but we cannot miss the problematic character of such an enterprise. More reasoned, more pragmatic, more agile understanding indicates an interpretive maneuverability (slippage?) between theological affirmation and political enactment. The prophetic dissenters may make a powerful force in opposition; as we shall see with Jehu (see 19:16), when such dissent takes power, the outcomes tend to be neither pretty nor affirmative.

NOTE

[1]Klaus Koch, *The Prophets: I, The Assyrian Period* (Philadelphia: Fortress Press, 1982) 5 and *passim*.

A CLASH OVER LAND

1 Kings 21:1-29

The ideological war we have seen in chapters 18–19 and chapter 20 continues, only now framed by property rights. The narrative divides into two parts, the dispute over land (21:1-16) and the prophetic response to the royal practice of land (21:17-29).

COMMENTARY

Naboth against the Crown, 21:1-16

The dispute about land is presented as a dispute between one seemingly defenseless man, Naboth, and the crown (21:1-16). But the personal confrontation is in fact a dispute between conflicting theories of land ownership. Naboth represents, in the narrative, an ancestral notion of land whereby land and owner are inseparable; the land is an "inheritance" and the family belongs undeniably with and upon the land. The alternative theory, embraced especially by Jezebel the non-Israelite, views the land as at best a commodity to which the crown has special and privileged claim. Ahab, it seems, is ambiguous about the matter. While he acquiesces in the scheme of his wife the queen, he himself does not resist Naboth's refusal to trade land.

The king proposes a trade of properties (21:1-4). We have no hint that the proposed trade was in any way unfair. Ahab seems to make a reasonable offer and gives a reasonable motivation for the offer (21:2). Naboth's refusal, however, indicates the problem with the offer. The property is "inheritance" (*nahalah*) and cannot be traded. Ahab has wrongly seen the land as a tradable commodity, and made an offer that must on principle be refused. [Property as Inheritance] Ahab is not coercive and does not press the point. But he is enormously unhappy. The phrase "resentful and sullen" is reiterated from 20:43. Ahab is undone by the vision of radical Yahwism, whatever form it may take.

Jezebel, great foe of Yahwism, intervenes and refuses to give Naboth the last word…or the property (21:5-14). When she learns the detail of the rejected trade (21:5-6), she invites the king out of his depression (21:7). The rhetorical question she asks him is both a

Jean Francois Millet. *The Angelous*. 19th century. Oil on canvas. Museé d'Orsay, Paris, France. (Credit: Giraudon/Art Resource, NY)

AΩ Property as Inheritance

The notion of inheritance *(nahalah)* is intimately linked to a tribal notion that land and its occupants are inseparable. [On this notion of land, see W. D. Davies, *The Gospel and the Land: Early Christianity and Jewish Territorial Doctrine* (Berkeley: University of California Press, 1974) especially 3-48; Gerhard von Rad, "There Remains Still a Rest for the People of God: An Investigation of a Biblical Conception," *The Problem of the Hexateuch and Other Essays* (New York: McGraw-Hill, 1966) 94-102; and Johs. Pedersen, *Israel: Its Life and Culture I-II* (London: Oxford University Press, 1926) 81-96.] In the social processes of economic transaction, however, deals are made that eventually separate some people from their land. Two texts indicate practices (or at least notions) of how elemental land rights may overcome the consequences of other modes of economic life. In Jer 32, Jeremiah is mandated to secure the land of his family:

> Hanamel son of our uncle Shallum is going to come to you and say, "Buy my field that is at Anathoth, for the right of redemption by purchase is yours." Then my cousin Hanamel came to me in the court of the guard, in accordance with the word of the LORD, and said to me, "Buy my field that is at Anathoth in the land of Benjamin, for the right of possession and redemption is yours; buy it for yourself." (Jer 32:7-8)

[See Walter Brueggemann, "A 'Characteristic' Reflection on What Comes Next (Jeremiah 32:16-44)," *Prophets and Paradigms: Essays in Honor of Gene M. Tucker*, ed. Stephen Breck Reid, JSOT Supp. 229 (Sheffield: Sheffield Academic Press, 1996) 16-32, on this text.

The ensuing narrative describes in detail how the land must be protected and secured. Notice that the family agent is a "redeemer" who refuses the usurpation of land by others.

More grandly, Lev 25 proposes a practice of *Jubilee*, wherein land is returned to its proper owner every forty-nine years. Sharon Ringe has suggested that such a radical notion of land management was operational in the horizon of Jesus.

Sharon H. Ringe, *Jesus, Liberation, and the Biblical Jubilee*, OBT (Philadelphia: Fortress Press, 1985).

While questions remain about the historical practice of land redemption and Jubilee, there is no doubt that the Naboth narrative is situated in such an ideological point of reference that intended to resist commoditization.

reprimand and an invitation: (a) Shame on you for not being king! (b) Be the king that you are! She immediately resolves to secure the land, by hook or by crook. It may be that she is simply ruthless and dishonest. More likely she assumes that a king, like her father the king of Sidon, is entitled to whatever land he wishes. [Royal Claims on Land]

Her plan is to frame Naboth so that he must be executed, whereupon the land will revert to the crown (21:8-14). The royal act of instigation is to write letters. It likely should be recognized that writing is a skill of the privileged, a way of enacting formidable power in a benign and invisible way. The act of writing may suggest an important analogue to 2 Samuel 11:14, where David writes what turns out to be Uriah's death warrant. In both cases, shameless "reasons of state" evoke hidden violence through writing. The queen offers concrete instruction to create a mob scene built around the prohibition of Exodus 22:28. The plan (21:9-10) is precisely executed (21:11-13). Naboth is dead! The owner of the land is eliminated!

All that remains is royal confiscation (21:15-16). Jezebel, in v. 7, had commanded Ahab to "rise *(qûm)* and eat." She is the one who commands; the king obeys. Now, with success in hand, she says a second time "arise *(qûm)*, possess the land." He silently obeys, thus appropriating the land he has wanted since v. 2. The narrative is complete. The royal claim is undeniable. Everything works as planned by the queen. Without any visible activity, Ahab receives land denied him by old peasant land theory. The score: king 1, peasants 0.

Prophetic Judgment on Land-Grabbing Royalty, 21:17-29

Now, as the royal story ends, the prophetic narrative begins (21:17-29). Just when Jezebel had imagined royal authority to be absolute comes the counterauthority of "the word of the Lord" (21:17). Yahweh addresses Elijah with the same imperative verb that Jezebel twice spoke to Ahab: "Arise *(qûm)*, go down." The king is to be found in the newly confiscated vineyard still called "the vineyard of

---

📖 Royal Claims on Land

The king came to stand at the apex of a practice of land confiscation, but the king was by no means its only practitioner. The prophetic polemics of eighth-century prophets protest vigorously against acquisitiveness that destabilizes and displaces:

> Ah, you who join house to house,
>   who add field to field,
> until there is room for no one but you,
>   and you are left to live alone in the midst of the land!
> (Isa 5:8, see Mic 2:1-4)

See D. N. Premnath, "Latifundialization and Isaiah 5:8-10," JSOT 40 (1988): 49-60.

We may also notice the assumption that the kings can redeploy land at their will, as in 1 Kgs 9:11-13. More specifically, we may notice that the narrative of Ziba and Mephibosheth (2 Sam 9:1-13; 16:1-4; 19:24-30) readily assumes the capacity for David to reassign land. It is this theory of land that Ahab and Jezebel seek to enact and Naboth resists.

Naboth." Royal manipulation does not alter the true identity of the land!

Yahweh instructs the prophet to give the king a simple speech of judgment (21:19):

Indictment (in the form of a question): *You have killed and taken possession.* The rhetoric is parallel to the indictment uttered by Nathan to David, though the wording is different (2 Sam 12:9). The two charges are murder and taking what is not rightly his. The second indictment may appeal either to the commandment about stealing or about coveting. Either way, the king has violated Torah: Naboth was killed on phoney charges of Torah breaking, but the king and queen are the real Torah breakers.

Sentence: The king will die an ignoble death as has Naboth. [Sin and Judgment in Prophetic Theory]

Sin and Judgment in Prophetic Theory
The working of vv. 20-21 is not completely clear in the NRSV; for in fact the conduct of v. 20 and the threat of v. 21 are parallel:

…to do evil in the sight of the LORD your God
…I will bring evil on you….

The evil Ahab has practiced is to displace and kill Naboth. The evil Ahab will now receive is displacement and death, so that deed and consequence are completely commensurate. Ahab will have done to him (in spades) what he has done to his neighbor.

Patrick D. Miller, *Sin and Judgment in the Prophets : A Stylistic and Theological Analysis* (Chico: Scholars Press, 1982) has demonstrated the close and intentional correlation between affront and punishment in much of prophetic discourse.

Upon divine instruction, the prophet meets the king (21:20-29). In their first meeting, Elijah had been the "troubler" (18:17). Now he is "my enemy" (21:20). And of course Ahab has seen correctly what Elijah is up to. Elijah, rooted in Yahwism and committed to the peasant community, is indeed a determined adversary of royal ideology. Now the prophet proceeds to declare to the king a speech of judgment (21:20-24). While Yahweh has instructed the prophet (21:19), Elijah takes liberties to offer a much more insistent and unflinching statement than the one given by Yahweh.

The speech against the king has escalated matters. The indictment is "evil in the eyes of Yahweh," a rhetorical advance beyond v. 19. The sentence is "evil" (disaster) so that the *evil* of the king evokes the corresponding *evil* of Yahweh. The verbs "consume" and "cut off" are brutal and decisive, more violent than the divine sentence of v. 19. Now the threat is not only to the person of Ahab (as in v. 19), but concerns the entire dynasty and entourage of Ahab. (The same escalation of rhetoric happens with Amos and Amaziah in Amos 7:10-17.) The dynasty will end as the two previous Israelite dynasties of Jeroboam (14:10-14) and Baasha (16:3-4). We might have expected "the House of Omri" to be more durable than the preceding dynasties, but the practice of a public ethic of exploitation is the death knell for any regime in Israel. The prophets regularly place monarchy in deep jeopardy because the stubborn purposes of Yahweh will not tolerate royal exploitation.

The sentence against Jezebel, the number one enemy of Yahweh, is a considerable advance beyond v. 19, where she is not even mentioned (21:23-24). The threat against Jezebel is conventional and comprehensive. The pairs "city-country," "dogs-birds" echo the prophetic threat of 14:11 (against the house of Jeroboam) and 16:4 (against the house of Baasha). The terms mean to be inclusive, everything from A to Z. The judgment is massive and without qualification. While prophetic rhetoric is familiar to us, it is important to see how the *destruction of one peasant* evokes *total dismissal of the dynasty.* Parallel to the old Jewish saying "to save one life is to save the world," now the destruction of one life is as though the crown had ravaged all of creation. It will not be tolerated by Yahweh.

The text must at some point have ended with the devastating termination of the dynasty in v. 24, for the verse has a tone of finality. The present text, however, includes two other addenda. The first, in vv. 25-26, intensifies the condemnation of Ahab. As the parentheses of NRSV indicate, vv. 25-26 appear to be an explanatory editorial note, designed to make sure no one misunderstands why this massive judgment has been unavoidable. Ahab is trapped in his evil, and Jezebel is implicated with him. The narrative strives for hyperbole and can hardly find a reference point for such appalling evil. Appeal here is beyond appeal to the ignoble precedents of Jeroboam and Baasha. The narrative must go outside of Israel to find a comparison bad enough: it is the Amorites, the ones so evil they merited expulsion from the land. The inference is that Ahab and his ilk are justifiably "driven out." The notice includes the irony that the very action of *seeking to secure land* produces the most massive *expulsion from the land.* The historian perhaps has an eye on the coming expulsion from the North in 2 Kings 17:

> Then the king of Assyria invaded the land and came to Samaria; for three years he besieged it. In the ninth year of Hoshea the king of Assyria captured Samaria; he carried the Israelites away to Assyria. He placed them in Halah, on the Habor, the river of Gozan, and in the cities of the Medes.
>
> This occurred because the people of Israel had sinned against the LORD their God, who had brought them up out of the land of Egypt from under the hand of Pharaoh king of Egypt. They had worshiped other gods and walked in the customs of the nations whom the

LORD drove out before the people of Israel, and in the customs that
the kings of Israel had introduced. (2 Kgs 17:5-8)

The second addendum of vv. 27-29, curiously enough, in a modest
way mitigates the harsh prophetic judgment above; oddly this *mit-
igation* is in tension with the *intensification* of vv. 25-26. This final
paragraph was perhaps added to acknowledge the (inexplicable)
fact that Ahab was not immediately "cut off," thus to bring the
prophetic verdict into harmony with the visible data.

The addendum that qualifies prophetic judgment is of interest
on theological grounds, whatever may be the historical grounding
for it. Ahab is presented as deeply penitent in response to prophetic
judgment (21:27). This itself is unexpected, for Ahab had been
seen as grossly resistant and recalcitrant. We have noticed, however,
that in vv. 1-4, he did not himself have the stomach for usurpation
that was engineered by Jezebel. While he gladly receives the outcome of her devious work, he does not undertake it himself. This
may suggest that he himself, distinct from Jezebel, is recognized as
having some sensitivity to Yahwistic claims, though he does not signal that in any earlier action. In any case, the narrative is at pains to
certify his penitence by heaping up five terms: *he tore; he put on; he
fasted; he lay; he went.* He gives visible expression to his turn to
Yahweh, even though the prophetic speech of judgment had held
out no hope for rescue by any eleventh-hour act of remorse.

In any case, Ahab's act of repentance is enough to convince
Yahweh of the seriousness of the king, so that the immediate threat
of judgment is modified. The judgment holds, to be sure, so that
the dynasty will end in disaster (see 2 Kgs 10:1-17). Judgment pronounced by the Yahwistic party against a dynasty of compromisers
does not surprise us. Rather, we take notice of the modicum of graciousness on the part of Yahweh. Two texts occur to me that
contain parallel accounts of Yahweh's openness and graciousness. In
the book of Jonah, the prophet announced the destruction of
Nineveh:

Forty days more, and Nineveh shall be overthrown! (Jonah 3:4)

In response the people of Nineveh and the king commit acts of
penitence, not unlike those of Ahab. Indeed, the king seizes upon
the theological chance:

Who knows? God may relent and change his mind; he may turn
from his fierce anger, so that we do not perish. (Jonah 3:9)

In response, God revoked the intended punishment:

> When God saw what they did, how they turned from their evil ways, God changed his mind about the calamity that he had said he would bring upon them; and he did not do it. (Jonah 3:10)

[God's Change of Mind] The God of Israel is not bound by decree, even God's own decree, but responds on the spot to the emergent in the relationship.

A more symmetrical, reflective statement of this same dimension of Yahweh is offered in Jeremiah 18:7-10:

> At one moment I may declare concerning a nation or a kingdom, that I will pluck up and break down and destroy it, but if that nation, concerning which I have spoken, turns from its evil, I will change my mind about the disaster that I intended to bring on it. And at another moment I may declare concerning a nation or a kingdom that I will build and plant it, but if it does evil in my sight, not listening to my voice, then I will change my mind about the good that I had intended to do to it.

God's Change of Mind

The evidence of this text indicates, but does not say, that Yahweh has had a change of mind. This is no problem in the narrative presentation of Israel. Such a conviction, at which the narrative expresses no surprise, is however a problem in some scholastic forms of theology that imagine that since God knows all, God need never change. Perhaps the most interesting text related to this term is 1 Samuel 15. Verses 10 and 35 affirm that Yahweh's mind has changed; but v. 29 asserts that God will not "recant." The relation of these texts to each other requires some considerable interpretive agility. Readers for whom this issue is problematic may benefit from the exposition of Terence Fretheim and Francis I. Andersen and David Noel Freedman.

Terence E. Fretheim, *The Suffering of God: An Old Testament Perspective*, OBT (Philadelphia: Fortress Press, 1984); Francis I. Andersen and David Noel Freedman, *Amos: A New Translation with Introduction and Commentary*, AB 24A (New York: Doubleday, 1989) 638-79.

Consistent with this quite intentional theological affirmation, Ahab gains a respite from the judgment. As we shall see in the next chapter, the delay in punishment is less than convincing. In the event, however, we are able to see an important dimension in Yahweh's inclination toward Israel and its rulers.

CONNECTIONS

This narrative is a clear model of the ideological battle in ancient Israel that swirls around the figure of Elijah. The struggle has many dimensions to it; in the end, however, the radical Yahwists hold to a deep and uncompromising "either/or" that is identified in a variety of cases. Here we may note three aspects of that struggle.

First, the story of Naboth turns on conflicting theories of land possession. Naboth embodies and articulates a theory of land inheritance whereby land belongs in and with and for a family, tribe, or clan as its inalienable place of belonging, living, and safety.

Thus he is unable to sell or trade his land, because his land is not a commodity but a "place to come to." Against such a view, Jezebel, reflective of the non-Israelite world of Sidon, understands land to be a tradeable commodity over which the royal house has privileges and rights. It is completely beyond her understanding why Naboth will not or cannot trade or sell, and therefore she undertakes "radical measures." In the framing of the narrative, it is unmistakable that a tribal notion of land as inheritance is seen as integral to revolutionary Yahwism, and conceiving land as commodity is a practice of exploitative Baalism. [Competing Systems]

While the issues take somewhat different shape in the contemporary world, the fundamental disputes about land persist. Capitalism, now taking the form of a global economy, threatens to reduce all holdings to tradable commodity. In the face of such a system, "holdouts" for tribal lands are at an immense disadvantage. The conflict has been decisively chronicled in another context by John Steinbeck in *Grapes of Wrath*, which portrays depression-crippled, propertyless Okies reduced to virtual slavery and complete economic helplessness when all the land is owned by growers. The problem is exacerbated, as Steinbeck has shown, by the power of absentee owners who care neither for the land nor for the workers. In our time, it is the endless force and authority of *commodity* that threatens to undo the fabric of community. All of that is in the early stages of development and is present in our narrative.

Second, the struggle is presented as one between king and prophet, who are taken throughout the Elijah narratives as representative figures bespeaking social perspective and social interest. The king, reenforced by his wife, speaks and acts for a usurpative theology of land. Our narrative is arranged so that this "royal narrative" is complete at v. 16. It appears to be a complete narrative in and of itself. The tone of v. 16 is one of finality.

The exception is that v. 16 is followed immediately by another narrative, beginning in v. 17, that features the prophet as the key player, consequently reducing the king to an object of prophetic-divine action. The shape of the final form of the text is to insist that kings cannot have a complete narrative of their own without prophetic intrusion. From that we may derive the conclusion that the commodity theory of land will always be disrupted by a distributional insistence. The point is urgent in contemporary society in which bureaucracy and technology together would seem to make the commodity system immune to dissent and disruption. This ancient story insists that the commodity theory will never be safe and uninterrupted, precisely because disadvantaged persons make common cause with the power of Yahweh through the unintimidated voice of the prophet.

Third, a minor note is to observe this tension between harsh, insistent judgment and a hint of forgiveness and reconciliation. In the Elijah verses, to be sure, the speech of judgment predominates, so that the prophetic utterance against Ahab (21:20-24) is even more severe than the word offered by Yahweh in v. 19. The rhetoric of judgment is escalated in prophetic implementation. The tension, however, is in the curious addenda of vv. 27-29. This note suggests that even Ahab, the one under deep prophetic threat, the one likened to the Amorites, can turn and be forgiven. It is possible for practitioners of commodity theory to change and become obedient to the truth of distributional theory. It is possible...the sanctions here are not lifted, but they are postponed and to that degree qualified. The concession is modest, but it is significant when we consider the intensity of the struggle. An analogue might suggest that, in our time, we are not fated to destructive commodity theory. Different choices could be made; different policies could be implemented. Different gods could be served.

Competing Systems

Marvin Chaney comments on this dominating tension in ancient Israel:

As long as the freeholding peasants of premonarchic Israel retained their own "surpluses" and were bound together in a covenant of mutual assistance, such crises could be weathered, albeit with difficulty. Once the monarchic state and its ruling elite began to extract "surpluses" to pay for luxury and strategic items, however, the peasants' margin grew slimmer. Peasant producers were forced to borrow if natural disaster struck, and the only surpluses to be borrowed were in the hands of the large landlords. For collateral a freeholding peasant family had only its land and its persons. Usurious interest rates insured frequent foreclosures, debt instruments thus serving to transfer land from redistributional to patrimonial domain and to reduce previously free and independent peasants to landless day laborers or debt slaves ...more and more of what had once been considered *Yahweh's* land passed into fewer and fewer *human* hands.

Marvin L. Chaney, "You Shall Not Covet Your Neighbor's House," *Pacific Theological Review* 15 (Winter, 1982): 11-12.

Thus our chapter must not be read as a simple one-on-one confrontation but as a decisive clash of systems.

AHAB'S LAST VENTURE

1 Kings 22:1-53

Ahab, son of Omri, king in Samaria, is reckoned to be a great king, but also a target of revolutionary Yahwism. His reign begins, in this narrative, in 16:29-34. It has featured Elijah, great champion of Yahwism and great adversary to Ahab and his compromising faith. In the present chapter, the reign of Ahab is brought, by the narrator, to an ignoble end. The present chapter consists in the juxtaposition of *prophetic intervention* (22:1-28) and *military report* (22:29-40). The chapter concludes with two notes on the monarchy concerning, in turn, Jehoshaphat of Judah (22:41-50) and Ahayiah of Israel (22:51-53).

COMMENTARY

Prophetic Intervention against Royal Plans, 22:1-28

The presenting problem of the narrative is Israel's seemingly endless war with Syria (Aram) over disputed territory that lies between them. War with Syria was an enduring preoccupation of the Northern Kingdom (see chapter 20), and continues even now over what is more or less the same disputed territory (the Golan Heights). The narrative begins with royal consultation between Ahab and his Southern counterpart, Jehoshaphat (22:1-4). It is worth noting that the long-standing war between North and South has abated (see 12:24), so that the two kings may now act as allies. It is clear, moreover, that Ahab is the initiator of the military alliance in which Jehoshaphat willingly participates, perhaps because Israel is so much stronger that he has no option. The exchange between the two kings is brief. Ahab asserts that the disputed territory of Ramoth-gilead belongs to Israel and not to Syria (which of course is what disputatious kings always say) (22:3). Jehoshaphat does not dissent but pledges his complete military cooperation (22:4). The struggle over land here, as often, is seen to be worth dying for and killing for. Thus the mounting of the campaign is quick and without elaboration.

But this narrative is not in fact a story about a war. That is only the presenting problem. The real issue, as in the preceding chapters, is the deep struggle for Yahwism in the face of compromised alternatives championed by Ahab and Jezebel. In this narrative, Jehoshaphat (who appears abruptly and has not yet been formally introduced into the narrative) is the vehicle whereby the question of Yahwism is introduced into the narrative. Against Ahab's sheer pragmatism, Jehoshaphat asks about *the will of Yahweh* (22:5). Perhaps Jehoshaphat is genuinely pious, or the narrative wants us to see a Judean king at his Yahwistic best, or this is only a narrative device for posing the question. In any case, his insistence in v. 5 is a huge turn in the narrative, opening the way for the prophetic confrontation to follow. His insistence, moreover, invites us immediately to a radically different notion of public power. Yahweh is a key player in international affairs! Yahweh has a purpose in international transactions. The mobilization of state power is made penultimate by his awkward insistence. The remainder of vv. 6-28 are an implementation of the king's uncompromising requirement for divine approval. When the issue of Yahweh is raised in this narrative, a prophet will not be long in coming, for it is *the human agency of prophets* that makes available *the transcendent will of Yahweh*. All parties agree to the linkage of Yahweh and prophets. For that reason, prophets must be mobilized in order to satisfy the enquiry of the king. The insertion of *prophets* into royal *war making* is a characteristic maneuver of this Deuteronomic narrative. But beyond that, it is a characteristic move in the biblical insistence that the public realm—as in royal war-making—is an arena in which Yahweh's purposes are decisive.

"The king of Israel" is responsive to the insistence of Jehoshaphat. (It is instructive that in this long narrative Ahab is not mentioned by name until the concluding formula of v. 39. It is as though the narrator, finally, cannot bear to say his name.) The conclave between the kings is conducted in Samaria, Ahab's home turf,

---

Zedekiah and Hananiah

This particular Zedekiah, a stooge for the crown, appears only here (22:11, 24). In addition to his commitment to establishment policy, he is of interest because he engages in "street theater," a prophetic symbolic act. His action in making "iron horns" to signify Ahab's capacity to "gore" Syria is illuminated by the street theater of Jeremiah and Hananiah in Jeremiah 27–28. In that narrative, Jeremiah wears a wooden yoke to signify submission to Babylon as the will of Yahweh (27:2). His adversary, Hananiah, believes that the "yoke of Babylon" is temporary and fleeting and so dramatically breaks the yoke of Jer (28:10). In response, Jeremiah now offers an iron yoke that cannot be broken, in order to signify the durability of Babylonian domination (28:13-14). In both narratives, the horns or yoke of iron articulate the inescapable outcomes of public policy, in each case with a claim linking policy to the will of Yahweh. While the iron yoke of Jeremiah is bad news and the iron horns of Zedekiah are intended to be good news, in both cases the prophets make policy claims for Yahweh.

for Jehoshaphat "came down to the king of Israel" (22:1). Consequently, Ahab is able to respond to the request that Jehoshaphat makes for prophets. Indeed, he has 400 of them at hand, a number that echoes the large round numbers of 18:19. Ahab is flooded with prophets! These prophetic figures are friendly to Ahab and therefore, from the perspective of the narrative, they are accommodating prophets who echo what the compromising king wants to hear. The policy question is mobilization for war: "Shall I go to battle [for disputed territory], or shall I refrain?" (22:6). The answer is prompt and unambiguous: "Go to war." The prophets are amenable to war fever. The national mood—always pumped up by royal propaganda—is always in favor of taking [back] territory. The prophets voice no more than conventional jingoistic support for royal policy. They have no critical distance from the king, and therefore they offer no serious second opinion.

Jehoshaphat, loyal Yahwist that he is (see v. 43a), insists on a "prophet of Yahweh" (v. 7), a characterization not assigned to the preceding prophets. While Micaiah, the one who operates with critical distance rooted in Yahweh, is summoned, we are told about other prophets, including Zedekiah, who appear in the throne room to advocate war. [Zedekiah and Hananiah] The throne room is busy with advocates: "Go up, go up, go up!"

Micaiah, the one already known to be contrary (22:8), is summoned (22:8, 13). The royal messenger who summons him to court offers to the prophet a little friendly royal advice: "The king needs your support; make it easy on yourself" (22:13). The messenger assumes, as did everyone at the court of Ahab, that prophets exist in order to advance royal policies. (Obviously the messenger did not know about Elijah and had not yet read chapter 21.) But Micaiah, completely in character, resists any such buy-off and asserts his freedom from royal manipulation and his singular commitment to Yahweh (22:14). [On Prophetic Freedom and Prophetic Mandate] The brief exchange of vv. 13-14 provides an epitome of the deep ideological struggle of king and prophet that is a battle for the future of Israel.

When Micaiah comes before the two kings, he is completely unintimidated and unaccommodating (22:15-28). Indeed, it is clear that he seizes the initiative and dominates the consultation. Ahab puts to him the same policy question already posed for the 400: "Shall we go up?" Micaiah, moreover, gives the same response as the 400: "Go up and triumph." He seems to have taken the advice given in v. 13. He is favorable to the king's war policy. That should have been the end of the matter, for prophetic opinion is unanimous, just as the kings wanted it to be.

Ahab, however, is not fooled (22:16). He knows better. Perhaps he knows better because there are still traces of awareness of Yahweh in his consciousness. Perhaps he knows better because deep down the war effort is not justified. More likely, he knows better because the guileless, simple, direct, uncompromising quality of the prophet is irresistible. The prophet cannot lie with a straight face. And so the king, hearing what he wants to hear, knows better and rejects it. He insists on "the truth" in the name of Yahweh. That, of course, is what Jehoshaphat wanted and what Micaiah had come to say. We are treated to prophetic playfulness that delivers severe judgment. Micaiah, now mandated to tell the truth, opens with a quick vision report (22:17). He saw a *scattering*. The word is ominous. It refers to exile, displacement, and defeat. "No shepherd"

On Prophetic Freedom and Prophetic Mandate

Prophets in Israel utter words that are often outrageous and beyond social acceptability. Such prophets regularly insist, however, that such utterances are not by their choice. Rather they are mandated and compelled and have no option. They must speak the word given them. This inescapable requirement is acknowledged by Balaam:

> Whatever he shows me I will tell you.... Must I not take care to say what the Lord puts into my mouth?... Did I not tell you, Whatever the LORD says, that is what I must do?... Did I not tell your messengers whom you sent to me, If silver and gold, I would not be able to go beyond the word of the LORD, to do either good or bad of my own will; what the LORD says, that is what I will say? (Num 23:3, 12, 26, 24:12-13)

The situation is no different with Amos (3:8) and Jeremiah:

> But if they had stood in my council,
> then they would have proclaimed my words to my people,
> and they would have turned them from their evil way,
> and from the evil of their doings. (Jer 23:22)

One may understand this conclusion in some formal, mechanical way, as though God has the prophet by the throat and forces the utterance. It is, however, also possible to understand the compulsion as a deeply felt sense that the word is so urgent and the truth so obvious (even if rejected), that one dare not keep silent. One's whole life is focused on this utterance that simply must be said out loud. This is not an attempt to reduce theology to psychology, but to recognize that the compulsion is a felt sense of self as a voice preoccupied with God's resolve:

> Because they have spoken this word,
> I am now making my words in your mouth a fire,
> and this people wood, and the fire shall devour them. (Jer 5:14)

means the death of the king and the termination of the dynasty. [On Shepherds and Scattered Sheep] He imagines a scene of social chaos in which reliable order has completely broken down. In the larger narrative, Micaiah is anticipating the end of Samaria. In our narrative, he speaks of the defeat and death of Ahab. Now the king has "the truth" according to "the word of the Lord." But of course he does not welcome it and will not receive it, accusing the prophet of an inability to voice any good news (22:18). The prophet, characteristically, is in a bind. His offer of *good news* has been rejected as phoney. His offer of *bad news* is rejected as hostile.

He is, however, undeterred in his resolve. Now he explicates the vision of v. 17 (22:19-23).[1] He reports a meeting of the "Divine Council." [The Divine Council] Like other faithful prophets, this prophet claims to be given access to the arena of "the gods" who meet in concert and determine policies that will be enacted in the earth. In the vision, Yahweh (of course) is the lead God who presides. All other gods are attendants and advisors to the true God. In the vision, it is Yahweh who wants Ahab to go to war. The key term is "entice"

AΩ **On Shepherds and Scattered Sheep**

The imagery of *failed king* (=shepherd) and *exiled people* (=scattered sheep) is engaged in vv. 35-36. Without the royal leader, the army disintegrates. On a larger scale, the same twofold imagery is used to indict the kings of Jerusalem (see Ezek 34:2, 5-6). This reference is to the exile to Babylon as a result of failed kingship. The same imagery is utilized in Jesus' great feeding miracle, where he gathers the scattered to feed them as a shepherd should feed the flock:

> He had compassion for them, because they were like sheep without a shepherd. (Mark 6:34)

In this latter case, the enactment of Eucharist is seen, in Christian tradition, as an exile-ending miracle (22:41).

This mosaic fills a lunette on one of the walls of a mausoleum which was built for the Roman Empress Galla Placidia, who was buried there in 450.

Good Shepherd. 425–450. Mosaic. Mausoleum Galla Placidia, Ravenna, Italy. (Credit: Alinari/Art Resource, NY)

AΩ The Divine Council

This peculiar vision reported by the prophet is the most graphic offer of a "council of the gods" in the Old Testament, a portrayal of an arena of decision making beyond human decision making. But there are recurrences of the same motif in other places in the text (see Jer 23:18-22, Amos 3:7, Ps 82:1). The most graphic presentation is in Isa 6 wherein the prophet is given access to the heavenly throne room where the fate of Israel is sealed. It is suggested, moreover, that the many voices reported in Isa 40:1-11, together with the plural imperative of v. 1, reflect a like conversation. The negotiation between God and Satan in Job 1:6-12; 2:2-7 surely reflects such imagery and the chorus of "angels" at Bethlehem are likely announcing a decision of the divine council concerning the appearance of King Jesus (Luke 2:9-15). The imagery attests to a will other than our own operative and decisive in the world.

See Patrick D. Miller, Jr., *Genesis 1-11: Studies in Structure & Theme*, JSOT Supp. 8 (Sheffield: Dept. of Biblical Studies, 1978) 9-26, E. T. Mullen Jr., *The Divine Council in Canaanite and Early Hebrew Literature* (Chico: Scholars Press, 1980).

This panel focuses upon doxological utterance, with angels raising their voices in praise of humankind's redemption through the lamb of God.

Jan van Eyck. *Musical Angels* from the Ghent Altarpiece. Cathedral of St. Bavo, Ghent, Belgium. (Credit: Scala/Art Resource, NY)

(pathah). It is neither wise nor sensible that Ahab should undertake war. Indeed, it is a foolish policy that cannot succeed. But Yahweh wants the war to happen in order that Ahab may be killed in battle, for the real intention of Yahweh's foreign policy is the death of Ahab and the defeat of the party of theological compromise. Ironically, Ahab, at the outset, has already been "enticed" and is already determined to go to war, that is, already determined to go to his foolish death.

The prophet reports the vision of a general discussion among members of Yahweh's government seated in heaven. For the moment, the decision to be made is not obvious to the council; therefore a lot of opinions are offered by members of the council. In the end, one "spirit," that is, one of the lesser members of the body, volunteers: "I will seduce him." In answer to Yahweh's query about method and strategy, a plan is offered: "I will cause prophets to lie to him." The plan is approved by Yahweh, who authorizes the policy and anticipates its success (22:22). The concluding verse 24 is a subsequent comment by the prophet to the king: "The plan has worked." Yahweh has beguiled Ahab, who is, in the face of wiser policy, resolved to go to war…and to death. The vision of the prophet is offered as a teasing retrospective on what has already been enacted; Ahab has already been seduced toward his death. In prophetic clarity, however, "Yahweh has spoken evil for you." The vision is a remarkable narrative achievement. The vision of Yahweh moves at every point to parallel and undermine the royal deliberations of Ahab. The outcome is to show that Ahab's deliberations are, in the end, irrelevant. The decrees that count are made elsewhere, beyond the reach of the king. Ahab is caught up in the tides of policy under the authority of Yahweh, the very God whom he has, through all of these narratives, refused to acknowledge. Micaiah is as good as his word: "Whatever the Lord says to me, that I will speak" (22:14).

Micaiah is clearly an enemy of the regime (22:24-28). He is first taunted by Zedekiah, the one who has predicted a Syrian defeat (22:24-25; see v. 11). But the prophet is unintimidated and stands his ground against prophetic challenge. And after prophetic challenge comes royal detention (22:26-28). The king imagines, as kings always imagine, that to restrain the prophet is to deter the oracle. The king attempts silencing. [On Silencing] But again, the prophet is bold and defiant (22:28). The only possible negation of his prophetic word would be *shalom* (= peace, victory). Micaiah has anticipated *disaster (ra')*, the very antithesis of *shalom* (22:23). The prophet is very sure. As we shall see, shalom is completely beyond Ahab. The seduction has worked! Ahab is enticed to his own destruction. The war fever out of which he acted is a consequence of divine connivance!

On Silencing

King Ahab thought to eliminate the Word of the Lord by imprisoning and abusing the prophet. It is of course a recurring strategy among Israelite kings to imagine they can eliminate the superseding purpose of Yahweh by silencing the messengers. The most dramatic parallel case in the Old Testament is that of Jeremiah. He is brought to trial for his sermon threatening Jerusalem and is saved only by the intervention of "village elders" (Jer 26:10-19). On other occasions he is imprisoned, accused of deserting (37:13-16), accused of treason (38:4), and is assigned to a cistern (38:6; see Luke 13:34).

But of course, such a practice of silencing is not limited to the ancient world. It is, in our own time, the predictable practice of established power to silence contrary voices, hoping to eliminate the subverting threat of their words and symbolic actions. It is easy to observe, in retrospect, the silencing of the Soviet Union (chronicled by Solzhenitsyn) and in its satellite in such spectacular cases as that of Havel. [See especially Alexander I. Solzhenitsyn, *Gulag Archipelago* (San Francisco: Harper Collins, 1991); and Vaclav Havel, *Open Letters: Selected Writings 1965–1990* (New York: Vintage Books, 1992).] But we do not need to go abroad for we can, closer home, observe the fearful treatment of Daniel and Philip Berrigan. [On the Berrigan brothers, see M. Polner and James O'Grady, *Disarmed and Dangerous* (New York: Basic Books, 1997). For an even more relentless effort at silencing, see Taylor Branch, *Pillar of Fire: America in the King Years 1963–65* (New York: Simon & Schuster, 1998), an exposé of the single-minded resolve of J. Edgar Hoover and the Federal Bureau of Investigation to silence and destroy Martin Luther King, Jr.] In our own time, moreover, the church has found it prudent to silence those who question long-standing authority. Of course, in every case, as in the case of Micaiah, imposed silence does not work, because the truth has a life of its own.

In this engraving, Ahab is shown in his chariot, located at the pinnacle of a hillside in the field of battle. His head is backlit by the sunset upon which he gazes as he clutches his chariot.

Gustave Doré. *Death of Ahab* from the *Illustrated Bible*. 19th century. Engraving. (Credit: Dover Pictorial Archive Series)

Military Implementation of Prophetic Verdict, 22:29-40

The battle report is nothing more than an artistic enactment of the divine decree (22:29-36). The two kings go to war, heeding the advice of the accommodating prophets. The story, however, does not concern a war of people against people or state against state. On both sides, the combat is intensely personalized. Everything pivots on King Ahab, who is to die. Ahab seems to know. He disguises himself as an anonymous soldier, in contrast to Jehoshaphat, whom he sets up as the highly visible royal target. The Syrian army, moreover, is commanded to focus only upon Ahab; never mind anyone else. Evidently the Syrian army has been recruited into Yahweh's scheme to depose Ahab. It turns out that Ahab's demise is the single, prior purpose of the entire war effort!

Jehoshaphat, who seems always the lesser party in the coalition and submissive to Ahab, does not protest and offers himself as the visible king (22:32-3). By any ordinary outcome, Jehoshaphat should have been promptly killed. But this is no ordinary struggle. This is a battle designed from on high for a single purpose. And so, remarkably, Jehoshaphat is exempted from the killing. But the more staggering turn of events is the killing of Ahab, now masquerading as a peasant soldier. There is, it turns out, nowhere for Ahab to hide; he cannot hide from the relentless negative purpose declared by Yahweh:

> But a certain man drew his bow and unknowingly struck the king of Israel between the scale armor and the breastplate. (22:34)

It was all "an accident." The NRSV inserts the term "unknowingly" so that we do not miss the point. The soldier had no notion whom he had killed. But Yahweh knew, because Yahweh was singularly devoted to this assassination.

The story of Ahab ends with a bit of royal bravado (22:35-36). Ahab stayed in his chariot, propped up because he would not quit. Even mortally wounded, he would not yield to purposes beyond himself. And so he died thick in his own blood, shed according to divine decree. By the end of the day, his troops get the point: The king is dead, the battle is lost…retreat! "Let each go *in peace*" (22:36; see v. 17). Of course this is not the peace of which Micaiah defiantly speaks in v. 28. It is only escape from battle and the death-dealing policies of Ahab. It was intended by the gods to "go up to Ramoth-gilead"…but not "to succeed." God has intended otherwise! The narrative adds a summary formula for the reign of Ahab that began in 16:29-34. He has been an important king, attested by his "ivory house" and "all the cities he had built," emblems of royal achievement and success. The success, however, is incidental. The narrative is focused elsewhere. They took his blood-ied chariot back to Samaria. They hosed it down and the blood —the blood of the king!—ran off to the ground. The dogs came and lapped it up. Royal blood for dogs! This is exactly what Elijah had promised:

> In the place where dogs licked up the blood of Naboth, dogs will also lick up your blood. (21:19)

The total "disaster" *(ra')* to come upon the dynasty is still in the future (21:29). But there is enough disaster for the king (21:23). The word of the Lord has prevailed. Ahab's venturesome alternative to Yahwism has failed. Some might have thought his death was simply the turn of state policies. But our narrator knows better.

With the death of Ahab, the great ideological struggle is nearly over. The tension that has brought us to the end of 1 Kings is now somewhat relaxed. The narrative has yet to add only two royal notations in order to keep the royal timeline complete and symmetrical.

The Good King Jehoshaphat, 22:41-50

First, we are offered a quick summary of Jehoshaphat, king of Judah for twenty-five years (22:41-50). Even prior to this formal introduction, we have already seen him early in the chapter as the submissive partner to Ahab. Aside from a religious verdict, we are given here only one curious piece of data from his reign (22:47-50). He equipped a fleet for international commerce, based in Ezion-Geber in the South and headed for Ophir. The reference to Tarshish-type ships may suggest that Jehoshaphat was seeking to revive the commercial enterprise of Solomon before him. For reasons not revealed to us, the venture failed. Of interest to us is his refusal to join in the commercial enterprises of his Northern counterpart, Ahaziah. The narrative is terse, but we may suggest that the refusal is part of his attempt to separate himself from the Northern regime so bent on self-destruction. It may be that the insistence of v. 5 reflects the same differentiation on the part of the Southern king, but we are told nothing. We are told only that he "made peace" with Samaria (22:44). That "peace" was surely necessary in order to have freedom for commercial ventures. The narrative seems to hint, however, that it was an uneasy peace, perhaps only prudential, perhaps leveraged by the greater power of the North.

The theological verdict on Jehoshaphat is cautiously affirmative (22:41-46). He is, from the perspective of this narrative, not a purely Yahwistic king, for the "high places" lingered (see 1 Kgs 3:2). For the most part, however, he "did not turn aside" from Yahweh (22:43). Most particularly he exterminated heterodox cultic practices offensive to Yahwism (22:46). He reigned twenty-five years and perhaps accomplished more than interested our narrator. [Jehoshaphat's Judicial Reforms]

> **Jehoshaphat's Judicial Reforms**
> Our narrative has no principal interest in Jehoshaphat beyond his engagement with Ahab and Ahab's son. The more extended account of his reign in 2 Chronicles 17–20 offers a more vivid tradition about him, though important questions of historical reliability of the text must be faced. Whatever may be decided about the historicity, it is evident that the memory of Jehoshaphat provided important energy for Israel's enduring imagination. Specifically attention may be called to 2 Chr 19:4-11 where it is reported that the king instituted an important judicial reform (see vv. 6-9 and compare Exod 18:13-27).

The Quick Reign of Ahaziah, 22:51-53

The second king mentioned as an addendum is Ahaziah, son of Ahab, who reigned two years in Samaria (22:51-53). We are told nothing of him here, beyond a negative theological verdict. 2 Kings 1 ends his narrative account with his concluding formula in 1:17-18. Here we know only that he continued the political-theological practices of "his father and mother" (Ahab and Jezebel), thus he was as objectionable to this narrator as were his parents.

The reports on Jehoshaphat (22:41-50) and Ahaziah (22:51-53) interest the narrator only incidentally. The ending of the scroll of 1 Kings and the literary break in the continuing story between 1 Kings and 2 Kings refer to the death of Ahab. The ideological dispute enacted by Elijah (and Micaiah) swirls around him. His death effectively ends the dynasty of Omri with the story of his two sons given only as a mop-up action for this narrator. The death of Ahab "according to the word of the Lord" effectively ends the struggle and therefore the literary unit.

CONNECTIONS

The heated ideological struggle we have observed since chapter 17 continues here and reaches its culmination. For that reason, previous "connections" I have suggested pertain here as well.

It is important to recognize that this is no ordinary account of public history and it does not intend to be. The narrative contains a deep and determined dimension of unfamiliarity, and we must not seek to domesticate it according to our commonsense categories. The first "unfamiliarity" is the interplay of royal and prophetic perspectives. The royal perspective—that may be understood as ordinary, commonsense establishment thinking—is not at all odd to us. We inhale it every day. It is the assumption that dominant state power and dominant economic power allied with the state power needs always to act to protect its own interests, to sustain its honor and to maintain its credibility. All manner of brutality and stupidity can be done in the interest of such "reasons of state." Even in a democracy, moreover, permission and support for such ventures is relatively easy to muster, given propaganda, sloganeering, and manipulation of public opinion. As with the 400 prophets, the religious leadership is widely expected to follow the line of dominant ideology...and almost always does. "The interests of the dominant class become the dominant interests."2 This is completely familiar to us.

What is unfamiliar to us is the prophetic resistance of Elijah and Micaiah and the ground for such resistance. The resistance itself is the insistence that Yahweh's purposes are not readily collapsible into state policy, thus countering the royal assumption. Yahweh is not simply an echo of dominant opinion and is not primarily a legitimator of entrenched power. Micaiah's opening self-announcement in v. 14 is about an unfettered word that will not be accommodated. The claim is an affirmation that there really is a communicated will of God standing outside public control that can be and must be announced.

More odd for us than the claim itself, moreover, is the way in which that claim becomes known, by entry into the "divine council." We may admit, on the face of it, that the imagery of "divine council" is a mythic construction or an act of poetic imagination. We may see in it the attempt of the prophetic traditions to find a way to voice, imagine, and portray an authorization that supersedes all worldly authority. Having said that the imagery is mythic or poetic, however, is not to dismiss the claim. This is the way in which the prophetic tradition rather consistently imagines, because it holds, without compromise or embarrassment, that Yahweh administers a deciding mechanism for the future of the world over which the kings

The Limits of Human Wisdom

Undoubtedly human learning and human reflection are crucial for statecraft. Public leadership does not need any "dumbing down." That fact was fully appreciated in ancient Israel. But the same wisdom traditions that celebrated the human capacity for governance also recognized that such human capacity finally comes face to face with the inscrutable ways of God that make all human wisdom penultimate. Gerhard von Rad has recognized a series of powerful wisdom sayings that attest to this important awareness (Prov 16:2; 16:9; 19:21; 20:24; 21:2; 21:30-31). [Gerhard von Rad, *Old Testament Theology vol. 1* (San Francisco: Harper & Brothers, 1962) 439, *Wisdom In Israel* (Nashville: Abingdon Press, 1972) I:97-110.]

It is astonishing but regularly the case that human power succumbs to arrogance and hubris that culminate in destruction. In our time the most dramatic cases, of course, are those of Adolf Hitler and Joseph Stalin.

have no control and to which kings have no direct access. Given a rationalistic view of the world, such a claim is outrageous. But for any one who has a notion of *holiness* at the core of *human history*, an even more outrageous claim is the ready assumption of modernity that powerful people and governments (and corporations) are the ultimate deciders of human history who can plan so well and own so powerfully and implement so carefully that there is no slippage. The "divine council" is a rhetorical strategy for deabsolutizing human pretense and for allowing a willful instability at the center of world history. [The Limits of Human Wisdom] The temptation to absolutize visible authority is a very old temptation of public power.

The End of Human Control

Those with great power regularly imagine they will have it their own way. In the Old Testament, the quintessential figure with such "an attitude" is Nebuchadnezzar as portrayed in the book of Daniel. Reduced to animal life, he did indeed learn otherwise the hard way that,

> the Most High has sovereignty over the kingdom of mortals, and gives it to whom he will. (Dan 4:25)

In our own time, an example of such hubris is voiced in the book of Francis Fukuyama, *The End of History*, that celebrates the end of Western democratic capitalism in the world. [Francis Fukuyama, *The End of History and the Last Man* (New York: The Free Press, 1992).] Such an illusion does not reckon with the irreducible surge of people—a God-given undeniable urge of people—toward freedom and justice that will not finally be held in thrall by "our victory." The theological dimension of such a limit is nicely voiced by Stacy Johnson in his commentary on the work of Karl Barth:

> Perhaps it is this interplay between the real and the problematic, between the call for confession and the need for ongoing construction, that has caused some interpreters to see a permanent instability in Barth's theology.... It is true that Barth sought to reclaim the biblical story; but it is not true that the biblical story forms a theological resting place or "given." If there is an "instability" in Barth's theology, it is there for a reason. "The truth," Barth said, "demands complete openness."

The apparent instability that Barth maintains between realism and constructivism, ironically, is actually meant to provide a stability of a certain sort. The interplay between the real and the problematic, which is ceaseless, assures that we will neither deny the mystery of God nor presume to reduce that mystery to our own fallible constructions. In the first place, the category of "mystery" is not an abstraction void of content, as though mystery signaled a blank ignorance of God, but represents concrete Christian conviction. Against the sort of untethered constructivism that would dissever the task of theology from its nexus in Christian meaning, the mystery is that God is "for" us and "with us" in Jesus Christ, and the grace of God is mediated "in" and "among" us by the power of the spirit.... In the second place, there always remains more about God that needs to be said. The grace of God is "for" us; but there is always more to learn about the depths of that claim.

William Stacy Johnson, *The Mystery of God: Karl Barth and the Postmodern Foundations of Theology* (Louisville: Westminster/John Knox Press, 1997), 188-89.

And with recent technological developments, the temptation becomes even more acute. The political-economic-military planners know much and do much. But, insists this narrative, not finally. Finally there is another power at work before whom all other power must yield, willingly or not. [The End of Human Control]

It may disturb us that the divine deployment of "lying spirits" is so ruthless and unprincipled. Such a worry, however, is to hold the mystery of God's governance to our particular standards of morality. This text does not argue for morality. Rather, it argues for willful inscrutability that operates in, with, and under human events in order to curb and finally overthrow excessive human ambition.

This leads to our second major "connection." The *prophetic narrative* (22:1-28) and the *battle report* (22:29-36) are oddly and loosely connected. The prophetic narrative decrees the death of Ahab (22:23). But the narrative resolve is hidden and unclear. It is not straightforward and it is not highly transparent. Thus the way in which this resolve of heaven is implemented is through an "accidental" arrow shot by an unwitting archer at an unidentified soldier that finds its way through layers of armor to create a pool of royal blood. How odd! How odd indeed! The workings of God in human history could be explained in other ways, perhaps easier, more credible ways. That chance killing, however, is sufficient for our narrator. This account dares a connection between *divine resolve* and a *chance arrow*. It could be accident. It could be (bad) luck. It could be fate. Here it turns out to be active divine governance. No doubt this odd claim challenges the reasonable among us, as it must have in ancient days. Such is the scandal of faith where "God acts in history." The ideological revolution, against the great odds of the military-political establishment, proceeds in such inscrutable ways, leaving only blood for dogs and a demanding interpretive task.

NOTES

[1]It is plausible that the vision is a deliberate stratagem to parallel the "royal council" of Ahab and to show that at every turn the "divine council" overrides and negates the "royal council" that in truth has no authority.

[2]The statement is a programmatic insight of Karl Marx. See David McLellan, *The Thought of Karl Marx: An Introduction* (London: Macmillan, 1972) 46.

2 KINGS

ONCE MORE,
KING OVER PROPHET

2 Kings 1:1-18

Elijah continues to dominate the narrative. He has been in deep conflict with the Omri dynasty and especially with Ahab, son of Omri (1 Kgs 18:17-18). Indeed, he has long since pronounced a death sentence upon the dynasty, a death sentence our narrative takes with complete seriousness (1 Kgs 21:19-24). In the present chapter, the prophet confronts one of the sons of Ahab, Ahaziah, who lasted on the throne only two years (1 Kgs 22:51). He is inconsequential to the royal narrative and serves only as an occasion for the exhibition of prophetic authority.

The chapter is introduced by a curious note about Moab, but nothing is made here of that data (see 3:4-5). The chapter is organized around a prophetic death sentence pronounced against the king (1:2-4) and the implementation of that death sentence (1:17-18). Between the two, the narrative features a fourfold interaction between king and prophet who at first meet only through the mediation of royal messengers and then finally face to face. Notably, the royal party to the confrontation is never named, but is only "the king." The fourfold dramatization in fact does not advance the plot at all, but only heightens the tension and delays the outcome of v. 17.

COMMENTARY

The Initial Prophetic Sentence, 1:2-4

The king is injured in a fall. The fall is of no interest to the narrative, but only creates the circumstance for what follows; apparently in the end the king dies from that fall. Everything turns on the royal strategy for healing: Appeal to Baal-zebub! [Baal-zebub] Very little may be said specifically about this god, nor for that matter do we know anything about the religion of Ekron, a Philistine city. What counts for the action is that the king has sought help outside Israel and outside the governance of Yahweh. The narrative is indifferent to the particular identity of the god of Ekron in any particular way. This

Baal-zebub

This particular name for a god is known nowhere else. We are therefore left to speculate about its meaning. The first part of the name, "Baal," is of course well known, the god who is Lord and Master, who fructifies, gives life and health. Thus appeal to this god for healing must have seemed unexceptional. Plausibly, "zebub" is simply a subset for a local version of the Baal who is known more broadly. The term "zebub," however, is difficult. It is possible that the term means "fly," thus "Lord of the Flies." [Reference might usefully be made to William Golding, *Lord of the Flies*, Penguin Books (New York: Viking Press, 1997) that tells an unbearable tale of dehumanizing anarchy. Golding apparently has in mind that the "Lord of the Flies" is an instrument for unlivable chaos.]

The alternative is that "zebub" is a deliberate mistake for *zebul* (prince) a mistake designed to denigrate the god. In fact we do not know the meaning of the term. For our purposes, it is enough that this god, an opponent of Yahweh, is rejected by the narrative and defeated in the narrative, shown to be useless and powerless.

---

god belongs to the generic Baal that endlessly tempts and propels the dynasty of Omri (see 1 Kgs 16:31-32). The act of appeal to Baal-zebub signifies a royal disregard of the singular claim of Yahweh who, according to this narrative, is the only legitimate resource of life or healing in Israel.

The royal management of the process of healing for the king is ominously interrupted: an angel! Elijah is an inexplicable character in the narrative and an unfathomable presence in this royal history. He lives in another zone, reachable by divine messengers who deabsolutize royal authority. The point is intensified when we remember that the term "angel" is also "messenger," so that the *messenger of Yahweh* dispatches Elijah to meet *the messengers of the king*. The Samaritan king and King Yahweh both have messengers, so that the encounter is "royal power" versus "royal power."

A Death Sentence

The particular phrase, "surely die," is repeated three times by the prophet (1:4, 6, 16). While the phrase looks commonplace in English translation, it is in fact a quite severe, absolute, and formal pronouncement of a death penalty from which there is no escape or reprieve. The same formula is used in a series of commandments in Exodus 21:12-17, weakly translated in NRSV as "put to death." The formula is also the pronouncement of Yahweh to the first couple in the garden (Gen 2:7; echoed in 3:3). These parallels attest to the severity and firmness of the prophetic utterance to the king.

Elijah is given the exact terms of a prophetic speech of judgment he is to pronounce when he meets the messengers of the king. The *indictment* in v. 3 takes the form of a question. But it is no question. The prophet knows: "Yes, you did appeal to this other god! Yes, you acted as though Yahweh had vacated office as God." The sentence of v. 4 is inescapable, introduced by a characteristic "therefore": "You shall surely die." [A Death Sentence] The die is cast. This king, like his father Ahab, is on notice. There is no viable alternative to Yahweh.

The Drama of Confrontation, 1:5-16

Now begins a fourfold series of meetings, carefully conducted on the part of the king, through surrogates and mediators. There is a great deal of coming and going, of ascending and descending, since the awesome prophet is located in a high place. In the first narrative account (1:5-8), the royal messengers report back to the king the exact words of the prophetic indictment and sentence (v. 6). The king asks only one question and promptly identifies the source of the threat to the royal house: It is Elijah (1:8)! The king recognizes the appearance of the hairy man who dresses like an untamed outsider. [The Untamed Outsider] But the king also recognizes the cadences of Elijah's speech. Who else would assert the death of the monarch?! The royal identification of the prophet means that the king now knows what every hearer of this story already knows. The Great Destabilizer is on the move. The son's identification of the prophet echoes the verdict of the father, Ahab: Elijah is "Troubler" (1 Kgs 18:17), "Enemy" (1 Kgs 21:20).

The second moment of drama is a royal summons to the prophet (1:9-10). The king dispatches fifty men to the prophet. While we might take this as a negotiating party sent by the king, the number fifty suggests a military expedition. The king utters an imperative: "Come down." The utterance is terse. It might be an invitation to parlay. The flat imperative, however, suggests it is a command, designed to apprehend, perhaps silence, perhaps eliminate the prophetic threat.

The Untamed Outsider

Elijah is here portrayed as "hairy with a leather belt." That is, he is something of a wild man not readily conformed to civil society. This is in keeping with his initial entry into the narrative in 1 Kings 17:1-6 where he is the characteristic outsider reliant upon food outside the royal domain.

Christian readers will not fail to make connection to John the Baptist, Jesus' forerunner. John is characterized in a parallel way as an outsider:

Now John wore clothing of camel's hair with a leather belt around his waist, and his food was locusts and wild honey. (Matt 3:4)

Subsequently Jesus celebrates John by contrasting him with any accommodation to "soft robes":

What then did you go out to see? Someone dressed in soft robes? Look, those who wear soft robes are in royal palaces. What then did you go out to see? A prophet? Yes, I tell you, and more than a prophet.... Truly I tell you, among those born of women, no one has arisen greater than John the Baptist. (Matt 11:8-11)

In both cases, Elijah and John, the quintessential outsider brings the message that ordered society can scarcely bear. Nothing here of "soft robes"!

The prophet, however, is immune to royal imperative. He does not even acknowledge the summons. He disregards it and asserts his own counterauthority. Elijah, so sure of his dignity, is willing to be tested. He—and the narrative—regard the title "man of God" as one of immense authority, well beyond royal control. The prophet, moreover, will not only talk. He will act. He summons fire and devours the fifty men of the king. The prophet controls the very powers of creation! The royal house should have known this, because the narrative has long since made clear that the dynasty has not even power to overcome the drought (1 Kgs 18:1-6). Moreover, Elijah is unlike the priests of the royal house who are helpless to summon any powerful gods (1 Kgs 18:26-29). Here the prophet inflicts on the king an embarrassing defeat, obliterating his troops. Everyone can see where real power resides.

The third dramatic moment is an exact replay of the second (1:11-12). Again the king dispatches fifty men. Again the royal summons is issued. Again the prophet counters with fire. Again the royal troops are destroyed. Everything is the same, except the royal imperative. In v. 9 it was "come down." Now in v. 11, it is "come down *quickly.*" The adverb intensifies royal urgency, no doubt because of the intensification of royal anxiety. But to no avail. Royal imperative will not impinge upon prophetic authority. Again the prophet beats the king in a humiliating way.

AΩ Messengers

It is important to recognize that "messengers" (those who run for the king) and "angel" (as carrier of the word of Yahweh) are rooted in the same Hebrew term. The juxtaposition of messengers of two kings nicely dramatizes the power struggle between two "kings" (Yahweh and Ahaziah), each of whom dispatches couriers and each of whom claims to be "the true government." In the end, of course, the messengers of the Samaritan king are helpless and must plead to the prophet for their lives. The plea of v. 13 serves to show that the authority and power of Ahaziah is nil before Elijah who represents the only authority that matters in this narrative.

The narrative has three times delayed a settlement of the dispute between king and prophet. Narrative art will characteristically not permit a delay longer than three times. And so, in the fourth wave of the drama, the tone has changed (1:13-16). A third time a captain with fifty is sent on a mission. But this captain of fifty knows of his predecessors and their sorry fate. He knows that demanding royal imperative is futile with this untamed, unresponsive character. Now the tone is a desperate, fearful plea to the prophet. The captain is in an impossible situation: Either he disobeys his king or he is wiped out by the prophet. So he petitions the prophet. The verb "entreated" in the NRSV is the verb *ḥanan* ("to show grace"); he begs for graciousness, twice asking the prophet to value the lives of his soldiers.

Elijah, so it appears, is unmoved by the captain's appeal. The angel (= messenger) of Yahweh, however, inclines to save the messengers of the king. [Messengers] The messenger of Yahweh assures Elijah that he will be safe if he "goes down" to the king. The hearer of the text suspects that the king wants to kill the prophet; but divine assurance is enough. The prophet is assured and so is unafraid. Remarkably, we are told nothing of the meeting of king and prophet that follows. All we are told is once more the speech of judgment (1:16). The prophet reiterates in v. 16 what was already authorized in vv. 3-4 and announced in v. 6. A third time the narrative culminates, "surely die." Notably, the narrative has no interest in the fall of the king with which the narrative began (1:2). The king will not die from his injury. He will die, rather, because Yahweh plays for keeps, and will tolerate no alternative loyalty. The narrative is abrupt. In v. 7, the king responds to the prophetic declaration of death. But here there is a tone of finality to the prophetic word. The king does not speak, offers no rebuttal. He promptly dies in the next verse!

The Word Enacted, 1:17-18

The narrative account ends, as surely it must according to the larger horizon of the Elijah story. The king dies. The king dies "according to the word," the same word of the same prophet whose word brings life (see 1 Kgs 17:24). But of course the prophet is only instrumental. Yahweh, who will tolerate no rival, is the real cause of the king's death.

Verses 17b-18 are a standard formula of conclusion that introduces the king's brother Jehoram, a final, ineffective gasp of the Omri dynasty. The announcement of the brother is so formulaic that it requires no special comment, except that the narrative observes, "no son." No future, no heir, no offspring. Perhaps the court record only gives us a fact. But when the narrative is loaded, as is this one, with talk of Baal, we notice. Baal is the one who allegedly fructifies and is expected to give new life. But of course Baal does not, yet another evidence that Baal is a futile force, unable to produce sons; the future and its generativity are under the sure aegis of Yahweh and none other. The contrast between the failure and impotence of Baal and the narratives of birth and new life in Genesis that occupy Israel's imagination is complete. Yahweh gives a future. None is on offer from any other source. The royal family never understood, but the narrative permits us to notice what it failed to grasp.

The dark colors create a romantic mood and shading provides sublime depths. Doré shrouds the chaotic scene with smoke from the fire that has come down upon the soldiers.

Gustave Doré. *Fire Consumes the Soldiers of Ahaziah* from the *Illustrated Bible*. 19th century. Engraving. (Credit: Dover Pictorial Archive Series)

CONNECTIONS

This text is on the one hand very odd. On the other hand it is quite simple. The oddity is that in the uneven struggle between Elijah and the king, Elijah plays by no rules, certainly not those of the king, and appears to have no restraints on what is possible. We surely do not know what to make of a story in which the main character can summon destructive fire at will. At the same time, the story is direct, straightforward, and simple. The mediating drama of vv. 5-16 accomplishes almost nothing. What counts is only the prophetic instruction from the angel (1:3-4, reiterated in 1:6, 16) that becomes public history (1:17a). The simple matter is that the prophet prevails over the king, a theme already evident in the earlier stories. The oddity and simplicity of the narrative make clear that we should not anticipate any close "connection" to our time and place. We may limit ourselves to two comments.

First, Elijah is larger than life and must be accepted, in terms of the narrative, as a character and agent that fits none of our categories of explanation. This feature is not an accidental by-product of the narrative, but its main point. We must take care not to

In this painting, Elijah returns and drinks from the cup that is customarily left for him during Passover.

Anonymous. *Passover Feast in Russia.* 1949. Judaica Coll. Max Berger, Vienna, Austria. (Credit: Erich Lessing/Art Resource, NY)

A Mistaken Elijah

In a remarkable interpretive move, unlike the Jewish Bible, the Christian Bible ends with an affirmation that Elijah is a *coming, future* figure:

Lo, I will send you the prophet Elijah before the great and terrible day of the LORD comes. He will turn the hearts of parents to their children and the hearts of children to their parents, so that I will not come and strike the land with a curse. (Mal 4:5-6)

On this basis in times of acute need and therefore acute hope Jews expected Elijah to "come again" as a harbinger of Yahweh's full rule. It is from this claim that the New Testament reflects the mistaken opinion that Jesus was Elijah returned (Matt 11:14; 16:14) or that Jesus was in the company of Elijah (Matt 17:3-13), or that Jesus was thought to appeal to Elijah (Matt 27:47-49).

The many references to Elijah in the Gospel narrative reflect a deep expectation and an awareness that in Jesus, as in Elijah, someone larger than life is on the scene. Thus the hope of Elijah becomes an interpretive device for identifying and glorifying Jesus, the embodiment of Yahweh's full power become visible and active.

reduce this awesome character or explain him away in order to fit our timid reason, because if we do, we miss the point and the story evaporates. One strategy for handling this odd story that is common in the face of such a character is to settle that the narrative is a "legend," that is, a fantasy that moves beyond reality. Such a labelling, however, tells us nothing and only resists its larger-than-life subject.

The story insists that once there was indeed a *larger-than-life* character who dominated both the imagination of the community and its actual circumstance. This singular quality of "larger than life" is not an offer of a new category or model to be replicated. Elijah in memory and imagination is who he is. But his presentation in this narrative helps us see why those who subsequently witnessed Jesus of Nazareth on occasion mistook him for Elijah. [A Mistaken Elijah]

It is a challenge to our reductionist reason to host a larger-than-life character. The biblical narrative—in other places as well as here—champions precisely such characters who defy our familiarity and our reason:

On the one hand, he is absolutely, unquestionably submissive to Yahweh's directives. On the other, he is completely immune to pressures from the human side.[1]

Receiving this story depends upon our willingness to forego our controlling interpretive categories.

Second, there is more here than a simple, direct contest between king and prophet. The king and the prophet are dramatic ciphers whose action and articulation embody competing views of reality. That is, the king is not simply a more-or-less anonymous ruler; instead, in the narrative, he represents the entire royal enterprise of self-aggrandizement attached to Baalism, a strategy for security and prosperity. Elijah, in like manner, is not simply a singular man of power, though he is that, as is evident in the king's verdict in v. 8: "It is Elijah the Tishbite!" Rather, Elijah carries an entire view of reality rooted in Mosaic covenantalism and linked to Yahweh, the

📖 **Israel's Two Histories**

Ahijah and Elijah represent two narrative construals of reality that continue in deep dispute in Israel. That same deep contrast is expressed succinctly in Jer 9:23-24:

> Do not let the wise boast in their wisdom, do not let the mighty boast in their might, do not let the wealthy boast in their wealth; but let those who boast boast in this, that they understand and know me, that I am the LORD; I act with steadfast love, justice, and righteousness in the earth, for in these things I delight, says the LORD.

In the book of Jeremiah, the prophet again carries the covenantal traditions of justice and righteousness that compete with the royal accouterments of wealth and power. With Jeremiah, as with Elijah, the ostensive power of monarchy is shown to be feeble, ineffective, and finally irrelevant, even though it always appears otherwise.

See Walter Brueggemann, "The Epistemological Crisis of Israel's Two Histories (Jer. 9:22-23)," *Old Testament Theology: Essays in Structure, Theme, and Text* (Minneapolis: Fortress Press, 1992) 270-95.

God of prophetic insistence concerning justice and righteousness. Thus the narrative presents to us a deep dispute about conflicting metanarratives that touch every facet of Israel's public life. [Israel's Two Histories]

When the feeble king and the enigmatic prophet are seen as carriers of mutually exclusive symbol systems, we can observe a "connection" to our own time and place where the dispute continues.

If "the king" is understood as the administrator of a technical system of self-security (Baalism), then it is not much of a leap to see a counterpart in the glorification of *technique* and its commoditization of human reality, now expressed as the "global economy."[2] This theory of reality has no tolerance of human questions or human worth or human needs. It depends upon productivity to establish worth. In such a scenario, "Elijah" may be seen, in our time, as emblematic of human passion, human suffering, and human compassion that resists the dehumanization of social processes so that technique replaces political processes. Among others, we may identify Philip Berrigan, Martin Luther King, Jr., and Nelson Mandela as highly visible representatives and embodiments of a theory of reality that centers in the bodily reality of pain and possibility. This latter "theory" we may identify as a "prophetic" view of reality. [A Prophetic Countertheme]

To be sure, the move from (a) Elijah vs. "the king" to (b) Berrigan, King, and Mandela vs. technological society is a huge interpretive leap. It is, however, a leap invited by the narrative itself. Surely the narrative is not intended simply as concrete reportage on something past. It is, rather, a summons to and affirmation of on-going generations of listeners. In our common life, the king almost

A Prophetic Countertheme

The prophetic tradition, ancient and contemporary, may be summarized around a series of quite specific claims. I have elsewhere offered these as characteristic marks of a prophetic counterinterpretation of human history:

1. The prophetic tradition is against idols, and consequently against self-serving, self-deceiving ideology.
2. The prophetic tradition refuses, then, to absolutize the present, any present.
3. Prophetic speech characteristically speaks about human suffering.
4. Prophetic speech characteristically takes a critical posture over against established power.
5. Prophetic speech...is an act of relentless hope that refuses to despair, that refuses to believe that the world is closed off in patterns of exploitation and oppression.

These claims of course are not all explicit in our chapter. But I suggest they are implied and coded in the Yahwism that runs from Moses to Jeremiah, with Elijah occupying a middle position with great authority and consequence. It is this counterview of human history that is championed in the narrative through the person of Elijah, a view that continues to be the burden and wonder of prophetic faith.

Walter Brueggemann, "The Prophetic Word of God and History," *Interpretation* 48I (1994): 244-45.

always defeats the prophet. In our own horizon, the powers of technology always appear to be stronger and more durable than those "drummer boys" for humanity. The story stands as a powerful affirmation that prophetic claims are not always defeated, that prophetic urges are not to be silenced.

It is precisely the oddity and unfamiliarity of the story that matters most. In the conventional and familiar, such a countervoice has no chance. Precisely for that reason, generations of listeners who care about human dimensions of life cling passionately to this narrative and others like it. This narrative is, in the end, a life-and-death dispute about the nature of social reality. It insists that wisdom, might, and wealth finally cannot defeat steadfast love, justice, and righteousness, the most elemental marks of Yahweh's way in the world:

For God's foolishness is wiser than human wisdom, and God's weakness is stronger than human strength.... But God chose what is foolish in the world to shame the wise; God chose what is weak in the world to shame the strong; God chose what is low and despised in the world, things that are not, to reduce to nothing things that are, so that no one might boast in the presence of God. He is the source of your life in Christ Jesus, who became for us wisdom from God, and righteousness and sanctification and redemption, in order that, as it is written, "Let the one who boasts, boast in the Lord." (1 Cor 1:25-31)

The king, emblem of power and wealth, is dead, unable to resist the harsh pronouncements of the God of countertruth.

NOTES

[1]Christopher T. Begg, "Unifying Factors in 2 Kings 1.2-17a," JSOT 32 (1985): 79.

[2]See Jacques Ellul, *Technological Society* (New York: Random House, 1967).

A TRANSITION
IN PROPHETIC AUTHORITY

2 Kings 2:1-25

Elijah has dominated the narrative since his abrupt entry in 1 Kings 17:1. According to this rendering of Israel's public life, Elijah has dominated the political life of Israel as he has dominated the narrative, preempting any initiative that might have conventionally belonged to the monarchy. But now it is time for Elijah's "departure," with the transfer of prophetic authority to his disciple and successor, Elisha. The text accomplishes the transfer of prophetic authority, while at the same time further acknowledging and enhancing the enduring preeminence of Elijah. The text centers in vv. 9-12 with the "ascent" of Elijah. Before that dramatic moment is the preparatory interaction of Elijah and Elisha (2:1-8). After that moment comes the exhibit of Elisha's new authority and the beginning of his career of "wonders" in Israel (2:13-25).

The placement of this chapter is especially noteworthy. The death of Ahaziah and the concluding formula of his reign is given in 1:17-18. The introductory formula for his brother and successor, Jehoram, is provided in 3:1-3. The end of one reign in 1:17-18 and the beginning of the next in 3:1-3 means that chapter 2 stands between the two reigns, that is, outside them, outside "royal time." It is likely that the text is intentionally placed as it is, in order to suggest that the remarkable moment of prophetic transition is so odd and so exceptional that it cannot be held in royal time or understood in royal rationality. This text is something deeply "other" and so it is placed "otherwise."

COMMENTARY

Preparatory Interaction, 2:1-8

Elijah is about to "ascend," to be taken up to heaven (2:1)! How is that for openers?! Elijah's career and life are about to end...but he is not to die. Most remarkably, the narrative evidences no wonderment or curiosity about this staggering claim. He is to "go up" to heaven where the gods live. Israel has not known of such a "departure" for anyone heretofore, not even Moses. The "ascent," moreover, is to be in a storm, the special kind of storm of theophanic proportion that signifies Yahweh's peculiar and powerful involvement. Elijah will be as special and peculiar in departure as he has been odd and problematic while on earth.

Elijah, however, is not yet finished. Before he ascends, he itinerates the central territory of Israel: *Gilgal* (2:1), *Bethel* (2:2-3), *Jericho* (2:4-5), and finally the *Jordan River* (2:6-8). We are not told why he goes; we are told only that he is "sent" by Yahweh (2:2, 4, 6). Elijah is still commanded by Yahweh and until the last is obedient. He goes where he is sent.[1]

For reasons we do not understand, he proposes in each case to go without Elisha, whom he has already summoned and given his mantle (1 Kgs 19:19-21). In this particular case, however, Elisha will not do as Elijah commands. He says three times, "I will not leave you" (2:2, 4, 6). The verb "leave" has the force of "abandon." The subordinate refuses to leave his master alone, and so goes with him. The exchange between the two is three times stylized, not unlike the threefold repetition in 1:5-16.

In each of the three locales visited by the two prophets, there is also a "company of prophets." [The Company of the Prophets] This larger band of prophets undoubtedly regards Elijah as their great master, and so meet him in deference as well as curiosity. They know, moreover, that he is about to be "taken." The company of prophets in Bethel does not surprise us when we recall the prophetic narrative of 1 Kings 13 concerning the prophet from Bethel. Jericho, by contrast, is completely new with respect to prophetic presence. (The number of fifty at Jericho surely is a counterpoint to the fifty messengers of 1:5-16.)

Elijah acts in what must be a prophetic, symbolic way, although the significance of his act escapes us (2:8). The mantle, already mentioned in 1 Kings 19:19, an object invested with enormous significance and power, is again in play; Elijah parts the waters of the Jordan, an act reminiscent of Moses' great act of dividing the waters in Egypt. [The Jordan as the Red Sea] The two of them now

---

AΩ **The Company of the Prophets**

The "company of the prophets" apparently was an informal group that stood outside normal social transactions, a group peculiarly open to invasions of the spirit that lived together under the discipline of a leader, at different times including Elijah and Elisha. Robert Wilson comments:

Seen from a sociological perspective, the sons of the prophets closely resemble members of a peripheral possession cult. Although there is no direct evidence on this point, members of the group were presumably peripheral individuals who had resisted the political and religious policies of the Ephraimite kings and who had therefore been forced out of the political and religious establishments. After having prophetic experiences these individuals joined the group, which was under the leadership of Elisha. In the group they found mutual support and were encouraged to use prophecy to bring about change in the social order.

Robert R. Wilson, *Prophecy and Society in Ancient Israel* (Philadelphia: Fortress Press, 1980) 202.

cross the Jordan together, departing the settled land governed by the king into the wilderness, the inscrutable land of mystery. In this territory Elijah began his own dangerous ministry that refused any royal authority (1 Kgs 17:1-6). That the two of them go into the untamed land parallels the entry of Moses into the wilderness where reliance upon the raw power of Yahweh is a necessity (Exod 15:22).

> **The Jordan as the Red Sea**
> The Jordan River in this narrative clearly provides something of a crucial boundary between *the wild* where God's power prevails and *the domesticated land* west of the Jordan. It is possible, moreover, to recall Josh 4:21-24 and to notice that the Jordan is there regarded as a replication of the Red Sea, the water of the Exodus. Seeing the Jordan in this way is yet one more indication of the way in which Elijah replicates Moses by the dividing and crossing of the waters.

This entire narrative unit is deeply enigmatic. It is impossible to understand what is happening or why the narrator includes it. Clearly, the company of prophets is aware of the near departure of a great man, so they act in awed deference. That awed deference, moreover, is matched by the wonder of v. 8. Whatever may be intended, Elijah, until the last, is capable of high drama in which he replicates the wonder of Moses.

The Ascension, 2:9-12

With the enigmatic preparation of vv. 1-8, the narrative now presents Elijah's actual departure. As in a deathbed scene (though he is not to die), Elijah grants Elisha one last wish. His request is bold and prompt, a "double share" of Elijah's spirit. The "double share" is one more portion than is normally distributed (see Deut 21:15-17; 1 Sam 1:5). The phrasing is odd, because "double share" refers to something quantifiable, but Elisha asks for *rûah*, for the force and vitality, energy and authority of Elijah, none of which is quantifiable. He asks to be invested with Elijah's power as prophet. Perhaps he knows that the external sign of the mantle by itself (19:19), without a match of intrinsic force, is meaningless and powerless. Elijah's response to the request is less than reassuring. Apparently he does not know whether the request of his disciple can be honored, for he is not the one to assign *rûah* (see Mark 10:40). He only states a criterion to determine whether the gift of the spirit is genuinely given (2:10). It will be known when it is determined what the younger prophet saw.

In vv. 11-12, the narrative reports on the actual ascent of Elijah. Every part of the account is loaded with force beyond the conventional. The text is bold: "Elijah ascended." [The Ascension] He went up in a storm (see 2:1), indicating that the turbulence of his departure is an element in the invasive force of Yahweh. Elijah is in the storm, but between him and Elisha comes a chariot of fire and

The Ascension

The ascent of Elijah into heaven is without parallel or precedent in the Old Testament. The narrative description surely means to portray the movement of the unparalleled prophet into the realm of the gods beyond the reach of human affairs. The only other like ending to a human life on earth is that of Enoch of whom the text says tersely, "Then he was no more, because God took him" (Gen 5:24). That account of Enoch, however, provides no image of any ascent. There is no doubt that this report on Elijah stands in the background of the New Testament account of Jesus' departure. While the report may trouble our rationality, the narrative clearly intends to place Elijah well outside our rationality.

Of the many versions of Elijah ascending, the version by Nicolas of Verdun effectively communicates the demarcation of the separation between Elijah and Elisha.

Nicolas of Verdun. *Ascension of Elijah* from the Verdun Altarpiece. 12th century. Sammlungen des Stiftes, Klosterneuburg Abbey, Austria. (Credit: Erich Lessing/Art Resource, NY) horses of fire. Contrary to common portrayal in religious art, Elijah is not riding in the chariot. The chariot functions, rather, not as transport but to separate the two, separating the one upon earth and the one in heaven, the one left with prophetic responsibility and the one taken up into the awesome realm of the divine. Verse 11 does not tell us what Elisha "saw," the condition of a double portion in v. 10. But v. 12 says he "could no longer see," making clear that he had seen and thereby was qualified for a double portion of the enduring power and authority of Elijah.

Elisha knew that Elijah would depart. Nonetheless he is not prepared for it in the event. His cry of v. 12 seems to be one of salute but also of loss. He uses two titles for the departing prophet. First, "father, father," perhaps a title used in the "company of the prophets" to characterize their master and leader. Elisha expresses filial devotion. But then, second, "The chariots of Israel and its horsemen." The phrasing is perhaps triggered by the vision of v. 11. In any case, the use of armaments as an image for the prophet indicates that Elijah has been the powerful guarantor and indomitable protector of Israel. A negative implication is that the military apparatus of the monarchy has been an irrelevance that plays no role in the real securing of Israel. The ascent narrative is in every part inscrutable, indicating that Elijah in his departure is seen to be unlike anyone else in Israel. Elisha tears his clothes, a gesture of grief at loss.

The Newly Authorized Prophet, 2:13-25

In Elijah's absence, the man of the hour, the man of the narrative, is Elisha. Elisha is slightly more credentialed than was Elijah, for we know his father (Shaphat) and his locale (Abel-meholah) (1 Kgs 19:16). But what we mainly know is that his name means "my God saves." His name embodies the peculiar claim of Yahwism; it is Yahweh who can emancipate, heal, rescue, and transform. At the beginning of his work, now without Elijah, Elisha is at the Jordan. He is at the boundary between the wild zone of Yahweh's direct power and the controlled territory of the monarchy. He wears the mantle, insignia of newly authorized power. He seeks after Yahweh whom he identifies as "the God of Elijah." His first utterance is an enquiry and a petition. For without Yahweh, he has no power and no authority. He receives no answer. But his third act is to strike the water of the Jordan. He strikes the water; and then strikes it again. The narrative detail suggests that unlike Elijah in v. 8, his first striking is not effective and he must do it twice. Thus his power may be less than that of Elijah. But it is adequate. He does

The artist has used the arched building as an ingenious device to divide the 2 scenes: the Ascension and the boys who mocked Elisha. Here, Elisha has now become bald, which is being indiscreetly pointed out by the jeering, taunting children exclaiming, "Baldy, Baldy!" (2 Kgs 2:23). Though the scale and proportions of the figures are distorted, the drift of the narrative is explicitly communicated; Elisha looms larger than life, dwarfing both the children and the vengeful bears. This size differential is a medieval construct which also creates a hierarchy of importance.

Anonymous. *Elijah Ascends to Heaven in a Whirlwind; The Boys Who Mocked Elisha Are Eaten by Bears.* Illustration from the *Nuremberg Bible* (Biblia Sacra Germanaica). 15th century. Victoria & Albert Museum, London, England. (Credit: Art Resource, NY)

part the waters of the Jordan, replicating Elijah who, as we have seen, replicated Moses. Elisha crosses back over the Jordan, now entering into the land ostensibly governed by the monarchy.

Upon reentry to Jericho, a characteristic point of entry from the wilderness, Elisha meets the community of the prophets, exactly as had Elijah. They come out to meet him, perhaps in deference as they came out to see Elijah. They affirm that "the spirit" has indeed been transferred to Elisha. They accept his empowerment and his preeminence among them.

But for all of that, they are not yet finished with Elijah. While they do not doubt that Elijah's departure was an awesome work of Yahweh, they apparently cannot believe he has arisen to heaven. They fear for him a lesser fate, namely, that he was dropped or thrown somewhere in the land. Their response is a mix of devotion to Elisha and skepticism about the wonder of the ascent.

Even in their zeal, however, they obey Elisha who must now issue appropriate directives. First, he forbids them to search, being fully confident of Elijah's "ascent." There is nobody to find. But then he abruptly reverses field and authorizes a search, perhaps recognizing that the suspicion and yearning of the prophets could not be satisfied in any other way. They search, for three days. But of course they do not find Elijah because "he is risen." Elisha is vindicated and his authority is strengthened. He knew all along and never doubted. But he cannot resist one final "I told you so" (2:18). The episode may constitute the narrator's acknowledgement that the ascent is indeed strange and inexplicable. The other prophets have no categories for it. In order to reassure those who hear the narrative, this three-day search is one additional assurance. The entire exchange serves, in the end, to enhance the authority of Elisha.

With the establishment of authority in his "inner circle," Elisha now becomes more public in his assertion. In vv. 19-22 he rescues the water supply of Jericho. We are not told why the water supply is spoiled, but clearly the condition is a severe emergency as is any such water crisis. Elisha responds promptly and effectively to the emergency and cleanses the water with salt. He "healed" the water which from that day was healthy and reliable. This is Elisha's "coming out" miracle. We notice only how terse the narrative is, how understated is his debut. The narrator knows that this is an agent now laden with uncommon powers.[2] Our reading must explain no more than does the narrator. It is a wonder! From such an act explanation can only detract.

The public "healing" is matched by a public massacre instigated by the prophet (2:23-25). On the way from Jericho to Bethel (thus a reversal of the journey from Bethel to Jericho with Elijah in vv. 2-5), the rising prophetic figure is accosted by small boys who mock him, "baldy, baldy," thus ridiculing him when they should have known better. As the prophet has enacted a blessing on the waters of Jericho, so now he declares a curse on the mocking boys. She-bears, the most ferocious kind of bears, appear abruptly and kill the boys, all of them. Notice how elliptical is the statement. There is a curse, and then there are bears. The narrative does not explicitly connect the two, thus adding to the inscrutability of the prohetic claim. The incident puts Israel on notice. This Elisha is dangerous and is not to be trifled with, not by small boys, not by kings, not by anybody, for he has the spirit of Elijah.

The concluding itinerary of v. 25 shows the prophet stopping at Mt. Carmel, scene of Elijah's great triumph (1 Kgs 18:36-40, 42), and ending in Samaria, home city of the Omri dynasty. The emergence of Elisha moves in four concentric circles: (a) he is alone (2:13-14); (b) he is with the sons of the prophets (2:15-18); (c) he is in the city (2:19-22); and finally (d) he is on the road to the king (2:23-25). In each case, his authority and awesome power are attested. By the end of the narrative, he is fully established as the new prophetic force in Israel.

CONNECTIONS

The plot of this narrative is the transition of power and authority from the master to the disciple, from Elijah to Elisha. At the beginning, Elijah is clearly the dominant force as Elisha, seemingly unwelcome on Elijah's farewell tour, trails along. By the end of the narrative, by contrast, Elijah is absent (even if yearned for), and Elisha takes up all the room in the narrative. Thus we might think of this narrative as a careful, imaginative transfer of power. Dennis McCarthy, in a study of Deuteronomy 31:23, finds a literary genre of "installation" that concerns the transfer of authority from Moses to Joshua.[3] The genre concerns how continuity of authority and leadership is assured in the community, something like "apostolic succession." Our present text, however, is more problematic; it does not admit to institutional protocols or procedures or guarantees. Everything depends upon the gift of the spirit that Elijah cannot guarantee to Elisha, because it is a "hard thing" beyond human control (2:10). While we may think of continuity and transfer of authority, it is important to recognize that this text reflects no routinization of a conventional, institutional practice.

Perhaps the most important factor in interpreting this text is the recognition of its wild, inscrutable quality that refuses any explanatory approach. The better perspective is simply to track the odd drama and to be amazed at the surge of power upon "the new man" that defies our rationality. The proper response is one of dazzlement that the spirit, beyond every human domestication, adds a disconcerting plus to the human enterprise.

It does not surprise us then that this "story beyond reason" hovered in Israel's life and haunted Israel's imagination, precisely because it refuses routinization. That hovering and haunting, for the Christian reader, shows up in the attempt of the New Testament church to witness to the transhistorical, larger-than-life characters of John and Jesus.

1. Concerning John the Baptist, we have already noticed in 1 Kings 1:8 that Elijah is replicated in John, and that some identified John with Elijah (Mark 6:18). In the present chapter I wish to note only that in v. 8 the two prophets cross the Jordan River into the untamed wilderness where the untamed power of God is palpable, and in v. 14, Elisha—now without Elijah—recrosses the Jordan back into royal, tamed land. It is the untamed place from which prophetic counterpower comes. Notably, in Luke 3:1-2, John is presented as a contrast to all settled power. The taming governance is fully identified:

> In the fifteenth year of the reign of Emperor Tiberius, when Pontius Pilate was governor of Judea, and Herod was ruler of Galilee, and his brother Philip ruler of the region of Ituraea and Trachonitis, and Lysanias ruler of Abilene, during the high priesthood of Annas and Caiaphas. (Luke 3:1-2a)

By contrast, John receives only a terse introduction:

> The word of God came to John son of Zechariah in the wilderness. (Luke 3:2b)

The subversive word appears "in the wilderness," beyond the reach of established power, the same wilderness where Elijah's preparation for witness is located in 1 Kings 17:1-6.

2. The claim that Elijah was "taken up" into heaven permits him to be a continuing figure in the faith and hope of Jews. There is no doubt that this strange account of ascent makes Elijah available in the hopes of the Jesus narrative. The story of "transfiguration," as an anticipation of the resurrection of Jesus, is an "out of time" occurrence peopled by Elijah along with Moses (Luke 9:30-33). The presence of Elijah with Jesus on the mountain surely attests to the church's conviction that Jesus is now the carrier of the same awesome force that marked both Elijah and Elisha.

As the "transfiguration" anticipates in narrative fashion the culmination of Jesus' life, so Luke's account of the ascension of Jesus is one more retelling of the moment of God's power and splendor, which operate outside of royal time and beyond royal reason:

> Then he led them out as far as Bethany, and, lifting up his hands, he blessed them. While he was blessing them, he withdrew from them and was carried up into heaven. (Luke 24:50-51)

So when they had come together, they asked him, "Lord, is this the time when you will restore the kingdom to Israel?" He replied, "It is not for you to know the times or periods that the Father has set by his own authority. But you will receive power when the Holy Spirit has come upon you; and you will be my witnesses in Jerusalem, in all Judea and Samaria, and to the ends of the earth." When he had said this, as they were watching, he was lifted up, and a cloud took him out of their sight. While he was going and they were gazing up toward heaven, suddenly two men in white robes stood by them. They said, "Men of Galilee, why do you stand looking up toward heaven? This Jesus, who has been taken up from you into heaven, will come in the same way as you saw him go into heaven." (Acts 1:6-11)

The end of Elijah's life is narrated so that *he did not die!* His life continues in the splendor of God's presence. So also after the wonder of crucifixion and resurrection, Luke has found the most dramatic narrative way to assert that *Jesus did not die* but lives in the splendor of God's presence. We can see that in both narratives the witnesses in rather unsure and clumsy ways make an affirmation beyond all credible affirmations, because the person and event at issue are beyond all credible affirmation. [Appeal to "Historical Reason"]

3. This peculiar turn of affairs, as narrated, permits two derivative points of interest. First, the whole matter of ascent needs to be considered. To say the least, the ascension of Elijah is "irregular." As a result, fifty of the "strong men" of the company of the prophets spent three days searching for the body. They did not believe he had died—nobody thought that. But they fantasized that Yahweh may have dropped him—as from a helicopter—in some mountain or valley. It took the search to convince them that he had "risen."

This reservation about the wonder of ascent is echoed in the Jesus narrative in two ways. First, outsiders were doubtful and imagined that the body had been hidden. Indeed, even the disciples must lie about the body in order to be safe from "the authorities" (Matt 28:12-15). In both cases, Elijah and Jesus, the wonder of ascent and resurrection, respectively, are too demanding, too outrageous, too astonishing to be accepted. The same is true of the insider (Thomas) who is

---

📖 Appeal to "Historical Reason"

The account of Elijah is not a case in a larger genre, but is a distinctive, one-time event. It is important to engage a very different mode of reason to deal with such a one-time occurrence for which no parallels can be cited. Richard R. Niebuhr has termed such a rationality "historical reason."

Richard R. Niebuhr, *Resurrection and Historical Reason: A Study of Theological Method* (New York: Scribner's, 1957). See also W. B. Gallie, "The Historical Understanding," *History and Theory,* ed. George H. Nadel (Middletown CT: Wesleyan University Press, 1977) 149-202.

unable to open his life to the miracle of newness and must be reassured "fleshly" (John 20:24-29).

The second derivative point is that ascension as alternative to death means that the ascended figures are not finished. In each case, he continues a life with the potential of descending with power into the life of the world. In the case of Elijah, this continuing potential is articulated at the end of Malachi, happily, the end of the Christian ordering of the Old Testament:

> Lo, I will send you the prophet Elijah before the great and terrible day of the LORD comes. He will turn the hearts of parents to their children and the hearts of children to their parents, so that I will not come and strike the land with a curse. (Mal 4:5-6)

Extraordinarily, Elijah is nowhere mentioned in the Old Testament outside the Kings narratives until this Malachi reference. That oracle clearly has turned the departed, past Elijah into the future, expected Elijah who will come into the vexed world of conflict with transformative, healing power. In the case of Jesus, the Lukan portrayal of ascension ends on a parallel note:

> ... will come in the same way as you saw him go into heaven. (Acts 1:11)

The one who ascended "will come again in the same way." And therefore the church, in its great Eucharistic affirmation, asserts:

> Christ has died,
> Christ is risen,
> Christ will come again.

Perhaps a parallel to the Elijah ending of the Old Testament in Malachi is the New Testament ending in Revelation:

> Amen. Come, Lord Jesus! (Rev 22:20)

The church's hope, prayer, petition, and expectation are that the risen Christ who sits in glory will come to the earth again.

To be sure, there are deep and difficult questions for modern rationality in the face of this primitive, poetic vision. To linger there, however, is to miss the point. The point is that the vexed earth is open to the transformative visitation of the heavenly power of God that will come and make all things right:

> With the spirit and power of Elijah he will go before him, to turn the hearts of parents to their children, and the disobedient to the wisdom of the righteous, to make ready a people prepared for the Lord. (Luke 1:17)

Such interpretation goes beyond our narrative but explicates what is already inchoate in the ascent. In the narrative, as the story continues, Elisha ministers on earth in place of the departed Elijah. In the meantime he heals the water supply of Jericho. In the meantime he crowds royal authority with transformative acts. In the meantime he is the focus of the narrative, as Israel continues to be dazzled and disrupted by him. In parallel fashion, the book of Acts portrays the church responding to the departure of Jesus. The church is, in the meantime, to do its testimony and its mighty works. The church is situated like Elisha: Elisha has the spirit to do wonders. It is not different in Acts, a people propelled by God's Holy Spirit that is the spirit of Jesus:

> When the day of Pentecost had come, they were all together in one place. And suddenly from heaven there came a sound like the rush of a violent wind, and it filled the entire house where they were sitting. Divided tongues, as of fire, appeared among them, and a tongue rested on each of them. All of them were filled with the Holy Spirit, and began to speak in other languages as the Spirit gave them ability. (Acts 2:1-4)

None of this is explained. All of it is narrated and enacted. Elisha had detractors but the bears came against them. The early church had its detractors. The lions came. But the church persisted:

> He lived there two whole years at his own expense and welcomed all who came to him, proclaiming the kingdom of God and teaching about the Lord Jesus Christ with all boldness and without hindrance. (Acts 28:30-31)

The story ends "without hindrance."

NOTES

[1]Richard Nelson, *First and Second Kings,* Interpretation (Atlanta: John Knox Press, 1987) 158-59, terms the journey "pointless, silly."

[2]Burke O. Long, *2 Kings,* The Forms of the Old Testament Literature vol. 10 (Grand Rapids: Eerdmans, 1991) 31, likens Elisha's work on the water to the work of Moses in Exod 15:22-25. As this is Elisha's first wonder, so for Moses the act is his first in the wilderness outside Egypt.

[3]Dennis J. McCarthy, "An Installation Genre?" JBL 90 (1971): 31-41. McCarthy also cites 1 Chr 28:10; 2 Chr 19:5-7; 32:6-8; Hag 2:4; perhaps Ezra 2:4.

A MISCALCULATED WAR

2 Kings 3:1-27

After the hiatus in royal history for the narrative in chapter 2 of the ascent of Elijah that stands outside "royal time," the royal narrative here resumes. The fourth and final king of the Omride dynasty (after Omri, Ahab, and Ahaziah) is Jehoram who reigned twelve years (849–842) and is killed in a palace coup (2 Kgs 9:24).[1] We know him only from this chapter, except for the report of his death. Like his brother Ahaziah in chapter 1, he is of interest only as a foil for the prophet—in this case Elisha—the real focus of the narrative.

Royal history here, as so often, is preoccupied with military adventurism when military stratagems become the total expression of foreign policy. After the royal formula of vv. 1-3, the remainder of the chapter concerns war with Moab, Israel's near neighbor (3:4-27).

COMMENTARY

A Not-So-Bad Omride, 3:1-3

We are now introduced to the tail end of the Omride dynasty, a regime toward which our narrator has strong antipathy. Along with a standard chronological note, we are also given a predictable theological verdict upon the king. The verdict, however, is more than a little ambiguous. The first part of v. 2 is conventional—because every Northern king and certainly every Omride king did evil. What is interesting is that vv. 2b-3 follow this sweeping verdict with a double preposition of qualification (*raq*), the first rendered as "though," the second given as "nonetheless." That they are the same Hebrew term is suggestive. The first qualification in v. 2b is positive. This king is much better than either father Ahab or mother Jezebel because he curbed the emblems of Baal. This is a most remarkable concession by our narrator to an Omride king, and likely squares with Elisha's positive response to the king later in our narrative.

But the narrator cannot tolerate the positive qualification of v. 2b as the final word. It is qualified in turn by the "nonetheless" of v. 3. This verse disputes the positive note of v. 2b and returns to the more predictable negative verdict of v. 2a. One gains the impression that

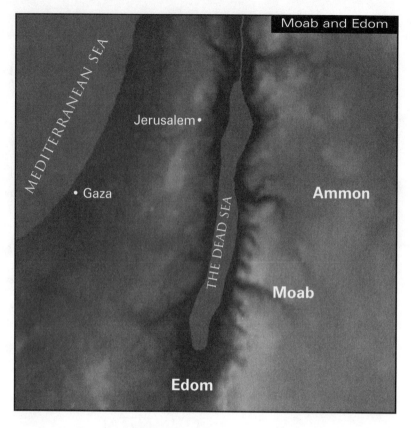

the truth about this king was more positive than the ideology of the narrator could bear. At best, the data on the king is mixed.

The Moabite Expedition, 3:4-27

The remainder of the chapter is taken up with an account of Israel's aggressive military action against Moab, a state across the Jordan to the east of Israel. [Map: Moab and Edom] We have earlier been put on notice that a dispute with Moab was inevitable (1:1). That signalling verse indicates that under the reign of Ahab, the Israelite king has been strong enough to dominate Moab and make it into a client state. As so often happens, however, the death of a dominating king is an occasion when things become unglued and oppressed parties may reassert themselves (see Exod 2:23). Such is clearly the case here.

Initial Success and Jeopardy, 3:4-12

Mesha is Jehoram's royal counterpart presiding over a semi-nomadic economy in Moab. The principle industry is sheep and the principle products are wool and lamb. The opening of the narrative suggests that Mesha and Moab were quite subordinate to what must have been the formidable power of the state of Israel, and regularly sent produce as a tributary tax. (See a comparable arrangement in 1 Kgs 4:21.) The statement suggests that the fixed and agreed upon tax is considerable. It was apparently routinely paid without protest, an acknowledgement of a dependency relationship between the two states. [When the Shoe Was on the Other Foot] Worth noting is that the statement of the amount of tribute money does not offer a time frame. Perhaps we are meant to interpret "per year."

When "the king" (Ahab) dies, the Moabites may judge that Israel is so weak or so distracted that Moab can safely risk withholding the expected payments, thus asserting independence from Israelite domination (see 1:1). One is struck by Jehoram's quick (and as it turns out, ill-considered) response to the Moabite refusal to pay (3:6). Perhaps a prompt show of force was felt necessary to make clear that the death of Ahab in fact had changed nothing about the dominating policy and expectation of Israel. Israelite power and demand would continue.

As the king of Israel makes military preparation, a first step is to enlist his Southern counterpart, Jehoshaphat of Jerusalem, as his ally and accomplice (3:7-8). Jehoram "inquires" and Jehoshaphat responds positively with exaggerated assent, prepared to risk everything in order that the Northern regime can retain its colony. The immediate response of Jehoshaphat indicates a complete willingness to go to war; his response suggests that he was firmly under the thumb of the North, so that Jehoram's question in v. 7 is in effect a requirement of his subordinate ally.

The response made here by the Southern king from Jerusalem (3:7) compares to the response he made earlier to Ahab (1 Kgs

---

When the Shoe Was on the Other Foot

Moab was never a major political, military power, but it was a pesky near neighbor of Israel and Judah with whom it characteristically had troubled and vexing interactions. As a consequence, Moab is a recurring subject in Israel's prophetic Oracles Against the Nations, wherein Israel anticipates Yahweh's mighty judgment of Moab (Isa 15–16; Jer 48; Ezek 25:8-11; Amos 1:1-2; Zeph 2:8-9).

The narrative of Judges 3:12-30 tells of a time when the shoe was on the other foot, when Moab was the stronger party and Israel was the client community. In that narrative, the Israelites send "tribute" to Moab (3:15), though the amounts are not specified as in our present narrative. The submission of Israel to Moab, moreover, was at the behest of Yahweh (vv. 12-14). The narrative that follows tells of the daring and trickery by which Eglon, king of Moab, is killed by a "message" from God (v. 20), a message that in turn produced a great Israelite victory (vv. 29-30). That immense success over Moab, surely available in Israelite lore, makes the ultimate defeat of Jehoram in our present text all the more unexpected. In both cases, the hiddenness of God works outcomes that conventional politics could not have anticipated.

22:4). The important difference is that, in the Ahab incident, the response of willingness is promptly qualified in 1 Kings 22:5 by the requirement of a consultation with Yahweh. In the present narrative there is at the outset no such requirement. There is only a query about chosen strategy, ceding to Jehoram the authority to decide (v. 8). The reference to Edom as the chosen route in v. 8 and the mention of the king of Edom in v. 9 are almost incidental. The latter reference indicates that Edom, another state to the east of the Jordan and to the south of Moab, is also a vassal state of Israel, so that the choice is to proceed against Moab through friendly territory. Thus the expedition of the three kings is quickly under way.

The expedition advances for a week, and then crisis: *no water!* (v. 9). The territory east of the Jordan is notoriously arid. It appears that Jehoram's excessively eager military mobilization was poorly planned. Perhaps the narrative is reminiscent of the drought that Elijah had announced and then ended (1 Kgs 17:1; 18:45), reminding that the Omride dynasty is endlessly vexed by drought and is not good at water management.

The king's response to the drought is gratuitous and self-serving: it is Yahweh's fault! (The response is not unlike the quarrelsome response of the Israelites upon first reaching the wilderness after the Exodus; Exod 16:3.) So, says the king, Yahweh has summoned and now Yahweh will give over the three kings to the enemy. Except that the king's reference to Yahweh is decidedly late in the process. Indeed, this is the first mention of Yahweh in the narrative, for Yahweh had not earlier been on the king's horizon. There has been no summons to battle by Yahweh. There has been no inquiry to Yahweh about the expedition. The initiative has not been at all Yahwistically framed. Perhaps Jehoshaphat has been remiss in not making the same insistence to Jehoram that he had earlier made to Ahab about an inquiry to Yahweh (1 Kings 22:5).

Only now does Jehoshaphat intervene with an appeal for prophetic counsel (3:11). It is, belatedly, the same appeal made in 1 Kings 22:5, but here out of a very different motivation, no longer piety but practical emergency. The two kings quickly agree that Elisha is the acceptable nominee for the role of prophet (3:10-13). This quick agreement is again contrasted to the earlier Ahab episode wherein Ahab deeply resisted the nomination of Micaiah ben Imlah.

Prophetic Assurance, 3:13-20

Elisha is clearly on better terms with Jehoram than Micaiah had been with the king's father. Nonetheless Elisha at first resists the tricky assignment as theological advisor to the king. Because the military mobilization was not, at the outset, Yahweh-propelled, the military crisis can have nothing to do with Yahweh or with Yahweh's prophet. It would be better, urges Elisha (perhaps sarcastically) to consult with the gods of Ahab or Jezebel, since the monarchy is so notoriously prone to Baalism. But of course, since we know of the dramatic failure of Baal at Carmel in 1 Kings 18:25-29, Elisha's dismissive counsel is a counsel of despair, for the narrator, and perhaps the king, already knows that Baal cannot save.

Jehoram, however, persists. He insists, with the same misrepresentation uttered in v. 10, that the entire effort is a Yahweh-project. Yahweh should finish what Yahweh has begun. If it is a Yahweh project, then the prophet of Yahweh must be engaged and take some responsibility. Remarkably, neither Jehoshaphat in v. 10 nor Elisha in v. 13 objects to Jehoram's false revision of the facts. His appeal to Yahweh is, in the end, accepted at face value. The prophet has finally been recruited to assist in the crisis.

Elisha agrees only reluctantly (3:15). There is no love lost toward the Omrides, and a prophet of Yahweh can hardly afford any longer to be seen in public with the Israelite king. Elisha's aversion to Jehoram, however, is overridden by his high regard for Jehoshaphat, a genuine Yahwist. The dismissive rhetoric at the end of v. 14 is daring indeed; the prophet is carelessly indifferent to the Omride king.

The assurance of the prophet to the three kings constitutes the center of our narrative and is another attestation to the remarkable power and authority of the prophet who carries the "spirit of Elijah" (2 Kgs 2:15). The consultation requires music; apparently the prophet submits to an out-of-consciousness experience, a trance. [On Prophetic Consciousness]

On Prophetic Consciousness

The peculiar behavior of Elisha under the impetus of music is beyond our explanation. There is evidence, as in 1 Sam 10:9-13; 19:23-24, that behavior beyond the realm of normal consciousness was not regarded as excessively odd or uncommon. The prophets (including Saul as a prophet) who experienced such "trances" were persons who were uncommonly available for the intrusion and invasion of "the spirits," or Yahwistically, "the spirit" or "the hand" of Yahweh. In that "primitive" world, the boundary between managed, rational human life and the odd dynamic of "the gods" is not tightly sealed off. Such "prophets" are access points through which the intention of God may be operative in real life. [On issues related to prophetic consciousness, see Robert R. Wilson, *Prophecy and Society in Ancient Israel* (Philadelphia: Fortress Press, 1980) and the older study of J. Lindblom, *Prophecy in Ancient Israel* (Philadelphia: Muhlenburg Press, 1962).]

Such conduct seems to us, in our urbaneness, at least primitive if not irresponsible. We may dismiss it as primitive in terms of being ancient or "prescientific." Or we may treat it as an outcome of being ignorant and "uneducated." We may, however, be given pause to notice that it is this same intrusiveness of the spirit that is the taproot of Pentecost that powered the early church in Acts (Acts 2:1-13). And in contemporary reference, we may pause to notice that it is such "Pentecostalism" that is now seeding the spectacular growth of the world church. [See Walter J. Hollenweger, *Pentecostalism: Origins and Developments Worldwide* (Peabody MA: Hendrickson Publishers, 1997).] It may be that what is to be reassessed is not such "primitivism," but our modern rationality that seeks to seal off such access to the inscrutable.

In Doré's engraving of *The Pentecost*, a trance-like obedience is emphasized as the Holy Spirit has "intruded" upon them. Rather than wild-eyed disbelief, here the viewer is privy to the quiet power of holy communion.

Gustave Doré. *The Pentecost*. From the *Illustrated Bible*.19th century. Engraving. (Credit: Dover Pictorial Archive Series)

It is important that the peculiar and extraordinary experience of the prophet is taken at face value by all parties to the consultation. A condition evoked by music makes Elisha peculiarly susceptible to and available for a divine assurance beyond conventional royal reckoning.

The remarkable prophetic assurance given to the three kings is in two parts (3:16-19). First, the immediate crisis of water shortage will be resolved (3:16-17). The announcement from Yahweh is astonishing. The NRSV does not render it correctly, for in v. 16 there is no first person verb. It is not "I will make," but it is the wadi that will produce "pools and pools." There will be ample water. There will be water for the troops, for the cattle, and for the animals of transport. The threat of v. 9 will be completely overcome. The water, moreover, will be given in no ordinary way. There will be no wind and no rain, that is, no storm, so that all will know that the water is a spectacular wonder of Yahweh's generosity that will well up in the wadi. Perhaps the double negative of v. 17 is reminiscent of 1 Kings 19:11-12; there will be no storm, a usual vehicle for water. Yahweh will work otherwise, outside human explanation and conventional expectation. That is, Yahweh will perform a miracle.

But second, the real assurance is not simply the resolution of the water problem; the big issue is the war itself (3:18-19). Yahweh will not only give water; Yahweh will give victory. The water miracle pales in impressiveness when compared to the military miracle to come. The promise is that Moab and its cities will be completely in the power of the royal coalition, so that the three kings will be able and free to do what they want toward their enemy, to work fierce devastation without restraint against the rebel state. Notice how the prophetic oracle, as Yahweh's own assurance, is deeply marked by the kind of devastating resentment and thirst for vengeance that can lead to military brutality beyond the requirements of simple victory. The kings are authorized to devastate Moab: (a) to cut down every good tree, in violation of the "rules of war" from Deuteronomy 20:19-20; (b) to block up every spring of water, and this after their own water crisis; (c) to ruin good agricultural land with rocks. The damage is clearly well beyond victory, an act of vengeance that is perhaps both "instruction" to the enemy as well as retaliation. The prophet, seemingly, is led by the power of Yahweh to confirm the most rabid sensibility of war, and to sanction the kind of environmental disaster that regularly accompanies war. Following the oracle of two assurances, we are told that the first assurance is immediately enacted (3:20). There is water! Not only is the crisis overcome, but the implementation of the first assurance provides ground for assuming that the second assurance of victory will follow promptly in good order.

Prophetic Vindication and Then Disaster, 3:21-27

The Moabites, apparently bold and unafraid, mobilize to resist the three kings (3:21). The narrator, however, is not yet finished with the water so wondrously given by Yahweh. The Moabites see the water. They should have been dazzled that there was water at all, without wind or rain, a confounding miracle. But they see more than water; the water is "red as blood." [Red as Blood] The narrative offers no explanation for this strange appearance,

AΩ **Red as Blood**
It is odd that the text gives us no hint as to what caused this strange coloring of the water. We go beyond the text if we explain. It is at least worth noting that the term "red" (*'adûmim*) is the same Hebrew term as *Edom*, perhaps referring to red soil that may have colored the water. (On the term see Gen 25:25, 30, noticing that Esau is Edom). In any case, the coming of red water in the narrative is bound to remind an Israelite listener of the plague narrative of Exod 7:14-25. In that narrative, however, the water is not "red *as* blood" but it is "turned *to* blood." Both cases bespeak a wonder beyond explanation. Because Yahweh is at work in Jehoram's aggression, moreover, we are permitted to believe that the redness is here the inexplicable work of Yahweh as it was in Egypt.

📖 As Yahweh Intended

In a characteristic way, the oracle of Elisha asserts Yahweh's resolve without any hint of "how." That, of course, is the way of Yahweh in the rhetoric of Israel, long on resolve, reticent about means, because the means are regularly beyond Israel's awareness. That is part of the glory and power of such rhetoric; it can say more than it explains, perhaps more than it knows. We may notice two other uses where Yahweh's unexplained resolve is decisive:

> For the LORD had ordained to defeat the good counsel of Ahithophel, so that the LORD might bring ruin on Absalom. (2 Sam 17:14)

> So the king did not listen to the people, because it was a turn of affairs brought about by the LORD that he might fulfill his word, which the LORD had spoken by Ahijah the Shilonite to Jereboam son of Nebat. (1 Kgs 12:15)

The rhetoric is Israel's recognition that more is at work in the human enterprise than is susceptible to human explanation. The inscrutable is alive and well in Israel's self-articulation, an inscrutability that the world of technique will not overcome.

---

and exhibits no curiosity about it. The appearance as blood is a stratagem of Yahweh, linking the miracle of water to the miracle of victory. Quite clearly, the Israelite war effort has been taken up in Yahweh's inscrutable operations. What started out as an impulsive royal act has become, for the moment, a manifestation of Yahweh's power.

The appearance of water "red as blood" completely confounds the Moabites. They interpret the "blood" to be the spilled blood of the three kings and their soldiers. They imagine deep division in the fighting force of the coalition, so that the enemy has been in conflict and has self-destructed. And so, in a relaxation of military vigilance, they enter the enemy camp and become themselves sitting ducks. Yahweh, through Elisha, had given an assurance to the three kings. But Yahweh had kept this cunning stratagem secret from the three kings and, we may believe, even from the prophet. But since no other explanation can be offered for "red as blood," this must be a secret plan of Yahweh on behalf of Israel. And it works!

Because the gullible Moabites are so vulnerable, their slaughter is inevitable. The three kings now work a massive devastation against Moab, exactly as Yahweh had intended: [As Yahweh Intended]

> The Moabite cities are overturned;
> the land is filled with rocks;
> the springs are stopped up;
> the good trees are felled. (3:25)

The fourfold devastation matches the prophetic oracle of v. 19 point by point. War works its predictable destruction and death, sure to ensnare the civilian population. There was only one exception to the devastation, the city of Kirhareseth, not yet overcome like every other Moabite city. [Kirhareseth] This exception, however, is only short-term. As soon as the Israelite archers come, zap! What a victory! It is exactly as Elisha had said. Yahweh is vindicated; Jehoram is triumphant; Moab has learned a costly lesson; Elisha is reliable. All is well!

It would be terrific for all Israelite parties and their allies, including Yahweh and Elisha, if the narrative ended with the attack on Kirhareseth in v. 25. But of course the story does not end there (see 3:26-27). Mesha, the Moabite king, is not so easily defeated, even if he faces the power of Yahweh; he has some resources of his own

Kirhareseth

Nothing is known of this city, the site of Israel's last success in this military campaign. However, the mention of the city in Isa 16:7, 11; Jer 48:31, 36 as a poetic parallel for "Moab" suggests that it was a major site, certainly a freighted item in Israel's poetic imagination.

Chemosh

The Moabite god to whom Mesha made sacrifice is not named, but is commonly taken to be Chemosh, a god known in Israelite poetry (Jer 48:7, 13, 46). Special reference should be made to the Moabite Stone, a remarkable stone inscription reporting on Mesha:

Mesha Inscription, stone slab also known as the Moabite Stone, 3'x2'. Discovered in 1868, slab tells of the revolt of Mesha.

Mesha Inscription. c. 830 BC. Louvre, Paris, France.

I (am) Mesha, son of Chemosh-[...], king of Moab, the Dibonite—my father (had) reigned over Moab thirty years, and I reigned after my father,—(who) made this high place for Chemosh in Qarhoh [...] because he saved me from all the kings and caused me to triumph over all my adversaries. As for Omri, (5) king of Israel, he humbled Moab many years (lit., days), for Chemosh was angry at his land. And his son followed him and he also said, "I will humble Moab." In my time he spoke (thus), but I have triumphed over him and over his house, while Israel hath perished for ever! (Now) Omri had occupied the land of Medeba, and (Israel) had dwelt there in his time and half the time of his son (Ahab), forty years; but Chemosh dwelt there in my time.

And I built Baal-meon, making a reservoir in it, and I built (10) Qaryaten. Now the men of Gad had always dwelt in the land of Ataroth, and the king of Israel had built Ataroth for them; but I fought against the town and took it and slew all the people of the town as satiation (intoxication) for Chemosh and Moab. And I brought back from there Arel (or Oriel), its chieftain, dragging him before Chemosh in Kerioth, and I settled there men of Sharon and men of Maharith. And Chemosh said to me, "Go, take Nebo from Israel!" (15) So I went by night and fought against it from the break of dawn until noon, taking it and slaying all, seven thousand men, boys, women, girls and maid-servants, for I had devoted them to destruction for (the god) Ashtar-Chemosh. [James Pritchard, *Ancient Near Eastern Texts Relating to the Old Testament* (Princeton: Princeton University Press, 1955) 320.]

The stone, likely dated about 830 BC, names the god of Mesha. Scholars have noticed that except for the names, the religious assumptions reflected in the script are exactly like those of Israel. It is for that reason that we will not be clear on who is wrathful in v. 37.

not yet tapped. He is fighting on his home turf for his own land, and will not yield easily. His first effort against the onslaught of Israel is military: 700 soldiers, a huge force, but a futile effort (3:26). The coalition of three kings will not be defeated in a straight face-to-face contest.

Mesha, however, is not yet finished. He is now a determined man, driven to desperate measures (3:27). As his final effort, he sacrifices his firstborn son, his heir apparent, as a burnt offering to his god. The text uses the technical term for "burnt offering," *'olah* (see Lev 1:3-17). He commits an act of intense piety. Oddly the narrative does not name the god to whom the son is offered, but it was surely the national god of the Moabites, Chemosh. [Chemosh] This act by King Mesha may be one of genuine piety; it may, however, be an extreme form of jingoistic militarism. Either way, it is the "supreme sacrifice." [Sacrifice of the Firstborn] It is, from this distance, an outrageous act, but one regularly replicated in the madness of war. The sacrifice itself is reported without comment in the narrative (3:27).

Then the narrative makes a huge leap, completely without explanation: "Great wrath!" Israel was forced to retreat, driven from the field. The leap made in the midst of v. 27 witnesses to a deep

---

Sacrifice of the Firstborn

The sacrifice of the firstborn by Mesha is the pivot point of this narrative. We might reflect on the phrase "firstborn" in other texts. In Exod 4:22, Israel is Yahweh's "firstborn," especially prized. If that identification persists in our narrative, then it is Yahweh's firstborn versus the firstborn of Mesha. The same juxtaposition is evident earlier in the Exodus narrative; there all the firstborn of Egypt are eliminated by Yahweh in defense of Yahweh's own firstborn, Israel (Exod 12:29-30).

Particular attention should be paid to the close study of Jon Levenson, who argues persuasively that the sacrifice of the firstborn was not common in Israel, but was surely known and practiced. [Jon D. Levenson, *The Death and Resurrection of the Beloved Son: The Transformation of Child Sacrifice in Judaism and Christianity* (New Haven: Yale University Press, 1993).] Levenson insists, moreover, that it was this Israelite-Jewish practice and this rhetoric that has been taken over by Christian interpretation of Jesus. Jews and Christians together continue to ponder the narrative of Genesis 22 and the struggle for the firstborn. Mesha's act in any case cannot be dismissed in condescension as a "primitive act." The act of Mesha is not so much removed from the pondering of Micah:

With what shall I come before the LORD,
   and bow myself before God on high?
Shall I come before him with burnt offerings,
   with calves a year old?
Will the LORD be pleased with thousands of rams,
   with ten thousands of rivers of oil?
Shall I give *my firstborn* for my transgression,
   the fruit of my body for the sin of my soul? (Mic 6:6-7)

reversal in the fortunes of the battle. Israel, who had been winning, as the prophetic oracle had assured, is now routed. The only conclusion to draw, is it not, is that the Moabite god, Chemosh, is motivated by the sacrifice and is activated on home ground against the invader? The most remarkable fact about the narrative is that everything we would most like to know is left unsaid. In fact, the unsaid is the most demanding and remarkable theological data in the narrative.

In the face of such an enigma, it is plausible that the Moabite god defeated the God of Israel, and the narrator could not bring himself to say so. Or perhaps Yahweh had turned against Israel and belatedly fights for Moab, though there is no hint of this. It is in any case worth noting that we are not told whose "wrath" this is. Perhaps the narrator is as dumbfounded as we are. The narrative leaves us hanging, without resolution. Elisha is nowhere to be found when we need him most.

CONNECTIONS

This narrative is built around a massive lie (self-deception?) twice voiced by Jehoram: that it was Yahweh who instigated Israelite military action (3:10, 13). A careful reading of vv. 6-8 indicates that Yahweh had nothing to do with the decision to invade. The initiative is taken solely by the king. This falsehood, implicating Yahweh in actions chosen independently, is characteristic, especially in the formation of public policy, especially military policy. Every regime likes to claim theological legitimacy for its actions. Like much military policy, the ill-advised, knee-jerk reaction of Jehoram is undertaken in order to recover *lost resources* that the king of Moab will now withhold, or *lost face*, whereby Israel "loses Moab" the way the U.S. "lost China" in the late 1940s. By this lie, the policy of Jehoram is at the same time escalated (now a matter of divine concern) and made to appear virtuous. This fundamental theological dishonesty that makes the war in the end unwinnable is a characteristic act of mixing self-serving aggressive policy with the will and purpose of Yahweh.

We may be astonished at the king's capacity for dishonesty, seemingly without a second thought. But we are more amazed at the collusion of Elisha in the war project, for his oracle commits Yahweh entirely to the project. Even beyond our astonishment at the king and our amazement at the prophet, we may be more deeply appalled by Yahweh's ready collusion in the process. Yahweh has been invited late into the "war effort," but even late, Yahweh engages it fully, even to an escalation of the rhetoric of violence that goes beyond simple victory (3:19).

In this connection we may ponder a general theological problem and a more specific temptation in our own U.S. culture. The theological problem is that Yahweh is often, if not characteristically, a party to public violence. One may argue that it is human violence imposed upon Yahweh but, as the text stands, it is Yahweh's own violence. And surely Yahweh's engagement in violence has created a legacy of religious violence that operates even until now.

Concerning the more specific temptation, we may ponder the propensity of U.S. policy, not unlike that of Jehoram, to turn military aggressiveness into a Yahwistic crusade. Thus, for example, it is now clear that the specific warrant for U.S. action in Vietnam was a trumped-up incident in the Gulf of Tonkin that created a cover of virtue for aggression. More recently, in the so-called "Gulf War," there is no doubt that the U.S. motivation was in part presented as a noble effort in the interest of "Western Civilization," even though the U.S. government regularly and easily cavorts with petty tyrants who administer oil. As Reinhold Niebuhr has seen so well, the capacity for self-deception is a defining characteristic in mixing public policy with religion.

The narrative takes an odd, unexpected, and quite inexplicable turn in v. 27, where the military success of Israel is abruptly thwarted and Israel is driven from the field. Three observations occur to me that require some consideration:

1. The trigger for the reversal is apparently the sacrifice of "his firstborn son," the supreme sacrifice in such an intergenerational society committed to the principle of primogeniture. The crude action of Mesha is, I assume, repugnant to us all. Surely such a sacrifice is ignoble, the sort of practice that "pagans" might do, but that Israel has foresworn (see 2 Kgs 16:3; 17:17; 21:6; 23:10). We may wonder, moreover, what kind of god the Moabite god is to be bribed or moved by such a gross act.

The act of child sacrifice ought readily to appall. But then it should give us pause, precisely because "the war effort" always requires the sacrifice of our beloved sons (and now daughters) in ways that are characteristically futile and barbaric, but that we decorate with noble, patriotic rhetoric. One may think, perhaps, that "child sacrifice" is too remote from forced conscription of the young into military service for a valid connection to be drawn. Both acts, however, may be based on a decision that a "larger cause" warrants such sacrifice. Our repugnance at Mesha's act should cause us to examine closely such acts of brutality in the service of victory.

2. The strange outcome of v. 27 indicates that the determined oracle of Elisha in vv. 16-19 is either wrong or has been superseded by something else. In this particular case, Elisha is not vindicated by events. Perhaps we should have been suspicious of his oracle, for it is so unlike the resistant utterances of Micaiah and Elijah in like circumstance. Indeed Elisha's oracle is more in keeping with the prophets in 1 Kings 22:6 who easily and readily support the war effort. In this case, Elisha is not said to be "false," but perhaps it is a case in which even this prophet is caught up in war fever. Perhaps the music that entranced the prophet consisted of marches played by John Philip Sousa that are sure to make the blood run patriotic! In any case, the narrative does not comment on the peculiar turn whereby our prophet hero turns out to be unreliable.

3. The enigmatically expressed outcome of v. 27 witnesses the enigma of the historical process that runs beyond royal planning and prophetic anticipation. The text says only, "Great wrath came upon Israel." Significantly, there is no hint of the source of the wrath. On the face of it, it is the wrath of Chemosh, the god of Moab. In that case, the narrative suggests that *in Moab* the Moabite god prevails, thus putting Israel and the God of Israel to flight. But because the narrative is reticent, the source of wrath may perhaps not be Chemosh. Perhaps it could be Yahweh who prevails even in Moab, even against Israel. Or perhaps there is collusion between Yahweh and Chemosh against Israel. We do not know and are not told. Israel from time to time must reckon, in retrospect, with its defeat and the defeat of Yahweh (see 1 Sam 4:10-22). What Israel knows is that history has its own untamed quality:

> No word, no understanding, no counsel,
>   can avail against the LORD.
> The horse is made ready for the day of battle,
>   but the victory belongs to the LORD. (Prov 21:30-31)

On occasion, victory is beyond the war planners. This enigmatic outcome to the war renders the theological certitude Elisha offered the king, at best, penultimate. In parallel fashion, it makes reliance on military technology less than sure.

One connection might indeed be the enduring, haunting time of the Vietnam War. The unexpected, and to some incomprehensible, defeat of the U.S. in that war is surely an abiding scar and wound on the public imagination of the U.S. There is something beyond rationality in that war, for the U.S. effort had all the blessings of good Western theology in its "final solution" to the problem of Communism. And surely the U.S. had all the technical capacity that could be imagined. And yet they could not prevail! Because the Western God has turned to wrath? Because the gods of Southeast Asia were afield and powerful? Until now, at least, our judgment about Vietnam is not unlike v. 27. That is, we do not know what to say.

(I understand that in a commentary like this one, a focus upon Vietnam is too pointed and too remote and comment serves to open old wounds. I do so only because Vietnam is an open sore in our body politic. It is an enduring undermining of our self-confidence and self-righteousness. It is a deep case in point of having first mobilized and then belatedly imagined God's initiative. As in our text, moreover, there were ample prophets to certify the war in Vietnam.)

Chapter 3 has no closure, even as the Vietnam War in many ways lacks closure for the U.S. For some, who lost sons and daughters to the war effort, it was a story of immense "child sacrifice" and "great wrath." Surely God has been implicated in the tragedy and the sorrow. As of this late date, we are unable to say how, even as our text does not know how.

Military Funeral Procession. (Credit: Department of Defense. USA)

NOTE

[1]Notice that the text allows him twelve years. The chronology I am following is reconstructed and necessarily approximate.

ELISHA AS A TRANSFORMATIVE FORCE

2 Kings 4:1-44

We have now seen Elisha as a powerful prophet endowed with the spirit of Elijah. In chapter 3, we have witnessed the prophet engaged in public activity, authorizing the coalition of three kings to war. In the present chapter, the prophet continues his awesome work, only this time engaged in pastoral activity toward needy people, without reference to the king. The narrative consists of five "wonders" that invite astonishment (4:1-7, 8-17, 18-37, 38-41, and 42-44). Of these, the second and third episodes (4:8-17, 18-37) are interconnected and deal with the same person, the woman from Shunem. The wonders are designed to evoke amazement at Elisha's inscrutable and awesome capacity to invert circumstance.

COMMENTARY

An Escape from Enslaving Poverty, 4:1-7

Elisha is like a magnet. He draws needy people to himself. In this narrative he is approached by a woman married to one of the "company of the prophets," presumably one of Elisha's disciples. That she is married to such a man surely earns her special attention from the prophet. But her connection to prophetic circles is not important to the narrative, and is not mentioned after v. 1. What counts is that she is a helpless, vulnerable widow, not helpless as "an inept silly woman," but helpless as a woman without a male advocate in patriarchal society. It should not surprise us that v. 1, where she is identified as a widow, mentions a *creditor*, for creditors characteristically show up around widows, like buzzards circling near-prey. [Creditors and Debtors] In that ancient society, one is forced into "debt slavery" in order to pay off standing accounts. Because the woman has no reserves, her two children are about to be reduced to debt slavery. She faces an acute economic crisis.

Elisha commands her in her acute scarcity to prepare for unthinkable abundance: summon all the pots and pans and buckets in the

Creditors and Debtors

The world about which this story is told is a real economic world of creditors and debtors. There are of course no isolated economic acts that take place in a vacuum of equity. Every economic act takes place in a world already disproportionate, where the cards are stacked. In that world of economic reality, creditors regularly gain more and more at the expense of debtors who soon have nothing. There is a long history of reading the Bible as an innocent book about religion. But of course it is not. The ministry of Elisha, moreover, is no idyllic religious enterprise. Coping with debt is a defining problem for a widow in a patriarchal society; she is lost and hopeless without a male advocate. The story is about a prophetic intervention that quickly redefines economic reality for all parties.

Reference might be made to Jesus' parable in Luke 7:41-50, wherein Jesus connects *forgiveness of sins* and *forgiveness of debt*, the two forgivenesses being of a piece. Jesus teaching on forgiveness, moreover, is in the Jewish context of "release" (Deut 15:1-18) and Jubilee (Lev 25).

See Sharon H. Ringe, *Jesus, Liberation, and the Biblical Jubilee: Images for Ethics and Christology,* OBT (Philadelphia: Fortress Press, 1985).

---

neighborhood…and start pouring (4:3-4)! She obeys (4:5). The neighbors help her; they bring every container they can muster. Only when there were no more containers did the oil stop. [Oil as Commodity] The movement of the narrative is from *prophetic command* (4:3-4) to the *obedience of the woman* (4:5-6) that transforms her situation. But the structure of command/obedience is framed with reference to *creditors* (4:1) and *debt* (4:7). The woman is admonished to sell the oil, pay the debts, and thus to rescue her children from economic bondage, and then to live on the residue. Elisha engages in *debt cancellation*. He has broken the cycle of poverty in this case, and placed the woman and her children beyond the grasping power of acquisitive economics. *In nuce*, the prophet introduces an alternative economics. We may notice the laconic style of the narrative. No curiosity is exhibited about the abundance of oil. No special acknowledgement is made of prophetic authority. All we have is a restored woman. She has been "released" from her life-threatening debt. [Debt Cancellation]

Oil as Commodity

In our contemporary world, of course, "oil" is the elemental commodity that drives the postindustrial economy and that fuels much of U.S. foreign policy. Some argue that it is for that reason the U.S. often intervenes in the "Mideast" to protect oil intrests. In the ancient world of the widow, oil has not yet become such a formidable public issue. There is no doubt, however, that even in that simpler economy, oil is a necessity; it is hard to come by and widows are likely to be without. While oil is indeed a gift from God (see Jer 31:12; Joel 2:19; Ps 104:15), it is also a prized commodity of royal interests (2 Kgs 20:13; Isa 39:2; 2 Chr 11:11; 32:28). Thus it is a free gift of the creator; in a demand economy, however, it will tend to become the commodity of a monopoly that in turn produces desperation. Elisha enters "the oil crisis" at the point of desperation.

Thus the prophetic supply of free oil is a radical redefining of economic relationships. Reference can be made to the narrative of Luke 7:36-50. The entire story concerns "ointment" (v. 46), and reference is also made to oil (v. 46), here perhaps a less valuable commodity.

See Luke 7:37-38: "And a woman in the city, who was a sinner, having learned that he was eating in the Pharisee's house, brought an alabaster jar of ointment. She stood behind him at his feet, weeping and began to bathe his feet with her tears and to dry them with her hair. Then she continued kissing his feet and anointing them with the ointment."

Philippe de Champaigne. *Feast in the House of Simon*. 1656. Oil on canvas. Musée des Beaux-Arts, Nantes, France. (Credit: Giraudon/Art Resource, NY)

The Gift of a Son, 4:8-17

Whereas in vv. 1-7 Elisha dealt with a poor, nameless widow, now he deals with a wealthy woman who had befriended him. In vv. 8-14 the narrative describes the uncommon generosity toward the prophet by the woman from Shunem. [Map: Shunem] It is astonishing that nowhere in the narrative is she named, perhaps because the interest of the narrative is completely on the prophet. In any case, the woman wants nothing and needs nothing from the prophet, not even an intervention on her behalf with the king (4:13).

Remarkably, the identification of her "need" upon which the story focuses comes not from her, but from Elisha's attendant, Gehazi (who is named). Gehazi verbalizes what the woman would not verbalize: "No son" (see 1:17;

Debt Cancellation

The "sabbatic principle" in Israel's legal imagination stretched from sabbath through the "year of release" to Jubilee. [On the "sabbatic principle," see Patrick D. Miller, Jr., "The Human Sabbath: A Study in Deuteronomic Theology," *The Princeton Seminary Bulletin* 6/2 (1985): 81-97.] Israel at its best is determined that debt should not define social relationships. At the end of this narrative, the widow is freed from debt; she is able to "pay [her] debts" (4:7). The intervening activity of Elisha makes such a payment possible. His action is best understood as a strategy for "release." [On the defining claim of "release" for Israel's ethical vision, see Jeffries M. Hamilton, *Social Justice and Deuteronomy: The Case of Deuteronomy 15*, SBL Dissertation Series 136 (Atlanta: Scholars Press, 1992).] Elisha adheres to the deep Israelite conviction that debt must not finally be the decisive factor in social organization. Such a conviction requires the transformative interventions that the prophet boldly enacts.

3:27). [No Son] We do not know why the woman never asked for a son, because in a patriarchal society (on which see v. 1) a son is a *sine qua non* for a secure life. Perhaps she did not ask because she was otherwise secure in her wealth. Perhaps she was simply no whiner; or perhaps in her judgment a son was beyond even the capacity of Elisha. For whatever reason, she did not ask; but he promises anyway.

No Son

It is impossible to overestimate the cruciality of a son in that ancient, patriarchal world. A son guaranteed economic surety in time to come, and lack of a son was a social stigma to a woman. It may well be that the woman in our narrative thinks otherwise, but Gehazi voices conventional perceptions. In his purview this woman joins the long line of Israelite women nearly shamed in their lack: Sarah (Gen 11:30), Rebekah (Gen 25:21), Rachel (Gen 29:31), and Hannah (1 Sam 1:2).

The pivotal exchange between Elisha and the barren woman is given in three quick lines:

1. *The prophet:* In due time you will have a son;
2. *The woman:* Do not deceive me;
3. *The narrator:* She bore a son at the time he had declared to her.

The exchange is reminiscent of the promise of the LORD to Sarah:

1. *The LORD:* In due season, Sarah will have a son;
2. *Sarah:* I did not laugh;
3. *The narrator:* Sarah bore Abraham a son at the time of which God had spoken (Gen 18:10-15; 21:2).

As with the birth of Isaac, this son is clearly a gift of God's peculiar generosity, implemented through the promise of Elisha, man of God. Indeed, such a gift is a quintessential exhibit of Elisha's authority. Remarkably, unlike Sarah in Genesis 21:6, the woman expresses no gratitude or delight, indeed makes no statement at all. The prophet who can produce oil (4:4-6) can produce a son. As he created a future for the poor widow, so now he creates a future for this wealthy woman.

Life Restored, 4:18-37

This narrative of a wonder of Elisha is related to vv. 8-17 in the same way that the episodes of 1 Kings 17:8-16 and vv. 17-24 are related to each other in the work of Elijah. In each case a preliminary miracle is seconded by a follow-up deed. While the pattern is the same, it is to be observed that Elisha's initial miracle of a son dramatically surpasses the initial wonder of Elijah toward the women; Elijah's deed in 1 Kings 17:8-16 is a close parallel to Elisha's miracle of oil in 2 Kings 4:1-7. Thus the tradition has perhaps scrambled and displaced what may have been free-floating and unconnected prophetic narratives that could be arranged in a variety of configurations.

In any case, the son wondrously given in v. 17 is dead in v. 20. We are told only that his head hurt acutely, but the narrative lacks any explanation of his death in which the narrator has no particular interest. The mother's response to the death, resistant to her husband's counsel, is to rush to see Elisha (4:21-25). The prophet is at Mt. Carmel, perhaps the home of the prophetic community (see 2:25), certainly the emblem of dramatic prophetic authority (see 1 Kgs 18:42). The woman has no doubt that Elisha is the one who can deal with the emergency she now faces. He has been established as a source of life, and she herself knows of his odd power for life.

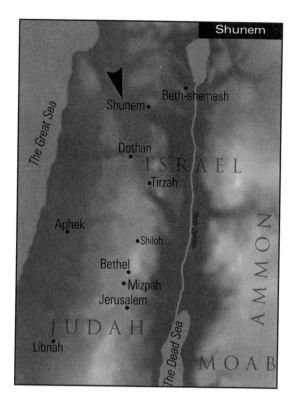

Her initial response to Gehazi, as he rushes to welcome her, is enigmatic. The servant asks about the well-being of her son and of herself (4:26). She answers, "It is all right." In Hebrew the exchange is dominated by the term *shalom*. He asks, "Is it *shalom* to you? Is it *shalom* to your husband? Is it *shalom* to your son?" She answers, "It is *shalom*." It is the same answer she gave to her husband in v. 23. Five times the term *shalom* is utilized, three as a question by the servant, twice in her response to her husband and to the servant.

The question Gehazi asks is appropriate. Her reply is completely unexpected. Indeed her own hurried journey tells against her verbal answer. Nothing is *shalom* for her. It is surely not *shalom* when one's only son, miraculously given, has died. Perhaps the woman is only offering conventional responses, or she is engaged in denial. Much more likely, she has deep confidence in Elisha, deep faith that he can reverse the death as he had overcome her barrenness in order to make all things new. Entirely credible within the narrative is that the inexplicable power of the prophet (already experienced by the woman) should be matched by her limitless trust in him.

She throws herself in need at the feet of the prophet, suggesting that she is neither voicing convention nor engaging in denial. The attendant of the prophet tries to protect the prophet from her, but he insists upon being available to her. In this instance, Elisha is a remarkably responsive giver of pastoral care. He recognizes her deep anguish, the same anguish mother Hannah felt in barrenness and that priest Eli failed to recognize (1 Sam 1:12-13). Elisha confesses, moreover, that he has failed to understand her need (4:27). The woman is beside herself in grief and engages in accusation against the prophet for having given her a son that she does now not have. The prophet has toyed with her! The accusatory tone of the bereft woman matches the mother's assault on Elijah in 1 Kings 17:18.

Elisha's response to her is immediate. He dispatches his servant, Gehazi, to the dead boy. The prophet proposes that his "staff" should be an instrument of effective healing power, that it should work new life by the hand of Gehazi, even if he himself is not present. This is an extraordinary act of self-confidence on the part of the prophet. But it does not work! The staff by itself could do nothing. Perhaps the woman knows this, for she refuses to leave the presence of the prophet. She understood that it is the person of the prophet who carries authority that cannot be extended beyond the prophet's own person. There is no transfer of power to a totem, for this power is a person-to-person phenomenon.

Having failed with such a secondhand stratagem, the prophet now engages directly against the power of death. There is no one in the room except the prophet and the boy. Nonetheless our narrator gives us a play-by-play account of what happened. First, the prophet prayed to Yahweh. Second, he engages in physical gestures that can perhaps be understood as something like artificial respiration, though his motions are not clear in the report. In any case, the prophet pled for Yahweh's action and then he himself acted. His direct intervention, unlike his ineffective staff, works the wonder of life. Seven sneezes and the boy is alive. This is indeed a resurrection! New life is given to the son.

Elisha returns the son, now alive, to the mother with the same terseness as Elijah's parallel in 1 Kings 17:23. Unlike her counterpart in 1 Kings 17:24, this woman is speechless. Saying nothing, she falls at the feet of the prophet, an action parallel to her desperation in v. 27. Her action now expresses unutterable gratitude and joy, but also acknowledges the incomparable authority, power, and generosity of the prophet. The prophet is not "a god," but he is the next best thing, a human person who carries God's life-giving power that lies beyond the scope of any normal human capacity. (See Acts 10:26.) The son is twice-given by the power of the prophet, given first in a wondrous birth, given second in an astonishing healing. This is a son "born again" to new life.

Another Rescue from Death, 4:38-41

These verses relate yet another wonder of the prophet, whereby life is given in the place of death. This brief narrative is placed after the resurrection narrative of vv. 18-37 and parallels its action of wonder; the storyline itself is more closely parallel to the episode of 2:19-22. But the ordering of the different narratives makes little difference, because they all attest to the uncommon power of Elisha.

The crisis is evoked by a famine, undoubtedly the result of a drought. Though nothing is made of it here, the famine-drought circumstance evidences continuity with the Elijah narrative (1 Kgs 18:1-6), and continues the attestation that the Omride kings are ineffective in their public responsibility. The famine, in this narrative, has resulted in a desperate scavenger search for food. Such desperate actions are likely to be careless, because anything edible looks good. As anyone knows who picks greens or mushrooms, some are not edible. Not surprisingly, the resulting stew is poisonous. The eaters recognized immediately its ominous character, a pot filled with the power of death.

The antidote to "death in the pot" is the prophet who exudes the power for life. His response, as with salt in 2:20-21, is to transform the poisonous food with flour. His action works! Death is overcome. The food is edible and so fends off the famine. He is indeed a bringer of life, capable of turning curse to blessing.

Food in Abundance, 4:42-44

A man brings "first fruits" to Elisha: that is, from the first and best barley and grain, bread is offered to the prophet. Perhaps the grain produces better bread than will a later crop. More likely the bringing of first fruits is simply a gesture of gratitude, affection, and honor. The prophet receives the bread, but he will not eat it or save it for himself. He consigns it to all "the people." He intends that what he has should be shared, no doubt with reference to the famine of v. 38. His servant (Gehazi?) resists: "There is not enough. What are twenty loaves among so many?" The prophet, however, is undeterred by caution, and yet overly impressed with scarcity. He knows more than his servant. He knows that bread shared will multiply. He promises his servant that there will be enough to go around and bread left over. The statement of the prophet is a quote, perhaps a reference to the manna narrative of Exodus 16. In any case, the servant complies; the bread is distributed. The crowd is fed. Outcome: they had some left over! Of course they did, because this is no ordinary bread, given out by no ordinary man. This is bread by "the word of the LORD." There is a power that readily overrides famine and scarcity.

The five wonders in this chapter—oil, son, son again, stew by flour, bread—are of different kinds enacted for different constituencies in different circumstances. They are, however, all of a piece. All attest to the peculiar significance of Elisha and to the recognition that when the powerful purpose of Yahweh sets down in human life, nothing is normal; nothing is as it was. Everything is changed. Everything is different. Everything is new. And all the powers of death are feeble and helpless before this determined will for life.

CONNECTIONS

These prophetic wonders, given here in an uninterrupted series, offer a welcome world of life, but seem contradicted by our ready-at-hand world where death seems to prevail. That contradiction raises the difficult question of how we are to understand and appropriate these stories. The conventional approach, taken by almost all scholars in a way that may be the best we can do, is to regard these stories as "legends," that is, memories that have been greatly enhanced beyond "what happened" by a vivid and energetic imagination. That is, imagination carries the narrative well beyond anything credible as a happening.

Such a procedure serves to explain away the text. I have no interest in championing the historicity of the narratives that surely seem to us implausible. We ought, however, at least to struggle with the intention of the text. I suggest that in these stories—and more largely the corpus of stories of Elijah and Elisha—an argument is being made that there is an alternative world of reality beyond royal control and royal reason. Our problem with these stories, characteristically, is that we are wont to "explain" them in terms of royal reason, which quickly renders them incredible.

We do know, however, that what is *seen* and what *happens* are largely determined by the social framing of reality, so that in communities not enthralled by Enlightenment reason, things happen that such reason dismisses in principle. I suggest then, that these stories invite and enact a contest between frames, a dispute between perceptions of reality that comes down to a controversy between texts as competing scriptings of reality. This set of stories scripts reality in a way taken as unreal by royal reason. Conversely, royal scripting of reality may strike this "community of astonishment" as flat, sterile, and productive only of despair. Readers of the Bible must contend with the fact that the Bible characteristically rescripts and reconstrues reality in different categories. That, however, does not automatically make it fanciful "legend." Were one to step outside our controlling reason, we may find, as some always have, a world where our declared impossibilities take on the quality of the possible.[1] Now to the detail of this alternative possibility:

The narrative of vv. 1-7 is clearly linked to Elijah's wonder in 1 Kings 17:8-16. Notably, however, the Elisha account is more rigorously framed by "creditor" (4:1) and "debt" (4:7). This is not simply a tale of charity to the needy. This is rather to plunge the prophet into the deep economic crisis of the day in which an indifferent economy was permitting the big ones (creditors) to devour the little ones (debtors). The tale will surely be misunderstood unless it is read in terms of economic crisis, a point that brings the narrative very close to our own time of economic crisis. In order to read the narrative biblically, reference might be made to the "year of release" (Deut 15:12-18) that eschews a permanent underclass, to the demanding economic program of Nehemiah wherein creditors and debtors form an economic alliance (Neh 5:1-13), to Jesus' dangerous teaching concerning the entitlement of the poor (see Matt 20:1-16 concerning bold gospel arrangements of first and last). Elisha is a force who functions as the Great Equalizer in the social arrangements of his context, bringing equalization by denying the claim of scarcity that drives an economy of greed.

The narrative of the Shunemite woman warrants most of our attention, since it is the most complex of these episodes and claims the deepest wonder of resurrection. The story is of course linked to Elijah's miracle in 1 Kings 17:17-24; only this account is more complex. It is, moreover, echoed in the wonder enacted by Jesus (Mark 5:21-24, 35-43, see John 11). This entire sequence of texts attests to the claim, well outside the scripting of royal reason, that Yahweh's power for life is not defeated by the claims of death. Here and there, that intrusive, irresistible power for life has been entrusted to those who act outside the bounds of accepted reality.

Beyond that general, dazzling claim—that for Christians culminates in the joy of Easter—I wish to observe two points. The first is this: while the story is, in the end, a celebration of the power of

Elisha, we should not miss the decisive role played by the woman who is the mother of the dead son. At the outset she regards the offer of a son, when her husband is old, as foolish nonsense (4:16). When her son dies, she is filled with resolve and will not be deterred. Right from the beginning, she aims at *shalom* that can only mean the well-being of her son (4:23, 26). Her determination is of course linked to Elisha; she is adamant in holding him to his power and in ensuring that he will do the wonder of which he is capable. She is for an instant a more powerful, determined figure than the prophet. She grasps him in insistence (4:27). She accuses him of betrayal (4:28). She refuses his ploy of sending his staff, knowing before he does that the gesture is futile (4:30). She is vindicated as a woman of *shalom*; for she departs only when she has her living son restored. Burke Long has seen the power of her character well:[2]

> The writer...draws the human, male shape of wonder-worker in Jehoram's kingdom over against an unnamed, assertive woman who turns aside protocol and moral obtuseness...one's adulation [for the prophet] is cooled by the mother's experience of loss and the knowledge or Elisha's astonishing blindness.... As a sort of new miracle, Elisha is taught the lesson (or does he get the point after all?) by a woman without lineage, emboldened only with passion and determination born of her desperate bereavement.

Long has helped me see that the power of the prophet, wondrous as it is, is mobilized only by the insistent, contentious woman who in her hope and her anger refuses to let things be. The "voice of pain" mobilizes the power of God to newness; we may believe that without such voicing, the prophet may have quit in resignation after Gehazi's futile effort with his staff.[3]

The particular action of Elisha over the boy is described in great detail but is far from clear (4:34-35). It seems plausible that he breathed life into him, transferring his own breath to become the new breath of the boy. While this may be understood simply as a physiological transaction, reference to "breath" draws us close to a theological aspect of a biblical understanding of life. In Genesis 2:7, inert matter is breathed upon in order to make human life possible, so that Elisha in our story does what the LORD God does in the creation narrative. The Psalmist is aware, in a most specific way, that life is indeed the gift of God's breath:

When you take away their breath, they die
 and return to their dust.
When you send forth your spirit, they are created.
(Ps 104:29-30)

Elisha enacts a miracle of creation, making *shalom* available for
mother and son (see also Ezek 37:1-14 on the power of God's
breath).

The final narrative of vv. 42-44, in which the prophet creates
abundance where there was none, nicely parallels the prophetic
abundance of oil in vv. 1-7. The two narratives frame the entire
collection of wonder stories, thus constituting a collage of abundance (*shalom*) in a world too much defined by scarcity and its
consequent death. Elisha's presence reconfigures the world according to the abundance of Yahweh that redefines every sphere of
existence. In this final narrative, the emphasis is on "had some left,"
a residue after feeding a hungry people (4:44).

Such a narrative about "wonder bread" must surely be linked to
the manna narrative of Exodus 16 which reports no surplus, but
enough for all:

> The Israelites did so, some gathering more, some less. But when
> they measured it with an omer, those who gathered much had
> nothing over, and those who gathered little had no shortage;
> they gathered as much as each of them needed. (Exod 16:17-18;
> see 2 Cor 8:15)

The claim of a surplus created by the prophet in the face of skepticism like that of his servant is of course echoed in the "feeding
miracles of Jesus" (Mark 6:30-44; 8:1-10). In both these narratives,
the disciples of Jesus, like the servant of Elisha, are practical people
who can count and who are impressed with the evident shortage of
food. In their practicality, however, they miss the point of Jesus'
capacity to enact abundance (Mark 6:42-44; 8:8-9). [A New Testament
Replica] No, they did not understand, any more than those around
Elisha understood. Nothing is as it seems,
because in this concrete prophetic character, a world of abundance is unleashed into
the world that makes available a context of
shalom. In that alternative world, concretely given in these narratives, the claims
of creditors, barrenness, death, famine, and
hunger are ruled to be completely irrelevant. No wonder they were amazed!

A New Testament Replica

"Do you have eyes, and fail to see? Do you have
ears, and fail to hear? And do you not remember? When I
broke the five loaves for the five thousand, how many
baskets full of broken pieces did you collect?" They said
to him, "Twelve." "And the seven for the four thousand,
how many baskets full of broken pieces did you collect?"
And they said to him, "Seven." Then he said to them, "Do
you not yet understand?" (Mark 8:18-21)

NOTES

[1]See Walter Brueggemann, "'Impossibility' and Epistemology in the Faith Tradition of Abraham and Sarah (Genesis 18:1-15)," *The Psalms & the Life of Faith* (Minneapolis: Fortress Press, 1995) 167-88.

[2]Burke O. Long, *2 Kings*, The Forms of the Old Testament Literature, volume X (Grand Rapids: Eerdmans, 1991) 61-62.

[3]On the defining, restorative "voice of pain," see Elaine Scarry, *The Body in Pain: The Making and Unmaking of the World* (Oxford: Oxford University Press, 1985).

Jacopo Tintoretto. *Multiplication of Loaves and Fishes*.1578–1581. Oil on canvas. Scuola di San Rocco, Venice, Italy. (Credit: Cameraphoto/Art Resource, NY)

THE LEPROSY OF NAAMAN, HEALED AND REASSIGNED

2 Kings 5:1-27

We have seen Elisha operating politically with the coalition of three kings (3:13-20), and we have seen him engaged pastorally with needy persons in more local, domestic circumstances (4:1-44). In the present chapter we observe him in yet a third arena, international politics: he deals with Naaman, a top-ranking Syrian general, not only an outsider to Israel but a prominent agent of Israel's perennial enemy. This long chapter divides into two distinct narratives, the complex account of the healing of the general (5:1-19a) and the follow-up narrative of Gehazi who tries to exploit Naaman (5:19b-27). The two episodes are interrelated: (a) the afflicted one is healed, (b) the exploitative one is afflicted. The two characters, in the end, exchange positions (5:27).

COMMENTARY

The Healing of Naaman's Leprosy, 5:1-19a

This narrative traces the miracle from leprosy to healing, accomplished by the prophet, so that it exhibits yet another example of the wonder of Elisha's power. The wonder is made all the more spectacular by the reluctant but complete submission of the mighty military man to the authority of the prophet of Yahweh, God of Israel.

Since we already know of the prophet, the narrative begins with the military man. He is a Syrian, an outsider to Israel's faith and servant of a foreign king. He is a successful and great man with victories to his credit. But already in v. 1, we are offered two qualifiers about him. First, he is the one that propels the story: he has leprosy. Not only is his life under threat, but he is socially unacceptable, thus unable to enjoy his success. [Leprosy as Social Disease] His leprosy becomes the pivot point of the narrative. Second, his military victories are a gift of Yahweh. This remarkable claim identifies the God of Israel as the source of Syria's military success. Nothing is subsequently made of that claim, except that we are on notice from the outset that

Leprosy as Social Disease

Leprosy was a deeply feared skin disease in the ancient world. It is important to remember that the ancient world had no access to any of our medicines and therefore an epidemic of a deeply contagious disease was a great threat. The primary strategy for coping with the infected was isolation and exclusion, thus cutting off the infected from normal social intercourse and certainly from participation in worship activities. Thus the threat is social as well as physical. The social threat, moreover, was managed by rules of purity that excluded the "contaminated" who endangered the community. The long exposition of Leviticus 13–14 indicates the enormous attention given to skin infections before which the community was largely helpless.

While an approach to leprosy through purity may be seen as "primitive," it is important to recognize that (a) priestly activity, as in Leviticus, was the primary form of medical practice of the day, and (b) that our own contemporary response to AIDS infection is, in a parallel fashion, driven by fear coupled with ignorance. Given the serious sense of threat attached to the disease and the social danger seen to be inherent in it, the narratives of healing and the agents of healing are, for that reason, all the more spectacular.

Yahweh has been at work behind the scenes on Naaman's behalf long before the present crisis.

Naaman is a larger-than-life military figure. The turn toward well-being in his life that he so much wants, however, is accomplished through a nameless Israelite girl taken as a prisoner of war by the Syrians (5:2-4). She waits on the general's wife. In passing she observes that in Israel there is a prophet who could heal the general. The young girl—nameless and inconsequential, but Israelite!—knows what the great general does not know and needs to know. In response, the general secures permission from his king and commander to go abroad on sick leave, away from military duties, to seek healing that will permit him to enjoy his career success to the full (5:5a).

The Syrian king and the Syrian general, characteristically, misunderstand (5:5b-7). The young Israelite girl had referred the general to "the prophet who is in Samaria," but the king assumed it was "the king who was in Samaria." Men of power are accustomed to dealing only with other men of power. The young girl suggested a visit to an uncredentialled healer; but the general, to the contrary, makes it a showy visit of state, general to king, with silver, gold, and cloth, surely bribes in exchange for the favor of healing. As the Syrians have misunderstood, so the Israelite king misconstrues, and perceives the military mission of the Syrian general as provocation. Verses 5b-7 do not advance the plot, but make clear that the pursuit of healing will carry the general into unfamiliar territory where he is out of his element and cannot control what happens. The miscommunication of the power men only accents how odd the prophet is; the reader knows that we must simply wait until the men of power come to realize, against their better judgment, that they do not have among them what is needed for healing.

With the failure of royal engagement, the prophet must take the initiative (5:8-14). He gently chides the general for seeking healing outside the matrix of prophetic reality. Indeed, all the prophetic narratives witness to the conviction that public life understood apart from prophetic reality is a hopeless enterprise. With the royal failure, the general's second effort is, finally, toward the prophet. The general arrives with "horses and chariots," still

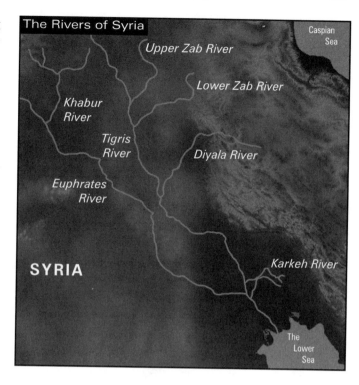

The Rivers of Syria — Caspian Sea, Upper Zab River, Lower Zab River, Khabur River, Tigris River, Diyala River, Euphrates River, Karkeh River, SYRIA, The Lower Sea

emblems of his immense importance, emblems congruent with the silver and gold itemized in his approach to the king. He still does not get it! The general continues to operate as though he is the key player, for he has the most stars on his shoulder; surely the prophet will be impressed.

Elisha the healer, however, does not make housecalls (5:10). He simply relays his strategy for healing to the general, not appearing to be much interested in what the general takes to be his deep crisis. (The doctor is never as interested as the needy, sick person, so the directions are rather like "take two aspirins.") His instruction is terse and enigmatic: cleanness, the antithesis of the infection of leprosy, is available, on Israelite terms. The cleansing must be at the Jordan, the prophetic boundary beyond royal administration (1 Kgs 17:3; 2 Kgs 2:7-9, 13-14). "The seven times" is surely folk practice that hardly conforms to the reasonableness of royal expertise! The foreign general is offered an Israelite folk remedy! The prophet sounds almost casual, as though the treatment is obvious and unexceptional.

The general is indignant. He has better rivers than the Jordan. [Map: The Rivers of Syria] After all, he is a great man (5:1), with silver and gold (5:5), with horses and chariots (5:9), not to be trifled with. The flip casualness of the prophet seems to mock the general, as though the prophet is unaware of his station. Only the general's

AΩ **Baby Flesh**
It is important to recognize that the Hebrew for "young girl," *na'arah qetannah* (5:2) in the feminine is the same Hebrew as "young boy" *(na'ar qaton)* in v. 14 in the masculine form. The utilization of the same Hebrew phrase cannot be happenstance. Thus the girl is presented in the narrative as an innocent, trusting, whole person, as an earnest of what the general will become through the ministration of Elisha. The healed "flesh" of the general is like the flesh of the young, perhaps the very young, thus "baby flesh."

commonsense aides prevail upon him to accept the prescription (5:13-14). The general had hoped for something more dramatic, a bigger river, a more direct intervention of the God of Israel of whom he has heard so much. The general wanted something appropriate to his own social standing. But he has now been reduced to his true status as a suppliant who comes to the healer as a leper "without one plea." Finally, grudgingly, chastened, he obeys the prophet. And he is healed! He is made clean. He is restored to full life. He is made socially acceptable. He can now be his true, public self… "according to the word of the man of God" (5:14). The story is simple. It moves from leprosy (5:1) to healing (5:14), with two delays of misunderstanding (5:5-7) and resistance (5:11-12). Neither the misunderstanding nor the resistance of the powerful can stop prophetic power. The skin of the general, we are told, is like "baby flesh," soft, supple, sweet smelling, a new gift of innocence. [Baby Flesh]

Only after the healing will the prophet meet the general (5:15-19). The attitude of the general is now completely reversed. Recalcitrance has become gratitude. In this face-to-face meeting, the Syrian general now acclaims the God of Israel as the God of all the world. [Say among the Nations] Naaman belongs to that company of outsiders, along with Laban (Gen 30:27), Jethro (Exod 18:10-11), and Rahab (Josh 2:9-11) who confess the God of Israel. The general wants to give payment to the healer, a

Cornelius Engebrechtsen. *The Prophet Elisha Heals the Syrian Captain Naaman.* 1520. Oil on panel. Kunsthistorisches Museum, Vienna, Austria. (Credit: Erich Lessing/Art Resource, NY.)

barakah (blessing). The prophet, however, is no hired doctor, runs no HMO. He refuses the offer.

But then, upon his unrestrained confession of Yahweh, the general reverses field, in two ways seeming to qualify his extravagant doxology to Yahweh. First, he requests to take Israelite soil back to Damascus, as though Yahweh pertains only to the territory of Israel and not to the territory of Syria, even though he has just commended Yahweh as God "of all the earth." Second, he anticipates, with regret, that when he is back home in his restored public stature, he will of necessity continue the state rituals to the Syrian god Rimmon. [Rimmon] The general is embarrassed to notify the prophet of his realism about his return to his social routines and obligations as a great man:

Say among the Nations

Naaman's acclamation of Yahweh (5:15) is not a studied affirmation of theoretical monotheism; it is, rather, an exuberant doxology of gratitude that moves easily and freely beyond the conventional theological categories of his previous faith. Thus the narrative places in the mouth of the foreigner the unrestrained affirmation of Yahweh as the God of all creation. What is here expressed narratively is a common theme in the Psalter. In Psalm 96:10-13, for example, the liturgy of the Jerusalem temple makes sweeping claims for Yahweh among the nations:

Say among the nations, "The LORD is king!
   The world is firmly established;
   it shall never be moved.
   He will judge the peoples with equity."
Let the heavens be glad,
   and let the earth rejoice;
   let the sea roar, and all that fills it;
   let the field exult, and everything in it.
Then shall all the trees of the forest sing for joy
   before the LORD; for he is coming,
   for he is coming to judge the earth.
He will judge the world with righteousness,
   and the peoples with his truth.

In doxological summons that are daring but have come to look to us like clichés, the nations are invited to join the doxology of Israel:

Let the peoples praise you, O God;
   let all the peoples praise you. (Ps 67:5)

Praise the LORD, all you nations!
   Extol him, all you peoples. (Ps 117:1)

The nations are, it is assumed, able to see the goodness and generosity, the faithfulness and reliability of Yahweh and therefore gladly join in Israel's songs of praise. It is certain that Naaman could join such a song precisely because he knows of Yahweh's transformative goodness in his own body (flesh).

The conviction that the God of Israel reaches beyond Israel to be the God of those outside Israel is reinforced by the single mention of Naaman in the New Testament. In Jesus' announcement of the jubilee for the poor and excluded, Jesus mentions two foreigners who are clearly within the scope of the goodness of the gospel. First he mentions Elijah's ministry to a widow at Zarephath in Sidon (Luke 4:26; see 1 Kgs 17:8-24). And then, in the same declaration to the angry assemblage who resist such openness, he says:

There were also many lepers in Israel in the time of the prophet Elisha, and none of them was cleansed except Naaman the Syrian. (Luke 4:27)

In our narrative, Naaman gladly counts himself in the sphere of the rule of Yahweh. And then Jesus, among the people of Yahweh, refers to Naaman in order to make the point that the governance and goodness of Yahweh cannot be monopolized by Yahweh's own people.

Rimmon

The present narrative is the only mention of this Syrian god in the Bible. The name is known elsewhere in connection with Hadad, Syrian god of storms. It is likely that Rimmon, a derivative from Hadad, participated in the common functions of divine power that are broadly associated in Israel with Baal. For the purposes of this narrative, such particulars are not important. What counts is that the general must, because of his public office, reengage in the "civil religion" of Syria addressed to a god who competes with Yahweh. Rimmon's importance here is only that this god is *not Yahweh*. In our narrative, it is noteworthy that the prophet, even given the harsh, exclusive Yahwism of these narratives, accepts such "civic obligation" on the part of Naaman and considers it no affront to Yahweh.

Thus Naaman seeks pardon in advance for these unavoidable semblances of his old self when his heart is newly, and really, wed to Yahweh.[1]

The prophet understands and takes no umbrage at the political realism of the general. He dismisses the healed man with his blessing (5:19).

This story perhaps stands in some intentional relation to the narrative of chapter 3. In both, Yahweh and the prophet are engaged in international affairs. In this narrative, it is clear that Yahweh governs in the affairs of other nations, especially Syria. In chapter 3, as we have seen, the engagement of Yahweh in Moab is somewhat enigmatic, because we cannot make out 3:27b. In any case, it is clear in both cases that the God of Israel will not be safely contained as the God of Israel; nor does the prophet of Yahweh operate on a small, restricted scale.

The Infection of Greedy Gehazi, 5:19b-27

Gehazi, Elisha's servant, has not been mentioned in this narrative, though we have encountered him in chapter 4. Clearly he had observed the actions of healing and the concluding meeting of vv. 15-18. Upon reflection, he decides that Elisha's refusal of the general's offer of a gift is inappropriate and he will redress the mistake. Verse 20 is remarkable, because it is not often in these narratives that we are given such direct access to cunning motivation. The resolve of v. 20 is more abrupt than the English may suggest: "I will take something from him."

Gehazi's initiative toward Naaman works perfectly. Naaman is generous and grateful, as we might expect after v. 15. He suspects nothing and gives to Gehazi even more than he asks. Naaman's innocent generosity is contrasted with Gehazi's greedy duplicity. He claims to have come on behalf of Elisha. He claims a special need in the community of the prophets. When he arrives back home, moreover, "He stored them in the house" (5:24). The deed is done; the narrative proceeds without comment, permitting us to observe the contrast between the two players and the way in which Gehazi's covetousness has spoiled a narrative of innocent healing.

The shameful deed of vv. 19b-24 is complete in itself. No narrative in this cluster, however, is complete until the prophet appears, as surely he will here. Elisha now interviews his servant. The questions he asks seem to be innocent probes; they are in fact accusations, because the prophet already knows. Gehazi adds to his troubles by lying in the face of Elisha's knowledge. He denies, but the prophet has traveled "in his heart" all the way into Gehazi's exploitative deed. After his denial in v. 25, Gehazi speaks no more. He has nothing else to say. Now Elisha will do all the talking in order to utter a speech of judgment:

> *Indictment:* "You have taken." The NRSV "accept" is a weak translation, because it suggests passive receptivity rather than aggressive appropriation. While the narrative says only that Gehazi took silver and clothing (gifts fit for a king in v. 5), the prophet extrapolates to every other form of wealth that might be confiscated. He delivers a broadside against corrupting acquisitiveness.

> *Sentence:* "Therefore"…leprosy, that is, social rejection and exclusion from the community. The narrative adds only that the word of the prophet came to be enfleshed in Gehazi (see 5:27).

The foreigner is on his way home, healed and rejoicing. The servant is now repudiated and brought under severe judgment. This narrative deals with two characters, Naaman and Gehazi. At the center as the key character, of course, is Elisha. The destiny of both the general and the servant is at the behest of the prophet. The general prospers, because in the end he submits to the prophet and to the God of the prophet; he moves *from leprosy to well-being.* The servant, in a spasm of amnesia, forgets who he is and where he is. Specifically he forgets the world of Yahwism in which he belongs to and with Elisha; he moves *from well-being to leprosy.* Thus the narrative tells of a deep reversal that may be enigmatic to an outsider. To those who "know" (5:15), both the blessing and the curse follow obviously. Naaman submits to the prophet. Gehazi contradicts the prophet (5:16, 20). The rest follows for both.

CONNECTIONS

This narrative teems with themes that are defining for the faith of Israel. These themes testify to inscrutable gifts given by Yahweh. We may mention first the "young girl" in vv. 2-3. She has only a bit part and is not mentioned again. She is one of the "little ones" who are so characteristic and decisive for biblical faith, not unlike Puah and Shiphrah in Exodus 1:15-22. She asserts that the healing of Yahweh happens outside the precincts of grand order. She is a prisoner of war; and yet even in her abusive dislocation, she has not forgotten or given up on the particularity of her Israelite, prophetic faith. In this narrative, as we have seen, her very characterization as "young girl" is a direct anticipation of the restoration of the general who will be restored to "baby flesh." The news of the God of Israel is characteristically enacted in, with, for, and through "little ones," judged by the world to be of no account (see Judg 6:15; Matt 18:1-4; 19:13-15; 1 Cor 1:27-29).

The royal miscalculation of vv. 5-7, in which both king and general collude, is perhaps intended as a humorous detour. The truth is that none of the power people "get it." They are excessively impressed with their own wealth and power and status, and imagine that in the midst of their grandeur dwells the power to heal. But of course they have it all wrong, as the self-impressed always do. That same false assumption is dramatically presented in Matthew 2:1-6 where it is assumed by all parties—the magi and Herod—that the new king of the Jews would be birthed in royal

---

📖 Elisha Redux

As we have seen, in much of the Gospel narrative Jesus replicates these prophets. Jesus also is a healer of lepers (Luke 7:22). As with Elisha, the Jesus narrative makes the crucial point that God's healing force does not reside in "official channels," but in this uncredentialled force. Thus in Luke 5:12-16, Jesus touches a leper and heals, a risky action because in the touch, Jesus may become as impure as the leper. More important, in Luke 17:11-19, Jesus heals ten lepers. This healing is more congruent with that of our narrative, because Jesus only gives directives for conventional procedures of healing ("show the priests"), without any direct contact. But the point of the narrative is that only one of the ten returned in gratitude. For our purposes it is of enormous importance that the one who came back in gratitude is a foreigner, albeit a Samaritan:

> Then Jesus asked, "Were not ten made clean? But the other nine, where are they? Was none of them found to return and give praise to God except this foreigner?" Then he said to him, "Get up and go on your way; your faith has made you well." (Luke 17: 17-19)

The narrative makes no explicit reference to Naaman the Syrian. We cannot, however, miss the parallel, even as Jesus' formula of dismissal in v. 19 echoes that of Elisha in 5:19. In both cases, the healed foreigner praises the God of Israel. It is not much of a stretch to imagine that the healed man in Luke 17:19 might have reuttered Naaman's doxology from 5:15. In both narratives the wonder of newness wrought by Yahweh's uncredentialled agent is celebrated, a wonder declared impossible by frightened society.

📖 An Alternative to Coveting

In the Gospel narrative Jesus warns of the destructiveness of covetousness:

Take care! Be on your guard against all kinds of greed; for one's life does not consist in the abundance of possessions.... Therefore I tell you, do not worry about your life, what you will eat, or about your body, what you will wear. For life is more than food, and the body more than clothing. Consider the ravens: they neither sow nor reap, they have neither storehouses nor barns, and yet God feeds them. Of how much more value are you than the birds! And can any of you by worrying add a single hour to hour span of life? If then you are not able to do so small a thing as that, why do you worry about the rest? (Luke 12:15, 22-26)

Jesus contrasts the deathliness of acquisitiveness and the generative power of God's limitless, alternative generosity.

---

environs. The Gospel of Matthew delivers one of the great jolts of the narrative by asserting that the prince of the future is in Bethlehem, not Jerusalem, among peasants and not kings. The citation of Micah 5:2 in the Matthew narrative, moreover, is a telling assertion that the power of the future lies outside the loci of ostentation, so also with the general and Elisha.

Too much should not be made, perhaps, of the contrast of rivers in vv. 11-12, a contrast that is yet another example of *little* Israelite claims against *big* claims otherwise made. We may notice a like appeal to rivers in the oracle of Isaiah 8:5-8 that contrasts "the gentle waters of Shiloah" and the mighty "flood waters of the Euphrates." The river imagery there contrasts the offer of Yahweh's peace and the threat of Assyria. The imagery serves a very different purpose here, but the river imagery in both cases witnesses to the modest means in Israel for the powers of Yahweh.

The tale of Gehazi, after the story of healing, is a counter-narrative on the destructiveness of covetousness.[2] The verb "take," in the NRSV regularly rendered as "accept," is an aggressive verb of coveting (see 5:15, 16, 20, 23, 26). The verb warrants considerable study, with special attention to 1 Samuel 8:11-17 where the power to take is accented; it is, moreover, enacted by David in 2 Samuel 11:4 in a "taking" of the woman that sets in motion the destruction of the monarchy. [An Alternate to Coveting]

In our narrative, the covetousness of Gehazi that leads to his demise is contrasted with the generosity of Elisha who heals without a charge, and with the gratitude of Naaman who responds appropriately to generosity and accepts a new faith. In an acquisitive society like ours, propelled by a determined ideology of consumerism, the odd offer of free healing is an occasion for gratitude, praise, and amazement, not for cunning exploitation. [Elisha Redux] The deep choice of faith is spelled out:

Put to death, therefore, whatever in you is earthly: fornication, impurity, passion, evil desire, and greed (which is idolatry). On account of these the wrath of God is coming on those who are disobedient. These are the ways you also once followed, when you were living that life. But now you must get rid of all such things—anger, wrath, malice, slander, and abusive language from your mouth. Do not lie to one another, seeing that you have stripped off the old self with its practices and have clothed yourselves with the new self, which is being renewed in knowledge according to the image of its creator. In that renewal, there is no longer Greek and Jew, circumcised and uncircumcised, barbarian, Scythian, slave and free; but Christ is all and in all! (Col 3:5-11)

The overcoming of such conduct (including greed) is the overcoming of all social divisions, even between foreigners and insiders.

NOTES

[1]Burke O. Long, *2 Kings,* The Forms of the Old Testament Literature, vol. 10 (Grand Rapids: Eerdmans, 1991) 73.

[2]On the ethical trajectory of greed in the Bible, see Walter Brueggemann, *Finally Comes the Poet: Daring Speech for Proclamation* (Minneapolis: Fortress Press, 1989) 99-110.

IRON FLOATS

2 Kings 6:1-7

COMMENTARY

This brief narrative again features Elisha as one with uncommon power to transform a circumstance of trouble and negativity. Robert Culley has nicely traced the movement and structure of the passage that closely parallels the miracle accounts of 2:19-22 and 4:38-41:

1. A party falls into a problem situation. The party brings this to the attention of the prophet.
2. The prophet responds with a request for essential information, which he receives and then takes a material and applies it to the problem.
3. The result is a miraculous occurrence, which solves the problem.[1]

The setup of the narrative is the decision to build "a place," a house, which requires securing lumber from the vicinity of the Jordan River (6:1-4). In cutting down trees, the ax head fell off the ax handle, a mishap common enough. The loss of the ax head means that the entire project is hampered. The response of the one who lost the ax head is a characteristic utterance in time of great distress, "Alas" (6:5). It is most remarkable that the distress expressed is not over the impediment to the project, but that the damaged tool is borrowed. That note suggests an intensely self-conscious moral community that is especially attentive to neighbor rights.

In any case, the cry of distress (6:5) evokes a characteristic and magisterial response from "the man of God" who restores the ax head and rights the situation (6:6). The final verse gives closure to the narrative by the prophet's terse instruction to pick up the recovered ax head and resume the work (6:7).

This brief narrative proceeds according to a standard "trouble-rescue" pattern. We may be especially impressed with the terseness of the account and with the acceptance of the wonder wrought by Elisha as a routine activity that does not evoke any particular curiosity or amazement. It is merely "business as usual" for the prophet. Given that, however, we should not miss the extraordinary claim made for Elisha in such ordinary rhetoric. This is "the man of God" filled with the spirit of Elijah and the power of Yahweh who yet again enacts what may be routine in this circle but that everywhere else is judged impossible.

CONNECTIONS

The abrupt affirmation of v. 6 is "made iron float." That "iron floats" is an attention-getter, because the verb does not fit with the noun in our common horizon. The narrative articulates a wonder that must be taken for a miracle and nothing less. Our interpretation may resist any attempt at rational explanation such as that offered by John Gray:

> The actual basis of the "miracle" of the floating ax head may be that Elisha with a long pole or stick probed about the spot indicated (an important point in the text) until he succeeded either in inserting the stick into the socket, or, having located the hard object on the muddy bottom, moved it until the man was able to recover it. In the circles in which the Elisha-hagiology took shape simple instances of prophetic sagacity were soon exaggerated to miracles.[2]

Such an account is hardly convincing. If it were, moreover, it goes completely against the grain of the narrative itself. "Wonders" are not to be explained; they are to be wondered at. The Elisha narrative resists such explanation that detracts from the claim that here the inexplicable power of God is at work.

We are clearly into the category of *miracle* that evokes amazement. [Abiding Astonishment] We may not, in my judgment, soften the dazzling claim of the text. As Richard Nelson comments about the whole collection of biblical stories,

> God's power invades the world of the ordinary to effect strange reversals. The lowly are raised to places of honor (Luke 1:51-53). The unrighteous are justified (Luke 18:9-14). The lost are found (Luke 15:3-10). The dead are raised. These are as much incredible reversals as is iron that floats.[3]

It will not do, moreover, to say that we are "rationalists" who cannot enter the narrative. It is exactly the opposite: we as readers are

Abiding Astonishment

Martin Buber comments on the character of the miraculous:

The concept of miracle which is permissible from the historical approach can be defined at its starting point as *an abiding astonishment*. The philosophizing and the religious person both wonder at the phenomenon, but the one neutralizes his wonder in ideal knowledge, while the other abides in wonder; no knowledge, cognition, can weaken his astonishment. Any causal explanation only deepens the wonder for him. The great turning-points in religious history are based on the fact that again an ever again an individual and a group attached to him wonder and keep on wondering.... They sense and experience it as a wonder.

Martin Buber, *Moses: The Revelation and the Covenant* (Atlanta; Highlands NJ: Humanities Press International, 1946; 1988) 75.

---

invited into the narratives of wonder and out of our technological, explanatory modes of life that miss the oddness of God's power in the world.

The doing of "wonders" is the defining work of Yahweh in the lyrical world of Israel's praise:

> One generation shall laud your works to another,
>   and shall declare your mighty acts.
> On the glorious splendor of your majesty,
>   and on your wondrous works, I will mediate.
> The might of your awesome deeds shall be proclaimed,
>   and I will declare your greatness.
> They shall celebrate the fame of your abundant goodness,
>   and shall sing aloud of your righteousness. (Ps 145:4-7)

1. Yahweh is a doer of wonders.

2. Elisha does the wonders of Yahweh. The entire collection of stories about him is a collage of acts that the world thinks is impossible. The defining miracle may be the restoration of the dead (2 Kgs 8:4-5), but that miracle is powerfully seconded by a series of others.

3. In this particular narrative, it is important to recognize that the miracle is "in the woods" with working people. Moreover, this wonder concerns the most advanced technology available (iron), so that the miracle is preoccupied with Israel's material means of production. The capacity of this community of marginalized people to have an iron ax head must have been remarkable. As marginalized hill-country people, the early Israelites had no control over their technology and were dependent upon others. [On Needing a Blacksmith] While the text purports to report ninth-century affairs two centuries after the Philistine monopoly of iron (1 Sam 13:19-22), an ax head must have been a rare and valued tool, so that its loss was

On Needing a Blacksmith

In a statement that pertains to the control of material and technology, an early narrative in Israel asserts:

Now there was no smith to be found throughout all the land of Israel; for the Philistines said, "The Hebrews must not make swords or spears for themselves"; so all the Israelites went down to the Philistines to sharpen their plowshare, mattocks, axes, or sickles; The charge was two-thirds of a shekel for the plowshares and for the mattocks, and one-third of a shekel for sharpening the axes and for setting the goads. (1 Sam 13:19-21)

This citation is enough to indicate that the matter of iron tools was an item of some importance in early Israel, and that the loss of such a tool would matter a great deal, given their scarcity.

---

an emergency. Thus the capacity of technology is here contained within prophetic wonder. Finally, those with technical capacity are drawn beyond their technology to appeal to and rely upon the God of all wonder.

4. Jesus is presented in the testimony of the Gospel narratives as a doer of wonders that transform life:

Go and tell John what you have seen and heard: the blind receive their sight, the lame walk, the lepers are cleansed, the deaf hear, the dead are raised, the poor have good news brought to them. (Luke 7:22)

Jesus, in the same testimonial genre as that of Elisha, does what God does. While Christian confession assigns a deep distinctiveness to Jesus, it is evident that in the Elisha stories the same power is seen to be at work in the world where people live their lives.

It is, I suggest, the work of synagogue and church to invite folk into the narratives of wonder as an act of resistance against the world of technology that wants to reduce all possibility to human explanation and human control. Those who cherish this narrative and others like it know that human life cannot be lived in its fullness, except by appeal to and reliance upon the power of transformative wonder that is in, with, and under our best explaining, controlling technology.

NOTES

[1]Robert C. Culley, *Studies in the Structure of Hebrew Narrative* (Philadelphia: Fortress Press, 1976) 82.

[2]John Gray, *1 & 2 Kings: A Commentary,* OTL (Philadelphia: Westminster Press, 1963) 460.

[3]Richard Nelson, *First and Second Kings*, Interpretation (Atlanta: John Knox Press, 1987) 185.

HIDDEN ALLIES

2 Kings 6:8-23

Conflict with Syria (Aram), in abeyance since the death of Ahab in 1 Kings 22, resumes. There is perennial conflict between the two states, so that the narrative can pick up the account of the hostility at any time. This narrative identifies neither the "king of Aram" nor "the king of Israel," so we can fix the report historically only by literary context. Clearly, Elisha (and neither king) is the key character in the story. The narrative may be divided into three parts, the pursuit of "the spy" (6:8-14), the decisive and peculiar action of Elisha (6:15-19), and the happy consequence of prophetic activity (6:20-23).

COMMENTARY

The Pursuit of "the Spy," 6:8-14

The ongoing war between these two traditional enemies is here focused on a particular crisis. There is a steady and rapid "leak" in Syrian intelligence. Israel knows Syria's battle plans as soon as they are formulated in Damascus. It turns out that the intelligence leak is due to Elisha, man of God, who has penetrated the Syrian planning system and reports promptly to the king of Israel on Syrian military plans. We are not told how the prophet manages such access and, characteristically, the narrative expresses no interest in the question. This odd form of knowledge is a given of prophetic inscrutability, suggesting that the hidden ways of Yahweh endlessly subvert human power and human planning. This remarkable disclosure of the leak is given in two distinct ways in the narrative. In vv. 8-10, the narrative tells the reader about this movement from Syrian planning to Israelite response. Then in vv. 11-14, what the reader knows is learned belatedly by the Syrian king as well. The king imagines that there is a traitor in his camp. His advisors, however, know better and correct his false impression. The king's response to the identification of the prophet as leak and

Dothan

Dothan, the locus of the prophet, is mentioned only in Gen 37:15-36; Judith 3:9; 4:6; 7:3-18; 8:3, and in no other source. It is thought by scholars to be the mound of Tell Dothan, fourteen miles north of Shechem. The site does not figure elsewhere in Israel's life, and has no special significance here. Its mention is a characteristic practice of concrete particularity in the biblical material.

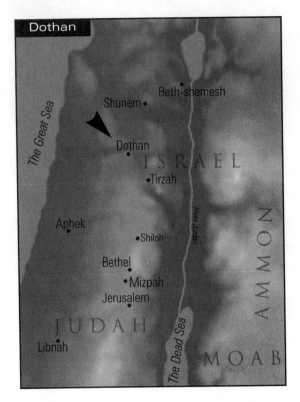

threat is to mobilize a large, impressive military force of horses and chariots in order to seize the prophet in Dothan. [Map: Dothan] The king's approach is not unlike that of the Syrian general to Elisha in 5:9. No doubt the great mismatch between the Syrian military party and the lone figure of Elisha, meant by the Syrians as intimidation, is designed by the narrator to evoke humor at the pitiful, frightened, futile effort of Syria against Israel's prophet.

The Decisive, Peculiar Action of Elisha, 6:15-19

While the king's party makes its rough and rowdy approach, we readers are transported to the inside of the prophet's house. While the king of Syria is "greatly perturbed" (6:11), things are peaceful in the chambers of the unnamed prophet. His servant (Gehazi?) was awake early, perhaps before his master. Outside the house he found an encampment of threatening horses and chariots. The place was surrounded by a hostile force. Not without reason, the servant is alarmed. His response to what he sees is exactly parallel to the outcry of the man who lost the ax head in 6:5: "Alas Master!" It is a cry of great fear and helplessness, demanding a response.

The prophet, unlike the king or the servant, is unperturbed and completely confident. He speaks a "Do not fear" to the servant, the proper and reassuring response to a cry of distress. [Do Not Fear] The assurance rests on a basis that the prophet utters: We outnumber them. The statement must have bewildered the servant, because he can see and he can count. There is a large host outside and two inside. The prophet's arithmetic is clearly out of touch with reality. The prophet and his servant are hopelessly outmanned.

Elisha nonetheless prays that the servant may see differently (6:17). His prayer is answered immediately. The servant gains second, prophetic sight, so that he now sees what was invisible to him in his cowardly common sense. What he now sees is that the mountains and hills all around Samaria are occupied with "horses and chariots of fire," that is, arms and weapons of a luminous quality that lie outside conventional weapons. The servant is granted a vision of transhistorical reality or, as I choose to think, the servant can now see what conventional discernment misses in its self-assured blindness. Either way, the prophet's count of allies and enemies is validated and his "fear not" is grounded in reality. The allies of the prophet and his servant massively outnumber those of Syria.

The prophet, however, is not yet finished. He prays a second time that the Syrians should be struck blind (6:18). This prayer is also answered promptly, and the Syrians are reduced to helplessness. The two prayers and Yahweh's two powerful responses to the prayers are perfectly symmetrical. The servant, who was blind to the allies now sees; the Syrians who discerned according to their power can now see nothing. The prophet has, by prayer, completely inverted the military realities of the situation.

The Happy Consequences of Prophetic Action, 6:20-23

Having created the new circumstance by rendering the powerful powerless, Elisha undertakes a follow-up action. He leads the Syrians, now completely in his power, to "the man whom you seek," presumably the king of Israel in Samaria. The Syrians had indeed wanted to get to the king in Samaria, but only so they could attack him. The Syrians never intended to be led to the Israelite king helpless. (The situation of the Syrians is parallel to that of the Syrian king in 1 Kings 20:31-34 where he is also a helpless suppliant. In that episode his life is spared by the Israelite king. The Syrians in our narrative, however, have no reason to expect the same mercy from the king of Israel, especially since the prophet in

---

AΩ **Do Not Fear**

Elisha's formulaic response to his frightened servant is a standard response to petition in the Old Testament. It is evident in Lamentations 3:57 that the phrase "Do not fear" is an answer to prayer, commonly thought to be utterance by an authorized human person on behalf of Yahweh:

I called on your name, O LORD,
    from the depths of the pit;
you heard my plea, "Do not close your ear
    to my cry for help, but give me relief!"
You came near when I called on you;
    you said, "Do not fear!" (Lam 3:55-57)

Elisha's utterance is a recognizable way in which the prophet redefines the situation of apparent threat for the servant; the formula assures divine presence and readiness to help. The distress of the servant is a fear of isolation, abandonment, and helplessness, all overridden by Yahweh's presence effectively assured in utterance and in act.

On the phrasing and significance of this response in Lam 3:57, see Patrick D. Miller, *They Cried to the Lord: The Form and Theology of Biblical Prayer* (Minneapolis: Fortress Press, 1994) 141 and his more extended discussion of the form, 135-77.

20:42 had severely reprimanded the Israelite king for his mercy shown to the Syrian king.)

Elisha leads the impotent Syrian troops into Samaria blind. There he prays a third time, this time to permit the Syrians to see the sorry situation in which they have landed (6:20). To be "inside Samaria" means that they are captives, at the mercy of Samaria's king. The king, moreover, is eager to dispose of the Syrians in a way normal among military disputants: "Take no prisoners." The king, however, is a latecomer to the narrative. He has been mentioned in vv. 9-10, but has had no part in the capture of the Syrians. The king's address to the prophet is properly deferential, on which see 2:12.

The prophet, however, will not yield his captives to the king and the king's urge to kill them. The prophet rebukes the king and reminds him that the Syrians are not the king's prisoners, so he may not decide their fate. The Syrians are, rather, the captives of the prophet and he, not the king, will decide their future. The prophet's resolve to decide the matter is fortuitous for the Syrians, for he will let them live. More than that, he will offer them a great feast before they return to their king. The purpose of the feast is not overt. The narrative conclusion of v. 23b, however, states the consequences of his action. The raids stopped! At least provisionally, the feast produced a momentary pause in the hostilities, an occasion of friendship and peaceableness.

This is a narrative account of a remarkable inversion, all accomplished by the prophet. At the center is the move of the servant *from blindness to sight*, complemented by the Syrian experience *from sight to blindness to sight*. A narrative pattern is wrapped around these core actions so that the larger move of the story is *from hostility to peaceableness*. The key character around whom all the other characters revolve is the prophet. He has, in this narrative, the authority to shape the future, and is engaged in public activity that decisively impinges upon large policy questions. He is shown to have authority unmatched by either king. He is, in this episode, a force for peace.

CONNECTIONS

The entire narrative turns on a visionary moment permitted to the prophet's servant wherein the servant (and we) become aware that things are not as they seem in a world where the prophet is on the loose. There is a force from Yahweh at work in the world that is not subject to the policies or maneuvers of ordinary politics. Attempts to "explain" this vision are futile. As in so many of these prophetic narratives, we face here again an elemental claim about effective power in the world, power not measured by scientific precision or political concreteness. The intent of the narrative is to assert that there are indeed allies offered in the world to those who are outnumbered and helpless.

This confident, enigmatic awareness leads to the recognition that,

No wisdom, no understanding, no counsel,
   can avail against the LORD.
The horse is made ready for the day of battle,
   but the victory belongs to the LORD. (Prov 21:30-31)

Things do not work out as planned or predicted. Great power and wealth and intelligence do not always prevail. What others may term "luck" is taken in prophetic rhetoric to be the normally hidden, occasionally visible way of Yahweh that defies human control and overrides human reason. In the end, the faithful appeal to this rhetoric in times of deepest distress:

No, in all these things we are more than conquerors through him who loved us. For I am convinced that neither death, nor life, nor angels, nor rulers, nor things present, nor things to come, nor powers, or height, nor depth, nor anything else in all creation, will be able to separate us from the love of God in Christ Jesus our Lord. (Rom 8:37-39)

While this Pauline lyric is remote from the battle field, it is telling that the imagery is military: "In all these we are *more than conquerors*," more than conquerors because the hidden forces of Yahweh cause outcomes of well-being not otherwise explicable.

Elisha's decisive prophetic action revolves around three prayers that in turn produce,

- sight for the servant,
- blindness among the Syrians, and
- sight among the Syrians.

The prophet governs who sees what and when.

It is clear in many other places in Scripture that "sight" is a way of speaking about discernment informed by faith so that the world looks different. [The Light That Lets Us See] The mandate of Isaiah, in his call experience, is to urge Judah and Jerusalem to obdurancy so that they cannot notice:

> Keep listening, but do not comprehend;
>   keep looking, but do not understand.
> Make the mind of this people dull,
>   and stop their eyes,
>   and shut their eyes,
> so that they may not look
>   with their eyes,
>   and listen with their ears,
> and comprehend with their minds,
>   and turn and be healed. (Isa 6:9-10)

In this text, Yahweh wills that the people of Israel should not see, because if they see, they will turn and be healed.

In Jesus' great denunciation of scribes and Pharisees, the language of sight is crucial for the articulation of obdurancy and resistance:

> Woe to you, blind guides, who say, "Whoever swears by the sanctuary is bound by nothing, but whoever swears by the gold of the sanctuary is bound by the oath." You blind fools! For which is greater, the gold or the sanctuary that has made the gold sacred? And you say, "Whoever swears by the altar is bound by nothing, but whoever swears by the gift that is on the altar is bound by the oath." How blind you are! For which is greater, the gift or the altar that makes the gift sacred? (Matt 23:16-19)

The ones who should be discerning in fact miss everything important.

The complicated narrative of the "boy born blind" in John 9 makes clear that "blindness" is a metaphor for failure to discern the truth of God in Jesus. The narrative moves from the physical blindness of the boy to the spiritual obtuseness and recalcitrance of Jesus'

AΩ **The Light That Lets Us See**
Gail O'Day comments:

Sin is defined by neither the presence of an illness (John 9:2, 34) nor the violation of the law (9:16, 24) but by one's resistance to Jesus. Throughout the preceding dialogue, the Jewish authorities, who have their physical sight, repeatedly insisted on their knowledge about who Jesus could and could not be (vv. 16, 24, 29) and by so doing showed themselves to be closed to Jesus as the light of the world and hence blind. By contrast, the man who had been born blind received his physical sight, but his true sight came as he moved through his ignorance (vv. 12, 25) to recognize Jesus as the Son of Man, as the light of the world. In their immovable insistence on their own rectitude, shown once again in their question of v. 40, the Pharisees demonstrate their own blindness and hence judge themselves (cf. 3:19-20).

Gail R. O'Day, "The Gospel of John: Introduction, Commentary, and Reflections," NIB (Nashville: Abingdon Press, 1995) IX: 661.

The finality of death in the midst of famine conditions is portrayed in this print. The scene is shrouded in murky, expressionistic darks as the hand of death, clutching and covering an empty bowl, is complemented by the other hand which falls on the deceased father.

Käthe Kollwitz. *Death,* from the series *The Weavers' Revolt*. 1897. Etching. Fine Arts Museum of San Francisco, CA. (Credit: Fine Arts Museum of San Francisco. Achenbach Foundation for Graphic Arts, Gift of Alfred Fromm)

opponents. The way in which the Bible proceeds, as in our narrative, is to keep the word pair "blind/sight" open so that it refers variously, at the same time (?), to physical and spiritual discernment. The gift of sight is that the world may be *seen differently,* according to Yahweh's governance that Elisha here embodies.

The gift of unseen alliances and the restoration of sight to the Syrians lead to Elisha's third unexpected action, the great feast for the Syrians. This is a most remarkable gesture, surely against the expectations of both the Syrians and the Israelite king. The captives are Elisha's to do with as he chooses. The prophet seems to know that there is something elementally transformative (and therefore sacramental) about shared food. In the end, because of the great feast, Elisha is a peacemaker who turns hostility into provisional friendliness.

This brief narrative exhibits an alternative way in the world, alternative even in the close context of many other, more violent Elisha stories. For an instant, the Near East is changed. For a moment enemies eat together and have no will to continue further raids. This is surely what Paul means by "be transformed." [Life over Death] Elisha transforms the way of his people, for one episode, away from fear and killing. The faithful are always deciding whether the hidden resources of God are an adequate ground for acting differently in a world of hostility and danger. One never knows who is being fed in such a feast (see Matt 25:34-40).

Life over Death

This alternative way in the world, here enacted by Elisha, is exposited by Paul:

If it is possible, so far as it depends on you, live peaceably with all. Beloved, never avenge yourselves, but leave room for the wrath of God; for it is written, "Vengeance is mine, I will repay, says the Lord." No, if your enemies are hungry, feed them; if they are thirsty, give them something to drink; for by doing this you will heap burning coals on their heads. Do not be overcome by evil, but overcome evil with good. (Rom 12:18-21)

GOOD NEWS AMID
THE VAGARIES OF WAR

2 Kings 6:24–7:20

The truce accomplished by Elisha in the feast in v. 23 did not hold. Hostility between Israel and Syria (Aram) was old and well established, and persisted long past any peacemaking effort on Elisha's part. This extended, complicated narrative tells of the resumption of the war and its wretchedness, of the duplicities required by war, and of the resolute ways in which the promises of Yahweh become "good news" in the midst of such wretchedness.

COMMENTARY

The High Cost of War, 6:24-25

The king of Syria invaded Israel and laid siege to the capital city of Samaria. The name of the Syrian king, Ben-hadad, is already known in 1 Kings 20:1; there is a series of royal Ben-hadads in Syria, and this narrative has no interest in further identification of him, for that is beside the point of the story. The siege sounds like an all-out war effort. A primary consequence is famine. The war-induced famine is the defining factor for the narrative that follows. As we will see in v. 33, it may be that v. 2 skips over the cause of the famine, or it may be that the drought of the previous chapters is operative, or it may be that the disturbance of food production and distribution is an unexceptional consequence of sustained hostility. Verse 25 lays out the consequence of famine, namely, the exorbitantly high price of food, much too much for the desperate purchase of a donkey's head or "dove's dung." [The High Cost of War] The intention of v. 25 is completely clear; but the specifics of the statement are not clear at all. The purchase of a "donkey's head" is an act of desperation, at best the food of needy peasants. The purchase of "dove's dung" may indicate the desperate situation of eating manure (see Ezek 4:9-15). Two alternative explanations are possible. First, the "dung" may have been used for fuel for cooking, and not as food. Second, John Gray suggests that the term we read as "dove's dung" may refer to a plant elsewhere termed "roasted chick peas."[1] The measure *kab*, moreover, is unclear; Gray suggests a measure of two liters.[2] While it is unfortunate that we cannot be more precise, the characterization of desperate need is unmistakable.

Notably, these are the prices "in Samaria." While no comment is made, we are free to conjecture that this desperation was not operative in royal environs, but only among the peasant poor who suffer first from the vagaries of royal policies of war.

The High Cost of War

Any state is aware of the costs of war that show up in the budget for weapons and troop support. This narrative makes clear that such budgetary items are only the surface costs of war, for this war, like every war, sends out a ripple of costs that finally settles on vulnerable women (6:26-29) and resourceless lepers (7:3-4). The conduct of the women, moreover, suggests the wretchedness and degradation that follow the ruin of the economy and the destruction of the infrastructure of society. Such costs, of course, never show up in budgetary summaries.

War Among the Most Vulnerable, 6:26-31

The prospect that we are to make class distinctions in the cost of war between those who *enact* war in the royal house and those who *suffer* war in lesser places is made clear in these verses. The king, perhaps inspecting fortifications, is addressed in urgent petition by a nameless woman: "Help!" [The Petitioning Woman] She asks help from the king because she is desperate. She asks help from the king because it is the king's business to care for the needy:

> Give the king your justice, O God,
>   and your righteousness to a king's son.
> May he judge your people with righteousness,
>   and your poor with justice....
> May he defend the cause of the poor of the people,
>   give deliverance to the needy,
>   and crush the oppressor. (Ps 72:1-4)

The Petitioning Woman

It is clear that the woman's petition in v. 26 triggers the narrative that follows. Jacques Ellul writes:

What brought on the whole train of events was the woman's cry, "Save me." The king was then reduced to despair by the full horror of the situation. Then the prophet stepped in. There is a kind of parallelism with the story of Naaman. The general, too, was crying out: "Heal and save me." The king was again in despair and rent his cloths. In both cases he proclaimed that he could not respond to the cry, "Save me." In both cases the prophet stepped in. In answer to the scandalous question of the woman, to her ignoble and yet desperate situation, the prophet gave God's answer—a positive answer.

Jacques Ellul, *The Politics of God & the Politics of Man* (Grand Rapids: Eerdmans, 1972) 51-52.

The woman speaks an imperative to the king: "Save!" (*yasha*). [Save] She expects the king, as he is obligated by office to do, to intervene and right the circumstance of famine. The Israelite king is unnamed, though in context we are to believe it is Jehoram. In any case, his conduct is characteristic of the dim view this literature has of the Omride kings. He refuses to help, that is, he denies the responsibility of his royal government for the needy woman. He wants to "separate religion and politics" and leave the trouble to Yahweh. The grammar of the king's statement suggests an "if-then" structure with the "If" not stated but implied: "[If Yahweh will not help] …then, How can I help?" That is, from what source? The king pleads that he cannot get food for the woman from the threshing floor or from the wine press, for there is none there. The king has no resources with which to respond to the trouble of the woman or, more widely, the trouble of his realm.

Save

Larry L. Lyke has observed that the woman's petition here is an example of a characteristic type scene of a woman petitioning before a king. [Larry L. Lyke, *King David with the Wise Woman of Tekoa: The Resonance of Tradition in Parabolic Narrative,* JSOT Supp. 255 (Sheffield: Sheffield Academic Press, 1997), 90-126.] Included in the cases he cites are the following:

- the two women before Solomon (1 Kgs 3:16-28);
- Esther (Esth 5:1-8);
- Abigail (1 Sam 25:23-35);
- Bathsheba (1 Kgs 1:15-21).

Cases might also be cited in the ministry of Jesus, as in Mark 5:28.

The petition characteristically addresses the king as judge who is able and expected to intervene on behalf of the weak to right a situation of injustice and exploitation. The women characteristically find voice to insist upon justice.

In this painting, the mother and child on the left are the real victims of war. The primal scream of a mother for her dead child is disturbingly portrayed in this powerful work, which was based on the destruction of the Spanish town, Guernica, by the Germans in 1937.

Pablo Picasso. *Guernica.* 1937. Oil on canvas. Museo Nacional Centro de Arte Reina Sofia, Madrid, Spain. (Credit: John Bigelow Talyor/Art Resource, NY)

On the Mother's Protest

The protest of the mother is deep and pathos-filled. But behind her desperate protest was the fact that the two needy women had perpetrated violence upon each other and their sons, a violence between them that left the patriarchal configuration of power unchallenged. Of that fact, Gina Hens-Piazza shrewdly observes:

> How is it that stories of women at odds with one another become instrumental in a tale that highlights monarchy? Does the endurance of monarchy or any form of hierarchical government necessitate women's remaining in conflictual relationships? Is the maintenance of enmity between women essential for the maintenance of the ethos of power and domination? To put it another way, do women working together gravely threaten to upset and dismantle such hierarchical forms? [Hens-Piazza, "Forms of Violence and the Violence of Forms" 24.]

The king states his inability (not his unwillingness) to come to her aid.

But then, acting in his royal office as judge, he does listen to her case, and some case it is! These verses are a concrete manifestation of the depth of the famine. The famine is so acute that two mothers have conspired to cannibalism, the eating of their own treasured sons. The woman does not even bring cause against the king for the famine, as she might have done or as the king had assumed. Nor does she blink in her statement at having shared her son as food with the other woman. Her cause is only that the second woman has reneged on her promise to provide a second meal of her son, and so she has acted unjustly. That the woman takes the famine and cannibalism for granted and only protests against the woman who would not share, that she has come to this sorry state in her perspective attests to the degradation of war and extreme poverty, whereby she is ground down to such an ignoble condition. (Her statement reflects the kind of desperate concern for survival in the Jewish death camps, wherein for some the aim of survival overrode all that might be called moral, because survival itself becomes, in such circumstance, a moral agenda. As it was in the death camps for some, so it is here for this woman.) She intends to survive, no matter what the cost may be. [On the Mother's Protest] She is an unexpected witness "from below," a marginalized woman who attests to the deep cost of famine and war brought about by patriarchal power. Indeed, the makers of war rarely pay the costs of war regularly borne by the voiceless, surely the poor, always the mothers.

The king's response is perhaps predictable (6:30-31). Give him this: he was already dressed in sackcloth kept hidden from the public. That is, he already grieves the cost of war and famine, which are on the way. The king already knows the dire suffering his policies have produced. His response, however, is hidden until now, rather like the leadership knowing beforehand that the U.S. war in Vietnam was lost, while the "war effort" and the killing continued.[3] The consternation of the mother has forced the king to come clean by exhibiting his grief-dress to the public.

Beyond that, however, the response of the king is inappropriate to his petitioner. In the phrasing of Gina Hens-Piazza, he interrupts "emotional discourse" and insists instead upon "hegemonic discourse."[4] Indeed, he never responds to the plight of the woman. He has no sensitivity to the killing costs to her of his war. His response is focused instead on the larger contest between king and prophet in which he can never prevail. In such a larger context, moreover, the voice of such a pitiful entry from the woman goes unheard; and when heard it is completely unacknowledged. The woman is the unacknowledged but nonetheless highly visible, expendable financier of the king's war.

The king's diversionary response is to apprehend Elisha and seek to execute him. He holds the prophet responsible for the trouble, completely unwilling and unable to recognize his own deep complicity in the suffering just reported. So it goes regularly with makers of war; so bound are they to the categories and cliches and statistics that the human cost of policy is simply screened out. The king cannot think of his subjects at all, but only of his sorry throne, made pitiful by his own policies. His response is like blaming war protesters for the failure of the enterprise.

A Prophetic Intervention, 6:32–7:2

The scene shifts abruptly to Elisha who knows immediately of the king's pursuit of him and his deadly "contract" on him (6:32; see vv. 9, 12). The king finds the prophet and addresses Elisha as his father before him had addressed Elijah (see 1 Kgs 18:17), even though the word for "trouble" here is a different one. It is, according to the king, Elisha who has brought the evil of the famine upon Samaria, an assumption repeated from 6:31 and perhaps implied in v. 25. This king, like every Omride king, is so unsure of Yahweh that he threatens the prophet not only with his own death, but with abandonment of Yahweh. The God who sends famine (through his prophet) is scarcely the God from whom to expect relief!

The prophet and the king's aide engage in an argumentative exchange. The key element is the prophetic announcement in v. 1: *Tomorrow* things will be drastically changed. *Tomorrow* the high cost of food reflected in v. 25 will be relaxed because there will be ample food. *Tomorrow* meal and barley, the staples of life, will be readily available, no need for desperate cannibalism. The prophet declares that in the immediate future, the immense, hidden power of Yahweh will decisively reverse the circumstance of Israel. The military aide, the third ranking man, of course, does not believe the prophet (7:2). Even a miracle could not accomplish what the prophet promises. The rhetoric of the prophet and the response of the aide lead us to expect a miracle like manna, or a jar of oil and a river of meal like those in which these prophets seem to specialize. The military man knows: it is not possible! The prophetic rejoinder is quick, harsh, and enigmatic: "It will happen…but you will not see it" (v. 2). No explanation is given.

Clearly, the prophet (and the narrator) have led us—and the king and the aide—to an expectation that will be fulfilled in an odd, unanticipated way. We look for "a miracle of nature," but we are to witness "a turn of history." Yahweh has a myriad of ways in which to transform and bring newness. It may be implied but not stated that the coming abundance will relieve the woman who protested. She is, however, no more present in prophetic speech than in royal discourse. Likely the prophet who traffics in needy women lingers longer over her, but there is no hint of that here; we readers, in any case, will not forget her haunting, enduring intrusion into royal, hegemonic discourse, regardless of her disposition by these two disputants.

Either/Or

The wager of the lepers is a desperate one, with no assurance that one option is any better than another. But their third option, to flee to Syria, has a chance of life unlike the other two choices. That chance is more than Kierkegaard holds out in his famous no-win either/or:

Marry, and you will regret it. Do not marry, and you will also regret it. Marry or do not marry, you will regret it either way. Whether you marry or you do not marry, you will regret it either way. Laugh at the stupidities of the world, and you will regret it; weep over them, and you will also regret it. Laugh at the stupidities of the world or weep over them, you will regret it either way. Whether you laugh at the stupidities of the world or you weep over them, you will regret it either way. Trust a girl, and you will regret it. Do not trust her, and you will also regret it. Trust a girl or do not trust her, you will regret it either way. Whether you trust a girl or do not trust her, you will regret it either way. Hang yourself, and you will regret it. Do not hang yourself and you will also regret it. Hang yourself or do not hang yourself, you will regret it either way. Whether you hang yourself or you do not hang yourself, you will regret it either way. This, gentlemen, is the quintessence of all the wisdom of life.

Søren Kierkegaard, *Either/Or*, trans. Howard V. Hong and Edna H. Hong (Princeton: Princeton University Press, 1987) I:38-39.

The Prophetic Word Enacted, 7:3-20

The narrative turns upon the prophetic promise of v. 1 that the military man has declared impossible (7:2). The fulfillment of the prophetic word happens in a complicated, quite unexpected way in which lepers, as silent and voiceless as the protesting woman of 6:26, play the key role.

The lepers carefully assess their situation of famine and commit to a wager (7:3-5).[5] [Either/Or] They reason that they will surely starve to death if they stay in Samaria where the famine is acute and where the king has no resources. If they stay "outside the city" (where lepers belong!), they will surely die. Their third alternative is to desert to the Syrians where they may also die; but with the Syrians they have a chance, may find food, and may not die. It is their only possibility for life. Unbeknownst to them, the lepers are a key part of Yahweh's devious, hidden strategy for fulfilling the prophetic promise of v. 1.

The second hidden stratagem of Yahweh is reported in vv. 6-9. The lepers find the Syrian camp—where they thought they may have a chance for food and for life—deserted. The camp is empty. The Syrians have fled. They have fled, mistakenly, because Yahweh has deceived them. The interpretive comment of v. 6 is remarkable: Yahweh *"caused the Syrians to hear."* The causative verb explains nothing; what the Syrians mistakenly heard was a Yahwistic ruse, the "voice" of chariots, the "voice" of horses, the "voice" of a great army. The threefold "voice" matches the threefold negation of 1 Kings 18:29. While Baal, in that contest, has no "voice," Yahweh sounds in many effective voices. Moreover, the sound Yahweh caused to be heard by the Syrians recalls the vision of 6:17. In the prophetic world of Elisha, there are ample resources for the friends and allies of Yahweh. In the present reference, the voices and the sounds they produce are enough to frighten the Syrians. We are not told if the sounds have the substance of the military behind them, or if these are only illusionary noises. Either way, the Syrians flee. The matter is perfectly orchestrated. They flee so quickly that the lepers find everything in place…food, drink, silver, gold, and clothing, and in v. 10 horses, donkeys, and tents. (On the triad of gold, silver, and clothing, see 5:5.) The lepers find the residue of a formidable economy, now all abandoned in fear of Yahweh's might.[6]

The lepers take counsel in the midst of their new find (v. 8). They know that they have stumbled on data that is important to their home state. They know, moreover, that the data on which they have stumbled cannot be kept to themselves. It is "good news"

AΩ **The Gospel**
The technical term used here for "gospel" (on which see Isa 40:9; 52:7) refers to an actual change of circumstance evoked by Yahweh. [On the theological use of the term *basar* ("gospel"), see Walter Brueggemann, *Biblical Perspectives on Evangelism: Living in a Three-Storied Universe* (Nashville: Abingdon Press, 1993), 14-47.] It is misleading and unfortunate that the church characteristically turns "gospel" into something spiritual when at bottom the term refers to changed material circumstance.

(7:9). [The Gospel] This is good news of a theological kind, known in the realm of material transformation. The news to be relayed to the Israelite king is that Yahweh has defeated the enemies of Israel, and Israel is safe. This turn of affairs, caused by Yahweh's inexplicable activity, puts Israel in a wholly new situation of well-being (see 7:6).

The news is brought to the king in Samaria so it can be acted upon (7:10-15). The "good news" will be told *(nagad)* to the king (7:9). It is told *(nagad)* to the gatekeepers (7:10), who "proclaim" *(nagad)* it to the king's household (7:11). Finally the king is told *(nagad)* and given verification (7:15). The four uses of the verb *nagad* show the way in which good news travels all the way from the lepers to the king. The news is everywhere to be told, because it decisively contradicts what had been anticipated in the negative judgment of the captain in v. 2.

The king is incredulous (7:12). He cannot believe or rely upon Yahweh's decisive subterfuge. He believes the deserted camp is a Syrian trick. He accepts the advice of his aide, who urges that the data be tested by sending a scouting party to visit the deserted Syrian camp (7:13). These spies do not merely find the testimony of the lepers to be true. In addition to a deserted camp, they find the path of Syrian retreat littered with valuable items that the Syrians have dropped and abandoned in their panic (7:15). The Syrians have fled from imagined Hittites and Egyptians, completely taken in by Yahweh's manipulation. They are gone, utterly gone, having left everything in their fear.

The consequence is a glut of goods that vindicates the prophetic word (7:16). The abandoned Syrian camp is plundered by the astonished Israelites. Lots of meal and lots of barley! So much food that it is suddenly cheap, an oversupply. The famine is ended. The high price of food is overcome. It is in v. 16 exactly as the prophet had said in v. 1. It is all "according to the word of the Lord," enacted by desperate lepers, frightened Syrians, and verifying spies. Elisha is indeed a true speaker of promise. The captain of v. 2, as might any of us, expected the prophetic promise of good to be fulfilled in a miracle from the sky. Nobody thought that Yahweh's abundance would be from the Syrian camp; but it is so.

A harsh addendum to the prophetic word of v. 1 is given in v. 2: "You shall not eat from it." The final paragraph of our narrative recalls and enacts that dreadful, threatening qualification

(7:17-20). That same captain from v. 2 is still in charge, still doing his duty, still trying to contain and direct the flow of people. The flow of people, however, is not about to be controlled. These are desperate, starved people, perhaps including the two women who ate the son, eager for the raw food of the enemy. They will not abide by royal control or protocol. This is relentless energy in desperate hunger. The military man is trampled by the frantic crowd "as the man of God said" (7:17). This text is of special interest because the prophetic word of v. 2 is first alluded to in v. 17 and then quoted in vv. 18-19. The narrative is at pains to make the connection: it happened so! (7:20). The final refrain of v. 20b reiterates v. 17, to be sure that the promise-fulfillment linkage is not missed. The famine is overcome. The "trouble" is ended (6:33). The agent of new food is Elisha. It happens in a way no one expected. Food is plentiful and cheap, for this God gives food to the hungry (see Ps 146:17).

CONNECTIONS

This is a narrative of radical reversal that moves from famine to abundant food. The radical reversal includes the hidden, inexplicable action of Yahweh that is effected through unwitting human agents, all in the service of a prophetic word that is oddly brought to fruition.

The problem of famine, that is, the desperate needfulness of an abandoned, wretched society, is sketched out in 6:24-33. This sketch is an illumination of many like scenarios that take place in our own contemporary world, scenarios that devolve around three features.

First, there is the war that is conducted by the men of power, the king of Syria (Ben-hadad) and the unnamed king of Israel. For them, the war is standard operational procedure to sustain the long-standing hostility between the two states. It is simply policy. We have no hint that either of the kings suffered or was even inconvenienced by the war. War-makers tend to live outside the consequences of their actions.

Second, there is famine. We are not told that the war produced famine; but it does, as surely as v. 25 follows v. 24. The war disrupts the economy, damages the environment, and, through the siege, produces a food shortage in Samaria. The long-term consequences of war are not confined to injuries and body counts. Wars, as here, characteristically leave abiding scars on the body politic.

Third, there are the unnoticed, unvalued victims of war-generated famine, in this case two women. [Products of War and Famine] One of the women here petitions the king. But they are usually invisible and completely absent from the reckoning of the particularities of war. Their "maternal discourse" disrupts "hegemonic discourse," but only briefly. Verses 24-33 give us a world without God and without hope, in which taken-for-granted human evil shapes social relationships. The king is helpless in the face of what he himself has brought his people. The story turns, as does the story of the world, with the prophetic utterance of 7:1, according to which food is on the way. It is impossible to overestimate the impact of gospel utterance upon the narrative of the world, even if that world requires a complicated, hidden enactment. The third officer of 7:2-3 plays the role of an unbelieving world that does not trust that gospel announcement can impinge upon a world seemingly closed to the power of life.

In the end, the deliverance of food will overcome the problem of famine (7:3-16, with 7:17-20 as a negative addendum to complete the warning of v. 2). In this part of the narrative, we may notice the following features. First, the action is taken up by four lepers, men outside the city gate. The lepers function in the narrative as a counterpoint to the women who enact the nadir of the negative narrative. That is, their discovery of bread matches the deep hunger of the women.

> **The Gospel of Bread Found**
> D. T. Niles, the great twentieth-century Christian ecumenist from Sri Lanka, has famously said, the practice of Christian evangelism is "like a beggar who has found bread telling other beggars where there is bread." So these lepers who found bread tell the others.

It is staggering that the move to well-being reached in v. 16 is enacted by the socially unacceptable who are excluded from the normal life of the royal city. It is they who declare "the gospel" of v. 9, a gospel that the enemy is gone and there is food. [The Gospel of Bread Found] The entire narrative pivots on this gospel announcement from an unlikely source.

Second, the strategic importance of the lepers for the narrative is matched by the odd working of Yahweh, especially through the "sounds" that frightened the Syrians, sounds reminiscent of the threat of the greatest empires. The odd articulation of v. 6, culminating in the sorry retrieval of v. 15 and in the miracle of v. 16, is key to the passage, laconic as it is. We are told nothing of what happened in the sound nor how it happened. It is clear, nonetheless, that it is this act of "sound" that triggered the retreat of the Syrians, out of which has come great abundance for Israel.

The hidden Yahweh and the visible lepers operate synergistically. The ruse of Yahweh's sounds would be incomplete without the reporting lepers. But the lepers by themselves, without the antecedent sounds of Yahweh, would have had nothing to report. The inversion from famine to food can happen only because of the twin efforts of Yahweh in hiddenness and lepers in astonishment. The miracle does not come from the sky but from the vagaries of the historical process. The narrative celebrates the concreteness of historical happenstance that makes food abundant in the face of famine. History is not a straight line of managed outcomes, as our Western optimism might suggest. The turn wrought by Yahweh in this narrative disrupts all the war planners. Food came, perhaps too late for the women, but it is good news for lepers and many other survivors of war and famine. The resistance of the military officer and his subsequent trampling assert that the doubt of a nontrusting world will not deter the feeding surprise of Yahweh. The captain, man of power, could not believe what the lepers, in their desperation, were ready to affirm. At the outset the lepers are excluded and the captain is a man of power. By the inversion of the narrative, the lepers may now gorge themselves on the abundance while the captain is trampled and killed by the parade of people on their way to the food he had doubted.

NOTES

[1]John Gray, *1 & 2 Kings: A Commentary*, OTL (Philadelphia: Westminster Press, 1963) 467.

[2]Ibid., 471.

[3]The classic example is the confession of Robert M. McNamara, *In Retrospect: The Tragedy & Lessons of Vietnam* (New York: Random House, 1995).

[4]Gina Hens-Piazza, "Forms of Violence and the Violence of Forms: Two Cannibal Mothers before a King (2 Kings 6:24-33)" (unpublished paper). I am grateful to Kathleen O'Connor for this reference.

[5]The "wager" of course calls to mind for us the famous wager of faith by Pascal.

[6]Gerhard von Rad, *Holy War in Ancient Israel* (Grand Rapids: Eerdmans, 1991) 41-51 has proposed that in the practice of holy war in ancient Israel, Yahweh characteristically sends terror and confusion into the camp of the enemy, causing the enemy to lose heart and retreat. Our narrative bears none of the marks of holy war, but the parallel is worth noting.

LAND RESTORED

2 Kings 8:1-6

The woman of Shunem from 4:8-37 now reappears in the narrative. This odd episode resituates Elisha back in his pastoral ministry, after he has invested for several chapters (5–7, except for 6:1-7) in more public matters of royal policy. In fact the prophet plays only a minor, preliminary role in this narrative. He is present in v. 1 only to create the problematic of the story, after which he does not appear again. The story continues, in his absence, in the departure of the woman from Israel at his behest (8:2), and her return and recovery of property (8:3-6).

The prophet's opening announcement to the woman indicates both the decisive governance of Yahweh (instead of the king) over matters of life and death, and Elisha's role as the one who knows and asserts Yahweh's future. We are not told Yahweh's motivation for causing a famine. Famine can be a curse from Yahweh, and especially a curse to punish royal figures who have been disobedient (see 2 Sam 24:13). [Famine as Curse] It is credible to imagine that Yahweh's antipathy to the continuing Omride dynasty might occasion such a judgment against the regime; but no such claim is given here. It is, in any case, an uncommon act of concern and compassion on the part of the prophet to warn the woman so that she may flee in order to be free of the threat of famine.

The woman is given no specific direction by the prophet, but she finds her way to the coastal area of the Philistines, an area to which the famine apparently did not extend (8:2). This verse is rather incidental to the narrative, rather like "travelling music." We note nonetheless two motifs that echo the narratives of Genesis. First, the

---

📖 Famine as Curse

It is not the case that famine is always curse. But in Israel's two great recitals of covenant curses, famine is a prominent threat:

When I break your staff of bread, ten women shall bake your bread in a single oven, and they shall dole out your bread by weight; and though you eat, you shall not be satisfied. But if, despite this, you disobey me, and continue hostile to me, I will continue hostile to you in fury; I in turn will punish you myself sevenfold for your sins. You shall eat the flesh of your sons and you shall eat the flesh of your daughters. (Lev 26:26-29; see Deut 28:56-57; Amos 4:6; Jer 15:2)

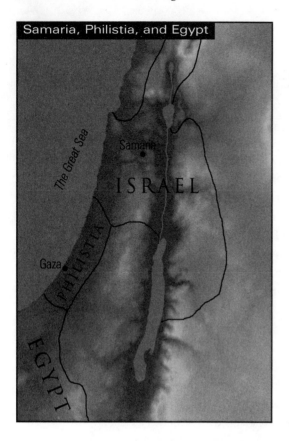

Samaria, Philistia, and Egypt

seven years of displacement during the famine match the seven-year cycle of famine reported in the Joseph narrative (Gen 41:25-30). Probably the number is an approximation meaning "a very long time for a famine." Second, the ancestors in Genesis regularly flee from famine to the breadbasket of Egypt (Gen 12:10; 42:1-2). The woman in our narrative does not flee so far, but she goes in the direction of Egypt, perhaps into the Egyptian sphere of productivity and abundance. [Map: Samaria, Philistia and Egypt] The place of her temporary settlement was a place of safety where she survived outside the devastation of famine. Oddly, the narrator says nothing about the specifics of the famine. We may, however, refer back to 6:24-29 as a clue to its potential deadliness. The prophetic office of v. 1 has protected the life of the women in a circumstance of deadliness.

The point of the narrative is the return of the woman to Israel after the famine. During her absence, her land apparently had reverted to the crown. (Though her husband is mentioned in 4:9, 18-22, he is not mentioned here; she is, however, nowhere called a widow, though her loss of land might suggest her economic vulnerability as a widow.)

AΩ **The Petition**
It is likely that the petition of the woman constitutes a formal court procedure. It is important, nonetheless, that the word "appeal" is *za'aq* "cry out." [See Patrick D. Miller, *They Cried to the Lord: The Form and Theology of Biblical Prayer* (Minneapolis: Fortress Press, 1994) 55-134.] Patrick Miller has noticed that in Exod 22:23, 27, those who are abused or oppressed, especially the poor, may "cry out" to Yahweh against the abuser, that is, file a claim with Yahweh. Miller suggests, moreover, that what is *authorized* in the Torah commandment is what the poor and needy *verbalize* in the Psalter when they "cry out" to Yahweh for help (see Pss 5:2-3; 55:16-17; 57:2). The ultimate petition, wherein Israel makes formal appeal for help, is to Yahweh. But the political process is the same as such address to Yahweh. The cry insists upon redress, in this case granted by the king.

The resolution of her problem of land loss entails a petition to the king (8:3) and the positive royal verdict whereby the king restores her land (8:6). [The Petition] That exchange between woman and king, however, is intruded upon by another conversation in which the king engaged Gehazi whom we know from a previous episode with the woman (4:25-37).

At the outset that royal conversation does not at all concern the woman or her land, but is about Elisha who now interests the king (8:4-5). The king inquires of Gehazi for a narrative account of the "miracles" of Elisha. [A Recital of Miracles] The king knows that Elisha is a wonder-worker, but asks for specifics. The recital perhaps included a number of the stories we have considered—the bad water, death in the pot, recovery of an ax head. The deed that is most prominent, perhaps Elisha's most startling and most celebrated miracle, is the raising of the dead boy in 4:32-37. That act may not have been the focus of the recital of Gehazi, but it is the topic of this conversation that converges with the other narrative thread of the woman and her land. The woman is only incidental to the story of the resurrection, but it is enough to situate her, for the king, in the midst of the wonder of Elisha.

The king, upon having her identified in the midst of Elisha's miracles, interviews her. We are not told if the questioning concerned the wonders of Elisha or if it addressed the loss of land. Either way, the king is satisfied about the legitimacy of her petition and grants the recovery of her land by royal fiat:

> Restore all that was hers, together with all the revenue of the fields from the day that she left the land until now. (8:6)

The major theme of the story concerns the woman and her land. In it Elisha figures only incidentally and is not an agent for her restitution of land. In context, however, the story concerns the wonder-worker whose reputation endures and perhaps impresses the king, perhaps moving the king to enact his own political wonder of restoration.

A Recital of Miracles

The Old Testament has a variety of terms for miracle, for mighty acts that defy conventional categories. In our text, the term *gadol* is "great deeds." Elsewhere the term is often "wondrous works" (*paloth*).

But sir, if the LORD is with us, why then has all this happened to us? And where are all his *wonderful deeds* that our ancestors recounted to us, saying , "Did not the LORD bring us up from Egypt?" (Jud 6:13; see Jer 21:2; Pss 9:2; 26:7)

Such wonders are beyond explanation and constitute the "stuff" of biblical faith.

CONNECTIONS

We may focus upon the two predominant themes of this brief episode. First, at the center of the text lie the "great things" that Elisha has done. The phrase suggests a self-consciousness on the part of the narrator that the incidental and likely distinct tales of Elisha are now thought of as a catalogued group that is available for recital. That is, the incidental acts of Elisha, any one of which is beyond explanation, now have been grouped for cumulative impact, in which the detail of the drama is taken up into a larger sweep.

This grouping of individual acts in a common recital is a characteristic way in which Israel expresses its faith. I may mention four examples of this maneuver:

1. In Psalm 136, Israel recites its faith in a form whereby each first half-verse is a deed, followed in the second half-line by the refrain, "Yahweh's steadfast love lasts forever." That is, each specific item is presented as a sign and embodiment of Yahweh's fidelity.
2. In Psalm 107:4-32, four particular "rescues" are named in a stylized way: being lost, being imprisoned, being sick, and being at sea. In each case, Yahweh has acted in faithfulness that evokes gratitude.
3. In Luke 7:22, in response to John's question, Jesus' ministry of wonders is recited and summarized in a stylized fashion. This recital clearly gathers together individual miracle stories and generalizes.
4. In my church tradition, the United Church of Christ, our Statement of Faith has as its preamble:

We believe in you, O God, Eternal Spirit,
God of our Savior Jesus Christ and our God,
and to your deeds we testify.

The "deeds" to which the church testifies are the entire story of God's life in its Trinitarian casting.

People of faith live by collages of wonders, of which the inchoate recital pertaining to Elisha is an early example.

Second, the narrative concerns disposition of land. Though there is no concrete adversarial tension at work here, the story does reflect the play between two theories of land, that of *inalienable inheritance* in a tribal society and *crown land* in a monarchy. The woman's petition to recover land concerns its inalienable quality. [Inalienable Land and Jubilee] Conversely, the unnamed

---

Inalienable Land and Jubilee

The land theory of market capitalism acknowledges no land to be inalienable inheritance. All land is "available" for purchase. That theory of land in our own time has made all land a tradable commodity. An alternative view of land, in its extreme expression, is the year of Jubilee:

The land shall not be sold in perpetuity, for the land is mine; with me you are but aliens and tenants. Throughout the land that you hold, you shall provide for the redemption of the land. (Lev 25:23-24)

The act of "redeeming" the land recovers or retains family possessions when the next of kin is obligated to buy the land in order to keep it in the family; see Ruth 4:5-6; Jer 32:6-15. In our narrative the woman acts to redeem her land. It is impossible to overestimate the radicality of the Jubilee tradition of land that curbs all commoditization.

See John Howard Yoder, *The Politics of Jesus: Vicit Agnus Noster* (Grand Rapids: Eerdmans, 1972) 64-77.

king in this narrative assumes the capacity both to *preempt* her land and to *restore* it to her.

Two other examples of this crown privilege may be cited. David spends energy adjudicating the continuing land claims of Saul's family and Saul's grandson Mephibosheth (2 Sam 9:1-13). When David thinks the grandson has been disloyal to him, the land is reassigned by royal fiat to Ziba (2 Sam 16:1-4). But when Mephibosheth can establish his innocence and his loyalty toward David, the land is again redeployed by royal verdict (2 Sam 19:24-30). Second, it is plausible that the narrative of Naboth's vineyard and the seizure of land by Ahab and Jezebel by murder (1 Kgs 21:1-16) are in the background of this narrative. [Echoes of Naboth]

Echoes of Naboth

We have seen in 1 Kings 21 how the notion of crown privilege overrode the inalienable claims of Naboth and produced a hard prophetic denunciation of the Omride dynasty:

Thus says the LORD: In the place where dogs licked up the blood of Naboth, dogs will also lick up your blood. (1 Kgs 21:19)

With such a narrative ringing in his ears, the present unnamed son of Ahab on the throne makes no such claim for the crown. The woman's land claim is honored, even in the face of what may have been accepted royal prerogative.

The tension between individual inheritance and public, eminent domain is endlessly reenacted, when malls buy up land, when land are "condemned" for public projects. The old Torah and old wisdom side with the small ones about land:

> You must not move your neighbor's boundary marker, set up by former generations, on the property that will be allotted to you in the land that the LORD your God is giving you to possess. (Deut 19:14)

> Do not remove the ancient landmark
>   that your ancestors set up. (Prov 22:28)

> Do not remove an ancient landmark
>   or encroach on the fields of orphans,
> for their redeemer is strong;
>   he will plead their cause against you. (Prov 23:10-11)

The power of the "big players" nonetheless often leaves the little ones denied. The issue in our narrative has a better outcome for the woman, perhaps because of the power of the wonder-worker that intimidated or persuaded even this belated son of Ahab, the coveter.

THE SORRY FUTURE
OF THREE KINGS

2 Kings 8:7-29

In this extended narrative, three kings are linked to the demands and expectations of prophetic faith, Ben-hadad of Syria (8:7-15), Jehoram in Jerusalem (8:16-24), and his son Ahaziah (8:25-29). The earlier, peculiar mandate to Elijah in 1 Kings 19:15-17 clearly looms in the background as a prophetic force that endlessly destabilizes royal power.

COMMENTARY

A Syrian Assassination, 8:7-15

In this episode our text begins a series of reports on the unstable, fluid, and violent political situation in Israel, Judah, and Syria, a situation evoked, according to our narrative, by the agitation and empowerment of Elisha. In the first report in this series of violent acts, these verses focus upon Aram (Syria) in whose internal life Elisha is implicated. The narrative moves through three scenes: (a) the dispatch of a Syrian messenger, Hazael, by King Ben-hadad (8:7-8); (b) the exchange of Elisha and Hazael (8:9-13); and (c) the consequent action of Hazael who seizes royal power (8:14-15).

The presenting problem is the illness of the Syrian king, Ben-hadad (vv. 1-2), whom we have already encountered in 1 Kings 20 and 2 Kings 6. Since the healing of Naaman in 2 Kings 5, the Syrians have known of Elisha's capacity for healing, though here the Syrian king asks not for healing, but for knowledge about his prospects. The Syrian king designates Hazael, apparently one of his trusted servants, to meet with the prophet. [Hazael] The enquiry is not unlike that of Ahaziah in 2 Kings 1:2, suggesting that the enquiry about illness and healing is likely a common literary convention.

Hazael dutifully approaches the prophet "armed," as is royal custom, with an enormous array of gifts, perhaps an antecedent of later "high costs" of medical care (see 5:5). The address to the prophet by the Syrian royal messenger is deeply deferential. The king of Syria is

Hazael

Hazael is an uncredentialled latecomer to power in Syria. Apparently he has no proper claim to power and no pedigree that would give entitlement. While we lack concrete data, he apparently had a long reign in Damascus and mounted a sustained and vigorous political, military front against Israel. As a consequence, for forty years (about 840–800), the Syrian front was a central preoccupation of the government in Samaria. Hazael was important enough to be named in the annuls of Shalmaneser III, a great Assyrian ruler, albeit dismissively:

Hazael, a commoner (lit. son of nobody), seized the throne, called up a numerous army and rose against me. I fought with him and defeated him, taking the chariots of his camp. He disappeared to save his life. I marched as far as Damascus, his royal residence [and cut down his] gardens. [The comment from the records of Shalmaneser III is presented in ANET 280.]

Israel received respite from the Syrian threat after 800 only because Assyria to the north defeated Syria. But that defeat of Syria brought no real relief to Israel; instead, it was to go from the frying pan into the fire, for Assyria was a greater, more durable, more ruthless, and more costly threat than was Syria.

---

identified as a "son" of the prophet, this man of God who has become "father" in Israel (see 2:12). All parties affirm that Elisha knows to what extent Yahweh will heal, and perhaps controls the healing processes.

The prophet's response is prompt, even if duplicitous. The deception the prophet now authorizes is underscored by two infinitive absolutes in the Hebrew that are perfectly complementary: (a) "*surely* live," (b) "*surely* die." [Infinitive Absolutes] The prophet is terse and explains nothing. His point, however, is unambiguous. The fate of the Syrian king is sealed, though the messenger is to conceal what is sealed. The king may recover from illness but he will die anyway. Verse 11 is difficult, because the antecedents to the pronouns are unclear. It seems likely that the prophet gazes and the messenger is ashamed. Some interpreters suggest that Elisha is testing the nerve and the ambition of the messenger. Perhaps the gaze is a nonverbal communication to ask, "Do you get the point?" The messenger is perhaps "shamed" because he has been inducted all at once into political intrigue that he had not yet contemplated.

AΩ Infinitive Absolutes

A fine grammatical point may tax the reader but can also be illuminating. The "infinitive absolute" is a feature of Hebrew grammar whereby the verb is repeated in different forms for purposes of accent. In English translation, the usage is rendered as "surely." Thus, in our case, "live, live" becomes "*surely* live" and "die, die" becomes "*surely* die." The parallel intensification in this case is noteworthy.

The weeping of Elisha abruptly changes the subject of the narrative (8:11). We might have thought he was weeping over the Syrian king whose death sentence he has just pronounced. But no, he has no emotion to spare for Ben-hadad. He is finished with the Syrian king, having disposed of him. Elisha weeps, rather, for Israel. For he knows, as he always seems to know beforehand, that the messenger who stands before him will be the Syrian king, and that he will work a deep, long, barbaric cruelty against Israel; for in the next forty years (roughly 841–800), Syrian military policy will endlessly harass and devastate Israel. Well beyond any thought or plan by Hazael, the prophet anticipates the next generation of trouble for Israel.

The prophetic discourse then addresses the soon-to-be king of Syria in the formal utterance of v. 12 with its series of direct "you will" statements:

> You will do evil;
> You will burn fortresses;
> You will kill young men (soldiers),
> You will mutilate children,
> You will savage pregnant women.

The language parallels the indictment of Amos 1:3-4, but see also Amos 1:13 where rhetoric like our oracle is related to Ammon. This barbarism is indeed the nature of war in a cultural environment where there are no military protocols, where war is not only about winning, but about savage violence, devastation, and humiliation. The prophet is a realist about the brute capacity of unrestrained military violence.

In response to the prophet, the messenger demurs from the prophetic anticipation in deferential fashion. He identifies himself to Elisha as "your servant" and claims for himself the lowly status of "dog," that is, one completely unworthy and without standing (8:13). The self-defense made by Hazael to Elisha is not to claim he is too civil or too innocent to work such violence, but that he is too insignificant and is incapable of enacting it. Hazael acknowledges that such a devastation of Israel would be a "great thing" (see 8:4 with a different term), but well beyond his powers. Elisha refutes his demurral with the assertion that by Yahweh's will Hazael will be king in Syria. In this anticipation Elisha recalls the mandate given to Elijah to anoint Hazael (1 Kgs 19:15), and apparently moves to complete the unfinished work of his predecessor. The inference to be drawn is that when Hazael is made king, he will indeed be both able and willing to enact the horrors of v. 12. The utterance of the prophet sets in motion futures that were not available until the awesome opening of the future by prophetic oracle.

This narrative account concludes with Hazael returning to Damascus to report to his master, Ben-hadad (8:14-15). Hazael has understood Elisha well. He faithfully reports the deception offered by the prophet in v. 10: "surely live." The lie is for the king's consumption and false assurance. The lie is in the verbiage of v. 14. The truth of "surely die" (8:10) is in the action of v. 15. The terse conclusion of the narrative is that the king's trusted servant smothered the king, enacting the prophetic word. The report ends with what Elisha had anticipated: "Hazael has become king." The Israelite reader is on notice that the threats of v. 12, given in prophetic utterance, are close at hand. It is the prophet who has evoked the coup of Hazael. The narrative never says so, but we are left with the impression that becoming king was a new idea for Hazael, an idea upon which he acted promptly and violently, at the behest of the prophet.

Two Kings in Judah, 8:16-29

In short order these verses trace the reign of two undistinguished Judean kings, Jehoram, son of Jehoshaphat (8:16-24), and Ahaziah, grandson of Jehoshaphat (8:25-29). As is regularly the case, the narrative offers occasional reportage on the two reigns, but is primarily concerned with theological assessment.

Jehoram reigned in Jerusalem eight years (849–843).[1] The theological verdict on him is as negative as we have come to expect of Northern kings, even though he rules in Jerusalem as a son of David and not in the North (8:18-19). The ground for the negative judgment is clear: he is son-in-law of Ahab and presumably participates in the theological waywardness of the Omride kings for whom our narrator has no appreciation at all. The condemnation of the king in v. 18 is familiar, suggesting, as in 1 Kings 11:1-8, that the king disastrously followed the lead of his wife, an Omride. The qualifying "yet" of v. 19 is an echo of the "yet" spoken over Solomon (1 Kgs 11:12). Yahweh's old, durable commitments to the Davidic house here still override the concrete data that justifies the termination of the dynasty. Yahweh has promised "forever" to the Davidic house (2 Sam 7:11-16). Up to this point in our narrative (though not to the end of 2 Kings) that promise of Yahweh to David holds. The Davidic family has "the lamp" given them by Yahweh. [The Lamp]

Image of lamp as "cult object symbolizing divine presence" As discussed in the Oriental Institute's archaeological description: lamps such as this one consist of a bowl to hold fuel, which was usually olive oil, and a spout to support a wick, which was probably made of flax. The burning wick blackened the spout and must have produced a rather smoky light.

Oil Lamp from Megiddo, ancient Palestine. 8th century BC. Baked clay, 4.5cm x 13.5cm.

(Credit: Courtesy of the Oriental Institute of the University of Chicago)

It is evident that Jehoram was a weak, ineffective king. The measure of his failure is his loss of colonial territories (8:20-22). We have seen in chapter 3 that Edom was a willing, perhaps coerced, ally of Israel and Judah, likely a client state. Now, in the time of Jehoram, Edom rejects that status and revolts against Judah, its overlord. And while the Judean king tried a nighttime stratagem against Edom, it failed. Edom got free of Judah and stayed free, at least for the horizon of this narrator. Our text adds laconically the loss of Libnah, apparently another client state that provided revenues for the government in Jerusalem.

AΩ **The Lamp**
The term "a lamp" here is apparently a metaphor for the divine investment in the dynasty that makes the dynasty itself a source of life in the community:

Then David's men swore to him, "You shall not go out with us to battle any longer, so that you do not quench *the lamp* of Israel." (2 Sam 21:17)

Yet to his son I will give one tribe, so that my servant David may always have *a lamp* before me in Jerusalem, the city where I have chosen to put my name. (1 Kgs 11:36)

In the latter text, the term perhaps refers to a cult object signifying divine presence, but surely in the service of the dynasty.

[Map: Libnah] The narrative does not explicitly suggest that international weakness on the part of the king of Judah is linked to the theological failure of v. 18. The narrative only sets the two awarenesses—loss and theological failure—side by side; the reader can decide about their possible connection.

Ahaziah, son of Jehoram, reigned in Jerusalem one year (843–842), hardly enough to count (8:25-29). Whereas the origin

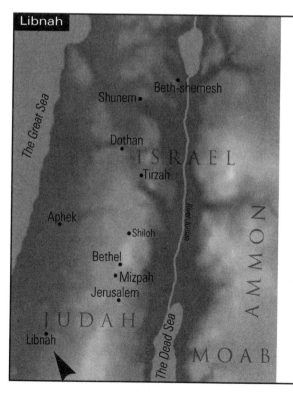

Libnah

Libnah
It has not been possible for scholars to locate the ancient city of Libnah with any certitude. The best guess is that it is a site on the southeast boundary of Judah toward the area of the Philistines. Other than boundary lists in Numbers 33 and Joshua 10–15, the site is mentioned primarily in the Kings narrative (19:8; 23:31; and 24:18) and related texts. In our text, its importance does not depend upon geographical location but serves to signal the military weakness of the regime.

(8:16-17) and demise (8:23-24) of Jehoram are given all in a piece, here we are given only the opening data on Ahaziah (8:25-26), and must wait until 9:27-28 for closure to his reign. The defining fact of the reign of Ahaziah is that, like his father Jehoram, he is married into the Omride family of Samaria and embraces the disastrous ways of his in-laws. The intermarriage of the two regimes in Jerusalem and Samaria is indicated by the use of the same royal names in both families, a use that makes the data sometimes difficult and confusing. The interrelatedness of the two regimes, moreover, indicates the solidarity in religious inclination and political policy, a solidarity that will only end in grief and failure for both.

In the present case the twin regimes must fight against Hazael of Syria, now ensconced as king in Syria as the prophet has anticipated in v. 13. While this is a paragraph about Ahaziah the Judean, the data in fact concerns his kinsman Joram of Samaria whom the Syrians have wounded in war.[2] While there is nothing as strikingly heroic in his woundedness as the combat death of his father Ahab in 1 Kings 22, the parallel between the two narratives is obvious. Joram is wounded and is visited by his Southern counterpart, Ahaziah, apparently his cousin. As we shall see in the next chapter, the purpose of this visit is apparently to situate both kings at the cursed location of Jezreel, to prepare for the royal killing that is to follow. The report suggests the closeness of the two and may suggest that the Northern king is the dominant force in the relationship, as was Ahab over Jehoshaphat in an earlier time. In any case, the wounding of the king once again suggests the vulnerability and precariousness of the regime in Samaria, a regime surely without the protection of Yahweh, endlessly exposed to prophetic disturbance.

The narrative, without calling attention to it, plants in these lines two tag words for what is to come later in the story. Ahaziah is the son of *Athaliah*, the Omride who will be crucial for the dynasty in Jerusalem. In texts to come he will occupy a large and troublesome role. The wounded king, moreover, is at *Jezreel*, a place freighted with heavy implication. [Jezreel] It is clear that this paragraph is not mere reportage. The narrator is inconspicuously signalling themes

---

Jezreel

The mention of Jezreel here is simply an identifiable place of royal occupancy. This usage, however, is sandwiched between the dreadful anticipation of Elijah (1 Kgs 21:23) and its fulfillment in 2 Kings 9:30-37. Placed as our reference is, even such an innocent-looking citation is a hint to the reader of terrible things yet to come upon the regime at prophetic instigation.

that will be the material out of which this sorry dynastic story comes to its bloody denouement.

CONNECTIONS

The Israelite narrative dips into Syrian history only as it is useful for this narrative, with no intrinsic interest in Syria. The succession of Ben-hadad by Hazael and the new aggression toward Israel under Hazael are the necessary historical backdrop for the prophetic narrative.

But clearly this particular narrative is concerned to exhibit the prophet as the pivotal character in the deep revision of international politics. Royal coups do happen and new oppressors do emerge, here and there, as matters of state. Our narrative, however, has no interest in such affairs of state as such. What counts for this narrative is Elisha's provocative announcement that surely legitimates, authorizes, and seems to evoke political activity of a quite violent kind. Thus the larger theme that pervades many of these narratives is the relationship between *prophecy and politics*, an exceedingly tricky, dense interaction. The narrator proposes no theocracy whereby the prophets should assume power and govern. That is why there are kings who must do what prophets do not do. But the narrative also eschews any notion of an autonomous, self-propelled royal governance. This "theory of history" believes that the seriously uttered claims of the prophets, perceived to be utterances beyond conventional history, do indeed turn the course of public events. To be sure, the narrative is not interested generically in such utterance, but only in utterance on the lips of this man of God who manifestly delivers a word other than his own, a word seen to be effectively a word from beyond the historical process. The narrative invites us to ponder how it is that such utterance "turns" public power.

The Bible is a disclosure of such utterance, all the way from Moses' demand of emancipation based on "Thus says the Lord" (Exod 5:1) to Jesus whose utterance trembled the powers of Rome. In the trajectory from Moses to Jesus (and beyond), there are many prophets in Israel whose words are remembered as future-shaping gifts.

It is not easy in modern, "rational" discourse to entertain the same interplay of word and power as these "primitives" practiced. And yet every extreme regime, even now, is profoundly frightened by poets who imagine public reality beyond given power arrangements, for such poetry seems to create openings in the public

Havel on Hope
Vaclav Havel writes of the possibility of hope:

> Hope is definitely not the same thing as optimism. It is not the conviction that something
> will turn out well, but the certainty that something makes sense, regardless of how it
> turns out. In short, I think that the deepest and most important form of hope, the only one
> that can keep us above water and urge us to good works, and the only true source of the
> breathtaking dimension of the human spirit and its efforts, is something we get, as it
> were, from "elsewhere." It is also this hope, above all, which gives us the strength to live
> and continually to try new things, even in conditions that seem as hopeless as ours do,
> here and now.

Vaclav Havel, *Disturbing the Peace: A Conversation with Karel Hvizdala* (New York: Knopf, 1990) 181-82.

process where newness may come as gift. Among the obvious examples of such utterances in our time are Martin Luther King, Jr. in this country, Nelson Mandela and Desmond Tutu in South Africa, who were so effective because they were able to claim such high moral ground, and Vaclav Havel in Czechoslovakia, who, by his faithful utterance, created an option that the regime could not tolerate. [Havel on Hope] Elisha is a model for irresistible truth and possibility. His utterance is marked by anticipated violence. Such utterance that has no self-serving dimension characteristically occupies high moral ground that conventional, violent politics finds irresistible. [On High Moral Ground]

On High Moral Ground
It is clear that from a Yahwistic perspective, the prophet characteristically holds high moral ground against the monarchs. On standing for truth before people of power, as Elisha stood before men of power, Jesus admonishes his disciples:

> Make up your minds not to prepare your defense in advance; for I will give you words and a
> wisdom that none of your opponents will be able to withstand or contradict. (Luke 21:14-15)

Of that strange advice, Choan-Seng Song writes:

> You were not after political power. The secret police who arrested you know that. You did not
> try to form an opposition political party. The prosecutor who conducted the interrogation is
> aware of that. And the authorities do not believe you have the power to overthrow the govern-
> ment. The state power is not reckoning with your political power. You do not have political
> power. The church has little to do with political power…. The state does not have to worry
> about your political power. But there is one thing the state must worry about: the moral power
> that comes from your faith in Jesus. That they have to reckon with. It is as formidable, if not
> more formidable than state power. It speaks the truth and not lies. It does not call evil, good
> and good, evil. It echoes the agonies of men and women under the heavy burden of life. And
> above all it calls for people to have a greater share in political decisions that affect their lives
> and future.

Choan-Seng Song, "The Politics of the Resurrection," *Proclaiming the Acceptable Year,* ed. Justo L. Gonzalez (Valley Forge: Judson Press, 1982) 32-33.

Kings must of course practice foreign policy, then as now much reduced to military enterprise. All around the realities of policy, however, this narrative raises issues about theological requirements present in such policy issues. The truth of the case is that both dynasties, North and South, have a sorry record of their commitments to Yahweh. Both royal families are much attracted to alternatives that, in the narrative, are taken as the ground for governmental failure. The narrator insists that an elemental Yahwistic perspective pervades the conduct of foreign policy. That perspective is always operative, even if it is not always visible; the demand of Yahwism, moreover, is the property of no single party, but pervades all those in power.

There is not any simple "connection" from that ancient context to our own present reality. If, however, the issue is Yahweh vs. Baal, as the narrative strenuously insists, then we in our belated time and place may observe that Baalism is ever again a system of self-securing through technological capacity that screens out large issues of fidelity and of Holy Purpose that make concrete covenantal demands. It is not difficult to see that by the end of the twentieth century, all parties of power, including the "last superpower," were and still are deeply committed to self-securing through technological capacity in a way that screens out large issues of fidelity, of Holy Purposes that make concrete covenantal demands. Our narrative is restrained about making any connections for us, but offers data for our own imaginative, interpretive connections.

NOTES

[1] The chronology of the kings cannot be established with any precision. I am citing dates that reflect a primary scholarly reconstruction of the chronology.

[2] It is important to recognize that Joram and Jehoram are variants of the same royal name.

A BLOODY, PROPHET-PROPELLED REVOLUTION

2 Kings 9:1-37

This narrative makes a decisive turn in this history of the monarchy in both North and South. The account of the revolution is military, ruthless and bloody, featuring the death of three royal persons (9:14-37), action propelled by a secret prophetic anointing, freighted with sufficient sacramental power to legitimate and sustain public acts of violence (9:1-13).

COMMENTARY

A Prophetic Act with Public, Violent Consequences, 9:1-13

The prophetic movement, led in turn by Elijah and Elisha, has, over all its time of effectiveness, been deeply antagonistic toward the Omride dynasty in the North and its derivative replication in the South among the heirs of David. The narrator who reports on the prophetic movement, moreover, views the Omride dynasty as the quintessential expression of disobedience that earns the dreadful opposition of Yahweh. The long prophetic narrative, beginning with the rise of Omri in 1 Kings 16:23, moves slowly and determinedly toward this startling moment of overthrow. It is likely that the events that come to fruition in our present narrative have their narrative or oracular seed in 1 Kings 19:15-16, wherein Elijah is empowered by Yahweh to three acts:

(a) the anointing of Hazael, on which see 2 Kings 8:12, an empowerment by Elisha, even if not an anointing;

(b) the anointing of Elisha, on which see 2 Kings 2:9-12, also not an anointing but an act of empowerment, and

(c) the anointing of Jehu, the culminating event of the prophetic movement, enacted in our present chapter.

The narrative concerning the prophetic anointing of Jehu takes place in three successive scenes, in each of which the term "anoint" figures centrally (9:1-3, 4-10, and 11-13).

In the first scene, the prophet Elisha takes the initiative by instructing one of his cohorts (9:1-3). Notably, Elisha here has no mandate for this dangerous act, but presumably acts to complete the mandate given to Elijah in 1 Kings 19:16. No reason is given here for the act, though the reader may understand that both Yahweh and Yahweh's prophet have had more than enough of the Omrides. The prophet gives his aide quite explicit directions (9:2), and understands that the proposed act is indeed a dangerous one (9:3). The agent who anoints Jehu must run for his life, because he will anoint a king when there is no vacancy in the office. (See the parallel risky action of Samuel in 1 Sam 16:1-13). Notably, the act of anointing includes both (a) word: "Thus says the Lord, 'I anoint you'," and (b) sacrament: "pour it on his head." The instruction of v. 3 makes clear that it is Yahweh's own utterance and Yahweh's own self who anoints. This revolutionary act is from Yahweh.

The deed anticipated in vv. 1-3 is enacted in vv. 4-10. Up through v. 6, the agent of Elisha follows his instructions precisely. But then, in the oracle of vv. 7-10, the aide goes well beyond explicit directions and verbalizes concretely what had only been implied in vv. 1-3. Verses 7-10 in fact interpret the act of anointing so that the newly anointed one, plus the reader, will be in no doubt about the importance or the requirement of the sacramental act.

Jehu, already nominated in the oracle to Elijah in 1 Kings 19:16, is to do the work of eliminating the Omrides, the task that Yahweh and the prophets and the Deuteronomic editors have long regarded as inescapable. The target of the act of anointing is not just the incumbent king, Joram, but the entire dynasty of Omri. The act of killing the prophets, especially by Jezebel, is here only a reference point for the total, massive, wholesale reaction of the dynasty to Yahwism. And now that reaction must be answered, totally, massively, and wholesale.[1] The oracle of instruction to Jehu echoes the prophetic oracle of Elijah in 1 Kings 21:21-22. With the reference to "the house of Jeroboam" (on which see 1 Kgs 14:13-16) and "the house of Baasha" (on which see 1 Kgs 16:1-7), it is clear that the narrative thinks in terms of successive dynasties, each of which and all of which are dismal failures of disobedience. The cumulative effect of dynastic dismissal is to formulate something of a philosophy of history: dynasties against Yahweh cannot endure; all Northern dynasties are against Yahweh; all Northern dynasties are under violent, certain judgment.

Along with the judgment pronounced on the "house of Ahab," the present oracle to Jehu includes a personal addendum in v. 10: "the dogs shall eat Jezebel." That queen, wife of Ahab and mother of Ahaziah and Joram, must have been the driving force of the regime (or as least is portrayed as such) so despised is she by the prophets. In any case, she is the point of preoccupation in the narrative and oracle; Jezebel draws the great venom of the prophets. It is she who hunted for Elijah (1 Kgs 19:2). In 1 Kings 21:23, moreover, Elijah has already declared, "The dogs shall eat Jezebel," so that the phrase became a slogan against the queen mother and her house. No wonder our scene ends, "He opened the door and fled" (9:10).

The anointing of Jehu happened in secret as Elisha had planned. It did not, however, stay secret for long. Now Jehu must return to his fellow officers at the officers club (9:11-13). Of course the other officers are curious about the message brought by the strange intruder. They refer to the prophetic messenger as a "madman," and Jehu agrees with that characterization. [Prophet as Madman] But of course the other officers do not believe Jehu's dismissive report on the secret encounter. Finally he must tell them what happened in secret, so that the narrative can repeat, for a third time, "I anoint you king over Israel." The other officers are now completely credulous when they hear his report. They accept his royal designation at face value. Or perhaps their response is one of half mock humor in which they go along with the gag. Either way, for real or for fun, they enact a small ceremony of acclamation with the usual trimmings, a "red carpet" of their uniforms, a blast of trumpet, and an

---

AΩ **Prophet as Madman**

Undoubtedly some prophets in ancient Israel operated in trances: they were seized by God's spirit and consequently acted in ways that might be regarded by well ordered society as "mad." See 1 Samuel 10:9-12; 19:18-24. Prophets sometimes acted outside conventional social orderliness, conduct that bespoke special power and authority but that also made them a threat to society. Thus a prophet may be dismissively termed a "madman" (see Hos 9:7; Jer 29:26).

In our text, the comrades of Jehu comment on the apparent madman, one outside socially accepted convention, who called upon Jehu. Jehu's response to his comrades, moreover, confirms such a dismissive view of the prophet. In truth, the idea of Jehu's anointing was "crazy," for he had no royal claim to make.

It is surely more than coincidence that the same term as "madman" (*shûggah*) in v. 11 is used to characterize Jehu who rides "like a maniac" (9:20). In context the term means, as it is usually taken, that he rides with great speed, carelessly and dangerously, so as to be unsafe. Along with the term used in v. 11, the usage in v. 20, in my judgment also reflects the wild, nonconventional political reality that Jehu embodies in the desire to overthrow legitimate, established authority. Jehu is indeed as "crazy" as the prophet who authorizes him.

See Phyllis Trible, "Exegesis for Storytellers and Other Strangers," JBL 114 (1995): 3-19.

acclamation assertion, now out loud, "Jehu is king!" Whether that scene is serious or only for amusement, the soldiers have now signed on with Jehu in a daring act of treason, for the acclamation implies that Joram is no longer king! [From Anointing to Acclamation] The prophetic act of anointing has set in motion a decisive, sure-to-be-bloody break in royal governance.

Violent Enactment of the New Rule, 9:14-37

The anointing and acclamation of Jehu are the easy parts. Now begins the political, military reality of the coup. In turn Joram, king of Israel (9:14-26), Ahaziah, king of Judah (9:27-29), and Jezebel, the hated queen mother and symbol of blatant disobedience (9:30-37), must all be destroyed.

Because Joram, king in Samaria, is the target of the Northern coup, his elimination receives most detailed coverage in the narrative (vv. 14-26). We have already seen in 8:29 that Joram was recuperating in Jezreel from wounds earned in the Syrian War, and that his Southern ally, Ahaziah, was there commiserating with him. Jehu is at Ramoth-gilead with the troops on the Syrian front (9:14; see 8:28), and must now travel in secret from Ramoth-gilead to Jezreel in order to enact his now prophet-legitimated rule. He "plans" (9:14; better, "conspires") for the death of the king who has now been delegitimated as far as the Yahweh-movement is concerned. In v. 15, he apparently plans with his fellow officers to whom he says, "If this is your wish.... " That is, he clearly intends this beginning of his rule to be a collegial matter, and all his men

---

AΩ **From Anointing to Acclamation**

The anointing of Jehu is in secret so that not even his military comrades know. The "making of a king," however, is not completed in a secret anointing, but is done only with the public acclamation of his troops who in their acclamation reject old royal authority, acknowledge new authority, and therefore commit treason against the present king. Public acclamation completes kingmaking and sets in motion the overthrow of old authority.

The formulation of acclamation is the actual "performance" of kingmaking, the utterance that has the force of coronation and empowerment. While the anointing is "from above," from God, the acclamation is "from below," from the subjects. The same linkage of anointing and acclamation is evident in the "kingmaking of Solomon that we have considered in 1 Kings 1:39. Nathan anoints Solomon, but Beneniah the military man, pronounces something like an acclamation, making the event loudly public. The people echo Beneniah in v. 39.

One other aspect of the formula of acclamation that has occupied Old Testament scholarship may be mentioned. The formula of acclamation, "Jehu is king" (*malak Jehû*) (9:13) surely means "is just now made king." That same understanding of the formula has been taken by some scholars concerning Yahweh who "is king =" has just now been made king" (see Pss 96:10; 97:1; 99:1; Isa 52:7). In public utterance, the emphasis is characteristically upon the "performative" power of acclamation.

AΩ The News

The phrase "tell the news" in v. 15 in fact translates the verb "proclaim" *(nagad)* that has no direct object. That is, the term "the news" is not in the text. The usage of the verb, however, is reminiscent of 7:9-15 which, as we have seen, has the same verb a number of times, plus the term "news" (gospel) in v. 9. The point I wish to notice here is that in our verses the notion of "telling the news" refers to the acclamation of Jehu as king, the declaration of a coup that treasonably overthrows old royal power. That of course is indeed news in any society. The same sort of acclamation is employed in Ps 96:10 and Isa 52:7, to assert Yahweh's newly established kingship in Israel and over the world. The rhetoric of Israel is derived from commonsense political usage, so that the theological "gospel" is news of a change in governance. The same usage is reflected in Jesus' initial announcement in the Gospel of Mark:

Jesus came to Galilee, proclaiming the good news of God, and saying: "The time is fulfilled, and the kingdom of God has come near; repent, and believe in the good news." (Mark 1:14-15)

---

support him in his murderous plan. He must keep "the news" of the coup secret from Joram so that he may take him by surprise. [The News]

The account of Jehu's approach to Jezreel, where rests the convalescing Joram, is saturated with *shalom* (9:17-20). A watchman sees him approaching. He is instructed to ask, "Do you come in *shalom?*" (9:17). That is, is this a friendly approach? Joram had every reason to anticipate a friendly visit, for Jehu was one of his own officers (see 9:25). And yet the question itself suggests anxiety, for the king is surely not unaware of the agitation against the dynasty by religious "conservatives." The guard asks Jehu as instructed, "Is this *shalom?*" In brusque fashion Jehu rejects the question and invites the messenger to ride behind him, that is, to join his cause against the king who had just dispatched him. The clear unspoken implication is that this is not *shalom.* Immediately and silently the messenger joins Jehu, that is, changes sides against the king. Little is said and little needs to be said, for the point of the "conspiracy" is abundantly clear. Joram's own house guard begins to abandon him for the new cause. All this is reported to Joram by the watchman.

The king sends a second messenger to whom the same thing happens. He asks, *"Shalom?"* Jehu again refuses *shalom.* The second messenger also joins the new cause, as is again reported to Joram. The watchman, moreover, guesses that the approaching rider is Jehu, riding like a maniac. Apparently Jehu has a reputation in the army for speed, daring, and recklessness. He is a "maniac" *(bishg'on).* And now he rides like a crazy man on a crazy mission instigated by a crazy prophet. King Joram is about to be to be broken in upon by a highly irregular, highly motivated, volatile force that comes as a threat. For all of the use of the term in the account, there is here not a hint of *shalom* in the events narrated.

The approach of Jehu is ominous because of his speed and because he evidently recruits the two messengers of Joram to his side; that is, they quickly abandon the king who sent them, perhaps sensing that momentum for the political future has shifted abruptly. In response, Joram, with his sidekick Ahaziah of Judah, rides out to meet Jehu. While the narrative presents the royal response as consisting in an approach by the two kings, it is likely that they are accompanied by a military group, at least a bodyguard. The king puts to Jehu the same question of *shalom* (9:22). Jehu issues his same defiant answer, only this time adding the reasons why there can be no *shalom*: "whoredom and sorceries." [Whoredom and Sorceries] The terms are not explicated, but as elsewhere everything is focused on the queen mother, Jezebel. She is for this text the focal point of all evil that must be eradicated. Joram, upon hearing such a phrasing, recognizes immediately that this is the stuff of military coup and dynastic overthrow, and seeks to flee for his life (9:23).

He is, however, too late. He is killed by Jehu with one shot of an arrow (9:24), a death not unlike that of his father Ahab in 1 Kings 22:34. For our text, however, the act of killing is matched and overwhelmed by the speech Jehu makes to his aide (9:25-26). What can be seen is a royal assassination. What is to be understood, however, is an enactment of the old pronouncement of Elijah against that royal house in 1 Kings 21:19. It is telling that, here, that oracle is "uttered by the Lord," with Elijah not even mentioned. The death of Joram is closely linked to the specific violation of Naboth by Ahab and Jezebel. Royal history turns on one pivotal violation to

---

📖 Whoredom and Sorceries

This phrasing is a savage summary assessment of the Omri dynasty. Clearly, the phrasing intends to be as derogatory as possible. Beyond that, however, its precise meaning is not obvious. The conventional term used here for "harlotries" (meaning betrayal of a defining loyalty) is linked to worship Jezebel and may refer to some practice of Baal-zebub worship (1 Kgs 16:31; 18:4, 13, 19; 19:1-2; 21:5). If that connection is valid, then it refers to the trust that the dynasty has placed in a certain Baal who is a rival to Yahweh. The second term, "sorceries," refers to manipulative technical modes of religion designed to bring religious mysteries under control. (See Deut 18:10-12.) It may be that the terms refer to quite specific practices in ancient Israel considered by this tradition to be affronts to Yahwism. In our narrative, however, the force of the phrase is cumulative, so that the intent of the whole is greater than the naming of all of its parts. This is a decisive indictment linked to Jezebel concerning a regime that deliberately and continually acted in ways contrary to Yahwism and in defiance of Yahweh. In v. 23, Joram's recognition of "treason" borders on the ironic, for the term used by the king bespeaks treachery, when the Omri dynasty itself has been endlessly treacherous and duplicitous toward Yahweh.

which is gathered all the resentment and hostility of the "true Yahwists." Everything happens "in accordance with the word of the Lord." It may be that Jehu is simply an ambitious, bloodthirsty, military killer. By this oracle he is transposed into a key player in a Yahwistic-prophetic drama much larger and more formidable than he as a military man could ever claim. He is the right man at the right time, caught up in forces and purposes of which he apparently knows or cares little. It is, in the end, Yahweh who "kills and makes alive" (Deut 32:39).

The death of Ahaziah is, by contrast to the Joram narrative, reported in a terse account (9:27-29). We may note that nowhere is Ahaziah or the Southern dynasty mentioned, neither in the governing oracle of Elijah (1 Kgs 19:15-16) nor in the specific mandate to Jehu (2 Kgs 9:6-10). Ahaziah is apparently implicated in the "sins of the North" and therefore is killed alongside Joram for his collusion and the broader collusion of the Southern dynasty in the vagaries of the Omri dynasty in the North. No extravagant prophetic rhetoric is used of him in order to justify his death, simply, "Shoot him also." He is wounded, but unlike Joram, he escapes with his wounds to die later at Megiddo, perhaps a royal fortress (see 1 Kgs 10:16). Because he is from the Davidic line, moreover, he is given an honorable royal burial in Jerusalem, in deep contrast to both the sorry disposal of Joram's body (v. 26) and the ignoble desecration of Jezebel's (9:35-37). One has the impression that the narrator has no real interest in the death of Ahaziah; it is reported simply to complete the picture. The odd note in v. 29 seems misplaced and is in any case a variant for the same data in 8:25. The verse is as close as Ahaziah comes to having the concluding formula to which every Southern king is entitled.

Finally this bloody turn of affairs reaches it culmination (and goal?) in vv. 30-37. Unlike the terse account of vv. 27-29, here the narrator warms to the subject and leads the reader into every savored detail concerning this queen whom we are to despise. The mandate under which Jehu operates had concluded with particular reference to Jezebel (v. 10, on which see 1 Kgs 21:23). Jehu now proceeds, with great dramatic effect, to enact his mandate. Jezebel awaits him in Jezreel. She knows the score and knows her time is up. She is, however, not a coward or a wimp. She meets Jehu defiantly, both by appearing at the royal balcony dressed like the queen she is (v. 30), and by mockingly addressing him (9:31). She asks "the *shalom* question" as had the messengers (9:17, 19) and Joram (9:22). But she knows the answer; for that reason she does not hesitate to assault and goad Jehu by linking him to Zimri, who killed

Elah, son of Baasha, and destroyed that dynasty (1 Kgs 16:8-16). Jehu, like Zimri—says the queen in jeopardy—is a king-killer and a dynasty destroyer. Now, he brings no *shalom*, and everyone involved knows that he brings no *shalom*.

Jehu, however, is a man on a mission. He is not deterred by the defiance of the queen. He has no hesitation and no interest in responding to the woman he has come to kill. Ignoring her, he bids for the loyalty of the court functionaries (eunuchs) who stand beside her in the window: "Who is with me? Who?" Like the messengers in vv. 17-20, the attendants to Jezebel can spot the new winner. They say nothing for the record in response to Jehu, but they act promptly according to his command. They throw the queen down to an ignoble death, to be trampled by horses. [An Ignoble Death] The narrative is at pains to exhibit the humiliation of Jezebel, in an instant transformed from a narcissistic queen to a piece of rubbish in the street.

Jehu is quick and ruthless. He eats and drinks, ostensibly occupying the royal quarters, all at once eating and drinking like the king he has just become. And then, now exalted with a show of success and arrogance, he remembers the trampled, discarded queen. His directions for her burial are enigmatic. Does Jehu, now royalty himself, begin to ponder that royalty must respect royalty, for she is "a king's daughter" (see 1 Kgs 16:31)? Or does he cynically know beforehand that with trampling horses and hungry dogs it is much too late for royal honors? When told that the dogs had done their predictable work on the discarded royal carcass, the new, violent king never misses a beat. As in vv. 25-26, he here situates his violence as an enactment of divine oracle (9:36-37). No wonder the violence has happened to the queen! No wonder the queen's

---

📖 An Ignoble Death

The narrative is at pains to portray the death of Jezebel dismissively with as much shame and humiliation as can be mustered. Her death contrasts with that of Ahaziah who is accorded the honors befitting a king (9:28). The contrast is that the body of the despised queen is not only dishonored and turned over to the most brutalizing and ignoble of all animals, but is left without a trace for any possible burial rite. Her "burial," or one like it, is perhaps a basis for Jeremiah's anticipation for a disgraced king in Jerusalem:

They shall not lament for him, saying,
    "Alas, my brother!" or "Alas, my sister!"
They shall not lament for him, saying,
    "Alas, lord!" or "Alas, his majesty!"
With the burial of a donkey he shall be buried—
    dragged off and thrown out beyond the gates
    of Jerusalem. (Jer 22:18-19)

Here, the ghastly immediacy of the event is captured as Jezebel, kicking and screaming, grasping and grappling, is pushed from the window. Jehu is shown calmly seated on his horse below. Also, emerging from the gloom and darkness of Doré's dark shadows for those who have eyes to see, a pack of dogs await the "offering" of Jezebel as they are interspersed among the soldiers. This image of the dogs provides a foreboding sign of events to come.

Gustave Doré. *The Death of Jezebel* from the *Illustrated Bible*. 19th century. Engraving. (Credit: Dover Pictorial Archive Series) body is gone. No wonder the hungry dogs are triumphant. Elijah knew all this eleven chapters ago (1 Kgs 21:23). Her body is quickly dissolved into manure. She is removed from the history of Israel with no visible trace, not to be honored, not to be remembered. Jehu has no regret and no remorse. The entire deed is done at Jezreel, all forespoken by the prophet, all willed by Yahweh. In the providential governance of Yahweh, all is beyond sorrow, all a good thing for the future of Israel now to be presided over by the family of Jehu.

CONNECTIONS

The details of the killings are graphic, designed to match human ruthlessness to divine purpose. While the chapter is extensive and both parts—the narrative of anointing and the cycle of assassinations—are slow paced and deliberate, the plot line of the chapter is clear and simple. Prophetic *instigation* leads to *bloody political revolution.*

The large theme of this narrative is the rise and fall of the dynasty of Omri that has featured four kings and that has had a deep impact upon Israel. That deep impact—deep enough to evoke this long narrative account of the prophets—apparently included considerable political-economic achievement, none of which is valued by this partisan prophetic narrative of 1 and 2 Kings. The overthrow of the regime is effected by an odd and uneasy convergence

---

The Rise and Fall

Paul Kennedy writes of the rise and fall of nation-states without reference to moral or theological considerations. Given the categories in which he operates, the judgments are somewhat different but not, I suggest, wholly without resonance:

The feat demanded of most if not all governing bodies as the world heads toward the twenty-first century is therefore a *threefold* one: simultaneously to provide military security…for its national interests, *and* to satisfy the socioeconomic needs for its citizenry, *and* to ensure sustained growth, this last being essential both for the positive purposes of affording the required guns and butter at the present, and for the negative purpose of avoiding a relative economic decline which could hurt the people's military and economic security in the future. Achieving all three of those feats over a sustained period of time will be a very difficult task, given the uneven pace of technological and commercial change and the unpredictable fluctuations in international politics…the basic argument remains: without a rough balance between these competing demands of defense, consumption, and investment, a Great Power is unlikely to preserve its status for long.

Paul Kennedy, *The Rise and Fall of the Great Powers: Economic Change and Military Conflict from 1500 to 2000* (New York: Random House, 1987) 446.

of prophetic authorization and unrestrained military ambition and violence. That convergence, seemingly irresistible, causes a powerful regime to fall abruptly.

Thus our exposition may consider "the rise and fall" of these dynasties and, by extrapolation, the "rise and fall" of mighty powers in ways that surprise and bewilder. According to the wisdom of this world, powerful, wealthy regimes should be able to defeat all opposition and sustain themselves in power indefinitely. And of course many regimes do precisely that. Here and there, however, as with the dynasty of Omri, they disappear abruptly when they are expected to continue. While the demise of such a regime may be the result of complex factors, the surface representation of the fall—such as our narrative provides—is simple and dramatic. There is something loose in the public process, as this narrative testifies, that may be available for analysis but that in the end defies understanding.

Public history is not finally contained in or explained by sheer power, but by a kind of inscrutability that believers—such as the makers and keepers of this narrative—link to the hidden workings of God. [The Rise and Fall]

In the last years we have witnessed such dramatic falls from power of the totalitarian regimes in the Soviet Union and the apartheid government in South Africa, to name the most dramatic cases, though we may also mention the petty dictatorships of Marcos in the Philippines and Suharto in Indonesia. In each case, the reason for collapse (which has been without much violence) is surely complex. Obviously explanatory dimensions include the relation of economic and military power. In each case, however, the demise surely included a moral dimension not explained by military excess or by economic foolishness. There was and is something else at work that is too easily harnessed for aggression and ambition. In our narrative, as in other cases that might be cited, it is clear that the military violence is completely unchecked and there is a certain bravado reflected in its enactment. At the same time, however, we notice that Jehu (or the narrator) is careful to link the violent overthrow of monarchy twice to the prophetic oracle of Elijah. It is this linkage that makes this portrayal of public power so demanding and so enigmatic.

The connection between violent overthrow and prophetic instigation, moreover, is specified in v. 7. It is worth noting that Elisha, the prophet of import here, is present only in vv. 1-3 in his dispatching of the "young prophet" who will do the act of anointing. After that initial mandate, the narrative seems to develop according

The Bishop and the President

The collusion of the anointing prophet and the murdering king suggests the necessary interface between sacramental power and state leverage in the making of governance. There are of course many such examples of this interface. Here in the interest of considering the founding of a viable state revolution I cite the odd case of South Africa in recent decades in which the "front men" have been Bishop Desmond Tutu who brought the moral leverage of the church and President Nelson Mandela who understood well how to manage the powers of the state. The revolution in South Africa that overthrew the apartheid state is of course complex and multidimensional. It does seem clear that it would not have happened, for all the implied violence of the African National Congress that Mandela led, without the belated moral courage of some elements of the church. In a rough parallel, the revolution of Jehu is indeed bloody and rooted in violence, but it depended upon the legitimacy of the anointing.

---

to a momentum all its own, without further appeal to the instigating prophet. Undoubtedly the act of anointing is to be understood as a freighted symbolic gesture that we may say is filled with sacramental power. That is, it is a solemn religious act that overflows with significance, authority, and power well beyond the act itself. It is possible, of course, to regard the prophetic act as a cynical show to legitimate a military coup that was in any case waiting to happen. In terms of the narrative itself, however, there is no hint of such a cynical deployment of sacramental significance. The act perhaps takes Jehu by surprise and motivates him in directions he would never have otherwise gone, perhaps so unlike the prophetic announcement to Hazael in vv. 12-13. Such interventions by "holy men" characteristically pose a potential threat to established power because they unleash subversive authority and evoke subversive imagination that does not readily yield to established categories of what is proper and what is possible. Such gestures create imaginative space in which one may entertain a scenario of public power that does not conform to present givens. It is clear in this episode, and in the prophetic narratives of Elijah and Elisha more generally, that prophetic gesture keeps the Omride dynasty off balance and makes it a constant candidate for destabilization and finally overthrow. It is important not to underestimate the force, power, and importance of such sacramental gestures in the redeployment of public power. [The Bishop and the President]

The specificity of prophetic instigation is matched in Jehu's pronouncements by the specificity of the royal offense. While the prophetic-Yahwistic opposition to the dynasty of Omri might be quite general and programmatic, it is important that according to vv. 26, 36-37, the destruction of the kings is linked to Elijah's oracle concerning Naboth. That quintessential act of royal usurpation has become the sign and symbol of this regime, a royal usurpation for which answer must be given. Prophetic opposition and eventual public fervor against a regime are characteristically focused upon a particular affront, an affront so violent and offensive and unbearable that it can mobilize moral passion and fearless armed resistance. There are limits to what royal regimes can perpetrate with impunity. Such a limit is reached here, a limit reflected in the directness of prophetic authorization and in the vigor of Jehu's violence.

NOTE

[1]See Robert R. Wilson, *Prophecy and Society in Ancient Israel* (Philadelphia: Fortress Press, 1980) 229-30.

THE END OF THE
BLOODY REIGN OF JEHU

2 Kings 10:1-36

Setting political violence in motion by a sacramental act of anointing (9:6) is easier than curbing that violence. In chapter 9 Jehu had already committed three acts of regicide: the murder of Joram (9:14-26), the murder of Ahaziah (9:27-29), and the murder of Jezebel (9:30-37). In the present chapter the killing, justified as the elimination of Baalism, is continued in four acts: the house of Ahab (10:1-11), the house of Ahaziah (10:12-14), the residue of the house of Ahab (10:15-17), and the prophets and worshipers of Baal (10:18-27). The chapter ends with a concluding assessment of the violent reign of Jehu (10:28-36).

COMMENTARY

Death to the House of Ahab, 10:1-11

These verses tell of two waves of killing, first the members of the royal family and then the royal household, twin acts made possible by the duplicity and cunning of Jehu. The royal family of Ahab was a complex extended family, apparently of many branches, any one of which could still rise with power against the coup of Jehu. The number of sons, seventy, is perhaps not a precise count but may mean "many" (10:1). Jehu's stratagem is to move against all of these potential challengers, wholesale but not directly. In his cunning, he invites the royal officials (not the family) to send a "champion" son of Ahab against Jehu, a controlled, planned contest, perhaps reminiscent of the David-Goliath contest of 1 Samuel 17 (10:2-3). We cannot know if Jehu's goading invitation is serious or if it is only a ploy. If it is a ploy, it is a successful one. The royal entourage, not unlike the servants of Jezebel in 9:32-33, promptly recognize that Jehu will win any such contest and any other struggle, and that to oppose him is suicidal. [The Steward of the Palace] Without delay, the palace officials (including "the steward of the palace") refuse to take the bait of the invitation, quickly surrender, and declare themselves adherents of the new regime:

> We are your servants; we will do anything you say. We will not
> make anyone king; do whatever you think right. (10:5)

The response to Jehu from the palace is almost obsequious toward
the king-killer, surely a response made in fear.

Jehu immediately follows this decisive capitulation with a test of
this newly declared loyalty (10:6). To prove their loyalty to Jehu
(exactly like the attendants to Jezebel in the previous chapter), they
must kill the seventy sons of Ahab, thereby eliminating all the
princes who still may threaten Jehu. Jehu's vigorous intimidation of
the royal officer is effective. The deed is done. The heads of the seventy are brought to Jehu at Jezreel (where else!?) as attestation of
loyalty to the new power. Jehu has had seventy killed (10:6b-8) and
in so doing Jehu has, so to speak, "killed two birds with one stone,"
being assured of loyalty and eliminating the opposition.

In his cunning, however, Jehu is not yet finished. First, he attests
that he himself killed the king; the royal entourage is innocent of
that (10:9, on which see 9:14-26). But then, before the verse is finished, Jehu reverses field with a taunting, accusatory question:
"Who killed all these seventy?" The implied answer for Jehu is
"Certainly not I." Thus he has tricked and seduced the royal
entourage into killing the royal family, binding them irreversibly to
himself. Their innocence is limited to the death of the king. They
must answer for all the other deaths.

Jehu's verdict in v. 10, in yet one more appeal to the oracle of
Elijah, does not follow from v. 9. The guilt or innocence of the others is irrelevant to the outcome, because they themselves are to be
slaughtered in any case. The reference to the oracle in v. 10 is used
to justify the action of v. 11. The roster of the slain in v. 11—
leaders, close friends, and priests—roughly approximates the leadership mentioned in vv. 2 and 5. In the end all that counts in the
narrative summary is this: no survivors (10:11). The line is a characteristic marker for Jehu.

AΩ The Steward of the Palace

Among those included in Jehu's cunning invitation is the "Steward of the House." On this
office see Isaiah 22:15-25. It is likely that this person is a major official in the realm, perhaps the integral manager of royal affairs, not unlike Joseph in the household of Pharaoh (Gen 41:41-45;
47:13-26). The title gives specificity and weight to Jehu's ambitious strategy.

Death to the Family of Ahaziah, 10:12-14

As the death of Ahaziah in 9:27-28 receives lean attention from the narrator, compared with the death of Joram (9:14-26), so the follow-up killing of members of the Davidic dynasty (10:12-14) is less conspicuous in the narrative than the slaughter in the North (10:1-11). Jehu meets the Southern royal entourage on its way to visit members of the Northern royal family. The term rendered "visit" in v. 13 is *shalom*, "come down for peace." The Southern royals apparently are completely innocent and uninformed about the previous killings. They do not even know they are in danger or that a coup is under way. They are on their way to visit sons of the queen mother, Jezebel, who appears in the narrative yet once more. The outcome of their confrontation with Jehu is quick and expected: *not a survivor* among them (10:14).

More Killing in Samaria, 10:15-17

It is as though Jehu cannot stop the killing and the narrative cannot stop the telling. The follow-up action of Jehu in these verses should not have been necessary after the finality of v. 11. Here it is nonetheless. The variation in this particular episode of bloodiness is an encounter with Jehonadab (elsewhere Jonadab) the Rechabite. [The Rechabites] Jehonadab is the leader of a zealous community (sect?) of passionate Yahwists who oppose any compromise with Baalism, and who are therefore likely to be in complete sympathy with the coup of Jehu. The violent new governance of Jehu surely needs all the supporters it can muster, and so to be seen in public with the leader of the Rechabites is an important public relations gain for Jehu. We may imagine that the mustering of an ally was an informal matter between leaders of small movements who signed on their followers for "the cause." We are not told that Jehonadab or his followers participated in the killing of v. 17, but we may surmise that they approved the killing and perhaps lent the legitimacy

---

AΩ **The Rechabites**

The Rechabites, an informal religious community (sect?) with conservative Yahwistic commitments, is known only here and in the related passage of Jeremiah 35. In the second passage where Jonadab (Jehonadab in 2 Kings) is again the head of the community, the ethic embraced by the community is the most stringent kind of Yahwism, a commitment that surely would be resistant to any compromise with Baalism. The rule of the community included the following:

You shall never drink wine, neither you nor your children; nor shall you ever build a house, or sow a seed; nor shall you plant a vineyard, or even own one; but you shall live in tents all your days. (Jer 35:6-7)

of their special reputation for Yahwism. Indeed Jehu's zeal for Yahweh is a gesture of solidarity with the pure zeal of the Rechabites. [Yahwistic Zeal] That zeal is a refusal to compromise, precisely the zeal required for a revolutionary movement that seeks to overthrow established power. The conclusion of this killing in v. 17 echoes 9:26, 36-37, and 10:10. Strikingly, in all this series of killings, the formula of appeal to Elijah's oracle is absent only in 9:27-28 and 10:14, the two acts of violence against the Southern dynasty. Jehu clearly has no mandate from Elijah for an action against the Southern monarchy, a lack evident already in the mandate of 1 Kings 19:15. In these cases, Jehu must act out of political necessity, clearly beyond his theological warrant.

> **Yahwistic Zeal**
> The notion of "zeal for the Lord" is almost like a mantra for the movement of prophetic Yahwism, a passion that would find resonance with the Rechabites. Apparently the term came to refer to unrestrained violence against the religious compromisers. In his use of the phrase Jehu echoes the usage of Elijah (1 Kgs 19:10, 14); that prophet had already made the rhetorical move to transpose religious devotion into violent politics.

Death to Baalism, 10:18-27

After the finish of the royal family and the royal household, the circle of violence now includes all those who adhere to Baalism, the functioning religion of the regime. This longer account of death is divided into two parts: the pretense of Baal worship (10:18-24a) and the slaughter (10:24b-27).

Jehu is "cunning" in his plan to gather all the worshipers of Baal into one place (10:19). The term "cunning" is the term 'aqob (= jacob), used to refer to Jacob as the cunning brother in Genesis (27:36). Jehu's deceptive plot is to pose as an adherent to Baal and as a sponsor of a great festival for Baal. He is concerned that *all* adherents to Baal must be present, on pain of death (10:19). They *all* come. They *all* crowd into the temple of Baal. Jehu provides liturgic vestments suitable for the occasion. Jehu also takes care to exclude all who worshiped Yahweh, ostensibly to keep the worship pure, in fact to exempt them from the killing. He appears in the crowd with Jehonadab; that should have been a clue to the plot, for Jehonadab was apparently a known Yahwistic zealot. In any case, a great sacrifice is offered to Baal (10:24). [Whole Offering...Holocaust?] Jehu is true to his word; he did indeed offer the burnt offering. Except that if we wait two verses, we shall see the true character of the sacrificial killing that apparently none of those involved expected. The entire account of the offering is given as an ironic act; we readers know better, Jehu and Jehonadab know better, but the attendees themselves suspect nothing.

Michelangelo Buonarroti. *Jehu Destroying the god Baal*. 1508–1512. Fresco. Medallion located above the Erythraean Sibyl in the Sistine Chapel, Vatican Palace, Vatican State. (Credit: Scala/Art Resource, NY.)

The tone of the narrative changes abruptly in the midst of v. 24. Now Jehu is back in his killing posture. He orders that none escape; and if any escape, his officers will pay with their lives, "a life for a life" (10:24). This is a "ritual cleansing" of the community. The officers of Jehu are obedient; they kill all the gathered adherents of Baal and expel their bodies from the temple, tossing out the slain.

After the killing, Jehu and his forces move against the symbols and furniture of the shrine to Baal. They seize the pillar, central liturgical symbol of Baal, an act not unlike seizing the flag of the enemy. The narrator uses three strong verbs to characterize the destructive action undertaken: they *burned*...they *demolished*...they *destroyed*. The action reflects the use of pent-up hatred against the symbols of the despised regime that had been oppressive and exploitative.

Whole Offering...Holocaust?

Perhaps there is irony in the report that they offered "whole offerings" just before the complete slaughter of the worshipers. To be sure Jehu has engaged in great deception to arrange this slaughter. Given that dishonesty, the slaughter in the name of Yahweh is closely linked to the ruse of sacrifice. The connection between the two acts offers an eerie suggestion of a reference to the slaughter of six million Jews that we have come to call "holocaust." It is the slaughter of the people that is the "burnt offering." While we must be concerned primarily with the twentieth century massacre, we must pay attention to this episode as among the antecedents of such action in the name of ideology.

The overthrow of the temple is the overthrow of the entire liturgical apparatus that served as support and legitimation of what must have been an exploitative regime. The final line describing the devastation tells all (10:27): They took the holy place of Baal and made it into a perpetual "latrine." The term used in its masculine form is regularly "dung" (see 2 Kgs 18:27). This is the only feminine use of the term that may be rendered "cesspool." We may understand, "place of dung," thus "latrine." The narrator exhibits deep contempt for all that is of Baal, now reduced to a scatological reference to the community of Baal. The reversal of fortunes from the Omri regime to the rule of Jehu is now complete: the defeat of adherents to Baal, the elimination of princes, and the obliteration of symbols, all these waves of violence undertook and justified from (a) the act of anointing and (b) the oracle of Elijah. The revolution of Jehu in 842 is understood in the narrative as a moment of complete discontinuity in the political life of northern Israel. We are now ready for a concluding assessment of Jehu. On the basis of the data we have considered, it is clear that all that Jehu enacted was a season of unrestrained violence, nothing more.

The End of Jehu, 10:28-36

Jehu had a long reign of twenty-eight years, 842–815 (10:36). That is a long time for a Northerner, all of whom are in principle condemned in this larger narrative. Given that prior judgment on all Northern kings, we may expect a mixed and delicate theological verdict on Jehu, and that is what we have. The verdict begins in v. 28 with an affirmation: Jehu "wiped out" Baal. Indeed, the series of violent acts in the last two chapters is aimed at adherents to Baal, royal and otherwise. Jehu has won a great and decisive victory for the pure Yahwists, enacting in bloody fashion the most passionate hopes of Yahwists like the Rechabites. In terse fashion the narrative almost gives Jehu two cheers. Before a third cheer can be added, not surprisingly, along comes v. 29. This verse is negative and qualifies v. 28.

Characteristically, the narrative looks back to the founding of Northern shrines by Jeroboam in 1 Kings 12. The real and enduring sin of Jeroboam and all after him in the North is that he refused to submit to the one true shrine in Jerusalem. Of course, in principle, the Northern kings could not submit without ceasing to be kings in the North. Thus, in principle they must bear condemnation in this narrative simply for holding power in the North.

As indicated in this relief monument of the Assyrian ruler, Israel has yielded to Assyria (2 Kgs 10:32).

Jehu, King of Israel, Prostrating Himself Before King Shalmaneser III of Assur. 841–840 BC. Basalt bas-relief. Black stele of Shalmaneser III. British Museum, London, England. (Credit: Erich Lessing/Art Resource, NY)

The judgment of v. 29, however, is almost formulaic because v. 30 follows the more positive inclination of v. 28: Jehu has done *well!* Imagine that! He has been obedient in crushing Baalism, a much more severe problem for this narrator than the shrines mentioned in v. 29. That act of obedience on the part of Jehu earns him a durable dynasty of four generations:

Jehu 842–815 (2 Kgs 9–10),
Jehoahaz 815–802 (2 Kgs 13:1-9)
Jehoash 802–786 (2 Kgs 13:10-13)
Jeroboam II 786–746 (2 Kgs 14:23-29)

This is an exceedingly long period, the longest by far in the North, for a dynasty that became effective and most prosperous. Jehu gets credit for its founding.

The promise of v. 30 nicely corresponds to the actual longevity of the dynasty. In v. 31, however, the narrator returns to a negative judgment according to the tilt of v. 29, linking Jehu to Jeroboam of an earlier, failed, and condemned dynasty.

Before moving to the concluding formula on Jehu in vv. 34-36, we are given one other piece of information, namely, the loss of

Israelite territory east of the Jordan River. The narrator does not suggest that the loss reported in vv. 32-33 is punishment for the indictment of vv. 29 and 31, but characteristically leaves that connection for the reader to determine.

Whatever is to be made of the matter theologically, these verses reflect the expansionism of Hazael as king of Syria, an expansionism that required the brutal policies of Hazael as anticipated by Elisha in 8:12. The biblical perspective on international transactions is shot through with prophetic judgments. Those judgments are made to match the realities on the ground, for in the long period of the second half of the ninth century, Syrian expansionism was a central policy preoccupation of the Northern Kingdom. The phrase "trim off" (v. 32) suggests a theory of interpretation of Israel's history that the loss of territory to Syria is part of an ongoing process whereby the sphere of influence of the Northern state gradually would diminish until it was limited to the environs of the city of Samaria, a diminishment that was the will of Yahweh.

The reign of Jehu, set in motion by prophetic anointing, is now ended. From the perspective of the narrative, he has accomplished a "good thing," the eradication of Baalism. If, however, we consider the force of his entire two chapters, he was clearly and solely a military man whose reign is marked by relentless violence, military violence propelled by religious fervor, what Richard Nelson terms "snowballing violence."[1] Seen from a different angle, his time in power must have been experienced as a "reign of terror."

CONNECTIONS

To overstate the gravity of the turn Jehu accomplished in political history is impossible. Or put differently, it is impossible to overstate the appreciation this narrative has for the violent end of Baalism. The revolution he enacted created a deep break in governance patterns, whereby a strong, compromising dynasty (that of Omri and Ahab) is replaced by an uncompromising, relatively weak dynasty (Jehu). Seen religiously, such a trade-off is a gain. It might indeed be viewed otherwise from the perspective of political reality.

I suppose the key reflection to be made concerning this narrative is the odd relationship between *revolutionary vision* grounded in faith and *revolutionary violence* undertaken in service of such a vision. When faith turns to politics, matters are complex and by no means obvious or benign. In this narrative presentation, Jehu no doubt acted at the behest of Yahwistic authority. There is equally no doubt that he enacted the revolution in a season of ruthless violence. One may say that the revolution got out of hand. But one may also conclude that the God of the revolution is a God of violence, for the action here authorized against Israelite rulers is of a piece with the earlier Yahwistic violence worked against the Canaanites in the book of Joshua.[2] Perhaps the connection of *God and violence* is a huge misperception on the part of the prophet, on the part of Jehu, or on the part of the narrator. If it is a misperception, then it is a mistaken discernment that is deep in biblical piety and imagination and persists even now with recurrent violence in the name of this same God. If not misperception, then the theological problem is even more acute: for the linkage, if truly perceived, draws Yahweh shamelessly close to violence.

As a consequence, Jehu himself is an ambiguous figure, at the same time *obedient and violent*. That ambiguity is well rehearsed by Jacques Ellul, so that only thirteen pages apart he offers a positive portrayal of Jehu as "the earthly representative of God," then "as a man who interposes himself while pretending to be accomplishing the purpose of God."[3] Ellul imagines that by separating these two statements in his analysis and commenting on different initiatives by Jehu, the trouble is overcome. [The Ambiguous Jehu] But of course this is no real solution, not even in the hands of Ellul, for the deep linkage is there in the narrative as it is in so many places in the biblical text. [Current Interpretations of the Theological Problem of Violence]

The Ambiguous Jehu

Ellul's fuller statement on the two pages cited below is this:

All this notwithstanding, Jehu is temporarily, before men, the earthly representative of God, of the true God. He is chosen by God and anointed king on God's behalf…. He has a scrupulous regard for the Word of God and the prophecies of God. He wants to obey these and fulfil them. He offers himself to the people as the man who will reestablish God's rights on earth…. He does not allow us to see the work of God and the love of the Lord through these terrible and tragic actions. This is why Elisha is silent during his reign. The Word of God is no longer spoken. Jehu's revolution is not really religious. It makes the presence of the Lord more incomprehensible to men. For in it man is fully the master of his own life.

Jacques Ellul, *The Politics of God & the Politics of Man* (Grand Rapids: Eerdmans, 1972) 104, 117.

Current Interpretations of the Theolgical Problem of Violence

There is no doubt that the violence Jehu enacted in the name of Yahweh with the support of both the prophets and the Rechabites may be a metaphor for religious violence generally. This text may invite a broad, critical reading on the subject. Among the more important studies of the problem, see David R. Blumenthal, *Facing the Abusive God: A Theology of Protest* (Louisville: Westminster/John Knox Press, 1993; Regina M. Schwartz, *The Curse of Cain: The Violent Legacy of Monotheism* (Chicago: University of Chicago Press, 1997); Renita Weems, *Battered Love: Marriage, Sex, and Violence in the Hebrew Prophets*, OBT (Minneapolis: Fortress Press, 1995); Walter Wink, *Engaging the Powers: Discernment and Resistance in a World of Domination* (Minneapolis: Fortress Press, 1992); *Naming the Powers: The Language of Power in the New Testament* (Philadelphia: Fortress Press, 1984); and *Unmasking the Powers: The Invisible Forces That Determine Human Existence* (Philadelphia: Fortress Press, 1986).

📖 Democratic Containment of Violence

Reinhold Niebuhr has especially appreciated the emergence of democratic institutions and procedures under the influence of Calvinism that broke with authoritarian patterns that fostered the legitimacy of violence (the record of Calvinism is not clean in this regard, but is a trajectory that continues to develop in liberating directions):

> The development of Calvinistic thought from a conservative justification of political authority to a living relation with democratic justice deserves special consideration because, in its final form, Calvinistic theory probably came closest to a full comprehension of all the complexities of political justice.... Thus justice, rather than mere order and peace, became the criterion for government; and democratic criticism became the instrument of justice. The difference between the democratic temper of later Calvinism and the undue and uncritical reverence for political authority in the early Reformation, both Lutheran and Calvinistic, is well illustrated in John Knox's interpretation of Romans 13.

Reinhold Niebuhr, *The Nature asnd Destiny of Man* (New York: Charles Scribner's Sons, 1951) 2:281-83.

When religious passion is transposed directly into political-revolutionary action, violence driven by religious passion becomes a terrible enterprise. In that regard, the massacre by Jehu is a harbinger of the many and strange ways in which religion fuels political revolution in our own time. The easy transposition of religion to revolutionary action benefits from a heavy dose of critical realism that recognizes the need for an important distance between the two, so that one cannot move easily and directly from religion to revolutionary action. Reinhold Niebuhr warned often about "the Children of Light" who failed to recognize ambiguity in their own political enterprise, and who moved simply and innocently to public action, almost always with disastrous results. [Democratic Containment of Violence]

This chapter provides opportunity to think about faith, warrants for revolution, and the need for political imagination beyond

✏️ Variables in Revolutionary Theory

Because political revolution is an available, legitimate option in this faith tradition, it is important to think clearly about the conditions that make revolution theologically acceptable. Paul Lehmann has provided an inventory of the "uniformities" and "variables" in revolutionary theory and practice. Among the latter he lists the following:

1. The identification of the major counterrevolutionary realities and patterns of power;
2. The relations between leadership and the people, especially with reference to guerrilla warfare and contradictions in society; and as its corollary:
3. The uses of ideology;
4. The inevitability of violence;
5. The relation of religious resources to revolutionary endeavor.

Paul Lehmann, *The Transfiguration of Politics: The Presence and Power of Jesus of Nazareth in and over Human Affairs* (New York: Harper & Row, 1975). See Lehmann's longer analysis, 103-226, and the more recent discussion of Michael Walzer, *Exodus and Revolution* (New York: Basic Books, 1985) which makes important distinctions among types of revolutions.

📖 **Calvin's Appeal to Peter**

It is of great importance that in his final discussion of Christian obedience to government, on the very last page of the *Institutes*, Calvin appeals to Peter's verdict: "We must obey God rather than man" (Acts 5:29). [John Calvin, *Institutes* 2, 1521.] There is no doubt that Calvin's remarkable judgment lies behind the subsequent Enlightenment theory of John Locke.

---

simple religious fervor. [Variables in Revolutionary Theory] Revolutions, by their very nature, are not easy. As Israel discovered with the coming of the new regime of Jehu, revolution leaves the difficult work of recovery of what the violence has destroyed. In the case of the dynasty of Jehu, it was a very long time before the dynasty returned to the effectiveness and prosperity that it had destroyed.

Revolution is always an extreme but available option in this faith tradition. In the presence of Jehu, it is instructive and important that John Calvin, that great voice of orderliness, ends his *Institutes* with a warrant for revolution in the extreme case:

> But in that obedience which we have shown to be due the authority of rulers, we are always to make this exception, indeed, to observe it as primary, that such obedience is never to lead us away from obedience to him, to whose will the desires of all kings ought to be subject, to whose decrees all their commands ought to yield, to whose majesty their scepters ought to be submitted.... The Lord, therefore, is the King of Kings, ...next to him we are subject to those men who are in authority over us, but only in him.... If they command anything against him, let it go unesteemed.[4] [Calvin's Appeal to Peter]

NOTES

[1]Richard Nelson, *First and Second Kings,* Interpretation (Atlanta: John Knox Press, 1987) 200.

[2]See Regina M. Schwartz, *The Curse of Cain: The Violent Legacy of Monotheism* (Chicago: University of Chicago Press, 1997).

[3] Jacques Ellul, *The Politics of God and the Politics of Man* (Grand Rapids: Eerdman's, 1972) 104, 117.

[4]John Calvin, *Institutes of the Christian Religion 2,* Library of Christian Classics (Philadelphia: Westminster Press, 1960) 1520.

BEGINNING AGAIN
WITH A CHILD KING

2 Kings 11:1-20

The story of the Omride dynasty and its full, abrupt end at the bloody hands of Jehu had effected a deep discontinuity in the governance of northern Israel. The matter was only somewhat different in Judah in the South, a subject that occupies the present chapter. The power and attractiveness of the Omride dynasty had made the kings in Jerusalem—seemingly willing—allies and cohorts of the North. The ways of Jehu, moreover, cost the life of King Ahaziah in the South along with King Joram in the North. While the break in the South is not as decisive because of the durability of the Davidic dynasty, there was nonetheless a deep break. Indeed the discontinuity in Jerusalem—as presented in our narrative—is so deep that the present chapter—not unlike chapter 2—occurs "outside time," that is, outside the containment of royal formulae. The last king, Ahaziah, has his conclusion in 9:27-29, and the next king—the boy king—has a beginning formula only in 11:21–12:1. This chapter concerns the attempt at *discontinuity* by Athaliah, mother of Ahaziah, and the *continuity* worked by the priest, Jehoiada. As Athaliah seeks to kill the heir to the throne, so Jehoiada protects the heir and brings him to power.

COMMENTARY

A Desperate Act of Hiding, 11:1-3

With the murder of Ahaziah, the Jerusalem palace is filled with dangerous intrigue among the various factions. Athaliah, the queen mother, is a major and desperate player. We have already seen that queen mothers are formidable operators in royal politics, and we have seen that Athaliah is a link to the disastrous Northern dynasty, a granddaughter of Omri. We are not told why she undertook the work of destroying the royal family and the narrator does not speculate on her motives. Perhaps she, like the entire situation, was marked by insanity. Or perhaps she sought vengeance for some internal dispute. More likely she stands at the head of a pro-Baal movement in violent resistance against the zealous Yahwists. We do not know; we only know that she seeks to continue the brutal work of Jehu.

The important point is that Jehosheba, sister to the slain king Ahaziah, counters the murderous intention of Athaliah. Jehosheba is possibly the daughter of Athaliah, more likely a stepdaughter, acting on behalf of a rival palace faction. She rescues the baby heir from the killing and hides him. The text says, literally, she "stole him away" (kidnapping?) in order to keep him safe. Because she kept him six years, he was seven when he was made king (11:21), suggesting he was a one year old at the moment of the hiding. In any case, the plot of Athaliah is thwarted and the monarchial line is kept intact. We are to understand then that Athaliah ruled in Jerusalem for six years, though she has no royal formula in the narrative and thus is never regarded as legitimate. She stands as a disruption of the royal line, in deep defiance of the Yahwist purge that Jehu tried to work in the South as well as in the North.

The New King, 11:4-12

Jehosheba was probably connected to a network of folk in the palace entourage who were committed to preserving the Davidic royal line and who cared intensely about the Yahwistic commitments of that dynasty. One of her accomplices in this work, as the narrative tells it, is the priest Jehoiada. At the right time—we do not know why this particular time—Jehoiada initiates the coronation of the seven-year-old boy now long in hiding.

These verses culminate with the act of enthronement (11:12), but the comments leading up to the act of enthronement are of interest for their remarkable detail. The priest takes great pains to assure maximum security for the boy; the image that emerges is that this royal personage is surrounded by layers and layers of security officers who "cover" him in his every exposed move. The detail of security suggests that the boy is known to be in immense danger. The reason for the danger is that Jehoiada and his cohorts are enacting a coup against the reign of Athaliah, an act that seeks to replace her, her entourage, and her ideology with the "legitimate" line of Davidic Yahwism. The careful action portrayed in these verses suggests startling tension in the palace, no doubt among competing factions who vied for control of the government. Thus the act of enthronement is no routine, innocuous matter, but a dangerous commitment that sees to "lock in" the government in one way rather than another. The risks are very high, commensurate with the stakes in the dispute.

It is most likely that the ceremony of kingship in v. 12 was not a public spectacle, but a closely guarded palace act conducted in the company of only reliable adherents to this party of royal power and religious passion. The act of king-making includes the two ingredients we have seen heretofore: *anointing*—no doubt done by the priest as a gesture of divine authorization—and *acclamation* by those who constituted the approved crowd that day. The detail of the ceremony and procession shows that it is most carefully choreographed, perhaps in the interest of security. Of particular interest is the special notice that the new king receives "the covenant." The term here is not very clear. It may refer to insignia of office. Or it might more precisely refer to a scroll, a written charter delineating both the prerogatives and requirements of power, a document that situates royal power in something like a constitutional frame of reference that precludes undefined royal arbitrariness. If it is a scroll, some scholars speculate that it delineates the powers and limits of royal office in the terms championed by this narrative with an appeal to Deuteronomy 17:14-20. [A Royal Charter] The term, however, offers only hints with nothing specified.

Death to Athaliah, 11:13-16

Royal ceremony is of immense importance, for it firmly seals the future and ends whatever may have been the threat. Thus the actual enthronement of the boy king was a strategic response to the

---

A Royal Charter

Deuteronomy 17:14-20 is commonly regarded as the Deuteronomist's guiding statement of political theory:

Negatively: [The king] must not acquire many horses for himself, or return the people to Egypt in order to acquire more horses…and he must not acquire many wives for himself, or else his heart will turn away; also silver and gold he must not acquire in great quantity for himself.

Positively: He shall have a copy of this law written for him in the presence of the levitical priests. It shall remain with him and he shall read in it all the days of his life, so that he may learn to fear the LORD his God, diligently observing all the words of this law and these statues, neither exalting himself above other members of the community nor turning aside from the commandment, either to the right or to the left.

This theory of royal power is determined to subsume royal power under the claims of Torah. It is surely this subsummation that David in 2 Sam 11 and Solomon in much of his reign did not embrace.

Gustave Doré. *Death to Athaliah* from the *Illustrated Bible*. 19th century. Engraving. (Credit: Dover Pictorial Archive Series)

threat from Athaliah. A fully inaugurated king indicates that the struggle for power is over; out of such an act there is a visible winner and, consequently, losers. Athaliah, it appears, is the last to know of the royal act. From her perspective, it is likely that the battle for the shape and control of the royal future was still underway. She was still competing and did not know that she had been outflanked and defeated by careful planning and tight security. She heard the noise of celebration from the winners; she could tell that the noise was celebrative and she wondered what was to be celebrated.

When she looked in upon the ceremony in the temple, what she saw stunned her, for there was the boy of seven, the new boy king, standing in the place of honor with all the markings of royal office and royal authority. She could tell at a glance what had happened without her knowing. The little boy who had been hidden now was available in public as an agent of power. Perhaps he had been so well hidden that she had forgotten him; certainly she had not seen him since the early days of his life. In a flash, she knows everything. Above all, she knows her own ambitions are finished and her life is now in jeopardy. She knows what winners do with losers in ruthless royal combat, for she knew about the North and the ideological passion embraced there by Jehu.

The response of Athaliah to the scene of triumph, as she assessed the noisy arrival of the young royal alternative, echoes Joram: "Treason! Treason!" (see 9:23). She quickly deduces that the palace faction that opposes her, by secret maneuver moreover, has pre-empted power on behalf of the boy king. The priest Jehoiada, clearly the one in charge, also recognizes that the time has come for a showdown. Except, of course, he gives an opposite reading of the events she observes. Athaliah regards the anointing of the boy king as a betrayal. Conversely, the priest regards the presence and conduct of Athaliah as completely unacceptable and worthy of death. These people do not fool around, but play for keeps. In the space of two verses, the priest sentences her to death, and the sentence is promptly enacted. She is a faction leader who will never accept the boy—her own grandson—as king. Because she is a leader in a palace dispute, it follows almost inevitably that she must be executed. The death of Athaliah has a significant parallel to the death of Jezebel in the North, except that the death of Athaliah is not so much marked by religious justification as was that of Jezebel. Her execution is for political reasons. She threatens the new order and will continue to threaten it as long as she is alive. Hence she must go! And she does!

The Beginning of the New Order, 11:17-20

The twin events of *anointing the boy king* in the temple amidst the royal entourage—an event enacted at great risk—and *the killing of Athaliah* as the symbolic focus of a rival palace faction prepares the way for the more public presentation of the new king. Jehoiada, sponsor of the boy king and guarantor of the process of political renewal, takes the initiative yet a third time.

The operational term here is "covenant" as the foundation for a new start in Jerusalem after the long deterioration of royal leadership in the collusion of the dynasty in the heterodoxy of the Northern regime. The making of covenant in this great ceremony has two dimensions to it. First, there is a *theological* dimension that binds both king and people to Yahweh, the God of covenant. This motif is of primary importance to the Deuteronomic shapers of this tradition, who insist that the covenantal agreements and conditions voiced in the book of Deuteronomy are indeed foundational for public life, definitive and nonnegotiable for Israel.[1] For that perspective, moreover, behind Deuteronomy stands the elemental agreements of Mt. Sinai wherein Israel has sworn full obedience to the purposes of Yahweh. This particular episode at the beginning of the reign of Jehoash is a prime example of the way in which this narrative seeks to situate monarchy in Torah and redefine the David traditions according to the claims of Moses. [Sinai and Zion]

The covenant of v. 17, however, is also an agreement between "the king and the people," so that the covenant enacted by the priest has an important *horizontal, political dimension* to it. This means that the Davidic kings are understood, at least from now on, as having contractual obligations to the public. The royal rule in Jerusalem is not a unilateral act imposed upon the public by divine fiat—or by ideological royal self-assertion or by a flat act of power. The notion of covenant suggests that both parties to the new governance—king and people—have obligations and entitlements, thus curbing any despotic inclination. It may be that this insistence of the Deuteronomic interpreters is a late retrospective limit on kingship (as in Deut 17:14-20). But this remarkable limitation upon royal power might also be understood as a response to the recent period of monarchy when the Southern dynasty seemed to imitate its Northern counterpart in its commitments to Baalism; that accommodation brought with it not only religious distortion, but also produced an exploitative sense of royal power that understood monarchs as unfettered in their capacity for self-enhancement.

The most blatant example we have of this ideology is the shameless act of Jezebel and Ahab in the usurpation of the property of Naboth, an act that evoked the oracle of Yahweh and ultimately the action of Jehu. To be sure, we have no parallel account of such actions by the Southern kings, but such exploitative ways of power were surely in the air. It is not difficult to imagine Athaliah as the Southern Jezebel, and so to imagine such possible actions in the South's regime, which had lost its focus. If this is so, then the political agreement in v. 17 embodies an important evolvement in political theory about the Davidic kingship.

The renewal of covenant among Yahweh, king, and people required the purgation of all in Jerusalem who had been anticovenantal, that is, linked to the anticovenant, anticommunity symbolizations of Baal (11:18). According to this narrative,

---

Sinai and Zion

It is clear that this literature is occupied with adjudicating the competing claims of the Sinai and David traditions with a resolve to make the David claims subordinate to the claims of Sinai, even if the David royal claims were historically autonomous of Sinai. Harmut Gese has gone so far as to suggest that one can see in the traditioning process the way in which the Torah of Sinai was relocated and recharacterized as the Torah of Zion.

Harmut Gese, "The Law," *Essays on Biblical Theology,* trans. by Keith Crim; (Minneapolis: Augsburg Publishing House) 60-92. See the more recent and more general discussion of the relation of these themes by Jon D. Levenson, *Sinai & Zion: An Entry into the Jewish Bible* (New York: Winston Press, 1985).

alongside the "house of Yahweh" where Jehoash was enthroned, there was a "house of Baal," a rival temple that is a measure of the heterodox distortions of the Davidic regime. That "house of Baal" was an important symbolization of how the monarchy understood itself—remote from old Yahwistic promises, equally remote from Torah obligations.

The covenant renewal of Jehoiada is the refounding of governance on the basis of Yahwism, a reordering that evokes a purging more modest but parallel to the purgation worked in the North by Jehu.

That negative act of "cleansing," apparently done with considerable energy and the emotional force characteristic of reformers, is matched by the great procession of the boy king and his royal, military entourage from the temple to the "king's house," that is, to the throne room (see 1 Kgs 7:7). The procession of a clearly Yahwistic king, bound by Torah obligation, must have been immensely reassuring to the old political opinion of Jerusalem that had never been persuaded of the heterodox, exploitative alternative into which the Davidic regime had fallen. It is clear in v. 20 that the execution of Athaliah is not merely the removal of one person, but the elimination of an entire symbol system of an alien account of reality that had encroached upon the Yahwistic enterprise. No wonder there was rejoicing!

The assertion that the "city was quiet" is more important than the simple phrasing might suggest (11:20). The term "quiet" (*shaqath*) is the same term used in the book of Judges in the recurring phrase "the land had rest" (Judg 3:11, 30; 5:31; 8:28). The term in such usage does not mean simply a stillness at the end of the day. Rather it means the restoration of the elemental, reliable, reassuring governance of Yahweh after things had fallen into chaos and confusion. Thus the term makes a profound theological claim for "the God of order" with a reestablished governance and control. The world is again seen to be coherent. The center will hold. The processes of chaos and disorder have been overcome. All is well and all shall be well. That the boy king is seven years old offers a hint that the city is now positioned for a long period of well-being.

We cannot fail to notice that the "*tranquility*" of the city is achieved through an act of *violence*. The text, however, sees nothing ironic in the juxtaposition of violence and tranquility, for Athaliah represented and embodied the powers of chaos—linked to the claims of Baal—the elimination of which is a precondition of the restoration of order. Building upon the daring act of Jehosheba who hid the child, Jehoiada and the Yahwistic party in Jerusalem have, according to this narrative, made possible a new beginning in Jerusalem, a beginning that parallels the work of Jehu in the North, but surely on a more reliable dynastic foundation in the South.

CONNECTIONS

This royal baby, Jehoash (= Joash), represents and embodies a chance in Jerusalem for newness. He is, however, exceedingly vulnerable and at great risk from powerful palace forces that oppose him and his party. He must for that reason be hidden and protected. When I read this account, I think of Anne Frank, a treasured child in Amsterdam who was, along with her family, at great risk. She also was a child who had to be hidden and protected, but who in the end was not kept safe.

A new chance in history is often carried by a child, innocent and endangered, who has to be protected from a ruthless, destructive world. In the Old Testament, the protected child upon whom the entire future turns is Moses (Exod 2:1-10). He also is rescued by a daring woman, a member of the royal family. Out of that vulnerable process of birth and nurture, moreover, comes a new chance for Israel. In the New Testament, the protected child upon whom the future (of the entire world!) turns is Jesus (Matt 2:13-23). This vulnerable baby is protected by mother and father, but also by angels, and is hidden away in Egypt (like Moses), until it is safe to return (see Hos 11:1 quoted in Matthew).

Of course Jehoash turns out not to be as pivotal for the future as either Moses or Jesus. The issues, however, are the same; the threat is as great, and the stakes are as high. Pharaoh, Athaliah, and Herod all engage in measures of violence in order to maintain themselves and their power. The baby, in the face of such a threat, is greatly endangered. But so it is with innocence that is the foundation of newness. The wonder of our story, as with the other narratives, is that risks are run by those willing to run such risks for the sake of newness they cannot yet see. The hiding of the baby is an act of profound hope that refuses to give in to the fearful brutality of the status quo.

Jehoiada has his brief moment of historical prominence. We have of the priest only the reform movement of the next chapter. But his work is pivotal in the larger plot of Israel's life. We may reckon him to be a faithful functionary, diligent and dutiful, utterly determined and resolved, all the while looking beyond himself, knowing that he has the opportunity to "shepherd newness" in Jerusalem, a dazzling newness that has not much to do with him.

His role in this narrative has set me to thinking about the almost unnoticed "shepherds of newness" who have their brief moment that they enact with courage and resolve, and quickly let the large matter of newness run past them. The case in point that occurs to me in recent public life in the U.S. is Gerald Ford, short-term U.S. president. Ford is a modest man who as president of the U.S. had no real mandate from the public, having never been elected to the office of president. He did, however, preside with great wisdom and dignity over the end of the "nightmare" of the presidency of Richard Nixon when the constitutional foundations of the State were apparently in jeopardy. By his act of

Ford Pardons Nixon (Credit: Gerald R. Ford Library)

pardon for Nixon—which apparently cost Ford dearly in the next election when he lost to Jimmy Carter—he permitted the political process to begin afresh in the U.S. As he himself declared at the moment of the pardon, "the long nightmare is over." Ford did his courageous deed when the credibility of government was almost nullified; by his act he opened the way for the restoration of confidence.[2] I suggest that the work of Jehoiada is to be understood in a parallel fashion, more risky and more violent to be sure, but he, too, was a modest figure making way for newness.

The violent destruction of the symbols of Baalism, done in the North by Jehu (10:26-27) and now in the South by Jehoiada, may strike us as fanaticism that does not contribute effectively to policy formation but only permits an emotional catharsis of orgiastic proportions. A parallel to such destructive activity may be the pillaging of churches and religious statuary by Oliver Cromwell in the English revolution against the Stuart monarchy. Indeed, I have more than once heard English tour guides polemize against Cromwell's senseless destruction of religious art. Within the confines of artistic sensitivity, Cromwell's action is surely to be condemned; no doubt there were those in Jerusalem who made the same judgment about Jehoiada and the Yahwistic zealots.

Such a critique, valid on its own terms, however, fails to take into account the enormous power of such religious symbolization inescapably tied to certain political practices that were found, in both the cases of Omride Baalism and the Stuarts, to be exploitative and oppressive. It is important not to miss the deep and powerful linkage between symbolism and power, for without the legitimating significance of symbols, the exploitative power of the regime could not be sustained. It is worth noting that in the case of Cromwell the zeal about hated symbols is finally coupled with regicide. In the case of Jehoiada, a like act of violent death is perpetrated against Athaliah, although not crowned, certainly the de facto monarch. Regicide strikes us as more violent than the purging of symbols, but the two are of a piece.

Therefore we are to notice that such a destruction of symbols is not simply an emotive frenzy, but a programmatic commitment of the Deuteronomists, placed at the very beginning of Deuteronomic commands in Deuteronomy 12:2-3:

> You must *demolish* completely all the places where the nations whom you are about to dispossess served their gods, on the mountain heights, on the hills, and under every leafy tree. *Break down* their altars, *smash* their pillars, *burn* their sacred poles with fire, and *hew down* the idols of their gods, and thus *blot out* their name from their places.

One may notice the sequence of strong, negative verbs in the command of Moses, the very verbs enacted by Jehoiada.

Covenantal Power and Authority

The theme of covenant as a theory of social power has been well traced by Charles S. McCoy and J. Wayne Baker in a study with roots in Heinrich Bullinger, sixteenth-century successor to Zwingli in Zurich:

> As the federal tradition comes back into view, its basic ideas about human nature will be a surprise to those brought up on the curiously mistaken notion that Western societies are founded on liberal individualism. Johannes Althusius, the first systematic expositor of federal political philosophy and one whose thought has pervasive direct and indirect influence on European and American political orders, understands humans as existing only in symbiotic relationship…. It may come as new information to some that government based on covenant or compact was thoroughly embedded in the federal tradition prior to Hobbes and Locke, who probably may best be regarded as later variants of federal thought. And not everyone may be aware that federalism had well-articulated notions of the division of powers and their limitation through checks and balances before Montesquieu formulated them so well that federalists quoted him to bolster convictions they already held, not to attribute their origin to him.

Charles S. McCoy and J. Wayne Baker, *Foundations of Federalism: Heinrich Bullinger and the Covenantal Tradition* (Louisville: Westminster/John Knox Press, 1991) 9. For derivative comments on covenantal modes of public power, see Robert N. Bellah, *The Broken Covenant: American Civil Religion in Time of Trial* (New York: Seabury Press, 1975) and Michael Walzer, *Exodus and Revolution* (New York: Basic Books, 1985).

It is not a "clear and present danger" that religious passion in our time might so directly assault the symbolization of the ideology of consumerism as it is lived out in television commercials and more general programming. It is clear nonetheless that what was symbolized in the ancient text by "altars and pillars" is matched by the logos of beers, shoes, soft drinks, and cars. Those symbols, like ancient pillars, make false promises of security, joy, and well-being that completely distort reality and seduce into false reality in our own time. Thus it is important to understand that the zeal of Jehoiada is not simply a simple-minded primitivism, but the outgrowth of a social analysis that seeks to break the social power of a certain oppressive kind by an assault upon ideological symbols. The same crisis of symbol and power is posed directly in the emperor worship of Daniel 3:1-18, and no doubt subtly posed to Jesus in the question of "rendering to Caesar" (Mark 12:13-17), for emperor worship and acknowledgement of the ultimate power of the emperor were a live option and a powerful seduction in the time of Jesus and the early church.

Most probably, too much should not be made of the reference to covenant "between king and people" (11:17). We may nonetheless recognize this verse as pivotal in the Deuteronomic theology of power, as this narrative concerns the reconstitution of social power in Israel.[3] Beyond that, it is important that "covenant" is taken up from Deuteronomic theories of social power and eventually mediated through Calvinism to become the basis of democratic social theory whereby the governed not only have a stake but a voice in governance. Such a theory of governance is of course here completely inchoate, but the seed is planted that sprouted as a powerful Western theory, eventually appearing in John Locke's idea concerning the consent of the governed. [Covenantal Power and Authority]

Thus I propose that the reconstitution of the Davidic enterprise through the boy king, and the visionary courage of the priest is certainly a major turning point in Israel's self-presentation of monarchy. In that reconstitution and reordering, moreover, are the beginnings of a social theory that began to curb absolute royal power toward a public practice of power. The act of Jehoiada is congruent with the covenantal reality of 2 Samuel 5:1-3 as a Northern phenomenon. It apparently took much longer for the same concessions and visions to operate in the more stable and more self-assured throne of the South.

NOTES

[1]Ernest W. Nicholson, *God and His People: Covenant and Theology in the Old Testament* (Oxford: Clarendon Press, 1986) has provided the most helpful and comprehensive study of recent work in covenant. His final chapter is an excellent statement of the theological aspects of the theme.

[2]It is more than a little ironic that in the late 1990s President Ford issued a statement suggesting that President Clinton should receive a "rebuke" from Congress, thus averting the savage political cost to all parties of impeachment proceedings. Again Ford in his modest way thought beyond party and self to larger social vision.

[3]Norbert Lohfink, "Distribution of the Functions of Power," *Great Themes from the Old Testament* (Edinburgh: T. & T. Clark, 1982) 55-75 has seen that Deuteronomy 16–19, in which the commandment on monarchy is embedded, proposes a separation of powers in a very early move from tyranny.

THE LONG REIGN
OF JEHOASH

2 Kings 11:21–12:21

The reign of Jehoash, whom we have seen coronated as a boy of seven, was quite long: forty years (837–800; 12:1). The present chapter is completely concerned with his long reign. The chapter frames his reign with an introductory formula (11:21–12:3) and a concluding formula (12:19-21).[1] Between these two formulae, the narrative is preoccupied with two agenda, the internal problem of temple repairs (12:4-16) and the external problem of Syrian diplomatic and military pressure (12:17-18).

COMMENTARY

The Introductory Formula, 11:21–12:3

The introductory formula provides the usual information about the king. We may notice two elements in particular. First, his mother, Zibiah, is named, again calling our attention to the prominence of that role in palace politics. The several queen mothers are of interest to us because they often become centers and rallying points for palace factions that decisively influence political and religious policies. Second, the theological verdict on the present king is "yes, but." The king did what was right according to Deuteronomic theory, most especially paying attention to the temple; but like almost every king in Jerusalem, any positive assessment is promptly qualified. According to v. 3 the king lamentably permitted worship in "high places," likely rural shrines that were not as fully committed to Torah practices as Deuteronomic theory required.

Temple Repairs and Financial Problems, 12:4-16

According to this narrative, the central occupation of the long reign of Jehoash is temple repairs. While we may assume that the king in fact had many other enduring and important preoccupations, temple repairs peculiarly concern our narrative. The Jerusalem temple, its building and ultimate demise, provides the story line for the books of Kings.

The report on the crisis of temple repairs indicates that the king was fully committed to temple reform and was prepared to commit public funds to the project. At the outset it is important to recognize that temple building and renovation are in principle an evidence of piety in that ancient world. [Temple Reform as Piety] It is important to recognize that Jehoash is the leader of the reform party who had a great personal "career" stake in such repairs. Beyond that, moreover, he had been long tutored by the priest Jehoiada whose actions in chapter 11 attest to his passion for things Yahwistic. The parallel narrative of 2 Chronicles, moreover, attests to the decline of the temple under the previous rulers, so that Jehoiada's zeal is surely designed to contrast him with them:

> For the children of Athaliah, that wicked woman, had broken into the house of God, and had even used all the dedicated things of the house of the LORD for the Baals. (2 Chr 24:7)

We may believe that the "house of Yahweh" was in disrepair because funds and energy had been diverted to the "house of Baal."

The king, however, is said (as almost anyone could be who intends such a building project) to be thwarted by finances and frustrated by the unresponsiveness and lack of effort by the builders. We are not yet told why there is such inactivity. The priests were apparently "sitting on" the money collected for the project and were not mobilizing the workmen. The king finally intervenes, raises difficult questions, and prohibits the priests from receiving any more money. There is no hint in the text of

---

Temple Reform as Piety

There is no doubt that temple renovation was viewed not only as a proper work for the king but as an act of quite public piety. Thus, in the royal annuls of the Old Testament, "good kings" reform the temple. It is immediately evident that the temple is an ambiguous symbol; the king's engagement with the temple shows the deference and submission of the king to the high purposes of God. At the same time, however, it is clear that such public action also enhances the power and prestige of the monarchy, for the king shows himself to be intimately linked to the lord of the temple. Thus the ambiguity of the king's piety in this chapter can hardly be missed.

As a state institution, the Temple thus represented the intersection of the ideological values and religious beliefs of the nation with the social, political, and economic aspects of its organization.... It was instrumental in establishing both divine and royal power:

Carol Meyers, "Temple, Jerusalem," ABD 6:361. See also John M. Lundquist, "What Is a Temple? A Preliminary Topology," *The Quest for the Kingdom of God: Studies in Honor of George E. Mendenhall*, ed. H. B. Huffmon et al. (Winona Lake: Eisenbrauns, 1983) 205-19.

mishandling or misappropriation of money, but the king is surely presented as growing impatient with the inexplicable delays.

In response to the royal intervention, Jehoiada, the "Mr. Reliable" of Jehoash's reign, takes an initiative for new monies that can be moved along readily to the workmen. The detail of vv. 11-12 suggests that there was a large, specialized workforce at the temple project. The relay of the money, moreover, suggests that it was the priests who delayed matters by withholding money. Clearly the artisans would not work without payment, for which the priests held ample funds.

The positive engagement of the workmen in vv. 11-12 is matched by the sorry observation of v. 13. The house of Yahweh was impoverished. It was clearly no longer the posh, well-appointed arrangement given us in the report on Solomon (see 1 Kgs 7:50). We have no clue why the temple lacked all this equipment, having been given no report on the loss of what Solomon purportedly provided. We may assume either (a) the temple equipment was lost as Judah was a vulnerable state and used temple wealth as protection money (on which see v. 18) or (b) the temple equipment was redeployed under those clustered around Athaliah for the "house of Baal." Either way, political or religious, the diminishment of the temple reflects a diminished zeal for Yahweh. Even the investments of Jehoash and the insistence of Jehoiada did not overcome that diminishment. The narrative, in any case, painstakingly shows that the money was honestly handled, especially by the workers (v. 15). Whatever the problem may have been, it was not a problem with the artisans. [The Artisans] In the end the king has apparently accomplished a financial reform, curbing the autonomous power of the priests and establishing a procedure whereby priests and royal officers together oversee the expenditures on repairs. The end result is that the king is effective in his purpose and manages to recruit for his major enterprise the loyalty and effectiveness of both priests and workmen.

The vindication of the workers in v. 15 makes one wonder what we are to make of the notice concerning the priests in v. 16. It is of

The Artisans

In this chapter, the workmen who restore the temple are fully appreciated and honored as honest. They were surely gifted artisans who had great aesthetic sensitivity. On such extraordinary artisans in another context, see Exodus 35:30-35. It is evident that in ancient Israel the temple (tabernacle) is taken to be the primary expression of beauty in the realm. That aspect is important, because in much theological sensitivity, the ethical completely vetoes the aesthetic.

It may be that these craftsmen who renovated the temple for the king were at the same time coerced workers for the state. If the artisans are placed in such an ambiguous position as state slaves, then it may be that the regime suffers as does every such coercive regime that wants beauty to have an ideological thrust for the enhancement of the regime. Such an ambiguity is plausible, for this is clearly a royal chapel in the service of the state. In any case, the report invites us to think clearly about artistic service both in the glorification of Yahweh through temple construction and in the enhancement of the regime that administers the temple.

course possible that v. 16 simply reports a fact that deferral of certain funds to the priests is a long-standing and continuing provision. It may not mean more than that. In light of the vindication of the workers, however, it may be that this notice points fingers at the priests who were much too occupied with their own income and consequently not so devoted to or generous with the temple project.

The Continuing Threat of Syria, 12:17-18

We have seen that Hazael of Syria continued to pressure Israel, taking from Israel all the territory east of the Jordan River, pushing the shared border of the two states to the West. Now, in a parallel report, it becomes clear that Hazael also threatened Jerusalem. That he conquered Gath, a coastal city of the Philistines, suggests that Syrian troops had gone far toward the defeat of Judah. Hazael's capacity to threaten Jerusalem indicates Syria's strength and, conversely, Judah's weakness and vulnerability.

The measure of the threat and the inability of Jehoash to respond or resist are evident in v. 18. The temple treasury is being used to bribe the enemy to withdraw. The king is willing to spend the treasury in such a way. Beyond the clue as to the political-military weakness of Judah, the offer of temple gold is indeed a deeply humiliating turn of affairs. It is no wonder that Hazael withdraws. He has received all that he had wanted, in fact, a surrender. Worth noting is that the narrative nicely but silently juxtaposes the crisis of temple reform and the threat of Syria. No explicit connection between the two is made here, although, as can be seen in 2 Chronicles 24, a connection can indeed be made. The two narrative episodes, temple reform and payment to the Syrian, seem to balance out. In the first, the king is heroic in his commitment to the temple. But in the second, he uses the very materials of the temple to bribe an invader, thus indicating his weakness. Likely the narrator intends to present a balanced or ambiguous view of this king who is commended, but only with significant reservation.

The Death of Jehoash, 12:19-21

The concluding formula on this king contains all the usual information. The peculiar element is the report that the king was killed in a process of palace intrigue and conspiracy. The term to describe the assassination of the king, "conspiracy," is the same term used in 11:14 (but there translated "treason") by Athaliah. The fact that it was "his servants" who killed the king suggests that within the palace, acute tension continued between factions competing for control of the levers of power. Given what we know of Jehoash as a protege of Jehoiada, who executed Athaliah, we may believe that the dispute that erupts in regicide is a continuation of the old dispute between Yahwists and would-be Baalists. These could be the terms of dispute even if the tension is no longer over religious loyalty, but about a complex of issues that appeals to religious loyalty but in fact masks other concerns.[2] Given such a possibility, we may suspect that as the Yahwists killed Athaliah, so "the favor is returned" as the continuing party of Baalists retaliates with the death of the boy king, now a seasoned adult.

The murder of the king in v. 20 may cause us to reconsider what looks like the innocuous report about temple repairs. While it is not at all clear that the parallel account in 2 Chronicles 24 is "historically" reliable, this different rendering of the same data suggests how the texts of Israel are open to ideological pressure. In the account given in Chronicles, Jehoiada figures more prominently in the narrative, as the great guarantor of Yahwism. Upon his death, he is buried "among the kings" because of his immense public service (24:16).

But the death of Jehoiada leaves a huge ideologic void and makes the king susceptible to other "officials of Judah" who lead the king, astray, even as the king, without the backbone of Jehoiada, reverts to idolatry. In this reading, Zechariah, son of Jehoiada, is a powerful advocate of Yahwism, but is murdered at the behest of the king, who is no longer a passionate Yahwist. On this reading, moreover, it is Judah's heterodoxy that causes Syria to defeat Judah as a Yahwistic punishment. In a final element of irony, in this version, the Yahwists murder the king to avenge the death of Jehoash, whereas in our Kings passage, it seems more likely to be the other party, the Baalists, who kill the king.

I do not suggest that the version of events in 2 Chronicles is preferable to the Kings narrative or that it is historically reliable. My point rather is that the story likely hints at deep ideological issues, suggesting that the "Yahweh alone" party continues in deep and dangerous tension with a party of religious compromise.

CONNECTIONS

While matters are highly stylized as a familiar sort of royal report, we may note several aspects of the story that remind us not to read the Bible innocently. The text is loaded with ideological interest, parties jockeying for position, power, and influence, so that one must pay attention to the subtext while following the main story line. The complicated statement about finance for the temple suggests that king and priests are in some tension, while Jehoiada seems to be a free agent, not fully aligned with either party. We may imagine heated tension over how to deal with the Syrian threat, whether to appease (as the king did) or to withstand. And certainly the assassination of the king suggests acute internal tension in the royal household. It will not do to read this royal history as though it were all neat and tidy. The vision of a well-governed Jerusalem is not easy to maintain. The city is subject to jeopardy from many threats, internal and external. As we can identify such powerful vested interests in the text, we may take their presence as a learning more generally about the Bible. Much of the time those interests are kept hidden, but we do better with the Bible if we recognize that the truth of faith is carried by interested parties who inevitably mix their interest with their faith.

The overriding theme of the chapter is the temple and its rich treasury. This powerful institutional presence looms largest in both episodes of temple reform and Syrian appeasement. In the first episode, the temple and its repair are a central passion of the king. The crisis of temple repair opens the way for serious reorganization of financial management in the regime. In the second episode, the temple is the repository of riches that serve to buy off the Syrian assault. There is no doubt that the temple is a serious, formidable theological institution, guaranteeing and making visible the power, presence, and mystery of Yahweh. We may even think that the king's public exhibit of piety is authentic. The temple is exactly a place of presence. At the same time, however, we are made inescapably aware that in a deep crisis any awesome transcendent symbol becomes a convenient bartering chip. Thus the temple treasury, a depository of holy things, becomes simply a tool of weak foreign policy with only instrumental value.

This narrative report is an invitation to ponder the deep intertwining of the *transcendent* and the *pragmatic* in the very same objects and practices. We cannot live without the transcendent, but the transcendent would seem to be a luxury we enjoy in good times. When the crunch comes and issues are demanding,

Praise and Swords
More anciently the Psalmist declares:

Let the high praises of God be in their throats
    and two-edged swords in their hands,
to execute vengeance to the nations
    and punishment on the peoples,
to bind their kings with fetters
    and their nobles with chains of iron,
to execute on them the judgment decreed.
    This is glory for all his faithful ones.
Praise the LORD! (Ps 149:6-9)

we may put our best transcendence to instrumental use in order to accomplish other goals and objectives less noble than the pure presence of Yahweh. The clearest example of the transcendent transposed into the pragmatic is what characteristically happens to religion in time of war. In dire circumstance, the large vision of faith is easily and most often co-opted into a tool and rationale for aggressive military policy, so that the transcendent is lost and given up for prudential "reasons of state." The easy usurpation of the temple as a tool is readily heard in the war song of the Second World War, "Praise the Lord and Pass the Ammunition." [Praise and Swords]

NOTES

[1] Kings 11:21 is 12:1 in the Hebrew text and obviously belongs to the paragraph that follows.

[2] It is entirely possible that religious dispute may no longer pertain to religious questions but has to do with power and control for which religion is a front or surrogate. Such a state seems obviously to pertain in Northern Ireland where "Catholics" and "Protestants" clearly dispute over economic and political matters rather than religious. The violent disputes in Jerusalem may have been of the same sort.

KINGS, PROPHET, AND WAR IN THE NORTH

2 Kings 13:1-25

After the establishment of Jehoash and the restoration of Yahwistic "purity" (chapter 11), chapters 12–16 provide a narrative account of the twin monarchies. The present chapter continues the narrative account of the public events of northern Israel. It deals in turn with the reign of Jehoahaz, second in the dynasty of Jehu (13:1-9), the reign of Jehoash, third in the dynasty of Jehu (13:10-13), the death of Elisha the prophet (13:14-21), and the Israelite war with Syria (13:22-25). This narrative account is relatively undistinguished, primarily designed to preserve continuity in the royal record and to reiterate themes of particular concern to the narrator.

COMMENTARY

The Long, Devastating Reign of Jehoahaz, 13:1-9

We learn very little here about the rule of Jehoahaz, even though he was on the throne for seventeen years (815–802). After the introductory formula (13:1), we may distinguish two patterns of theological assessment (13:2-5, 6-7), followed by the concluding formula (13:8-9). The introductory and concluding formulae are unexceptional, suggesting that after the violent coup of Jehu, a measure of orderly governance was reestablished in Samaria so that kings can begin and end their reigns in relatively stable fashion.

We may thus focus on the two evaluative statements in turn. The first of these is a formula in four parts:

(a) This king did the characteristic *evil* of Northern rulers, retaining the Northern shrines as an alternative to the Jerusalem temple and all that it signified for the Davidic house (13:2).

(b) Yahweh is angry about that evil and *punishes* Israel by making Israel vulnerable to Syria under Hazael and his son, Ben-hadad (13:3). This statement reflects the general international situation of the period, wherein Syria, with strong military pressure, encroached on Israelite territory (see 10:32-33). This narrative characteristically

AΩ **Savior**
The notion of a savior sent by Yahweh is a common idea in the Old Testament. The term itself is clear enough. It is derived from the verb "deliver" and refers to a human agent who intervenes for the sake of Israel. There are many other texts in which God's own role is that of savior. God has here intervened in a situation where Israel itself is helpless. The identity of the "savior," however, is not so clear. It is possible to imagine that it is an Assyrian military figure who attacked Damascus and so took the pressure off Israel. But one might also imagine that in context the prophet Elisha is the one sent by Yahweh to make a difference on behalf of Israel. The text is unclear even though the point that Yahweh saves Israel is clear enough.

matches theological assessment to political reality.

(c) The king, Jehoahaz, *petitions* Yahweh to relieve the pressure of Syrian encroachment (13:4a).

(d) In response to the petition and because Syrian pressure on Israel is acute (see 14:26-27), Yahweh *delivers* Israel from that Syrian pressure by means of a "savior" (13:5). The text gives no specificity, but we may take the term "savior" to refer to a human, military agent who is strong enough to push back the Syrian threat. [Savior] This human agent of Yahweh could be the king himself (though nothing is said to that effect), or some other military figure who is left unnamed.

What interests us is that this fourfold report is highly formulaic, reflecting exactly the "theory of history" of the book of Judges—perhaps by the same narrative tradition—that sketches the political

---

📖 **A Patterned Sequence of Interpretation**
The fourfold pattern of sin-punishment-entreaty-rescue is common in the book of Judges, the editors of which may be akin to the shapers of the narratives of Kings. The simple, unambiguous example of Judges 3:7-9 may be cited as characteristic:

> The Israelites did *what was evil* in the sight of the LORD, forgetting the LORD their God, and worshiping the Baals and the Asherahs. Therefore the *anger of the LORD* was kindled against Israel, and he sold them into the hand of King Cushan-rishathaim of Aram-naharaim; and the Israelites served Cushan-rishathaim eight years. But when the Israelites *cried out to the LORD*, the LORD raised up a deliverer for the Israelites, who *delivered* them, Othniel son of Kenaz, Caleb's younger brother.

The formulation, often repeated in the book of Judges, amounts to an entire philosophy of history that insists that Yahweh stands at the center of the process and that coming to terms with Yahweh is the decisive ingredient in communal well-being.

On a more personal level, the same general movement is evident in the Song of Thanksgiving of Psalm 107.

> Some were sick through their sinful ways,
>   and because of their iniquities endured affliction;
> they loathed any kind of food,
>   and they drew near to the gates of death.
> Then they cried to the LORD in their trouble,
>   and he saved them from their distress;
> he sent out his word and healed them,
>   and delivered them from destruction. (vv. 17-20; see vv. 4-9, 10-16, and 23-32)

life of Israel in terms of evil-punishment-repentance-rescue. [A Patterned Sequence of Interpretation] We may believe that Israel's public life under this king was (a) a compromise of pure Yahwism and (b) engaged in big trouble with Syria. It is the work of the theological formula to tie together *religious compromise* and *military defeat* as cause and effect. Such a rhetorical, interpretive connection not only brings coherence to the internal and external life of Israel, but it presents Yahweh as the key and defining character in the entire process. Thus Yahweh is not only a religious reference point in the narrative, but is offered as the decisive agent in both the trouble and the well-being of Israel. It is Yahweh who judges and who saves. [Yahweh Gives Death and Gives Life]

📖 Yahweh Gives Death and Gives Life

At the core of biblical faith lies the conviction that Yahweh, the one God confessed in Israel and in the church, gives life and gives death. To be sure, there are difficulties in this claim, but it is the characteristic claim of the text. Thus in our narrative and in the formula that governs it, the same Yahweh brings trouble and delivers from trouble. Explicit statements of this twofold capacity of Yahweh include the following:

See now that I, even I, am he;
    there is no god beside me.
I kill and I make alive;
    I wound and I heal;
and no one can deliver from my hand. (Deut 32:39)

I form light and create darkness,
    I make weal (*shalom*) and create woe;
    I the LORD do all these things. (Isa 45:7)

The second rhetorical pattern of theological assessment varies on particulars, but insists upon the same accents (13:7-8). The introductory "nevertheless" of v. 6 is necessary because the preceding v. 5 has just celebrated Yahweh's deliverance. The new pattern of vv. 6-7 follows a standard form of "prophetic speech of judgment."[1] The *indictment* of v. 6 again concerns the "sins of Jeroboam" with the additional particular reference to the "sacred pole," a sign of departure from Yahweh through alternative cultic practice. [The Asherah] That is, the affront to Yahweh is liturgical. The *sentence* of v. 7, however, is military, so that *liturgical* waywardness eventuates in a *military* disaster. Israel suffers a devastating and humiliating defeat at the hands of Syria, a defeat that our narrative attributes to the displeasure of Yahweh, displeasure that the regime in Samaria did not submit and succumb to Jerusalem. Israel's military capacity

---

🏛 The Asherah

This term refers, in a variety of uses, to both a female deity and a cultic pole affirmed in Canaanite worship. It is likely that the polemical allusion to "the pole" in texts like this one has no specific reference but is a generalized polemic against any cultic practice not devoted to Yahweh. It may be that the pole and the other symbols associated with it were an affirmation that the forces of generativity and fertility were available apart from the Torah requirements of Yahweh. In a general way, the polemic refers to the religious attempt to have the gift of life apart from Yahweh, here affirmed as the only true giver of life.

See John Day, "Asherah," ABD 1:483-87

Asherah was honored as a sacred tree, with upright posts or living trees used to represent her. Here, she is shown holding plants, perhaps suggesting her affinity with the tree of life.

Asherah. 1300 BC. From Minet el Beida. Ugarit, Syria. Louvre, Paris, France (Credit: Giraudon/Art Resource, NY)

was nullified so that it could not defend itself. Later on, in 2 Kings 18:23, we shall see that Assyrian rhetoric tauntingly offers to provide 2,000 horses for Israel's military if Israel can supply cavalry riders, with the clear understanding that Israel is so decimated that it lacks such a number of men. Thus in our text the Syrians (and later on the Assyrians) reduce Israel to helpless military impotence so that Israel is incapable of defending itself. The "savior" of v. 5, who belongs to the first wave of rhetoric, is nowhere to be seen in this second, more severe judgment. Israel is now hopelessly lost, without a "savior."

The Long Unreported Reign of Jehoash, 13:10-13

Jehoash is now the third king in the dynasty of Jehu. It is clear that this narrative is not much interested in this king or his reign, for the report is exceedingly brief and consists almost completely of formulaic data. He, like every Northern king, persisted in the separatism of Jeroboam and so stands under judgment.

The single detail in the report that departs from predictable formulae is the note in v. 12 of war with Amaziah, his Southern counterpart. Even that matter of civil war, moreover, is briefly reported. Our narrator has opted to provide more detail on that conflict in 14:8-14 under the rubric of Amaziah, the Judean king, who is clearly the aggressor. But while the Southern king is the aggressor, it is Jehoash of Samaria who prevails, who devastates Amaziah, and who plunders the royal treasures of Jerusalem. Clearly the sorry military status of Jehoash in v. 7 has now been quickly overcome, so that Israel has adequate military power of horses, chariots, and soldiers. This conflict of North and South, of course, resumes the ancient dispute that had earlier occupied Rehoboam and Jeroboam, suggesting that the alliance of convenience between the two states during the Omri dynasty has been an interim disregard rather than a settlement of the issues between North and South. This brief report suggests, moreover, that by this time Israel had a respite from the Syrian threat, enough to turn its military energy toward the South. And indeed, Syrian power had apparently waned by this time (see vv. 22-25). What is perhaps most remarkable is that the terse report of v. 12 not only does not indicate the victory of Jehoash over Amaziah, a report withheld for one more chapter, but also does not suggest any theological judgment about the matter.

The Death and Continuing Power of Elisha, 13:14-21

Of much more interest to the narrator (and therefore to us) is the death of Elisha, for in the horizon of this narrator, prophets are certainly more interesting and more important than kings, especially Northern kings. According to our narrative, Elisha has dominated the public scene of Israel for a very long time, since his distinctive empowerment during the reign of Jehoram (2:9-12).

Elisha's final illness that frames vv. 14-20 is a matter of immense concern to Joash (Jehoash) who regards the prophet as a powerful resource and mainstay for his regime. Indeed, the dynasty, like the reader, is not unaware that it is at the behest of Elisha that the dynasty of Jehu has come to power and remains in power (9:1). The king's lament in response to the prophet's illness is both a statement of need and a tribute to his importance (v. 14). The wording of the lament echoes the words Elisha spoke at the departure of Elijah (2:12). The formula expresses not only loyalty and deference toward the prophet, but royal dependence upon him. In addition, the phrase "chariots and horses" should perhaps be linked to the absence of chariots and horsemen in v. 7. If that connection is intended by the narrative, then the claim is that the power of the prophet is more than adequate to compensate for a lack of conventional arms. Of course it is plausible that the line uttered by the king is a conventional lament over a great person, and is not to be taken with any such precision.

In any case, even if terminally ill, Elisha is not finished yet with the exercise of decisive public power. In a strange but characteristic prophetic maneuver, the prophet authorizes the king to enact a symbolic gesture that anticipates (and assures?) the destruction of Syria and the victory of Israel. (It is clear that power relations with Syria have been completely inverted since the devastation of Jehoahaz in v. 7.) Now Israel can legitimately expect the defeat of Syria.

> **Aphek**
> This town was apparently on the border in the territory claimed by both Israel and Syria. The reference to the place in 1 Kings 20:26-30 suggests that it was at the boundary between the plains and the hill country. Such topographical data, however, is not precise and the exact location of the place is uncertain. It functions in the story as the place of dispute over territory and a place of confrontation that characteristically concerns the control of land.

We have no clue about the intention or significance of the shooting of the arrow, except that the gesture is a prophetic harbinger of the end of Syria in a battle at Aphek (13:17). [Map: Aphek] The king, however, fails to enact fully the intention of the prophet, though characteristically the prophet is elusive and unclear about his intention or requirement. Perhaps the king thought the gesture of an arrow foolish, perhaps he thought "three times" was enough, given prophetic power. Only after the "three strokes" does the prophet

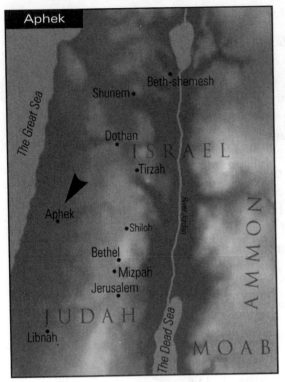

respond to "explain" that the symbolic strikes will match the number of military strikes against Syria, and three is not enough. The enigmatic quality of the act defies explanation and likely was completely enigmatic for the king as well.

The death of Elisha permits yet one more startling report (13:20-21). This brief passage, without context or explanation, speaks of marauding "bands of Moabites" who are incidental to the quickly told plot. We have heard nothing of the Moabites since chapter 3 and may be surprised that they are in this narrative. We have no indication about the military or political importance of their presence here. Such "invaders" are important in the narrative only to create confusion and anxiety among Israelites, so much confusion and anxiety that a funeral is disrupted and a corpse was put into the grave of Elisha, a grave that apparently was still open and uncovered. We do not know if the corpse was mistakenly put into the grave, or if the corpse was put there for safekeeping until the threat of the Moabites had passed. Either way, what counts is that contact between the corpse and the bones of Elisha causes a restoration and resurrection of the dead man. The narrative is not interested in the Moabites and does not comment on them again, for the focus is upon Elisha, or at least his powerful bones.

As is characteristic in such presentations, the narrator gives us the "data" without explanation, without curiosity, and without regarding the report as exceptional or problematic. It is clear that the report intends to assert, and to claim without question, that even in death, Elisha is a life-bringer. His "afterlife" is operative in the community of Israel. Like Elijah before him, Elisha has been a powerful force for life with a capacity to transform circumstances of death. Thus he is the one who turned deathly water whole (2:19-22), who gave life to the besieged widow (4:1-7), who rescued the pot of food from death (4:38-41), who fed the hungry (4:42-44), who healed the foreign leper (5:14), who recovered a lost ax head (6:1-7, who turned war to feast (6:7-23), who provisionally ended famine (7:1), and who turned out the deathly dynasty of

Omri (9:1-37). Quintessentially, he is the one who raised the son of the Shunammite woman from death to life (4:32-37), a wonder subsequently reckoned as a "great thing" in Israel (8:4-5). The present text functions as something of a reprise on this entire memory of ministry. The power of life has been operative in Israel through this enigmatic figure and is at work yet. The public memory of Israel has inexplicable wonder at its center![1]

Yahweh Trumps Hazael, 13:22-25

Hazael the Syrian has been an endless scourge against Samaria, a threat anticipated by Elisha (8:12; see 10:32-33; 12:17-18). Syrian policy of a push into Israelite territory is a recurring and durable challenge to Israel. Hazael is indomitable and will not quit his campaign against Israel, because it is the cornerstone of his policy (perhaps not unlike the intransigence of contemporary Syria toward Israel). There was, however, a shift in geopolitical fortunes by the end of the ninth century. Seen in the perspective of our narrator, the Syrians had failed to reckon with Yahweh, who is a major player in the geopolitical fortunes of Israel. Verse 23 is a most remarkable theological statement that our narrator puts down in the midst of geopolitical data.

We may notice three elements in this carefully nuanced statement. First, Yahweh is "gracious and compassionate" toward the Northern Kingdom. This is something of a surprise to us, because we know that the narrator (and Yahweh?) disapproves of the Northern regime in principle. Yahweh's character, however, is to be gracious and compassionate toward Yahweh's people, even in the North. [Yahweh Gracious and Compassionate] Yahweh extends Yahweh's own self in caring ways, so the narrative offers, that are effective in public life. Second, we are told the most elemental motivation for Yahweh's present positive inclination toward the Northern Kingdom. It is because of Abraham, Isaac, and Jacob! This motivational clause is not an unfamiliar one, being offered even in Exodus 2:24, 3:6 as the ground for the Exodus emancipation, thereby linking ancestral promises in Genesis to the Exodus narrative.[2] To find this motivation in the context of Northern royal history, however, is unprecedented and completely unexpected. The oldest commitments of Yahweh concerning graciousness and compassion are here said to be operative on behalf of this doubtful regime!

Third, however, the final phrase of v. 24 adds a profound reservation to the first two statements of assurance. The *graciousness and compassion* of Yahweh, rooted in *promises to Abraham, Isaac, and*

Yahweh Gracious and Compassionate

The usage of this word pair in this narrative is remarkable. It is a familiar word pair in the Psalms where Israel meditates upon the character of Yahweh. The terms refer to Yahweh's self-giving intention toward Israel and especially toward those in need. The term "gracious" is the root term of the name of "Hannah" in 1 Samuel 1 and refers to Yahweh's free gift that is not earned or deserved. The second term, "compassionate," derives from the term "womb" (*reḥem*) and has been interpreted to mean "womb-like mother love," on which see Isa 49:14-15. The usage seems to be rooted in what may be the old cultic recital of Exod 34:6-7, and can be used in the Psalms both as ground for praise of Yahweh in hymns and as a basis of petition that asks Yahweh to be Yahweh's true self.

On the terms, see Walter Brueggemann, *Theology of the Old Testament: Testimony, Dispute, Advocacy* (Minneapolis: Fortress Press, 1997) 216-24, and "Crisis-Evoked, Crisis-Resolving Speech," BTB 24 (Fall, 1994): 95-105.

Jacob, are "until now," until the end of the ninth century, until this point in the telling of the royal tale, until now, but not to perpetuity. The narrator knows where the royal history terminates and knows that this telling of royal history will come to a devastating end in four more chapters (17:5-6). Thus "graciousness and compassion" rooted in the ancestral promises offer relief but not finally pardon. This carefully nuanced theological statement takes into account Israel's short-term success and Israel's long-term failure.

Hazael is succeeded by his son Ben-hadad. Hazael is an upstart without pedigree (8:13). By the end of his aggressive reign, however, he is legitimated and can give his own son a throne-name belonging to the legitimate dynasty that he has displaced (see 8:14-15). Hazael's bequeathal of such a name is a standard example of how yesterday's terrorists become tomorrow's legitimated establishment. In the face of such Syrian legitimacy, however, Israel is now militarily strong. Jehoahaz, third in the line of Jehu, can now push Syrian troops back and recover territory across the Jordan River, territory previously taken by Syria (10:32-33). This success, of course, matches Elisha's enigmatic assurance in vv. 17-19. Thus the military success of Israel fulfills prophetic anticipation. The final notice of "three times," however, also ominously recalls the previous prophetic exchange about the arrows. Apparently Israel in this period conducted three successful assaults on Syria, three times victorious. Three times, however, is not enough. Elisha reckoned "five or six" to be adequate (13:19). Thus even in success, the regime fails to enact the full prophetic promise. The narrative is restrained and tells us nothing more of the matter. The wording of the last sentence, however, suggests that three-times success carries in it long-term failure. Kings should pay more attention to prophets!

CONNECTIONS

The fourfold formula of vv. 2-5—evil-punishment-entreaty-savior—is a remarkable summary of a Yahwistic discernment of public history. To be sure, the formula that recurs often in the book of Judges, is so familiar as to be a cliche, and appears excessively simplistic and familiar. Nonetheless, it brings together in a fresh configuration crucial aspects of Israel's faith. The first two elements of the formula—evil-punishment—together articulate the most insistent prophetic claim of the *speech of judgment*, whereby prophetic *indictment* for disobedience leads to prophetic *sentence* concerning Yahweh's punishment. [The Prophetic Speech of Judgment] This rhetorical convention asserts Yahweh's moral claim over Israel's public life. The third and fourth elements—entreaty-savior—articulate the elemental claim of Israel's piety in the book of Psalms. When Israel prays or cries out to Yahweh in need, it is regularly an act of desperation as well as an act of faith. Characteristically, Yahweh hears the cry of petition on the lips of Israel and intervenes in responsive ways to right an unbearable wrong and to rescue Israel from its trouble. The claim is that Yahweh answers prayer and effectively intervenes. [Israel's Conviction of "Cry-Save"]

The formula of vv. 2-5 thus joins a *prophetic speech of judgment* focused on Yahweh's sovereign insistence together with Israel's pious conviction of *prayer answered*.[3] The combined form enables Israel to affirm both *deep accountability* for its culpability and *deep hope* that Yahweh will move beyond judgment to rescue. The repeated use of the formula permits Israel endlessly to reread its life and its public experience with decisive reference to Yahweh.

AΩ **The Prophetic Speech of Judgment**
Among the most important studies of prophetic rhetoric is the work of Claus Westermann. [Claus Westermann, *Basic Forms of Prophetic Speech.*] He has argued that the most basic form of prophetic speech, that can be expressed in a wide variety of ways, is the "speech of judgment" that includes both the *indictment* (of what Israel has done wrong) and the *sentence* (of what Yahweh will do as punishment). Westermann's study tabulates the evidence for this most prominent of speech forms that is utilized in our text. The theological importance of the form is to insist upon the context of accountability in which Israel's actions operate. The actions of Israel evoke from Yahweh blessing and curse.

Claus Westermann, *Basic Forms of Prophetic Speech* (Philadelphia: Westminster Press, 1967).

AΩ **Israel's Conviction of "Cry-Save"**
The work Westermann has done on prophetic speech is matched by his remarkable study of the Psalms. Claus Westermann, *The Praise of God in the Psalms* (Richmond: John Knox Press, 1965).] Westermann has been able to show that the faith of the Psalms characteristically begins in a cry of need and distress resolved by the response of Yahweh who hears, answers, intervenes, and saves. This convention is evident, for example, in Exodus 2:23-25 and often in the patterned speech of Psalm 107. The theological import of the rhetorical convention is to assert that Israel must speak its need to Yahweh and that Yahweh characteristically (but not always) answers such a prayer.

The final episode in the larger-than-life phenomenon of Elisha shows him to be decisively involved in the *public agenda* of war with Syria (that ends in a wistful allusion in v. 25—three times and no more), and in the strange *pastoral act* of a resurrection. Of course the two aspects of his presence are not commensurate beyond the claim of Elisha's dominance in every circumstance of the life of Israel. The wonder of the resurrection of the man ready for burial is Elisha's final, most breathtaking wonder. While the wonder strikes us as deeply primitive, its placement as his final act asserts narratively that Elisha's enduring power and presence are at work in Israel's life. That durable, transformative presence, moreover, makes clear that Israel's life is not closed, not reduced to royal options, not shrivelled to despair. Yahweh's power for life, intensely present in this Elisha, is abidingly present in Israel in ways that yield unexpected newness. This "resurrection" is not simply a tale of primitive miracle (though it is that), but it is a claim that Israel's life and the life of the world are kept open beyond what the world judges to be possible. Thus this small, sparsely expressed wonder keeps the horizon of faith and life open.

That this little episode has "futures" suggests that it is not unlike "Easter" in Christian faith. No trusting Christian denies that in some decisive way the wonder of Easter is a happening whereby the life of Jesus resumes in the world. Beyond that claim, however, is the larger claim that this event in the story of Jesus is a paradigmatic event that insists that all of creation under the rule of Yahweh is open to the new gift of life. Easter faith, a claim surely rooted as concretely as the wonder of Elisha, insists that this God has the capacity to call into existence things that do not exist. [The Wonder of Life Restored]

The Wonder of Life Restored

The wonder of life restored is pivotally expressed in Christian faith with reference to Easter. It is important, however, to see that the same wonder at Yahweh's miracle of new life is everywhere in these texts of faith. Perhaps as a clue we may especially cite Romans 4:17 wherein Paul brings into convergence, "grace alone," "creation from nothing," and the resurrection of the dead. These are all forms of the claim that Yahweh can begin again with newness rooted in nothing more than Yahweh's own generative resolve.

This narrative that juxtaposes Elisha with Joash's war effort (13:14-19) and the resurrection (13:20-21) culminates in an assertion of the "graciousness and compassion" of Yahweh. In this word pair, the narrative appeals to what is perhaps the most elemental claim that Israel makes for Yahweh: that Yahweh is a generous, self-giving God who overrides negative circumstance to make all things new. That quality in Yahweh, moreover, is linked to Israel's oldest ancestral promises from the book of Genesis, signifying that Israel's entire memory is deeply marked by Yahweh's life-giving graciousness. This formulation, a most recurring and familiar cadence in

Israel's faith, puts to rest any mistaken notion that Israel's faith is marked by anything other than Yahweh's transformative graciousness. Finally, moreover, it is noteworthy that here Yahweh's graciousness and compassion are at work in the public arena. The peculiar life of Israel and the public life of the world are not, in the end, reduced to power or to that false conviction that "might makes right." The claim made here is that the life of the world is under another governance, propelled by promise and aimed at well-being.

The final comment concerning "three times" (13:25) is a wistful reference back to the action of Joash who struck the ground only three times (13:18). In context, this enigmatic matter asserts that Yahweh's full exercise of grace and compassion in the public domain depends on *agents of power* (the king) heeding the *voice of open wonder* (the prophet). The king did not trust the prophet enough to strike more. The implied outcome of v. 25, implied but not stated, is that the king quit too soon in his obedience to the prophet. As a result, the three strikes of the arrow and of the army are not enough.

This entire narrative of closure to the life of the prophet is difficult and lacking in a smooth story line. Its odd articulation, however, is an unsettled recognition that history has been visited by the voice of wonder. Neither the king nor one who reads this text can ever again imagine that our life in the world is reduced to "guns and butter." There is more, and the "more" of Elisha eludes either explanation or control.

NOTES

[1]See Walter Brueggemann, *Abiding Astonishment: Psalms, Modernity, and the Making of History* (Louisville: Westminster/John Knox Press, 1991) and Yosef Hayim Yerushalmi, *Zakhor: Jewish History and Jewish Memory* (Seattle: University of Washington Press, 1982).

[2]See R. W. L. Moberly, *The Old Testament of the Old Testament: Patriarchal Narratives and Mosaic Yahwism,* OBT (Minneapolis: Fortress Press,1992).

[3]See Walter Brueggemann, "Social Criticism and Social Vision in the Deuteronomic Formula of the Judges," *Die Botschaft und die Boten: Festschrift für Hans Walter Wolff zum 70. Gebürtstag,* ed. Jorg Jeremias and Lothar Perlitt (Neukirchen-Vluyn: Neukirchener Verlag, 1981) 101-14.

ON AMAZIAH
AND JEROBOAM II

2 Kings 14:1-29

The twin accounts of Southern and Northern royal history continue with an extended narrative concerning the reign of Amaziah in the South (14:1-22) and Jeroboam II in the North (14:23-29).

COMMENTARY

Amaziah, Practitioner and Victim of Violence, 14:1-22

Amaziah, son of the boy king Joash/Jehoash, receives an especially long narrative report, framed with an introductory formula (14:1-4) and a concluding formula (14:17-20). Of particular interest in this account are two diversions from Amaziah, one concerning Jehoash (14:15-16), one concerning Azariah, son and successor to Amaziah (14:21-22).

The account of Amaziah's reign begins with a characteristic report: a reign of twenty-nine years, 800–783 (14:1-2). His theological verdict is a characteristically mixed one, doing right, *but* leaving the high places (14:3-4). Nothing exceptional is reported in the beginning.

What strikes one most is that the reign of Amaziah is dominated by acts of violence. His first act reported here is to execute the assassins of his father Joash (14:5-6). We are given no details of that assassination here, but must refer to 12:20-21 where the royal killers are named, Jozacar and Jehozabad. Both the killing of Joash and the responding killing of the killers indicate that the throne in Jerusalem is not completely secure, very probably a condition reflecting old and enduring disputes in the larger royal family, perhaps partly driven by ideological conflict (Yahweh vs. Baal). Retaliation on the part of Amaziah against the killers of his father would seem to be studied royal common sense. His action is in the train of Solomon, who at the outset of his reign enacted the violence necessary to his security (1 Kgs 2:5-46). The notice of vv. 6-7 is less expected than the murder of v. 5. It suggests that King Amaziah's retaliation was a reasoned act of vengeance with a limit, so that the vengeance did not extend beyond the killers themselves. The notice is designed to portray the king as a Torah-keeper restrained by the limitation of Deuteronomy 24:16:

> Parents shall not be put to death for their children, nor shall children be put to death for their parents; only for their own crimes may persons be put to death.

The commandment is no doubt an attempt to curb an older, long-standing practice of blood feud whereby the killing may go on and on from one generation to the next.[1] (See also the same limitation on well-known proverbial wisdom in Jer 31:29 and Ezek 18:2.)

With his internal rule secure, King Amaziah turns to foreign policy which for him is reduced to military ambition. We have seen Edom, an eastern neighbor of Judah, mentioned only sporadically in the text (3:8-26; 8:20-22). Amaziah apparently conducted a major incursion toward Edom in the valley south of the Dead Sea and won a major victory. [Joktheel] The notice of the military slaughter is terse and undeveloped. As we shall see, the mention of this victory is for the sake of the next episode.

The major episode given us from Amaziah's rule is his challenge to his Northern neighbor, Israel and its king, Jehoash (14:8-14).

Joktheel

This is a new name given to the Edomite stronghold of Sela (modern Petra) after the conquest by Amaziah. The change of name is to indicate new governance; given Amaziah's next venture in the narrative, it is likely that the name change was also a bit of public relations to celebrate himself and his success. The site is not to be confused with the town mentioned in Joshua 15:38, located in the southwest of Judah.

Amaziah is clearly the aggressor who challenges the North to conflict (14:8). It is possible that the invitation in v. 8 is not yet a military challenge but only a request for a "summit meeting." The same phrasing in v. 11, however, is clearly military. The challenge is remarkable, because during the Omride dynasty it was consistently made clear that the Northern state was the stronger party with whom the South was docilely cooperative.

The challenge of Amaziah is rebuffed by Jehoash in two ways. First, the Northern king responds in a somewhat enigmatic parabolic form (14:9). It is most plausible that the roles in the parable are:

(a) thorn bush, a lowly unattractive growth = Amaziah;
(b) cedar, an impressive, stately growth = Jehoash;
(c) wild animal = an unnamed third party who destroys.

The relation of the first two suggests that Amaziah as thorn bush is unattractive, unimpressive, and unwanted, and is reaching beyond true character by engaging a superior. Jehoash as "cedar" is the appropriate and attractive growth vastly superior to the unwanted

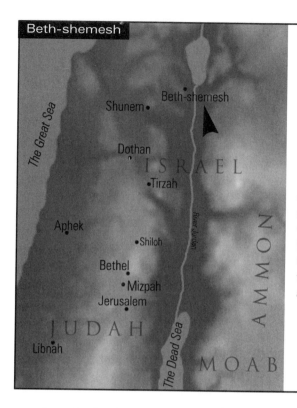

Beth-shemesh

The town of Beth-shemesh is located in the northeast corner of Judah. It is a border town that was strategically important as it stood at the head of the valley of Sorek. Its strategic importance suggests that it was likely in disputed territory even if our narrative assigns it to Judah.

thorn bush who merits only contempt. Both, however, are exposed to and vulnerable before a "wild beast," perhaps a reference either to the near menace of Syria or the rising menace of Assyria. Either way, the engagement between the first two parties (here war) is not viable or wise, given the threat of the third party. The parable not only reflects the challenge but answers Amaziah with dismissive contempt.

The second response of rejection by the Northern king is more direct but equally contemptuous (14:10). The Northern king reminds his Southern counterpart that the victory over Edom in v. 7 has given the Judean king unreal notions of his military capacity, so that one can see why v. 7 is placed where it is by the narrator. The Southern king is invited to enjoy his "glory" from that success over Edom and not to squander his recent victory by an attack on the North where he will surely be defeated. The Northern king speaks confidently and contemptuously, but seeks to avoid conflict. It is clear that the narrative is arranged to show the Southern king in a bad light.

Amaziah, however, will not accept such sober advice, and mounts an attack against Israel, a battle at Beth-shemesh. [Map: Beth-shemesh] It is worth noting that the battle is joined in Judean territory, indicating that Amaziah could not even move quickly or powerfully enough to reach Israelite territory.

The battle is joined; it turns out that Amaziah is foolish and Jehoash's previous advice to Amaziah is well founded. The Southern army is routed. The king is captured, Jerusalem is occupied, and the temple vessels are taken. Hostages are secured. The Southern king is totally humiliated. Perhaps the king from Jerusalem counted on the Davidic promise of Yahweh to see through to victory; it is an understatement to say that the promise did not work!

Lachish

Lachish was a major fortress city of Judah located on the road to the coastal plain in southwest Judah; the most likely identification of the site is Tell el-Duweir. That Amaziah fled from Jerusalem to Lachish may indicate that the threat to him was most acute in Jerusalem. It may also indicate that the fortress of Lachish was regarded as a safer place for the king, a judgment that proved to be false. See map page 443.

In vv. 15-16, we reach one of the two interruptions in the Amaziah narrative. We are offered, a second time, the concluding formula on Jehoash, data we have already encountered in 13:12-13. This curious repetition is no doubt evoked by the military success of Jehoash in vv. 8-14. Whether the statement is reiterated as an editorial mistake evoked by vv. 8-14 or whether it is reiterated for accent upon the victorious king, we cannot say. In any case, this king is twice saluted in the narrative for his victory over Amaziah.

The concluding formula of vv. 17-20 completes the report on Amaziah. In addition to the usual data, we learn only that he, like his father Joash, is murdered, yet more evidence for the instability of the throne and the continuing conflict in palace officialdom, perhaps reflecting old, ideological disputes. The locus of the regicide is Lachish, Judah's most important fortification. [Lachish] The royal flight to Lachish suggests that Amaziah was exposed and sought a safe place; but even Lachish was not safe enough. Amaziah's regime is remembered for only three pieces of data, (a) the avenging of his father, (b) his victory over Edom, and (c) his loss to Israel. He was only a military man, an unsuccessful one at that.

Elath

Elath is a fortress city that gave Judah access to southern trade routes via the Red Sea. Because it is the single point of access to the south, it was a matter of perpetual concern for the economic, political well-being of the Kingdom of Judah. The capacity of Judah to control and use the site, however, was intertwined with Judah's larger relations with the Edomites who also vied for control of the port. Thus when Judah was able to overcome Edomite control, it had access; but when Edom was stronger than Judah, Edom controlled the port and Judah had no access. In the kingdom of Judah, Solomon first captured and built Elath (Ezion-Geber at Eloth, 1 Kgs 9:26). During the reign of Joram, the Edomites regained the city, and only with the defeat of Edom by Amaziah in 14:7 did Judah regain control, permitting Azariah to rebuild and restore. That period of control, however, proved to be brief, for the port was lost again by Ahaz, grandson of Azariah (2 Kgs 16:5-6). Thus the site is an indicator of Judah's political power and economic capacity.

The narrative moves, as quickly as it can, to Amaziah's son Azariah (14:21-22). This next king will not be formally introduced in the narrative until 15:1-4. The narrator, however, cannot wait until then, so that as a conclusion to the sorry tale of Amaziah, we already learn of Azariah's restoration of the southern port of Elath. [Elath] We are led to anticipate an economic recovery in Judah, for in one verse Azariah has already done more good than his father Amaziah during his long reign.

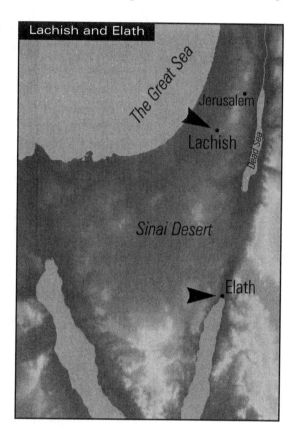

Lachish and Elath

The Great Sea

Jerusalem

Lachish

Dead Sea

Sinai Desert

Elath

The Fourth of Jehu's Line, 14:23-29

In 10:30, Yahweh promised Jehu a dynasty of four generations. We now reach the fourth king in the line, Jeroboam II, who takes the name of Jeroboam I (see 1 Kgs 12), but is not related to him. The introductory notice on this fourth king is conventional (14:23-24). He enjoyed a long reign of forty-one years, 786–746. Like every Northern king, he is condemned by the narrative as theologically and liturgically heterodox, that is, outside the sphere of Jerusalem.

It is astonishing that this king receives only seven verses, for his reign was not only long but greatly effective (14:25-27). Jeroboam's great achievement, according to this narrative, was the recovery of a great deal of territory that the Northern state had lost in its long-standing and losing disputes with Syria. Specifically the recovery of Lebo-hamath to the north up to the "sea of Arabah," was a recovery of land commensurate with the ancient Solomonic notion of "Greater Israel." In this instant Israel was stronger than its erstwhile enemy who had previously defeated Israel's claim to the territory.

The narrative, moreover, is careful to give a theological basis for the military success of Jeroboam (14:25b-27). On the face of it, from a theological perspective, this military success is remarkable, because we have already been told that Jeroboam was a bad king. The success and recovery of territory, however, have nothing to do with Jeroboam or even with the dynasty of Jehu, but only with Yahweh's commitment to Israel. Yahweh saw that Israel's "distress was very bitter." Yahweh saw the humiliation, suffering, and resourcelessness of Israel and so acted to rescue. The response to suffering by rescue is not unlike the formula we have discussed in 13:4-5. Yahweh can watch and see and care and notice and respond, and does so "by the hand of Jeroboam."

Yahweh's transformative action in the world is accomplished by empowered human agents. It is perhaps even more noteworthy that Yahweh still continues to regard Israel as Yahweh's peculiar people to whom Yahweh is attentive, so that Yahweh intervenes when there is no other source of help. Jeroboam thus is to be understood as the single resource of a diminished and humiliated Israel, a resource directly from Yahweh. The deep and immediate linkage between *Jeroboam's military, political success* and *Yahweh's attentive intervention* is established by the work of Jonah the prophet. The prophet is mentioned only in this single narrative, and the later book of Jonah may be reckoned to be a derivative commentary from this single verse. The prophet (whose words are not given to us) is the characteristic *connector* between *political reality* and *Yahweh's intentionality*. For all the waywardness that the narrator reads in Northern history, Yahweh nonetheless regards the Northern state as a proper object of caring attention.

The concluding verse of this theopolitical statement of recovery is odd, because it is stated negatively.[2] It is not claimed that Yahweh would protect Israel, but only that (so far!) Yahweh had refused, for

---

Yahweh's Recruitment of Power People

In this text, Jeroboam is seen to be an agent and instrument of Yahweh's foreign policy. Of course it would have been enough to identify Jeroboam simply as "the next king." But the theological claim of the narrative is that Jeroboam is especially recruited for this function of Yahweh's graciousness toward Israel. That Yahweh should accomplish such a work "by the hand" of a human agent is characteristic of the ways in which Yahweh's purposes are effected in history. In the memory of Israel, Moses is forcefully recruited for Yahweh's rescue mission of the slaves from Egypt, even though Moses refuses that recruitment as strongly as he possibly can (Exod 3:10-4:17). In 3:7-9 Yahweh asserts all that he will do; but then in v. 10 it is clear that Yahweh's way of working is to dispatch Moses as human agent who will effect the liberation of the slaves.

In like manner, Cyrus, a Persian and non-Israelite, is identified as Yahweh's "messiah" (Isa 45:1). In reference to Cyrus, the poet has Yahweh say:

> I stirred up one from the north, and he has come,
> from the rising of the sun he was summoned by name.
> He shall trample on rulers as on mortar,
> as the potter treads clay. (Isa 41:25)

Yahweh engages and presses into service various human agents who enact a will other than their own. Jeroboam is among such agents.

the sake of a promise, to "blot out" Israel; and if not "blot out," then "save;" if not negative destruction, then positive restoration. In the end, the entire episode is governed by Yahweh's verb "save" in v. 27. Yahweh saves Israel. Jeroboam is Yahweh's agent. Biblical, prophetic faith has a characteristic way of recruiting into Yahweh's work those who are unaware of selection, but who act unwittingly and effectively. [Yahweh's Recruitment of Power People]

The conclusion of the reign of Jeroboam is typical, though two points are worth noting (14:28-29). Though the narrative has already commented on the recovery of Lebo-hamath, the point is repeated. The added reference to Damascus, capital of Syria, must have been a peculiarly important and gratifying gain for Israel, for it means that Israel has been able to penetrate to the very core of Syrian power. It has been from Damascus that Syria has harassed and troubled Israel for half a century. The present reversal is enormously significant. Jeroboam is effective, but we already know he is only an instrument of Yahweh. It is Yahweh who is generous in rescue.

The final line of the report mentions Zechariah, son of Jeroboam, as his successor (14:29; see 15:8-12). This may be only an ordinary historical note. But because we are aware of the primal promise to Jehu in 10:30, we pay special attention to the addendum of v. 29. It has been promised that there will be a secure dynasty for four generations. There have now been the four generations assured by Yahweh: Jehu-Jehoahaz-Jehoash-Jeroboam. The dynasty has prospered, culminating in the success and stability of Jeroboam. The problem is that Zechariah to come is the fifth generation of a four-generation dynasty, not a good role to play. As we shall see, he plays but briefly. Time will have run out, even on this successful dynasty.

CONNECTIONS

This chapter, concerning both Amaziah of Jerusalem, who is defeated by the North and then assassinated, and Jeroboam of Samaria, who is a winner who regains lost territory, plunges us into international affairs and military adventurism. Aside from the theological verdicts that preoccupy the narrative, these kings are situated in the political, military world of power, violence, aggression, and suffering. They pose the large issue of how *faith* operates in a world of real *power*, even though neither king is particularly championed as a man of faith. The issue is not the personal

On Counting the Cost

Obviously waging war is a costly business, costly in terms of money, equipment, and lives. One can imagine that Solomon, the quintessential planner in ancient Israel, must have done careful cost estimation for everything he did. Amaziah, by contrast, is one who did not reckon with the costs of this war, for it cost him not only profound humiliation, but also quite concrete costs as his treasury was looted by the winners.

In Luke 14:31-32 Jesus speaks of counting the cost of going to battle; the specific reference means to weigh the odds of available troops against the available troops of the enemy. It is clear that in the teaching of Jesus this reference is only a figure for the "cost of discipleship." The teaching is an acknowledgement that discipleship is costly and a warning against a foolhardy commitment to Jesus without being prepared for the cost. [The theme of course has received its most poignant voicing by Dietrich Bonhoeffer, *The Cost of Discipleship* (New York: Macmillan Company, 1957).]

It is clear that Jesus moves beyond the literal reference of military preparedness. We cannot, however, understand the reference Jesus makes unless we take concretely the meaning of his image, a meaning clearly reflected in the Amaziah refusal to count the cost.

---

inclination of the characters but the theological insistence of the narrative. The latter is resolved to present public history as an arena of Yahweh's governance, and to reflect upon the quotidian conduct of human power in the service of Yahweh's abiding claims.

Remarkably Amaziah receives a qualified affirmation from the narrative (14:3-4), but then is presented as an astonishingly violent king who lives by the sword and who dies by the sword. Indeed, Amaziah, heir of David, may be a prize example of Nathan's verdict on the dynasty in 2 Samuel 12:10, "The sword will never depart from your house."

The focus of the Amaziah report is, of course, the challenge to Samaria by Jerusalem (14:8-14). As the Northern king recognizes in v. 10, it was a military success against Edom in v. 7 that seems to impel Amaziah to do more. We are not told for what "reasons of state" Amaziah challenges the North. Of course, there was always the Southern sense that the Northern regime was really "occupying" what was properly Southern territory, a view agreed to by the narrator. But the territorial realities between the two states have been settled and stable for a long time.

One gains the impression that Amaziah's challenge to Jehoash is frivolous, a king who goes forth to war and does not count the cost. [On Counting the Cost] The parabolic response of the North suggests that the North hardly takes the matter seriously. And indeed the defeat of Amaziah suggests that had he counted the cost, he would not have advanced to war. His action is indeed a folly that apparently has no chance of succeeding. [On Public Folly] Thus I suggest his policy might be entered as "war as folly," an interesting, playful pastime that is not serious, planned, or calculated, and that brings untold suffering upon others.

"War as hobby" is an endless temptation to governmental leaders who feel strong, need to flex their muscles, and imagine that such posturing makes them important and/or secure in office. A prize example of such "war as hobby" might be World War I, a war clearly unjustified and unneeded and without clear aims of state, a war stumbled into by careless posturing among royal cousins across Europe. A more immediate point of contact may be the endless military posturing of the U.S. as "the last superpower" that maintains endless expansionism and, in this judgment, endlessly unnecessary military preparedness, especially to move against small, weak adversaries, many of whom control oil. And if "war as hobby" is too much to say of such public posturing, then such posturing may at least be seen with war as a first diplomatic impulse, without due regard for long-term policy or the durable costs of war.

It is not for nothing that Barbara Tuchman terms Vietnam a "march of folly" that was propelled by unarticulated reasons of state.[3] While I would not draw the analogy too closely, one can argue, given the residue of unfinished business in the U.S. concerning Vietnam, that the "vessels of democracy" have indeed been forfeited in an avoidable war with incalculable, abiding losses and jeopardies. It is worth noting that there is no impetus from Yahweh for this war of Amaziah, only the slow, reliable way in which the public processes put foolishness to work at its own costs, no matter the powers of "wisdom" and technology at work in the foolishness. By the end of the narrative, the foolish sword of Amaziah has come round to his own belly (v. 19). History of this kind watches over its perpetrators and gives back in kind, the narrative quietly observes.

The account of Amaziah's "war as hobby" is quite in contrast to the report of the successful recovery of territory by Jeroboam II in the North. The "factual report" of that recovery (14:25a) is, according to the horizon of the narrative, illuminated in vv. 25b-27. These verses are a remarkable assessment of events, both because Yahweh is credited with the success of the Northern king, and because Yahweh is gracious and generous toward the Northern regime that the narrator characteristically condemns. It is Yahweh, represented by the prophet Jonah, who

On Public Folly

Barbara Tuchman, in her famous phrase "The March of Folly," refers to public policy decisions made despite evidence and quite visible advice to the contrary. The decision to make such a decision against advice and data is an act of deliberately chosen folly. Amaziah's decision to go to war would seem to fall into that category, even though it is not a case that Tuchman mentions. It is noteworthy that in her introduction to such acts of foolishness Tuchman explicitly refers to the foolish policy decisions of Rehoboam in 1 Kings 12, one among many such follies that she terms "Pursuit of Policy Contrary to Self-Interest." [Barbara Tuchman, *The March of Folly*, 8-11.] Amaziah's decision to attack the North would seem precisely to be such a "pursuit of policy contrary to self-interest."

sees the "bitter distress" of Israel, presumably the distress caused by endless Syrian harassment.

This God notices suffering and responds to distress. Indeed, this God notices public, corporate distress. Yahweh has noticed that the population of Israel is decimated, almost wiped out, *none* left strong, *none* left free, *none* left to help. The condition of Israel is indeed dire. More than that, however, that dire condition is noticed. More than that, the dire condition of Israel evokes Yahweh to action. The linkage offered between dire Israel and noticing Yahweh is not unlike the initiatory engagement of Yahweh with Israel:

> After a long time the king of Egypt died. The Israelites groaned under their slavery, and cried out. Out of the slavery their cry for help rose up to God. God heard their groaning, and God remembered his covenant with Abraham, Isaac, and Jacob. God looked upon the Israelites, and God took notice of them. (See Exod 3:7-8)

In the case of the Exodus, Yahweh's ground for notice is a memory of a promise to the ancestors in Genesis. In our text, Yahweh's notice arises from Yahweh's freedom to act because Yahweh has not resolved to blot out the North. For all of the predictable, formulaic condemnation of the North, these are still Yahweh's people; Yahweh still notices, cares, intervenes, and rescues. The theological implication, not unlike 13:5, substantiates Yahweh's lingering graciousness toward a people already in principle rejected, but not yet "fated" for "blotting out." It is this lingering graciousness over the North that is verbalized in the pathos-filled poetry of Hosea and Jeremiah:

> My heart recoils within me;
>   my compassion grows warm and tender.
> I will not execute my fierce anger;
>   I will not again destroy Ephraim;
> for I am God and no mortal,
>   the Holy One in your midst,
>   and I will not come in wrath. (Hos 11:8-9)

> For the hurt of my poor people I am hurt,
>   I mourn, and dismay has taken hold of me.
> Is there no balm in Gilead?
>   Is there no physician there?
> Why then has the health of my poor people not been restored?

O that my head were a spring of water,
    and my eyes a fountain of tears,
so that I might weep day and night
    for the slain of my poor people! (Jer 8:21–9:1)[4]

The remarkable claim made in our text is that the pathos of Yahweh is specific and powerful, and turns up in places where we might have expected only Yahweh's indifference and disregard. The good and kind impulses of Yahweh operate fully well beyond our expectations suggested by the moral calculus of the narrative.

It is worth juxtaposing the defeat of Amaziah (14:8-14) and the success of Jeroboam (14: 25-27), because the interaction between the two reports is suggestive:

(a) The narrative of Amaziah's defeat is devoid of any mention of Yahweh. Power politics and war work out their own consequences. By contrast, Yahweh is said to be the key player in the North, the one who intervenes decisively and positively.

(b) The absence of Yahweh in the first story is not what we expect, precisely because Yahweh has already sworn fidelity to this regime. [A Pledge to David] Conversely, Yahweh's disfavor toward the North is well documented in our narrative so that we expect it here. Thus this narrative contradicts what we might expect in terms of Yahweh's disposition and deployment; Yahweh can act freely beyond any predictable or imposed formula.

(c) Both the absence and presence of Yahweh in the narrative attest to Yahweh's decisive and free engagement in the historical

---

A Pledge to David

A major theme in royal history in the Old Testament is the apparently unconditional promise to David and his dynasty. That promise is formally articulated by Nathan in 2 Sam 7:11-16 and echoed in the poetry of Ps 89:1-37. That promise, of course, has theological rootage, but it also surely served important political purposes. It is nowhere explicit that Amaziah relied on such an ideological assurance, but it stands to reason that such an assurance taken with seriousness would encourage risky, venturesome policy that seemed to be warranted by an unconditional assurance. The promise in poetic rendering must have been familiar to the ears of Amaziah:

Once and for all I have sworn by my holiness;
    I will not lie to David.
His line shall continue forever,
    and his throne endure before me like the sun.
It shall be established forever like the moon,
    an enduring witness in the skies. (Ps 89:35-37)

Gerhard von Rad has shown how this promise impacts the presentation of the monarchy in our narrative tradition. [Gerhard von Rad, *Old Testament Theology I: The Theology of Israel's Historical Traditions* (New York: Harper & Brothers, 1962) 334-47.] It may well be that as the promise impacts the view of the narrator, so it also impacted policymakers in Jerusalem.

process. Yahweh will not be reduced to conventional expectations nor to reasons of state. The course of public history, given Yahweh's irreducible freedom, is more open than predictable theology or self-serving patriotism can ever allow.[5] That violation of convention, of course, does not deter our narrator who is intent on testifying to the odd singularity of Yahweh before whom all royal power is provisional and penultimate.

NOTES

[1]On vengeance, see George E. Mendenhall, "The 'Vengeance' of Yahweh," *The Tenth Generation: The Origins of the Biblical Tradition* (Baltimore: Johns Hopkins University Press, 1973) 69-104.

[2]For the notion of "theopolitics," see Henning Graf Reventlow et al. (eds.) *Politics and Theopolitics in the Bible and Postbiblical Literature,* JSOT Supp. 171 (Sheffield: Sheffield Academic Press, 1994).

[3]Barbara W. Tuchman, *The March of Folly: From Troy to Vietnam* (New York: Ballantine Books, 1984) 233-377.

[4]The most complete statement of the pathos of Yahweh is by Abraham Heschel, *The Prophets* (New York: Harper & Row, 1962).

[5]William Stacy Johnson, *The Mystery of God: Karl Barth and the Postmodern Foundations of Theology* (Louisville: Westminster/John Knox Press, 1997) has nicely exposited the surplus mystery of God beyond controlling categories in the work of Karl Barth. Thus, "there always remains more about God that needs to be said" (189). Part of the wonder and greatness of our present narrative is that Yahweh is not controlled by neat editorial formulations but acts, according to the narrative, in freedom beyond what we expect. In this text that mystery of God is effected as rescue.

TWO JUDEAN KINGS, A SERIES OF NORTHERN NONDESCRIPTS

2 Kings 15:1-38

This chapter continues the chronicle of the twin monarchies. The chapter is bracketed by reports on two Judean kings, Azariah (15:1-7) and his son Jotham (15:32-38). Between the narrative account of the two, father and son, five Northern kings—well, scarcely kings—are treated in turn, Zechariah (15:8-12), Shallum (15:13-15), Menahem (15:16-22), Pekahiah (15:23-26), and Pekah (15:27-31).

COMMENTARY

Azariah, a Great King in Miniature, 15:1-7

Azariah, also called Uzziah, was one of the great kings of Judah. [Uzziah] His long reign of fifty-two years is staggering in length (783–742) and, according to 2 Chronicles 26, staggering in success; he is portrayed as a great builder, a great warrior, and a great developer. That his reign is nearly coterminal with the long, successful reign of Jeroboam II in the North indicates that the two realms enjoyed a long season of peace and prosperity (see 14:23-29).

One would not, however, guess such achievements from our narrative that is divided into three brief parts. We are offered an introductory formula (15:1-2), a theological verdict of qualified approval (15:3-4), and a concluding formula (15:7-6). The only particular item beyond conventional formulation that interests the narrator is in v. 5. The king was leprous; his contagious skin disease made him disqualified for the sacral functions of kingship and so

---

Uzziah

This same king, Azariah, is elsewhere referred to as Uzziah (see 2 Kgs 15:13, 30-34; 2 Chron 26, 27:2; Isa 1:1; 6:1; 7:1; Hos 1:1; Zech 14:5). It may be that the two names are simply slight variants in the single name; or it may be that one name is a personal name and the other a throne name. Nothing is to be made of the distinction, but it is important to recognize that the two names refer to the same king so that all of the traditions can be properly related to a single person.

disqualified him as king. As he retained his titular role as king, his son Jotham was apparently coregent and effectively the ruler of the realm for much of his reign.

While the parallel account of 2 Chronicles 26 is beyond the scope of our work here, its variation from our report is so remarkable that attention must be paid to it. That longer account is divided into two symmetrical parts. First, Azariah (Uzziah in 2 Chron) is positively portrayed with great appreciation. He is given a positive theological verdict without any qualification (26:4-5). He is celebrated for his great building activities and his successful conduct of war, his mustering and equipping of a great military force. In particular we may observe three celebrative affirmations of the king:

> The Ammonites paid tribute to Uzziah, and his fame spread even to the border of Egypt, for he became very strong. (2 Chron 26:8)

He is known abroad for his great political, economic, and military strength. Second, he developed agriculture, perhaps operating an early "A & M" school, because, says the narrative, "he loved the soil" (2 Chron 26:10). Third, the concluding affirmation is a remarkable theological statement with a passive verb:

> And his fame spread far, for he was marvelously helped until he became strong. (2 Chron 26:15)

He was "marvelously helped." The text does not identify the agent of the verb, but it is clearly Yahweh, as in 2 Chronicles 26:5: "God made him prosper."

In 2 Chronicles 26:16, the narrative abruptly reverses field and offers one of the harshest judgments on any king (2 Chron 26:16-23). He was "proud" in his strength; he was "false" to Yahweh. He sought to usurp priestly prerogatives. (It is important to remember that the Chronicler's version of Israelite kings is focused on the role, responsibilities, and rights of priests, on which see 2 Kgs 12:9-16). As a consequence of his usurpation, he became leprous, clearly here understood as punishment from Yahweh. The punishment led to his acute isolation and removal from effective royal power (2 Chron 26:21). In the end he is given a dismissive verdict echoing the "old" laws against uncleanness that put the rejected outside the community and beyond the pale of Yahweh's presence and mercy. [He Is Leprous]

When we read the presentation of Azariah/Uzziah according to the Chronicler, we may be impressed with the great restraint of the Kings version. In our text, there is no heavy theological judgment attached to his leprosy, which is treated in a much more minimalist way. Nonetheless, because his leprosy is the only datum given us beyond the conventional formulae, we may conclude that his leprosy was indeed a defining mark of his long rule, a defining mark that made his rule a deep shadow on the history of kingship.

The Fifth Generation: Zechariah, 15:8-12

In 10:30, it is declared that the Jehu dynasty will last only four generations. Thus far it has: Jehu, Jehoahaz, Jehoash, and Jeroboam. The point is recalled in verse 12. Zechariah, son of Jeroboam, is fifth in a line of four. He is beyond the promise of Yahweh and cannot succeed. This is the most important claim made for him. Thus he lasts on the throne only six months, is a victim of a conspiracy, and is "struck down in public." His short reign once more attests to the instability of the Northern throne. For our narrator, what counts is the limit of Yahweh's promise to the dynasty, beyond which royal power is impossible.

A King a Month, 15:13-15

Shallum is the killer of Zechariah and the terminator of the dynasty of Jehu. That is all he is, nothing more. He lasted a month in power. His month begins with his killing. That same month ends in his being killed. His "reign," if it can be called that, is reminiscent

---

He Is Leprous

The matter of leprosy is, of course, a physical condition that threatened the health of the community. But along with its force as a condition, it is also a verdict uttered by an authoritative priest, a diagnosis that consigns the victim to a certain social status. Thus it is likely that the king was not only seen to have leprosy, but was *declared* a leper and thereby marginated in the community. The status of a leprous king is surely related to the priestly regulations:

> The priest shall make an examination, and if the eruption has spread in the skin, the priest shall pronounce him unclean: it is a leprous disease. (Lev 13:8; see Lev 13:15, 17, 25, 28, 37, 44, 45, 46)

Gerhard von Rad has suggested that this uttered verdict, "He is leprous, he is unclean," is reflected in the verdict declared in Gen 15:6, "He is righteous." [Gerhard von Rad, "Faith Reckoned as Righteousness," *The Problem of the Hexateuch and Other Essays* (New York: McGraw-Hill, 1966) 125-30.] Very much depends upon uttered verdict by an authorized official. This king was given a verdict that excluded him from royal function.

of Zimri who lasted only a week (1 Kgs 16:15). Yahweh is nowhere mentioned in connection with him. He is a man of violence, remote from any intention Yahweh may have for kingship. The monarchy in Israel is clearly an institution that has lost its way, even its *raison d'etre*.

Menahem: Enter Assyria, 15:16-22

The parade of violence continues. Menahem—next in succession, next in violence (see v. 14), next without pedigree or legitimacy—of course receives a wholly negative theological verdict, even though he lasted as long as ten years.

The defining fact of his reign, however, has nothing to do with him. The defining reality is Pul, king of Assyria. [Tiglath-pileser III]

During the reign of Menahem, Tiglath-pileser III comes to power in Assyria. He is a great imperial leader, one of the great ones of the ancient Near East. He transforms the kingdom of Assyria into the dominant power of the Fertile Crescent, a power distinguished in its brutality, that will, at its zenith, extend its control into the far reaches of Egypt. From this point on, for over a century, Israel and Judah are drawn definitively and irresistibly into Assyria's sphere of influence. For all practical purposes, the kings in Samaria and Jerusalem are puppet figures who have no autonomy but who govern according to the little maneuverability left them by Assyrian policy and Assyrian capriciousness.

The aggressive moves of Tiglath-pileser III in and through Israel can be understood as commonsense imperial expansionism and a desire to reach the Mediterranean Sea, and so to open up huge commercial and military opportunities. Indeed Tiglath-pileser made thirty-eight military drives in the direction of Israel and the Sea. The policies and conduct of the Assyrians, moreover, were oppressive, exploitative, and brutalizing, all of which is readily understood in terms of a characteristic superpower unchecked either by any moral sensitivity or by any counterpower. As Assyria comes to loom large on the screen of biblical awareness, we watch the muscle flexing of the "last superpower" left standing. It is striking that in our text, no particular theological role or dimension is assigned to Assyria (as it is in

Tiglath-pileser III

This king rules in Nineveh for a long period (745–727 BC) and is one of the greatest kings of the ancient Near East. He is also mentioned in the biblical accounts by his nickname, Pul. While the biblical narrative has him preoccupied with Israel and Judah, in fact he had no continuing interest in such small states. His policy aims were to have access to the Mediterranean Sea and to establish trading lines with Egypt. It so happened that it was necessary to pass through (and control) territory in the states of Israel and Judah in order to achieve larger policy aims. He is the first in the line of Assyrian kings who will dominate these smaller states in brutal ways for the next century.

In this relief, Tiglath-pileser receives three emissaries while a warrior prostrates himself at his feet. Such limestone reliefs were located along the courtyard walls of his royal palace at Nimrud and were used to impress and intimidate the visitors to the palace. Above the figures cuneiform inscriptions describe a military campaign.

Tiglath-pileser III Receiving Homage from a Vanquished Warrior. 745–727 BC. Limestone. South-west palace, Nimrud (Kalah) Mesopotamian, Neo-Assyrian period. The Detroit Institute of the Arts, Detroit, MI. (Credit: The Bridgeman Art Library/Founders Society, Ralph Harman Booth Bequest Fund)

Isa 10:5). What we have in the text is a matter-of-fact report on the irresistible military power of the empire.

Also matter-of-factly, we are told that Menahem, the weak and vulnerable king in Samaria who is without legitimacy beyond the capacity to kill his predecessor (15:14), coped with Assyrian aggression by offering a huge amount of "protection money," one thousand talents of silver. The money can be perceived simply as buying off Tiglath-pileser as a kind of bribe. Put in more political language, this is "tribute money" that a client state pays to the patron state for protection. (See 1 Kgs 4:21 when the money flowed to Jerusalem under Solomon and not the other direction, out of Israel.) The wording of v. 19 suggests that Menahem willingly entered the Assyrian sphere of influence and accepted his role as a puppet figure for the Assyrians. Clearly Menahem served only by their leave and as long as his conduct befitted their policies. Indeed it is difficult to imagine what alternative to accommodation Menahem might have had. It would seem that if he had resisted Assyria—refused to pay and to cooperate—the Assyrians might have readily and easily replaced him with a more pliable accommodator.

The narrator, moreover, remembers that Menahem paid protection money to Assyria in the only way possible, by taxation upon the wealthy. Indeed, the narrative even remembers the amount of taxation. It is plausible to imagine that Menahem, on account of the taxes, could not have been a popular figure among wealthy

A Prophetic Anticipation

The prophetic connection made between internal antisocial behavior and the external threat of Assyria is remarkable; the prophets insist on the moral, covenantal linkage between the internal and external. The point is made clear in the rather characteristic prophetic speech of judgment in Amos 4:1-3:

Hear this word, you cows of Bashan
   who are on Mount Samaria,
who oppress the poor, who crush the needy,
   who say to their husbands:
   "Bring something to drink!"
The Lord GOD has sworn by his holiness:
   The time is surely coming upon you,
when they shall take you away with hooks,
   even the last of you with fishhooks.
Through breaches in the wall you shall leave,
   each one straight ahead;
   and you shall be flung out into Harmon, says the LORD.

---

opinion-makers in his realm. Perhaps he lasted on the throne as long as he did, ten years, because not even his opponents could think of a better alternative response to the empire.

Son of Menahem, 15:23-26

Menahem had no claim to legitimacy as king, only a fragile hold on power due to his uneasy accommodation to Assyria. His son Pekahiah had even less claim to the throne and is dispatched in short order by a conspiracy. The narrator knows the names of the king-killers, not only Pekah who succeeded to the throne, but also Argob and Arieh (15:25). The narrative is terse; we are not told the reason for the regicide. Two alternative explanations occur. First, because Menahem is an accommodator to Assyrian policy, it is possible that Pekah represents a counter political opinion that Israel should not so readily submit to Assyria, but should enact a policy of independence. Such an explanation is possible (a policy apparently urged by the prophet Isaiah in the South), and we may suppose that this entire series of conspiracies in the royal household reflects policy disputes. That explanation, however, is doubtful in this case, because Pekah rules, apparently without distraction, for twenty years, a situation Assyria would not likely accept were he a confirmed anti-Assyrian.

An alternative explanation for the conspiracy is that governmental matters in Samaria had completely deteriorated (as in recent Beirut), so that different groups of thugs simply competed for power; no faction had any claim to legitimacy more than any other, and no faction in fact had a policy proposal beyond the desire to exercise power. It is at any rate important to recognize what must have been the near-chaos of politics in Samaria, partly caused by the growing and inescapable threat of Assyria, and partly produced, as the prophecies of Amos and Hosea had anticipated, by the unravelling of the social fabric of Samaria (see Amos 4:1-3, 6-16; Hos 8:4-6; 9:16-17; 10:7-8; 13:1-3). [A Prophetic Anticipation] It is noteworthy that the murder of Pekahiah occurred "in the citadel of the palace," suggesting deep internal tension and intrigue in the royal entourage.

Assyrian Domination, 15:27-31

Perhaps we are to think of Pekah, Argob, and Arieh as a junta that seized the government, and Pekah as not more than the titular head of the junta (15:25). In any case, Pekah made his power seizure in Samaria stick for twenty years. In the end, he is killed, even as he killed his predecessor. The tail end of the royal timeline in Samaria makes no pretense of legitimacy for any of its occupants, none of whom has a chance to found any dynasty with any stability. In this case, the king-killer is Hoshea, on whom see 17:1-4.

The dominant fact of the twenty years of Pekah, as with Menahem before him, is Tiglath-pileser and the Assyrians. Now, compared with the earlier years of Menahem, Assyrian pressure is more constant and more immediate. Now the empire will not be bought off with tribute money. Now there is conquest and occupation, so that the governable land of the Samarian ruler is sharply reduced. [Map: The Loss of Territory] Samaria is reduced so as to be confined to the territory immediately around the city of Samaria. The Assyrians, moreover, enacted their recurring policy of deportation. The empire displaced the population of leading citizens, likely as a device to prevent any challenge to the imposed domination. The Assyrians are determined to preclude any movement of agitation toward independence from the policies and requirements of the empire.

Jotham, Son of Azariah, 15:32-38

We are now permitted to take a break from the dizzying instability of the Northern government to take up again the Davidic line in Jerusalem that still has the appearance of stability. We have already seen that Jotham acted as regent for his disqualified father, Azariah (15:5). Now Jotham becomes king in his own right. His theological

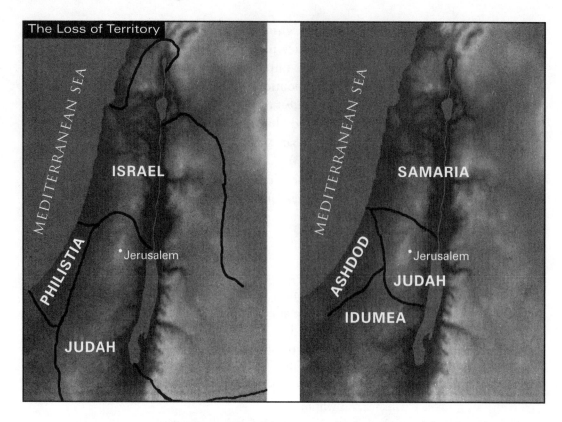

The Loss of Territory

verdict is among those most surely approved by the narrative, though with the qualifying "nevertheless" that we have come to expect. His reign of sixteen years, 742–735, was a prosperous one, continuing the prosperity of the long reign of his father over which he had presided.[1] He is noted in the narrative as a builder. In our text, only one project is mentioned to his credit, "the upper gate of the House of the Lord" (15:35). The parallel account of 2 Chronicles 27:3-6 offers more detail, suggesting that Jotham's extensive royal building enterprise is related to his military successes that assured both the stability and the necessary financial resources for the building projects. Clearly, the Southern regime, the one in whom our narrator is finally interested, enjoys, for this brief moment, a period of stability quite in contrast to the anarchy of the North.

That stability, however, is characteristically at risk. In v. 37, our narrative signals a threat against the Jerusalem government from the small states of Israel (and its king, Pekah) and Syria (and its king, Rezin). These small states to the north of Judah are, of course, increasingly aware of and alarmed by the increasing pressure and presence of Assyria. They propose to form a coalition of small states in order to resist the encroachment of the empire. They offer the Jerusalem government poor choices, *either* to join the alliance and resist Assyria *or* to reject the alliance and enlist with Assyria. There is no good choice. Jotham, cleverly, declines the choice and leaves the terrible question to his son, Ahaz. While Assyria has not yet reached the gates of Jerusalem—as it has the suburbs of Samaria— the empire is nonetheless the defining fact for South as for North. The options for Jerusalem are not good, and the future holds only deep trouble for the regime and the city.

CONNECTIONS

The narrator has chosen to present the downward slide of Israel and Judah into defeat, exile, and deportation piecemeal, one king at a time. In tracing the distinct periods of rule by different kings, it is important not to miss the big picture. The narrator renders explicit verdicts only upon individual kings. The unstated subtext, however, is that the narrative offers a harsh, negative verdict upon the entire royal history of Samaria and Judah. Thus it is important to see each of the rulers as a part of the larger judgment made in this rendition of Israelite history.

We may comment, in that light, upon three themes in this chapter.

1. Azariah is surely one of the greatest kings of the Davidic dynasty in terms of both length of reign and success. And yet all we are told is that he is ritually unfit for office because of leprosy. Leprosy is a "disease of impurity" that means that the king is cut off from all formal access to Yahweh. Lepers are precluded from the holy place. The holy people of Yahweh are presided over by a dis-qualified king. His son and regent, Jotham, may have conducted the affairs of state effectively, but the condition of leprosy means that Judah is presided over by a king absent from Yahweh's pres-ence. In the total narrative, this leprosy that "exiles" Azariah from Yahweh is a foretaste of the coming exile of Judah when the entire community will be alienated from Yahweh's presence in Jerusalem. This narrative foretaste invites wonderment about *power* cut off from *holiness*, a situation destined for despair and death.

2. The rapid and apparently meaningless succession of illegiti-mate and violent kings in the North after Jeroboam II—Zechariah, Shallum, Menahem, Pekahiah, Pekah, and Hoshea—is surely a pic-ture of instability, a deep disorder that is a harbinger of exile. To be sure, not all these reigns are brief, Menahem lasting ten years, Pekah twenty years; and Hoshea nine years (17:1). But all are ille-gitimate; all are without legitimate successors, save Menahem

📖 **The Force**

I use the term "the force" to refer to the sense of power and legitimacy that has theological dimension, as one "approved of God." In the Saul and David narratives, this force of legitimacy is termed "the spirit," that may be given or withdrawn as God chooses (see 1 Sam 10:6; 11:6; 16:13-16, 23; 18:10; 19:9, 20, 23). In all four gospel accounts, the same imagery is used to characterize the legitimacy of Jesus when the spirit comes down "like a dove" (Matt 3:16; Mark 1:10; Luke 3:22; John 1:32). With the series of kinglets we are presently studying and with all of the Northern kings, there is never any hint of such divine favor or legitimacy. Of course we no longer speak of the legitimacy to rule in this way. In the demise of the presidency of Richard Nixon, however, it was evident that the force had departed him, rendering him incapable of governance. In the late 1990s some of the same questions arose over Bill Clinton's legitimacy and capacity to govern.

whose son lasted only two years. Such illegitimacy surely suggests that "the force" of Yahweh has not been with the Northern governance, so that the judgment against Samaria coming in chapter 17 is already visible in these narratives—for anyone with eyes to see. [The Force]

3. As leprosy foreshadows exile and as royal instability anticipates the chaos of exile, so the arrival of Tiglath-pileser in the home territory of Menahem and Pekah makes the concrete historical agents of exile altogether visible. It is important to recognize that the Bible—and its construal of history—is the tale of a small, vulnerable people whose states are continuously exposed to the policies, aggressions, and whims of the great states. It becomes clear in this chapter that the little states (here Israel, in the next chapter Judah) have little choice, opting, wisely it would seem, to be "Red rather than Dead," that is, choosing to submit rather than to be destroyed. [On Submission as Faith]

Thus the North becomes a puppet state as a way of coping with the resolute imperial threat of Tiglath-pileser. The puppet state is neither as bold or courageous as our narrator would prefer, but kings—or what now pass for kings—have little option, and do not seem to have the theological nerve that the narrator characteristically recommends.

The reader may more fully appreciate the narrow policy options available if we consider, in recent memory, the ways in which the Soviet Union imposed its will on the puppet governments of the Warsaw Pact. The courage of the Czechoslovakians and the Hungarians surely evoked the harshness of the Soviet military. In Prague it was Alexander Dubček who boldly imagined a socialist government "with a human face," only to be immediately and

📖 **On Submission as Faith**

Our narrator inclines to regard resistance to foreign occupation and assertion of independence as acts of fidelity toward Yahweh. Sometimes, however, circumstance dictates otherwise. The most prominent case of submission as faith is in the dominant attitude of the book of Jeremiah toward Babylon. The tradition of Jeremiah, as interpreted by the Deuteronomists, makes resistance to Babylonian power not only foolish politically, but an act of covenantal disobedience; see especially Jeremiah 37:17; 38:1-4, 17-23. Clearly, in the prophetic traditions, what constitutes faithfulness is endlessly disputed; there is no single pat answer to the question which must be discerned and answered according to circumstance. That is, faithfulness is contextual for the prophets.

brutally crushed by tanks. Little states have little choice in the face of big, exploitative states.

The shoe on the other foot is not different. In the West, the U.S., like the Soviet Union in the East, is often seen as replicating the intrusive, demanding quality of Assyria in our narrative.

Power looms large in the interplay of imperial advance and dependent state. We likely miss much of the point if we read our chapter simply as a dismal recital of petty kings. In truth the names of all of these kings do not count for much. What counts is imperial power that preempts the life of the two small states. Biblical faith—as long ago as Egypt and as soon to come as Babylon, Persia, and Rome, even without pondering the great modern empires culminating in the U.S.S.R. and the U.S.—always lives in the face of such threatening power. These great powers are dominant, even if one cannot determine if they are the great *nemesis* of Yahweh's purposes in the world or if they are, unwittingly, the severe *tool* of Yahweh's purposes in the world. On occasion they play both roles in biblical construal.[2] All such interpretive options are beneath the surface of our narrative or even just beneath the surface of our own life in the world. The great powers move partly by force, partly by hegemonic seduction, partly by idolatry that seems true. All the while, the believing community must find its way amid accommodation, compromise, and resistance. In these two small states, the next moves are up to Ahaz (16:1-20) and Hoshea (17:1-6). In our own time and place, the same issues and dangers operate. There is enough evidence to believe that such leprosy and alienation endlessly bespeak a coming disorder of uncontrollable proportion, all in the name of power. The narrator, from a perspective of convinced faith, tells a sorry truth about then…and about now.

NOTES

[1]The dates for the rule of Jotham are uncertain. It is evident that the dates given in the text are at great variance. Perhaps the longer period of rule assigned to him also reflects the period of his regency for his father Azariah. As elsewhere, it is evident that the dates given us require critical review and assessment.

[2]On Yahweh's governance of the nations, see Walter Brueggemann, *Theology of the Old Testament: Testimony, Dispute, Advocacy* (Minneapolis: Fortress Press, 1997) 492-527.

AHAZ AS A WILLING ACCOMMODATOR

2 Kings 16:1-20

By the time of the death of King Jotham (15:38), Judah—like Israel—was left in a terrible policy bind. Ahaz, son of Jotham, became king and resolved the policy bind. His resolution must have seemed inevitable at the time; in retrospect it was an act of great foolishness. Ahaz receives an unusually long report in our narrative, a report comprising this entire chapter. It begins with a deeply negative theological verdict (16:1-4), offers a statement of the policy problem (16:5-6), and a long review of the royal solution (16:7-18), plus a concluding formula (16:19-20).

COMMENTARY

A Harsh Royal Verdict, 16:1-4

Ahaz's reign in Jerusalem lasted sixteen years though the chronological figures are uncertain, perhaps 735–715. After a sequence of Davidic kings who receive a "yes, but" positive verdict from the narrator, Ahaz is rated as unqualifiedly bad. Indeed, he is as negatively judged as any Northern king. The data, moreover, suggests policies and conduct more resonate with the Omride dynasty before the purge of Jehu, for Ahaz is indicted for religious practices that are deeply inimical to Yahwism. He (a) engaged in the "abominable practices of the nations" (on which see Deut 18:9-12); (b) practiced sacrifice indiscriminately in many places without due regard for the distinctiveness of worship in Jerusalem; [Under Every Green Tree] and (c) specifically made his "son pass through fire" (see Deut 18:10). [Passing through Fire] The narrator is repelled by what is reported, and intends that the reader should be repelled as well. The *theological verdict* of vv. 1-4 provides a context and anticipation for the *political judgment* rendered in the remainder of the chapter. In the judgment of the narrator, infidelity to Yahweh is characteristically linked to weak political leadership that characteristically compromises Jerusalem's independence, that is, that fails to champion the distinctiveness and,

Under Every Green Tree

This phrase has become a slogan in the Old Testament polemic against religious practices that are regarded from the perspective of strict Yahwism to be heterodox. The phrase likely refers to Canaanite religious practices in which the gods of fertility and productivity were associated with green growth, so that religious attentiveness could be exercised anywhere there was green growth. But where the phrase is used in a stylized way in the Old Testament, it likely has no such specific content but refers to any departure from Yahwism. The notion of "fertility religion" may strike the contemporary reader as a practice of sexuality. More likely it is to be understood as any technology or technique designed for self-securing. Taken in that way, the entire enterprise of TV advertising is an offer of products that by themselves will create safety and well-being. Every such ad approximates such "green trees."

See Susan Ackerman, *Under Every Green Tree: Popular Religion in Sixth-Century Judah,* (Harvard Semitic Monograph (Atlanta: Scholars Press, 1992).

---

therefore, the independence of the political realm as a realm fully obedient to Yahweh alone.

The Problem Faced by Ahaz, 16:5-6

The foreign policy problem faced by Ahaz and the Jerusalem government was the one left him by his father Jotham (15:37). The small states of Syria and Israel attacked Judah in an attempt to force Judah into an alliance against the looming imperial threat of Assyria. That assault against Jerusalem in 734–732 is termed by scholars "the Syro-Ephraimite War" (Syro = Syria, Ephraimite= North Israel). [The Syro-Ephraimite War] What must have been a major crisis in Jerusalem at the time is passed over quickly by the narrator; we must, however, notice the deep threat of that war or we will not appreciate the desperate action Ahaz took in response to it. It is clear that military preoccupation detracted and weakened the Jerusalem establishment from other matters, for it is at the same time that Jerusalem lost territory to the south to the kingdom of Edom (on which see 14:7). Clearly Ahaz was not able simultaneously to maintain two military fronts toward the alliance to the north and toward Edom to the south.

AΩ **Passing through Fire**

This phrase refers to the sacrifice of a child in an act of religious devotion. Certainly by the time of our text it has become a slogan used as a polemic against non-Yahwistic religious practices that were regarded as manipulative acts without theological seriousness. Jon Levenson has provided a subtle argument that in the early practice of Israel, before such phrasing became polemical, there may have been the offering of sons in devotion to Yahweh.

See Jon D. Levenson, *The Death and Resurrection of the Beloved Son: The Transformation of Child Sacrifice in Judaism and Christianity* (New Haven: Yale University Press, 1993). The point is a vexed one, but this text entertains no such vexation in its simple polemic.

We may cite two matters to indicate the importance of the military threat against Jerusalem. First, Pekah is twice referred to in the context of the war as "son of Remaliah" (15:37; 16:5; see 15:27). It is probable that this is his father's true name. Reference to it nonetheless

The Syro-Ephraimite War

This phrase is used by scholars to refer to the brief military encounter between Syria and Israel on the one hand and Judah on the other. The aim of the two northern states was to force Judah into an alliance to resist Assyria that is the looming threat to all of these states. While the skirmish between these states is of interest to us, the entire crisis needs to be seen as a subset to the overall Assyrian threat. Specifics about the war are largely uncertain, both because the relation of Old Testament prophetic texts to the war is largely conjectural, and because extrabiblical texts are far from clear.

Henri Cazelles, "Syro-Ephraimite War," ABD 6:282-85, has summarized the text and data available on the subject from nonbiblical sources. For a more detailed discussion, see M. E. W. Thompson, *Situation and Theology: Old Testament Interpretations of the Syro-Ephraimite War,* Prophets and Historians Series (1 Sheffield: Sheffield Academic Press, 1982).

---

reminds every hearer that he is an illegitimate upstart with no authentic royal claim or pedigree. He is in fact a nobody and, therefore, not to be taken with excessive seriousness. The citing of the "nobody pedigree" is perhaps war propaganda, not unlike the current fashion in the U.S. to refer to President Hussein of Iraq only as "Saddam," that is, by his first name as a way of demeaning the enemy.

Second and more important, the particular data of 15:37, 16:5 is taken up by the prophet Isaiah in what must have been his intense engagement in the crisis of 734–732. The prophet also alludes specifically to the two kings, Rezin of Damascus and "the son of Remaliah" (Isa 7:8-9). In the latter case, the prophet does not even call Pekah by his name, thus becoming even more dismissive of the upstart. The prophet addresses the king, Ahaz, and assures the king that these two upstarts to the north are not a durable threat and the king should not base policy on that momentary threat:

It shall not stand,
    and it shall not come to pass.
For the head of Aram is Damascus,
    and the head of Damascus is Rezin.
(Within sixty-five years Ephraim will be shattered, no longer a people.)[1]
The head of Ephraim is Samaria,
    and the head of Samaria is the son of Remaliah. (Isa 7:7-9b)

The oracle intends to assure Ahaz that the threat from the North "shall not stand...shall not come to pass." This famous prophetic oracle is matched in the preceding prose that is addressed to the king in his moment of anxiety when he examines the water supply of the city:

Take heed, be quiet, do not fear, and do not let your heart be faint because of these two smoldering stumps of firebrands, because of the fierce anger of Rezin and Aram and the son of Remaliah. (Isa 7:4-6)

What the prophet apparently knows is that if the king in Jerusalem is excessively anxious about this threat, he is likely to make an appeal to Assyria, an appeal the prophet regards as disastrous (an appeal that the king does in fact make). To appeal to Assyria against these petty kings is a decision to go from the frying pan into the fire.

With this analysis of the situation, the king is confronted with difficult policy options: (a) surrender to the coalition of states, (b) appeal to Assyria, or (c) as offered by the prophet:

If you do not stand firm in faith,
　you shall not stand at all. (Isa 7:9c)

The alternative is *faith*, to count on the reliability of Yahweh as a matter of policy, to reckon Yahweh to be a real player in geopolitics, a force stronger than either the coalition or the empire. [Faith as Policy] The prophet addresses the king in a way that our narrative would approve by appealing to serious Yahwism. "Faith" here is not assent to doctrine nor is it an easy piety. It is rather an elemental confidence in the trustworthiness of the promise and presence of God, so that policy need not be an enactment of fear, anxiety, or compromise that causes the king to violate the very character of the community over which the king presides.[2] Isaiah speaks out of the depth of biblical tradition that characteristically asserts that the public processes include the inscrutable, decisive

---

Faith as Policy

Gerhard von Rad has seen most clearly that the prophecy of Isaiah in the context of the Syro-Ephraimite War is the matrix in which a firm understanding of faith has emerged. [Gerhard von Rad, *Theology of the Old Testament II* (San Francisco: Harper & Row, 1965), 160-61.] Faith means "leaving room for God's sovereign action, desisting from self-help…. Isaiah demanded of his contemporaries that they should now make their existence rest on a future action of God." While that option is not explicit in our text, it is clear that Ahaz represents the complete antithesis to such a notion. Von Rad has suggested that the emergence of faith in such a national emergency is informed by the old practice of "holy war" when trust meant to rely upon Yahweh to fight battles for Israel. The classic text to which von Rad appeals is Exodus 14:13-14, 31:

But Moses said to the people, "Do not be afraid, stand firm, and see the deliverance that the LORD will accomplish for you today; for the Egyptians whom you see today you will never see again. The LORD will fight for you, and you have only to keep still…. Israel saw the great work that the LORD did against the Egyptians. So the people feared the LORD and believed in the LORD and in his servant Moses."

The Virgin as Time Clock

The prophet's estimate of the Syro-Ephraimite War occurs in Isaiah 7, the text that has been crucial to biblical evidence for "the virgin birth" (on which see Matt 1:18-25). It is important, in the context of the war, to see clearly the use made of "the virgin." Whoever she may be, her function is to bear a son who will know "good and evil," a time usually reckoned for a child as two years. That is, the entire reference to mother and child is simply a poetic, prophetic way of setting a time limit on the threat from the north. The intent is that the threat will last no longer than the first early moral awareness of a child, that is, the limited span of two years.

participation of Yahweh, so that the future of public matters is not to be reduced to visible power players. While Isaiah's oracle is not present in our chapter, it makes most sense to assume that in the purview of our narrator, who always affirms that trust in Yahweh matters decisively, the invitational oracle of Yahweh through Isaiah must be heard just at the end of our verse 6. One policy option open to the king in Jerusalem is to remain steadfast and not to panic in the face of the immediate threat.

The Solution Chosen by Ahaz, 16:7-20

We already know from vv. 2-4 that Ahaz is not a reliable Yahwist. He is an accommodator and compromiser; we might term him a religious pragmatist. Such pragmatism will never evoke hard, courageous acts or policies that rely upon a single, overriding commitment. Thus, it does not surprise us that Ahaz will not listen to Isaiah, will not govern out of confidence, but will make the crucial policy decision on the basis of short-term anxiety. The rejection of Isaiah's word is not only a rejection of Yahweh. It is also a rejection of Isaiah's political analysis. The prophet had declared that the coalition to the north is a momentary threat that will evaporate within two years, so that policy based on that threat is foolish and near-sighted. [The Virgin as Time Clock]

As our text has it, however, it appears that Ahaz did not even weigh political alternatives. He did what he had decided to do long before any critical reflection. He did what he had decided to do through the process of accommodation and compromise. When the crunch time came, he had no way to appeal to a sturdy Yahwism he had already refused; consequently he looked outside Yahwism for help. All that was out there beyond Yahweh was Assyria. He appealed to Tiglath-pileser! (16:7). [Tiglath-pileser III] This is the same Tiglath-pileser whom Menahem had bought off (15:19-20) and to whom Pekah had lost territory (15:29). The Northern population was already well-schooled in the fierce and demanding ways of Tiglath-pileser and had witnessed the deportation from

Samaria. Now Ahaz, shamelessly and without seeing beyond his own nose, appeals to the very force that was the primal threat to his throne. Because of Ahaz's appeal, Tiglath-pileser need not force his way into Judah. He is invited in by the king, devoured by anxiety, devoured by anxiety because he has long since expelled any serious Yahwism that might counter his anxiety. The narrative intends us to sense his dismay: He sends to Tiglath-pileser!!

The message of Ahaz to Tiglath-pileser, his desperate S.O.S., is terse and telling:

> I am your servant and your son. Come up, and rescue me from the hand of the king of Aram and from the hand of the king of Israel, who are attacking me. (16:7)

The self-identification of Ahaz as "your servant and your son" is a formula of submission and surrender, a deep act of self-abasement. From the rigorous Yahwistic perspective reflected in our narrative, the Davidic king can only be *son and servant* of Yahweh (see Ps 2:7; 2 Sam 7:14; Ps 89:20, 26). Thus the submission of the king to Tiglath-pileser is a direct repudiation of the identity of the Jerusalemite king and a rejection of the only theological rationale for the Davidic kingdom. As the roles, son and servant, are misappropriated in this act of surrender, so the two imperatives "come up" and "rescue" are verbs that characteristically belong in an address to Yahweh. Ahaz, however, has no knowledge of or confidence in Yahweh, and so must redirect the verbs of petition to the only source of help he can envision. This speech is a stunning departure from and rejection of not only Isaiah's counsel but the entire ideological apparatus of the Jerusalem kings. Ahaz has traded sovereigns and has done so in a moment of anxiety that, from a Yahwist perspective, is insane and suicidal.

Tiglath-pileser III

This Assyrian king, also called Pul in the text, dominated the Fertile Crescent for the period of his rule, 745–727 BC. It is therefore not surprising that he is the defining power and presence in the foreign policy of Israel and Judah. As he seized land from Israel during the time of Pekah (15:29), so he intimidated the South under the rule of Ahaz. His successors on the Assyrian throne terminated the government of Samaria and, as we shall see, displaced its leading citizens. That Judah was able to withstand the Assyrian threat is a cause for wonder and is regarded in the Bible itself as a miracle of Yahweh's deliverance. As becomes immediately evident in 20:12-19, escape from the threat of Assyria only postponed Judean fate until the rise of Babylon whose policies replicated those of Assyria. Thus Tiglath-pileser may be reckoned as the primal agent in initiating the imperial process that eventually caused the termination of both states.

The verbal appeal to Assyria requires only one verse. By contrast, the enactment of allegiance to Tiglath-pileser and the payments of the requisite costs require a long narrative account (16:8-18).

Tiglath-pileser, like every leader of a superpower, is not impressed with words from a lesser power. It takes deeds, specifically economic deeds, "tribute," because empires are fundamentally money-collecting machines for the benefit of those who control power. The term used in v. 8 in NRSV is "present." That is what Ahaz sent to Assyria, valuables from the entire royal establishment, including the temple. The Hebrew term is *hohad*, elsewhere rendered "bribe." The "present" was sufficient; Tiglath-pileser moved promptly against Syria, sacked Damascus, and killed the Syrian king. That part of Isaiah's analysis proved correct. Half of the threatening coalition is gone in quick order. That much of the alliance is an illusion. All it took was a little cash from Jerusalem to Nineveh.

Ahaz, however, goes further to assure solidarity with Assyria, the "big kid on the block." He goes to Damascus where Tiglath-pileser is ensconced in victory as an occupying force. We may believe that in Damascus papers were signed; agreements were reached, and promises were made between the winner and the petitioner. The actual physical journey to Damascus was a dramatic act of submission by the "son and servant" to Judah's new "master and father."

Such a political act, in that ancient world and perhaps always, has a religious, ideological dimension. King Ahaz was attracted to the altar in Damascus (v.10). The altar is not described. But we may believe it was not an altar of the defeated Syrian apparatus, but an altar on which offerings were made to the victorious Assyrian gods. That is, Ahaz's attraction to the altar is not simply aesthetic; it is political. The new alliance must allow for religious affiliation to the gods of Tiglath-pileser.[3] The "model" for the altar is sent to Jerusalem. The altar is quickly replicated in Ahaz's city. Upon returning to Jerusalem, Ahaz must promptly, publically enact his new, defining loyalty, a public enactment that he appears to undertake with zeal.

Upon return from his submissive parley in Damascus, the king must promptly act as high priest. (Jerusalem kings are always high priests, but normally in the service of Yahweh.) Here an old role is devoted to a new god.

The redeployment of royal loyalty is so intense that the old bronze altar to Yahweh is sidelined to make room, liturgical room, for Ahaz's new devotion. Nothing could more dramatically enact changed loyalty than a transfer of altars. "The great altar," the one imitating the imperial altar in Damascus, now claims the king's religious energy and passion (16:15): morning burnt offering, evening grain offering, king's burnt offering, grain offering, burnt offering, grain offering, drink offering, burnt offering, all the blood of sacrifice. The recital is punctilious; this is passionate, exaggerated, overstated religious enthusiasm. Everyone can see; hopefully the empire receives a report on the zeal of this "new convert."

The footnote of v. 15 is odd and noteworthy. As though as a modest gesture to the old Yahwistic ways, the old bronze altar is allowed one function; "enquiry" whereby the king receives guidance on policy. It is as though Ahaz cannot quite shake off the old Yahwism retained in an unnoticed corner of his practice. The empire would not like that perhaps, so it is a quiet report at the end of the bombast. Even after the big extravaganza of the new altar, the king dissembles, as will a coward without any genuine faith.

Ahaz, however, is not yet finished (16:17-20). Before he finishes, the king will sack his own temple in Jerusalem and strip it of its valuable and impressive adornment in order to send the valuables of bronze to Assyria as another gesture of appeasement and compliance. The statement is governed by verbs of strong action, "cut off,…remove,…remove." The temple that his Davidic ancestors had worked so hard to beautify, that had come to symbolize not only well-being but also presence, that was "beautiful in elevation…the joy of all the earth" (Ps 48:2), all that is now dispatched by the very king who benefitted from the temple and who was sworn to protect and enhance it.

The narrator is, I suggest, scandalized and astounded at the practice that must be reported. The inevitable question is, why would a king sack his own temple? The answer of course is, "because of the king of Assyria" (16:18). Perhaps Tiglath-pileser's demands for valuable goods from Ahaz as protection money were limitless. Likely the king was so anxious to please that he operated with a zeal beyond the demands of the empire in order to protect himself and to impress his new overlords. No doubt the king was driven by anxiety so acute that it amounted to a paralysis of policy. Indeed, the king imagined that he had no option. Read theologically, the king had no option because he had exchanged the sovereignty of Yahweh for the sovereignty of Assyria (see Jer 2:11). Given this theological commitment that is a commitment beyond political convenience, it followed that one must take the valuables dedicated to Yahweh (already in 1 Kgs 8) and "rededicate" them to the new overlord, Tiglath-pileser and his imperial gods. The narrative, in its understatement, will not let us separate political pragmatism from theological commitment. As Ahaz had political commitments to Yahweh, so now he enacts theological loyalty to Tiglath-pileser.

The concluding formula of vv. 19-20 is lean and sober. But perhaps it is its very leanness that is to be noticed. The two verses by themselves suggest that all is in order. Following what has gone before, however, the two verses ironically insist that everything is in disarray. It is time for the king to die, because he has completed his scandalous work of alienating his throne from the God who guarantees it.

CONNECTIONS

Like his father Jotham before him (15:37), Ahaz was confronted with a terrible policy decision. He either had to capitulate to the threatening alliance of small states (Syria and Israel), or he had to sign on with the rising empire. It was a terrible either/or. He chose "or," appealing to the big power against the immediate threat of the small powers. In fact, Ahaz unwittingly chose long-term trouble of immense proportion instead of the short-term threat that quickly evaporated. On geopolitical grounds, he chose badly.

If, however, we permit the prophet Isaiah to have his say during that Syro-Ephraimite War, then the theological issue is not a wrong political choice among available options. The theological issue is that the king failed to consider all of his options. He thought, by a study of the map, that he had two options, small coalition or large empire. It is the insistence of prophetic faith that beyond the two obvious policy options there is a third policy choice of trust in Yahweh that is not simply pious talk. It permits the conduct of power with unflappable courage in an act of confidence and independence that refuses any of the other choices, all of which are foolish and destructive. The hard case to make, which prophetic faith always seeks to make, is that this third option is a real option in the world of *Realpolitik.*

> For thus said the Lord GOD, the Holy One of Israel:
> In returning and rest you shall be saved;
> > in quietness and in trust shall be your strength.
> (Isa 30:15)

The policy option of the prophet is to act soberly, with discipline and without panic. But, says the tradition, Judah refused that option and so was routed:

> But you refused and said,
> "No! We will flee upon horses"—
> therefore you shall flee
> and, "We will ride upon swift steeds"—
> therefore your pursuers shall be swift!
> A thousand shall flee at the threat of one,
> at the threat of five you shall flee,
> until you are left
> like a flagstaff on the top of a mountain,
> like a signal on a hill. (Isa 30:15c-17)

The theological point is that faith is always a third option in the real world.[4]

Such a claim must not be made lightly, because it insists that the force of Yahweh's will for the world counts in crises. The urging of prophetic faith upon Ahaz is not unlike counseling occupied Poland not to appeal to the Soviet Union in the face of disorder, like advising Panama—let us say—fearful of a threat from Cuba, not to appeal to the U.S. for intervention, because such intervention brings with it unending occupation from "the Colossus of the North." In the crisis of deciding for or against a superpower, it is "natural" (as for Ahaz!) to conclude there are only two options.

More broadly and beyond questions of geopolitics, faith in Yahweh is presented in prophetic tradition as a third alternative that is always choosable, a choice the world would think foolish. Faith is the capacity to believe and act upon the reality of Yahweh's guaranteeing presence in contexts where we lack a capacity for self-guarantee. [Faith as Alternative Choice] Finally we are driven to ponder the decisions of faith made in the Bible's narrative account:

Faith as Alternative Choice

Faith is a conviction that God offers a guarantee of the future:

Now faith is the assurance of things hoped for, the conviction of things not seen. (Heb 11:1)

In the context of Ahaz around whom hovers the alternative of faith offered by Isaiah, it is important to see faith clearly. On the one hand, faith as the prophet characterizes it is a capacity to act differently in the world. On the other hand, it is important to recognize that this faith is in the real world, for faith does not change the hard and dangerous circumstances in the midst of which faith must act. It is unfortunate that in the history of Christian faith, especially under the impetus of the great Luther, faith has been largely reduced to a narrow relationship with God through Jesus. [For an example of such a restrictive view see, Gerhard Ebeling, *The Nature of Faith* (Philadelphia: Fortress Press, 1961). Ebeling offers a magisterial exposition of faith, but the scope of his presentation is narrow indeed and lacks the daring offered in Isaiah's matrix.]

By faith Abraham obeyed when the was called to set out for a place that he was to receive as an inheritance; and he set out, not knowing where he was going. By faith he stayed for a time in the land he had ben promised, as in a foreign land, living in tents, as did Isaac and Jacob, who were heirs with him of the same promise. For he looked forward to the city that has foundations, whose architect and builder is God. By faith he received power of procreation, even though he was too old—and Sarah herself was barren—because he considered him faithful who had promised. Therefore from one person, and this one as good as dead, descendants were born, "as many as the stars of heaven and as the innumerable grains of sand by the seashore."

All of these died in faith without having received the promises, but from a distance they saw and greeted them. They confessed that they were strangers and foreigners in the earth, for people who speak in this way make it clear that they are seeking a homeland. If they had been thinking of the land that they had left behind, they would have had opportunity to return. But as it is, they desire a better country, that is, a heavenly one. Therefore God is not ashamed to be called their God; indeed, he has prepared a city for them. (Heb 11:8-16)

Israel's memory is populated by such enactments of faith. The community knows many of the names of those who chose a third way. In this presentation, King Ahaz is offered by the narrative as a quintessential non-truster who chose foolishly and destructively for his people.

The third option never seems viable in a pragmatic world. It is a viable choice only among those so committed to the tale of faith that Yahweh is known to be a force and agent who matters decisively. The tale of faith, that King Ahaz had long since abandoned, is the story of how Yahweh makes "a way out of no way." The world calls such a "way out of no way" a miracle or even a mirage. The faithful, unlike Ahaz, know better. ["A Way Out of No Way"]

"A Way Out of No Way"

This phrase, as Andrew Young has shown, is a classic articulation of African-American Christian faith that trusted that when there were no resources for life or well-being, God would give a way not yet seen by human agents. [Andrew J. Young, *Way Out of No Way: The Spiritual Memoirs of Andrew Young* (New York: Nelson, 1995).] Young uses the phrase to explicate the work of the Civil Rights Movement in which he was crucially involved. That movement saw doors open when the advocates themselves did not know what to do next. While the phrase arises from the resourcelessness of that community kept largely powerless in the ways of the world, the same phrasing approximates what Isaiah has in mind that Ahaz rejects. The only way he can trust is what he can see, i.e., the way of Assyria. The prophet insists against such a stance that trust in Yahweh will be open to a third way between narrow options.

Such a claim makes no "logical sense" in the corridors of power, but is attested amply by those who have no access to worldly power. Ahaz is a resister to such God-offered openness in the world.

NOTES

[1]The reference to sixty-five years is clearly an intrusion in the text and refers to subsequent matters not available to us. It has no bearing on the proclamation in the oracle itself.

[2]On the matter of faith, reference should be made to the three taunting speeches of the Assyrians to Hezekiah in chapters 18 and 19. It is clear that Assyria is cast in the text as the voice urging unfaith. In response, Hezekiah is portrayed as a model of faith, quite the antithesis to his untrusting father, Ahaz.

[3]It is likely that the Assyrians were not coercive about the embrace of imperial religion by Judah. Rather Judah willingly chose it under Ahaz as a signal of compliance. On this judgment see John McKay, *Religion in Judah under the Assyrians*, SBT, Second Series 26 (Naperville: Allenson, 1973) and Morton Cogan, *Imperial Religion: Assyria, Judah, and Israel in the Eighth and Seventh Centuries BC*, SBL Monograph Series 19 (Missoula: Scholars Press, 1974).

[4]A convenient and accessible review of the issues related to this crisis is offered by Norman K. Gottwald, *All the Kingdoms of the Earth: Israelite Prophecy and International Relations in the Ancient Near East* (New York: Harper & Row, 1964) 148-62.

THE END OF THE
NORTHERN KINGDOM

2 Kings 17:1-41

This extended chapter narrates, with heavy theological accent, the dismal, sorry end of the Northern Kingdom. It divides into two unequal parts. Verses 1-6 provide the concrete data concerning the imperial onslaught against Samaria. It quickly completes the time line of Northern kings with the disposal of Hoshea (17:1-4; see 15:30) and summarizes the harsh policies of the empire (17:5-6). The long second part of the chapter is a theological reflection considering, in turn, the fate of Israel and the fate of the disobedient nations (17:7-41). This latter part of the chapter reflects at great length on the reasons for the concluding devastation of Israel, rereading the history of Israel according to Torah requirements (17:7-22). In this latter section the theological commentary of our narrative is able to look beyond Israel, now devastated, to include other nations in the vast panorama of Yahweh's Torah (17:24-41).

COMMENTARY

The Termination of the Royal Time Line of the North, 17:1-6

The last king of the Northern Kingdom, Hoshea—like Shallum (15:10), Menahem (15:14), and Pekah (15:25) before him—seized the throne in Samaria by violence (15:30). Hoshea has no more legitimacy or claim to the throne than any of his recent predecessors. He is, moreover, ironically named "deliverer," on which see the same name in Matthew 1:21. The verdict he receives on his nine-year rule (732–724) is a mixed one (17:2): *evil* like all of the Northern kings, *yet* not so bad. The verdict is a surprising one, given the fact that the string of kings runs out with him. Perhaps vv. 3-4 hint at the reason Hosea receives a positive "yet" from our narrator. Like his predecessor and like Ahaz in the South, Hoshea knuckled under to Assyria and paid tribute as had they. Indeed, he would have thought, like them, that he had no option but to pay tribute. The only difference is that now he must deal with Shalmaneser V who has

Shalmaneser V

The probable dates of this Assyrian ruler are 726–722 BC. Thus his reign is short and in the overall reality of the empire, he is not very important. Nonetheless he exercises an important impact on Samaria and the kingdom of Israel, for he completed the conquest and destruction of Samaria. Most probably he simply continued the brutal and determined policies set by Tiglath-pileser III; the destruction of Samaria, from an imperial perspective, simply served long-standing imperial purposes of colonization. The view of the narrator, of course, is very different and from a Yahwistic perspective.

---

succeeded Tiglath-pileser III on the Assyrian throne. [Shalmaneser V] The leaders change but the policy of the empire is unaltered. Assyria wants to control access to the Mediterranean Sea. Hoshea, it would appear, is a docile, accepting vassal of the empire.

Verse 4, however, undercuts that relationship of docility and may suggest why Hoshea receives a grudgingly positive affirmation from the narrator. The term rendered "treachery" in NRSV is *qeṣer*, the same term used often for internal "conspiracy" (see 15:10, 25, 30) and now used to characterize resistance to the empire. Hoshea withheld tribute money from Assyria, tribute money that is the measure, guarantee, and purpose of the vassal relationship. Withholding tribute is an overt act of defiance, sure to evoke retaliation from on high, that is, from Nineveh. The narrative suggests that Hoshea felt strong enough to defy Assyria because he had been negotiating with So, Pharaoh of Egypt. [So, a Belated Pharaoh] It is plausible that this act of defiance is the ground for the positive verdict offered in v. 2. Thus our narrator seems regularly to correlate:

So, a Belated Pharaoh

Nothing certain is known of this pharaoh. There is ample scholarly speculation about his identity, but it is no more than speculation. His importance in this narrative is that the pharaoh embodies and typifies the endless capacity of Egypt to intrigue against the power of the North, in this case Assyria. Egypt often played a clever and subtle diplomatic game, seeking to destabilize Northern imperial control. At times Israel and Judah were taken up in such projects. In this case, the Egyptian option turned out to be ineffective. The prophet Isaiah, in this same period, warns that Egypt is an unreliable source of help and alliance (Isa 31:1-3).

> trustworthy Yahwism = political independence;
> compromised Yahwism = accommodation to imperial power.

Given such a correlation, Hoshea may be seen to have a little spine, though as the text has it, his reliance is on Egypt and not on Yahweh, thus hardly meeting the prophetic requirements of faith. In any case, the act of defiance fails and Hoshea pays dearly along with his realm. He is imprisoned by the Assyrians and never heard from again.

His act of defiance, moreover, evoked not only an action against the king, but a decisive, terminating action against the regime in Samaria and the state over which it presides. The empire had concluded that the regime in Samaria would never be a reliable vassal state and so crushed it. The fortified city of Samaria was difficult to take, but Assyria was persistent as well as formidable. The siege of three years (725–722) was successful. The king of Assyria, now Sargon, took the city and deported the leading Israelites, presumably including Hoshea. [Sargon]

We have already seen Assyrian deportation enacted in 15:3, and now it appears to be more wholesale. [Assyrian Deportation] The purpose of deportation, the relocation of large numbers of people, was apparently to dislocate leadership in order to assure that no local movement of resistance or rebellion could ever be undertaken. The leading citizens of the Northern state are scattered across the Fertile Crescent, surely "the Lost Tribes of Israel," simply gone!

A Prophetic Reflection: A Population Removed, 17:7-23

The narrative now reaches a pivotal point in theological reflection upon the sorry story of northern Israel that ends in an ungrieved absorption into the Assyrian empire. This long commentary is verbose and repetitious, but can be read clearly by recognizing two points. First, this commentary is saturated with the most poignantly insistent phrasing of the book of Deuteronomy that is the norm and interpretive standard for this commentary. Second, the thematic development of this theology of Deuteronomy sounds the two characteristic accents of a prophetic speech of judgment, indictment and sentence. Reduced to its most simple claim, the argument is:

Indictment: violation of the first commandment of Sinai;
Sentence: rejection and therefore exile.

The commentary moves through a variety of rhetorical developments, making the

Sargon

Sargon succeeded Shalmaneser V on the throne of Assyria. He was a usurper who seized the throne by violence. He is only mentioned in the Bible in Isa 20:1, and is reckoned the one who completed the conquest of Samaria and the Northern Kingdom after Shalmaneser. In the Assyrian Royal Annals, Sargon boasts:

I besieged and conquered Samaria, led away as booty 27,290 inhabitants of it. I formed from among them a contingent of 50 chariots and made remaining (inhabitants) assume their (social) positions. I installed over them an officer of mine and imposed upon them the tribute of the former king.

ANET 284-85.

Assyrian Warriors. c. 710 BC. Palace of Sargon II at Khorsabad. Iraq Museum, Iraq. (Credit: Scala/Art Resource, NY)

Sargon continues the propagandistic tradition of the Assyrian kings by inundating the walls of his palace at Khorsabad with scenes of his reign. Through the use of limestone reliefs, attention is focused upon the power and fury of his warriors, his ability to rule over his officials, his ability to transport goods, and the tributaries that pay homage to him.

King Sargon II and Official. c. 710 BC. Palace of Sargon II at Khorsabad. Louvre, Paris, France.(Credit: Erich Lessing/Art Resource, NY)

Assyrian Deportation

The imperial strategy of deporting large numbers of peoples was prominent in the regime of Tiglath-pileser III and continues after his time. The purpose of such deportation apparently was to displace potential leaders of rebellion against imperial governance, so that potential leaders were situated in publics that were not their natural constituency. That policy, evidenced in the termination of both kingdoms in ancient Israel, reflects the oppressive capacity of regimes to dominate and control the lives of persons without thought or concern. Perhaps the contemporary counterpart is the endless production of refugees and displaced persons by aggressive military efforts. In the U.S., one might think of "deportation" as a governmental policy with respect to Native Americans who were forcibly deported to "reservations." Special attention might be given to the displacement linked to the "Trail of Tears." Less directly but still on the screen of the same project, one might also consider the U.S. interment of Japanese-Americans during World War II and the endless relocation of poor people and African-Americans in restricted urban zones. Taken most broadly the policy of deportation is still operative wherever government or the corporate economy impinges on the location of people.

---

matter more interesting and more complex, but not departing a great deal from this simple plot line.

In large sweep, the indictment extends from v. 7 through v. 17, governed by the "because" of v. 7. The cause of the sorry crisis of 722 in Samaria is rooted in the will of the Exodus God who at Sinai had said, "No other gods, only Yahweh" (Exod 20:1). The command is total and uncompromising, reflecting Yahweh's jealous character that is defining for the life and faith of Israel as understood by this interpreter.

That single, uncompromising demand of "Yahweh alone," however, was not the way of Israel. Indeed, it has been the purpose of the long recital of Northern kings since 1 Kings 12 to exhibit the characteristic departure from the requirement of Sinai. Israel was endlessly attracted to other loyalties, other gods, and other forms of security. The polemic, characteristically, is against "high places, pillars, and sacred poles," all markers of other religious options, all taken as substitutes for Yahweh. We have already seen in 2 Kings 11 that this vocabulary is rooted in the commands of Deuteronomy 12 that seeks to assert "Yahweh alone."[1] We have seen, moreover, that these religious symbols (that we do not understand in any detail) are not narrowly "religious," but have wide and deep dimensions related to the socioeconomic, political, and moral life of the community. They signify alternative forms of sexuality, economics, and well-being that compromise the single demand of Yahwism.

Israel, says this commentary, is addicted to compromise about fundamentals upon which the well-being of the realm depends. This long commentary functions as a *theodicy*, as a theological justification for the destruction of Israel and its abandonment by Yahweh. The burden of the argument is to establish that Israel

Turn, Listen

It is likely that the two imperative terms, "turn, listen," are thematic and programmatic for the theology of the Deuteronomist:

Indeed, we find the theme "return" in almost all of the important passages which enable us to recognize DtrH's [Deuteronomic Historian's] intention…. In a decisive passage, 2 Kings 17, where DtrH pauses to mediate on the end of the state of Israel, he summarizes (vs. 13) the message of Yahweh spoken "by all prophets and seers of Israel and Judah" as the single word *shûbû*!

Hans Walter Wolff, "The Kerygma of the Deuteronomic Historical Work," *The Vitality of Old Testament Traditions* by Walter Brueggemann and Hans Walter Wolff (Atlanta: John Knox Press, 1982) 90-91.

---

deserved such abandonment and that Yahweh, in this act of termination, has not been fickle or unreliable. That point is especially clear in vv. 13-14, a slight interruption of the indictment. Yahweh has tried, tried repeatedly and incessantly, to warn Israel of its waywardness and to persuade Israel to return to Torah obedience. Yahweh's strategy has been to dispatch numerous prophets—note especially Elijah and Elisha—who incessantly summon Israel away from Baalism and back to Yahwism. It is clear that Deuteronomic theology has here somewhat stylized and programmed prophetic declarations that were not always so clearly a call to "turn." In the hands of this interpreter, however, all prophetic intervention in all of its variations has the single purpose of bringing Israel back to its Yahwistic commitments. Yahweh has tried! The termination is not the fault of Yahweh, who has given ample notice (17:13-14), but the fault of Israel who would not listen. [Turn, Listen]

In v. 14 the indictment against Israel, momentarily interrupted by v. 13, continues. Israel did not "believe" Yahweh. The phrase is better rendered, "did not trust in, did not rely upon, did not see Yahweh as a real alternative." Lacking confidence in Yahweh, they placed their trust elsewhere. [Luther on Trust]

The latter part of the indictment resumes the accusation, and again becomes quite specific (17:15-17). The bill of particulars again includes a sacred pole, but now shows the "true colors" of Jerusalem with the practices of divination, augury, and passing children through fire, all condemned in Deuteronomy 18:9-11, all attributed especially to Ahaz of the South. It is not likely that this inventory of affronts

Luther on Trust

In his famous comment on the first commandment from Sinai, Martin Luther links obedience to the commandment with the capacity for trust amidst the threats of life:

Whatsoever your heart clings to and relies upon, that properly is your God.

That is, adherence to Yahweh does not have to do with formal profession but with the actual living of life according to the will and assurance of God. Given such an understanding of compliance to the commands, this text reflects the judgment that Israel was completely unwilling and unable to practice the commandment of Yahweh's exclusive claim to loyalty.

AΩ **Vapor**
The term "vapor" (that I cite) does not occur in this text but in Jer 2:4, where it is translated "worthless things." This is also the term rendered "vanity" many times in Ecclesiastes. It refers to an emptiness without substance. The gods Israel has worshiped are nothing but vapor, and as a consequence, Israel vaporizes into nonexistence. The term refers to a lack of substance, a quality of the false gods and then, derivatively, a quality of Israel that disappears from the map of the world.

against Yahweh is to be taken with detailed exactitude. Rather we have here a torrent of Deuteronomic phrases, an avalanche of rage in which the punishment "throws the book" (the book of Deuteronomy) in the face of northern Israel.

The outcome is predictable. They worshiped "vapor" and they became "vapor" (17:15). [Vapor] They worshiped unreality and they became unreal. They trusted in phantom promises and became a phantom in the Near East with no bodily, identifiable substance, simply gone, carried away by Assyria and at the behest of Yahweh. The text acutely observes that Israel became like its gods, taking on the quality of that in which it trusts. This is a deep prophetic discernment:

> But they came to Baal-peor,
>   and consecrated themselves to a thing of shame,
>   and became detestable like the thing they loved. (Hos 9:10)

> They went far from me,
>   and went after worthless things,
>   and became worthless themselves. (Jer 2:5)

> Those who make them [idols] are like them;
>   so are all who trust in them. (Ps 115:8)

They have committed to what is unreliable and have, consequently, become unreliable. The term "vapor," what they worship and now embody, functions in v. 15 of our text as an antithesis to the term "believe/trust" (17:14). That Hebrew term means "reliable, trustworthy." Israel had a chance for *trustworthiness* and instead opted for *vapor.*

The sentence of the speech of judgment is sure and harsh (17:18-23). It is introduced by the characteristic, strong, prophetic "therefore" (17:18). Yahweh was angry and departed Israel. Note well, in this reading it is not Sargon or any other Assyrian who did this to Jerusalem. It is the harshness of Yahweh, whose patience had run out on this recalcitrant partner. The last line of v. 18, a recurring note on the horizon of the narrative, is that thus far, Judah is a protected exception (see "yet" in 1 Kgs 11:13). The recognition that Judah will continue when Israel is terminated leads to the momentary digression in v. 19, acknowledging that Judah's survival is not based on obedience, for Judah has been rashly disobedient, as much as has Israel (see Jer 3:6-11). Verse 19 is laid down as a marker, as though the narrative provides a hint of what is to come in the remaining chapters of this narrative that terminates in deportation. That, however, is not a theme developed here.

The sentence continues and now draws to its conclusion (17:20-23). The condemning action of Yahweh is summarized in a series of harsh verbs: reject, punish, gave into, banished, removed. The deportation is not an accident. It is not a matter of Assyrian policy. It is the sure and inevitable enactment of covenant curses that have been known from the outset at Sinai. Yahweh is more harsh than anything the Assyrians could think to do. The punishment is severe and relentless because Israel has continued its scandalous response to Yahweh for a very long time, since Jeroboam in 1 Kings 12. That long time of recalcitrance has finally come to fruition in Yahweh's harshness. That harshness of Yahweh, however, is not a new idea. The prophets have been saying as much incessantly for a long time:

> Therefore thus says the Lord GOD:
> An adversary shall surround the land,
>   and strip you of your defense;
>   and your strongholds shall be plundered. (Amos 3:11)

> The Lord GOD has sworn by his holiness:
>   The time is surely coming upon you,
> when they shall take you away with hooks,
>   even the last of you with fishhooks.
> Through the breaches in the wall you shall leave,
>   each one straight ahead;
>   and you shall be flung out into Harmon, says the LORD.
> (Amos 4:2-3)

> Therefore they shall now be the first to go into exile,
>   and the revelry of the loungers shall pass away. (Amos 6:7)

To be sure, a great contrast exists between these daring prophetic utterances in poetry and the formulaic style of our narrative. In the end, however, they are of a piece. In the end they attest to the shared conviction that life outside Torah will create for Israel an unbearable future of humiliation, suffering, and dislocation. It remains only for the commentator to draw the clear, unambiguous conclusion toward which the entire narrative thus far has led:

> So Israel was exiled from their own land to Assyria until this day. (17:23)

History, so it is asserted, moves from an indictment of "because" to a sentence of "therefore." There is delay in that movement, but there is finally no escape and no slippage. Anyone who looks, the commentator contends, can see that the claims of this speech are abundantly clear on the ground—no apology, no grief, no softness, no giving in. The commentator is as hard and relentless as the God to whom he bears witness.

A Prophetic Reflection on the New Population, 17:24-41

Deportation is a two-way street. Not only was the land "emptied" of Israelites, according to this theory of deportation. Other populations in the empire, who for the same reasons "needed" to be moved out of their homelands, were moved by the Assyrians into the environs of Samaria. They came from all over the empire and, of course, they brought with them their religious convictions and practices. Indeed, we may imagine that every displaced people hold even more closely to their religion when they have nothing else for sanity and assurance. The narrative is tenaciously Yahwistic and has no sympathy for the new arrivals in the land of Samaria. The narrator expects that the new arrivals will promptly and gladly give up all such "disapproved" religious practices and embrace Yahwism as the proper religion of the territory. Naturally, Yahwism is the only religion the commentator can countenance as legitimate.

The new population, predictably, will have none of it and fails completely to meet the rigorous requirements of the narrator. They persist in old practices, a clear violation of Sinai's primal requirement. This long discussion, filled with much haranguing repetition, is essentially a condemnation of the heterodoxy of the new population. They continue "former customs" that are an abomination to this commentator. In the midst of that heavy, relentless rhetoric, we may notice four interpretive variations:

(a) At the outset, Yahweh is as upset and intolerant at the new pluralism as is the narrator (17:25). In a heavy-handed maneuver Yahweh dispatches lions who kill some of the recalcitrant ones. The extremity of this response indicates the extremity of Deuteronomic passion for "Yahweh alone." Yahweh is known to be a harsh enforcer who will tolerate no rival. These lions from Yahweh may indeed be the same lions who devoured the young deriders of Yahweh's prophet, Elisha (2 Kgs 2:23-25), or the one who dealt decisively with the false prophet (1 Kgs 13:24-28). Yahweh's land is occupied with Yahweh's ferocious agents, a measure of the emerging passion in this narrowing interpretation of Yahwism.

(b) The king of Assyria, perhaps still Sargon, is as concerned as is Yahweh and Yahweh's interpreter, about the refusal of the new inhabitants in Samaria to come to terms with the God of the land (17:26-28). As given here, the Assyrian is well-versed in the claims of Yahweh, but takes less violent steps, not a lion, but a priest who will teach Torah. If there really was a priest dispatched from the Jews in exile to instruct the new population, an anticipation of Ezra in Judah, we may imagine that the Assyrian is not concerned with Yahwism but with civil order and the need for the deportees to come to terms with a new environment and its requirements. The explicit reason given for that emissary is to stop the killing by the lion, which was too violent and destructive even for the Assyrians, who specialized in violence and destructiveness. At its best, the Assyrian seems to accept the principle that religion must be suited to the territory [A Formula of Accommodation], an acknowledgement that Yahweh is the titular ruler of the land and must be accepted. The Assyrian, on such a basis, does not mind an alliance with Yahweh if it will produce order and tax revenue in the colony.

(c) The narrator seems uncommonly well-informed about other religious claims and knows the names of the other gods (17:29-34). Of course, the narrative will concede nothing to those gods and knows them to be manufactured and so without power or authority (see Isa 44:9-20; Jer 10:1-16; Ps 115:4-8). The commentary concedes that the new population in Samaria is indeed willing to worship Yahweh, to include Yahweh among its loyalties. What they cannot accept and what infuriates our commentator is their failure to acknowledge the jealous, exclusive claim of Yahweh, already stated at Sinai, a claim that excludes the other gods and their worship. It is this "Yahweh alone" accent that is defining for the commentary and characteristically the stumbling block with "other religions."

A Formula of Accommodation

In order to curb the religious violence in Europe, the Peace of Augsburg in 1555 enunciated the principle of *cujus regio, ejus religio*, that is, "who rules determines the religion." In each case the religion of the ruler determined the religion of the realm. That principle was reiterated in the Peace of Westphalia in 1648 at the end of the Thirty Years War. I mention it because, though not articulated in the ancient world, it was surely practiced. Thus the Assyrians, through the eyes of our narrative, concede that the territory of Israel belongs to Yahweh and those who live there should be instructed in Yahwism. This is no serious affirmation of Yahwism by the empire, but a standard imperial principle of maintaining order. It seems, moreover, to be the policy adopted by Cyrus the Persian, who later helped fund the rebuilt temple in Jerusalem for Yahweh. Thus we must see that the apparent cooperation of Assyria in this text reflects political reality more than it does religious commitment.

As agents of Yahweh, the lions are purging Samaria of the many foreign deportees who show no awareness of the God of Israel.

Gustave Doré. *Foreigners Devoured by Lions in Samaria* from the *Illustrated Bible*. 19th century. Engraving. (Credit: Dover Pictorial Archive Series)

(d) Most remarkably, the commentary includes an invitation to the new population (from Yahweh) to enter into covenant with Yahweh, that is, a chance to become Yahweh's own people (17:35-39). This articulation sounds the most characteristic sounds of Israel's faith, a *rootage in Exodus* (v. 37) and a *declaration of Torah requirements* (17:35, 37-39). Clearly, the language is highly stylized, for the Exodus rhetoric makes no acknowledgement that this body of potential Israelites is not "from Egypt." That rhetoric, however, defines Israel, and so the new population must in some way imagine itself as an Exodus people and embrace the rhetoric of Exodus as its own. These verses attest to Yahweh's generous inclusiveness, but at the same time to the uncompromising insistence of the narrator that there is only one valid formulation of matters.

This new population is invited in. But it refuses: "they would not *listen*" (17:40). The enlisting of this new population for Yahwism is not unlike the enlisting of the old population for Yahwism (17:14). Neither would do the one thing required in Deuteronomy 4:4-5, that is, listen. The old, enlisted population has vanished from Samaria. The new population now invited to join is under enduring judgment. The commentary ends on a note of wistfulness, convinced that it did not need to be this way (17:40-41). Listening (to Torah) is the way to well-being. Apart from listening, public life is without positive possibility.

CONNECTIONS

This chapter is a great pivot point in the entire narrative of Kings. In it, primary themes of the whole are drawn together in a sweeping justification of the destruction of the Northern Kingdom. The central portion of the text (17:7-18) is a stern, uncompromising speech of judgment, the purpose of which is to hold Israel itself responsible for its termination and conversely, to clear Yahweh of any charge that Yahweh might have unfairly enacted the destruction. This chapter specifically states the speech of judgment (indictment and sentence) that has been slowly building through many bits and pieces of the foregoing narrative.

The thrust of this claim of justification for the destruction is to insist that history—in its large, international scope—is ordered by Yahweh according to ethical, covenantal norms. That is, history in all its parts—including the deployment of Assyria, the superpower—moves according to the intention of Yahweh, so that Assyria here does not at all undertake any autonomous, imperial action. There are, to be sure, immense problems with such a claim that are not difficult to identify. We must, however, understand this elaborate statement as a thematic resistance to the fragmentary meaninglessness of the public process, and to the counterclaim that the destruction reflects either the weakness, infidelity, or unfairness of Yahweh. The *reliability of Yahweh* and the *coherent meaningfulness of the public process* converge in this great statement. Rough and problematic as the claim is, in our contemporary situation, it is a powerful alternative to the reduction of the public process, either to "a tale told by an idiot signifying nothing" or to a kind of atomization as though no large purposes but only private moral preferences propel the public process. In the end, I suggest, such a sweeping claim as offered here is an antidote to absurdity, despair, and resignation.

Two important qualifiers to this sweeping statement of closure are offered us concerning Israel and Judah. First, this is not an action by Yahweh out of the blue. There have been a series of warnings and alarm bells that might have been heeded, that is, the prophets. If this speech of judgment is made contemporary, I may suggest that the public processes of acquisitiveness and violence in which we are engaged in the U.S. constitute a self-chosen death sentence for this society. Verse 13 and its reference to prophets might be taken as an invitation that there are signs of protest, dissent, and warning all around from "prophetic voices," which the dominant forces of acquisitiveness and violence do not notice or want to heed. They are nonetheless all around, providing alternatives in a society that does not realize how late it may be in its life with God.

Second, the exemption of Judah (17:18) is a temporary and provisional one. The favoritism toward Judah stated here has been a recurrent theme up until this time in the narrative. By now, however, the narrative knows where it is going…to the demise of Judah as well as Israel (see 17:19-20). Thus the good news for Judah is exemption; the bad news for Judah is that the exemption is temporary.

Judah's "exceptionalism" might be a way to think about the *privileged U.S.* as a surviving superpower while "the wicked superpower" (U.S.S.R.) has happily been destroyed.[2] Or it might be a way to consider the *privileged Christian West* while other parts of the world seem so much worse off. There are exemptions and survivals and remnants by Yahweh's favor. These exemptions, it is here suggested, are provisional, conditional, and not to be presumed upon. Thus Judah is an exception from judgment that turns out, very soon, to be no exception at all. In the wake of Judah, every other sense of "exception" (including the U.S. and the Christian West) might also be reconsidered as provisional and conditional.[3]

The second focus of the chapter is upon "the new population" that has been imported into Samaria that does not know Yahweh and does not understand the rigorous conditions of survival in a world where Yahweh rules. The new population is offered status as Yahweh's covenant people and is sent a priest to instruct in the faith.

It is not much of a stretch to suggest that in the U.S., "the new population" consists of the sons and daughters of believers who now suffer from amnesia, who are self-preoccupied, and who live by a creed of narcissism. [A Creed of Selfism] "The new population" knows less of the rule of Yahweh, even if the faith of the "old population" was largely formal and pro forma.

We may consider this new population and the points made with reference to it. First, the new population is offered status as the covenanted people of Yahweh. The fact that they were not indigenous to the old faith does not matter, because Yahweh is generous.

Second, the specific strategy is to dispatch a priest from the exiles to instruct in the faith (17:27). While the text is likely a claim for the orthodoxy and primacy of exilic Judaism against homeland Judaism in a later period, we may use the reference in order to reflect upon "North America as a mission field."[4] In current missiology, North America is now regarded not as the font of true faith and teaching, but as a territory now largely inhabited by non-believers to which emissaries of faith must be sent from other churches in other lands long thought to be benighted. Thus in the interaction of Samaria with Assyria (Babylon?), there is role reversal between homeland Jews and Jews in foreign lands. We are now facing the same role reversal in the U.S., as a land to which emissaries of faith must come. The church in the U.S., as the community in ancient Samaria, now faces a "new population."

Third, the new population stands under threat if it does not listen. The

A Creed of Selfism

In writing of "The New American Consensus," Nicholas Lemann offers the manifesto of the new population in the U.S., that is, the sons and daughters of older "believers":

We, the relatively unbothered and well-off, hold these truths to be self-evident: That Big Government, Big Deficits, and Big Tobacco are bad, but that big bathrooms and 4-by-4's are not; that American overseas involvement should be restricted to trade agreements, mutual funds, and the visiting of certain beachfront resorts; that markets can take care of themselves as long as they take care of us; that an individual's sex life is nobody's business, though highly entertaining; and that the only rights that really matter are those which indulge the Self.

Nicholas Lemann, "The New American Consensus: Government of, by, and for the Comfortable," *The New York Times Magazine* (November 1, 1998) front cover.

Whether such a perspective in any way matches that of the "new population" in Samaria is of course beyond us. But the text does suggest religious practice that is pragmatic and not too keen on costly commitment.

generous God is as demanding of the new population as was the case with those deported. Yahweh extends generosity for either the old faithful or the new faithful folk only to those who "get it" about Yahweh's singular requirements. This chapter, for both the old regime now displaced and for the new population, is uncompromising. Such a stance only makes sense if Yahweh is indeed such a God with such an expansive rule. Otherwise, it is all theological posturing. We seem always to find out very late when the claim is real and not posturing.

NOTES

[1]On passion for the notion of "Yahweh alone," see Morton Smith, *Palestinian Parties and Politics that Shaped the Old Testament* (New York: Columbia University Press, 1971).

[2]In a quite sophisticated way this seems to be the argument of Francis Fukuyama, *The End of History and the Last Man* (New York: The Free Press, 1992). Every surviving superpower imagines that it is the culmination and end point of the historical process.

[3]Paul M. Kennedy, *The Rise & Fall of the Great Powers: Economic Change & Military Conflict from 1500 to 2000* (New York: Random House, 1987) has considered the role of the military in international domination. For a case study, see his student, Fred Zakaria, *From Wealth to Power: The Unusual Origins of America's World Role* (Princeton: Princeton University Press, 1998).

[4]On "North America as a Mission Field," see George R. Hunsberger et al., eds., *The Church between Gospel & Culture: The Emerging Mission in North America* (Grand Rapids: Eerdmans, 1996) and Darrell Guder, ed., *The Missional Church* (Grand Rapids: Eerdmans, 1998).

HEZEKIAH'S REFORM
AND THE ASSYRIAN THREAT

2 Kings 18:1-27

THE FINAL DAYS OF JUDAH, 2 KINGS 18–25

After chapter 17, it remains only for the narrative to detail the final
failure of the Jerusalem regime. To do so, the material is organized
around three set pieces with each king being treated in a paradigmatic way. (a) King Hezekiah is presented as the pious, obedient king
who *relies upon the prophet* (chapters 18–20); (b) King Manasseh is
offered as the paradigmatic bad king, the *cipher of Torah rejection* that
bespeaks the Torah rejection enacted by the entire sweep of royal history (chapter 21); (c) King Josiah is presented as the paradigmatic
good king who *submits eagerly to the requirements of Torah* (chapters
22–23). By these three royal episodes, the narrative dramatically
articulates the decisive importance of *Torah* and *prophets* and the ines-
timably high cost of Torah disobedience and disregard of the
prophets who advocate the Torah. The accent of these three episodes,
moreover, negatively alludes back to Solomon as the purveyor of heterodox worship (23:13). By the dramatic judgments made upon
Hezekiah (+), Manasseh (-), and Josiah (+), together with the culminating narrative of 23:31–25:26, the narrative skillfully matches the
ending of 18:1–25:26 to 1 Kings 1–11 at the beginning, thus
enveloping the entire royal history as a bracketing of Torah compromise. The long telling of this tale of disobedience (that the piety of
Hezekiah and Josiah could not counter) makes clear that David's
remarkable advice to Solomon at the outset has been treated by the
kings with long-term disregard and disdain:

> Be strong, be courageous, and keep the charge of the LORD your
> God, walking in his ways and keeping his statues, his command-
> ments, his ordinances, and his testimonies, as it is written in the
> law of Moses, so that you may prosper in all that you do and wher-
> ever you turn. Then the LORD will establish his word that he
> spoke concerning me: "If your heirs take heed to their way, to walk
> before me in faithfulness with all their heart and with all their soul,
> there shall not fail you a successor on the throne of Israel. (1 Kgs
> 2:2-4)

As a consequence, there will be "no heir on the throne" (2:4). David's rejected counsel to his son surfaces negatively in the concluding addendum to our narrative in 2 Kings 25:27-30. In the end there is the pitiful boy king, Jehoiachin, now become a man, with no prospect of "an heir on the throne." This total account of monarchy concludes with "no heir," no prospect, no future. With Torah attentiveness, it could have been otherwise. But it is not!

COMMENTARY

The Good King Mocked along with His God, 18:1-27

With the nullification of the Northern Kingdom by Assyrian invasion in 721 (17:5-6), our narrator is able to abandon the tricky project of telling in tandem the deeply intertwined tale of the two kingdoms. The narrative can now, for the remainder of 2 Kings, focus singularly on the Kingdom of Judah, the only one remaining. The story line of 2 Kings 18–25, with some other miscellaneous detail, is organized around four accent points: (a) the reign of Hezekiah (18–20), (b) the reign of Manasseh (21), (c) the reign of Josiah (22–23), and (d) the final days (23:31–25:30). The story of Jerusalem moves inexorably to its sorry end; these three kings— Hezekiah, Manasseh, and Josiah—become the models and reference points of *faith and unfaith* in this ending.

The narrative account of Hezekiah occupies an inordinate amount of material (chapters 18–20), not only because he, along with Josiah, is regarded by the narrator as the only fully faithful king in Judah, but because the narrator utilizes the materials of Hezekiah as an opportunity to witness to the faithfulness of Yahweh and the commensurate faithfulness of Judah under Hezekiah. That is, the material is apparently an opportunity for theological reflection and instruction on the nature of faith.[1]

Chapter 18 plunges Hezekiah and his kingdom deeply into a crisis with Assyria. It is clear that the appeasing policy of Ahaz, Hezekiah's father, was not sufficient, even though it amounted to a humiliating surrender to the empire (16:7-18). Like every rapacious empire, Assyria always wanted more, and what Judah had to offer to the empire was never enough. The chapter begins with an introductory formula, a summary review of the rule of Hezekiah (18:1-8); this is followed by a brief reprise concerning the destruction of the North (18:9-12), an initial diplomatic confrontation with Assyria (18:13-27), and a second confrontation between the same parties (18:28-37). The entire chapter witnesses to the dire crisis of Jerusalem, and offers as yet no hint of a resolution to the crisis.

Introduction and Summary Report, 18:1-8

Hezekiah had a long reign of twenty-nine years, though the exact chronology is taken by scholars to be problematic. The probable dates may be 715–686, but the precise dates are impossible to determine. The theological verdict on Hezekiah is without precedent in the books of Kings (18:3-6). He is the best! He did what was right as had David, although unlike David, Hezekiah had no embarrassing "except" as did David with Uriah (1 Kgs 15:5). That is, Hezekiah is like David, only more so!

His doing "right" consisted (as commanded in Deuteronomy 12:3 and as done by Jehoiada before him in 11:18) of destroying all the emblems of non-Yahweh worship: high places, pillars, sacred pole, and bronze serpent (18:4). [Nehushtan] The verbs are vigorous: "remove, break down, cut down, break." Hezekiah is an assertive reformer of whom the narrator completely approves. The ground of reformist zeal, the willingness to take sides and refuse every compromise, is his trust (*batah*) in Yahweh. The king is willing to risk all on his conviction that Yahweh is a good and reliable force in the world, so that he rejects every alternative form of support (other gods). He is in every way, according to the narrator, scrupulously attentive to the Torah of Moses, here referring to some form of the book of Deuteronomy. He is the model for our narrator of conforming public policy to Torah requirements.

After such an unprecedented affirmation of the king, it is completely predictable that our narrator will say in the next verse, "Yahweh was with him...he prospered" (18:7a). Of course! It could not be otherwise. Deuteronomic conviction, here fully voiced, is that *obedience* produces *prosperity*. [Deuteronomy 30:15-20] The unspoken negative counterpart that we have seen in Ahaz (16) and will see in Manasseh (21) is that *disobedience* produces *disaster*. This

---

Nehushtan

The term as a proper name apparently refers to a lesser god eliminated by Hezekiah. Nothing is known about this god. The name itself seems to be a play on "bronze" (*nahash*) and "serpent" (*nahash*), thus a "bronze serpent." Judging from Num 21:8-9, the bronze serpent was a cult object, the purpose of which was to protect from snake bites. While this lesser god may have been thought to be subordinate to Yahweh and so compatible with Yahwistic claims, in the "Yahweh alone" perspective of our narrative, such an underling must be dismissed as heterodox. Thus its elimination as a cult object evidences Hezekiah's singular, uncompromised devotion to Yahweh.

theory of moral coherence is fully embraced by Hezekiah, to the great benefit of the king and his realm (18:7b-8). He became so strong and so effective, precisely because *obedience* produces political *independence*. Hezekiah became strong enough to defy Assyria, that is, to refuse the submissiveness of his father Ahaz, apparently to withhold payment of tribute (see 17:4). Alongside defiance of Assyria, moreover, Hezekiah was able to advance boundary lines to the southeast and to recover territory along the Mediterranean Sea. Our narrative is preoccupied with the Torah, but does not miss opportunity to attest the concrete, pragmatic gains of such Torah obedience.

A Memory of Israel, 18:9-12

These verses reiterate the sorry demise of Samaria at the hand of Shalmaneser the Assyrian (see 17:3-6). Apparently the data is repeated, along with the verdict of 18:12, "because" (on which see 17:7), in order to contrast *obedient* and prosperous Hezekiah with *disobedient* and failed Hoshea. The clue to well-being, the contrast suggests, is to *hear and do*. [Hear and Do] Thus vv. 9-12 provide a clear and simple contrast to the piety of Hezekiah in vv. 3-8, a contrast at the center of the testimony and conviction of our narrator.

The First Diplomatic Confrontation, 18:13-27

In these verses, the political, diplomatic power of the government of Hezekiah must come face-to-face with the arrogant military threat of Assyria voiced by haughty diplomats, a haughtiness befitting the power and capacity of "the only surviving superpower." The context for the encounter is Hezekiah's defiance in v. 7

Deuteronomy 30:15-20

This text is the clearest either/or statement of the tradition concerning the requirements of "Yahweh alone":

> See, I have set before you today life and prosperity, death and adversity. If you obey the commandments of the LORD your God that I am commanding you today, by loving the LORD your God, walking in his ways, and observing his commandments, decrees, and ordinances, then you shall live and become numerous, and the LORD your God will bless you in the land that you are entering to possess. But if your heart turns away and you do not hear…. I declare to you today that shall perish; you shall not live long in the land that you are crossing the Jordan to enter and possess…. Choose life so that you and your descendants may live…so that you may live in the land that the LORD swore to give to your ancestors, to Abraham, to Isaac, and to Jacob.

AΩ **Hear and Do**

These two terms together concern all that belongs to obedience, both active listening and then real, concrete practice of the commands. The terms are already uttered together in the vow taken at Sinai in Exodus 24:7. It has long been observed that the sequence of the two verbs in that oath are contrary to what we might expect. We might anticipate that Israel would first hear and then do. But the sequence in the text suggests that it is in actual concrete practice that Israel knows itself to be addressed and knows what is commanded. The accent is on the concrete practice out of which comes the depth and power of the relation of lord and people.

(18:13-18). The Assyrian diplomat issues an ultimatum to Jerusalem (18:19-25), which is followed by an anemic, fearful response from Jerusalem (18:26-27). While the narrative is framed as a historical happening, we should not miss that the reported exchange is a highly stylized piece of reflection and instruction. Indeed, we may say that it is a theological discourse on the meaning of faith in Yahweh.

An encounter with the imperial superpower has become inescapable after Hezekiah's rebellion against imperial authority (18:7). The empire expects to have local regimes that are completely compliant. When they are not compliant, the empire must perforce act as enforcer. The enforcement in our narrative takes place in the person of Sennacherib, who has now succeeded to the Assyrian throne. [Sargon and Sennacherib] The Assyrian ruler and his army have already penetrated Judean defenses, so that they are encamped at Lachish, Judah's strongest military installation. [Lachish] The Jerusalem king must send emissaries to Sennacherib at Lachish in a posture of subservience:

> I have done wrong; withdraw from me; whatever you impose on me I will bear. (18:14)

The speech of the Jerusalem king is a complete submission to Assyria, an abrupt reversal of the policy and action of v. 7. The assertion of independence symbolized by withholding tribute did not work. Assyria is too strong and too vigilant of its interests and too ruthless, so that for the moment, the simple formula of *obedience-prosperity* does not function for the king.

There is irony in the phrase, "I have done wrong" (literally, "I have sinned"),

Sargon and Sennacherib

The sequence of Assyrian kings and conquerors in this period is Shalmaneser-Sargon-Sennacherib. It is noteworthy that Sargon is nowhere mentioned in this text, even though he is thought to be the ruler who finally conquered Samaria. The lack of evidence in this particular matter is of a piece with the larger confusion concerning the incursions Assyria made against Jerusalem. It is thought by scholars that Sennacherib made two assaults on Judah, perhaps in 705 and 701; it is, however, not obvious how the several biblical texts relate to what may have been the historical data. Brevard Childs has sorted out the matter as clearly as is possible; but the only thing we can know for certain is that the Assyrian pressure in this period against Jerusalem was relentless and inescapable.

Brevard S. Childs, *Isaiah and the Assyrian Crisis*, SBT Second Series 3 (Naperville: Alec R. Allenson, 1967); see also John Bright, *A History of Israel*. 3rd ed. (Philadelphia: Westminster Press, 1981) 298-309.

Lachish

This ancient site is strategically located just at the transitional point between the hill country of Judah and the coastal plain. As a consequence, its control mattered enormously to the control of the larger area; it functioned for a long period of time as a major fortress. In the period of Judah's history that concerns us, the site was conquered by Sennacherib who created stone reliefs of the conquest of the site for his palace in Nineveh.

See David Ussishkin, "Lachish," ABD 4:121-24.

Typical of the plethora of Assyrian reliefs that inundated the palace walls of the kings, these limestone reliefs provide a visual account of the Assyrian destruction of the Jewish fortress at Lachish in 701 BC. One relief shows a battering ram mounted on a tower and Jewish prisoners being impaled. Another relief shows the prisoners being used as a work force.

Reliefs from the Palace of Sennacherib at Nineveh. c. 700 BC British Museum, London. (Credit: Erich Lessing/Art Resource, NY)

because it contradicts the statement, "He did what was right," in v. 3. What is *right* to Yahweh (independence) is at the same time *sin* to Assyria.[2] Just now Hezekiah faces Assyria and must "repent" of his defiance of the empire. For the moment, the requirements of Yahweh recede in the face of imperial demands. Hezekiah, good king that he is, wants the occupying troops of the empire removed, and offers tribute money to purchase their withdrawal, the very tribute money he had withheld in v. 7. Sennacherib is as ruthless and demanding toward Hezekiah as Tiglath-pileser III was toward Ahaz (see 16:17-18). In humiliating fashion, like his father before him, Hezekiah must take all the treasures of the temple, silver and gold, and give them to Assyria. Verses 14-16 are exact and tedious in detail, for the narrator wants us to experience the humiliation in the detail of the telling. Everything is "for the king of Assyria!" (18:16), having been removed from the "palace" of King Yahweh and dispatched to the palace of King Sennacherib.

Such submissiveness, however, is never enough, as it is never enough for any usurpatious empire (18:17-18). Sennacherib did not withdraw his threatening forces as Hezekiah had hoped. Instead, he sent his negotiators to Jerusalem to demand more. The empire is represented by three officers—the Tartan, the Rab-saris, and the Rabshakeh—accompanied by a great army. [The Assyrian Officers] Not only are they formidable, but they come with "a big stick" designed to intimidate the Jerusalem regime. They are met by Hezekiah's representatives, Eliakim, Shebnah, and Joah. [Hezekiah's Representatives] The two parties meet at the city waterworks, perhaps to call attention to the city's vulnerable water supply. (See Isa 7:3-9 for another desperate meeting at the same sight.) The exchange that

The Assyrian Officers

The three Assyrian officers who conduct negotiations for Sennacherib—the Tartan, the Rab-saris, the Rabshakeh—represent the high command of the Assyrian movement. The titles are names of offices and are not to be mistaken for personal names. It is likely that the three terms represent, in turn, the commander in chief, the chief eunuch, and the chief cupbearer. Those titles, however, do not in fact match their functions. It is enough to recognize that the Assyrian government, as might be expected from a great empire, had a well-delineated administration. The titles indicate, moreover, that this is a most high-level delegation capable of delivering the policies and threats they utter.

AΩ **Hezekiah's Representatives**

As though to match the three named negotiators of Assyria, Hezekiah has also dispatched three of his high-ranking officials, identified in turn as the one "in charge of the palace," the secretary, and the recorder. Again we are able to see the hints of an administrative organization. Surely these advisors are closest to the king. It is to be noticed that none of these titles to office have the prefix of two of the Assyrian titles, *rab*. That prefix means "chief" or "great," thus a claim of the great empire of Nineveh that Judah could not match and did not dare pretend to do so. These three are the best Hezekiah can offer, so that this is as close to parity as the king can come in a face-off with the empire.

follows is clearly between unequal partners, the intimidators and the intimidated.

The Rabshakeh, the third named of the Assyrian delegation, makes an extended speech of challenge to Hezekiah. The speech is highly stylized and articulates sound Yahwistic theology. In the horizon of our narrator, everyone is capable of being a Yahwistic theologian, as the narrative may require. The Rabshakeh speaks for "the great king." Like every diplomat, he speaks not for himself, but has the full weight of his government behind him. The formula is not unlike the familiar prophetic formula, "Thus says the Lord," and is echoed in United Nations enunciations. A diplomat never says "I," but, always, "My government...." The formula in v. 19 is perhaps designed to show that Assyria has more power than Yahweh, Hezekiah's patron.

In vv. 19-22, the Assyrian diplomat focuses on the issue of trust (*batah*). [Trust as Policy] Policy must be based on some elemental reliabilities. Hezekiah "trusts" Yahweh; it is the burden of the Assyrian speech to make the charge that the Jerusalem policy of resistance to Assyria is utter folly because no source of support is reliable in the face of the empire. In these verses, the term "trust" is used six times, not recognizable each time in English translation: "confidence, rely." The Assyrian shrewdly and methodologically names the candidates for trust and nullifies them: (a) "Mere words," rhetoric as a basis for trust? It will not work! (b) *Egypt* as ally? But Egypt has elsewhere been shown to be unreliable and treacherous (see 17:4, Isa 31:1-3). (c) *Yahweh* as a reliance? But, say the Assyrians, Hezekiah himself has already violated Yahweh in his stripping of the temple

Trust as Policy

It is the insistence of this narrator (and of Isaiah in a parallel tradition) that, in the unequal struggle between the empire and the government of Judah, Yahweh is the "great equalizer." That is, Yahweh must be taken into account in policy formation because the public, international process is not merely one of raw power. The capacity to take Yahweh into account as an active player goes under the rubric of "faith" or "trust." See the term in v. 5 and especially the oracles of the prophet Isaiah in 7:9; 30:15. It is easy for us to imagine that in the ancient world, such a dimension of faith was more credible than it would be in the modern world. But we must not misunderstand and assume that even in that ancient world, with its military, political, and economic realities, "faith" was such an obvious decision. It was then, as now, an act or a cluster of acts that ran against what seemed to be the pertinent factors of *Realpolitik*. That is, faith was no more an easy choice then than it might be now. Thus the text does not call for something easily embraced, but celebrates this king who took the hard choice. Indeed, this chapter and the ones that follow tell about the career of that hard policy choice taken by this king in his posture of unshakable faith.

(18:14-16). You cannot, reasons the empire, expect your God to save you when you have offended your God in such a visible way. Thus the diplomat names three possible sources of Judean nerve and eliminates each of them, clearly intending that the accent falls on the third nominee to make the point that reliance on Yahweh is indeed nonsensical. The purpose of the taunting speech is to erode Jerusalem's confidence, i.e., to undermine the courage it takes to mount a war effort, to make clear that resistance to Assyria is completely futile.

In v. 23, the Assyrian rhetoric changes, but not the intention of the speech. Verses 23-25 make two distinct points. First, Jerusalem is completely without military resources. It has no soldiers. The Assyrian mockingly offers to provide horses to Judah for Judah's war against Assyria, if Judah will provide the horsemen. But of course Judah cannot supply the men. That is the point of the offer. It indicates that Judah is bereft of manpower resources as well as every other kind of resource and therefore had better knuckle under to the empire. Indeed, Judah is so weak that its entire military force could not cope with one Assyrian military company. The odds are unthinkable for Judah, made more so by the fact that Egypt is no reliable military support. Judah is in principle defeated even before any conflict begins.

Second, the military point is matched by a theological point: Assyria has been dispatched by none other than Yahweh, because Yahweh wants recalcitrant Jerusalem to be destroyed, a point long anticipated by the prophets of Israel (18:25). This is the most daring taunt imaginable, that Assyria is a tool of Yahweh against Yahweh's own people. Clearly the prophetic intent of the text in the mouth of the empire is congruent with the theme of Isaiah who will appear later in our text:

> Ah, Assyria, the rod of my anger—
>   the club in their hands is my fury!
> Against a godless nation I send him,
>   and against the people of my wrath I command him,
> to take spoil and seize plunder,
>   and to tread them down like the mire of the streets. (Isa 10:5-6)

The challenge in the mouth of Assyria is sure to make Jerusalem hopeless—militarily, diplomatically, theologically—completely without resources. The Assyrian statement only gives name and visibility to what was in any case true. Jerusalem has no available way to withstand the imperial threat.

The Assyrian taunt of vv. 19-25 requires and receives an answer from the government of Hezekiah, the three Jerusalem officials named in v. 18 (18:26). But in fact they give no answer at all. Their response is nothing more than a pitiful plea for secrecy, since open conversation would make the desperate plight of Jerusalem public and known to "the man on the street," and thus rob the war effort of what little energy it had. Hebrew, the language of the people, was apparently what the Assyrian had used, and the plea is for Aramaic, the language of diplomacy not generally known. The request is a humiliating acknowledgement of the truth of the preceding Assyrian analysis. Such a plea permits a responding taunt by Assyria (18:27). The Assyrian speaker insists that what is to be said is not just for the diplomats but for everyone, for public consumption. Indeed, the public addressed over the head of the government is further identified as those who will be reduced to eating and drinking their own bodily waste. That is, the Assyrian answer contains one more assertion that the siege of Jerusalem will become so severe that the citizens of the city will be reduced to famine and will desperately eat whatever is available, recycling already digested food and surely recycling despair. The empire concedes nothing, continues its brutality, and refuses the request of the king's men.

A Second Exchange, 18:28-37

These verses, like vv. 19-27, offer again an Assyrian speech of taunting (18:28-35) and a response that is no response at all (18:36-37). The Assyrian speech goes over the same ground, again asserting Jerusalem's helplessness, this time with a different accent. Again the speech begins with a boasting claim for Sennacherib (18:28), wherein "The Great King" addresses the feeble king in Jerusalem. The Assyrian, moreover, speaks in Hebrew, the language of the people, and not Aramaic as requested in v. 26. The speech appeals to the people "over the head" of the government. While the word "rely" (trust) occurs in v. 30 as in the earlier speech, the dominant theme here is "deliver" (*nastal*). The term means to "snatch from danger," a term that can be used for military victory or escape, but also a term used for Yahweh's own work on behalf of Israel (see Amos 4:11).

The imperial speech, further seeking to erode public confidence in Jerusalem, first of all states its theme (18:30). Hezekiah "cannot save," Yahweh "cannot save." Neither king or God can withstand Assyria. Then the speech offers terms of surrender (18:31-32a). "Make peace" = surrender! The terms of surrender are in two phases. First, the threat of attack and siege will stop and there will be a period of security (18:31). That period may be brief, but the offer echoes the phrasing of the idyllic vision of a settled, agrarian economy of vine, fig tree, and water, all a peasant economy could desire (see Deut 6:11; Micah 4:4). But second, with the term "until" in v. 32, the terms of peace become both candid and ominous. The Assyrian candidly acknowledges an intention of deportation ("take you away"). The deportation, so says the voice of the empire, will be to a good land of grain, wine, bread, vineyards, olive oil, and honey, that is, a land of well-being and abundance. Perhaps; but it is an *alien land!* Thus the offer of well-being carries with it a deep threat of exile at the same time.

After the positive offer of vv. 31-32a, the speech concludes by a return to the insistence of vv. 29-30 (18:32b-35). These verses are dominated by the verb "deliver," with the repeated conviction that Yahweh "cannot deliver." The fivefold use of the term is arranged to link Yahweh to other gods:

> The LORD will deliver…
>   has any god delivered…
>   gods of Hamath, etc., deliver…
>   all the gods deliver…
> The LORD should deliver.

The opening and closing refrain concerning Yahweh concludes that Yahweh has not delivered because other gods do not deliver. None is powerful enough; therefore, Yahweh is not powerful enough. This is a perfectly compelling argument, if one agrees to the comparisons.

The chapter concludes with a report on Hezekiah's officials (18:36-37). They made no answer to the empire because their king had so instructed them. The same three officials report to the king. We are left waiting for the king's own response in 19:1-17. Our verses are quite terse and give us no hint of the felt response of Hezekiah's men. The last verse, however, may suggest that the Assyrian argument has hit its target, that the officials of Jerusalem were persuaded by the argument that diminished Yahweh. The narrative withholds judgment and the king's agents, good diplomats as they are, give no clue to their reaction. The impression, however, is a building sense of threat and danger.

CONNECTIONS

It is most plausible to conclude that these verbal exchanges are not in fact reports, but are imagined exchanges designed as testimony and instruction to the ongoing generations of the faithful. They portray Yahwism as a jeopardized faith and the community of Yahweh as a community short on worldly resources, exactly what we might expect among exiles. If that is the case, then we may conclude that this chapter, with its companion pieces in chapters 19–20, is an invitation to the community in many circumstances of threat, danger, and seduction to keep its faith in times of acute jeopardy.

This text attests not only that Israel's faith must be practiced in the midst of hostile nations. It argues beyond that, that other nations may be tools and instruments of Yahweh. Thus the text offers a sweeping geopolitical vision of Yahweh's sovereign governance, a large vision that precludes shrinking biblical faith to familiar and familial perspective. Thus the claim made by Sennacherib in v. 23—that Yahweh had dispatched him, the Assyrian, against Jerusalem—turns out in the prophetic horizon of Isaiah to be correct (Isa 10:5ff).[3] The picture given is of a God with a large international strategy that focuses upon "the chosen people," but that does not limit Yahweh's horizon to that people. The impetus for such bold thinking in the traditions of Isaiah and the Deuteronomist may be found in the large scope of the book of Genesis that not only presents a "map" of all nations (Gen 10), but that envisions Israel as an agent of Yahweh bringing "blessing" to all the families of the earth (Gen 12:1-3).[4] Indeed, Isaiah, closely linked to our text, finally entertains the grand outcome that Assyria and its counterpower Egypt will become—along with Israel—God's chosen peoples:

> On that day Israel will be the third with Egypt and Assyria, a blessing in the midst of the earth, whom the LORD of hosts has blessed, saying, "Blessed be Egypt my people, and Assyria the work of my hands, and Israel my heritage." (Isa 19:24-25)

This large vision of faith sounds awkward and unfamiliar to us, given the modernist tendency to confine the rule of God to safer, closer zones. The recovery of such a large-scale vision of faith is, in my judgment, an important aspect of contemporary biblical interpretation. It is, moreover, exceedingly difficult to make such a recovery in the contemporary scene because our vision of faith is always linked to the immediate demands of policy, politics, and interest. Nonetheless, the conviction that God is at work in public affairs is a challenge and affirmation of the Bible. Recent cases might be candidates for reflection: the fall of the U.S.S.R. and the emancipation of Eastern Europe, the fall of the apartheid government in South Africa, the potential peace agreement in Northern Ireland, all clearly made possible by international pressure and vigorous internal insistence. Of course, for U.S. interpreters, one must ask about God's work with "the last superpower" that is deeply bent on economic imperialism and about what happens when a nation-state—like Assyria (or the U.S.)—under Yahwistic mandate oversteps that mandate in self-aggrandizement. It may be that our reading in the U.S. should pay attention not to the destiny of Israel but to the fate of Assyria. The text offers no delineation of such an interpretation, but it invites daring analogies.

The first speech of Assyria focuses on the question of *trust*. The taunting speech of the empire argues that trust in Yahweh is foolish because Yahweh is untrustworthy. Of course the negative assertion of the Assyrian is a ploy by the narrator to make a positive invitation to trust as an affirmation that Yahweh is indeed trustworthy in every circumstance, even when apparent odds tell against Yahweh. One might indeed conclude that it is in the nature of faith in Yahweh that trust is not for complacent times when trust is easy and convenient, but it is precisely for times like the one in our text when trust contradicts data. Thus the Psalmist warns against "trust in princes," who are no reliable help, powers like Sennacherib; then the Psalmist offers Yahweh as real help:

> Do not put your trust in princes,
>   in mortals in whom there is no help.
> When their breath departs, they return to the earth;
>   on that very day their plans perish.
> Happy are those whose help is the God of Jacob,
>   whose hope is in the LORD their God. (Ps 146:3-5)

Another Psalmist, in a quite intimate crisis, can recall times past when Yahweh has been found trustworthy:

> In you our ancestors trusted;
>   they trusted, and you delivered them.
> To you they cried, and were saved;
>   in you they trusted, and were not put to shame. (Ps 22:4-5)

For this community of faith, the threat of the Assyrians is a characteristic circumstance in which the faithful count on Yahweh, even though Yahweh is not a visible power that the Assyrians would notice. Indeed, the Assyrian dismissal of Yahweh is not unlike the general comment of Joseph Stalin concerning the moral authority of the Pope: "How many military divisions does he command?" Sennacherib perceived Yahweh as helpless and unreliable, as Yahweh's detractors always do.

In the second Assyrian speech, the challenging empire verbalizes two huge misunderstandings that characteristically distort faith. The first is a misunderstanding of the land of promise given by God to Israel. The empire promises deportation to and settlement in "a land like your own land" (18:32). The decisive misunderstanding is to assume that any other land—no matter what it produces—could ever be like "the land of promise." There is no land like the land of promise, certainly not a land dominated by the empire. We may imagine that this text was an important one in the exilic community of those later carried away by Babylon. If so, it is an insistence and a reminder that "this land," Babylon, is not "our land," and Babylon must never be mistaken for home. This text is thus an important partner text to Jeremiah 29:5-7, which had enjoined exiles to settle in Babylon. Our text says, "Do not settle too much, for it is not home and will never be home." The "true home" of the faithful is never under imperial domination. Thus the text, by championing the antithesis of what it says, invites the people of faith to an endless restlessness in every circumstance of domination:

> But as it is, they desire a better country, that is, a heavenly one. Therefore God is not ashamed to be called their God; indeed, he has prepared a city for them. (Heb 11:16)

The second, even more gross misunderstanding on the part of the empire is the assumption of vv. 32b-35 that Yahweh is to be compared to other gods, that Yahweh belongs to a larger, commonly defined genre, "gods." If that assumption were granted, an endless temptation of the "history of religion," then the logic would be simple:

> all gods are powerless;
> Yahweh is a god;
> therefore Yahweh is powerless.

But of course Yahweh, in Israel's perspective, is not to be understood in terms of generic "godness," precisely because Yahweh is, so Israel endlessly confesses, incomparable in terms of power and in terms of solidarity with the poor and needy.[5] Thus Israel will endlessly assert, "There is none like Yahweh," or ask defiantly, "Who is like Yahweh?" It is this incomparability that makes arguments via comparison irrelevant and unpersuasive, and that gives Israel courage in the face of every circumstance. The incomparability of Yahweh is not voiced here in such a formula, but is implied by the very act of comparison done by the Assyrians. The argument Assyria makes is that Yahweh, like the genre of "god," is incapable of enacting the verb "deliver." Without that verb Yahweh is no god at all.[6] But of course that is exactly the point toward which chapters 19–20 will lead us.

The Verbs of the Easter God

The phrase in 1 Cor 15:54 echoes Isa 25:7. To be sure, those references in Isaiah are different from those found in our more sober text. I suggest, however, that the verbs utilized for the Easter testimony of the church appeal precisely to the powerful, death-defeating, life-giving ways of the God of Israel. More familiar than "swallow" is the verb "deliver," but that verb as well, when used of Jesus, carries with it the long history of Israel's prayer and praise, for Yahweh is characteristically the subject of such verbs of rescue and well-being.

See Walter Brueggemann, "Easter: Answer to Prayer," *The Living Pulpit* (forthcoming).

The attempt to deny Yahweh the verb "deliver" is a recurring enterprise of every form of philosophical theology in which Yahweh characteristically becomes object and not subject. Characteristically it is "primitive" testimony, uttered among primitive, unsophisticated, unaffluent people of faith that voices the raw claim of Yahweh's incomparable capacity. As our narrator—and the Assyrians—knows, everything depends upon Yahweh's capacity to enact this great verb in the face of Assyrian taunting. By the end of this chapter we are given no clue about Yahweh's ability against the Assyrians. But there is more in what follows.

The capacity of Yahweh against the Assyrians is a restatement—as Israel is always restating—of the ancient contest of Israel versus Egypt, of Yahweh versus the gods of Egypt. Each time the contest is reenacted, those who witness it do not know the outcome ahead of time. In Christian confession this same contest between the powers is enacted in the life of Jesus and especially in the death of Jesus wherein Jesus, it is confessed, defeats the powers of death. [The Verbs of the Easter God]

> Death has been swallowed up in victory.
>   Where, O death, is your victory?
>   Where, O death, is your sting?
>   The sting of death is sin, and the power of sin is the law. But thanks be to God, who gives us the victory through our Lord Jesus Christ. (1 Cor 15:54-57)

The enemies vary: Egypt, Assyria, death. In this testimony, Yahweh keeps showing up for the contest with the big verb—*deliver*—the very verb here denied Yahweh by the Assyrians.

NOTES

[1]Chapters 18–20 of 2 Kings have as their very close parallel the same text in Isa 36–39. On the latter text, attention must be given to Christopher R. Seitz, *Zion's Final Destiny: The Development of the Book of Isaiah: A Reassessment of Isaiah 36–39* (Minneapolis: Fortress Press, 1991). Seitz has shown what a pivotal place the chapters occupy in the total book of Isaiah. For our study of Kings, it is the great contribution of Seitz to show that the text is a profound theological statement and should not be treated in any thin way as historical reportage. Much of what Seitz has seen on these chapters in Isaiah applies equally well to the rendering in chapters 18–20, even though his interest is directly in the larger shape of the book of Isaiah.

[2]The rhetoric of "sin" in the mouth of Hezekiah as he addresses the Assyrians reminds us that "sin" has to do with disobedience to legitimate power. In the deferential statement of v. 14, Assyria is treated as the norm for the king's behavior. The use of sin in this way is an echo of the rhetoric of Pharaoh who acknowledges "sin" against Yahweh as the superior power whom he belatedly acknowledges. See Exod 9:27; 10:16.

[3]More generally on Yahweh's governance of the nations, see Walter Brueggemann, *Theology of the Old Testament: Testimony, Dispute, Advocacy,* 492-527.

[4]On a theology of blessing, see Hans Walter Wolff, "The Kerygma of the Yahwist," *Interpretation* 20 (1966): 131-58; and more broadly, Claus Westermann, *Blessing in Israel and in the Life of the Church* (Philadelphia: Fortress Press, 1978).

[5]See Brueggemann, *Theology of the Old Testament,* 139-44.

[6]Ibid., 173-76.

A FINAL THREAT AND COMPLETE DELIVERANCE

2 Kings 19:1-37

This chapter continues the account of the threat of Sennacherib against the city of Jerusalem. While the initial response of Hezekiah's government (18:36-37) to the second Assyrian speech of taunting (18:28-35) has been silence, now the king makes his own response to the saber rattling of the empire (19:1-7). This royal response is followed by the third address of Assyria (19:8-13) with the king's third response (19:14-19). The chapter turns abruptly with the assuring utterance of the prophet Isaiah (19:20-28, 29-31, 32-34). It concludes with a narrative report that vindicates the faith of the king and the assurance of the prophet (19:35-37).

COMMENTARY

The King Receives Prophetic Assurance, 19:1-7

At last Hezekiah appears in his own narrative. He has no doubt closely followed negotiations with the Assyrians at the wall, and now he responds to the ominous report of his three trusted officials.[1] He assumes a posture of grief and penitence, recognizing the deep danger to his realm and to his person (19:1; see 6:30).

The king sends an urgent, desperate request to the prophet Isaiah that he should pray on behalf of the realm (19:2-4). The messengers, like the king himself, take on appearance matching the depth of the emergency (19:2). The petition of the king to the prophet first of all describes the dire circumstance of the day, a day of "distress, rebuke, disgrace," of utter failure, emptiness, weakness, complete lack of vitality. [The Rhetoric of "The Day"] The rhetoric is extreme. It is as though a military defeat had already been suffered by Jerusalem. There is, however, yet a chance: "It may be!" The king still trusts, still hopes, still believes—but just barely. "It may be" that Yahweh will be moved to rescue because Yahweh is affronted by the mocking words of the empire.

AΩ The Rhetoric of "The Day"

The poetic rhetoric of Yahweh's intrusion and vindication echoes the stylized rhetoric of "The Day of the Lord" from other texts. That "Day" is a coming time when Yahweh will decisively act in powerful, brutal ways to defeat all enemies and protect the friends of Yahweh. That rhetoric is on exhibit in Zeph 1:14-16:

The great day of the LORD is near,
   near and hastening fast;
the sound of the day of the LORD is bitter,
   the warrior cries aloud there.
That day will be a day of wrath,
   a day of distress and anguish,
   a day of ruin and devastation,
   a day of darkness and gloom,
   a day of clouds and thick darkness,
   a day of trumpet blast and battle cry
against the fortified cities
   and against the lofty battlements.

Our text anticipates that such a day will befall the Assyrians in the interest of saving the city.

The empire has indeed "mocked the living God." This powerful phrase at the same time accomplishes two rhetorical purposes. First it asserts, against the testimony of the empire, that Yahweh is a living God, a God with energy, will, and capacity to make things new, a self-starter who can restart the public process. The phrase shows Hezekiah to be one who trusts in Yahweh, for Yahweh will not roll over dead like the non-gods whom the Assyrians have defeated.

Second, the empire has mocked the living God. One may mock the powerless gods with impunity; such mocking is appropriate and will evoke no punishment. But to mock the living God is to fly in the face of reality, to present one's self for severe judgment and punishment. [On Mocking Yahweh] On the basis of *the trust of the king* and *the blasphemy of the Assyrians*, the king bids the prophet to pray. The prayer is for "the remnant," for that part of Judah that still lives and hopes, and has not succumbed to the Assyrian threat. The prophet, apparently, is one who can pray powerfully, who prays for guidance and may receive, from Yahweh for the king, counsel on how best to deal with the empire. Via the prophet, the king places his realm in the sure hands of Yahweh.

The prophet's response to the request of the king is bold and direct (19:5-7). It takes the form of a salvation oracle: "Do not fear." [Salvation Oracle] Assyria is a cause for fear, but the assurance of Yahweh, the prophet affirms, is sufficient to override fear in trust and confidence. The prophet affirms back to the king that Assyria has "reviled" (mocked) Yahweh and Yahweh knows it, a ground for assurance. The true basis for the prophetic assurance is voiced in v. 7. Yahweh will act: "I myself." Yahweh is indeed "the living God" who takes initiative. Yahweh will do two interrelated things: (a) Yahweh will cause Sennacherib to hear a rumor and retreat

📖 On Mocking Yahweh

The theme of mocking is an especially grave concern in an honor-shame society. [On the rhetoric of honor and shame, see Thomas Jemielity, *Satire and the Hebrew Prophets*, Literary Currents in Biblical Interpretation (Louisville: Westminster/John Knox Press, 1992).] To mock is to diminish one's authority and capacity for influence. As concerns Yahweh, the theme is operative especially in terms of assaults on the temple in Jerusalem (as in our narrative), for the abuse of the temple is a defiance of the Lord of the temple; see Pss 69:10; 74:22; 79:12. The use of the theme in many texts (as in our text) intends to motivate Yahweh who will be offended by the mocking and so respond by decisive activity.

to go home, (b) where he will be violently killed. Yahweh is a major player in the destabilization and overthrow of the Assyrian regime—no explanation, only an assurance.

A Third Imperial Challenge, 19:8-19

The Assyrians proceed with their verbal (and military) attack on Judah, completely unaware of the decisive prophetic assertion of vv. 5-7. The third challenge to Hezekiah (after 18:19-25, 28-35) mainly reiterates the same negative themes that Yahweh is a false *reliance* (*bâṭaḥ*; v. 10) who cannot *deliver* (19:11), for no god can deliver from the empire. The same mistaken judgment about Yahweh is reiterated by Assyrian theologians who are informed by *comparative religion* but are completely ignorant of Yahweh's *incomparability*. The only new element here is that the Assyrian armies are on the move—from Lachish to Libnah—a move that evokes in turn the Ethiopian forces against Assyria. [Troop Movements] The evocation of Ethiopia, however, does not change the Assyrian threat against Jerusalem in any way.

We are now prepared for a third Jerusalem response to the Assyrian challenge, after the response that requests Hebrew language from the empire (18:26-27), and a response of silence (18:36-37). Hezekiah's response is one of passionate and devout prayer (19:14-19). This prayer reflects not only urgent need and deep faith; it also offers a clear model of true prayer that moves through deliberate rhetorical steps to ground the urgent royal petition.[2]

The prayer is framed by the parallel statements in v. 15 at the beginning and v. 19 at the end, "You alone...God alone." Whereas the Assyrians had dismissively lumped Yahweh with all other gods, the premise of the king's prayer is that Yahweh is unlike all other gods, the only real God, the only God with power, the one who governs all nations, to whom all nations must submit. The prayer is concerned to enhance Yahweh against diminishment by the empire; this enhancement is undertaken with the

AΩ Salvation Oracle

It is plausible that the "do not fear" spoken by the prophet to the king in v. 6 is the pivot point of the text and that the entire promise of vv. 20-34 is an explication of that assurance. [For an exposition of the salvation oracle, see Patrick D. Miller, *They Cried to the Lord: The Form and Theology of Biblical Prayer* (Minneapolis: Fortress Press, 1994) 135-77.] The salvation oracle is Yahweh's characteristic response to prayers of lament and petition such as the one the king has just uttered. Thus one must understand that this royal-prophetic exchange is cast in the rhetorical conventions of the liturgical practices of the temple.

Troop Movements

Libnah is a border town to the southwest of Judah. Reference to it in our text indicates that the struggle with Assyria was in part fought in this vulnerable region of Judah's territory. The reference to Tirhakah also focuses our attention on that area, for it suggests that, as usual, Egyptian policy was to destabilize territory in which its great imperial rival to the north was involved. Tirhakah (690–664) was a prominent and assertive Egyptian Pharaoh representing a dynasty from Sudan, hence "Ethiopian." His activity (mentioned only in our text) is a reminder that Judah was, as usual, embroiled in a complex set of geopolitical relations. It could be that this Pharaoh, like many before him, was simply an opportunist utilizing Judah as a foil against the empire to the north.

initial address of v. 15, an address appropriate to the claims and imagery of the Jerusalem temple. This God is enthroned above the cherubim, wood carvings in the Jerusalem temple that portray winged attendants to Yahweh (see 1 Kgs 6:23-35). The imagery is established as decor, but it operates in prophetic imagination, for example in Ezekiel 9–10, 43–44, bespeaking the vitality and lordly impressiveness of Yahweh. This God is God of all nations and creator of heaven and earth, and at the same time "God of Israel." Thus the prayer makes the most sweeping claims for Yahweh while drawing Yahweh close to the elemental needs of Jerusalem. It is this linkage of *cosmic and particular* that characterizes a prophetic claim for Yahweh. Assyria of course can understand neither the cosmic nor the particular claim.

After the address articulating the broadest of claims for Yahweh, the prayer moves through petition, motivation, and a final petition.[3] The first petition in v. 16 addresses Yahweh with five imperatives: "incline, hear, open, see, hear." The focus of Yahweh's attention is to be upon Sennacherib, who has "mocked the living God" (19:5). The motivation, already voiced at the end of v. 16, gives specificity to the mockery. The way of imperial mocking is not only in the verbalizations we have considered, but also in brutal military policies that have devastated nations and destroyed gods. The prayer presumably has no great sympathy for other gods, but "gods and nations" go together, and Yahweh as creator— already stated in v. 5—is God of all kingdoms. Thus the devastation of the lands is a concrete mocking of Yahweh's rule over those nations. The purpose of the motivational statement in v. 17 is to make clear to Yahweh that Sennacherib's actions are a direct and deliberate affront to Yahweh's own sovereignty. There is as much at stake in this crisis for Yahweh as there is for Hezekiah. Finally the prayer comes to its focal petition in v. 19: "Save us." The verb *yashah* is perhaps stronger than the oft used term "deliver" (*nastal*). This verb refers to a powerful intervention. This single petitionary imperative is the burden of the king's prayer. The rescue might well deliver Jerusalem and save Hezekiah. The prayer, however, concludes with the reminder to Yahweh that such a rescue would greatly enhance Yahweh's reputation among the kingdoms. That is, if Yahweh can and will crush Assyria, it will be everywhere evident that Yahweh does govern, and all other nations will know to worship and obey Yahweh, Yahweh alone. Thus the *particularity* of this rescue of Jerusalem is turned by this prayer into a *cosmic claim* for Yahweh. According to the prayer, Yahweh has as much at stake in this issue as does the king.

Prophetic Intervention, 19:20-34

We have seen the brief assurance of the prophet Isaiah in vv. 5-7. Now the prophet occupies center stage in the narrative. His principle oracle in response to the prayer of the king is in the poem of vv. 21-28. After that oracle are added two prose pronouncements (19:29-31, 32-34), perhaps a result of editorial addition but now a part of the prophet's decisive intervention.

The poem is on the lips of the prophet but is given to us as Yahweh's own response to the prayer of the king (19:20-28). The poem begins in v. 21, by way of introduction, with an acknowledgement that "she," the Assyrian empire, scorns and despises Jerusalem. By this lead statement, Jerusalem is presented as "the righteous sufferer" who endures the hate of detractors but who is the special object of Yahweh's attentiveness.

The first substantive element of the poem has Yahweh address Assyria, specifically Sennacherib as "you" (19:22-24). By its conduct Assyria thought it could mock and revile Jerusalem and Hezekiah with impunity because the powers of Jerusalem are modest and irrelevant to the great empire. Verse 21 has asserted that Assyria mocked "virgin daughter Zion." But the mocking of Jerusalem is in fact a mocking of Yahweh; Assyria mistakenly thought it could mock safely, but failed to reckon with Yahweh who is a force well beyond the visible capacity of Jerusalem. It is Yahweh whom Assyria has mocked, reviled, raised voice against, and lifted eyes in arrogance, exactly as the king has said (19:5, 16).

Because the God mocked is "the living God," the empire will pay dearly. This is none other than "the Holy One of Israel." This latter title is Isaiah's most formidable title for Yahweh, most sovereign, most ominous. Verses 23-24 specify the ways in which Sennacherib has mocked. The mockery has been by "messengers"= ambassadors, as in 18:19-25, 28-35; 19:8-13. The messengers have used a series of first-person pronouns of self-assertion for Sennacherib, as though Sennacherib were a free, unencumbered, autonomous agent in the world who could do what he wanted. Thus the braggadocio of the empire:

> my chariots,
> I have gone up,
> I felled,
> I entered,
> I dug,
> I drank,
> I dried up.

The empire, in its taunting discourse, clearly imagines itself—the last superpower—to be unanswerable to anyone in its aggressive use of all of its power. The references to Lebanon and Egypt refer to Assyrian military advances clear across the Fertile Crescent without hindrance or deterrence. It is to be observed that in the diplomatic arrogance of superpowers, such self-announcement seems ordinary and unexceptional. We must wait until vv. 25-27 to find out how it is that this "ordinary and unexceptional" rhetoric is in fact mockery, reviling, and haughty.

The reason for the disastrous Assyrian miscalculation about Yahweh is that Sennacherib did not understand that he himself is no self-starter. Such autonomy as he thought he possessed is in fact a gross illusion, even when it happens with a superpower. How could Assyria not know? In fact *Yahweh* planned and determined Assyria's actions. Sennacherib did not know it, but he is simply an instrument to act out in the world the long-held resolves of Yahweh:

It is Yahweh who determined that Assyria should destroy fortified cities;

It is Yahweh who causes inhabitants to be dismayed and confounded;

It is Yahweh who causes cities and inhabitants to be blighted and lacking in growth.

It is Yahweh! It is all Yahweh. It is not at all or ever Sennacherib. The Assyrian pretense of autonomy mocks Yahweh by failing to recognize that Yahweh is the one, the only one who takes initiative in international geopolitics. The illusion of autonomy causes Assyria to do crazy, destructive things. Moreover, such destructiveness will not be tolerated! [When Man Becomes God] Yahweh knows every move Sennacherib makes. Yahweh knows about Sennacherib getting up and sitting down, Sennacherib going out to battle and coming home in triumph (see Ps 139:7-12). Indeed, Yahweh knows about Sennacherib's defiant usurpation of Yahweh's preeminence in the world. Yahweh laughs cynically about such posturing:

> He who sits in the heavens laughs;
>   the LORD has them in derision.
> Then he will speak to them in his wrath,
>   and terrify them in his fury. (Ps 2:4-5)

Yahweh may laugh; but Yahweh is not amused!

When Man Becomes God

Donald Gowan has written clearly and eloquently on texts that show the arrogance of imperial powers that are taken to be rivals and therefore enemies of Yahweh. [Donald Gowan, *When Man Becomes God: Humanism and Hybris in the Old Testament,* Pittsburgh Theological Monograph Series 6 (Pittsburgh: Pickwick Press, 1975).] Gowan makes clear that the besetting temptation of superpowers is autonomy that shows up in policies of control, abuse, and exploitation that seem to serve state interest but are in fact superfluous to normal state interest. In such texts, Yahweh represents a deep, elemental resistance and curb to such aggrandizement.

The oracle of Isaiah concludes in v. 28 with an uncompromising speech of judgment:

> *Indictment:* because you have raged…

> *Sentence:* [therefore] I will put…I will turn.

Because Assyria is arrogant, the Assyrian armies will be tamed and bridled by Yahweh who will lead Assyria home—against its will—the way any master/trainer handles a subdued animal that has been out of control.

The poem is a remarkable example of prophetic assertion that defeats and curbs imperial autonomy. It is worth noting that this poem says nothing about the rescue of Jerusalem or about Yahweh's care for Israel or Hezekiah. All that counts here is the reassertion of Yahweh's magisterial rule against autonomy and imperial illusion. To be sure, answer to the king's prayer for rescue is an assured by-product of Yahweh's self-assertion, but it is clearly by-product and not intention. The point is to reassert "the Holy One." The arena of that assertion is Israel, so that the outcome is for "the Holy One *in Israel.*" In the same assertion, the rescue of Israel and the glorification of Yahweh over Assyria are accomplished in one rhetorical maneuver. The poem is a vigorous example of the biblical claim that the "kingdom, the power, and the glory" of Yahweh are indeed enacted in the earth. This, of course, is what "the messengers" of Assyria cannot understand, this upon which the king in Jerusalem must finally rely.

The splendid poetic assertion of the prophet is reinforced in a prose utterance that makes the promise of deliverance quite concrete (19:29-31). The narrative offers a "sign" as further verification that the poetic promise is reliable. This is an unrequested sign, as though the narrative tradition were resolved to enhance the pledge of Yahweh made through the prophet. While "signs" are often uncommon events that bespeak Yahweh's powerful commitment (as in 20:8-11), here the sign is simply the assertion that abundant agricultural produce will prosper in a three-year period. The sign attests that the creator is reliably at work causing the earth to produce.

The linkage in v. 30 moves from the sphere of creation to that of history, asserting that as the creator wills an abundant creation, so the redeemer wills well-being in history. Judah will prosper like good agricultural growth, rooted down into the earth, bearing fruit up into its branches. The use of such terms as "remnant" and "survivor" may appeal to the Isaiah tradition and its use of those terms, and likely reflects an exilic or postexilic context when the population had been decimated and the historical continuity of the community was seen to be in jeopardy.[4] In such a context, "rooted down" might refer especially to being securely in the land and not displaced. If the oracle does indeed concern a belated remnant community, then the break in time between the poem and the prose narrative of the sign is considerable, and suggests that the vindication of Jerusalem is not as decisive, visible, and glorious as the poem anticipates. [The Destruction of Sennacherib]

This in fact is not much of a sign when seen in the context of imperial threat. In the end, what counts is the final phrasing of v. 31, on which see Isaiah 9:7. It is the "zeal"—the passionate commitment—of Yahweh that will preserve the remnant community. Yahweh is here identified as "Lord of Hosts," a title bespeaking near-military capacity, set against the military capacity of the threatening empire. The entire three verses and especially this last statement assert that the empire in all its power is finally no match for Yahweh.[5] Yahweh, in resolve to *sustain*, will override every historical attempt to *nullify* Jerusalem. It is in Yahweh's passionate commitment that the future of the community rests. When heard in the context of Assyrian mocking, the oracle is a sweeping insistence that Yahweh is indeed *trustworthy* and will *deliver*, precisely the two points of the Assyrian taunt. The rhetoric of remnant may be a grudging concession to reality. The historical deliverance is not too soon (if exilic or postexilic) and not too grand. But it is undoubted and sure.

In the second prose oracle added to the poem, the promise becomes much more concrete (19:32-34). Now we are dealing with no "sign" that only indirectly makes a statement, but now we have a direct promissory speech from Yahweh. The preliminary statement concerns "the king of Assyria" who is unnamed (19:32-33). He will not enter Jerusalem! The

The Destruction of Sennacherib

The Assyrian came down like wolf on the fold,
And his cohorts were gleaming in purple and gold;
And the sheen of their spears was like the stars on the sea,
When the blue wave rolls nightly on deep Galilee.

Like the leaves of the forest when Summer is green,
That host with their banners at sunset were seen:
Like leaves of the forest when Autumn hath blown,
That host on the morrow lay wither'd and strown

For the Angel of Death spread his wings on the blast,
And breathed in the face of the foe as he pass'd,
And the eyes of the sleepers wax'd deadly and chill,
And their hearts were once heavend, and for ever grew still!

And there lay the steed with his nostril all wide,
But through it there roll'd not the breath of his pride;
And the foam of his gasping lay white on the turf,
And cold as the spray of the rock-beating surf.

And there lay the rider distorted and pale,
With the dew on his brow, and the rust on his mail
And the tents were all silent, the banners alone,
The lances unlifted, the trumpet unblown.

And the widows of Ashur are loud in the wail,
And the idols are broke in the temple of Baal;
And the might of the Gentile, unsmote by the sword,
Hath melted like snow in the glance of the LORD!

—Lord Byron

Julius Schnoor von Carolsfeld. *The Angel Smiting the Camp of the Assyrians.*19th century. Woodcut. From *Das Buch der Bucher in Bilden*. (Credit: Dover Pictorial Archive Series)

negative is a series of four verbs, each governed by a negative: *not* enter, *not* shoot, *not* come before, *not* cast up. Sennacherib is a big "not" by the decree of Yahweh. Instead of *attack* (now negated), the empire will *retreat* (19:33). Sennacherib is, in an unqualified utterance of Yahweh, simply removed as a factor in the future of the city.

The weight of this oracle, however, comes after the imagined departure of Sennacherib in v. 34. This verse is one of the most remarkable in all of Scripture, a simple, unqualified promise to save the city and to keep it safe. The motivation for this promised protection is twofold: First, *for my sake*, in the service of Yahweh's reputation. In an honor-shame society such as the ancient world, Yahweh's actions for victory are seen to enhance Yahweh's reputation in the eyes of other nations and other gods, a matter verbalized by Hezekiah in 19:19. Yahweh will save Yahweh's own city of Jerusalem because all will see in such a rescue Yahweh's power and fidelity. Second, the city is rescued *for the sake of David*, because of

Yahweh's commitment to David and to David's dynasty, thus enacting fidelity to very old commitments.

This amazing commitment on Yahweh's part is noteworthy because it is, in all of the Old Testament, the highest, simplest statement of the guaranteed safety and well-being of Jerusalem as "the city of David." We may derive two additional observations from this guarantee. First, Yahweh is here unqualifiedly committed to a historical-geographical structure, a divine absolutizing of human arrangements, a commitment that stands, in Christian tradition, as a threshold to "word become flesh." Second, the *my sake* and *sake of David* are an important convergence of divine and human agenda, so that Yahweh's righteous guarantee serves both agenda at exactly the same time in the same way. Such a convergence exhibits Yahweh as a God in specific historical form and negates any chance of Yahweh ever being misunderstood philosophically or generically as a god apart from this place and this people. In context, the phrase, "for the sake of David my servant," surely commits to Hezekiah who is the "model David" as a perfect Torah-keeper (see 18:3). This quite specific promise thus brings to completion the extended prophetic response to the king's prayer. In this oracle, Yahweh has disposed of the blasphemer Sennacherib and made safe the city that seemed so much in jeopardy from the Assyrians.

The narrator knows that in order for the prophetic promises to be fully convincing to later generations of readers, the promises must be matched by *narrative enactment*, offered in vv. 35-37. The narrative is terse and says nothing of Jerusalem or David. It is concerned only with the narrative nullification of the Assyrian threat, a threat that will appear no more in our larger narrative. The opening phrase of v. 35 is voiced as though in the same twenty-four hour period the prophetic utterance is enacted as historical fulfillment. As with Exodus (Exod 12:29) and Easter (Luke 24:1), the deliverance of Yahweh happens in the dark of night when no one can see or explain.

The deliverance is briefly given in v. 35. A *messenger* (angel) of Yahweh came and killed 185,000 Assyrian soldiers. The number is astonishing and is meant to be. There surely is irony in the work of a "messenger" to counter the Assyrian "messengers" who earlier were so arrogant but now are completely impotent and irrelevant. Yahweh's messenger is decisive because Yahweh has sent him. Conversely the Assyrian messengers do not matter now because—it turns out!—they were dispatched by impotent kings and feeble gods. In the night, the imperial messengers are nowhere to be seen when needed. Indeed, the night contest is a rout, no competition, no resistance, nothing left but "dead bodies." The rhetoric is surely designed to recall the narrative conclusion of the Exodus:

> Thus the LORD saved Israel that day from the Egyptians; and Israel saw the Egyptians dead on the seashore. (Exod 14:30)

This is another mighty deliverance, with an exodus from another oppressive pharaoh:

> Israel saw the great work that the LORD did against the Egyptians. So the people feared the LORD and believed in the LORD and in his servant Moses. (Exod 14:31)

Israel may now believe, that is "trust," for this is the work of Yahweh for the king who trusts and for the prophet who speaks the truth.

The narrative cannot end with the deliverance, but must mock the contemptuous Sennacherib all the way home, to make sure his evil fate is fully and deservedly enacted (19:36-27). The two verses are not essential to the narrative but show both the historian's need for completion and a theological passion to be sure the reader "gets it" about arrogant power. Sennacherib went home to Assyria. He had no choice. He had lost his army. Yahweh had wiped him out. Even Nineveh, it turns out, is no safe place for such a blasphemer. He is an idolater…what else could he be as an Assyrian? He is killed. He is superseded by his son. The dynasty of Sennacherib continues, but it is a dynasty of devouring internal violence that matches its external brutality. Sennacherib is a loser, losing to Yahweh in Jerusalem, losing to home folks in Nineveh, losing everywhere, a practitioner of imperial violence finally devoured by that same imperial violence. All the while Sennacherib suffers his fate in vv. 35-37, Jerusalem in v. 34 is utterly safe—just as the king had asked, just as the prophet had promised, just as Yahweh had intended. In the end, all is well, even if only for a remnant.

CONNECTIONS

Through v. 13 this chapter continues the reflection of chapter 18 on *faith* in *the incomparable God* who can *deliver*. Reference may be made to my comments on those themes in chapter 18.

While Hezekiah's prayer in vv. 14-19 constitutes an answer to the third Assyrian speech of vv. 8-13 and so corresponds to the previous answers in 18:26-27, 36-37, we may understand the prayer as a part of the large unit of vv. 14-28. This larger unit is shaped as *royal prayer* and *prophetic response*. The prayer revolves around the petition of v. 19, "save us," and is framed by doxological affirmation at the beginning and at the end. The doxologies make clear that Yahweh's self-interest is at stake in the rescue of Jerusalem.[6] The larger structure of the responding prophetic oracle (19:20-28) evidences the narrator's conviction that Yahweh decisively answers prayer in ways that effect historical transformations. The oracle of the prophet is rhetorically shaped as address to Sennacherib, but in fact functions as an assurance to Hezekiah. Thus the oracle matches the petition of the king and concerns the immediate reality of Hezekiah's crisis. Taken more broadly as Scripture to be heard and trusted long after the Assyrian crisis, the point is that Yahweh is decisive in public affairs and that particular engagement with Yahweh as sovereign is through the act of prayer. Thus prayer is dramatically linked to the outcomes of public issues, a daring literary and theological claim, characteristic of prophetic faith that is enacted liturgically and pastorally. One need hardly observe that the claims of this presentation, judged by Assyrian rationality or the rationality of modernity, are not credible and border on the absurd. That fact can be granted while we nonetheless insist that the narrative protests against the grain of imperial "common sense." This presentation insists that imperial common sense characteristically misunderstands precisely because Yahweh matters, because Yahweh must be taken seriously by the self-sufficient pride of the empire. Hezekiah is commended because he trusts and prays, contrary to the wisdom of the world.

The prophetic assurance of vv. 20-28 is vouched for in the sign of vv. 29-31 and made most explicit in vv. 32-33. Taken all together, vv. 20-34 constitute *a promise* from the prophet that is actualized in vv. 35-37 as *historical happening*. That is, the structure and movement of these verses are as *promise and fulfillment*. In the defeat of Assyria in v. 35, Jerusalem is miraculously, that is, inexplicably saved. The prophet is vindicated and Hezekiah is rescued. Yahweh does what Yahweh says! Without the narrative confirmation of

vv. 35-37, the promises would hang in the air as a rhetorical irrelevance.

To be sure, acceptance of this deliverance strains our modern credulity. Indeed, Richard Nelson readily acknowledges this issue:

> The major interpretive problem with this narrative is that most of its modern readers will simply be unable to believe that it actually happened.... According to his own reports, Sennacherib left Judah without capturing Jerusalem, but few historians would be willing to credit the angel of the Lord for a death toll of one hundred eighty-five thousand.[7]

To measure this rescue by such rationality however, is to miss the point completely, as Nelson well knows. The Bible hangs or falls on its attestation of the decisive difference Yahweh makes in real events.[8] Even Nelson concludes:

> In the end God will defeat them—Pharaoh, Sennacherib, Domitian. For Christians, the event which makes it possible to believe such incredible news is the resurrection of Jesus, the defeat of death itself. All the Old Testament victories of God, both historical and literary, serve as pointers to and signs of that cosmic Easter triumph.[9]

That is, Easter is the supreme miracle in a Christian reading of the Bible.

But Easter is simply the culminating act, according to this testimony, of a series of acts whereby God's holy power impinges upon lived history in transformative ways. In the end, it is asserted that the enormous, autonomous power of Assyria cannot resist the purposes of Yahweh who acts for "Yahweh's own sake." Yahweh is at work toward good ends, which the power of the world cannot stop. Such a claim violates all our modernity, but modernity (in this context) is simply our contemporary, belated form of Assyrian hybris.

The great beneficiary of this entire exchange is Jerusalem. It is impossible to overstate the great significance of the rescue of 701 (late in the career of Sennacherib) for the place of Jerusalem in biblical faith. This wondrous deliverance, however it is to be explained or understood, makes Jerusalem the locus of Jewish, Christian, and Muslim hopes and dreams.[Hymnic Reverberations]

In biblical and derivative Christian traditions, Jerusalem—the saved city of Hezekiah—has become metaphor and cipher for concrete historical hopes:

Glories of your name are spoken,
Zion, city of our God;
He whose word cannot be broken
Formed you for his own abode.
On the Rock of Ages founded,
What can shake your sure repose?
With salvation's walls surrounded,
You may smile at all your foes.[10]

The rescue signifies that well-being in the world is the free, inexplicable but deeply trustworthy and overwhelming gift of God:

1. There has been a huge tendency in Christian tradition to *spiritualize* Jerusalem so that it is not the concrete city, but the envisioned paradise of well-being signified by Jerusalem. Of course the sober realities of Near Eastern tensions over the city keep the church from too much spiritualizing, for the concrete city of Jerusalem continues to be a place of deep dispute and vexation.

2. There is a powerful urge—supported by Isaiah 65:17-25 and Revelation 21—to treat Jerusalem as an *eschatological* symbol, so that it is a future city of *shalom*, which will override the present troubled city.

There is no doubt that the notion of Jerusalem, out of this narrative, has become a freighted, rich image for faith. Without detracting from that interpretive inclination, the narrative itself always pulls us back to a real city facing a real empire, summoning always to costly faith in God, who acts, so says the text, decisively, wondrously, against all odds. The deliverance that stunned Sennacherib is not for explanation. It is for astonishment, amazement, gratitude, awe, doxology, and finally obedience. This concreteness braced with hope, or conversely that hope sobered by concreteness, invites the faithful, even in the face of Sennacherib, to exult, "Next year in Jerusalem."

NOTES

[1]See Walter Brueggemann, "The Legitimacy of a Sectarian Hermeneutic 2 Kings 18-19," *Interpretation and Obedience: From Faithful Reading to Faithful Living* (Minneapolis: Fortress Press, 1991) 41-69.

[2]See Patrick D. Miller, *They Cried to the Lord: The Form and Theology of Biblical Prayer* (Minneapolis: Fortress Press, 1994) 158-59.

[3]The presence of motivation in the midst of several petitions is not exceptional. Our more conventional notions of prayer focus rightly upon petition. The motivation is more surprising to us, and is often seen to be ignoble. The purpose of the motivation is to provide Yahweh reasons to answer the petition. One of the primary strategies of such motivation is to make a case that there is something at stake for Yahweh in the crisis as well as for the suppliant.

In this case, Yahweh's honor is at stake. If the Assyrians can abuse the holy city without punishment, Yahweh's credibility and authority are deeply undermined, so implies the prayer of the king.

[4]On the remnant as a theological theme with particular reference to Isaiah, see G. E. Hasel, *The Remnant*, 2d ed. (Berrien Springs MI: Andrews University Press, 1974).

[5]The same sort of combat that exhibits the other gods as powerless is in the narrative of 1 Samuel 5. During the daytime, Dagon, the god of the Philistines, is honored and taken to be victorious over Yahweh. But in the night, when no one can see, Dagon is shown to be powerless before the hidden, inscrutable but very real power of Yahweh who can "disarm" the Philistine god and finally rout that god completely. The defeat of Dagon is a fairly conventional way in which the narrative victories of Yahweh are presented by Israel.

[6]See the fine structural analysis of this prayer by Samuel E. Balentine, *Prayer in the Hebrew Bible: The Drama of Divine-Human Dialogue*, OBT (Minneapolis: Fortress Press, 1993) 95-96.

[7]Richard Nelson, *First and Second Kings* (Interpretation; Atlanta: John Knox Press, 1987) 242.

[8]On the characterization of the Old Testament text as attestation (testimony), see Walter Brueggemann, *Theology of the Old Testament: Testimony, Dispute, Advocacy* (Minneapolis: Fortress Press, 1997) 117-144.

[9]Nelson, *First and Second Kings*, 242-43.

[10]The original words of the well-known hymn—"Glorious Things of Thee Are Spoken"—are by John Newton.

THE END OF HEZEKIAH: THE LONG-TERM END OF JERUSALEM

2 Kings 20:1-21

This chapter contains two additional episodes concerning King Hezekiah, plus a concluding formula in vv. 20-21. The first episode concerns the personal illness of the king (20:1-11). The second is an oracle concerning the coming judgment upon the Davidic dynasty (20:12-19). The two episodes are quite distinct; their juxtaposition, however, may suggest a deliberate placement. The first episode makes clear that it is only by Yahweh's graciousness that Hezekiah lives; in the same way, it is only by Yahweh's decree that the dynasty will end. Thus the juxtaposition of mercy and judgment, shown respectively to king and dynasty, evidences the cruciality of Yahweh for the well-being of both king and dynasty. Yahweh alone has the whole of Jerusalem "in his hands."

COMMENTARY

Sickness and Healing, 20:1-11

We are not told what ails the king. Hezekiah's illness is the premise of the narrative, and apparently the motivation for the prophet's presence and pronouncement (20:1). The prophet is inescapably present and decisive in the crucial turns of the life of the king. (In earlier texts on prophets in the midst of illness, see 1 Kgs 14 and 2 Kgs 1.) Knowing that the royal illness is in the hands of Yahweh, the prophet declares that it is a terminal illness.

Hezekiah's response to the prophetic verdict is twofold, both in one sentence. He turns away from the prophet, perhaps in resistance to the verdict. In the same instant, however, he turns to Yahweh in prayer. We have already seen Hezekiah twice as a pious man of prayer, first urging the prophet to pray (19:4) and then uttering his own urgent petition that evoked the prophetic response (19:15-19). The present prayer is remarkable, for it addresses no explicit petition to Yahweh (20:3). It only appeals to Yahweh and offers a motivation to Yahweh, that the king has been utterly faithful and obedient to Yahweh (on which see 18:5-7). The tone of the prayer suggests that because of Hezekiah's genuine piety, Yahweh is obligated to respond positively to his need. We are not told the meaning of the king's bitter weeping. It is, in any case, a response very different from his first response in v. 2. Perhaps his great weeping is an acknowledgement of a lack of personal resources, and by implication, an acknowledgement of his unqualified reliance upon Yahweh.

In any case, the prayer is effective. As his prayer in 19:15-19 promptly evoked the assuring prophetic oracle of 19:21-28, so here his prayer evokes the remarkable prophetic response of vv. 5-6. The judgment made by the prophet in v. 1 that the king would die is not given as a prophetic judgment but only as a medical opinion. (It lacks the messenger formula.) That medical opinion, however, is countermanded by the intervening God who, in response to the pious, passionate prayer of the king, alters the future of the sick king. Not only has God heard his prayer, but God has seen the tears, apparently taking the tears as an elemental form of petition, so elemental as to be beyond utterance. Yahweh will heal! The king's capacity to return to his royal role in the temple is a measure of his full restitution. His restoration is a decisive contrast to the leprosy of Uzziah that precluded his ever returning to the temple (see 2 Kgs 15:5). The one set to die will live because of the resolve of Yahweh in response to prayer. Not only will the king be delivered from his ailment, but he may anticipate fifteen additional years of well-being, a remarkable gift.

The prophetic response goes well beyond the sickness of the king. The oracle, congruent with that of 19:34, also assures well-being for the city with two decisive verbs, "deliver, defend." In light of this utterance, there can be no doubt that the illness of the king is understood as an ebbing of the power of the dynasty. The motivation for the reversal on Yahweh's part, moreover, is for David's sake and for "my own sake," a phrase echoing 19:34. The double phrase suggests a remarkable feature of Yahweh's commitment to Jerusalem. Yahweh has indeed made promises to David and to David's dynasty that are now in play (see Ps 89:19-37). Yahweh will keep Yahweh's promises! Beyond that, however, Yahweh will save the city from Assyria for Yahweh's own sake, i.e., to defend the honor and reputation of Yahweh before the nations and the other gods. Yahweh's motivation is in part self-enhancement. The happy reality is that in this prophetic utterance, Yahweh's own sake and David's sake converge. The king will live and the city will be safe.

Yahweh is a guarantor of well-being. Verse 7 would seem to be simply medical advice for the specific illness of the king, but is an afterthought to the theological point of the oracle.

It is remarkable after such a resounding and reassuring oracle by the prophet upon whom the king has previously relied that the king asks for "a sign," for tangible evidence that the oracle of hope is reliable. There is no hint here that a request for a sign is an act of doubt—doubt by Isaiah or doubt of Yahweh—but in Isaiah 7:10-14, Ahaz, father of Hezekiah, refuses to ask a sign, for it would be regarded as an unnecessary challenge to Yahweh. Here Hezekiah has no such reservation or compunction. The king is filled with authority and is unabashed in his demand. He not only wants a sign; he specifies: turn time back. Let the shadows recede instead of advancing.

The request of the king is remarkable. But perhaps if Yahweh can interfere with his illness to bring healing, Yahweh can as well interfere with time and bring back lost time. The bold challenge by the pious king perhaps alludes to two old memories in Israel's lore. First, we are reminded of the moment in Joshua's battle against the Amorites when the darkness threatened to engulf the battle. Joshua asked for more time and he received it from Yahweh:

> Sun, stand still at Gibeon,
> 　　and Moon, in the valley of Aijalon.
> And the sun stood still, and the moon stopped,
> 　　until the nation took vengeance on their enemies.
> (Josh 10:12-13)

Remarkably the request of Joshua is granted. The sun stopped in its tracks in order to lengthen the day:

> The sun stopped in mid-heaven, and did not hurry
> to set for about a whole day. (Josh 10:13)

And then the narrator adds:

> There has been no day like it before or since, when the LORD heeded a human voice; for the LORD fought for Israel. (Josh 10:14)

In making this latter statement, the narrator apparently had not yet reckoned with the drama of Hezekiah, for not only does the sun stand still for the king, but for this beloved king it moves back.

Second, Hezekiah's double demand for a sign is closely reminiscent of the demand of Gideon. Gideon asks for a sign from the angel of Yahweh (Judg 6:17), and specifies the sign:

> In order to see whether you will deliver Israel by my hand, as you have said, I am going to lay a fleece of wool on the threshing floor; if there is dew on the fleece alone, and it is dry on all the ground, then I shall know that you will deliver Israel by my hand, as you have said. (Judg 6:36-37)

When that sign is given, Gideon reverses field:

> Let me, please, make trial with the fleece just once more; let it be dry only on the fleece, and on all the ground let there be dew. (Judg 6:39)

In each case, the sign is granted and Gideon is assured of Yahweh's solidarity with Israel. In like manner, Hezekiah receives confirmation of the oracle through sign. The prophet invokes Yahweh and time is moved back (20:11). The creator God has disrupted conventional sequence in order to reassure the Jerusalem king. The entire ordering of creation is mobilized and "reset" for the sake of Jerusalem. The king now knows for sure that healing will come to him from Yahweh.

An Oracle of Termination, 20:12-21

After the remarkable affirmation of vv. 4-11, we are scarcely prepared for the severe oracle that follows next. Whereas vv. 1-11 concerned the personal fate of the king (except for v. 6), this episode concerns the public future of the dynasty and the city.

Abruptly, Babylon enters the purview of the narrative in the person of Merodach-baladan, son of Baladan. [Merodach-baladan] We, along with the king and the prophet, have been completely preoccupied with the threat of Assyria (see v. 6). The appearance of Babylon in the narrative suggests anti-Assyrian intrigue, for Babylon was a stifled province of Assyria that ached for its autonomy. Perhaps the visit was an attempt to provoke Hezekiah into active rebellion against Assyria, surely a high-risk venture.

Whatever may have been the motivation for the visit, Hezekiah is an overly responsive host who welcomes the visiting dignitaries. (We note reference to his sickness in past tense in v. 12, suggesting the efficacy of the prophetic promise of healing.) Hezekiah's welcome includes a candid, perhaps exhibitionist, display of royal resources, both economic and military. It is the kind of exhibit that one might make only to one's most trusted allies, even though this is, as far as we know, a first meeting. One may suspect that discussion and negotiation may have moved far toward an anti-Assyrian conspiracy, though no hint of that is offered in the narrative.

When the envoys from Babylon have gone, the prophet and the king have a conversation, suggesting that Isaiah has easy and frequent access to the king.[1] The prophet asks two questions that the king answers without hesitation: "From Babylon." "They have seen everything." There is no hint in the prophet's questions nor in the entire exchange of any note of reprimand. It could be that this is only an innocent enquiry, a gathering of information among friends. The prophet, however, is always a prophet, always holding out to royal power (yet another dimension of governance to which the king has not adequately attended). What may have been simply an innocent act of friendship on the part of the king toward his new allies, in prophetic perspective, was a foolish and unnecessary exposure that makes Jerusalem freshly vulnerable.

Merodach-baladan

Merodach-baladan was a Babylonian sheikh who played a prominent role in the politics of the upper Fertile Crescent in the time of Hezekiah. He was a sometime subservient ally of Assyria, but used great energy and effectiveness in resisting Assyria and in staking out some independence for Babylon, at that time a subordinate power. His importance for our text and for the politics of Jerusalem is that he became a rallying point for opposition to Assyria. In the next century, at the time of Josiah, Babylon was to become more formidable and finally to displace Assyria as the dominant power (see 23:29-30).

In any case, the exchange between prophet and king promptly produces a prophetic oracle (20:16-19). The oracle is not connected to the immediately preceding meeting. There is no "therefore" of cause and effect, as though Hezekiah's careless exhibition would produce danger. Indeed, it may be that the oracle stands alone and would have come anyway. The narrative, however, arranges the materials to suggest more than that.

In contrast to the exchange of vv. 1-11, this oracle is harsh. There is no indictment, no reason given that appeals to the king's waywardness or disobedience. It is possible that this is simply, in context, a prophetic anticipation of what is inevitable in the rise and fall of great powers. In any case, the prophetic oracle looks ahead to the Babylonian sacking of Jerusalem and its treasury. [Anticipated Babylon]

The prophet declares that Babylon will come and seize everything. More than the loss of wealth, sons of the royal house will be taken away to the royal palace in Babylon. There they will be made subservient functionaries in the royal household of Babylon. That they are to be "eunuchs" in Babylon may be only a necessary sign of submissiveness; but the same noun bespeaks the termination of

Anticipated Babylon

With the resistance Merodach-baladan led in Babylon against Assyrian hegemony, one could anticipate the rise of Babylon as a major power to challenge and finally dominate Assyria. This did not happen, however, until the rise of a new dynasty in Babylon, founded by Nabopolassar (625–605 BC) who was succeeded by his more famous son, Nebuchadnezzar (604–562 BC). Babylon comes to dominate the Near East and certainly comes to dominate the imagination of ancient Israel in the period when it shaped its canonical text.

The first reference to the Babylonians in our text, perhaps appropriated from a like usage in Isaiah 39, is probably not a historical anticipation, for the text was written after the fact; but it is a rhetorical anticipation so that the reader in the time of Hezekiah can already see that the final trouble for Jerusalem comes from Babylon. Thus the introduction of the Babylonians in 20:1 is an ominous and irreversible turn in the narrative as it was an ominous and irreversible turn in the life of Judah. The prophet of course knew this long before the king recognized it.

the royal dynasty, for eunuchs, even royal eunuchs, do not bear royal heirs. The announcement bespeaks a sorry, humiliating termination of the monarchy. [Princes Become Eunuchs]

Hezekiah's response to the oracle is perhaps shameless, certainly pathos-filled (20:19). The first part of the response echoes the pious response of the priest Eli when told of the divine judgment against his priestly family:

It is the LORD; let him do what seems good to him.
(1 Sam 3:18)

That part of the royal response voices an unflinching piety and readiness to trust and submit to Yahweh's purpose in any case, exactly what we would expect from Hezekiah. The second part of the response, however, is less noble, suggesting that the king reckons his own life, and reign will be undisturbed, as though he had no care for what comes after.[2]

The oracle and response bring to a close the reign of Hezekiah, the most remarkable and approved of all of the kings in the narrative up to this point. While we cannot assess what is "historical" about the exchange between prophet and king, it is not difficult to see the function of the prophetic oracle in the longer sweep of the books of Kings. This oracle looks beyond Assyrian domination to the difficult final days of Judah, when Babylon will sack the city and deport the king (chapters 24–25). The narrator knows where the narrative is headed. The story, Hezekiah's piety notwithstanding, culminates in demise at the hands of Babylon. In the parallel account in Isaiah 39, the literary-canonical matter is arranged differently. In that text, the same words plunge Judah into the exile, so that a period of 150 years passes before the utterance of Isaiah 40:1. That utterance assumes not only the destruction here anticipated but the long period of displacement and exile that followed the destruction. Both accounts—in Kings and in Isaiah—mark the Babylonian appearance as a step toward the final termination.

The concluding formula concerning Hezekiah is conventional, anticipating his son Manasseh (20:20-21). The single point to be noted here is the reference to the improvements Hezekiah made in the water supply of the city. We have already seen Hezekiah preoccupied with the water supply (18:17), a note paralleled by his father Ahaz (Isa 7:3). The problem of water for the city was acute in the face of any prospect for a military siege against the city. In our text, it is likely that Hezekiah took concrete steps to enhance the water supply of the city by constructing a new conduit for water. Most remarkably, archaeologists have found an inscription celebrating the completion of the new water channel, surely an achievement welcomed in the jeopardized and exposed city. [The Tunnel Inscription] This achievement is yet one more indication of the formidable quality of Hezekiah's royal administration, a formidable rule soon to be squandered by his son Manasseh.

CONNECTIONS

We may in turn consider the personal and public aspects of this narrative. The personal account of the sickness of the king moves in quick sequence:

> sickness…healing
> > prayer…oracle.

At one level, the external matters of the king's personal condition, the movement is *from sickness to healing*. That by itself could yield a commonsense, albeit surprising, turn of affairs. The narrative,

---

AΩ **Princes Become Eunuchs**

It is possible that the term rendered "eunuch" (*sarîs*) may mean a castrated male, or it can mean simply "minor official." Either way it bespeaks subservience and humiliation. It is not clear what we may make of the term, but we may see in one moment (a) the deportation of Jehoiachin as a boy to Babylon together with (b) Jeremiah's anticipation that Jehoiachin would have no heirs (Jer 22:30), as real eunuchs would not. Moreover, attention must be paid to Isaiah 56:3-5 that clearly recognizes that such eunuchs were a part of the exiled community who want to be restored to and included in the community of faith. This cluster of texts in any case witnesses to the emergency created by subservience to Babylon, partly coerced and partly done willingly. The entire cluster of texts points to the deep humiliation that is seen to be part of the consequence of Yahweh's decision no longer to practice fidelity toward the dynasty.

The Tunnel Inscription

The mention in our text of Hezekiah's attention to the city water supply is explicated more fully in 2 Chronicles 32:4, 30. In 1880, archaeologists found an inscription carved on the wall of the water conduit. The inscription celebrated the achievement of the channel and tells how the workmen working from the two ends of the channel called out to each other, until finally the work converged on the completed tunnel. Robert B. Coote

Siloam Tunnel Inscription. c. 700 BC. Flat stone with inscription in ancient Hebrew marking the completion of the water tunnel under Hezekiah.

(Credit: Palestine Archaelogical Museum, Israel)

suggests that the calling from one side to another indicates that the final connection of the two crews was largely accomplished in the midst of uncertainty and confusion by responding to the sounds. [Robert B. Coote, "Siloam Inscription," ABD 6:23-24.] The inscription itself is a remarkable confirmation of the data given in the biblical texts concerning Hezekiah's achievement in the face of the vulnerability of the city's water supply.

---

however, insists that the primary elements in the event are *prayer and oracle*, so that the crisis is not simply a biological trouble, but an engagement with Yahweh, who has power to heal when evoked to pay attention. [Israel's Characteristic Prayer] Thus the narrative pivots on prayer, the daring capacity of an Israelite—any Israelite, but in this case the king—to impinge upon Yahweh by bitter tears of need and demand. It is certain that this narrative, and the Bible generally, offers no "naturalistic" account of such human crisis, but keeps issues of well-being intensely Yahwistic. It is not as though these characters live a "naturalistic" life and then, at the last moment, invoke Yahweh in an emergency as "the God of the gaps." No, it is rather that the entire life of Israel, according to this text, is framed, understood, and practiced as a covenantal transaction with the God of covenant, who issues commands and keeps promises. In such a world, it is unimaginable that illness—or any other condition—would not be understood in terms of covenantal transactions of prayer.

The public dimension of this narrative is to be understood in a way parallel to the personal arena of prayer. In the public as in the personal, the appearance of Isaiah reminds us of a surplus-defining dimension of reality not to be explained conventionally, neither the personal by biology nor the public by *Realpolitik*. Isaiah's oracle reminds the king and the reader that there are large, hidden processes at work in the public arenas of life that pertain to the rise and fall of nations.

In this particular case, it may well be that the books of Kings, like the book of Isaiah, simply knows in retrospect what is coming next. That is a perfectly credible way to think, since these books are designed to function as prophetic models for coming generations. If, however, we are to understand the prophetic oracle in vv. 16-18 in something like an Isaianic frame of reference, then one may say that prophetic faith wanted neither Judah's self-destructive defiance of Assyria (as here perhaps proposed by Merodach-baladan) nor compliance to Babylon as new ally that would promptly become a vigorous and vicious enemy as circumstance permitted. A prophetic assessment of foreign policy, exemplified by Isaiah, is not simply a juggling and weighing of geopolitical options—though the prophetic tradition is knowing and wise about such matters—but concerns the steadfastness of Yahweh as a key and operative factor in public decision-making. That side of Isaiah is more evidenced in the book of Isaiah that operates with what Klaus Koch terms a "meta-history."[3]

The juxtaposition of the two prophetic oracles—one on healing and one on exile—is, in the end, telling. The personal oracle of vv. 5-6 offers assurance; the public oracle of vv. 16-18 offers only threat. The two oracles together define life with reference to

---

📖 Israel's Characteristic Prayer

In a most helpful "theology of prayer," Patrick Miller makes the following pivotal points:

1. The active involvement of God in the human situation is evoked by cries to God, by prayers for help.
2. Petitionary prayer is fundamentally an act of persuasion, seeking to lure or coax God into responding to the cry for help.
3. The prayers of Scripture consistently expect and receive a response from God in a word that has a particular character to it and in help that transforms the situation, redeeming the one(s) in trouble. Such help may be perceived to a more-or-less degree as miraculous.
4. Trust in God is a dimension of the context of prayer and also a part of the transforming act.
5. The dominant language of prayer in the form of a cry for help that arises out of the pain of suffering and oppression, however responded to in the story, carries with it an implied claim that there is a moral ground to the universe.

Patrick D. Miller, "Prayer and Divine Action," *God in the Fray: A Tribute to Walter Brueggemann,* ed. Tod Linafelt and Timothy K. Beal (Minneapolis: Fortress Press, 1998) 212-29.

Given Miller's analysis (not all of which I have summarized here), two points become abundantly clear. First, Hezekiah's prayer is completely consonant with the characteristic practice of prayer in Israel and is unexceptional. Second, this entire practice, so crucial to faith, enacted by Hezekiah in this narrative, lives in a world totally apart from modern rationality and cannot be made sensible or credible in that latter, thin world. But men and women of prayer have always known that faith is practiced according to other categories of discernment and trust, and are not scandalized by that distinction.

On the different rhetoric of faith with its own credible reason, see John Wisdom, "Gods," *Logic and Language,* ed. Antony Flew (Oxford: Basil Blackwell, 1952) 187-206.

Yahweh. The king in and of himself has no resources for either personal or public well-being. All is gift. The gift, however, requires attentive responsiveness, a requirement not honored in Hezekiah's foolish courting of Babylon. What the tradition knows and what Israel learned late and repeatedly is that life, personal and public, will not be reduced to manageable proportions.

There is an *otherness* to life in the world that defies such control. In part that otherness is a wild capriciousness that refuses reduction. In part that otherness is a will and resolve that will not be mocked. Assyria had to learn that; Judah, with Hezekiah and after Hezekiah, learned it. Later Babylon learned it. And we, now, belatedly, learn it ever again. The very mocking against which the king prayed (19:4, 15-19) is a mocking that the king himself enacted with Babylon. Power always tempts to autonomy. The text sadly, resiliently declares, "It will not work!"

NOTES

[1]Robert R. Wilson, *Prophecy and Society in Ancient Israel* (Philadelphia: Fortress Press, 1980) 270-74 and passim, shows the ways in which Isaiah was a "central prophet." That is, not only did he have easy access to the king and the power elite, but he likely saw things from their perspective and according to their interest which he largely shared.

[2]Christopher R. Seitz, *Isaiah 1–39,* Interpretation (Louisville: John Knox Press, 1993) 263-66, offers a very different and quite suggestive interpretation of Hezekiah's response to the prophetic oracle.

[3]Klaus Koch, *The Prophets: The Assyrian Period* (Philadelphia: Fortress Press, 1983) 156 and passim.

MANASSEH
AND HIS SON

2 Kings 21:1-26

The account of the Judean monarchy continues in this chapter, dealing in turn with Manasseh (21:1-18) and his son Amon (21:19-26).

COMMENTARY

The Reign of Manasseh, 21:1-18

Manasseh, son of Hezekiah, had an exceptionally long reign of approximately 50 years, 687–642. Such a tenure might suggest a judgment that he was an effective ruler and maintained a high degree of governmental stability. Such a verdict, however, is remote from the one given in our narrative. Indeed, Manasseh is reckoned by the narrative to be the most evil of all of the Davidic kings, the one finally held responsible for the final failure of the Jerusalem establishment:

> Still the LORD did not turn from the fierceness of his great wrath,
> by which his anger was kindled against Judah, because of all the
> provocations with which Manasseh had provoked him. (23:26; see
> 23:32)

The negative judgment made against Manasseh is so intense and so full that beyond a theological verdict rooted in religious practice, we are told nothing about his long reign. Given what we know of the interpretive categories of our narrator, one may surmise that the religious compromises with which Manasseh is charged are complementary to willing political accommodation to the Assyrian empire; but we are told nothing of this. Beyond the conventional introduction (21:1) and the concluding formula (21:17-18), the entire Manasseh narrative is in fact one extended speech of judgment. While the rhetoric concerns the specific king, the son of Hezekiah, we may suggest that in our narrative this text is "the great speech of judgment" that pertains to the entire realm of Judah and so may be seen as a parallel to the great Northern indictment of chapter 17.

The speech of judgment features an extensive *indictment* of the king's accommodationist practices (21:2-11). The indictment is framed by general statements in vv. 2 and 11 with the ominous term "abomination," that is, practices most offensive and affrontive to Yahweh (or at least to this spokesperson for Yahweh). It is Manasseh's great failure that he did not enact or maintain the peculiar character of Judah by its commitment to the jealous, incomparable God, Yahweh. The verses bracketed by vv. 2 and 11, vv. 3-10, provide the particular charges against Manasseh concerning his openness to non-Yahwistic worship, surely for the narrative reflecting other compromises in the political realm. The references to high places, altars, poles, and Asherah, and the several practices—divination, passing a son through fire—are familiar to us as conventional and predictable heterodox practices. The rhetoric is intense, escalating the affront that the reader is expected to feel and embrace in the report.

That conventional inventory of scandalous liturgic acts and practices is intensified by two other rhetorical features. First, the intensification in a negative direction is made by connecting the policies of Manasseh to those of Ahab who, for this narrator, is a "worst case" example. Thus the Jerusalem royal cult is associated with the worst of the Omride practices in the North, worse than which is not imaginable to this narrative. The problem with Ahab—and thus with Manasseh—is that the distinctive character of Yahweh and Yahweh's distinctive requirements for Israel were forfeited in a broad-based readiness to accommodate other divine powers. Thus worship of "the host of heaven" likely refers to the stars, so that the phrase concerns astral worship, an aspect of Assyrian cultic influence. Thus what Ahaz began in chapter 16 is extended by his grandson, Manasseh.

Second, the intensification of the indictment of Manasseh in a positive direction is voiced in two allusions to the covenantal theology of Deuteronomy. In v. 4, Yahweh is remembered to have said of Jerusalem, "In Jerusalem I will put my name." The phrasing alludes back to the temple dedication under Solomon (1 Kgs 8:29) that in turn appeals to the "name theology" of the book of Deuteronomy.[1] The point of the alleged quote is to insist that if Yahweh is present in Jerusalem, it is inappropriate and impossible to erect symbols for any other deity. The alleged quote in v. 4 is matched in vv. 7-8 by a larger allusion to Deuteronomy that links *presence* (name) and *land* to Torah obedience. Torah obedience in Deuteronomic theory is the condition and prerequisite of the land, and the core facet of Torah is "no other gods." Manasseh has clearly violated that command, and so has placed both presence and land in deep jeopardy.

The two allusions to Deuteronomy are echoed and reinforced by the decisive condemnation of v. 9: "they did not *listen*." They did not need or pay attention to the singular requirements of Yahweh's Torah. The verb "listen" (*shema'*) is, of course, defining for the covenantal theology of Deuteronomy. "Listening" is the acknowledgement that one receives life in address from another who has the authority to call into existence by utterance. Failure to listen is an attempt at autonomy, an attempt by Manasseh in this case who, without adherence to Torah, has led his realm into massive violation of Yahweh's will.

This strong indictment is matched by an extended speech of sentence (21:12-14), introduced by a characteristic "therefore" that binds sentence to indictment as effect to cause. That is, the "wrath to come" is fully deserved by Manasseh. The coming punishment that Yahweh will enact is first stated in a series of suggestive images:

1. The intended evil to come will cause "ears to tingle." The phrase means that the things to happen are so unbearably menacing that announcement of them will cause a jarring reaction, a pounding in the head, an unsettling reverberation among those who hear it. The same phrasing is used in 1 Samuel 3:11 at the beginning of this royal tale concerning the demise of the priestly house of Eli that, in the tradition, is a foretaste of the demise of the Davidic house. (See a parallel usage in Jer 19:3.)

2. A "line and plummet" refers to a builder's measurement to determine what is truly straight. The imagery takes on force by being connected to Samaria and Ahab. The suggestion is that "Torah norms" applied to the North brought on the termination of the royal house that was found inadequate by Torah measurement, and now these same criteria used in the same way will terminate the royal house of the South.

3. The term "wipe" suggests the imagery of a towel drying a dish with such force that anything left is wiped away. That imagery, however, is a bit misleading, because the verb itself is the verb for "blot out, exterminate," suggesting the savage force of the larger statement.

It is noteworthy that with all three images—ears tingling, plummet measurement, wipes dry—we still lack a concrete statement of punishment. All we know is that what is to come is negative and severe. It is only in v. 14 that the threat becomes concrete: Judah and Jerusalem will cease to receive Yahweh's protection, and so will be exposed to concrete, historical threat. The verb "cast off" alludes to the deportation policies of the empire, already experienced in the North. The loss of land, safety, and well-being is the price of Torah neglect. The enemy is not named, but in the time of Manasseh, that threat is still Assyria. By the end of 2 Kings, Babylon has displaced Assyria as the great external threat, but the change has little theological significance. Such an imperial power is always a threat!

After the concrete threat of v. 14, the utterance returns to the indictment in vv. 15-16. In this statement of indictment that follows the earlier indictment of vv. 2-11, two additional factors may be noticed. First, the violation of Torah may be concentrated in Manasseh, but in fact it is the entire history of Judah since the Exodus that brings the coming judgment. Manasseh is only a representative figure of that broad and deep violation.

Finally, the indictment offers one particular element after a great deal of generalization, namely, "shedding innocent blood" (21:16). This rhetorical extremity imagines that under Manasseh the city of Jerusalem has been filled with innocent blood, rivers of blood. In the first instant, "innocent blood" refers to murder and related bodily violence. More broadly however, the phrase can refer to acts of systemic, institutional violence whereby the powerful prey upon the weak and vulnerable in exploitative ways. Thus the phrasing likely does not refer to bodily brutality, but to the exercise of social power in anti-neighborly ways. As illustration of this way of violence, the prophetic rhetoric of Micah and Jeremiah is instructive:

> Hear this, you rulers of the house of Jacob,
>   and chiefs of the house of Israel,
> who abhor justice and pervert all equity,
> who build Zion *with blood*
>   and Jerusalem with wrong!
> Its rulers give judgment for a bribe,
>   its priests teach for a price,
>   its prophets give oracles for money. (Mic 3:9-11)

> For if you truly amend your ways and your doings, if you truly act justly one with another, if you do not oppress the alien, the orphan, and the widow, or *shed innocent blood* in this place, and if you do not go after other gods to your own hurt, then....
> (Jer 7:5-7)

In both cases, "blood" is linked to the weak and marginated who are helpless before exploitative power. Thus v. 16 in our text may be a reference to political-economic aggression that is surely the practical side of the already condemned religious enterprise in which Torah responsibilities are disregarded.

The Manasseh narrative is thus framed in a chiastic fashion:

> introduction (21:1),
> > indictment (21:2-11),
> > > sentence (21:12-14),
> > indictment (21:15-16),
> conclusion (21:17-18).

Such a pattern is worth noticing because it places the harsh sentence of vv. 12-14 at the center: Manasseh's reign becomes an occasion for a narrative accent on the judgment of being "cast off."

The Short Reign of Amon, 21:19-26

This son of Manasseh scarcely figures at all, sandwiched as he is between the paradigmatically evil king, his father (Manasseh), and the paradigmatically good king, his son (Josiah). The theological verdict on Amon is stereotypical, associating him with the evils of his father (21:19-21). Of interest is the wording of v. 22 that echoes the cadences of Deuteronomy. The primal sin is to disregard "the way of the LORD." [The Way]

The most important aspect of this report on Amon is the narrative account of his demise (21:23-24). The report suggests an internal dispute between passionate parties in the government. Apparently the king is caught between two powerful, violent forces, "the king's servants" and "the people of the land." This narrative account concerns two steps of violence: first, the murder of the king by his servants; second, a responding violence against the servants of the king by the people of the land. While intrigue and violence are to be expected in the courts of power, this particular phrasing suggests an ideological dispute that in part turned on theological

AΩ **The Way**
The narrative uses the phrase "The Way of the LORD" to refer to the entire teaching of Torah that this narrator champions as the true ethic of Israel. Of the term "way," James Muilenburg has written:

The primary image to express conduct or behavior in the Old Testament is the "way" or "road" (*derek*). No other image was more rich and manifold, none more diverse in nuance and connotation. Hebrew words for road can be translated in a number of different ways, but it is the verbs of action associated with them that best reveal the versatility of usage and the dynamic character of the symbol, above all the verb "to walk" or "to go" and, indeed, the many different kinds of going and walking. The way of a man was the course he followed through life, the direction of his going, and the manner of his walking. It was a good word because it was drawn from the vicissitudes of daily life, from a land of many roads and paths in which walking was the usual manner of going from one place to another. It was a good symbol because it involved beginning and end and the intention which prompted the journey. There were different ways a man might take, and his journey involved decision or choice of the right or wrong road.... It was always a *particular* walking because the content of the intention was always particular. What makes this terminology of supreme importance in Israel's manner of thinking is that it is applied to God. [James Muilenburg, *The Way of Israel: Biblical Faith and Ethics* (New York: Harper & Brothers, 1961) 33-34.]

For our narrator, see especially Deut 30:15-20, on which see also Psalm 1. The same image is important in the self-presentation of the early church, Acts 24:14.

commitments that came to be expressed as policy proposals. It is plausible that "the servants" represent the palace clique that wanted to enhance royal authoritarianism, not unlike Rehoboam's "young men" (1 Kgs 12:8-11). If they killed Amon, it may have been that Amon was moving in a covenantal, Yahwistic direction, a move unwelcome in the palace clique.

If that tension is correctly understood in this way, then we may understand that "the people of the land" may be an alternative ideological force. "The people of the land" are commonly thought to be covenantal, conservative Yahwists of a political bent who resisted the enhancement of the royal office at the expense of the "elders."[2] If that is so, then the dispute reported here continues a very old quarrel about king and Torah, the servants wanting a *king uncurbed* by Torah and the people of the land concerned for *Torah restraints* on royal aggrandizement.

If this analysis is correct, we may learn something interesting about Amon. In the first instance he was perhaps not clear enough to satisfy fully any party opinion. But if our analysis is correct and he was slain by those who wanted a stronger throne, it may indicate that he had broken with his father and was moving in a reformist, Torah direction. That is, he may have been more like his reformist son, Josiah, than like his accommodationist father, Manasseh. Such a view helps us see why the avengers of his death (the people of the land) could welcome Josiah to the throne. (21:24). In any case, Amon's culmination in violence suggests that Jerusalem was a cauldron of competing ideological passions.

[Manasseh in Repentance]

Manasseh in Repentance

It is instructive that this heavy, unmitigated picture of Manasseh's evil is substantially corrected in the later rendering in 2 Chronicles 33:12-13. After reporting that the king was taken captive by the Assyrians into Babylon, a change of heart on the part of the king is reported:

While he was in distress he entreated the favor of the LORD his God and humbled himself greatly before the God of his ancestors. He prayed to him, and God received his entreaty, heard his plea, and restored him again to Jerusalem and to his kingdom. Then Manasseh knew that the LORD indeed was God.

This remarkable report removes Manasseh from Jerusalem and returns him there, no doubt functioning in Chronicles as an earnest of the exile and return of Israel from exile. This latter rendering, of course, has nothing to do with our narrative, but suggests how supple the data is to variant renderings.

CONNECTIONS

This narrative account of Manasseh reaches the apex of the ideological assertion of our narrative. It is clear that the narrative is not interested in Manasseh as a person or as a king, but takes the occasion of his reign to make the defining connection between a *chosen departure from Torah as royal policy* and a subsequent *forced departure from the land.* The narrative boldly presents the history of Judah and Jerusalem as a theodicy, as an argument that bad things happen to bad people according to the reliable rule of Yahweh. That view of public history is, to say the least, odd. It is odd because it insists on the defining linkage between Torah obedience and public destiny guaranteed by the Lord of the Torah as the defining reality in the history of Judah.

Such a claim, when stated so boldly, as does this narrative, is shocking in its simplistic insistence. And yet such a way of doing theology, with or without its bold articulation, is simply an insistence that public life is morally coherent and involves a discernable pattern of accountability. Such a claim might be stated with less clumsiness, but in whatever form it may be stated it stands, now as in the ancient world, as a contradiction to the two primary rival theories of public power. The first of these alternatives is that "power always wins," that is, "might makes right." Against such a view, this narrative insists that there are "Torah forces" at work beyond the simple capacity of power. The second of these alternate theories is that life is elementally absurd and there is no rhyme or reason to what comes next. Against such a view, our narrative asserts that there is a coherent purpose and a sustained will at the core of all futures that can be thwarted but not defeated. Whether or not one finds such a view convincing, here stated in bold simplicity, one must at least recognize that this is an alternative both to modernist rationality that reduces everything to power [Knowledge as Power] and to postmodernist irrationality in our assessment of public life. The claims of this tradition, moreover, are not primarily theoretical, but are practical and pragmatic in their interest and in their presentation. To say that Yahweh will not be mocked—even by the king in Jerusalem—is to say that the future has not been

---

Knowledge as Power

There is little doubt that modernist rationality aims at control, and that "knowledge as power" is a primary mode of such control in modernist perspective. This trajectory of control and the primacy of "man" (understood as maleness) can be traced to the rise of modern science in the sixteenth century, through the reasoning of René Descartes, and on to current technological control of "nature" by the last standing superpower and its immense military bureaucracy. [Brian Wren, *What Language Shall I Barrow? God-Talk in Worship: A Male Response to Feminist Theology* (New York: Crossroad, 1989) 232-55 and passim, has provided a quite practical consideration of this ideological heritage and its abiding power. See in more critical fashion, Stephen Toulmin, *Cosmopolis: The Hidden Agenda of Modernity* (New York: The Free Press, 1989).] The modernist enterprise has been able to exclude the rule of God from all public projects. This exclusion puts the modernist enterprise in deep contradiction to the claims of biblical faith which counters all such pretensions to ultimacy by the claims of Yahweh's rule. The matter explicitly pertains to international affairs.

ceded over to human control and that the future is not out of control.

The theodicy expressed as Yahweh's prophetic indictment of Judah and Yahweh's sentence of Judah is structurally litigious. That is, by placing fault upon Israel, the text serves to protect Yahweh's honor. Yahweh is about to abandon Jerusalem; the case made here is that the fault for such an abandonment lies clearly with Jerusalem and its recalcitrant leadership. It may seem odd to assign *fault* for the future. Such a question is inescapable, however, once one has asserted that public life is morally coherent, as Israel always asserts.

The litigious shape of theodicy voiced here is a backdrop for much biblical thought. In the Christian tradition, it is important to see that litigious theodicy lies behind Paul's great argument of justification by God's grace. "Justification" has become such a heavily freighted theological word that we often forget its forensic nature. The term refers to being found just or being declared just, that is, acquitted. Thus the "good news" of justification makes sense theologically, morally, and religiously only if the case has gone to court and the guilty are found guilty only to be declared innocent. While our theological sensitivities would not easily link the case of Manasseh to the argument of Paul, it is the structure and shape of our case that makes the news of free justification so powerful.

[Manasseh Seeks Forgiveness]

Manasseh Seeks Forgiveness

I have already called attention to the developing interpretive trajectory of Manasseh in 2 Chronicles 33:10-13. That development, in contradiction to the absolute condemnation of Manasseh, is further developed in "The Prayer of Manasseh." This late prayer in the Apocrypha further develops the initiative of 2 Chronicles 33 and presents Manasseh as a pious king who throws himself on the mercy of Yahweh:

> I pray and beseech thee,
> spare, O Lord, spare me,
> destroy me not with my transgressions on my head,
> do not be angry with me forever, nor store up evil for me.
> Do not condemn me to the grave,
> for thou, Lord, art the God of the penitent.
> Thou wilt show thy goodness towards me,
> for unworthy as I am thou wilt save me in thy great mercy. (Pr Man 13–14 NEB))

The tradition has placed in the mouth of the king a penitential Psalm not unlike Psalm 51 placed on the lips of another king. This development is clearly remote from the agenda of our narrator, for the prayer is for personal rescue and is uninterested in the judgment made in our text that the king has brought down upon the entire realm by his own failure to "listen."

The large public issue of theodicy concerns the *conduct* of Israel and the *future* of Israel. It does not in the first instance concern Manasseh per se. And yet it is clear that the narrator offers Manasseh as a representative figure of all that is wrong in Israel's life with Yahweh. Thus interpretation must move between public Israel and representative Manasseh. In order to understand Manasseh's literary-theological function in the narrative, it may be useful to consider other representative figures in our own public history who are held personally accountable and yet who embody a whole people in an entire era, and not just themselves. Thus one may think, in U.S. history, of the representative force of leaders like Washington (independence), Jackson (empire), Lincoln (pathos), Coolidge (business), Truman (Cold War), Reagan (free enterprise), each of whom is in part held accountable for setting forces in motion and in part is assigned a burden well beyond himself.

Of course one may go outside such official leadership and think of other figures on the underside of society who also formidably embody their time and place, figures such as Meriwether Lewis, Andrew Carnegie, Eugene Debs, Martin Luther King, Jr., who bring to visibility forces shaping the future in a larger-than-life way.

More specifically, to take Manasseh as a representative figure may be illuminated by juxtaposing him to his grandson Josiah:

> Before him there was no king like him, who turned to the LORD with all his heart, with all his soul, and with all his might, according to all the law of Moses; nor did any like him arise after him. (23:25)

Manasseh as representative disobedient king brought wrath while Josiah as representative obedient king brought what he could of well-being to his realm, though not enough (see Jer 22:15-17). In the end, so our narrator concludes, Manasseh's impetus prevailed over that of Josiah. In light of this juxtaposition, we might echo Paul:

> Therefore just as one man's trespass led to condemnation for all, so one man's act of righteousness leads to justification and life for all. (Rom 5:18)

The "one man" in our narrative is Manasseh who could not be overcome by Josiah, one man's righteousness that leads to life. On Paul's larger screen, the one man is Adam and the one man who prevails is Jesus. I do not intend to equate the two cases nor to introduce any Christological note here. By citing the Pauline argument about representative figures, however, we may see what the narrator in our case is doing. In the cases of these two kings, the narrator has very little interest in historical data, but is trading in models and paradigms that give shape to the data.

Finally the violence around Amon warrants comment. It suggests that Amon is yet one more victim of a deep and abiding dispute over the shape and character of Israel. We cannot precisely identify or characterize the parties to the dispute, but we can guess at the broad outlines. An argument that we might call "ecclesial" (= concern with the nature of the community of faith) is apparently under way. The "servants" of the royal clique might have wished for more accommodation while the people of the land might have wanted greater distinctiveness. In more recent parlance, this is an argument over *unity* and *purity* in the community of faith. Since there are two stages of violence and murder in this royal account, what we notice is that both parties, for unity and for purity, are quite capable of violence in order to advance their view. When advocates and ideologues vie for control, nobody is innocent, and nobody is safe. In this brief paragraph on this pitiful son of Manasseh and father of Josiah, I suspect we can see the accommodating party of Manasseh and the reformist party of Josiah at hard and vicious work against each other. Both parties will go to extremes in order to control the future. No doubt both thought they occupied high ground, either the high ground of *pragmatism* (so Manasseh) or the high ground of *fidelity* (so Josiah). Control of high ground seems always to cause a lot of hurt. Amon—perhaps still bleeding—is the body over which the parties disputed. The narrator is not neutral but is an intense advocate in the dispute. That advocacy notwithstanding, the sorry part is that nobody wins and everyone loses in the process. The narrative wants us to be sure to notice that Yahweh is not in fact involved in these conspiracies. I suspect that the actual disputants thought otherwise, thought they were recruits in Yahweh's very own party. About such a mistaken partisanship, Paul writes to a later community:

> What I mean is that each of you says, "I belong to Paul," or "I belong to Apollos," or "I belong to Cephas," or "I belong to Christ." Has Christ been divided? (1 Cor 1:12-13)

NOTES

[1]See Gerhard von Rad, *Studies in Deuteronomy*, SBT 9 (Chicago: Henry Regnery Company, 1953) 37-44.

[2]On the "elders" as carriers of a tradition alternative to monarchy, see Hans Walter Wolff, "Micah the Moreshite—The Prophet and His Background," *Israelite Wisdom: Theological and Literary Essays in Honor of Samuel Terrien,* ed. John G. Gammie et al. (Missoula: Scholars Press, 1978) 77-84. On the ideological dispute between royal perspective and the elders, see especially Jer 26:16-19.

JOSIAH, MAN OF TORAH

2 Kings 22:1-20

Finally the narrative arrives at King Josiah, the narrator's model king, the one upon whom rests all the hopes of Judah. This report on the celebrated king offers an introductory formula (22:1-2), a narrative on temple reform in which is embedded the report on the discovery of the scroll (22:3-10), the response of the king to the scroll (22:11-13), and the oracle of Huldah the prophetess (22:14-20).

COMMENTARY

The Good King, 22:1-2

Josiah enjoyed a long reign of thirty-one years, 640–609. He was placed on the throne by "the people of the land" (21:24), whom we assume to be the conservative, Torah-trusting, rural population. If this is a correct characterization of "the people of the land," then Josiah is correctly expected to be their man. That is, he is the quintessential royal Torah-keeper. Only Hezekiah receives such an unqualified affirmation from the narrator as does Josiah:

> *Hezekiah*: He trusted in the LORD the God of Israel; so that there was no one like him among all the kings of Judah after him, or among those who were before him. For he held fast to the LORD; he did not depart from following him but kept the commandments that the LORD commanded Moses. (18:5-6)

> *Josiah*: He did what was right in the sight of the LORD, and walked in all the way of his father David; he did not turn aside to the right or to the left. (22:2)

This introductory assessment concerning Josiah is matched by the verdict at the end of his narrative report:

> There was no king like him, who turned to the LORD with all his heart, with all his soul, and with all his might, according to all the law of Moses; nor did any like him arise after him. (23:25)

It is the intention of the narrative to situate kingship in Judah in the context of Torah and to show Torah as the defining characteristic of a proper king. [Torah and Kingship in the Psalms] Scholars increasingly think that the Josiah narrative, like much else in the books of Kings, is not historical reportage, but is in fact "model building" for what should be the case—not reportage, but advocacy. Such "model building" may, of course, appeal to actual historical data, but goes well beyond such data in the presentation of "the good king." Thus we read this narrative not primarily for historical data, but as a theological, ideological proposal for the proper, responsible relationship between *power* (monarchy) and *faithful obedience* (Torah). Josiah here is the prince made exactly for that relationship.

> **Torah and Kingship in the Psalms**
> The relationship between Torah and kingship is an endlessly complex one. In the Psalms, it is clear that Torah as signaled in Psalm 1 (see also Pss 19, 119) is a primary theme. The placement of Psalm 2 next is the beginning of the "royal Psalms" that focus upon the king who played a prominent role in the worship of Israel. The juxtaposition of Psalms 1 and 2 hold the two themes together and indicate that the entire book of Psalms is to be read with awareness of the interrelatedness of the two.
>
> See Patrick D. Miller, "The Beginning of the Psalter," *The Shape and Shaping of the Psalter,* ed. by J. Clinton McCann, JSOT Supp. 159 (Sheffield: JSOT Press, 1992) 83-92.

Temple and Torah, 22:3-10

These verses provide the narrative background through which we may understand the remarkable responsiveness and fervor on the part of Josiah in what follows. Two themes are skillfully interwoven, carried by two characters whom we have not previously encountered. First appears Shaphan who is a prominent and influential member of the royal entourage under Josiah. [Shaphan] He is the money manager for temple reform, the one entrusted by the king with proper payment to the workers who repair the temple. The rhetoric used to characterize temple renovation and payment for it is an exact replica of the same language in 12:11-15, suggesting that we are dealing with stereotypical royal rhetoric. That Josiah is funding temple renovation indicates his own pious commitments as a devoted Yahwist for whom the priest Hilkiah, the other supporting character, is the on-the-site royal agent.

> **Shaphan**
> There is no doubt that Shaphan, an influential member of the government and likely a scribe, occupies a prominent position in the life of official Jerusalem. Not only does he enjoy access to the king in this dramatic moment of scroll discovery, but his family also plays a decisive role in the presentation of the scroll of Jeremiah in Jer 36. Andrew Dearman has suggested that Shaphan and his family stand at the beginning of the Deuteronomic trajectory of literature and theology.
>
> J. Andrew Dearman, "My Servants the Scribes: Composition and Context in Jeremiah 36," JBL 109 (1990): 403-21.

The temple renovation, however, is a backdrop for what follows and is no primary interest of the narrator. Hilkiah the priest, our second character, stands in for the king who in theory is himself the proper high priest of the Jerusalem temple that is the royal chapel. Hilkiah, in the narrative, performs the crucial function of announcing the second and major theme of our narrative, namely, the book of Torah found in the temple:

> I have found the book of the law in the house of the LORD. (22:8)

This is the pivot point in the entire narrative and makes the Torah scroll the centerpiece of Josiah's reign and certainly the narrator's primary interest. The report itself suggests that the scroll had been hidden or discarded in the temple and had been long forgotten. [The Scroll] Shaphan, a faithful royal official who functions as the middleman between priest and king, summarizes for Josiah both themes of the present narrative: (a) the money has reached its destination (22:9); (b) the scroll has been found and is now read to the king (22:10). Thus all we know of the scroll is that it is found (22:8) and read (22:10). It is remarkable that neither Hilkiah nor Shaphan exhibits any emotional response to the scroll, but leanly enact their responsibilities for the king.

The Scroll
Since definitive research in 1805, scholars have assumed that the scroll found in the temple is some form of the book of Deuteronomy, and that hypothesis is still widely accepted as a key to interpretation. The specific parallels have been detailed by S. R. Driver and have been later reviewed by Henri Cazelles and J. Philip Hyatt.

S. R. Driver, *Deuteronomy*, ICC (New York: Scribner, 1895) lxxxvi-xcv; Henri Cazelles, "Jeremiah and Deuteronomy," *A Prophet to the Nations: Essays in Jeremiah Studies*, ed. Leo G. Perdue and Brian W. Kovacs (Winona Lake: Eisenbrauns, 1984) 89-111; J. Philip Hyatt, "Jeremiah and Deuteronomy, ibid., 113-27.]

The King Hears the Scroll, 22:11-13

The response of King Josiah to the scroll is in marked contrast to the flat response of the priest and the secretary before him. The scroll is read to the king, perhaps suggesting that the king cannot or does not read, but is dependent upon the skill of a trained scribes.[1] In any case, the king's response upon hearing the scroll is

AΩ **On Royal Tearing**
Scholars have noticed a remarkable parallel in two royal acts involving scrolls that are likely related to each other. In our text, Josiah, the good king, hears the scroll and tears his garment in a dramatic act of repentance (22:11). In Jeremiah 36:23, Jehoiakim, Josiah's son who is a bad king, hears the scroll of Jeremiah and "cuts" the scroll and not his garments; that is, he does not repent but seeks to dispose of the troublesome scroll. It is important that the term "tear" in our text and "cut" in Jer 36 are the same Hebrew term, *qara*. Given the close connections between the literature of Deuteronomy and Jeremiah and given the same term in both cases, it is likely that the two texts are interrelated, offering the two classic responses of resistance and repentance to the authority of the scroll.

On the relation of the texts to each other, see E. W. Nicholson, *Preaching to the Exiles: A Study of the Prose Tradition in the book of Jeremiah* (Oxford: Basil Blackwell, 1970) and Charles D. Isbell, "2 Kings 22:3-23:24 and Jeremiah 36: A Stylistic Comparison," JSOT 8 (1978): 33-45.

dramatic and intense: he "tore his clothes," suggesting a dramatic royal act of abasement and repentance (22:11). [On Royal Tearing] Josiah's response suggests that the Torah he hears is threatening and deeply unsettling to him. That is in part a comment on the nature of the scroll, and in part a comment on the king's readiness to hear. [On Hearing]

Josiah immediately dispatches his high royal advisors to "inquire," to receive oracular guidance concerning the meaning and prospects of the Torah. The king's fearful response is grounded in an astonishingly knowing assessment of the Torah and its significance. The king is alarmed because he knows the Torah includes a threat. He knows, moreover, that his realm is endangered because, since the beginning of Israel, the people have been either Torah-indifferent or Torah-defiant. It seems likely that the narrator has placed on the lips of the king a characteristic summary judgment on the theology propelling the entire royal venture, namely, that the entire history of disobedience is leading inexorably to exile (22:13). [The Threat of the Scroll]

The Prophetic Oracle, 22:14-20

The "inquiry of the Lord" that the king authorizes in v. 13 is to seek a prophetic oracle. It is remarkable that *Torah* requires *oracle*, thus nicely bringing together the authority and importance of "law and prophets."[2] The Torah announces threat and the oracle makes the threat of Torah quite concrete.

Huldah the prophetess belongs to the order of royal officers and appears to be well-known and well-connected at court.[3] Her oracle in two parts is given promptly. The first part concerns Jerusalem and its inhabitants, and consists in the two predictable elements of a speech of judgment (22:16-17). The sentence is all the "disasters" (evil) of the book, apparently referring to the massive inventory of covenant curses in Deuteronomy 28. The city is on notice and

---

AΩ **On Hearing**

It is important that the scroll is read aloud and that Josiah *hears*. Of course the term "hear" may only refer to a natural and unavoidable aural function. But the term in Hebrew, *shema*, characteristically means more than that, especially when used in contexts linked to the book of Deuteronomy. It is well known, of course, that Deuteronomy 6:4-5 is a key text in Deuteronomy (and for Judaism) that focuses upon listening to Torah which means both to "hear and to do." That is, the term implies obedience, readiness to act on what one hears. The act of listening with an intent to obey is a sharp alternative to autonomy that resists such address and assumes that one is unaddressed and therefore free to do what one will. Josiah is a model listener ready to submit his life to the demands of Torah. It is impossible to overstate the importance of Josiah's act of listening in the context of the theology of Deuteronomy operative here. It marks him as a man of obedience.

The Threat of the Scroll

Remarkably, there is no explicit threat quoted from the scroll in our text. Josiah, however, responds as though such a threat had indeed been read to him. Huldah, moreover, alludes to the "disasters" that are delineated in the text. Thus this entire drama assumes more of the text than is given us. In the book of Deuteronomy, presumably the scroll being read and heard, the threats are given in the long recital of covenant curses in chapters 27 and 28. The simple logic of the scroll is that disobedience to Torah places all of life in deep jeopardy. In the Books of Kings, the series of prayers offered in 1 Kings 8:22-53 roughly matches the threats and curses, so that the community is here seen to pray out of the condition anticipated in the threats. All of this is implied in Josiah's response and in Huldah's pronouncement.

---

under judgment (22:16). The indictment in v. 17 is stereotypical. Israel has violated the first commandment concerning exclusive loyalty to Yahweh by embracing other gods. The anger of Yahweh, who insists upon singular devotion, is massive. It will not be quenched. It is important to note that Huldah's oracle of judgment contains no conditional qualification, no suggestion of escape, no summons to repent. The "evil" to be enacted in Jerusalem is a done deal.

The second part of Huldah's oracle concerns the person of the king (vv. 18-20). The prophet allows that the personal destiny of the king can be differentiated from the sorry future of the city. The statement on Josiah is in "because-therefore" sequence, not unlike a speech of judgment, except that the verdict on the king is positive. The ground for the positive verdict is Josiah's capacity for repentance (22:19).[4] Josiah is penitent; he humbled himself; he tore his garments, and he wept. That is, he freely submitted to the demands of Yahweh and took the threat seriously, seriously enough to engage in acts of submissive self-abasement.

The result of Josiah's pious response, introduced by "therefore," is that in his life and in his death Josiah will not experience or witness the disasters of v. 16. The assurance that Josiah will have a peaceable death is not unlike Hezekiah's verdict in 20:19:

Why not, if there will be peace and security in my days?

The difference is that Hezekiah makes this short-term claim for himself that may sound cynical, whereas the verdict on Josiah is given by Huldah and so has a ring of genuine piety to it. The sum of Huldah's oracle is that Josiah's short-term well-being will be free of the long-term fate of the city. That long-term fate is massive and inescapable. The oracle serves to reinforce the most negative anticipation given in the Torah. Torah and prophet agree on the main point. Because Josiah is a model of piety, he will take with utmost seriousness, as we shall see, both Torah and oracle. [The "If" of a King under Torah]

CONNECTIONS

Two major accents occur to me out of this dramatic episode. First, the narrative asserts and makes clear that Torah is the ultimate clue to a good life with Yahweh, the only shape of faith that will finally prevail:

1. This claim, if taken with historical seriousness, makes the crisis of Josiah the defining moment in the emergence of Judaism as a community powered and authorized and summoned by the scroll of the Torah.

2. This claim, if taken as Deuteronomic imagination rather than history, serves to assert the ideological insistence of Torah against all alterative forms of faith.

3. This claim, if understood as a later realization in exile long after Josiah, enunciates and insists in any case that Old Testament faith is all about command and obedience, a covenantal, moral purpose that relentlessly shapes the future.

This narrative is able, in dramatic and deliberate fashion, to subordinate one by one all other modes of faith to that of Torah:

(a) The Torah prevails over *temple*. There is no doubt that in Jerusalem, the temple has loomed large since the work of Solomon. In our narrative, Hilkiah the priest stands in for the temple; Josiah, moreover, as every pious king, is a patron and benefactor of the temple. This temple is a great ideological support for the monarchy and a locus of presence and forgiveness. The Torah is found in the temple!

In a narrative instant, however, the temple is completely forgotten and disregarded. No more money or attention is given to the temple in this narrative. All effort and energy now go to coming to terms with Torah, for it is Torah-adherence that assures a future for the realm. In this horizon, the temple has nothing to offer the Jerusalem establishment. This theological claim resonates with the dismissal of the temple as a source for the future in the confrontation of Amos (Amos 7:10-17) and in the declaration of Jeremiah (Jer 7:12-15).

(b) The Torah prevails over the *kingship*. We are, after all, studying "kings." Among them, Josiah along with Hezekiah is the most enthusiastically commended by the narrator. We might expect that Josiah would be celebrated for his royal achievements or even for his fully attested temple piety. In fact, however, Josiah is here commended only for his total submission and response to the Torah. Thus his greatness as king is constituted by his readiness to submit his royal powers to the Torah. The upshot of this submission is that monarchy is totally beholden to Torah-obedience, exactly as the narrator wants us to notice.

(c) The Torah prevails over *prophecy*. The relation of Torah to prophecy is very different, in the horizon of this narrative, from its relation to temple or monarchy. For the latter represent and embody an accommodationist propensity that violates the "Yahweh-alone" perspective of the narrator. Unlike temple and monarchy, prophecy, as presented in the narrative, has no itch to accommodate, but is as zealously "Yahweh-alone" as the Torah. Thus Torah and prophecy are companions and allies in the uncompromising vision of this narrative; we have seen in the rendering of the great ninth-century prophets—Elijah, Elisha, Micaiah—that our narrator is fully appreciative of these prophets who also voice an insistent "Yahweh-alone" vision of Israel.[5]

This companionship and alliance, moreover, is fully exhibited in our text, for the immediate impulse of Josiah, upon hearing the Torah scroll, is to seek out a prophet:

> Go, inquire of the LORD for me, for the people, and for all Judah, concerning the words of this book that has been found. (22:13)

Huldah, the subject of the inquiry, receives considerable attention in this text. She pronounces two characteristic oracles, one a speech of judgment against the city, the other a speech of assurance to the king.

Having said this, it is clear that Huldah's prophetic function is to enhance and reinforce the Torah scroll. Everything turns on "the words of the scroll" (22:16). The threat against the city, she proclaims, is rooted in the scroll and is simply articulated by Huldah. The assurance to the king is because of "the words you have heard," words of Torah (22:18). Clearly Huldah as a prophetess has no autonomous function or voice, but is dependent on the Torah

📖 The "If" of a King under Torah

We can see this submission of monarchy to Torah in the movement from Psalm 89 to Psalm 132. In the former, the promise of Yahweh to the king is unconditional:

> Once for all I have sworn by my holiness;
> I will not lie to David.
> His line shall continue forever,
> and his throne endure before me like the sun.
> It shall be established forever like the moon,
> an enduring witness in the skies. (Ps 89:35-37)

In Psalm 132, however, the promise to the dynasty has been made conditional upon Torah obedience:

> *If* your sons keep my covenant
> and my decrees that I shall teach them,
> their sons also, forever more,
> shall sit on your throne. (Ps 132:12)

Josiah, in our narrative, is a model king. But that has nothing to do with royal achievements. It has only to do with his example as an unreserved Torah keeper, the true measure of kingship.

The promise of Ps 132:12 is that with the conditions met, there will be heirs to the throne. The statement is a counterpoint to the pathos-filled statement concerning Jehoiachin in Jer 22:30, the king who will have no heir. The entire future of the monarchy, like the family of promise in the Genesis narratives, depends completely upon an heir. Thus the heir given or withheld is of immense importance.

scroll and is in its service. Her role is to make the scroll immediately contemporary for city and for king.[6]

(d) I might add that if Shaphan belongs to a scribal tradition, as seems most plausible, then we may also see that even the scribal tradition, later to emerge with such importance, is in the service of the Torah.[7]

Thus without calling any particular attention to it, the narrative effectively claims preeminence for Torah at the expense of any rival claim of authority. We may see in this decisive maneuver (a) the beginning of the process of canonization whereby Israel became "a people of the book," (b) a harbinger of the defining role of Ezra in the shape of postexilic Judaism (see Neh 8), and (c) the creation of the categories out of which Pharisaic Judaism could become the preeminent mode of Judaism and of the practices that enabled Jewish survival as a religious community in contexts of brutality and persecution.

Second, I want to consider the relation between the two oracles of Huldah, concerning Jerusalem (22:16-17) and the king (22:18-20). I do so under the rubric of "the limits of personal piety." There is no doubt that Josiah is a good and obedient son of the Torah, good and obedient enough to shield his own eyes from the coming disaster in Jerusalem (22:20). The gain of his piety and obedience, however, is limited to his own destiny and has no impact upon the fate of the city mired in its own self-destructiveness. Thus Huldah and the tradition fully affirm and appreciate the king's personal piety. But they permit that piety no decisive impact on the public future.

Three interrelated extrapolations from this point occur to me:

1. The juxtaposition of the two oracles amounts to a deep judgment upon individualism, which is so powerful and attractive in the modern world. Classical liberalism assumes that the individual is the elemental unit of reality and that society is a sum of those individuals. Against that assumption, this juxtaposition of oracles insists that the body politic has a life of its own that is other than the sum of individual persons; the body politic thus stands under its own judgment and may have its own open future. The utterance of Huldah invites a radical reconsideration of the common assumption of individualism in our body politic.

2. This text might evoke a careful rereading of Reinhold Niebuhr's *Moral Man and Immoral Society*.[8] His shrill manifesto was a defining break with the illusions of liberalism that "good men" together would constitute "good society."[9] The Torah

tradition is not primarily about "good persons," but it is about the grand framing of social life. Thus Niebuhr:

> Our contemporary culture fails to realize the power, extent, and persistence of group egoism in human relations. It may be possible, though it is never easy, to establish just relations between individuals within a group purely by moral and relational suasion and accommodation. In intergroup relations this is practically an impossibility. The relations between groups must therefore always be predominantly political rather than ethical, that is, they will be determined by the proportion of power which each group possesses at least as much as by any rational and moral appraisal of the comparative needs and claims of each group.[10]

Niebuhr's stricture, so stunning when offered, has become commonplace, but it is in fact a mere footnote to the power of the ideology of individualism. If that ideology were true, Josiah's piety would have saved his city. But it did not!

3. The deep question of personal good and the public good has been a spectacularly dramatic issue in the U.S. during the presidency of Bill Clinton. None can gainsay the cruciality of personal integrity in public leaders. This juxtaposition of oracles by Huldah, however, may invite a refocus away from such personal issues to the public questions of justice, mercy, and compassion, for it is around these that the future of the realm is decided:

> Woe to you, scribes and Pharisees, hypocrites! For you tithe mint, dill, and cummin, and have neglected the weightier matters of the law: justice and mercy and faith. (Matt 23:23)

The narrative brings positive closure to the life of the king in 22:20 and 23:25. But the story does not end there, because the story is about "Immoral Society" that stands judged by Torah, even in the face of this "Moral Man."

NOTES

[1]On the connection of this tradition to scribal activity, see James Muilenburg, "Baruch The Scribe," *Proclamation and Presence: Old Testament Essays in Honour of Gwynne Henton Davies,* ed. John I Durham & J. R. Porter (London: SCM Press, 1970; new corr. ed.: Macon GA: Mercer University Press, 1983) 215-38.

[2]On the relation of the law and the prophets, see the novel and suggestive approach of John Barton, *Oracles of God: Perceptions of Ancient Prophecy in Israel After the Exile* (Oxford: Oxford University Press, 1986).

[3]No doubt important is that a female prophet is enlisted and obviously has authority in that environment. It is equally important that no special notice is taken of that fact, suggesting that Huldah's authority was not exceptional enough to evoke notice.

[4]Unfortunately Manasseh, before him, waited until the later literature of the Chronicles to repent. Had there been repentance in the Kings account of his rule, things might have turned out differently, according to the huge role assigned to him in the destruction to come.

[5]The cruciality of prophets for this narrative is so important that Walter Dietrich, *Prophetie und Geschichte. Eine redaktionsgeschichliche Untersuchung zum deuteronomistischen Geschichtswerk* FRLANT 108 (1972) can argue for a redaction of the literature that is primally interested in the prophets, that is, they have been edited into the narrative.

[6]Barton, *Oracles of God,* suggests that the prophet, not the scroll, is inventive and venturesome. That is, the commentary on the scroll makes the connections. That of course is exactly what Huldah does here by commenting on the scroll in a contemporary way.

[7]On the cruciality of scribes, see Philip R. Davies, *Scribes and Schools: The Canonization of the Hebrew Scriptures*, Library of Ancient Israel (Louisville: Westminster/John Knox Press, 1998).

[8]Reinhold Niebuhr, *Moral Man and Immoral Society.*

[9]See Robert N. Bellah, *The Good Society* (New York: Random House, 1992).

[10]Niebuhr, *Moral Man and Immoral Society,* xxii-xxiii.

THE RULE AND
DEATH OF JOSIAH

2 Kings 23:1-30

The oracle of Huldah in 22:14-20 had distinguished between the personal future of King Josiah ("gather to your grave in peace," 22:20) and the public fate of Jerusalem ("I will bring disaster," 22:16). This oracle provides a backdrop for the present chapter that details the reformist activity of Josiah during his long reign. His reformist activity begins in a dramatic act of covenant-making for the entire realm (23:1-3). This is followed by a long account of the purgation of worship by Josiah (23:4-20, 24), interrupted by a positive report on Passover (23:21-23). The account ends with an affirmative verdict on the king (23:25), a negative judgment on Jerusalem (23:26-27), and a report on the king's death (23:28-30).

COMMENTARY

Royal Covenant-Making, 23:1-3

Josiah's initial response to the newly found "book of Torah" (see 22:11-13) leads to a major royal initiative in religious reform. Scholars have for a long time been uneasy about the historical reliability of the entire report. An older critical view held that the finding of the scroll in chapter 22 was a "plant" of the scroll, but the ensuing reform was authentic. Subsequently, scholars were inclined to treat the entire sequence with historical seriousness. Currently, however, the strong interpretive opinion is that the entire account may not reflect history at all, but is simply an ideological statement by the narrators to model the sort of radical and passionate act of obedience that is essential to the future of the community of faith. For our purposes, one may bracket out the historical questions and pay attention to the content of the narrative itself. In one way or another, it is thought by most scholars that the narrative reflects a commitment to the theological requirements and vision of the book of Deuteronomy, so that at the very least this text is an imaginative act of what a Deuteronomy-propelled act of faith might permit and require.

The initial and defining act of reform is the reconstitution of the community of faith as one intentionally committed to Yahweh's Torah and to covenantal obedience of Yahweh. Thus Josiah assembles the leadership of the community and "all the people great and small." The purpose is to hear the Torah read and to pledge obedience to its radical vision of reality. Covenant-making, the submission to Yahweh's requirements and expectations, is deeply rooted in Israel's memory and imagination. The narrative surely appeals to the fundamental covenant-making of Sinai (Exod 24:1-8) and echoes the provisions in Deuteronomy for regular reconstitution of covenant (Deut 31:9-13), the practice of Joshua upon entry into the land (Josh 8:30-35; 24:1-28), and the covenant-making of King Jehoash and the priest Jehoiada (2 Kgs 11:17-20); it anticipates the work of Ezra in Nehemiah 8:1-12. All of these texts—and most especially our present text—understand that a covenantally constituted community is particularly linked to Yahweh, is committed to a radically alternative ethic, and is aimed at a quite alternative future in the world. We are here at the most distinctive ecclesial and ethical claim of the Old Testament.[1]

The negative counterpoint of the act, implied and not stated, is that over long years of carelessness and indifference, covenantal dimensions of life have been forgotten and neglected, so that through ethical carelessness, religious indifference, and theological heterodoxy, Israel's peculiar identity and vocation in the world have been abandoned. Thus, the narrative presents Josiah's act as an act of such profound importance that it parallels the founding act of Moses at Sinai and the renewing act of Ezra. This act is nothing less than the recovery of a lost destiny.

The Purgation of Alternatives, 23:4-14

As this narrative presents it, the Jerusalem temple—reflective of long-term religious carelessness and compromise—was saturated with symbols, images, emblems, and practices of alternative religious loyalties that contradicted covenantal Yahwism. Scholars have offered detailed analyses of (a) how these purging acts correlate with the demands of Deuteronomy and (b) the particular significance of the various symbols negated by the reform.[2] It is not necessary for us to reiterate these important and detailed analyses. For our purposes it is sufficient to notice two things: (a) the range of symbols mentioned that bespeak religious compromise against "pure Yahwism"—symbols that refer to Baal and Asherah, idolatrous priests who engaged in astral worship, male prostitutes bespeaking close linkage between religion and productive sexuality, "high places" long a target of this narrative, that is, country shrines and sanctuaries, and sun worship that likely reflects Egyptian influence connected to the macho imagery of horses, pillars, poles, and altars to other gods; (b) the zeal, passion, and completeness of the royal reform aimed not only at elimination but the public humiliation of all such imagery, so that the acts of purgation are intensive and extreme. The "geography of disposal" locates the Wadi Kidron and the valley of Ben-hinnom as the "dumps" where the dangerous pollutant materials are to be stored. [The Storage Dumps] Indeed this narrative regards these symbolizations as profound "health hazards" that will create a pathology of compromise, and therefore they must be eliminated in the most dramatic ways possible.

It is positively important that, in this recital, the narrator can polemically name the members of the royal line who have financed and sponsored these dangerous and destructive practices. One can see that the narrator readily situates Josiah (along with Hezekiah?) as militantly reformist, in contrast to the kings who have been slack and thereby placed the community in jeopardy. Not surprisingly, the report concludes with a reference to the work of Solomon and a mention of three rival gods—Astarte, Chemosh, and Milcom—respectively linked to the Sidonians, Moabites, and Ammonites, on which see 1 Kings 11:5-8. Thus we are able here to see some of the larger architecture of the narrative, so that the denunciation of Solomon in 1 Kings 11 is designed from the outset to point to Josiah as the healthy alternative. In this juxtaposition, Josiah to Solomon, the narrative makes clear the conviction that the entire temple establishment, since its posh origination by Solomon, has been a dangerous, destructive alternative to "pure Yahwism." This juxtaposition of kings nicely creates an interface between *Torah*

The Storage Dumps

The place for dumping these dangerous and despised religious symbols is variously "the Wadi Kidron," a ravine to the east and south of the city that turns out toward the east, "The Valley of Hinnom," a lesser locus to the south of the city, and the "Mt. of Destruction" (otherwise the "Mt of Corruption") where Solomon apparently had located his heterodox worship (see 2 Chr 28:5; 33:6; Jer 2:23; 7:31-32; 19:5-6). This general area to the south of the city had a reputation as the place where non-Yahwistic shrines were located. By the time of our narrator, the place names had taken on a symbolic significance as not only the place for such religious activity, but the place to preserve such emblems, far away from the ordered life of the Yahwistic cult. Because such religious practices jeopardized the community when seen in Yahwistic perspective, it is useful to see that these objects are regarded as dangerous pollutants that must be disposed of carefully and permanently. They have the power, so it is claimed, to bring death to the community, and so are embodiments of all that opposes the life Yahweh would give.

Greater Israel

Scholars commonly assume that Josiah, given the weakness of Assyrian power, did indeed recover territory to the north. While the recovery has important political and military dimensions, it is equally important to notice the power of a vision of "Greater Israel" that extends far to the north, beyond what the royal house could hope to control: (a) that vision of Greater Israel is rooted in the memory of Solomon who extended his borders as far as ever in Israel; (b) alongside what may have been the reality of Solomon, the vision of "Greater Israel" is linked to the old ancestral promises of Genesis (see Gen 15:18-21), a vision well beyond any political reality; (c) it is worth noticing that the same visionary rhetoric is sometimes at work in the policies of the contemporary state of Israel, so that more conservative politicians in Israel persist in utilizing ancient biblical names for contemporary political reality, thus infusing present policy with enduring ideological visions and promises.

---

faith enacted by Josiah and *temple* faith sponsored by Solomon, with no doubt as to which is proper to Yahwism and which is the indispensable summons for a durable Israel of faith. It may well be that this elaborate rhetoric of purgation is only rhetoric and not an actual political program. But even if that is the case, the text puts down a decisive marker concerning the true characterization of Yahweh's community.

The Recovery of Samaria, 23:15-20

No doubt the narrator, utterly committed to the exclusive theological claims of Jerusalem, has been vexed from the outset by the competing claims of the Northern Kingdom, its capital in Samaria and its pivotal shrine in Bethel. If we are to take these verses as historical reportage, they reflect a moment when the power of Josiah was strong enough to recover some of the territory that had been lost long ago in the cession of Jeroboam (1 Kgs 12). Such a moment of recovery may have been possible because by the time of Josiah, the enforcing, occupying power of Assyria that had reduced Samaria to a colony had waned and was no longer able to enforce its imperial claims. On that basis Josiah may have occupied a power vacuum and lived in a Jerusalem environment that had never lost its vision of a united monarchy.

Even if the report is not historical, from a theological, rhetorical perspective, these verses reflect the vision of a unified "Greater Israel" that properly belongs under the government of Jerusalem. [Greater Israel] Apart from any question of historicity, we can see a profound, self-conscious practice of intertextuality operative here. As vv. 13-14 allude to 1 Kings 11:5-8, so in like manner vv. 15, 19-20 allude to 1 Kings 12:25-33 and vv. 16-18 allude to 1 Kings 13:29-32.

We are permitted to see, moreover, that the three references to Jerusalem (23:13-14), Samaria (23:19-20), and Bethel (23:15-18) are not simply happenstance references to earlier texts, but that the earlier texts have been placed as they are in order to create a context for the distinctive work of Josiah. That is, in 1 Kings 11–12 (13), the narrative proposes, things went deeply wrong in both South and North from a Yahwistic perspective and have long remained wrong—until this drastic correction by Josiah.

Thus *Jeroboam* has led the North away from Jerusalem Yahwism. The *"man of God"* who protested against Bethel, is now honored so that his bones remain undisturbed. The *high places of Solomon* and their priests have enacted the destruction summarized so vigorously in 2 Kings 17 and that now receives violent correction by the work of Josiah. The purgation of the South under Josiah is matched by his harsh action against the North. The bones of the man of God exist, moreover, as a very old, incontrovertible witness against the entire Northern enterprise.

An Administered Passover, 23:21-23

These verses report the single positive act of reform in the entire account. It can be argued, on the basis of the liturgical practices behind Exodus 12–13, that Passover is the defining act of Israelite worship that is rooted in the old liberation narrative of the Exodus and that draws Israel closest to its miracle of origin. In that sense, the reassertion of Passover by Josiah fits well with the intent of his reform, for it invites Israel to reenact its most distinctive identity, celebrating Yahweh as the only giver of its life and, derivatively, the life of the world.

It is remarkable that in the long history of monarchy we have been studying, Passover has not heretofore been mentioned, not even once. Indeed, the most recent mention of the festival has been in Joshua 5:10-12, when Israel celebrated Passover just as it entered the land, thus claiming the land liturgically for the God of the Exodus. Claus Westermann says of this act, with particular reference to v. 12,

> The traditionists were fully aware that there was a change in the way Israel talked about God's working with the transition to set-tled life.... The bread of blessing now takes the place of the bread of saving.[3]

The Passover is an act of memory and of the redefinition of the land.

It is possible that the long silence regarding Passover means that the festival had been forgotten and neglected. It is more likely that it was regularly celebrated in homes, so that it was a "domestic" occasion not on the horizon of royal history.[4] The action of Josiah, however, does not look back to a Joshua celebration but alludes in v. 21 to the Deuteronomic regulation of Deuteronomy 16:1 in the context of Deuteronomy 16:1-17. The "calendar" of that passage seeks to regulate Israel's festival life in an orderly way. The effect of the regulation in this teaching is to make the festival a public affair that belongs to the more ordered life governed by a central government.

The Josianic maneuver in our text subscribed to the public practice of the festival, thus transferring a domestic festival to a regulated one that is, moreover, linked to "the book of the covenant." Josiah goes to great lengths to stamp out alternative acts of theological importance and concentrates them all in Jerusalem under royal supervision. Given that reality, it is suggested by some scholars that Josiah's work on the Passover is not an act of disinterested religious zeal, but that the concentration of the festival under royal surveillance assured that the central government would receive income by the collection of a festival tax.[5] This possibility suggests that the king, perhaps like any reformer, never operates with simple, unambiguous motivations. Just as the move back into northern territory meant the recovery of royal lands and their taxes, so this act of public administration may be designed to enhance the royal treasury. The narrator as a devotee of the memory of Josiah of course acknowledges no such mixed motive.

A Verdict on the Great King, 23:24-25

Verse 24 reprises on the purging activities expressed in such detail in vv. 4-20. The catalogue of abominations clearly alludes to Deuteronomy 18:9-13 and presents Josiah, negatively, as a zealous Torah keeper. That negative statement, however, is in the service of the positive assertion at the end of the same sentence. The point to celebrate is that in everything he did, Josiah "established the words," that is, enacted the requirements of the book of Deuteronomy. This verse then leads to the grand verdict on the king in v. 25.

Josiah is the only one of his kind, never before, never after. The nearest royal comparison is to Hezekiah:

He did what was right in the sight of the LORD just as his ancestor David had done. He removed the high places, broke down the pillars, and cut down the sacred pole. He broke in pieces the bronze serpent that Moses had made, for until those days the people of Israel had made offerings to it; it was called Nehushtan. He trusted in the LORD the God of Israel; so that there was no one like him among all the kings of Judah after him, or among those who were before him. For he held fast to the LORD; he did not depart from following him but kept the commandments that the LORD commanded Moses. (2 Kgs 18:3-6)

Josiah, moreover, outdid Hezekiah. The best comparison that might be made is to Moses:

Never since has there arisen a prophet in Israel like Moses, whom the LORD knew face to face. He was unequaled for all the signs and wonders that the LORD sent him to perform in the land of Egypt, against Pharaoh and all his servants and his entire land, and for all the mighty deeds and all the terrifying displays of power that Moses performed in the sight of all Israel. (Deut 34:10-12)

If a connection can be made to Moses, then the two together, Moses and Josiah, frame the larger historical account, placing a quintessential Torah keeper at beginning and end. There are no royal comparisons, and we must go outside royal categories to find a Torah companion. Josiah's distinctiveness is in adherence to the Torah, in the cadences of Deuteronomy 6:5 (see Mark 12:29-30). Josiah so keeps Torah as the model king that he is assured Torah blessings:

I will gather you to your ancestors, and you shall be gathered to your grave in peace. (2 Kgs 22:20)

Josiah Overridden, 23:26-27

Josiah not only prospered himself but did great good for his realm! Great good—but not enough. The realism of the narrator (who surely writes in light of the destruction of Jerusalem at the hands of the Babylonians) must acknowledge that Josiah's Torah-purity lacked sufficient saving power for the city. The reason that Josiah did not prevail through his piety, so says the narrative, is that the wholesale and programmatic Torah violations of his grandfather Manasseh were more powerful than his piety (v. 26). It is odd and noteworthy that in the end, the narrative can point to a single king as the cause of destruction, a curse more powerful than the enterprise of Josiah. From this one king proceeds everything, all the *removal* and the *rejection*, all the desolation that amounts to a termination of the old promises of Yahweh to David and to the city. In the end, the Torah prevails and overrides royal promises. Josiah is at best an encouraging episode, but only an episode and not a reversal of the inexorable demise brought on by Torah disobedience.

An Unexpected, Inexplicable End, 23:28-30

The narrator has yet more bad news for us. These verses begin with a standard formula of closure (23:28). We are nearly lulled by its familiarity. Beyond familiarity, moreover, we expect a good end to this king, based on both the oracle of Huldah (22:20) and the narrative verdict (23:25). We expect a good death well before any of the trouble that is already under way. If ever a good king warranted a good death, it is this Josiah.

We are ill-prepared for what comes next, both that it could happen and that our narrator will tell us of it. The life of this most pious and approved king culminates violently, presumably during a military expedition. Though the specifics are not clear, it is evident that Josiah took an initiative in the geopolitical upheaval underway. In the north, Assyria was an old, fading power that Jerusalem was glad to see go; Babylon was the rising power led by Nabopolassar from whom Jerusalem, at this early date, might expect relief from Assyria. In the south, the Egyptian pharaoh, Neco, was belatedly allied with Assyria, perhaps in order to resist the rising power of Babylon.

Apparently Neco and his Egyptian forces moved to the north in order to aid Assyria. Josiah, opposed to that old regime that had too long abused his realm, sought to intervene against Egypt, to intercept that force at Megiddo, a great and strategic military site. Neco had no designs against Josiah (see 2 Chr 35:21), but could not be detained by Josiah's intervention. As a consequence, Josiah was killed, a casualty of his war effort.

The geopolitical facts that resulted in the death of Josiah are complicated, but they are not difficult to understand. What is problematic about this death is not the external circumstance, but what we are to make of his death theologically, since our narrator insists upon thinking theologically. First, Huldah's oracle had promised Josiah, in contrast to the public fate of the city, a good death (22:20). Second, the extremely positive verdict of v. 25 should, by conventional theological reason, produce, as in the case of Hezekiah, a formula of prosperity (18:7). But it does not in the case of Josiah. Stanley Frost, most notably, has sensed that the death of Josiah is treated with stunning silence in the Bible, because "it is a recalcitrant fact" in a larger theological theory.[6] Indeed the narrator apparently can think of nothing to say that would resolve the problematic and therefore engages in a "conspiracy" (Frost's term) of denial. Frost understands that Josiah's death subverts all claims that life is morally ordered by Yahweh and that this death makes such claims impossible:

> The fact is that the death of Josiah proved to be the relatively small but sharp-edged rock on which the OT concept of divinely motivated history foundered.... Its effect was to destroy the premise on which all Hebrew historiography had been built.[7]

The narrator does seem to handle the problem in larger scope by making Manasseh's evil more powerful than Josiah's virtue. By the end of Josiah's reign, we are left with a foreshortened reign that is ideologically most important for the literature, but that has no effect at all on the larger pattern of demise and failure.

CONNECTIONS

Josiah is rightly known as a reformer. His reform, as reforms characteristically, aims to slough off an accumulation of excess baggage and distortion, and return to the most elemental claims of a focused, unambiguous identity. In the case of Josiah, the reform is to purge the religious practices of the realm of all that has been appropriated from non-Yahwistic religion in order to reembrace a single, covenant-oriented, commandment-based faith. (There are important historical questions that remain unanswered concerning whether such a seventh-sixth century move is a "return to purity" or whether it is in fact a new articulation of piety.) The intention of Josiah, in any case, as given in the narrative, is not difficult to discern.

The narrative invites reflection upon this sort of reform as it may occur in other contexts. Of course in Western Christianity one thinks first of the sixteenth-century Reformation that intended to liberate "gospel faith" from the distortions of the medieval sacramental system. While the main lines of that reformation are clear enough, it becomes more complicated to extend the same reformationist impetus into the twenty-first century because it will not do to reiterate the sixteenth century.

Many voices currently speak of "The New Reformation" that permits the notion of reform to be turned in a variety of directions. (a) It can be argued that Vatican II was a crucial reformist act that sought to permit an evangelical-catholic church freedom from the inherited postures of Trent. (b) It can be suggested that serious ecumenism (and many bilateral church agreements) are a reformist attempt to permit a united church to share in the elementals of faith, without all of the incidental traditions of accident that divide the church and hinder its missional freedom and energy. (c) It can be argued in some quarters that, in our postmodern culture, it is important to slough off the dominant mythical casting of gospel faith in order to focus on the crucial and simple claims of love of God and love of neighbor.[8] (It may be observed that such an inclination in Christian faith has important parallels to Reform Judaism that sought to purge Jewish faith of nonessentials in piety and practice). (d) In my mind, more important for contemporary life than any of these is the need to purge Western Christian practice of the accommodations long made to conventional politics and consequently to consumerist assumptions that have the force and authority of dominant power. That the community of faith may or may not be reformed, that is, given new form, is now an urgent question in light of the failure and inadequacy of old forms of Christendom and its accommodation to unexamined Western cultural assumptions.

For good reason, reformers are characteristically filled with energy and passion, for they would not be reformers were they not convinced that the distortions of faith and life block truth and justice. Such reformers know that return to elemental claims is an act of necessary discipline and obedience. Reformers characteristically have greater passion and authority than those who hold to old, unreformed postures, as is evident in the case of Josiah.[9]

At the same time, it is important to see in this narrative that, characteristically, reform is not disinterested but operates with inevitably mixed motives that may be kept hidden in the rhetoric of moral high ground. Thus Josiah's reform may have been in part about the recovery of territory or the control of festal receipts. And no doubt the Deuteronomic narrators, in championing such a memory, sought to enhance their own authority as the true carriers of emerging Judaism. In the later cases of Luther's alliance with German princes, and Cromwell's alliance to the commercial class against the feudal powers, the vested interests included as motivation for reform are evident. Thus one must always be alert to such ambiguity, without permitting such suspicion to subvert the authentic impetus to reform that may indeed be grounded well beyond vested interest.

Josiah is offered in the narrative as an exemplar of a Torah life, connected to Torah piety.[10] This theological tradition in the Old Testament believes that a life of simple trust and obedience is indeed possible:

> Surely this commandment that I am commanding you today is not too hard for you, nor is it too far way. It is not in heaven…. Neither is it beyond the sea…. No, the word is very near to you; it is in your mouth and in your heart for you to observe. (Deut 30:11-14)

The Torah is doable, and when done, it brings well-being and joy:

> Happy are those who do not follow the advice of the wicked,
>   or take the path that sinners tread,
>   or sit in the seat of scoffers;
> but their delight is in the law of the LORD,
>   and on his law they meditate day
>   and night….
> In all that they do, they prosper. (Ps 1:1-3)

At the same time, this tradition knows that such a life of Torah obedience may have only limited impact on public matters. [Moral Man and Immoral Society] Josiah is good without qualification. His goodness, however, cannot reorder public life, for public life has a form of its own. In this case, public life, for which Manasseh is a cipher, is bent on self-destruction. For that reason, Josiah's life is ultimately not determinative for his people. For the same reason, the narrator is not obligated to comment on or explain his death. [Bill Clinton]

Moral Man and Immoral Society
In the last chapter I commented on the phrasing that Reinhold Niebuhr used to distinguish and interrelate the personal and the social that comes to play acutely in the narrative of Josiah (see pp. 550-1). Josiah is indeed a "moral man," judged by Torah norms. At the same time, his society was, by the same terms, deeply immoral. The narrator, moreover, is not clear how to relate the two, a problem posed especially by the death of Josiah. Niebuhr warns repeatedly about illusions in the real world of power. In the end, one must wonder whether the simple theory of this narrator is an act of illusion or rather a daring act of faith that defies the illusions of control practiced by the power elite in Jerusalem.

The narrator leaves open and unresolved the delicate and enigmatic relationship between public and personal life. The narrative insists upon thinking about public life as a thing in itself that may not be reduced to a series of personal lives. It is a great tendency in the "liberal West" to eschew thought about public life in a passion for individualism. This text knows better. Thus it affirms at the

📖 **Bill Clinton**

In the late 1990s, America followed the Clinton impeachment and trial. Many commentators are of the opinion that the impeachment of President Clinton will stand as a deep question mark in U.S. society for a very long time. The connection to that issue here is that the personal integrity of a president is held up to public scrutiny. The case in defense of Clinton was that his public acts of government had been, from his perspective, adequate and effective and that in such a context, his personal life was irrelevant. Of course the opposition to Clinton took exactly the same view. Few would confuse Clinton with Josiah as a Torah keeper. In this case as in the ancient case, however, the distinction and the overlap between public and personal is operative. The narrator of Josiah in the end did not solve the riddle, and many in contemporary life have been unable to do so as well.

---

same time, (a) the limit of personal impact upon public life and (b) the cruciality of personal engagement that does not grow cynical in its limitation.

It appears that Josiah did leave a powerful legacy with his Torah commitment. In the end, the "people of the land," that body of opinion not controlled by urban, royal ideology, pick the next king by passing over the first candidate for a better choice (23:30). Josiah's crucial legacy that ends for now in death is not yet finished—indeed not yet finished even today, for the Deuteronomic narratives have their say and continue to have their Torah-toned say against all alternatives. On that ground, Josiah's life is not in vain!

NOTES

[1]See Ernest W. Nicholson, *God and His People: Covenant and Theology in the Old Testament* (Oxford: Oxford University Press, 1986) 191-217.

[2]On the linkages of this reform to the provisions of Deuteronomy, see my discussion of chapter 22 and the scholarly works cited there. On the meaning of the several symbols and objects mentioned in Josiah's purgation, ample references are offered in *Ancient Israelite Religion,* ed. Patrick D. Miller et al. (Philadelphia: Fortress Press, 1987). Special attention might be given to the discussion of Norbert Lohfink, "The Cult Reform of Josiah of Judah: 2 Kings 22–23 as a Source for the History of Israelite Religion," ibid., 459-75.

[3]Claus Westermann, *What Does the Old Testament Say about God?* (Atlanta: John Knox Press, 1979) 46.

[4]On the history of the Passover festival, see Roland de Vaux, *Ancient Israel: Its Life and Institutions* (New York: McGraw-Hill, 1961) 484-93.

[5]See W. E. Claburn, "The Fiscal Basis of Josiah's Reform," JBL 92 (1973): 11-22, and Shigeyuki Nakanose, *Josiah's Passover: Sociology & the Liberating Bible* (Maryknoll: Orbis Books, 1993).

⁶Stanley Brice Frost, "The Death of Josiah: A Conspiracy of Silence," JBL 87 (1968): 380.

⁷Ibid., 381-82.

⁸One can conclude that this is, in the end, the theological force of the trajectory of inter-pretation fostered by the Jesus Seminar. Particular attention in this regard should be paid to the work of John Spong on what he terms "The New Reformation."

⁹Allen G. Wehrli, "The Recurring Protestant Spirit," *The Heritage of the Reformation,* ed. Elmer J. F. Arndt (New York: Richard R. Smith, 1950) 14-34 has explored the ways in which the reform of Josiah stands at the fountainhead of an entire tradition of reform.

¹⁰See James L. Mays, "The Place of the Torah Psalms in the Psalter, *"The Lord Reigns: A Theological Handbook to the Psalms* (Louisville: Westminster/John Knox Press, 1994) 128-35.

FOUR PITIFUL KINGS

2 Kings 23:31–25:7

The narrative approaches its sorry end. The Torah obedience and piety of Josiah had little impact upon that future. More telling was the death of Josiah at the hands of Egypt, a harbinger of the way in which Josiah's sons and grandson, in royal succession, would be subject to the will and whim of the surrounding powers. The present verses tell of the final days and demise of Jerusalem, but are organized around the successive reigns of the heirs of Josiah: Jehoahaz (23:31-34), Jehoiakim (23:34–24:7), Jehoiachin (24:8-17), and Zedekiah (24:18–25:7). These verses tell a sorry tale with the sorriness intensified and extended by the detail of the telling. The sequence of the last days of Jerusalem narrated here has much in common with the sorry Northern tale of 15:8-31, 17:1-6. The distinction is that the Southern kings are all the legitimate heirs of David while their Northern counterparts had no claim to royal legitimacy recognized by the narrator. The distinction, however, is without a difference.

COMMENTARY

Jehoahaz for Three Months, 23:31-34

As we have seen in v. 30, the "people of the land" made Jehoahaz, son of Josiah, king in his place. "The people of the land" apparently embody a conservative political constituency that would have been sympathetic to Josiah's Torah religion and his anti-Egyptian policies. To that end, they apparently passed over the oldest son of Josiah in order to choose an heir more to their liking who would continue the policies of his father.

Jehoahaz (whose personal name is Shallum), whose mother was Hamutal, lasted only three months on the throne (609). [The Queen Mother] The brief verdict on him in v. 32 seems completely familiar and we learn nothing of his policies. It was inevitable that he should be driven into the Egyptian sphere of influence, and soon must face Pharaoh Neco at Riblah. [Pharaoh Neco] He is imprisoned by Pharaoh and promptly taken away to Egypt where he dies. It is not at all clear why he was in Riblah or why he must face Neco.

The Queen Mother

I cite in turn the queen mothers of all of these heirs of Josiah. It is entirely possible that the queen mothers are consistently mentioned precisely because they are prominent and influential royal figures. It is plausible that they were rallying points for very different policy opinions and options. Thus, for example, it may be important that Jehoahaz and Zedekiah had the same mother, setting them apart from Jehoiakim and perhaps indicating a different palace clique.

See the fine discussion of the theme by Christopher Seitz, *Theology in Conflict: Reactions to the Exile in the Book of Jeremiah*, BZAW 176 (Berlin: Walter de Gruyter, 1989) 52-55.

Most plausibly he was summoned there and removed from office because of an anti-Egyptian inclination. But John Gray offers the alternative suggestion that he had too readily submitted to Egyptian approval, a ground for the negative theological verdict of v. 32, that is, his "evil" is a refusal to be independent.[1] We lack the data to make a clear decision.

In any case, Neco had no particular interest in the Judean king, but wanted control of the territory and trade routes. He established control (a) by getting a Jerusalem king more to his liking (Jehoiakim, 23:34), and (b) by imposing tribute upon the land. Thus Jehoahaz's rule is brief and is to be understood completely in terms of irresistible Egyptian domination in a void left by the collapse of Assyrian hegemony.

The geopolitical reality of his brief reign is obvious enough. After that, however, we may pay particular attention to Jeremiah 22:11-12 where the prophetic tradition refers to him by his alternative name, Shallum. The facts summarized in this brief, pathos-filled statement correspond to what we already know. What interests us is that Jeremiah employs the term "exile" (*gōlāh*) for this king deported in 609:

> But in the place where they have carried him *captive* he shall die,
> and he shall never see this land again. (Jer 22:12)

The line is filled with characteristic Jeremianic pathos, grief for a king gone from his land, forever. It is clear that in such a phrasing, Jehoahaz is presented as a foretaste of the coming exile. He will die elsewhere as will the others. As he will never see his land again, so also the others. He anticipates and embodies the coming fate of Jerusalem. Such a pathos is not fully interested in geopolitics, but finally cares about the sad failure of the convergence of Torah-land-shalom. The prophetic articulation already verges on grief and tears that are not assuaged by geopolitical explanation.

Pharaoh Neco

Neco was an Egyptian Pharaoh who lasted on the throne for a considerable time, 609–595 BC. He was immensely influential during his time of power. He relentlessly pushed the boundaries and influence of his realm to the north, thus conflicting with the northern imperial powers and seeking to draw Judah into his orbit of influence. That he presided over his war effort at Riblah indicates how far north his influence had reached.

Josiah's Second Heir, 23:35–24:7

Josiah, and perhaps his son Jehoahaz, apparently followed a policy of *political independence*, celebrated by our narrator as *upright Yahwism*. That is, a political stance of independence is understood as an act of religious fidelity. The upshot of such policy earlier (in the time of Hezekiah) could have been anti-Assyrian policy (see 18:7). Now, a century later, given Assyrian collapse, the same policy of independence as fidelity is anti-Egyptian. But like Hezekiah's policy (see 18:14), the anti-Egyptian policies of Jehoahaz would not work because hegemonic powers are impatient and intolerant in this regard.

The outcome is that in an intrusive play of imperial power, Egypt and its Pharaoh Neco remove Jehoahaz from his throne and in his place situate Jehoiakim, another, older son of Josiah. As older son, he has an important claim to the throne. The introductory formula concerning his reign, that lasted eleven years (609–598), is given in 23:36-37. Like his brother in v. 31, he is given a terse, negative verdict. Of more interest is the name of his mother, Zebidah; thus he was only a half-brother to Jehoahaz, whose mother is Hamutal.

The report given on the reign of Jehoiakim may be sketched in three stages as he maneuvers in a minefield of international risks.

First, Jehoiakim is a submissive client of Neco and the Egyptians (23:35). He paid silver and gold tribute, for such imperial arrangements are always about money. There is no hint of reluctance or resistance on the king's part to such payments, though we may imagine that such payments were not popular on the home front.

Second, Jehoiakim changed loyalties after being submissive to Egypt for perhaps four years, 609–605. His change from one imperial loyalty to another is reflective of larger political changes in the Fertile Crescent, so that his change may be understood as quite pragmatic. The Kingdom of Babylon, led by Nabopolassar and then his son Nebuchadnezzar, emerged from a vassal position to the collapsing Assyrian empire and within a decade had achieved major power status. In 605 the rising power of Babylon fought Egypt at the famous battle of Carchemish and thereby established itself as a power to be reckoned with on a very large scale. This rearrangement of power in the Near East is reflected in the concluding statement of 24:7, so that v. 1 reports on Jehoiakim's policy in the context of the great changes stated in v. 7. Jehoiakim's loyalty to Babylon lasted three years, 605–602. [Map: Carchemish]

AΩ **Yahweh as a Textual Problem**
I am here following the Hebrew text that presents Yahweh as the subject of the verb "sent." There is a Greek manuscript tradition that omits the subject and permits the verb to be read with Nebuchadnezzar as its subject. The matter can be read either way. [See Mordechai Cogan and Hayim Tadmor, *2 Kings: A New Translation with Introduction and Commentary*, AB 11 (Garden City: Doubleday, 1988) 306.] It is worth noting what immense theological issues turn on such close textual issues. Perhaps the presence or absence of the subject evidences the hermeneutical play in the ongoing work of interpretation.

Third, after successive submissions to Egypt and to Babylon, in 602, Jehoiakim apparently felt strong enough to assert independence from Babylon and "rebelled," likely by withholding tribute money. In breaking free of imperial domination, perhaps Jehoiakim would earn the approval of the militant Yahwists of a certain ilk, but the act proved to be politically and militarily disastrous.

Babylon and its allies (or better, its puppet states), Syria, Moab, and Ammon, mounted an assault against Jerusalem and its government (24:2). All of this makes good sense in terms of *Realpolitik*, for empires are constantly vigilant about recalcitrant substates. It is noteworthy, though not unexpected, that our narrator is ultimately not interested in the vagaries of *Realpolitik*, but here, as is characteristic, understands these great public events Yahwistically. Thus in v. 2, Yahweh is the subject of the main verb "sent." [Yahweh as a Textual Problem] Yahweh, not Nebuchadnezzar, sends the attackers against the city and the king. Yahweh is fully able, according to this narrative, to mobilize other states in order to fulfill divine intentions in the life of Judah. The motivation for such action, moreover, is neither the enhancement of Babylon nor Babylonian punishment of

Judah as a recalcitrant puppet of the empire, explanations that
might be offered for the attack.

The entire violent military action against Jerusalem "to destroy
it" (24:2) is congruent with long-standing prophetic assertions that
Yahweh is against Yahweh's own city. The full reason for Yahweh's
assault is given in vv. 3-4. The case is introduced by "surely" (*'ak*),
the same particle used in 23:26 to introduce a statement of wrath.
The grammatical particle functions in both texts to signal Yahweh's
readiness to contradict Jerusalem's policies and to act for Yahweh's
own sake. The ground for the action against Jerusalem in 602–598
is Manasseh whom we have already seen in 23:26-27 as the culmination and cipher for the failure of the realm. Manasseh's policies
judged here, we have already seen in chapter 21, are conditioned by
political appeasement that enacts religious accommodation compromising Yahwism. In our text, however, another element of
Manasseh's failure is added along with appeasement and accommodation:

> For the innocent blood that he shed; for he filled Jerusalem with
> innocent blood.

In a rather uncharacteristic formulation, the narrative alludes to
Manasseh's internal policies of the exploitation of Judah's own citizens. While the language of "shed innocent blood" might indicate
violence and disorder, the same rhetoric is used by the prophets to
bespeak economic exploitation of the poor and disadvantaged:

> Hear this, you rulers of the house of Jacob
>   and chiefs of the house of Israel,
> who abhor justice and pervert all equity,
> who build Zion *with blood*,
>   and Jerusalem with wrong!
> Its rulers give judgment for a bribe,
>   its priests teach for a price,
>   its prophets give oracles for money. (Mic 3:9-11)

> For if you truly amend your ways and your doings, if you truly
> act justly one with another, if you do not oppress the alien, the
> orphan, and the widow, or *shed innocent blood* in this place, and
> if you do not go after other gods to your own hurt. (Jer 7:5-6)

Thus in this text the narrative echoes and reiterates what are more
likely prophetic themes, letting those concrete prophetic accents
impinge upon the more familiar formulations of the narrative. As
the prophets characteristically reason, the *external jeopardy* of the

city of Jerusalem is linked to *internal injustice*, a connection between *economic policies* at home and *military threats* from the outside. This stunning language, a commonplace in prophetic faith, is, of course, held together by the insistence that Yahweh governs both internal and external affairs; it is no stretch, given such an affirmation, that Syria, Moab, and Ammon are mobilized by Yahweh in response to exploitative economics in Jerusalem. Completely unexpressed but surely worth noting is the total sidelining of Nebuchadnezzar and all imperial players in this judgment. When Israel's theologians get down to particular cases, Yahweh is the decisive agent without any human agency being referenced.

The judgment voiced against Jehoiakim moves through the military threat of v. 2 to the indictment of vv. 3-4. The accent, however, finally falls on the concluding phrase of v. 4: Yahweh "was not willing to pardon" (*salaḥ*). This decisive formulation means, according to the narrative, that Yahweh's patience with Jerusalem had run out and that the judgment now enacted is final and irreversible. This is the full and inevitable outcome of Torah faith that the narrator has been lining out through all these chapters. Jerusalem is finally beyond the reach of Yahweh's forgiveness.

The term used for "forgiveness," astonishingly, is used in only one other passage in this entire history, namely, in Solomon's great prayer of temple dedication that makes the temple a locus for Yahweh's forgiveness:

> O hear in heaven your dwelling place; heed and forgive. (1 Kgs 8:30; see vv. 34, 36, 29, 50)

This prayer probably originated, along with our text, in exile, when the community stands in deep need, hopes for forgiveness, and counts on the God of Jerusalem to forgive. Our passage then trumps the prayer of Solomon to assert not only that the Jerusalem temple is no longer a place of forgiveness, but that it is itself beyond the possibility of forgiveness.

The prayer of 1 Kings 8 concerning forgiveness and our verdict against forgiveness both seem to be rooted in the curse formula of Deuteronomy 29:20:

> The LORD will be unwilling to pardon them, for the LORD's anger and passion will smoke against them.

That statement in the mouth of Moses can imagine Yahweh's people and Yahweh's place beyond forgiveness. And now a host of royal

AΩ Knowledge of God

It is not possible to reduce this phrase to a single meaning in its several uses. Among the important interpretations of the phrase are the following: (a) Hans Walter Wolff suggests that the term in Hosea refers to a confessional formulation of the canonical memory of "God's mighty deeds," so that it is a set recital of faith. (b) Herbert Huffmon has located texts in which "knowledge of God" means submission to and acceptance of God's sovereignty. (c) Jose Miranda, with special reference to this text, has shown how the term refers to concrete enactment of social justice. All of these interpretations are viable in context, but in our context there can be no doubt that the accent is upon the active engagement of the strong on behalf of the weak in matters of justice.

Hans Walter Wolff, "'Wissen um Gott' bei Hosea als Urform von Theologie," *Evangelische Theologie* 12 (1952/53): 533-54, Herbert Huffmon, "The Treaty Background of Hebrew *yada'*," BASOR 181 (1966): 31-37, Jose Miranda, *Marx and the Bible: A Critique of the Philosophy of Oppression* (Maryknoll: Orbis Books, 1974) 44-53 and passim.

---

failures culminating in Manasseh and Jehoiakim has brought Jerusalem to this sorry end.

The concluding formula on Jehoiakim follows immediately upon this verdict, as though the narrator can think of nothing to say about him after "not willing to pardon" (24:5-6). By his violation of Babylonian hegemony, Jehoiakim has set in motion a terrible attack on his city. He did not, however, linger long enough to pay for his failure. He died a peaceful death and left matters of consequence to his son and successor.

The remarkable theological judgment on Jehoiakim in vv. 2-4 with its references to the prophets permits us to pause over the prophetic characterization of this king in the tradition of Jeremiah. We have already seen in Jeremiah 22:11-12 a pathos-filled comment on Jehoahaz. The following poetic verses on Jehoiakim are fuller, both because Jehoiakim lasted longer on the throne and because his failures brought greater trouble on the city (Jer 22:13-19).[2]

(a) The king is condemned for his practices of exploitative injustice and unrighteousness, thus making him the appropriate target for the most characteristic prophetic agenda, and surely agreeing with the comment of 2 Kings 24:4 (Jer 22:13-14). The indictment is introduced by a characteristic "woe," suggesting coming death and sadness. The references to "spacious house," "large upper rooms," and "windows and cedar" are reminiscent of Solomon's self-indulgence and indicate the crass indifference of royalty to the lot of ordinary citizens.

(b) This condemned, self-indulgent king is contrasted with "your father," Josiah (Jer 22:15-17). Josiah is seen in every regard as a Torah keeper whose policies provided a "safety net" for the "poor and needy." Josiah's policies are here characterized as a full enactment of the Mosaic vision of a compassionate society with a justice-practicing economy. Indeed, such practice is the very "knowledge of God" about which the prophet Hosea speaks. [Knowledge of God] "Knowledge of God" is a sustained obedience in a life congruent with Yahweh's character and Yahweh's Torah of justice.

Jehoiakim, however, is the very antithesis of his father, thus a carrier of destructiveness for his society (Jer 22:17). He is a shedder of innocent blood, an oppressor who engages in policies of economic violence. The poetic critique summarized in our narrative is here given expansive poetic rendition in the Jeremiah text.

(c) The outcome of such a royal career is an ignoble death (Jer 22:18-19). The king, it is anticipated, will not be grieved or lamented in death, and will not finally be buried in royal fashion, but only like a despised donkey. The scenario offered calls to mind the ignoble death of Jezebel at the hands of Jehu, surely the most dishonored of all royal figures in our narrative (2 Kgs 9:30-37).

Our text in 2 Kings 24, however, contradicts this poetic anticipation and reports on the peaceable death of Jehoiakim (24:6). If that is the case, then we may observe these contrasting parallels with his father Josiah:

> Josiah: offered a *peaceable* death (22:20)
>   dies a *violent* death (23:29).

> Jehoiakim: offered an *ignoble* death (Jer 22:18-19)
>   dies a *peaceable* death (24:6).

We might notice, following Cogan and Tadmor, that there are alternative traditions about his death, no doubt in resistance to the easy conclusion that his death was a good one.[3]

In Jeremiah 26:20-23, this same king Jehoiakim is portrayed as a prophet-killer, surely deaths commissioned in an attempt to silence the Torah insistence on social justice and the prophetic warnings of the dire outcomes for disregard of Torah. Jeremiah's notice resonates closely with 2 Kings 24:2, "according to the word of the Lord spoken by his servants the prophets." Jehoiakim is clearly a practitioner of an anti-Torah, antiprophetic vision of social reality.

In Jeremiah 36, the contrast made in Jeremiah 22:15-17 between Josiah and Jehoiakim as "types" is explicated more fully. In Jeremiah 36:23, the prophetic scroll of Jeremiah is read aloud to the king. In an ostentatious act of contempt, the king defiantly cuts the scroll and burns it, an early example of "document shredding." As many scholars have noticed, the term "cut" (*qara*) is the same verb used in 2 Kings 22:11 wherein Josiah hears the Torah scroll read to him aloud, and "rends" his clothes in a dramatic act of royal

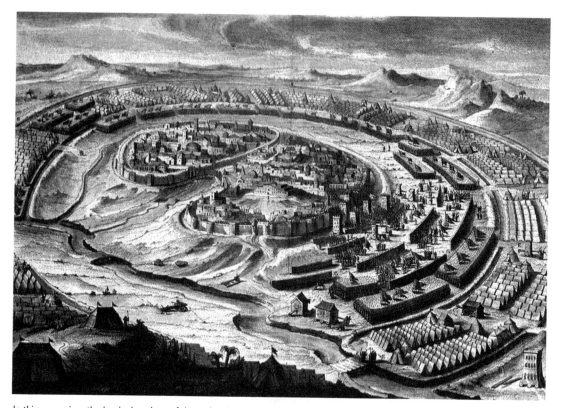

In this engraving, the beginning siege of Jerusalem is presented as a panoramic, geophysical unfolding as the Babylonian forces have surrounded the city.

Augustin Calmet. *Siege of Jerusalem by Nebuchadnezzar*. 1710. Engraving. (Credit: University of Florida. Map and Image Library)

repentance. The two acts of cutting, one to *eliminate the scroll* and the other to *obey the scroll* fill out the picture of the "typically good king" and the "typically bad king" who brings death to his city. In sum Jehoiakim is a remarkably crucial king, because he provides a dramatic interplay between the most expansive issues of international politics and the most acute Torah concerns of this narrative account. The narrator insists that the two sets of data converge completely in this reign, precisely because the Lord of the Torah is the Lord of all nations.

The Brief Boy King, 24:8-17

Jehoiachin, also named Coniah, became king in 598, just in time to preside over the disaster in Jerusalem that his father, Jehoiakim, had set in motion. He is the son of yet another royal mother, Nehushta; like his father Jehoiakim and his uncle Jehoahaz, he receives a terse, negative theological verdict (24:9; see 23:33, 37).

The important data of his three-month reign is that he presided over the loss of Jerusalem to the Babylonians when

Nebuchadnezzar came and conquered and sacked the city (24:10-17). In fact, Jehoiachin had no choice in the matter because, by 598, Babylon had become the unchallenged master of the land bridge of the Fertile Crescent. Its hegemonic policy required the crushing of any recalcitrant puppet state. The Babylonian policy of deportation simply followed the outlines of Assyrian policies of deportation that we have already witnessed in Samaria. We may identify three elements in the deportation:

1. The king himself is carried away to Babylon, where he will survive for a long, exilic existence (24:12).

2. The temple is sacked and the valuables are carried away, for imperial conquest is never far removed from money (24:13). The looting of the temple (on which see also 16:17-18) represents a practical loss plus a humiliating defeat for Yahweh, the Lord of the temple who is apparently not strong enough to defend Yahweh's own house. Besides these two points, Peter Ackroyd has suggested the way in which the loss of temple vessels (as here) and the recovery and restoration of temple vessels (in other texts) provided a way of commenting on the vexed questions of communal continuity

---

📖 The High Cost of Disobedience

In a very different mode of discourse, famine as a consequence of siege is vividly pictured in the covenant categories, perhaps in the very document that had moved Josiah with its threats in the first place:

> Because you did not serve the LORD your God joyfully and with gladness of heart for the abundance of everything, therefore you shall serve your enemies whom the LORD will send against you, in hunger and thirst, in nakedness and lack of everything. He will put an iron yoke on your neck until he has destroyed you. The LORD will bring a nation from far away, from the end of the earth, to swoop down upon you like an eagle, a nation whose language you do not understand, a grim-faced nation showing no respect to the old or favor to the young. It shall consume the fruit of your livestock and the fruit of your ground until you are destroyed, leaving you neither grain, wine, and oil, nor the increase of your cattle and the issue of your flock, until it has made you perish.... In the desperate straits to which the enemy siege reduces you, you will eat the flesh of your womb, the flesh of your own sons and daughters whom the LORD your God has given you. Even the most refined and gentle of men among you will begrudge food to his own brother, to the wife whom he embraces, and to the last of his remaining children, giving to none of them any of the flesh of his children whom he is eating, because nothing else remains to him, in the desperate straits to which the enemy siege will reduce you in all your towns. She who is the most refined and gentle among you, so gentle and refined that she does not venture to set the sole of her foot on the ground, will begrudge food to the husband whom she embraces, to her own son, and to her own daughter, begrudging even the afterbirth that comes out from between her thighs, and the children that she bears, because she is eating them in secret for lack of anything else. (Deut 28:47-57)

This text understands that famine follows siege; all of the suffering that follows is directly from Yahweh as a consequence of disobedience.

and survival.⁴ In our text, of course, there is no hint of any recovery or restoration, as here the concern is total, humiliating, irreversible loss. The "things of Yahweh" have been transferred to the gods of Babylon.

3. The leading citizens of Jerusalem are taken away to Babylon (24:14-16). This includes all those elements of society that make a society viable: the royal family, political leaders, soldiers, artisans, and craftsmen. The purpose of such deportation may be to enhance the Babylonian economy, for it is clear that the deportees did come to play a role in the imperial economy; the other purpose is to preclude rebellions such as Jehoiakim had mounted by taking away all political leadership. The text acknowledges that the "poorest" were left in the land, the ones who would not enhance the empire and who were unlikely candidates for rebellion. In any case, this reference acknowledges that the city is not "empty" or abandoned. We should also note, however, that such a labelling of "the poorest" may be self-serving on the part of the labellers, because the text is surely written among those deported, so that the labeling of the ones left behind as less significant may be a self-congratulatory way of enhancing the deportees.

That said, the tale of Jehoiachin is ended with the naming of his successor (24:17). It is most important to notice that the boy-king is given no formula of closure, precisely because he will outlive the monarchy in Jerusalem and come to occupy an important symbolic—perhaps political—role in the emergence of Judaism in the sixth century.

Though it lies outside our text, we may reflect on the textual traditions, both positive and negative, that are generated by the presence and significance of this boy-king who was carried away on behalf of his father's reckless royal policies.

First, Jehoiachin functions as a negative cipher, for which I again refer to Jeremiah 22. In Jeremiah 22:24-30, the tradition voices both a prose judgment against the king (22:24-27) and a poetic lament (22:28-30). The prose judgment asserts that Yahweh will abruptly and violently "tear off," "give," and "hurl" the king and the queen mother into "the hands of those who seek their life," that is, into the power of Babylon. The judgment anticipates deportation with a note of finality: "not return." In this utterance deportation is seen as termination, end of dynasty, end of city, end of promise, end! The lament that follows is even more pathos-filled, again employing the word "hurl," this time matched by "cast away…in a land you do not know"—Babylon (24:28-30). The imagery of a clay pot reinforces the verbs of rejection. In Jeremiah 18 and 19, the prophet has used the imagery of pottery in order to comment on this city and this people that is broken beyond mending (19:11). The same imagery is personalized with reference to the boy-king who is tossed off as a valueless, useless, discarded pottery shard, never restored, never valued, never returned, worthless.

The triad, "land, land, land," is an utterance of grief by a poet rendered speechless by the image of land without king, sheep without shepherd. While Jeremiah 22:28-29 offers such moving images, Jeremiah 22:30 comments according to the old promises made to the dynasty. The old tradition had heard Yahweh promise that there would always be an heir to David, assured and guaranteed (2 Sam 7:11-16; Ps 89:19-37; 132:11-12). Now comes the end of the line, because the promise is terminated and the dynasty is heirless. The promise had been unambiguous:

> I will establish his line forever,
>   and his throne as long as the heavens endure...
> His line shall continue forever. (Ps 89:29, 36)

Now in this pitiful boy-king comes a reneging:

> Record this man as childless,
>   a man who shall not succeed in his days;
> for none of his offspring shall succeed
>   in sitting on the throne of David,
>   and ruling again in Judah. (Jer 22:30)

This tradition can see no future; end of story, end of dynasty, end of promise, end! [The High Cost of Disobedience]

This, however, is not the complete tradition. In another context, likely in another generation, Jehoiachin is a positive force in tradition formation. He was deported but not terminated. He lived as an identifiable king in exile for a very long time. He is reckoned to be a legitimate king in exile who still controls lands and receives royal income. We may cite two texts that support the notion that Jehoiachin signifies a way into the future beyond exile. In Jeremiah 24, in a prohetic vision, he is the leader of the "good figs," the Jewish community in exile that will seize the initiative for the formation of Judaism. He is, unlike his uncle Zedekiah who is a bad fig, the reference point for renewed faith that aims at homecoming. In the book of Ezekiel (see 1:2), moreover, the exile of Jehoiachin in 598 becomes the reference point for the elaborate dating system of the book. This is remarkable, because the later destruction of Jerusalem in 587 under Zedekiah is commonly regarded as the pivotal date in the story of Jerusalem. In this exilic tradition, however, the clock of exile begins in 598, an exilic king who remains "in waiting" for Yahweh's future.

There is no way I know of to adjudicate between the pathos of Jeremiah 22:24-30 and the lively expectation of Jeremiah 24 and Ezekiel. Clearly, different voices in the tradition viewed the deportation differently and there is, in the end, no right answer. Because the matter is in dispute, our narrator provides a final note concerning the survival of Jehoiachin in exile after thirty-seven years (= 561). That text, however, does not speak clearly about either termination or possibility, a fact made clear by the remarkably energetic scholarly dispute on the passage. All that is certain is that the role of the boy-king has been defeated by Babylon in the service of Yahweh. Beyond that, the community waits, some in grief, some in hope, some in both. [The Proud Now Humiliated]

Zedekiah the Final King, 24:18–25:7

Zedekiah, also called Mattaniah, reigned eleven years, 598–587. The report on this last king consists in introductory matters, together with a most generalized verdict (24:18-20a), and a

---

📖 The Proud Now Humiliated

The flight in humiliating desperation is anticipated by Isaiah:

The haughtiness of people shall be humbled,
  and the pride of everyone shall be brought low;
  and the LORD alone will be exalted on that day.
The idols shall utterly pass away.
Enter the caves of the rocks
  and the holes of the ground,
from the terror of the LORD,
  and from the glory of his majesty,
  when he rises to terrify the earth.
On that day people will throw away
  to the moles and to the bats
their idols of silver and their idols of gold,
  which they made for themselves to worship,
to enter the caverns of the rocks
  and the clefts of the crags,
from the terror of the LORD,
  and from the glory of his majesty,
when he rises to terrify the earth. (Isa 2:17-21)

The escapees, however, did not get very far. The Babylonian soldiers caught up with the king's party by the time they arrived at Jericho. Now the king is abandoned to his fate, left alone and defenseless by his deserting guard. The glory of the Davidic monarchy has come down to this, a lone king without resources, taken in the night by pursuing imperial soldiers.

detailed account of his final apprehension by the Babylonians (24:20b–25:7).

Zedekiah, the third son of Josiah on the throne, is the son of Hamutal, thus a full brother to Jehoahaz (23:31). He receives a quick negative verdict as do all the heirs of Josiah (see 23:32, 37; 24:9). More important than his personal verdict is the generalized verdict of v. 20a: Yahweh's anger against Judah and Jerusalem is cumulative and now reaches full pitch. The history of monarchy is a history of disobedience which, for Yahweh, becomes a history of anger. It is this legitimate anger of Yahweh that produces expulsion from the land. The verdict, attributing exile to Yahweh, is a match for the summary statement of 25:21 that credits the deportation to Babylon. The narrator easily and without awkwardness appeals to double agency. It is no problem in prophetic horizon to credit exile to Yahweh (24:20) and to the empire (25:21).

In 24:20b–25:7 the empire acts with severity toward Jerusalem. Zedekiah rebelled against Nebuchadnezzar, likely by withholding tribute payment. There is an endless restlessness in Jerusalem with subservience to imperial power. The kings characteristically refuse such subservience whenever they think that they are strong enough to resist. Here we are not told the date of the rebellion. We do know, however, that political flux in Egypt in 593 created some destabilization of Babylonian control. It is more likely that Zedekiah's maneuver toward independence from Babylon is part of that more general picture of restlessness. Characteristically Egypt acts as an impetus toward rebellion against Babylon in Judah, but is not around to sustain those who run such risks of defiance.

Zedekiah has been placed on the throne by Babylon after the failure of Jehoiakim's rebellion in 598. Now the scenario of imperial military intrusion is reenacted a decade later. Nebuchadnezzar lays siege to Jerusalem in 589, a siege that lasts two years. The purpose of the siege is to starve out the city and to force capitulation. The siege works and by 587 the scarcity of food is severe. The famine is readily understood as a consequence of the siege. Our report is terse and gives no detail, except to indicate that the city populace was no doubt desperate.

Our more sober narrative indicates that the elite of the city, to say nothing of ordinary people, are so desperate that they manage an escape through enemy lines and flee to the south (25:4). The flight into the wilderness may have been an act of survival, but in poetic rendering, it is also an act of dreadful humiliation. For the sake of his life, the king in Jerusalem must flee the city of promise.

Zedekiah is taken to Riblah, as was his brother Jehoahaz before him (23:33). Jehoahaz had faced Neco the Egyptian. Zedekiah must face Nebuchadnezzar the Babylonian. Both Judean kings are deposed and humiliated. Both kings are utterly without resources. Both kings are deported, Jehoahaz to the south, Zedekiah to the north. In both cases, the kings are unprotected and uncared for. The only difference is that Zedekiah's captors are more ruthless and brutalizing. Unlike his brother, Zedekiah must watch the murder of his sons—presumably heirs and therefore potential threats to Babylon in the future. That is the last thing the king sees. The lights go out for him; he is blinded. The people who walked in light have come to an immense darkness beyond which they can see noting.

Zedekiah's narrative account is unremarkable and quite predictable, for all the heirs of Josiah suffer a bad fate. But of course there is more about Zedekiah than this lean narrative tells us; again we must refer to the tradition of Jeremiah. I will comment in turn on his political situation and then on a fuller religious assessment.

It will be recalled that Zedekiah's nephew, Jehoiachin, had briefly been king before him and had been deported to Babylon in 598. In exile, however, Jehoiachin continued to be recognized as king. Thus in the period 598–587, the time of the reign of Zedekiah, Jehoiachin was recognized as "king in exile." This means either that (a) there were two competing kings, each with claims to legitimacy, Zedekiah in Jerusalem and Jehoiachin in Babylon, or (b) Jehoiachin was in fact true king and his uncle Zedekiah was his regent in Jerusalem and not really king. Either way, Zedekiah had no time of uncontested authority on the throne.

Jeremiah 24, already mentioned, permits one characterization of this fluid and unsettled situation. In this rendering, the community around Jehoiachin (here Jeconiah) is the "good figs" and the wave of the future; conversely, Zedekiah and his entourage are "bad figs," of whom Yahweh has pronounced:

> I will make them a horror, an evil thing, to all the kingdoms of
> the earth—a disgrace, a byword, a taunt, and a curse in all the
> places where I shall drive them. And I will send sword, famine,
> and pestilence upon them, until they are utterly destroyed from
> the land that I gave to them and their ancestors. (Jer 24:9-10)

To be sure, the narrative verdict of Jeremiah 24 is not innocent; it no doubt reflects the political ascendancy and sense of theological legitimacy of the Jehoiachin community that subsequently emerged as the shaping force of Judaism. For Zedekiah, this means that while his nephew gathers himself for the future, he as king or regent (it does not matter which) is left holding the bag in the city that in principle is already lost on behalf of a dynastic line that is in principle already terminated.

The ambiguous and unsettled role of Zedekiah apparently produced a high and enduring level of anxiety and complete bewilderment about policy. Indeed, there is ground for anxiety and bewilderment in his situation, for Zedekiah arrived much too late to make a difference in the future of his city, even as his father Josiah arrived too late to make a difference (see 2 Kgs 23:26-27). In the case of Zedekiah, it appears that the die is cast for expulsion from the land, no matter what.

As a consequence of this bewilderment, this king-regent, without guidance or resource, according to the tradition of Jeremiah, appeals to that prophet for guidance, the very prophet whom his brother Jehoiakim had almost executed (Jer 26:1-24). [King and Prophet in a Desperate Situation]

King and Prophet in a Desperate Situation

In five reported encounters in Jeremiah that cannot be ordered sequentially, the king-regent five times engages the prophet, and receives either no answer, or an answer he cannot accept:

(a)   King: Please enquire of the LORD on our behalf.... Perhaps the Lord will perform a wonderful deed for us. (Jer 21:2)

Prophet: I am going to turn back the weapons of war that are in your hands and with which you are fighting against the king of Babylon and against the Chaldeans who are besieging you outside the walls; and I will bring them together in the center of this city. I myself will fight against you with outstretched hand and mighty arm, in anger, in fury, and in great wrath.... Afterward, says the LORD, I will give King Zedekiah of Judah, and his servants, and the people in this city—those who survive the pestilence, sword, and famine—into the hands of King Nebuchadnezzar of Babylon, into the hands of their enemies, into the hands of those who seek their lives. (Jer 21:4-7)

(b)   King: Why do you prophesy?...(Jer 32:3)

The prophet makes no answer, as the literary unit is terminated with the speech of the king.

(c)   King: Please pray for us to the LORD our God. (Jer 37:3)

Prophet: Do not deceive yourselves, saying, "The Chaldeans will surely go away from us," for they will not go away. (Jer 37:9)

(d)   King: Is there any word from the LORD? (Jer 37:17)

Prophet: There is!...You shall be handed over to the king of Babylon. (Jer 37:17)

(e)   King: I have something to ask you; do not hide anything from me.(Jer 38:14)

Prophet: If you will only surrender to the officials of the king of Babylon, then your life shall be spared, and this city shall not be burned with fire, and you and your house shall live. But if you do not surrender to the officials of the king of Babylon, then this city shall be handed over to the Chaldeans. (Jer 38:17-18)

While there are variations, the message of the prophet is clear. Jerusalem will be destroyed by Babylon as Yahweh wills. The only escape is to submit to Babylon and become a willing vassal. This policy of submission is pervasive in the tradition of Jeremiah. But of course such submission is precisely what the king cannot understand or stomach; in the end his defiance of Babylon brings the termination of the dynasty, the razing of the city, and the terrible fate of Zedekiah himself, echoed in Jer 39:6-7.

📖 A Divine Limit on Imperial Power

To be sure, that curb of Yahwism is characteristically voiced by Israel in the maintenance of its own interests in the face of imperial threat, as for example in these cases:

Ah, Assyria, the rod of my anger—
  the club in their hands is my fury!
Against a godless nation I send him,
  and against the people of my wrath I command him,
to take spoil and seize plunder,
  and to tread them down like the mire of the streets....
Shall the ax vaunt itself over the one who wields it,
  or the saw magnify itself against the one who handles it?
As if a rod should raise the one who lifts it up,
  or as if a staff should lift the one who is not wood!
Therefore....(Isa 10:5-6, 15-16)

The princes of Zoan are utterly foolish;
  the wise counselors of Pharaoh give stupid counsel....
Where now are your sages?
  Let them tell you and make known
  what the LORD of hosts has planned against Egypt.
The princes of Zoan have become fools,
  and the princes of Memphis are deluded....
The LORD has poured into them a spirit of confusion;
  and they have mad Egypt stagger in all its doings
  as a drunkard staggers around in vomit. (Isa 19:11-14)

I was angry with my people,
  I profaned my heritage;
I gave them into your hand,
  you showed them no mercy;
on the aged you made your yoke exceedingly heavy....
Now therefore hear this....(Isa 47:6-8)

Any serious reader of this text in the U.S. is in the demanding position of taking such a heavy critique of power, not from the vantage point of a little, vulnerable state, but from within the superpower itself. Thus we are required, in my judgment, to hear this curbing convergence from a perspective other than the one given in the text itself. Difficult as that is, it is for that reason no less urgent. Yahweh, so this text tradition insists, can work endings and terminations that violate even Yahweh's own assurances. In the context of advanced military-technological-bureaucratic power, the faithful are left to see how this old conviction may yet be truthful.

The Jeremiah tradition suggests that even as late as Zedekiah, the monarchy had a chance, but it was a chance strategically and emotionally unavailable to a royal party encased in Jerusalem ideology. The counsel of the prophet is "Better red than dead," but they did not believe it: "It cannot happen here." Clearly, ideological grounding in a certain form of faith precluded attention to the reality of the situation. And so the king, blinded by royal ideology, ends up blinded by the empire as well. [A Divine Limit on Imperial Power]

CONNECTIONS

This report of the sad demise of Jerusalem and the Davidic monarchy contains three recurrent elements of prophetic faith:

1. The story of faith takes place in the midst of the imperial realities of international politics. After the surge of independence in turn under Hezekiah and Josiah, the final days of Judah are in large part shaped by imperial powers. Thus each of these four pitiful kings is completely at the mercy of the whim of the superpower.

> Jehoahaz: *Pharaoh Neco* confined him at Riblah in the land of Hamath, so that the might not reign in Jerusalem…. He took Jehoahaz away; he came to Egypt, and he died there. (23:33-34)

> Jehoiakim: In his days *king Nebuchadnezzar* of Babylon came up. (24:1)

> Jehoiachin: At that time the servants of *king Nebuchadnezzar* of Babylon came up to Jerusalem and the city was besieged….The *king of Babylon* took him prisoner in the eighth year of his reign. (24:10, 12)

> Zedekiah: *King Nebuchadnezzar* of Babylon came with all his army against Jerusalem and laid siege to it…. the *king of Babylon* at Riblah, who passed sentence on him. (25:1, 6)

The dominance of Nebuchadnezzar, preceeded in the case of Jehoahaz by Neco of Egypt, indicates that only the names change in the power game. The power dimension of the real world persists. This recognition is highly important for these texts. It reminds us that biblical faith is never in a power vacuum and never primarily a religious or spiritual enterprise. This same acknowledgement of power realities as context for faith is nicely and unmistakably voiced in the Lucan narrative of the appearance of John the Baptist:

> In the fifteenth year of the reign of Emperor Tiberius, when Pontius Pilate was governor of Judea, and Herod was ruler of Galilee, and his brother Philip ruler of the region of Itruaea and Trachonitis, and Lysanias ruler of Abilene, during the high

priesthood of Annas and Caiaphas, the word of God came to John. (Luke 3:1-2)

When the rule of God appears, it is always in the presence of powerful people with impressive credentials and titles.

2. The power of empire is definitive in the narrative ending of each of these four kings. Thus the imperial powers are terminators of all the futures of the kings in Jerusalem:

Jehoahaz is taken to Egypt where he dies.

Jehoiakim, the worst of the lot, is the exception and dies a peaceable death.

Jehoiachin is taken prisoner to Babylon.

Zedekiah is taken prisoner (and blind) to Babylon.

It seems plausible that the narrator intends these accounts to betoken the exilic displacement of the whole people: "Like king, like people." Indeed, Jehoiachin and Zedekiah may be seen as important persons, but they lead and represent communities of exiles in 598 and 587 respectively. Everything moves to displacement.

3. For all the emphasis upon *Realpolitik* that operates in these texts, the narrative finally is not interested in such an account, but clearly offers a Yahwistic construal of the demise of the city. Thus the imperial leaders are at best tools and agents of Yahweh's purposes (see Jer 25:9; 27:6).[5] It is to be noticed that in three of the four cases (again Jehoiakim is the exception), there is no suggestion of divine judgment in the fate of the king, but the public process of imperial power simply plays itself out and the king in each case pays for that reality. We may, however, cite three attestations to prophetic conviction as clues to how the narrative is to be understood:

(a) The theological verdict of 24:3-4 (addressed against Jehoiakim though presumably it could have been voiced with reference to any of these kings) makes clear that the dispersal of Judah is indeed the will of Yahweh for which Nebuchadnezzar is simply the officer of the day.

(b) The sweeping conclusion of 24:20 is a generic judgment that is not specifically linked to any particular king; it is the decisive verdict of Yahweh on the entire royal process in Jerusalem.

(c) The capacity to correlate each of these kings with elements of the Jeremiah tradition, as I have indicated, keeps each of the kings in the context of the prophetic. Indeed, in the Old Testament royal power is never finally autonomous but is always linked to and judged by prophetic requirements.

The narrative then is a remarkable convergence of *Realpolitik* and *prophetic characterization*. This convergence sees no tension or problem in reporting the agency of empire and the agency of Yahweh in governing the affairs of Judah. The two are, in fact, varied ways of speaking about the one reality of Yahweh as a powerful player in the world of real power. This convergence is decisive and definitive for the entire account of royal history traced in 1 and 2 Kings. This conviction of ultimate accountability to Yahweh for power affairs in the world is an insistence that there are no autonomous zones of human power apart from the purposes of Yahweh. This deep conviction and convergence in biblical faith has been largely abandoned in the modern period. The upshot has been to confine the claims of Yahweh to private and interpersonal matters.

It is a difficult problem about how to recover in our time the conviction and/or rhetoric of biblical faith that dares to assert Yahweh's governance in the actual affairs of nation-states. And yet I judge such a recovery to be urgent and worth the effort. While the matter pertains everywhere in every configuration of public power, it may be particularly acute for readers and students who live and believe in the context of the United States. In terms of *Realpolitik*, it is now evident that the political, economic, military will of the U.S. is largely uncurbed and unrestrained by any counterforce in the world. Happily a residue of public morality is still present in U.S. public awareness. That residue, however, is thin and is able to exercise very little restraint in the face of economic momentum coupled to power characteristically reduced to amoral practices of technology.

Already in the Old Testament, the sovereign rule of Yahweh functions, among other things, precisely to set limits upon imperial actions that have no other curb or limit.

Finally, I will reflect upon the report of the text that there are two kings left, exiles but alive. We will have occasion to return to Jehoiachin at the end of chapter 25. It is for now exceedingly important that he is not killed by the empire: he is given no narrative closure. Likely this is strategically intentional on the part of the narrative, but it may also be the case that this narrative as of yet genuinely does not know the future of this boy-king. The text here only affirmed that he is still there. And if still alive, therefore still a carrier of hope, possibility, and royal legitimacy. In a story that kills kings off routinely, his very survival counts for a great deal:

> But whoever is joined with all the living has hope,
> for a living dog is better than a dead lion. (Eccl 9:4)

The case of Zedekiah is very different. He is alive, but blind. Unlike his nephew Jehoiachin, he will not reappear in this narrative again in any important way. We may nonetheless suggest that he also embodies his community in powerful ways.

1. In Jeremiah 24:8-10, he is taken to be representative of all those Jews after 597 who either stayed in Jerusalem or fled to Egypt, but were not taken to Babylon. Since the traditions are shaped by Babylonian Jews who established themselves as the legitimate carriers of Israel's faith, Zedekiah and all his ilk receive exceedingly bad press in the Bible. They are "not with the program" and so disappear from the screen of orthodoxy and legitimacy. Zedekiah may be remembered and valued as a sign of all those who are sloughed off and discounted by the historical process that validates and invalidates. Concrete historical reality is always given us through the lens of some orthodoxy or other. Zedekiah stands for all those invalidated who become "a disgrace, a byword, a taunt, and a curse in all the places where I shall drive them" (Jer 24:9).

2. Zedekiah is portrayed as an indecisive, anxious king who could not facilitate good policy in an impossible situation. We may cite two narrative evidences of his lack of courage and clarity. In Jeremiah 38:14-28 this sorry, final king has one of his several encounters with the prophet. Jeremiah is, as always, clear and unequivocal: surrender to Babylon for it is the will of Yahweh! Zedekiah's response is the voice of a leader who has lost self-confidence and authority, or as an earlier narrative might say it, "The spirit of the Lord had departed him" (cf. 1 Sam 16:14):

> I am afraid of the Judeans who have deserted to the Chaldeans,
> for I might be handed over to them and they would abuse me.
> (Jer 38:19)

Zedekiah is not afraid of the judgment of Yahweh or the treatment he may receive from Babylon; he is afraid rather of his own political constituency that would never accept such a policy of surrender. While Zedekiah is regularly castigated as a coward, perhaps he is better extended sympathy as one who must make hard decisions that offer no viable alternative. It is likely that the narrative is not especially focused on the king, but wants the reader to notice that Judah (along with its king) has arrived at a Catch-22, no-win moment.

The impossible situation of the king is further exemplified later on in the same chapter when Zedekiah, in great fearfulness, urges the prophet to join in a deception at the press conference:

Do not let anyone else know of this conversation, or you will die....you shall say to them, "I was presenting my plea to the king not to send me back to the house of Jonathan to die there." All the officials did come to Jeremiah and questioned him; and he answered them in the very words the king had commanded. (Jer 38:24-27)

That is, the king proposes that the real conversation must be kept secret and instead invents an alternative conversation to deceive his own officials. Amazingly enough, the prophet cooperates fully and does not blow the king's cover (Jer 38:27). Perhaps the prophet understood that the king and people were beyond a point of no return, and so acted generously toward a king already failed. [A Second, Puzzling Night Vision]

A Second, Puzzling Night Visit

This exchange in secret, at night, is hauntingly anticipatory of the night visit of Nicodemus in John 3. The teacher and representative of the bewildered Jews in that narrative probes in ways not unlike the ways of the king:

We know that you are a teacher who has come from God (v. 2).
How can anyone be born after having grown old? Can one enter a second time into the mother's womb and be born? (v. 4)
How can these things be? (v. 9)

Jesus is forthcoming, but not without some impatience:

Are you a teacher of Israel, and yet you do not understand these things? (v. 10)

The Pharisee did not get it.

In Jeremiah 34:8-22, the prophet takes a much harsher stance toward the king, perhaps because here the king plays fast and loose with Torah requirements. In what must be an elemental act of morality and generosity, the king issues a "proclamation of emancipation" for all slaves held in Jerusalem (vv. 8-9). This is understood in v. 14 as an implementation of the old "year of release" (see Deut 15:1). For that action, the king must have earned important political credibility with the old guard "people of the land" (see 2 Kgs 23:30) who know and honor the Torah.

Except that, the king promptly reneged on his own decree, nullified the old Torah command, and took back all those who were in slavery (v. 11). To this act of reneging, the prophet is harsh and adamant:

You have not obeyed me by granting a release to your neighbors and friends; I am going to grant a release to you, says the LORD—a release to the sword, to pestilence, and to famine. (Jer 34:17)

The prophetic response is a play on words, "release of slaves...release of sword, pestilence, and famine," the characteristic threats of war, that is, imperial invasion.

I cite this little episode because the king seems to embody a bewildered community of faith that stares at a real social circumstance and cannot make up its mind about obedience to the command of Yahweh because the command flies in the face of "realism." Thus the choice between command and "realism" is a fearful one. I cite the case because it appears to me that this is now exactly the ambiguous situation of much of the Western church, caught between commands well known and programmatic in a modern/postmodern context where it is not at all clear that the old command pertains or will produce any good. That is exactly the context of Zedekiah and his bewildered community. With backs against the wall, reliance upon the command of Yahweh seemed less than persuasive. The prophetic response to the king, harsh and not reassuring, insists that obedience in such circumstance is the only thing that could possibly count for anything. Any alternative is suicide (see Jer 34:21-22).

Finally a comment upon this same Zedekiah in Jeremiah 37:17:

> *King:* Is there any word from the LORD?
> *Prophet:* There is!

In our narrative, the king did not get it. "Power people do not get it" because the offer of Jeremiah and of Jesus is outside the bounds of conventional expectation. These texts bring the faithful to a crisis point where the offer of God is unbearable in its demand, its assurance, and its insistence. The words of Jesus might have been addressed to Jerusalem in its moment of collapse:

> Those who believe in him are not condemned; but those who do not believe are condemned already. (John 3:18)

Without adding the Christological specificity, the prophetic tradition knows that belief (trust) is the alternative to condemnation. And so the city stands condemned, the cost of lack of trust:

> Indeed, Jerusalem and Judah so angered the LORD that he expelled them from his presence. (2 Kgs 24:20)

NOTES

[1] John Gray, *1 & 2 Kings*, OTL (Philadelphia: Westminster Press, 1963) 681.

[2] On this text, see Walter Brueggemann, *A Commentary on Jeremiah: Exile & Homecoming* (Grand Rapids: Eerdmans, 1998) 199-202.

[3]See Mordechai Cogan and Hayim Tadmor, *2 Kings: A New Translation with Introduction and Commentary*, AB 11 (Garden City: Doubleday, 1988) 307.

[4]Peter Ackroyd, "The Temple Vessels: A Continuity Theme," *Studies in the Religious Tradition of the Old Testament* (London: SCM Press, 1987) 46-60.

[5]On nations as tools and agents for Yahweh, see Walter Brueggemann, *Theology of the Old Testament: Testimony, Dispute, Advocacy* (Minneapolis: Fortress Press, 1997) 492-527.

THE FINAL HUMILIATION

2 Kings 25:8-21

Since the account of the reign of Josiah that ended in 23:30, our narrative has been emitting obvious signals strewn across the account of Josiah's heirs about the final demise of Jerusalem:

> I will remove Judah also out of my sight, as I have removed Israel; and I will reject this city that I have chosen, Jerusalem, and the house of which I said, My name shall be there. (23:27)

> He sent them against Judah to destroy it, according to the word of the LORD that he spoke by his servants the prophets....the LORD was not willing to pardon. (24:2-4)

> Indeed, Jerusalem and Judah so angered the LORD that he expelled them from his presence. (24:20)

So far as our narrative is concerned, the destruction of Jerusalem is a done deal. In our present verses, it remains only to give the details of the Babylonian onslaught. The account begins with a general notice of the destruction and defilement (25:8-12), followed by two more specific accounts concerning, in turn, the temple treasures (25:13-17) and the royal officials (25:18-21). The impact of the whole is to exhibit the destruction as total, brutal, and irreversible.

COMMENTARY

Completion of the Babylonian Onslaught, 25:8-12

The policy of Babylon is unambiguous and is here pressed to its culmination. The agent of devastation is Nebuzaradan, a high-ranking military official of the empire. [Nebuzaradan] In the entire account, not only is Yahweh absent, but Nebuchadnezzar himself is also absent. His agent acts for him, even as Nebuchadnezzar had been an agent for Yahweh. Nebuchadnezzar is present—until v. 20—only as a reference for dating the final onslaught. The narrator—and everyone else!—knows exactly when it all happened. It was one of those events about which one remembers where one was, what one was doing,

Nebuzaradan

This Babylonian officer is known only in these biblical texts and seems to have had a role not unlike the Assyrian officials in chapters 18–19. While he is a military officer, he clearly had functions of a diplomatic kind that are often taken by high-ranking military officers. Of special note is his contact with Jeremiah in Jer 39:10-14. He clearly acts on behalf of his commander, Nebuchadnezzar.

and when it happened. Time is reckoned here according to the years of Nebuchadnezzar, here his nineteenth year. Since he came to power in 605, this yields a date of 586, though because of the details of calendar, it is frequently cited as 587.

Either way, what counts is that time is reckoned, even in this Israelite narrative, by reference to the reign of Nebuchadnezzar, who is now the defining and decisive criterion for chronology. We are accustomed, in the Christian West, to reckon "BC...AD" by reference to Jesus, who is taken as the true pivot of history. In the book of Ezekiel, moreover, the self-conscious chronology moves from Jehoiachin in 597, the beginning of his exile. But not here. Here it is all and only Nebuchadnezzar, as though this narrator took his rule with utmost seriousness. The narrative proceeds according to imperial time!

In that fateful year, the nineteenth of the defining regime, the high-ranking and ruthless military officer enacted fierce and brutal verbs:

He *burned*: Yahweh's house, the king's house, all houses, all great houses. Verse 9 is framed so that it has the verb "burn" at the beginning and the end. [The Fire Next Time] Burning is the stereotypical emblem of total mastery and complete lack of pity.

He *broke down*: the walls. The verb "break down" (*nts*) is a characteristic term of Jeremiah, anticipating the devastation of the city (Jer 1:10; 18:7; 24:6).

He *exiled*: The sentence in Hebrew is remarkable because, in unusual fashion, the verb "exile" is withheld until after the three phrases naming the objects of the verb: (a) the rest of the people remaining in the city, (b) the deserters, and (c) all the rest. The effect is comprehensiveness, by withholding the verb in order to accent that all are exiles—everyone! Nebuzaradan, like every imperial military officer who needs exercise no restraint, can enact every thinkable abusive verb: burn, break down, exile.

The Fire Next Time

The imagery of burning "the holy city" is dramatic in its termination of the city. Such conflagration is a usual act of conquest of fortress cities (as in Amos 1:4, 7, 10, 12, 14;2:5). [See Francis I. Andersen and David Noel Freedman, *Amos: A New Translation with Introduction and Commentary*, AB 24A (New York: Doubleday, 1989), 239.]

Fire as an image of total destruction along with humiliation and helplessness is a powerful metaphor that bespeaks apocalyptic totalism. [In contemporary usage: James Baldwin, *The Fire Next Time* (New York: Random House, 1995), and Kurt Vonnegut, *Slaughterhouse Five* (New York: Barron, 1985).]

Of special interest in the catalogue of deportees are those who "deserted" to the king of Babylon. This reference indicates that there has been in Jerusalem a deep and abiding policy dispute whether to *resist* Babylon or to *submit* to the empire. Those who wanted to submit were regarded by the resisters as traitors or deserters, even if political realities might have made submission a shrewd decision. The most spectacular case of submission is that of Jeremiah, who clearly belongs among those who urged submission, not only as a prudent act but as the will of Yahweh for the city:

> Those who stay in the city shall die by the sword, by famine, and by pestilence; but those who go out to the Chaldeans shall live; they shall have their lives as a prize of war, and live. (Jer 38:2)

> If you will only surrender to the officials of the king of Babylon, then your life shall be spared, and this city shall not be burned with fire, and you and your house shall live. (Jer 38:17)

As a consequence, Jeremiah is regarded as a traitor for undermining "the war effort" (38:4). And indeed, the reported consideration given to Jeremiah by Nebuzaradan indicates that Jeremiah's stance and his leadership were well-known, even to the Babylonians:

> Now look, I have just released you today from the fetters on your hands. If you wish to come with me to Babylon, come, and I will take good care of you; but if you do not wash to come with me to Babylon, you need not come. See, the whole land is before you; go wherever you think it good and right to go. (Jer 40:4)

It is not to be thought that Jeremiah was a loner or an oddball figure, but rather that he represented and spoke for a large body of influential opinion that opposed the royal policies perceived as suicidal.

In our text, however, the "deserters"—those friendly to the empire—are taken along with all the others. This is no time for friendly distinctions. This is a wholesale policy that includes everyone of every opinion.

But, says v. 12—not all! The narrative wants to make the deportation as comprehensive as possible, both to indicate its severity and to make the claim that the impetus for emerging Judaism was exclusively among those in Babylon (see Jer 24). That comprehensive claim, however, is modestly disrupted by the realism of v. 12. The land was not empty. There continued to be a rural population; it had to be rural, for the empire had eliminated the urban context for living. Indeed, we may imagine that as armies moved up and down the land, there was a rural population relatively untouched and surely indifferent to such urban posturing among the power brokers. Thus v. 12 reflects upon social stratification and the condition of "the poor." These are the uneducated, those without influence, who would have no voice in the future of faith or politics. They are only the slightest footnote to the large imperial totals. Nebuzaradan, at the behest of Nebuchadnezzar, has done exactly what Yahweh had determined:

> removed and rejected (23:27)
> not forgiven (24:4)
> expelled (24:20)

The Temple Treasury, 25:13-17

Imperial intrusion characteristically concerns money. Empires are always anxious about finance and particularly finance that makes possible an extravagant, exhibitionist public life. Tiglath-pileser III had already had a keen eye for wealth that, in a monarchial theocracy, is concentrated in the temple (16:17-18). Now Babylon will seize what Assyria had left behind in Jerusalem. Partly, the loss to the empire reported here is an actual monetary loss. But partly it is a huge political embarrassment because the loss indicates that Yahweh—the Lord of the temple—is unable to protect Yahweh's own house from Babylon. [A Power Struggle among the Gods]

The narrator provides something of a detailed inventory of what is seized by Babylon. The detail indicates both the monetary value of bronze, silver, and gold, plus the fine artistry represented in the temple artifacts. The most telling reference in the inventory is the direct connection made to Solomon in v. 16. We have already seen in 1 Kings 7:13-51 that the founder of the temple cult spared no expense and no artistic measure in bringing the temple to its full and splendid completion. The temple has immense symbolic power and importance for the dynasty as an appropriate place of residence for this God. And now, all of that is terminated: the claims of dynasty are thinned; absence looms in the place of presence; the temple is a marker for forgiveness no longer on offer.[1] The detail of the inventory is perhaps designed to let the reader, point by point, sense the loss, the degradation, and the hopelessness. The glory

A Power Struggle among the Gods

The seizure and later return of temple vessels are of course political and military actions that transpire between states. At the same time, such transactions are enactments of struggles among the gods to determine which god or gods are reliable and powerful. Thus the struggle is between Yahweh, the God in Jerusalem and the gods of Babylon. In Isaiah 46:1-2 the Babylonian gods are mocked in their defeat; Isaiah 52:11, moreover, suggests that the temple vessels are to be taken home by the returning Jews, a sure sign that Yahweh has been vindicated and has defeated the gods of the empire. Another tale of such dispute and struggle with another victory of Yahweh is given in 1 Samuel 4–6.

has indeed departed (see 1 Sam 4:21)! It is as the prophets had anticipated…a city forsaken.

The End of Bureaucracy, 25:18-21

The humiliation produced by the sacking of the temple is matched by the violent termination of the urban power structure. As with the detail of the temple furnishings, so now we are offered a detailed account of the end of the government apparatus and of the privileged urban elite in Jerusalem. The list of officials is careful and specific: chief priest, second priest, three keepers of the doorway, a commanding officer, members of the royal council, director of the military draft, and sixty "people of the land." The list details the entire power structure:

(a) the temple hierarchy;
(b) government officers closest to the king;
(c) "the people of the land."

This latter group refers perhaps to the rural population that was itself resistant to royal foolhardiness, perhaps that community of opinion closest to Jeremiah. Now, however, none of that matters. All are the same, all suffer the same fate:

> It is all one; therefore I say,
>   he destroys both the blameless and the wicked. (Job 9:22)

> I said in my heart, God will judge the righteous and the wicked, for he has appointed a time for every matter, and for every work. I said in my heart with regard to human beings that God is testing them to show that they are but animals. For the fate of humans and the fate of animals is the same; as one dies, so dies the other. They all have the same breath, and humans have no advantage over the animals; for all is vanity. All go to one place; all are from the dust, and all turn to dust again. (Eccl 3:17-20)

No doubt distinctions could be made among the deportees.[2] Empires themselves, however, have no time for distinctions. The empire makes sure that (a) no one is left who could effectively restore what was, and (b) these leaders exemplify the fate awaiting any who get in the way of the empire.

The story ends in Riblah (25:20-21). Riblah is not a good place for defeated people from Jerusalem. It was not a good place for Jehoahaz in the face of Neco (23:33). It was not a good place for

Our Little Systems
The phrases of Tennyson that have become a well-known hymn are pertinent to the crisis in Jerusalem:

Our little systems have their day;
They have their day and cease to be;
They are but broken lights of thee,
And thou, O Lord, art more than they.

Strong Son of God, Immortal Love

Jerusalem was, for ancient Israel, a "little system." It did have its day. And then, it ceased to be, according to this narrative of termination. It was at best a "broken light" of Yahweh. That is where we are left by this narrative. It is not stated here, but will elsewhere be affirmed that "Thou art more than they." The "Thou" of Yahweh is more than Jerusalem and not coterminous with the city, the dynasty, or the temple.

Zedekiah (25:5-6). Now it is not a good place for these leaders. Only now does Nebuchadnezzar appear in the narrative. He has been absent from Jerusalem. He has been waiting in Riblah for his moment of dramatic mastery. It takes a king to kill the best. And Nebuchadnezzar does kill, quickly, tersely, without comment or compunction "for reasons of state."

The narrative draws the conclusion already evident to every reader: exile (25:21). The story has been told so slowly and in such detail now to arrive at this verdict. We already have known that. The telling is rather, I suggest, so that the massiveness and brutality can sink in, from shovels to snuffers, everything, all, everyone, everybody, no mercy, no compassion, no exception. Only Babylon now. The story is finally about the killing. Jerusalem has been an odd experiment in human history, but it has failed. It did not work, and along the way we have been given ample evidence about why it did not work. Now the end is reached; that end has been many times deferred, but could not, at the last, be avoided.

CONNECTIONS

In this final accounting, we are in the field of public power where the great shapings of world history take place. The story reminds the listening community that the most preferred human arrangements of power and meaning are at best penultimate, even when we idolatrously invest them with ultimacy.

What we have in the text is the close, studied report of the ways in which this "little system" of Jerusalem is fully spent. Its termination invites reflection on our own "little systems" that soon or late will cease to be. [Our Little Systems]

The "system" in Jerusalem was the system of Solomon. It was he, according to our larger narrative, who made the city what it was. And now Solomon's edifice is, item by item, dismantled. One more time we may allude to the exposé of Solomon (and all that he represents) in the summation of Jesus:

Yet I tell you, even Solomon in all his glory was not clothed like one of these. (Matt 6:29)

Not clothed indeed, as in "The Emperor Has No Clothes." "Solomon in all his glory" is a passing arrangement, not to be taken with absolute seriousness. He is only a bit player in the total scheme of things over which Yahweh presides.

As we consider Solomon, we identify Nebuchadnezzar as the second player in this drama of "little systems." There is no doubt that Nebuchadnezzar is the defining force here, the cipher of absolute human power—the last superpower—who can proceed exactly as he chooses without any restraint of any kind. While we have noticed the murderous conclusion of v. 21, much more telling is the chronological reckoning of v. 8 wherein Nebuchadnezzar has become the clue to world history. It is no small matter to have world history marked by one's life. That is the astonishing symbolic claim Christians make in "BC–AD"; we unthinkingly and uniformly make of the high claims of Jesus the center of history. Given the power of Constantine to reorganize imperial reality around Jesus, such a claim is remarkable. Jesus is not, however, the only such marker available, and we may settle for lesser markers that become the pivot of our lives, markers such as:

> the day of the diagnosis,
> the day our child was born,
> the day the bomb was dropped,
> the day my spouse left,
> the day of parental rape,
> the day the market collapsed,
> the day Diana died, etc., etc.

The Gospel of Luke attests to such imperial marking, so attested that we do not notice:

> In those days a decree went out from Emperor Augustus....
> (Luke 2:1)

The decree is by Caesar. He is the marker of the day; in the poetic, liturgical imagination of the church, however, Caesar has yielded place to the Baby at Bethlehem. Caesar's "little system" ceased to be. Or in Luke 3:1-2, already cited, all the pedigrees of the system are recited. And then comes this John, uncredentialed, who defies all systems. The "little system" of Tiberius and Pilate has gone the way of the system of Pharaoh. We have watched the splendor of Solomon being dismantled in our narrative. For a believing reader, we know that Nebuchadnezzar's imperial-chronological system will cease to be, quickly and irreversibly:

> Declare among the nations and proclaim,
>   set up a banner and proclaim,
>   do not conceal it, say:
> Babylon is taken,
>   Bel is put to shame,
>   Merodach is dismayed.
> Her images are put to shame,
>   her idols are dismayed. (Jer 50:2)

It was quite a system—Babylon—a killing system at Riblah…and at Auschwitz, at Dresden, at Hiroshima, systems taking themselves seriously, too seriously.[3]

Nebuchadnezzar, on the horizon of this narrative, has displaced Solomon as the key dominant system. The wise reader, however, will remember that Nebuchadnezzar has been only an agent. In this final account, Yahweh is nowhere mentioned (except the allusion to "Yahweh's house" in vv. 13, 16). Yahweh is absent and Nebuchadnezzar is the key player; I think, however, that the narrator means for us to ponder Yahweh's powerful absence in this narrative. Yahweh does not need to be noticed or visible or active. Yahweh has decreed! Behind Jerusalem, the "broken light," is Yahweh who is "more than they." Yahweh is more, than Solomon, more than monarchy, more than temple, and in the end, more than Nebuchadnezzar and more than Babylon.

Yahweh did not need to stay around for the mop-up action completed by Babylon. Jeremiah, a close reader of these events, sees it all clearly:

> I am going to send for all the tribes of the north, says the LORD, even for King Nebuchadnezzar of Babylon, *my servant*.… (Jer 25:9)

> Now I have given all these lands into the hand of King Nebuchadnezzar of Babylon, *my servant*. (Jer 27:6)

Nebuchadnezzar implements Yahweh's dismantling work. But of course Jeremiah cannot resist a Yahwistic "until" in 27:7 that destabilizes Nebuchadnezzar. There is indeed raw imperial power in the world that must be reckoned with. But that is not all and it is not ultimate. Just beyond the impressiveness of such rulers there is the "more than" of Yahweh that is mobilized, a "more than" brutality that yields mercy, a "more than" judgment that yields hope, a "more than" termination that produces compassion. For that reason a later poet can say of Nebuchadnezzar:

> I was angry with my people,
>   I profaned my heritage;
> I gave them into your hand,
>   you showed them no mercy;
> on the aged you made your yoke exceedingly heavy....
> Now therefore hear this.... (Isa 47:6-8)

Mercy is just beyond the reach of our narrative that gives no hint of mercy. We cannot in this narrative rush to that mercy, for we are held focused on Riblah...all the while knowing that in the end Nebuchadnezzar counts no more than does Solomon. The loss bears witness to Yahweh.

The text invites reflection on this "little system," and on many other "little systems" that cease to be. We watched in the late twentieth century as the "little systems" of Soviet totalitarianism and South African apartheid ceased to be. At some point, the "little system" of Protestant hegemony in Northern Ireland may even cease to be.

Closer home, we are watching our little systems of racial and gender discrimination still operate but only as short-term systems of violence. We arrange our lives in power configurations on which we stake everything. We surround our power systems with symbols of transcendence, and they come to look permanent and ordered by God. It is so with capitalism in the West in its arrogant durability beyond socialist systems...for the moment. This "little system" of capitalism is currently invested with great ideological force that sweeps all before it.[4] It is, however, a little system. The problem, in ancient Jerusalem and now and always, is to reckon with little systems while remembering their penultimate quality. Solomon thought that with his temple he had arrived at "forever" (1 Kgs 8:13). And surely with the killing at Riblah, Nebuchadnezzar thought he had made himself lord and master forever. We covet our little patterns of privilege, certitude, and domination. We do careless, crazy, brutal things to our neighbors on behalf of Yahweh in the service of our little systems. On a good day we know, as our narrator knows, that in the midst of and behind our little systems is this One who is "more than they." Our narrator does not show us much beyond Nebuchadnezzar's bloody moment in defense of his system, only the hint of 25:27-30. But the attentive reader knows...and waits. In knowing and waiting, the reader may take fresh note of how temporary our own little systems turn out to be. The narrative is finally about the One who is "more than they."

NOTES

[1]On the powerful and defining absence of Yahweh, see Ezekiel 9–10.

[2]The deportees are all lumped together by the empire. But it is also the case that very soon the elites in exile were able to take the initiative and define themselves as the true carriers of Israel, to the exclusion of all others. See Norman K. Gottwald, "Social Class and Ideology in Isaiah 40–55: An Eagletonian Reading," *The Bible and Liberation: Political and Social Hermeneutics,* ed. Norman K. Gottwald and Richard A. Horsley, rev. ed. (Maryknoll: Orbis Books, 1993) 329-42.

[3]On the seductions of pride, arrogance, and autonomy in such contexts, see Donald E. Gowan, *When Man Becomes God: Humanism and Hybris in the Old Testament*, Pittsburgh Theological Monograph Series 6 (Pittsburgh: Pickwick Press, 1975).

[4]See the classic expression of such ideological totalism by Francis Fukuyama, *The End of History and the Last Man* (New York: The Free Press, 1992).

TWO PROXIMATE
CONCLUSIONS

2 Kings 25:22-30

The story of Jerusalem ends in v. 21. There is not any more to be said. The termination in exile has been the aim of the narrative. This is "the end of the world." The "end of the world," however, needs to be given nuance, since it has become such a religious cliche. As N. T. Wright has made clear, the phrase used in the Bible does not characteristically refer, even in apocalyptic context, to the annihilation of "space-time order," but to the present world order. In speaking of the Gospel narratives, Wright judges:

> The evangelists were not, then, expecting the immanent end of the space-time order. That is a simple misreading of their use of Jewish apocalyptic language, whose real reference is the end of the present *world order.*[1]

There is no doubt that the termination brought about by Nebuchadnezzar constituted an ending. There was, however, still soil to be tilled and vines to be dressed (25:12). There were still people living their lives, rearing their families, and holding their hopes. That which persisted in and through and beyond termination must needs be ordered. The order, moreover, is in the hands of Nebuchadnezzar. Thus, after the verdict of v. 21, we are given two episodes of ordering. The first, in vv. 22-26, is immediate and local. The second, in vv. 27-30, is long term and open-ended.

COMMENTARY

The Short, Failed Governance of Gedaliah, 25:22-26

Nebuchadnezzar, having destroyed the royal-temple system of order in Jerusalem, is responsible to fashion an alternative order. Like the Assyrians before him in Samaria and like every imperial occupying force, the desirable arrangement is to appoint a local who is directly and immediately accountable to the empire and who already has a propensity to cooperate with the imperial power. Thus empires

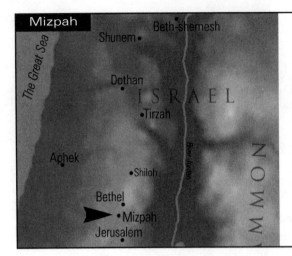

Mizpah

Mizpah is an ancient city in the territory of Benjamin. It appears to have been a major political and military locus in Israel's premonarchal period. For reasons not known to us, after the fall of Jerusalem, it became a major administrative post that housed the colonial governor. The report in Jer 41:1-6 suggests that it also functioned as a significant sanctuary, thus seeming to take over the principle functions of Jerusalem that were lost by default.

characteristically can identify puppets to govern, as the Soviet Union did in the Warsaw Pact nations and the U.S. has done for a very long time in the so-called "Banana Republics" of Central America.

Gedaliah is made governor at Mizpah. [Mizpah] The seat of government is dramatically relocated, thus making a statement about the cessation of the importance of the city of Jerusalem. Gedaliah comes to his post, well-credentialed, the son of Ahikam, the grandson of Shaphan. His grandfather and father before him have been influential functionaries in the royal government of Jerusalem. Thus Shaphan was the key agent in helping King Josiah find his way with the newly found Torah scroll (2 Kgs 22). Ahikam protected Jeremiah when he was at risk for his life (Jer 26:24). A member of the same family assisted in the scroll reading to Jehoiakim (Jer 36:10-12).

Thus this family is not only influential. It is present repeatedly in contexts where the scroll (of Deuteronomy) and the work of the prophet Jeremiah are in play.[2] This suggests that they are leaders of an important political movement in Jerusalem that was deeply critical of royal policies; they were grounded in the old Torah traditions that made them advocates of Deuteronomy and supporters of Jeremiah. All of this suggests a convergence in this family of theological and political forces that made them stand out in the crowd as the city was destroyed and the politics of the dynasty failed. As allies of Jeremiah, they were no doubt aligned with Jeremiah's judgment that obedience to Yahweh required submission to Babylon.

For these reasons, Gedaliah was a known entity and perhaps an obvious choice as the first Babylonian governor because he and his family had already publicly expressed openness toward Babylonian hegemony. He and his family had long been critical of the royal policies that were determinative in bringing imperial violence upon the city.

It was inevitable that Gedaliah, no more than established as governor, must deal with the unresolved issues of internal Judean politics (25:23-24). He receives a delegation of hard-liners, four leaders who were "captains of the guard," along with their men. For our purposes we need notice only the first two, Ishmael and Johanan. In these verses, we are told nothing of these men, but in v. 25 we learn that Ishmael is of the royal family. That identification, plus the military description of v. 23, indicates that these are partisans of royal policy, and therefore, long-standing opponents of Gedaliah who surely regarded him as an appeaser of the empire. Indeed, it is inevitable that those who cooperate with occupying powers are taken to be appeasers, even if they themselves regard their policies as the best among a spectrum of bad choices.

Gedaliah does not flinch but reiterates his pro-Babylonian policy (25:24). His policy is more fully stated in the parallel passage of Jeremiah 40:10:

> As for me, I am staying at Mizpah to represent you before the Chaldeans who come to us; but as for you, gather wine and summer fruits and oil, and store them in your vessels, and live in the towns that you have taken over.

Gedaliah assures his opponents that cooperation with the empire is a responsible way to reestablish peace and prosperity in a land devastated by combat. Gedaliah's policy is apparently a middle ground between two alternatives: (a) resistance to Babylon, a policy tried and now failed after the first deportation of 598, (b) an inclination to flee south to Egypt in order to escape the imperial power of the north. Jeremiah, surely a close ally of Gedaliah, had also faced both issues of resistance and flight. In Jeremiah 38:17-18, the prophet had dealt with the first policy alternative of resistance and had refused it. In Jeremiah 42:10-17, the prophet parallels the statement of Gedaliah and encourages his contemporaries to remain in the land, submissive to Babylon:

> If you will only remain in this land, then I will build you up and not pull you down; I will plant you, and not pluck you up; for I am sorry for the disaster that I have brought upon you. Do not be afraid of the king of Babylon, as you have been; do not be afraid of him, says the LORD, for I am with you, to save you and to rescue you from his hand. I will grant you mercy, and he will have mercy on you and restore you to your native soil. (Jer 42:10-12)

Gedaliah, like Jeremiah, has complete confidence that cooperation with Babylon is the proper policy, that Babylon will be benign and not abusive.

Such an assumption, predictably, was nonsense to his hearers, who resisted any such subservience (v. 25). In Jeremiah 40:13-15, Johanan, one of the four in the initial delegation to Gedaliah, reports to Gedaliah that Ishmael, with encouragement from the Ammonites, plans to assassinate him. But Gedaliah, perhaps in innocence, perhaps as an attempt to face down his opponent, refuses the warning and rejects Johanan's offer of a counterassassination (Jer 40:15). (The narrative of Jer 41:4-18 details the conflict and intrigue between Johanan and Ishmael, suggesting not only the social chaos of the moment, but the deep and abiding policy disputes that continued to surface.)

In any case, the upshot of the murder of the Babylonian governor, a cooperative Judean, makes the assassin and his company "wanted persons" in the purview of the empire. As a consequence, the whole company around Ishmael (including Jeremiah), carriers of dynastic pretensions, flees to Egypt, away from Babylonian power and danger. This is as much as the narrative tells us. No doubt the flight to Egypt was an act of prudence. No doubt it was an act of political realism, appealing to one great power against another. That flight, moreover, may have kept alive Davidic claims for restoration of monarchy, a claim in which the Torah-inclined party of Gedaliah had no interest.

Beyond that, however, the biblical narrative, formulated as it is by Babylonian sympathizers, regards the flight to Egypt as an evil act of disobedience. Thus the book of Jeremiah, closely linked to our text, is vigorous and redundant in its denunciation of the Egyptian remnant:

> Just as my anger and my wrath were poured out on the inhabitants of Jerusalem, so my wrath will be poured out on you when you go to Egypt. You shall become an object of execration and horror, of cursing and ridicule. You shall see this place no more. (Jer 42:18)

> I am going to send and take my servant King Nebuchadnezzar of Babylon, and he will set his throne above those stones that I have buried, and he will spread his royal canopy over them. He shall come and ravage the land of Egypt.... He shall kindle a fire in the temples of the gods of Egypt; and he shall burn them and carry them away captive; and he shall pick clean the land of

Egypt, as a shepherd picks his cloak clean of vermin; and he shall depart from there safely. He shall break the obelisks of Heliopolis, which is in the land of Egypt; and the temples of the gods of Egypt he shall burn with fire. (Jer 43:10-13; see 44:25-30)

The voice of Babylonian Judaism, now in its formative stage, is vigorous, vicious, and venomous toward Egyptian Judaism that is portrayed as heterodox and under deep and irreversible judgment. [Elephantine]

So the tale ends in Egypt. One may make the judgment that "return to Egypt" is the complete nullification of the story of faith that begins in the Exodus.[3] In this theological stylization of Israel's faith, all pharaohs, ancient and contemporary, are as one, and Egypt is always Egypt. Thus to return and submit to Pharaoh is to undo the exodus and to obliterate the entire story of Yahweh's covenantal deliverance. Our narrative itself is terse and makes no judgment on the matter. The allied account in Jeremiah tells us the opinion of the Gedaliah party. The debacle of Jerusalem is so massive and painful that the theological judgments about it are shrill and absolute. Our narrative, however, has no comment to make about the Egyptian development beyond the "brute fact" of departure.

Elephantine

Scholars have found an important collection of papyrus fragments of documents that evidence an important colony of Jews in the cite of Elephantine, on the upper Nile in the late sixth century. While that colony cannot be directly linked to the "flight to Egypt" we have just considered, it does attest to the fact that Jews must have retreated to Egypt in the face of pressure from the north. The evidence of worship in this community is that it was a form of compromised Yahwism, with the possibility that Yahweh was there understood to have a female consort. Such a possibility would illuminate the venom of the "Yahweh-alone" party of Babylonian Jews who sought to discredit those in Egypt. The evidence provides a context in which we may well understand the disputes reflected in the Jeremiah text and hinted at in our text.

Survival in Babylon, 25:27-30

Whereas the Egyptian contingent that fled Jerusalem is reported tersely and attracted no ongoing theological commentary, these verses provide a final comment on the Babylonian contingent of displaced Jews, which is suggestive and open-ended.

We have already seen in 24:12 that Jehoiachin submitted to Babylon in 598 and was carried away to Babylon. In our present verses, we are transported to 562, thirty-seven years after his deportation. The data is important because it marks the death of Nebuchadnezzar (562), and therefore, marks a decisive turn in imperial politics. Verse 27 suggests that Nebuchadnezzar had kept Jehoiachin "in prison" and that the new governance in Babylon, after Nebuchadnezzar, effects a major change in the treatment accorded to the exiled king. We may believe, moreover, that the change for the king amounted to a major change in the status and fortunes of the entire community of deported Jews as well.

Apparently there was a host of deported kings in Babylon, reflective of the military power and success of the empire and its widespread hegemony over many states. Among such deported kings, according to our narrative, Jehoiachin is well-treated and honored, albeit honored only as first among deportees. The new treatment of the deported king includes (a) speaking "good" to him, (b) giving him a role of relative prominence, (c) a change from prison clothes to clothes of royal dignity (see Gen 41:14), and (d) access to the royal dining room. All of these details together amount to imperial recognition of Jehoiachin's claim as the legitimate king over Jerusalem. The final verse of our text suggests that he was put on an imperial pension to maintain him in a status befitting his role as a king in exile.

The relatively positive note about the boy king now become middle-aged is intriguing and suggestive. It is important for what is not said. It is not said that Jehoiachin was offered any hope of restoration. It is not said that any provision was made by the empire of any recognition of any Davidic heir after the death of this king. It is not said that his access to the king's table was more than daily surveillance and hence a soft form of arrest. Because of so much that is not said, scholars are divided on what the paragraph might mean. Possibly, as Gerhard von Rad has forcefully suggested, this is a statement of hope, indicating that the royal line is alive, well, supported, and recognized, only awaiting the right time for restoration.[4] Such a view no doubt fed the messianic pretensions that turn up in a passage such as Haggai 2:20-23. Conversely, it is possible to conclude that the paragraph is simply an ending, playing out the tale of disasters and following the story of the last survivor in his long survival, but with nothing thereafter.[5]

Given the uncertainty about the meaning of this text, we may entertain the thought that the paragraph, offered both here and in Jeremiah 52:31-34, ends the royal narrative and is intentionally enigmatic because more could not be said. The narrator observes that the royal line is in jeopardy, but tells us no more than that. Thus whatever hope is offered here is unspoken—no blueprint, no firm design, no fixed assurance, but only "the conviction of things not seen" (Heb 11:1). The paragraph might do nothing more than confirm the flat verdict of v. 21: still in exile, still out of the land. But it might not!

CONNECTIONS

These two paragraphs state the parameters of Jews in exile, stretching from Egypt to Babylon, in both of which there emerged vital communities of faith. I will comment first on the Gedaliah passage (25:22-26). This passage first of all indicates that work toward the future must be done in the real world of political power with its limited options and possibilities. Indeed, the remainder of the Old Testament is a story about how Jews learned to practice faith in situations of endless compromise and accommodation.[6]

The other side of that work of the future is that one must work where one is and not somewhere else. This of course is precisely the insistence of Gedaliah and Jeremiah. The place where Yahweh had put them is in subservient, defeated Jerusalem, not a very good place to be. It was, nonetheless, their place of vocation and they could not seek otherwise. The most staggering embodiment of this conviction available to us is that of Dietrich Bonhoeffer, who could have stayed in the U.S., but who returned to his place in Germany in order to enlist in political conspiracy that led to his execution.[7]

This text, plus the evidence of Jeremiah, suggests that matters are highly disputatious in post-Jerusalem exilic communities. The resisters and the submitters are always vigorous and self-assured, perhaps in our time realigned in terms of the *unity* and *purity* of the community of faith. There is no doubt that in emerging Judaism the rivalry for defining power between Egyptian Jews and Babylonian Jews was immense and abiding. It turned out to be the case that Babylonian Jewry that presided over the formation of the canon was a party of "Yahweh-alone" voices, whereas Egyptian Jewry tended to be more open to cultural and theological accommodation. The lesson to be learned, I suggest, is that every theological passion is to some great extent context specific, if not context dictated. The biases of the received biblical text are all on the side of "Yahweh alone" as expressed in the traditions of Deuteronomy and Jeremiah. While the Egyptian party of Jews did not have a voice in the canon, it also was serious in faith as its context permitted and required. Indeed, there is no contextless Judaism even as there is no contextless Christian faith.

The paragraph on the emancipation of Jehoiachin, as it stands, is a statement of hope. It reminds us that hope is not a property, not a possession, but always a gift given generously and held loosely, always a chance and not an assurance, always a gamble against the staring face of reality. *Despair* is a disease in the modern world, a sense of closure already enacted against the world. *Nostalgia* is a pathology that imagines a possible return to the way it never was.

Optimism is a sickness that pretends and disregards how it really is. *Denial* is the stuff of refusal to live the life given us.

Taken all together—despair, nostalgia, optimism, denial—are all fashionable in a technically-ordered world that is thin on memory. But this boy king stands, as placed by the narrative, against all of that disengagement from the reality of exile. Hope, elusive and emancipatory, is a refusal to accept an end, a refusal to give Nebuchadnezzar the final word, a refusal to think that our defeats have in them the defeat of holiness, a refusal as it is more recently

The Long Saturday

I quote at length the terrible candor of George Steiner on this Jewishness that will refuse and not concede:

First, a question, almost taboo. Has the survival of the Jew been worth the appalling cost? Would it not be preferable, on the balance-sheet of human mercies, if he was to ebb into assimilation and the common seas? It is not only the horrors of our century, of the Hitlerite-Stalinist persecution and the mass-murder of Jews which enforce the question. It is not only the midnight of man at Auschwitz. It is the aggregate of suffering since, say, the destruction of Jerusalem and the second Temple in A.D. 70. It is the unending homicide, humiliation, pariahdom visited on Jewish men, women, and children nearly every day, nearly every hour, in some quarter of the "civilized" world. As consuming—the long history of flame climaxing in the Shoah—as the actual violence, has been the fear, the degradation, the miasma of contempt, latent or explicit, which has stained Jewish lives in gentile streets, institutions, and courts of law (Shylock on his knees). What Jewish child, across the millennia, has not known the gamut of threats and derision, of exclusion or condescension, which extends from blows, stones thrown, from being spit on, all the way to the urbane distaste, so the welcome "on sufferance" offered by the gentile? Every Jewish father is, at some point in his life and paternity, an Abraham to an Isaac on that unspeakable three-day journey to Mount Moriah. Genesis 22 is at the bruised heart of all Judaism....

Nonetheless, the enigma, the singularity of the survival of the Jew after the Shoah, persuades me of a purpose. Israel is an *indispensable miracle*. Its coming into being, its persistence against military,

geopolitical odds, its civic achievements, defy reasoned expectation. Today it looks with paradoxical satisfaction to normalcy: to the dosages of crime, corruption, political mediocrity, and vulgarities of the everyday which characterize nations and societies everywhere. Where Jeremiah thundered, there are topless bars.

This, precisely, is where I balk. It would, I sense, be somehow scandalous (a word with a theological provenance) if the millennia of revelation, of summons to suffering, if the agony of Abraham and of Isaac, from Mount Moriah to Auschwitz, had as its last consequence the establishment of a nation-state, armed to the teeth, a land for the bourse and the mafiosi, as are all other lands. "Normalcy" would, for the Jew, be just another mode of disappearance. The riddle, perhaps the madness, of survival must have a greater calling. One that is integral to exile....

It may be that the Jew in the Diaspora survives in order to be a guest—so terribly unwelcome still at so many shut doors. Intrusion may be our calling, so as to suggest to our fellow men and women at large that all human beings must learn how to live as each other's "guests-in-life." There is no society, no region, no city, no village not worth improving. By the same token, there is none not worth leaving when injustice or barbarism takes charge. Morality must always have its bags packed. This has been the universalist precept of the prophets, of Isaiah, Deutero-Isaiah, and Jeremiah in their ancient quarrel with the kings and priests of the fixed nation, of the fortress-state. Today, this polemic underlies the tensions between Israel and Diaspora.

George Steiner, *Errata: An Examined Life* (New Haven: Yale University Press, 1997) 56-62.

said, to give Hitler a posthumous victory. And so the boy king, now middle-aged, eats and waits, not knowing. The scene is so Jewish.

George Steiner takes one's breath away. [The Long Saturday] But even breathless, Jews and Christians arrive at the final chapter of the narrative, refusing to accept its finality. Jehoiachin is a "guest-in-life" in Babylon. The text says only, "As long as he lived." It does not say how many days, how long, long is. Clearly "long" is longer than the Babylonians ever guessed. This narrative is for the very long run.

NOTES

[1]N. T. Wright, *The New Testament and the People of God* (Minneapolis: Fortress Press, 1992) 401.

[2]There can be little doubt that the theology espoused by Deuteronomy and our derivative "historical" tradition constituted something of a movement in the final days of Judah. It is important to see that this literature reflects an important social reality of which the prophet Jeremiah is a crucial part. On this movement that he terms "Ephraimite," see Robert R. Wilson, *Prophecy and Society in Ancient Israel* (Philadelphia: Fortress Press, 1980) 135-252.

[3]See Richard Elliott Friedman, "From Egypt to Egypt: Dtr1 and Dtr2, "*Traditions in Transformation: Turning Points in Biblical Faith,* ed. Baruch Halpern and Jon D. Levenson (Winona Lake: Eisenbrauns, 1981) 167-92.

[4]Gerhard von Rad, "The Deuteronomic Theology of History in I and 2 Kings," *The Problem of the Hexateuch and Other Essays* (New York: McGraw-Hill, 1966) 219-21.

[5]See Martin Noth, *The Deuteronomistic History*, JSOT 15 (Sheffield: JSOT Press, 1981) 12, 74, 98.

[6]See Daniel Smith, *The Religion of the Landless: The Social Context of the Babylonian Exile* (Indianapolis: Meyer-Stone, 1989), and W. L. Humphreys, "A Lifestyle for Diaspora: A Study of the Tales of Esther and Daniel," JBL 92 (1973): 211-23.

[7]See Renate Wind, *Dietrich Bonhoeffer: A Spoke in the Wheel* (Grand Rapids: Eerdmans, 1990) 48-55.

SELECT BIBLIOGRAPHY

Ackerman, Susan. *Under Every Green Tree: Popular Religion in Sixth-Century Judah.* Harvard Semitic Monograph series. Atlanta: Scholars Press, 1992.

Balentine, Samuel E. *Prayer in the Hebrew Bible: The Drama of Divine-Human Dialogue.* Overtures to Biblical Theology. Minneapolis: Fortress Press, 1993.

Begg, Christopher T. "Unifying Factors in 2 Kings 1:2-17a." *Journal for the Study of the Old Testament* 32 (1985).

Bird, Phyllis A. *Missing Persons and Mistaken Identities: Women and Gender in Ancient Israel.* Overtures to Biblical Theology. Minneapolis: Fortress Press, 1997.

Bright, John. *A History of Israel.* 3rd ed. Philadelphia: Westminster Press, 1981.

Brueggemann, Walter. *Abiding Astonishment: Psalms, Modernity, and the Making of History.* Literary Currents in Biblical Interpretation. Louisville: Westminster/John Knox Press, 1991.

_____. "Abuse of Command." *Sojourners* 26/4 (July-August, 1997).

_____. "Crisis-Evoked, Crisis-Resolving Speech." *Biblical Theology Bulletin* 24 (Fall, 1994).

_____. "Faith with a Price." *The Other Side* 34/4 (July-August, 1998).

_____. *Finally Comes the Poet: Daring Speech for Proclamation.* Minneapolis: Fortress Press, 1989.

_____. "From Dust to Kingship (1 Kings 16:2; Genesis 3:19." *Zeitshrift für die alttestamentliche Wissenschaft* 84 (1972).

_____. *Old Testament Theology: Essays in Structure, Theme, and Text.* Minneapolis: Fortress Press, 1992.

_____. "The Legitimacy of a Sectarian Hermeneutic, 2 Kings 18–19." *Interpretation and Obedience: From Faithful Reading to Faithful Living.* Minneapolis: Fortress Press, 1991.

_____. "The Prophetic Word of God and History." *Interpretation* 48 (1994).

_____. *Theology of the Old Testament: Testimony, Dispute, Advocacy.* Minneapolis: Fortress Press, 1997.

_____. "When Jerusalem Gloats over Shiloh." *Sojourners* 19/6 (July 1990).

Brueggemann, Walter and Hans Walter Wolff. *The Vitality of Old Testament Traditions.* Atlanta: John Knox Press, 1975.

Buber, Martin. *The Prophetic Faith.* New York: Harper & Brothers, 1949.

Cazelles, Henri. "Syro-Ephramite War." *The Anchor Bible Dictionary.* 6 vols. New York: Doubleday, 1992.

Claburn, W. E. "The Fiscal Basis of Josiah's Reform." *Journal of Biblical Literature* 92 (1973).

Cogan, Mordechai and Hayim Tadmor. *2 Kings*. Anchor Bible 11. Garden City: Doubleday, 1988.

Cogan, Morton. *Imperial Religion: Assyria, Judah, and Israel in the Eighth and Seventh Centuries BCE*. Society of Biblical Literature Monograph Series 19. Missoula: Scholars Press, 1974.

Cohen, Martin. "The Role of the Shilonite Priesthood in the United Monarchy of Ancient Israel." *Hebrew Union College Annual* 36 (1965).

Conrad, Edgar W. *Fear Not Warrior: A Study of 'al tira' Pericopes in Hebrew Scriptures*. Brown Judaic Studies 75. Chico CA: Scholars Press, 1985.

Coote, Robert B. "Siloam Inscription." *The Anchor Bible Dictionary*. 6 vols. New York: Doubleday, 1992.

Culley, Robert C. *Studies in the Structure of Hebrew Narrative*. Philadelphia: Fortress Press, 1976.

Day, Peggy L., ed. *Gender and Difference in Ancient Israel*. Minneapolis: Fortress Press, 1989.

Fretheim, Terence E. *Deuteronomic History*. Nashville: Abingdon Press, 1983.

_____. *The Suffering of God: An Old Testament Perspective*. Overtures to Biblical Theology. Philadelphia: Fortress Press, 1984.

Frost, Stanley Brice. "The Death of Josiah: A Conspiracy of Silence." *Journal of Biblical Literature* 87 (1968).

Gottwald, Norman K. *All the Kingdoms of the Earth: Israelite Prophecy and International Relations in the Ancient Near East*. New York: Harper & Row, 1964.

Gowan, Donald E. *When Man Becomes God: Humanism and Hybris in the Old Testament*. Pittsburg Theological Momograph Series 6. Pittsburg: Pickwick Press, 1975.

Gray, John. *1 & 2 Kings. A Commentary*. The Old Testament Library. Philadelphia: Westminster Press, 1963.

Habel, Norman C. *Yahweh versus Baal: A Conflict of Religious Culture*. New York: Bookman Associates, 1964.

Harrelson, Walter. *From Fertility Cult to Worship: A Reassessment for the Modern Church of the Worship of Ancient Israel*. Garden City: Doubleday, 1969.

Hutton, Rod R. "Zimri." *The Anchor Bible Dictionary*. 6 vols. New York: Doubleday, 1992.

Isbell, Charles D. "2 Kings 22:3–23:24 and Jeremiah 36: A Stylisitic Comparison." *Journal for the Study of the Old Testament* 8 (1978).

Koch, Klaus. *The Prophets: I, The Assyrian Period*. Philadelphia: Fortress Press, 1982.

Levenson, Jon D. *Sinai & Zion: An Entry into the Jewish Bible*. New York: Winston Press, 1985.

Lindblum, J. *Prophecy in Ancient Israel*. Philadelphia: Muhlenburg Press, 1962.

Lohfink, Norbert. "The Cult reform of Josiah of Judah: 2 Kings 22–23 as a Source for the History of Israelite Religion." *Ancient Israelite Religion*, ed. Patrick D. Miller. Philadelphia: Fortress Press, 1987.

Long, Burke O. *2 Kings*. The Forms of the Old Testament Literature 10. Grand Rapids: Wm. B. Eerdmans Publishing Co., 1991.

McCarter, Kyle. *2 Samuel.* Anchor Bible 9. Garden City: Doubleday, 1984.

McCarthy, Dennis J. "An Installation Genre?" *Journal of Biblical Literature* 90 (1971).

McKay, John. *Religion in Judah under the Assyrians.* Studies in Biblical Theology, Second Series 26. Naperville: Allenson, 1973.

Mendenhall, George E. *The Tenth Generation: The Origins of the Biblical Tradition.* Baltimore: Johns Hopkins University Press, 1973.

Meyers, Carol. "Temple, Jerusalem." *The Anchor Bible Dictionary.* 6 vols. New York: Doubleday, 1992.

Miller, Patrick D. *They Cried to the Lord: The Form and Theology of Biblical Prayer.* Minneapolis: Fortress Press, 1994.

Montgomery, James A. *The Books of Kings.* International Critical Commentary. Edinburgh: T. & T. Clark, 1951.

Nakanose, Shigeyuki. *Josiah's Passover: Sociology & the Liberating Bible.* Maryknoll: Orbis Books, 1993.

Nelson, Richard. *First and Second Kings.* Interpretation. Atlanta: John Knox Press, 1987.

Nicholson, Ernest W. *God and His People: Covenant and Theology in the Old Testament.* Oxford: Clarendon Press, 1986.

Ollenburger, Ben C. Zion, *the City of the Great King: A Theological Symbol of the Jerusalem Cult.* JSOT Supplement 41. Sheffield: Sheffield Academic Press, 1987.

Pritchard, James B., ed. *Ancient Near Eastern Texts Relating to the Old Testament.* 3rd ed. Princeton: Princeton University Press, 1969.

Rad, Gerhard von. *Old Testament Theology.* Vol. I, *The Theology of Israel's Historical Traditions.* San Francisco: Harper & Brothers, 1962.

_____. *Old Testament Theology.* Vol. I, *The Theology of Israel's Prophetic Traditions.* San Francisco: Harper & Brothers, 1965.

_____. *The Problem of the Hexateuch and Other Essays.* New York: McGraw-Hill, 1966.

_____. *Wisdom in Israel.* Nashville: Abingdon Press, 1972.

Sakenfeld, Katharine Doob. *Faithfulness in Action: Loyalty in Biblical Perspective.* Overtures to Biblical Theology. Philadelphia: Fortress press, 1985.

Schwartz, Regina. *The Curse of Cain: The Violent Legacy of Monotheism.* Chicago: University of Chicago Press, 1997.

Seitz, Christopher R. *Theology in Conflict: Reactions to the Exile in the Book of Jeremiah.* Berlin: de Gruyter, 1989.

Shearing, Linda. "Queen." *The Anchor Bible Dictionary.* 6 vols. New York: Doubleday, 1992.

Smith, Morton. *Palestinian Parties and Politics That Shaped the Old Testament.* New York: Columbia University Press, 1971.

Thiel, Winfried. "Omri." *The Anchor Bible Dictionary.* 6 vols. New York: Doubleday, 1992.

Thompson, M. E. W. *Situation and Theology: Old Testament Interpretations of the Syro-Ephramite War.* Prophets and Historians Series I. Sheffield: Sheffield Academic Press, 1982.

Trible, Phyllis. "Exegesis for Story-Tellers and Other Strangers." *Journal of Biblical Literature* 114 (1995).

Ussishkin, David. "Lachish." *The Anchor Bible Dictionary.* 6 vols. New York: Doubleday, 1992.

Vaux, Roland de. *Ancient Israel: Its Life and Institutions.* New York: McGraw-Hill, 1961.

Wilson, Robert R. *Prophecy and Society in Ancient Israel.* Philadelphia: Fortress Press, 1980.

Wright, George Ernest and Norman C. Habel. *The Old Testament against Its Environment.* Studies in Biblical Theology 2. London: SCM Press, 1950.

Yerushalmi, Yosef Hatim. *Zakhor: Jewish History and Jewish Memory.* Seattle: University of Washington Press, 1982.

Zimmerli, Walther. *I Am Yahweh.* Atlanta: John Knox Press, 1982.

INDEX OF MODERN AUTHORS

1 KINGS
INDEX OF SIDEBARS

Text Sidebars

Art Side Bars

Map Sidebars

2 KINGS
INDEX OF SIDEBARS

INDEX OF SCRIPTURES

INDEX OF SUBJECTS DISCUSSED

J

1914:

Comment les Français sont entrés dans la guerre

Jean~Jacques
Becker

Contribution à l'étude de l'opinion publique
printemps~été 1914

presses de la fondation nationale
des sciences politiques

à mes enfants

TABLE DES MATIÈRES